The Classical World

LITERATURE AND WESTERN CIVILIZATION

The Classical World

GENERAL EDITORS

David Daiches
Anthony Thorlby

ALDUS BOOKS · LONDON

Aldus Editor   Kit Coppard

SBN 490 00240 4

Contents

General Introduction

General Introduction

David Daiches and Anthony Thorlby

The writing of literary history is a relatively late development in any culture. Long after a society has developed a sense of historical tradition and a curiosity about its relation to its past, the need to record the achievements of its writers can remain unfelt. This is partly because the concept of imaginative literature as a distinguishable cultural activity is itself a late growth. Neither the sacred texts of a people, preserved and interpreted by a priestly or scribal class, nor great national epics originating as heroic lays, transmitted orally for generations, and then put into a continuous, formal, and unified narrative and accepted as a central repository of traditional wisdom—neither the Bible nor Homer, to take the best-known example of each category in the West—could be put in a class containing other comparable works that chronologically preceded and succeeded it until long after the time when each was produced and first venerated. Even though the Bible and Homer both claimed to be works of history—or even in some degree because of this claim—they could not themselves be put in a historical context as long as they were regarded as unique.

It was the Christian humanists of the 16th and 17th centuries who, in their endeavour to reconcile their passion for the literature of ancient Greece and Rome with their veneration of the Bible, began to see both as literature and to compare them with modern works, as Milton did when he considered whether he should use as a model "the Epick form whereof the two poems of *Homer*, and those other two of *Virgil* and *Tasso*, are a diffuse, and the book of *Job* a brief model," and in doing so made a context for literary history possible. For literary history, as anything more than a list of names and works in chronological order, is essentially concerned with comparisons, with a noting of differences, and with the relating of those differences to other aspects of the culture out of which the literature arose. Thus the 18th-century concern with the origins of poetry, with the conditions that produced it, and with the functions it first served, led to a re-examination of both the Bible and Homer in the light of the time, place, and social conditions of their origin, which were discoverable from an examination of the works themselves and at the same time, when discovered, threw new light on those works. Robert Lowth's *De sacra poesi Hebraeorum* (1753) and Robert Wood's *Essay on the Original Genius and Writings of Homer* (1769) brought the subjects of their inquiry into literary history by demonstrating a connection between the language and ideas they exhibited and the geographical and cultural environment of their authors.

Interest in the origins of poetry, curiosity about what was considered to be "primitive" poetry, and concern with the history of poetry are thus interrelated, at least in the development of European literary historiography. But these are not enough to produce literary history, which finally emerges as a result of the confluence of many currents. One of those currents was the compendium of biographies of literary men, starting with the *De viris illustribus* (A.D. 106–13) of Suetonius and coming to the Middle Ages through St Jerome's *De viris illustribus*, a church history in biographies modelled on Suetonius and citing him. This biographical tradition was given new impetus with the development of the nation state, which encouraged such lists as a form of national pride; in the same way Renaissance Humanism encouraged eulogistic records of culture-heroes. In England the Reformation was also a factor, because the dissolution of the monasteries and the dispersal of their libraries led to realization of the need to preserve records before it was too late—a realization that lies behind the two pioneer works of English literary scholarship, John Leland's *Commentarii de scriptoribus britannicis* (written in the mid-16th century but not published until 1709) and John Bale's *Illustrium majoris britanniae scriptorum, hoc est, Angliae, Cambriae, ac Scotiae summarium* (1548–9). But such catalogues, although they may preserve and hand down information that the literary historian may eventually need, are not themselves literary history, even when they have developed (as they did in the 17th century) into lively and anecdotal biographical and even critical discussions of a large collection of writers.

Developing views of causation and historical movement represented another current that joined the confluence that produced literary history. Both the Suetonian tradition and its Renaissance development were atomistic in that they did not set their subjects in any moving historical context. But the sense of change and development produced by Renaissance scientific and geographical discoveries together with the characteristic Renaissance view of the educational value of history encouraged conceptions of historical movement and progress (or decline) and precipitated the 17th-century argument about whether the world was improving or worsening. This began as a great debate on the direction of human history, before it narrowed down, in the late 17th and early 18th centuries, to the antagonism between Ancients and Moderns and the Battle of the Books. Such arguments assisted the development of literary history, because they encouraged critical comparison in a historical context of the kind we get in the last two decades of the 17th century between Perrault and Fontenelle on the side of the Moderns and Boileau and Dacier on the side of the Ancients. By this stage a certain degree of critical sophistication had developed, representing yet another current that flowed into the complex of literary history, and the kind of comparison between the drama of different periods and different countries that we find in Dryden's *Essay of Dramatic Poesy* (1668) shows clearly how historical and critical awareness came to reinforce each other. Another factor became apparent by the end of the 17th century: literary history becomes possible only when a great deal of literature has been in existence for a long time.

Yet another current that first surfaces in the 17th century and becomes strong in the 18th is represented by theories of causation, linking causally the distinguishing features of the literature of particular periods and places to other factors—cultural, geographical, even climatic. Sir William Temple, in his essay *Of Poetry* (1690), which is full of historical reflections and comparisons, explained the superiority of English literature in that "which with us is called Humour" as perhaps proceeding "from the Native Plenty of our Soyl, the unequalness of our Clymat, as well as the Ease of our Government, and the Liberty of Professing Opinions and Factions. . . ." In the next century Vico in Italy and Montesquieu and Buffon in France took increasing interest in the real, historical foundations of culture, Vico in particular drawing attention to the function of the imagination and the significance of myths in the early history of mankind. In England Goldsmith argued strongly for the influence of climate on national character and therefore on national literature. It was still another century before such theories were refined and systematized by Taine in his view of literature as the product of "la race, le milieu, le moment" (*Histoire de la littérature anglaise*, 1863). But long before this another factor necessary for the production of literary history had developed, a factor that the student of literary historiography too often passes over: well furnished and properly catalogued libraries. Literary history is impossible if one has no access to the material, and even if the material exists it is

not much help to the potential historian unless it is well-enough catalogued for him to know that it exists and where it can be found. The
catalogue of the great Harleian Collection in the British Museum was
published in 1759; three years later Thomas Warton was reported by
John Nichols to be "in earnest with his project of the History of English
Poetry" (which was in fact the first English literary history). Uncata-
logued libraries produce antiquaries; catalogued libraries produce (or
may produce) historians: the difference between the antiquaries of 17th-
century England and the historians of the next century can be partly
explained by this fact. Yet England was not the pioneer here; France was
in the field as early as 1581, with Claude Fauchet's *Recueil de l'origine
de la langue et poésie française*, maintaining a continuous interest in the
historical interpretation of her own literature through the 17th century,
and (although not turning with sympathetic curiosity to mediaeval
literature in the age of Boileau) anticipating the English Richard Hurd
and Thomas Warton's historical interest in mediaeval literature with
Guillaume Massieu's *Histoire de la poésie française* (1739) and Sainte-Palaye's
Mémoires de l'ancienne chevalerie (1759).

A revival of an outmoded and rejected taste demands a historical
justification, or at least an effort of the historical imagination. This
explains the relationship between pre-romantic interest in the Middle
Ages and the quickening of interest in literary history throughout Europe.
A single ideal of civilization, such as that developed by the Enlightenment, can lie behind brilliant political history if that history takes as
its theme the rise, heyday, and decline of that ideal, as Gibbon's *Decline
and Fall of the Roman Empire* (1776–88) conclusively proves. But, as the
18th-century writers we mentioned in the opening paragraph of this
chapter clearly saw, the literary historian cannot successfully operate so
simple a dialectic. One reason why he could not do so, even in Augustan
England, was that the traditional veneration of the Bible and Homer
meant that two "primitive" works lay at the heart of a highly polished
and sophisticated culture. The strategies employed by Augustan writers
in reconciling appreciation of these works with the demands of an age of
self-conscious refinement were inevitably historical. Historical relativism,
of the kind so forcefully expressed in Hurd's *Letters on Chivalry and Romance*
(1762), was their way of having their cake and eating it—that is, of professing a neo-classical taste for the literature of their own day while
appreciating the literature of other periods that catered for quite different
tastes.

Historical relativism encourages, even forces, the use of historical imagination of a kind that Voltaire or Gibbon, who looked back on the past from the point of view of their own enlightened age, did not possess. Gibbon's brilliance, indeed, arises from the very fact that with consistently cool irony he judges the extravagances, follies, and superstitions of the past with the knowing confidence of a gentleman of his own day; and Voltaire's irony in discussing, for example, biblical history derives from a similar source. But you cannot for long impose a simple view of either progress or decline on literature because individual works speak out across the ages with persuasive elequence, sooner or later compelling the literary historian to cultivate the special kind of *Einfühlung* that enables him to see the world through an author's eyes. The cultivation of historical *Einfühlung* is a romantic trait: it distinguishes Barthold Niebuhr's *Römische Geschichte* (1811–32) from Gibbon's *Decline and Fall*, and Michelet's *Histoire de la révolution française* (1847–53) from Voltaire's *Essai sur l'histoire générale et sur les moeurs et l'ésprit des nations* (1756). But although for the political and social historian it is one of many viable attitudes, for the literary historian it is essential. It is a historical fact that the development of literary history is bound up with the development of critical relativism. Literary history matures with the enlargement of taste, with the ability to see mediaeval romance, for example, as in its own way as interesting and significant as modern prose fiction. So we have the paradox that, although the development of a critical tradition must precede effective literary history, literary history itself encourages or even perhaps in some degree depends on critical relativism, which is itself inimical to stable critical standards. You may despise the age of Gothic superstition and enjoy Boileau and Pope, but if you do you are not likely to be tempted to write literary history.

All this may help to explain why an age in revolt against critical relativism has also been an age in revolt against literary history. One of the features of the so-called "New Criticism" in the United States, at least in its early and most aggressive stages, has been its objection to literary history, its insistence that every work of literature be regarded ideally as contemporary and anonymous, a timeless structure of words to be examined and appreciated for its unique quality as an artifact rather than related to a chronological order or a cultural context. This ideal is incapable of realization because language, the medium of literature, itself exists in time; it is part of history, and even its primary denotational meaning, not to mention all those connotations and associations and echoes on which full literary meaning depends, can be determined only by knowledge of what *that* word meant at *that* time. But as an ideal it

15

makes sense: any work of art must seek to present a timeless pattern of significance, and if we look to history to help us see that pattern, we can argue that we are simply making a pre-critical discovery of the true text—an activity that, like the work of the bibliographer and textual critic, is not in any sense critical but may be necessary if we are to have before us the actual work of art created by its author. There is of course a tendency on the part of the literary historian to lose sight of value in stressing development, causation, relation to social and cultural context, and the degree to which a literary work reflects or responds to certain pressures of the time.

The purely evaluative critic may deplore this, however much he may depend on the historical critic for the information he requires to make sure that he reads a work of the past correctly. Of course there are purist evaluative critics who would deny any such dependence. But the proposition that any work can be profitably read by anybody, regardless of his knowledge of the language and of the conventions in which it was written, seems to us quite untenable. To a man who knows no Greek, a Greek text is a pattern of lines and curves; and to a man who hears a poem recited in a language he does not understand, the poem is only a vehicle for stimulating the vaguest and most random associations. Crucial passages in Shakespeare may be misread by a man who knows the English of today but knows no Elizabethan English. To deny this and to proclaim the total independence of the individual's reaction to a work of literature— that is, its independence of any relevant historical or linguistic knowledge —is to hold that any work may mean anything, depending on who reads it, and that literature is therefore merely a stimulator of wholly unpredictable ideas and emotions, none of which can be tested or checked by any objective reality that exists in the literary work. If literature is merely a hallucinatory drug, with effects on individuals depending entirely on their state of mind when they take the drug, then at best it is of very little value and at worst it may be harmful. But it seems perverse to hold the view of literature that implies this.

The critic may seek to avoid the problem altogether by turning to a kind of literary history that sees all literature as embodiments of certain primal myths corresponding to the most profound needs of human nature, but in charting the transmutations and varying manifestations of such myths the myth-critic runs the risk of ignoring precisely those qualities that distinguish one treatment from another, and, in so distinguishing them, produce fundamental differences in scope, richness, and quality. The myth-critic can see a nursery rhyme and *King Lear* as deriving from the same impulse, treating the same myth, belonging to the same seasonal or other sort of literary category. And so his criticism becomes reductive, and such evaluative gifts as he may possess become as unusable as those of the historian absorbed in influences, causes, and relationships.

One could perhaps say that one way out of these problems is for the literary historian to regard himself (as the editors of this work regard themselves) as charting an aspect of civilization, a central part of culture. This is what went on, he will say; this is how and what people wrote and this is how their writing is related to the kind of world they lived in. In taking this line, the literary historian will not necessarily be abrogating critical discrimination. He can be as discriminating as he likes, but he will take his criteria of discrimination not from history but from his knowledge of the nature of literature as an art-form. He will fully concede, for example, that Elizabethan and Jacobean drama is enormously superior in quality to the drama of any other period of English literature, and he will *use* his awareness of this superiority historically, by trying to show what it was in the whole social and cultural context of the time that channelled the greatest literary imaginations into this particular literary form, just as, when he deals with the flourishing of the novel at a later period, he will try to explain why this particular form captured so much of the highest literary vitality of the age.

This seems quite straightforward, but another paradox intervenes here to complicate matters. Literary history could not develop before some minimum amount of knowledge (philological, bibliographical, and biographical) had developed. But since these minimum conditions were reached, generally in Europe in the 17th and 18th centuries, such a massive amount of further scholarship has been built up that the literary historian finds it almost impossible to come to terms with the sheer quantity of knowledge available to him. In some cases, of course, generations of scholarship have made things much easier for the modern literary historian: he can take for granted innumerable bibliographical and biographical facts that at first had to be painstakingly established. He does not have to worry about establishing the canon of major writers or ascribing minor writers to their proper period. He finds that things have been shaped for him, whether he wishes it or not, so that he sees a pattern of, say, Enlightenment moving into pre-Romanticism and then followed by Romanticism (a pattern established by late-19th-century historians), which may determine his habits of thought about the past without his realizing it, unless he is sufficiently opposed to the established view to wish to attack it frontally, as some recent historians of culture have attacked the view that the Renaissance represented a real break with the mediaeval world view. Yet side by side with the common knowledge and commonly accepted patterns on which he can build, the modern literary historian is faced with an enormous quantity of unrelated scholarship and criticism in innumerable monographs written from every conceivable point of view.

The line of least resistance in such circumstances is to plod through as much of this material as it is physically possible to handle, and then employ it in a chronological march through each period and a biographical march through each author, listing, describing, evaluating, and then passing on to the next item. Sometimes the evaluation is omitted and literary history returns to the formless state out of which it originally emerged, not this time as a sparse catalogue but as a crowded jungle of undifferentiated information. A clear-cut ideology can, of course, solve the problem of formlessness by providing a standard of value and of significance that can enable the historian both to separate the sheep from the goats and to relate each author or group of authors to the charting of a presupposed progress or decline over a given period. In our experience, however, even the most rigorously ideological literary historian is not necessarily saved from the dull and crowded chronological catalogue to which (surprisingly) many Marxist literary historians are prone. There is an academic tradition that seems to intervene here, the concept of the professor doling out memorizable information about authors and their lives, works and their contents, periods and their characteristics: this concept took deep root in the 19th century and is partly responsible for the discredit into which literary history fell (in some quarters at least) in the 20th century.

Meditating on these and similar problems, the editors of this work firmly decided against a mere chronological plod through the literature of the western world, national literature by national literature. We also decided not to go to the other extreme and adopt a single, simple ideological framework in the light of which every work would fall into its proper place and every author be awarded so many good marks or bad. Contexts and relationships were what seemed to us most important in trying to define our approach. One of our main concerns was to place literature in its full human context so as to illuminate the relationship between literature and the various social and cultural forces from which it emerges. But in trying to place literature in its context, we soon found that no single definition of "context" would work for all phases and for all periods. Sometimes the most appropriate context is national, sometimes social, sometimes political, sometimes psychological. The relationship between the development of the acting profession and the flourishing of Elizabethan drama (which involves social and economic questions among others), or between the French Revolution and certain aspects of Romanticism, or between certain 19th-century nationalist movements and the development of national literary languages and literatures, or between violence in literature and the socio-psychological characteristics of an age—these are the kinds of questions that pose themselves, and no single set of questions is always applicable. Sometimes the organizing principle of a chapter comes from outside literature—from its social, national, or ideological environment—and sometimes from literature itself. The chapters that follow give neither pure history nor pure literary evaluation, but deal with topics arising out of the changing nature of literature and its changing place in a community in ways that seem most relevant both to a given time and place and to the modern reader's concern and curiosity.

This work makes no pretence, then, at giving a comprehensive history of western literature. It makes instead what is perhaps a more bold assumption that no such comprehensive history of literary products alone can any longer be very meaningful. The question that means most to our age is what are the foundations of civilized living, civilized thinking, civilized society. Literature can help us to answer that question. Indeed, unless the discussion of literature raises questions that are truly critical— critical for and of the way men live—it is not worth discussing at all. Nothing less than this deserves the name of criticism, for "to criticize" derives from a word meaning to judge, to pick out (and is cognate with the Latin for a sieve). Criticism and crisis are next of kin, not only etymologically, but in historical fact. In order to make judgments, the mind must separate and divide things. The mentality of criticism is necessarily different from that of imaginative creation; for great works of art aspire to an ideal of wholeness, which is doubtless a symbolic reflection of a wholeness in existence itself that only genius can intuit. Criticism is no substitute for doing or making. But just because of its more negative, divisive role, it may take the world to pieces in speculative thought, and measure the parts against one another. A critical age easily becomes pessimistically nostalgic for a state of the world that is ideally unified, whereas it is its own criticism that is putting it asunder.

The procedure followed in these volumes, of approaching literature in terms of critical topics, inevitably has the effect of dividing up books and authors and situations into rather arbitrary sections. For this no excuse need be made; it is necessary to the business of criticism. An encyclopaedic putting together again of the world's contents is not a task that any form of knowledge can accomplish. But this restriction on what knowledge can achieve does not render it useless. Montaigne declared that: "Most occasions of trouble in the world have to do with grammar." For him, this meant that one must be schooled in grammar in order to understand the world's troubles. But he was under no illusion that something more than grammar is needed to put them right. Thus, if the title of these volumes seems pretentious in bringing together two things of such evidently different magnitude, the understanding that is offered is like a reflection in a mirror: a glimpse of things that are really there, but not to be mistaken for the things themselves. For the things that we call "civilization" and "literature" are not, of course, material objects at all, but qualities, judgments. And how else should these be perceived except through studied moments of reflection?

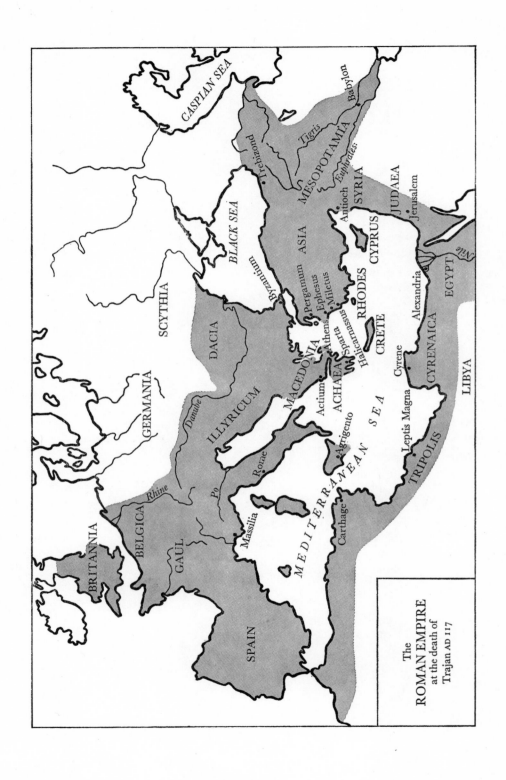

The
ROMAN EMPIRE
at the death of
Trajan AD 117

CHAPTER I

The World of Greece and Rome

M. I. Finley*

The Roman Empire reached its greatest extent at the death of the Emperor Trajan in A.D. 117. It then stretched from east of the Tigris River in Asia to the Atlantic Ocean, including all of Europe south and west of the Rhine–Danube line (and some important regions such as Transylvania on the other side), Britain to Hadrian's Wall, Egypt, and the coastal area clear across North Africa. Geographically, commercially, and culturally, the Mediterranean Sea bound together these million and a half square miles, inhabited by more than 50 million people. *Mare nostrum*, the Romans called it—"our sea."

More than 1000 years of complicated history led to this imperial climax. Although people speaking Greek (or proto-Greek, as contemporary linguists prefer to call it) entered the Greek peninsula before 2000 B.C., and migrants with Italic dialects, of which Latin was one, were in Italy by 1200 B.C., it is legitimate to begin Greek history with the "dark age" that followed the collapse of the Mycenaean civilization (say, from 1100 B.C.), and Roman history in the 8th century B.C., where their own tradition placed the foundation of Rome. In that century, Assyria was the great power in western Asia, an independent Egypt boasted a very long history of its own, the Etruscans were creating the strongest civilization in Italy, and Phoenicians and Greeks were making their first expeditions to the western Mediterranean, to be followed by permanent settlements. Most of Europe was forested and thinly settled by barbarous tribes. Neither the small Greek nor the small Latin communities foreshadowed the great things to come.

The long, slow process of absorption and integration that culminated in the reign of Trajan was very uneven, and it took different forms. Many peoples "disappeared" along with their languages, such as the Assyrians, the Lydians and Carians of Asia Minor (modern Turkey), the Samnites and Etruscans of Italy, the Sicels and Sicans in Sicily, and

* Professor of Ancient History, University of Cambridge.

numerous tribes of Spain and Gaul. These all became Hellenized* or Romanized. On the other hand, there were also peoples who did not disappear, who were absorbed politically but not, or at least not wholly, culturally. Even in the Roman Empire, Aramaic remained the language of everyday speech and of business affairs in a large area stretching eastward from Syria and Palestine. When Josephus, a member of the priestly class in Jerusalem, wrote his *Jewish War* in order to draw the lessons from the Roman conquest of Judaea in A.D. 70, he did so first in Aramaic, and only later in Greek, a language in which he was not altogether at home. And elsewhere there were tenacious pockets of native speech, especially among the peasantry.

Sociologically one sees essential similarities between the early Greek communities and the first Latin ones. Nevertheless, there were also important differences, both internally and in their environments, and then they took such different courses that it is impossible to discuss their historical development in tandem, until Rome conquered the Greek world in the 2nd century B.C. The very word "conquered" marks the first and clearest distinction. The Greeks, setting out from the peninsula to which they gave their name, gradually diffused east and west by small migrations. Sometimes they were able to establish new settlements peacefully, at other times they had to subjugate native tribes; but not until Alexander the Great were there marching armies like the Roman ones. The movement began a little before 1000 B.C. with settlements on the Aegean islands and the west coast of Asia Minor. Western "colonization," from about 750, led to the eventual Hellenization of Italy south of Naples, of Sicily except for a narrow stretch between Palermo and Marsala, of some of Corsica, of Cyrenaica (in Libya), and of Marseilles and its environs. And there was a steady progression along the Black Sea: in the Hellespont region up the western (Romanian) coast and beyond to the Crimea, and on the southern side all the way to Trebizond.

These far-flung settlements all clung to the coasts, though they often extended a few miles inland. The Greeks were not a maritime people in the sense that the Phoenicians were, and their literature reflects a profound ambiguity about the sea and seafaring: Poseidon (not only sea-god but also god of earthquakes) was a menacing deity who had to be placated all the time. But the sea was their life-line, along which men and goods moved, binding Hellas together, whereas the continental

---

* In their own language, past and present, the Greeks are "Hellenes," their country "Hellas." It was the Romans who called them "Graeci," whence their name in all western languages except their own.

interior was a reservoir from which to draw slaves, metals, and timber, but not a region for civilized living. This attitude held despite the agrarian basis of almost all the new settlements, which sprang from the land hunger of a growing population living on the poor, largely infertile soil of Greece. Trade considerations were also a factor but rarely a deciding one. Reggio and Messina were selected for settlement very early, presumably because they controlled the Strait of Messina, but the splendid harbour of Brindisi (on the outer "heel" of Italy) was passed by; some of the most flourishing new sites, such as Agrigento in Sicily, had no harbour worthy of the name, and in the east, Byzantium was a comparatively late foundation, and for long an unimportant one, despite its dominance of the Dardanelles.

The word "colonization," which modern historians conventionally use for this long-drawn-out process, is actually misleading on one fundamental point: the new communities were independent city-states. Men left the older Greek communities, not always voluntarily, to found new ones abroad, complete in themselves. They retained sentimental and religious ties with their mother-cities, but rarely anything more. By the end of the 6th century B.C. there were perhaps 1500 such small city-states from Trebizond to Marseilles, and collectively they were Hellas, an abstraction something like Christendom in the Middle Ages or Islam today, but with even less of a political accent. The remarkable fact is that, lacking a political centre, geographical unity, or a single religious authority, Hellas did not fly apart. To begin with, a Greek would have found his physical surroundings reasonably familiar wherever he went. Despite regional variations, the terrain, climate, and vegetation are similar all around the Mediterranean. Then, the Greek residential habit, like that of all Mediterranean people, was to crowd together in urban centres or villages, not to live in isolation on farmsteads. (In more hostile environments this preference would be strengthened by needs of defence.) Each city had its central square (*agora*), its unmistakably Greek stone temples and other public buildings, its cemeteries outside the walls, its lively and noisy outdoor life.

Cultural interchange was continuous and rapid. The speedy diffusion of the Homeric poems and of the Doric temple are examples enough. Both occurred early, in the archaic age,* when outbursts of creativity and

---

* It is the convention to divide Greek history into three periods: the "archaic" from 800 to 500 B.C., in round numbers; the "classical" from 500 to Alexander the Great; the "Hellenistic" from Alexander to the Roman conquest. The labels are not to be taken too seriously, but they are a convenient shorthand.

cultural leadership were as likely to emerge in the more outlying regions as in the old Greek heartland. Whereas life-size human sculpture seems to have received its early impetus in Crete, and the primacy in fine painted pottery shifted from Athens to Corinth and then back to Athens, lyric poetry counted among its first great figures (all active by 600 B.C. or earlier) Archilochus from the Aegean island of Paros; Stesichorus of Himera, in northern Sicily, and his disciple Ibycus of Rhegium (Reggio); and Alcaeus and Sappho of Lesbos. Philosophy and science originated in the speculations of the "Ionian school,"* begun according to tradition by Thales of Miletus about 600 B.C. Later in the century, refugees initiated a powerful western philosophical development—with the Pythagoreans, with Zeno and Parmenides of Elea near Naples, and finally with Empedocles of Acragas (Agrigento) in Sicily. Old (mainland) Greece seems to have played no role in this development before the middle of the 5th century B.C.

Geography and historiography were also Ionian creations (Herodotus was a native of Dorian Halicarnassus, but he wrote in the Ionic dialect). For this there is a simple and direct explanation in the Ionians' close contact with Lydians, Persians, and Egyptians. Wherever the Greeks migrated, they found themselves enmeshed with other peoples. In the end they called them all "barbarians"—a complex intellectual debate began later among the Greeks about the depth and implications of the Greek-barbarian dichotomy—but they could hardly avoid distinguishing between such advanced nations as Persia, Egypt, Carthage, or the Etruscans, and the more backward Scythians, Thracians, or Sicels. Political relations varied accordingly: the Persians forced Ionia into their empire and for a time threatened the independence of Greece as well; somewhat later, Carthage began to menace Greek Sicily, and the Etruscans were a block to further Greek expansion in Italy, whereas the weaker tribes were in the reverse position, often reduced to semi-slavery or pushed into the less-fertile lands by the technologically and socially more powerful Greeks. Cultural relations varied, too, but not along neatly parallel lines or in regular patterns. The Persians and Carthaginians, for example, welcomed Greek craftsmen, artists, and doctors, and the Egyptians employed Greek mercenaries at an early stage, but there seems to have

---

* Ionic was originally the name of one of the dialects of the Greek language. Then the Greek settlements in that sector of Asia Minor lying between Phocaea and Miletus (and the Aegean islands nearby) founded by Ionic speakers, came to be called Ionia; eventually, though loosely, the terms "Ionia" and "Ionians" were employed for Greek Asia Minor in general. Hence the "Ionic order" in Greek architecture points to its origins there, as the Old Testament "men of Javan" specifies the Greeks with whom the Hebrews had their earliest contacts.

been little lasting Greek influence on their institutions, beliefs, or arts.*
But the Etruscans were passionate importers and imitators of Greek
pottery and sculpture, and carried Greek cultural traits to the Romans.
The natives of Sicily were in the end so thoroughly Hellenized that their
native culture disappeared, whereas the Scythians seem to have been
relatively unaffected. Social relations were diverse. The early settlers
brought few women with them and customarily married native women;
in some places, such as Halicarnassus, intermarriage remained a common
practice into the classical age.

Perhaps the most fundamental distinction, in Greek eyes, between
themselves and the barbarians lay in their political structures. A tribal
monarchy was not an acceptable framework for civilized life; nor was a
tribal confederation nor a large territorial empire. Only the *polis*, which
we conventionally but not very happily translate as "city-state," was
suitable. When Aristotle defined man as a *zoon politikon*, a being who by
nature is designed to live in a *polis*, he meant that mankind could achieve
its full potential only at that stage of political development, which the
Greeks alone had reached (and in his view were alone capable of reaching).
Aristotle was writing at a time when the city-state was breaking down
under internal stresses and external aggression, but he had centuries of
history behind him. Attempts have been made to explain this insistence
on the small autonomous unit by reference to the broken terrain of Greece,
with its living space restricted by criss-crossing mountains. But this
factor, whatever its importance in the formative period, can scarcely
explain why the Greeks carried the *polis* idea wherever they went, to the
mouth of the Danube, to Sicily and Libya, under different and even
inappropriate conditions. Nor does geography explain the tenacity with
which many communities resisted attempts by powerful city-states such as
Athens or Sparta to impose some form of suzerainty on them. Even
Alexander and his successors met with continual resistance.

It is indeed arguable that the absence of political ties and controls
favoured the unity of old and new Greece. Men journeyed long distances
to consult the oracle at Delphi and less-renowned ones elsewhere, to
participate in the Olympic and other games, to trade in goods and ideas,
or to find employment on large temple projects, normally free from the
tensions and suspicions engendered by "imperial" ambitions or threats.
It can hardly be an accident that the greatest pan-Hellenic shrines—
Delos, Delphi, Olympia—were located in politically insignificant places.

* The radically changed situation begun by Alexander's conquests is not relevant at this stage
in the account.

Other states would surely have resisted the accumulation of so much awesome religious prestige by powerful communities.

It must be admitted, however, that even as an ideal the *polis* becomes rather elusive the moment one begins to analyse it in any detail. There were extensive backward areas in old Greece (rather than in the new regions) to which the application of the term *polis* was just a courtesy before the 4th century B.C. or later. Aetolia, Acarnania, and to a considerable extent Thessaly, with loosely federated tribal groupings under aristocratic clans or chieftains, were more like the world of the Homeric poems in their organization than like contemporary city-states. As for the city-states proper, they had a great incapacity to leave each other alone, to respect in others the autonomy they demanded for themselves as being the essence of civilized political organization. War was so much a part of their life that their own historians never thought to seek an explanation for the phenomenon, being content with the causes of specific wars. Often enough they were equally incapable of remaining at peace internally: what the Greeks called *stasis*, a word big enough to embrace the gamut from political faction to outright civil war, was their greatest malady, as their historians and political theorists acknowledged. And, finally, the tempo of development was uneven throughout, politically, economically, culturally, so that it is fallacious to take any one *polis* as a model. Above all, we must not generalize from Athens, about which we know far more than about all the others together. Nor was it simply a choice between the Athenian pattern and the Spartan one.

That said, some formal consideration of the *polis* as an ideal type remains the necessary starting-point of analysis. "A state composed of too many," wrote Aristotle in the *Politics*, "will not be a true *polis* because it will not have a true constitution. Who can be the general of a mass so excessively large? And who can be herald except Stentor?" A *polis* was not a place, though it occupied a defined territory; it was people acting in concert, a community (*koinonia*) in the full sense that scarcely survives in the modern world. Therefore the people must be few enough to assemble and deal with problems face to face. And they dealt with everything: religion and culture were as much public concerns as economics or politics. There were sacrifices in the home, and private poetry readings, but the great occasions for religious ceremonial, for music, drama, poetry, and athletics, were the public festivals, local or pan-Hellenic. With the state thus the universal patron, Greek tragedy and comedy, for example, were as much part of the process of face-to-face discussion as a debate in a legislative assembly.

The people were indeed few: the population of Athens at its maximum in the middle of the 5th century B.C. is estimated at about 250,000, possibly 275,000, of Corinth perhaps 90,000, of Thebes or Acragas (Agrigento) 40–60,000. From these totals one subtracts women, slaves, and in many cities a substantial number of immigrants. The *koinonia* was an exclusive community, which might welcome outsiders for their skills or their wealth, which might and usually did accept them socially and protect them legally, but which rarely extended to them actual membership—that is, the privilege and duty of sharing in the decision-making processes. Anyone who fails to contribute his share, said Pericles, the greatest Athenian statesman, "we hold to be not inactive but useless." He was thinking of the adult male citizens alone, 40–45,000 out of the 250–275,000, and then only in ideal terms. Even Athens had enough "useless" citizens, and Athens in the 5th century B.C. was the most democratic of Greek city-states, having travelled furthest from the days when Odysseus (in the *Iliad*) struck a commoner with his sceptre, "upbraiding him in these words: 'Good sir, sit still and hearken to the words of those who are your betters, you . . . who are not counted either in battle or in council.' "

The early archaic age had seen the disappearance of kingship, except for some curious and heavily modified exceptions, most notably in Sparta. Just how this happened is not at all clear: the Greeks, unlike the Romans, retained no legends or traditions about the overthrow of monarchy. Government became a monopoly of aristocratic clans, whose wealth came chiefly from their land and their flocks. Control of public religious activity gave them a moral sanction, symbolized by the divine or legendary heroic ancestry that they claimed, and they tended to congeal into a closed ruling group. Traditional ties binding the peasantry to their lords were strengthened by debt, the chronic malady of any peasant class lacking the resources to carry them through lean years. But, as the population increased, and as trade in luxuries, metals, timber, and grain grew to more significant proportions, new social tensions were generated. There was landed wealth outside the ruling aristocracy; now the urban sector provided outlets for some of the dispossessed or weak rural elements and for skilled outsiders. A revolution in military organization made its contribution. It was probably early in the 7th century B.C. that the massed formation of heavily armoured infantrymen (hoplites) was introduced, quickly to become the chief military arm of the city-state. Hoplites were not poor men—they were responsible for procuring their own equipment—and it was predictable that they would begin to demand a share in the political process of the states they defended with their arms. Peasants and urban proletarians began to be restless, too, and complicating dissensions sometimes arose within the aristocracies themselves.

All this complex history, spread over more than two centuries, has to be sketched in the broadest outlines, not only because of the paucity of evidence but also because of the uneven tempo of development already noted. Colonization was an early by-product, and it is revealing that not all the communities that were most active in this movement went through identical developments at home. It is also noteworthy that neither Athens nor Sparta was a colonizer, though for very different reasons.

Sparta, indeed, took a unique course, founded on helots (serfs). At a time too early to have left any reliable tradition, much of the population of Laconia, in which Sparta was situated, had been reduced to a servile status, not as chattels belonging to individual Spartans but as a subject "nation" compelled by the Spartan state to serve as the labour force. Eventually Sparta conquered the fertile district of Messenia and incorporated its population into the helot system. The effect was, by the end of the 7th century B.C., to shield Sparta against the civil strife of the day, at the price of converting the Spartan citizenry into full-time soldiers, moulded and trained from childhood, while the helots and another untypical group, the free men (known as *perioeci*) who lived in their own small communities, looked after the agriculture, trade, and manu-facture. In one sense, classical Sparta was thus the most complete and exclusive community of the city-states, managed by an assembly of all the citizens, elected executive officials, an elected council of elders, and that curious survival, two hereditary kings.

In time the legend arose that the Spartan system was the creation of one man, the "lawgiver" Lycurgus. Other city-states had their archaic lawgivers, too, some half-legendary, some, like Solon in Athens just after 600 B.C., fully historical figures. The one issue on which all the opponents of aristocratic monopoly could agree was the need for reform and codifi-cation of the law (whereas they diverged sharply on demands for cancella-tion of debts and redistribution of land). Hence, the rise of the lawgivers, who proposed new solutions to old human problems, with no models to follow, and nothing to guide them but public opinion, the collective experience of Greek city-states, and their own powers of rational analy-sis. Unlike the Hebrew lawgiver, they did not even claim divine inspiration.

They could not perform miracles, however. The economic position of the poor remained unrelieved; the aristocracies were themselves divided;

ambitious individuals turned to arms to back demagogic appeals, and struck out for personal power. In consequence, the last century and a half of the archaic period was an age of tyrants, who seized control in many city-states and sought to establish dynasties. The colouring that the word "tyrant" soon acquired conceals the fact that the best of them were able autocrats, not capricious despots. In Athens and elsewhere, the effect, though not necessarily the intent, of their rule was to destroy the old aristocratic monopoly once and for all, to advance the economy, and to incorporate the middle and lower classes much more fully than before into the community. By 500 B.C. the tyrants had been overthrown in all the advanced cities of old Greece (though not in the west), leaving the way open for an approximation of the ideal *polis*.

The end of aristocratic monopoly in politics did not mean the end of elites or of the old aristocratic values. There could be no better example than the poet Pindar, with his glorification of the victorious athlete, his saturation with myth and the divine ancestry of his heroes, his dislike of the new developments in philosophy and rational criticism, and his indifference to the aspirations and achievements of the common people, even to the great struggle for independence against Persia. Yet Pindar was a contemporary of Pericles, and died in 438 B.C. at the age of 80; and he had a busy life keeping up with the commissions of patrons throughout Hellas, among old aristocratic families and also among the tyrants of Sicily and Cyrene. Pericles had a far more aristocratic lineage than Pindar, but he represented those among the elite who accepted the new democratic *polis* and functioned within it. The history of the classical period has as one of its main themes the conflict between the two strains, represented in politics by a struggle between oligarchic and democratic forms of government.

Greek democracy was never egalitarian, even in Athens. "With us," said Pericles, "poverty does not stand in the way; no one is prevented from being of service to the *polis* by the obscurity of his station." Positive steps had been taken to give substance to this boast: office-holders were paid a small wage; most officials were chosen by lot and held their posts for only one year; everyone had the right to attend and speak in the assembly; and thousands of poor men earned their livelihood in the fleet. This was a direct democracy, not a representative system, and the proportion of the citizen body that was directly involved was high (without any parallel in modern history). The incorporation of the peasantry into the community was perhaps its unique and most notable feature. The whole conception was one of amateurism triumphant (as Plato never

31

tired of objecting), and in the end only men with sufficient private means had the leisure and the skills to give the state the leadership it required to function effectively. Athenian democracy lasted for nearly 200 years, and from all that period we know of no more than one or two men in major policy-making roles who came from the poorer classes. Some of the leaders belonged to old aristocratic families; others, such as Cleon, did not. But they all stemmed from the same social classes as the leaders of the oligarchic opposition (practical or theoretical) to democracy. The special virtue of Athens was that equilibrium among the classes was maintained, so that the system worked for a long time. Neither rich nor poor, it should be added, ever questioned the traditional exclusiveness of the *polis* or the right to use the full machinery of government to maintain it, through very strict laws of marriage, for example, which denied legitimacy, and therefore citizenship, to the children of a union between a citizen and a non-citizen. Pericles could associate freely with Aspasia, but could not marry her—not because she was a courtesan, however, but because she was a Milesian.

The most completely excluded were, of course, the slaves, whose numbers rose steadily from the late archaic period in precisely those states that were advancing most rapidly in urbanization and wealth, and whose citizens were moving toward self-rule. The impact of slavery was no simple one. Most free men, both on the land and in the cities, were poor, struggling for a livelihood through their own labour. Slaves impinged on them primarily in a negative way, as the customary labour force, at all levels of skill and responsibility up to managerial posts, in the workshops, the mines, and often the landed estates of the rich. The latter owed their leisure and their domestic comforts to their chattels—that was perfectly obvious and never disputed—and the attitude to work throughout the society was coloured by that fact. In his utopian dreams the little man looked to a time when he, too, could live off slaves. In real life, meanwhile, the majority had little scope for economic advancement, and the economy was kept at a rigidly low level, resting on a still primitive technology dependent on the muscle power of men and animals. Craftsmanship achieved great heights but it could never transcend the fixed limits. Shipping alone made extensive use of a natural source of power, the wind, but land transport and overland trade remained ponderous and prohibitively expensive. The bulk of the products of agriculture and manufacture were consumed locally: such famous exceptions as fine Athenian pottery merely prove the rule. Yet certain necessities for survival in the larger urban centres had to be procured from abroad, sometimes from great distances: metals and slaves above all, and, in many urban centres, grain, the staple food.

The *polis* thus rested on a fragile economic base. In the more backward, non-urban districts, with their traditional social relations and political structures, an equilibrium was easier to maintain. The greater the share of the common people in the community, the greater was the risk of conflict between "the many" and "the few" (to use Greek terminology). Classical Greek history is filled with civil strife. Where it was absent for long stretches of time, as in Athens during its imperial period, that is explained by special circumstances. The persistence of war between city-states was no doubt linked with the same difficulties, but it is not easy to say just how. Wars for territorial acquisition were rare: the Spartan conquest of Messenia and the expansionist moves among western Greeks, especially by Sicilian tyrants, were the main exceptions. A balance-sheet of the economic consequences of war cannot be drawn. On the one side was booty, sometimes a factor of considerable magnitude, especially if there were large numbers of captives who could be either ransomed or sold. On the other side was the waste of resources: crops were destroyed, quantities of equipment were expended unproductively, and there was frequent damage to the walls and buildings of cities.

It seems, then, that no mechanical economic explanation of Greek wars will do. Rather one should look to the chronic insecurity. Once Messenia was completely under control, Sparta made another unsuccessful expansionist effort in Arcadia and then changed policy radically. Thereafter Spartan military activity in the Peloponnese (and occasionally outside the peninsula), which was considerable, was directed to the creation of a network of defensive alliances, ultimately formalized in the Peloponnesian League. Thebes attempted the same with the Boeotian League. Neither grouping produced any direct enrichment of the dominant state, whatever the indirect benefits. Only the Athenians were able to convert a more or less voluntary league into a tribute-paying empire. In the dangerous situation left by the two Persian invasions of Greece, in 490 and 480 B.C., Athens mobilized the maritime city-states into a naval force that cleared the Aegean Sea and more or less eliminated the possibility of a third invasion. Then Athens not only refused to allow any state to withdraw from the league but compelled others to join, levied tribute (which added up to about as much as its own normal internal revenue), and asserted full authority over league affairs (and to some extent over the internal affairs of the tributaries). Other benefits to Athens included assurance, thanks to its navy, of vital corn imports from the Black Sea area, employ-

c

ment for thousands of poor citizens in the navy and on public works, and the consequent strengthening of the democracy in its most advanced, "Periclean" stage. More than 100 city-states were in the empire, encompassing the Greek cities in Asia Minor, the Aegean islands, and the mainland on the north side of the Aegean. The limits of Athenian ambition are indefinable. Military efforts to bring in Boeotia and other districts of mainland Greece were defeated, but there are signs that they would have been renewed if the opportunity had arisen.

By the middle of the 5th century B.C., therefore, much of old Greece was divided into two power blocs (with the western Greeks going their own way, as always). Together they damped down the endemic petty warfare, in their own interest, but between them there was an uneasy truce, punctuated by occasional fighting. This balanced situation came to an end with the outbreak of the Peloponnesian War (between Athens and Sparta) in 431 B.C., which dragged on for 27 years, and which even spread to Sicily in 415 when the Athenians sent a major expeditionary force there, with disastrous results. Sparta and its allies finally defeated Athens in 404 B.C., thanks to financial assistance from Persia in the last years. The Athenian Empire was dissolved, and Sparta then made a short-lived effort to establish a similar one, despite the "independence" slogan under which the war had been fought. But Sparta had neither the manpower nor the institutions with which to do this.

The ensuing half-century was a dreary one. The two power blocs had imposed a considerable measure of peace and, in one sense, a trend toward unification in Hellas. However, they changed nothing structurally or ideologically, and so their disappearance meant an immediate return to old habits, as autonomous city-states fought each other frequently and purposelessly. Sparta, Athens, and Thebes tried in turn to obtain some sort of hegemony, using the device of the league without tribute, and they all failed. Internally there were also signs of a breakdown of the former strong sense of community. The gap between rich and poor widened; their struggles were often violent, bringing about the exile of large numbers; there was greater mobility than before, as men sought their livelihood abroad, many as mercenary soldiers or sailors; responsibility for defence fell more and more on professional military men, breaching (though not totally destroying) the long tradition that this was one of the paramount duties of the citizens as citizens (and of their political leaders as well).

An apt symbol of the change in the tone of city-state life comes from comedy. The Old Comedy of Aristophanes, in the final third of the 5th century B.C., was exuberant and irreverent, taking its themes from current affairs, its characters from real life—Cleon, Socrates, Euripides—and expressing the self-confidence of the Athenian people by the very freedom with which their behaviour and values were mocked in public performances sponsored and financed by the state. A century later, Menander, the great name in New Comedy (known today chiefly through the Latin intermediaries Plautus and Terence), reveals the completion of a change already heralded in the last plays of Aristophanes, written after the Peloponnesian War. All the characters are stereotypes, the themes are personal and individual, never political, and the clever "solutions" are provided by slaves, as if to say that free men can no longer make the community work, but must seek inner peace and express their humanity in their relations within the narrow circle of friends and family.

Yet we must not exaggerate. Athens recovered rapidly from the heavy defeat by Sparta. Such 4th-century statesmen as Eubulus, Demosthenes, and Lycurgus, the latter a member of an ancient aristocratic clan, were able to give the *polis* a sense of direction, and in the end Athens made a stand against Philip and Alexander that revived some of the old spirit of the Persian Wars. Throughout, Athens was singularly free from the horrors of civil war; oligarchy was not a practical issue, although the political philosophers had little good to say for the democratic regime. The intellectual opposition made its home in Athens, where—after a repressive period during the Peloponnesian War, culminating in the trial of Socrates in 399 B.C.—inquiry and discussion were conducted freely and boldly in the schools of philosophy and rhetoric. Pericles had called Athens the "school of Hellas," and it was still that in the 4th century, though in a different and more literal sense. The city continued to attract large numbers of Greeks (and others) who came for profit or pleasure, among them artists, philosophers, and literati, in a flow no other Greek state could match.

Little notice was taken when Philip II became king of Macedon (in northern Greece) in 359 B.C. and rapidly converted his "semi-barbarian" tribes into a powerful, aggressive state. Demosthenes was an isolated voice of warning while Philip approached the Dardanelles, threatening the Athenian corn supply, and also became a factor in Greek interstate politics. Not the least cause of this indifference was Philip's repeated expression of phil-Hellenism coupled with his proposal for a coalition war against Persia. The opportunity for booty and for settlement was attractive. And there were those who said openly that the Greek city-states had themselves proved that they could not live peacefully together without a paramount authority (*hegemon*). Athens and Sparta had both failed in that role; now there was Philip, who promised to preserve city-state autonomy and freedom, to keep the peace, and to lead the crusade against Persia. In the end Demosthenes prevailed, but resistance came too late and Athens received too little support. Philip won a decisive battle at Chaeronea in Boeotia in 338 B.C., organized a "League of the Hellenes" with himself as head and commander-in-chief, and began preparations for the Persian campaign. Upon Philip's assassination in 336 B.C., his young son Alexander took over the programme, and before the latter's death in 323 B.C., the whole of the Persian Empire was in Macedonian hands and Alexander sat on the Persian throne.

The empire was too large to be held as a single unit. After a generation of internecine fighting among Alexander's generals and others, Ptolemy held Egypt, Seleucus a domain based on Syria and extending eastward, and Antigonus the territory of Macedonia and the old Greek world. The dynastic settlement was not altogether stable. The Ptolemies and Seleucids continued to fight for southern Syria; petty kingdoms arose in parts of Asia Minor; Rhodes maintained its autonomy; and some districts of Greece, notably Aetolia and the Peloponnese, kept up a continuous and fairly successful struggle for independence from the Antigonids, as did Epirus (on the modern Greek–Albanian border), where a tribal monarchy grew strong enough to permit King Pyrrhus to invade Italy and Sicily and to score several famous victories in the years 280–275 B.C., before being thrown back. This was Rome's first clash with Greeks other than those who had colonized southern Italy. The western Greeks remained outside the orbit of the new monarchies to the east, apart from diplomatic and commercial contacts, although the trappings of royalty were assumed by tyrants of Syracuse, who now openly called themselves "kings." By the end of the 3rd century, Rome was drawn directly into Greek affairs. A long series of wars followed. Macedonia was made a Roman province in 148 B.C., and the rest fell piecemeal until Egypt was annexed in 30 B.C. That date (or the Battle of Actium in the previous year) is usually taken to mark the end of the Hellenistic age.*

To rule their conquered eastern territories, the Hellenistic monarchs relied on a largely hereditary Macedonian–Greek bureaucracy and standing army composed originally of veterans of the campaigns, a considerable but unknown number of Greek migrants, and the rapidly

---

* Insofar as the "Hellenistic" label is used culturally, not just politically, it can fairly be attached to the Greek part of the Roman Empire long after 30 B.C.

Hellenized local aristocracies. The structure of government was autocratic, as it had been for many centuries in these regions. The cleavage between the ruling class and the rest of the population was very sharp, with little upward mobility, and it was intensified by the linguistic situation. Greek was the language of government and literate culture, but the peasantry clung to their native dialects. The Greek elite lived in cities, some of which were new foundations such as Alexandria, others old Syrian or Persian centres that had been enlarged and transmuted. These cities had many of the trappings of traditional *poleis* in their buildings, their educational and cultural institutions, their officials and administrative bodies, their formal citizenship regulations, and their political rivalries. They also had certain privileges that gave the illusion of autonomy: for example, their immunity from royal claims to ownership of all the soil.

In old Greece, where the population remained fairly homogeneous, the situation was necessarily different, although the Antigonids made the same autocratic claims as the Ptolemies and Seleucids, even introducing into Greece emperor worship, an almost universal characteristic of Hellenistic monarchy. Those city-states that succeeded in holding their independence maintained closer affinity to their past civilization. Yet even there the question arises of the extent to which one may still call them *poleis*, in Aristotle's sense. How much of the old community component was still alive and active? One negative clue is given by the common, though admittedly not universal, practice of charging quite high fees for citizenship. Another is provided by Hellenistic philosophy. Although Plato's Academy and Aristotle's Lyceum continued to flourish in Athens, the founders' successors turned their backs on the *polis*. And the new philosophies—Cynicism, Stoicism, Epicureanism—either were indifferent to politics altogether, holding that the good life was to be found in a spiritual withdrawal from society and its problems, or (notably with Stoicism) discovered in time that kingship was potentially the ideal form of government. The last important Stoic, appropriately enough, was the Roman emperor Marcus Aurelius, who died in A.D. 180.

Obviously the Greek cities inside the eastern territorial empires moved very much further from the genuine *polis*. Almost all that remained of the old community was its exclusiveness. A self-governing community in which a royal garrison is stationed, which is totally deprived of any voice in foreign affairs, in which even membership—that is, the gift of citizenship—is not always in its own control, is a contradiction in terms. Political ambitions and rivalries remained active and intense, but the issues were paltry, and usually came down to nothing more than personal honour and social status. All the important decisions were taken over their heads, by a ruler to whom they erected statues and made sacrifices exactly as did the non-Greek peasants, but much more lavishly. They had the right to petition him but not to debate, let alone to vote on, his edicts.

Yet, despite all the social and political differences, there was a common ruling-class culture, extending from the western Greeks to Egypt, Syria, and the borders of ancient Babylonia, that warrants the single label "Hellenistic." There was a common literary dialect, based on the Athenian one, that virtually obliterated all other Greek dialects. The same subjects were taught in the schools, from the same books, everywhere. Poets, philosophers, and scientists moved freely and were at home wherever they went. Among the heads of the royal Museum (really an institute of advanced study) and Library in Alexandria, founded by the first Ptolemy, were Zenodotus, a lexicographer and textual critic from Ephesus, Apollonius the epic poet, who was born in Egypt, and Eratosthenes of Cyrene, perhaps the greatest pan-Sophist and surely the greatest scientific geographer of the whole period. Other royal libraries were founded in Antioch and Pergamum, and philosophers continued to concentrate in Athens (to the end of antiquity), although at one time Rhodes became the leading Stoic centre. Among the outstanding Rhodian Stoics was Posidonius, who was born in Apamea (Syria) and who for a brief period had Cicero as one of his pupils in Rhodes. Hellenistic religion followed the same pattern. Although the old Olympic gods were still acknowledged, Greek religion was now most vital when it was infused in complicated ways with oriental notions and rituals. Zeus Sabazios was worshipped alongside Athena in her temple in Pergamum. The Egyptian Isis, duly Hellenized, appeared everywhere—under Roman rule, even in Britain.

How far any of this penetrated to the masses, or how rapidly, is not easy to say, because the common people left so few traces in the historical record. If we could answer, we should probably find considerable regional variation. The Egyptian peasantry, for example, appear to have been less affected than the Syrian. Nor was the Hellenization of the upper classes altogether uniform. Judaea, at least, was a major exception. Down to the time of Herod, in the final decades before Christ, there was not a single Greek city in Judaea, and the Hellenization of its aristocracy was but a thin veneer. Even this superficial assimilation aroused fierce popular opposition, mobilized by the Zealots in particular and contributing in the end to the revolt against Rome of A.D. 66–70. In the Jewish Diaspora, on the other hand, the cultural trends were in the reverse direction. Translation of the Old Testament into Greek—the Septuagint—began in Egypt before the middle of the 3rd century B.C., inspired by the inability of the Egyptian Jews to understand Hebrew. It was in Egypt, too, that the most coherent efforts were made to create a philosophical synthesis between Hebrew and Hellenistic Greek conceptions, climaxed in the many works of Philo of Alexandria, commonly known as Philo Judaeus, who was born in the year when Egypt was turned into a Roman province.

Two generations later, Josephus, who had become a Roman citizen living in Rome, published not only his *Jewish War* but also a lengthy *Jewish Antiquities*, written in Greek because its purpose was apologetic. The Hebrews, alone of the eastern peoples, had their own fully recorded account of their past, and had felt no need to produce one for their alien overlords. Not the least interesting consequence of the Graeco-Macedonian conquest was the discovery by the conquered people, no doubt restricted to a small circle, that they, too, had an ancient and honourable history worth preserving in books after the Greek fashion. So, early in the 3rd century B.C., a priest of Bel named Berossus wrote a history of Babylonia in Greek, and dedicated it to the Seleucid king Antiochus I; and an Egyptian high priest, Manetho, did the same for Egyptian history, with a dedication to Ptolemy II. Near the end of the same century, a Roman senator of high aristocratic lineage, Fabius Pictor, wrote the first history of Rome, also in Greek.

As has already been indicated, the Romans had responded to certain aspects of Greek culture at a much earlier date, but it was a less conscious process, often mediated by the Etruscans. The fact that early primitive Rome lived under the influence, and for a period the suzerainty, of more powerful, culturally and socially advanced people, guaranteed that its history could not follow the path of the Greeks, although Rome, too, was a city-state in the strict sense. In addition, there were important geographical differences: Greece had no terrain like the fertile coastal plains of central and southern Italy. But there were also broad similarities for a time, notably in the social conflicts. When Rome, still a tiny agricultural-pastoral community, broke from Etruscan domination just before 500 B.C., the aristocracy took full control of the machinery of government and of the public cults, and a struggle set in at once between the two orders—the closed elite of the patricians, and the plebeians. As in the Greek cities, the plebeians included not only the poor, often debt-ridden, peasants but also richer farmers and pastoralists who found themselves excluded from the ruling class. As in Greece, too, reform and codification of the law were central issues in the conflict, resolved in the first stage by the issue in 450 B.C. of the code known as the Twelve Tables.

Nor could the Latins and other Italic peoples remain at peace, and the league as an instrument of policy quickly made its appearance. The transition from league to empire was imperceptible and undatable. However, when in 343 B.C. the first of three wars broke out against the Samnites, with their main centre at Benevento (north-east of Naples), Rome was an imperial state in fact, if not yet in name, and a constantly expanding one: after the capture of Tarentum, an old Greek foundation, in 272 B.C., three years after Pyrrhus had been driven back to Epirus, all Italy south of the Po was under Roman control, exercised by a subtle network of treaties and nicely calculated statuses that left the "allies" with enough autonomy in return for their surrender of any independent foreign policy and their obligation to supply troops for Rome's wars. There followed the two bitter and exhausting Punic Wars against Carthage, from which Rome emerged with its first provinces (Sicily and Sardinia), some claims in Spain (later turned into a province), and control of the western Mediterranean. In the meantime the Hellenistic world had been weakened by the persistent efforts of important Greek cities and leagues to retain their independence, by wars among ambitious monarchs, and by dynastic disputes over the succession to various thrones. Hardly had Hannibal's army been annihilated in North Africa in 202 B.C., to end the second Punic War, when Rome received appeals to send an army to Greece. The Senate agreed, initiating the long, discontinuous series of wars that brought the Roman Empire to its maximum extent at the death of Trajan. Although henceforth Rome hardly needed any pretext to intervention or aggression, it should be said that the famed policy of "divide and conquer" was as much the doing of the conquered, who regularly divided themselves and then invited Rome to swallow them up. In 146 B.C. both Carthage and Corinth were razed with little justification. The velvet glove had been flung away.

The economic gains to Rome (or at least to some Romans) were enormous. In Italy, and to a lesser extent in Sicily and other conquered territories, much land was confiscated by the state and then leased out to senators and other members of the Roman upper classes, at nominal rents and *de facto* in perpetuity. The foundation was thus laid for the *latifundia* (large estates) that were the main source of large fortunes for the rest of antiquity. A cheap and abundant labour supply also became available through the rapid conquests. As early as the first Punic War, the Romans captured and sold 25,000 inhabitants of Agrigento, for example, and 13,000 from Palermo (where another 14,000 were permitted to ransom themselves). At the end of the third Macedonian War in 169 B.C., 70 towns and villages of Epirus were destroyed and 150,000 inhabitants enslaved. And when the armies left, private slavers moved in, sweeping a great net through Asia Minor and Syria in particular. Nor did pacification mean the end of financial exploitation: booty was then replaced by regular tribute. No province was exempt, but Italy enjoyed almost complete freedom from taxation. There were also substantial profits to be made, by a select circle of Romans, from the collection of the provincial taxes, from public works, and from arms supply, with extortion and corruption no small factor, especially in the provinces. At a lower social level, many thousands—Italian "allies" rather than Roman citizens— earned a good livelihood from the commerce in slaves and other goods that a rapidly growing standard of luxury was demanding. In the provinces themselves, finally, the local upper classes quickly adjusted themselves to the new situation and found in Rome a valuable support for their own economic superiority. Roman imperial rule proved to be a symbiosis between the ruling power and the provincial aristocracy.

The Italian (including the Roman) peasantry have been omitted from this survey for the good reason that as a class they alone seem to have lost rather than gained from the conquests. The Roman legions, like the Greek hoplite armies, were in origin citizen militias, recruited largely from farmers. As the wars were being fought farther and farther from Italy, and for much longer periods, owners of small or medium-sized farms often found it impossible to maintain their holdings. The slave supply had a bad effect on them in two ways: it made their plots attractive acquisitions for the large landowners, and it reduced their opportunity of finding employment or tenancies on the *latifundia* when they returned to civilian life. The result was a steady drift to the cities, especially to Rome, where opportunities for employment were sporadic and insufficient. Precise figures are unobtainable: some historians believe that the population of Rome eventually reached a million, and even if this is an exaggerated estimate, there can be no question but that by the middle of the 2nd century B.C. everything in Roman society was on a scale beyond anything the classical Greeks could have imagined. And the scale went on increasing. In the final struggle between Pompey and Caesar, the former's son enlisted 800 slaves from his shepherds and personal attendants to add to his father's army. Just to feed a city swollen to such proportions was a problem that exercised Rome's rulers to the time of Pope Gregory the Great (A.D. 590–604). Land transport was no better than before, and so

Sicily, then Egypt and North Africa, had to carry the burden of supplying Rome with corn by sea.

Institutionally and ideologically, Rome clung to the city-state during the centuries in which its rule spread to the Atlantic, the Sahara, and western Asia. Before Julius Caesar no one seriously challenged the axiom that provincials were excluded from the ruling power. Even the Italian "allies" did not gain Roman citizenship *en masse* until 88 B.C., and then only by going to war against Rome. Roman internal constitutional and political history may be summed up as a tortuous, continuous struggle to maintain the oligarchic system, the capstone of which was the Senate. Every popular or democratic concession was skilfully turned into yet another support for the oligarchy: witness the tribunes of the plebs. Not even the enfranchisement of the Italians or the strange practice of automatically granting citizenship to the freed slaves of citizens (who became numerous in the 1st century B.C.) provided an effective counterweight. The Roman "mob" became an instrument in the strife within the oligarchy, not a force mobilized in its own interest.* The oligarchy itself was no longer restricted to the ancient patrician families. There was a new nobility, which was also largely hereditary and which found place for wealthy plebeians, thereby depriving the opposition of its potential leadership. In the 100 years before the tribunate of Tiberius Gracchus (133 B.C.), nearly half the consulships were held by 10 families, 80 per cent by 26 families. And ex-consuls normally held the military and provincial commands as well as composing the Senate.

The tenacity of the oligarchic system can be explained by the unimpeded imperial progress of Rome. The subject territories grumbled from time to time when extortion was piled onto normal exploitation, but extended resistance to conquest (as in Spain) or sustained efforts to regain independence were remarkably rare. Between the destruction of Carthage and Corinth in 146 B.C. and the incorporation of Egypt in 30 B.C., Rome added to her provinces the territories of Greece, Tunisia and Libya, Asia Minor, Syria, and France, and controlled still further territory through "client-kings." Yet in the same period the Romans were busy fighting among themselves, beginning with the struggle of the Gracchi against the oligarchy, and followed by the civil wars between the factions of Marius and Sulla, Caesar and Pompey, and finally Octavian (the future emperor Augustus) and Mark Antony. One factor in provincial

---

* The free poor never combined with the slaves. The only large-scale slave revolts in antiquity occurred in Sicily between 140 and 100 B.C. and in Italy in 73–71 B.C. under Spartacus. They were symptomatic, but without lasting effect.

submissiveness, though not its sole explanation, was Roman non-inter-ference in their daily affairs (so long as the taxes were paid and Roman security was not threatened) and, above all, in their culture. Apart from southern Italy, which was rapidly and willingly Latinized, there was no replacement or dilution of the Greek language and religion in the Hellenistic lands, from Cyrenaica and Sicily to Asia Minor and Syria. On the contrary, Hellenism came to Rome: Horace's line, "captive Greece made captive her rude conqueror," has no doubt been quoted too often, but it is no less valid for that. The examples of Plautus and Terence, of Fabius Pictor, of Cicero in Rhodes, of the worship of Isis and other Hellenistic divinities, have already been given. Many educated Romans were henceforth bilingual. Only in the "barbarian" western provinces, Spain and Gaul, did Rome take steps to impose its own cultural identity abroad. The process was slow at first, and was usually set in train not by fiat but by the creation of urban nuclei of Roman veterans, from which civilized life was then diffused—by which they meant settled agriculture, the growth of cities, and the Romanization of language and institutions.

In the end, however, the political balance broke down inside Rome. Basic reforms were imperative, but the nobility refused to recognize the need, and their intransigence increased when men such as the Gracchi tried to force their hand. The citizen militia had to give way to a long-service professional army, who then required land settlements as bonuses on retirement. These changes were achieved, but only through the efforts of powerful politicians and commanders against senatorial opposition. The dispossessed peasantry and urban proletariat could not safely be left to starve. But, unlike the inadequacy of the old-style army, their misery did not immediately threaten the empire, and so, apart from sporadic land-distribution schemes, they had to be content with bread and circuses. That, too, played into the hands of ambitious individuals. Imperceptibly the political conflict that broke surface in the tribunate of Tiberius Gracchus was converted into factional strife, in which the only real issues were the power, honour, and profits of the rival leaders and their followers. Who was to rule Rome? That became the central question, though every-one denied it. Sulla abdicated, Pompey did not know what to do with the paramount position in the state when he had it, and Julius Caesar was assassinated. A century of bloodshed, extortion, conspiracy, and double-dealing went by before the permanent answer was found in the imperial regime created by Augustus. Honest men were voices in the wilderness. Cicero was put to death, though his strength lay only in his tongue and his pen. Shakespeare's *Julius Caesar* must not mislead us. The *libertas* of the assassins was merely the liberty of the old oligarchy to retain, and to enrich itself through, its monopoly of power. In 56 B.C. the Senate passed a special decree permitting Brutus, in violation of the law, to lend a large sum to the city of Salamis in Cyprus at 48 per cent compound interest. Salamis was then under the official protection of Brutus and his uncle, Cato the Younger.

To judge Caesar's long-range aims from the unsettled two years of his dictatorship would be folly. Nevertheless, it seems safe to assert that he had no intention of abdicating and that he had a vision of an empire in which Rome and Italy would no longer rule the rest. Augustus learned the lesson from his great-uncle's assassination. He, too, saw himself as a monarch, kept careful control of the armies, and worked all his life to create a hereditary dynasty. But he also went to great lengths to preserve the dignity and privileges of the Italian aristocracy and middle class, giving the "Senate and people" the opportunity in 27 B.C. to provide a constitutional basis for his power, and avoiding the hated titles of "king" and "dictator." Instead, he was *princeps* ("first citizen" is a rough approximation), *imperator* (commander), and, by a curious twist, Caesar. So were his successors.*

Genuine republican sentiment had been effectively destroyed by the endless civil wars. The smoothness with which Tiberius succeeded Augustus to the throne in A.D. 14 and the absence of republican moves after the suicide of Nero in A.D. 68 are proof enough. But the upper classes required the kind of treatment Augustus gave them: a share in the offices of government, a monopoly of privilege, protection of their wealth and opportunities to increase it, without any real authority. The difference between "good" and "bad" emperors—to descend for a moment to that tiresome but familiar terminology—was one of form rather than substance. From Augustus onward, every emperor was an absolute monarch. The Hellenistic world spontaneously offered the traditional ruler cult, and, although its diffusion to Italy and the west was resisted, it spread nonetheless as worship of the emperor's *genius* or *daemon* rather than of his person, and the Senate solemnly deified each emperor on his death (including Julius Caesar but excluding the "bad" ones). Open political debate was ended; it was replaced by conspiracies, real or imaginary, which became a structural element in Roman imperial history during

---

* One more historical convention must be noted. The period to the Battle of Actium is known as the Republic, the subsequent period as the Empire. The latter is then customarily divided at the reign of Diocletian (A.D. 284–305) into the Early and Late Empire, or the Principate and the Dominate (in French, the Haut and Bas Empire).

Augustus's reign. Not infrequently they originated within the emperor's own household.

Yet the adulation of Augustus by Virgil and other writers had its justification. The *pax romana* was a reality. Apart from the Jews there was no mass resistance or rebellion. There was a considerable re-settlement on the land. The undeveloped western regions were brought under cultivation and were urbanized on a scale still evident today in the Roman ruins in Provence and North Africa. The Augustan insistence on Italian primacy rapidly gave way. Citizenship grants to provincials were increasingly frequent; men of the upper classes, whether of old Roman veteran or of native ancestry, found their way into the imperial service and a few into the Senate. In the 1st century A.D. the western provinces produced some of the greatest Latin writers—Martial, Quintilian, Seneca and his nephew Lucan, perhaps Tacitus—and in the next century two emperors, Trajan and Antoninus Pius.

One question, however, remained open. Where did the Roman Empire end? Outside it at Augustus's death were Britain, continental Europe beyond the Rhine and the Danube, bits of Africa north of the Sahara, Arabia, and most of Asia. Augustus left behind a document advising his successors that the empire had reached its natural limits, a conclusion he presumably drew after his costly efforts to move one boundary from the Rhine to the Elbe had been smashed in the Teutoburg Forest in A.D. 9. It was impossible advice. So long as there were bordering inhabited lands, there would be war, and Rome would continue to conquer when it could, as it did at intervals until the death of Trajan. Then it could do so no longer, and Augustus seems to have had an early glimpse of the critical flaw when he stabilized the army at about 300,000 men, where it remained until Diocletian. Gibbon noticed that this figure was equalled by Louis XIV, "whose kingdom," as he said, "was confined within a single province of the Roman Empire." The static economy could support no more. This was still fundamentally a peasant society, which had made little technological advance in production or transport, and in which the tax burden lay on the poorest classes, while the costs of government and the good life kept going up.

No contemporary would have made such an analysis, of course, and only in Utopia could remedies have been found. The world seemed to have reached a permanent state of equilibrium, in which conspiracies and famines were unfortunate but momentary disruptions. The gloomy voices of Tacitus, Juvenal, and a few Stoics were not widely echoed. After the assassination of Domitian (the third emperor to be violently removed) in A.D. 96, the new regime introduced Gibbon's golden age of the Antonines. Eternal Rome now seemed a reality. Not even the revival, after nearly three centuries, of threatening Germanic activity on the northern frontiers looked too foreboding, although Marcus Aurelius had to devote all his energies to repelling them. And no one noticed, at a time when higher education was flourishing, when schools of rhetoric and philosophy were established in all the main centres and in many small towns, when the emperors and the aristocracy built great theatres and amphitheatres and patronized the arts and learning, that intellectual and cultural creativity had dried up. Everywhere, apart from some of the sciences—astronomy and mathematics, physics and medicine—there was a sterile academicism. After Tacitus, Plutarch, and Juvenal there was only an occasional exception, such as the Greek satirist Lucian or the Latin historian Ammianus Marcellinus. The future lay with neo-Platonism and Christian theology, and it is not irrelevant that their concern was with the souls of men in eternity. With the death of Marcus Aurelius in A.D. 180 the collapse began. The throne rapidly changed hands by purchase or by murder. After a period of relative stability under the North African dynasty of the Severi, which rested openly on the armies, there came a 50-year stretch during which 20 emperors were formally sanctioned by the Senate and as many more claimed the throne. Barbarian incursions grew heavier and more frequent. Much arable land was deserted, as peasants fled or revolted. Eventually Diocletian and Constantine pulled the empire together, but the steps they were compelled to take in order to do so all pointed ahead to the Middle Ages and Byzantium. The peasants were bound to the soil; other occupations and statuses were made hereditary. The establishment of the new eastern capital at Constantinople was the beginning of the division of the Empire into eastern and western halves. The conversion of Constantine to Christianity paved the way for the conversion of the whole empire. But the myth of eternal Rome stood fast. When the Visigoth Alaric sacked the city in A.D. 410, St Jerome in Bethlehem added these words to the *Commentaries on Ezekiel* he was then writing: ". . . the brightest light of the whole world was extinguished . . . the Roman Empire was deprived of its head . . . to speak more correctly, the whole world perished in one city. . . ."

Bibliography

A. ANDREWES, *The Greeks* (London 1967); *The Greek Tyrants* (London 1956).

E. BADIAN, *Roman Imperialism in the Late Republic* (Oxford 1968).

JOHN BOARDMAN, *The Greeks Overseas* (paperback: London 1964).

P. A. BRUNT, *Social Conflicts in the Roman Republic* (London 1971).

J. CARCOPINO, *Daily Life in Ancient Rome*, trans. by E. O. Lorimer (London 1941; paperback: London 1956).

J. M. COOK, *The Greeks in Ionia and the East* (London 1962).

J. A. CROOK, *Law and Life of Rome* (London 1967).

M. I. FINLEY, *The Ancient Greeks* (London 1963; paperback: London 1966); *Ancient Sicily* (London 1968); *The World of Odysseus* (London 1956; paperback, rev. edn: London 1967).

W. G. FORREST, *A History of Sparta 950–192 B.C.* (London 1968).

A. H. M. JONES, *Constantine and the Conversion of Europe* (London 1948).

F. MILLAR, *The Roman Empire and Its Neighbours* (London 1967).

C. MOSSÉ, *The Ancient World at Work*, trans. by Janet Lloyd (London 1969).

M. ROSTOVTZEFF, *Rome*, ed. by E. J. Bickerman (paperback: London 1965).

R. SYME, *The Roman Revolution* (Oxford 1956).

W. W. TARN and G. T. GRIFFITH, *Hellenistic Civilization*, 3rd edn (London 1952).

V. TCHERIKOVER, *Hellenistic Civilization and the Jews*, trans. by S. Applebaum (Philadelphia 1959).

CHAPTER 2

Language and Myth

Anthony Thorlby[*]

Language is the medium of man's civilized life. It "contains," therefore, the problems and the history of his attempts at civilized living: his attempts to achieve social order, to understand himself, and to depict the way self relates to the society of others—to men, to gods, and to things. This relationship, which is intangible and immeasurable, which is daily experienced but which no science can completely define, is the sphere of literature (more even than of the other arts), the sphere of imagination and belief, and of that meditation of the mind upon itself that has always been a major concern of philosophy.

This is not the place to do more than remind ourselves of the power that language has had since the earliest times: in magic, in religion, in politics. The Sophists, who dominated Greek education during the 5th century B.C., claimed that mastery of language, of the style in which a view is expressed and argued, is the key to its truth; and by "truth" they generally meant effectiveness in society. Their success was due to the unsettling of ancient religious and moral certainties under the impact of agnosticism, which itself had grown out of early speculation in physics. Plato owes much of his inspiration to his alarm at the dangers implied by a reduction of truth to a technique of words; and part of his notorious suspicion of literature stems from this. Socrates himself was misunderstood by some as being a Sophist, though he argued against them (only seeming thereby to argue "like" them), and was surely a man devoted to a truth that was a way of life rather than a form of words. How often this dispute about language has been repeated down the centuries: that education contributes to scepticism and to the disruption of the social order, perhaps by men who have made a business out of dealing with words, who are in effect mercenaries serving this or that vested interest, not least—as Socrates ironically made clear—their own.

[*] Professor of Comparative Literature, University of Sussex.

The interest of language for these volumes varies from century to century, and chapters on primarily linguistic matters will be given a different place accordingly. At no time has this interest been stronger than in the present, when a combination of academic and social circumstances has rejuvenated philology to form the new science of semantics. On occasions when semantic theory has acquired notions (and, just occasionally, some actual evidence) from cybernetics, such questions as whether a poem can be written by a computer even make headline news. Unfortunately, in the heat of polemical debate, just as much as in the dreary details of semantic research, the only civilized answer is lost sight of: namely, that no computer can *read* a poem in any human sense. That is to say, it cannot distinguish which, among the million variant lines it can produce in one minute, is really the best. And this is because what "the best" is, can only be a matter of personal experience, of taste nurtured within as well as a situation encountered from without—in a word, a matter of civilization.

Civilization is not assumed, in these volumes, to be equatable with a given state of society, past, present, or to come. Literature undoubtedly "reflects" society, but the interest it holds for us depends also on the civility of the literary medium, the quality of experience that the language conveys. The question, then, is not simply how "true" the reflection is, but how civilized. Words are chosen and enjoyed in works of literature. Doubtless the choice and enjoyment are to some extent a matter of fashion and individual taste. (Here, social influences are likely to be strong, and we shall often refer to them.) But deeper in the structure of language lies a given potential: something, however, that gives neither a simple rule nor yet arbitrary freedom about what makes sense and what does not; something that has been recognized from the earliest times as a necessary or binding quality, akin to that of religion (Lat. *religare*, to bind);* something that defies adequate explanation. For explanations have to be written in language, and cannot fully grasp themselves.

Explanations are still searched for, of course, and in rather differing terms on either side of the Atlantic, on either side of the Iron Curtain—indeed, on either side of the English Channel. The reason for this wide range of approaches lies in the nature of the subject itself. Words may be thought of as spoken or written, as parts of sentences and thoughts, or as noises made by men. Apart from these differences, there are others of a

---

* Cicero takes a more literary view of the etymology of *religio*, deriving it from *relegere* (to read over again); but the compulsion to "read again" points no less clearly to the spiritual power of words.

largely historical kind, caused by variations between one age and another, and one culture and another, in the assumptions and methods of study. Thus, the philology of ancient Hebrew and its literature was traditionally a sacred matter; so also was the linguistic research of Arab scholars in the Middle Ages, whose task was to preserve the purity of the language of the Koran which had to be interpreted to non-Arabic-speaking believers but was not allowed to be translated. Aristotle, on the other hand, approached language from the point of view of style—the question of what type of expression is *proper* to the occasion*—and also from the point of view of logic. The early Christian writers confronted a new conflict between the demands of sacred and profane languages, and repeatedly during the centuries that followed, even down to modern times, writers of all kinds have been conscious of similar conflicts between usage and tradition, private preference and public requirements, national identity and supra-national norms.

These, then, are the aspects of language study that will receive most attention here. It would be inappropriate to try to explore also the more modern, scientific approaches to language. Although no infallible distinction can be drawn at any period between philology that helps us to understand literature and philology that does not, a whole family of kindred subjects—such as literary history and criticism, semantics and linguistics, language philosophy and language psychology—have broken away in recent times from the single family name that once seemed capable of uniting our entire understanding of human culture: *philologia*, a concept that embraced generally the study of words, the study of texts, the love of learning. One of the last typical philologists to believe that linguistics and literary history, etymology and textual appreciation, form an ideal whole, and that "in all word-histories there is the possibility of recognizing the signs of a people at work, culturally and psychologically," was Leo Spitzer.[1] It should perhaps be added that he was besides a German and a "romantic" (the significance of which will be discussed later), who also believed in such things as the "soul" of a nation and the "spirit" of an epoch, and yet also in the unique inwardness of a literary experience.

This is not to say that the 20th century has shown less interest in lan-

---

* This question was important also, of course, for Cicero and subsequent schools of classical "good writing." It is discussed in Ch. 5, "The Latin Language," and Ch. 20, "The Two Cities: Christian and Pagan Literary Styles in Rome"; in Volume II in chapters such as "The Romance Languages" and "Medieval Rhetoric"; in Volume III in the Preface and in "The Grand Style" and "Humanism and Language"; and in Volume IV in "Language and the Intellectual in Italy" and "The Development of German Classical Style."

guage: on the contrary, it has shown more—but not always in literature as the most significant example of the way words speak to us. The study of language to which Claude Lévi-Strauss has given such remarkable impetus in Paris since the war[2] is for him the key not to literary understanding but to social science. Words are only one instance of communication by signs, and semiology is only one way of studying the structures of human existence, and all phenomena are grounded in structures. It is tempting to regard this preparedness to believe in a universal science, in the primacy of rational models, as being characteristically French. Certainly, some of Lévi-Strauss's assumptions about language as signs can be traced back to Saussure and, through him, back even to Condillac and the aspirations of the Enlightenment; and ultimately, of course, this confidence in an intellectually accessible key or plan, to which the mere material of the world is a secondary, almost superfluous, addition *in extenso*, has been associated (in the minds of outsiders, at least) with Cartesian rationalism and the dominance of French neo-classical culture.

Ferdinand de Saussure (1857–1913) introduced a quite new sense of method into the then German-dominated field of philology, and by "method" he meant nothing so imaginatively interesting as etymology, but a system as abstract as algebra or geometry. One of his favourite metaphors for language was a game of chess, in which the actual appearance of the pieces is not important, but only their functional relationships.[3] Saussure relates words not to things but to concepts, with the result that the relationship between *le signifiant* and *le signifié*, as he called the two faces of a language sign, is declared to be both arbitrary and indissoluble. This has important consequences for the sociological aspects of language study in which Saussure was, strange though it may appear, particularly interested, influenced no doubt by his great contemporary, the sociologist Durkheim. For Saussure's theory recognizes both that language is socially determined and that it is an autonomous institution with rights of its own. The logic of his categories is indisputable. What is less clear in Saussure's (never completed) system is the point where the relationship of a word to a concept meets the relationship of words to situations or things. Here the clarity of his analytical distinctions gives the impression that these two relationships are identical, but in fact no such identity has been established.* Again it is hard not to see from abroad a reflection here of a recurrent paradox in French political life: its passion for social

---

* Saussure introduces a special term to explain why words have a particular "value" when used in particular situations. This conception of value is not grounded simply in fact nor in logic, but seems to arise ultimately from a poetic or creative intuition.

liberty and its regard for rational order as an absolute, a fusion (or confusion) of the sovereign *peuple* with a sovereign ruler, in the manner represented by more than one autocrat in French history, and bequeathed to Europe in the most beguiling theoretical form by J. J. Rousseau. A romantic might be forgiven for seeing a symbol of the "soul" of a nation in Saussure's style, which is full of emotive—one might almost say poetic—metaphors to adumbrate a quite rationalistic system of linguistics. It was, significantly, a French writer, Mme de Staël, who once likened the use of rational speech to the use of alcohol. (Her analogy was, admittedly, meant to suggest that the way French intellectuals use their language is particularly artistic, but it also makes their art sound a particularly intoxicating one.)

> Language in France is not simply what it is elsewhere, a means of communicating ideas, feelings, and practical matters, but rather an instrument that it is a pleasure to play and that stimulates the wits [*ranime les esprits*], in the same way that music does for some nations and alcohol for others.*

Saussure was Franco-Swiss, though he taught for a decade in Paris and had studied in Germany—circumstances comparable with those of Mme de Staël, as well as with those of Rousseau. We may also note that the decisive period of inspiration in Descartes' life came while he, too, was abroad, and that his interest in and influence on the question of language was considerable. It is tempting to generalize, to the extent of formulating what is possibly no more than a truism: namely, that mental insight, like actual seeing, is much dependent on where one stands and how much one has seen—on what might be called perspective. Languages and local idioms are just as much types of mental perspective as are more specific "forms" of expression in literature or philosophy. Wilhelm von Humboldt was indicating this when he wrote: "Each language draws a magic circle around the people to whom it belongs, a circle from which there is no escape except by stepping out of it into another."[4] The importance of a second language during the formative period of the national literatures of Europe—apart from its educational importance in the lives of countless generations of civilized men—will be made repeatedly apparent in subsequent chapters of these volumes. Throughout large parts of Europe and most centuries of the Christian era, this language was Latin; but at later

---

* The relationship of an idea to the language in which it is expressed can be seen in even the harmless-looking phrase *ranime les esprits*. "*Les esprits*" immediately suggests a social context, the "minds" of a group talking together, and perhaps all (French) people's minds. "*Ranime*" means literally "revive," not merely in the English sense of bringing fresh life to a wilting body, but also in the sense of rousing the spirit.

periods and owing to different historical and national conditions, French or German or some other language played this role; for educated Romans themselves, the other language was, of course, Greek. Most recently, deliberate experiments in stepping out of the "magic circle" have been made by writers who have felt from within the decline or inadequacy of their native idiom, generally under the pressure of such social circumstances as war or exile, or for more complex sociological reasons—for instance, in the United States (these questions are raised again in Volume VI).

Preoccupation with the medium of expression has, then, increased in modern times, not only with regard to language but in the other arts besides, and not only among scholars and thinkers but also among creative writers. Some of them have developed a virtually mystical reverence for the form itself of language, which they have felt to be more real than anything that words refer to in the world.* This phenomenological tendency is perhaps the only one that could be said to give a semblance of unity to the mass of literary criticism in various countries that has broken away from earlier philological and historical approaches to literature. That the structure of a literary work presents an independent reality would be as acceptable a premise to many French "structuralists" as it would to Anglo-Saxon critics, who have long pursued image-analysis and textual "close-reading." A sense of national difference arises mainly from the more serious philosophical, even scientific, character of French research, especially that which has felt the influence of Gaston Bachelard (1884–1962), who was as interested in physics and psycho-analysis as in poetry. A similar difference of tone has marked also the manner in which philosophers on both sides of the channel have in recent decades tackled fundamental problems regarding the status of words. A socially relaxed, almost buoyant, unconcern has characterized British scepticism about the possibility of making universally binding statements about reality. A profounder, but creative and often potentially revolutionary, doubt has accompanied European uncertainties about the adequacy of conventional ways of conceptualizing and linguistically shaping the world.

The most striking example of the way national and ideological factors can influence the study of language may be seen in the Soviet Union. Just as artists and thinkers in the West have been castigated by Marxists for their preoccupation with the form itself of art or thought (instead of with social reality), so structuralism in linguistics and literary criticism

* See, in this connection, Volume V, "The Cult of Art."

was for a long period virtually banned in communist countries, where it was loosely associated with "Americanism" until about the time of Stalin's death. Various other factors have contributed to a growing interest in Western methods since then, chief among them being the realization that a systematic theory of the relationship of words to meaning is important for applied sciences such as electronic communication, machine translation, and so on. In addition, the "correct" ideological attitude toward language was itself not clear. The philologist who reigned supreme during most of Stalin's era, Nikolay Marr, developed various now discredited approaches to language, based on assumptions such as, for instance, that all languages derive from four basic elements, that national idioms have no particular importance and do not need to be compared, and that problems of communication and expression are merely marginal to non-linguistic sociological facts. In 1950 a scholarly dispute began when a Caucasian philologist attacked Marr on a number of etymological questions, and—for reasons that have remained unclear— gained Stalin's support.* The dispute, which reached the pages of *Pravda,* ended in the deposition of Marr and his school after personal intervention by Stalin, who laid down the doctrine that language must be regarded not as a mere fabrication of the social superstructure but as an essential product, inseparable from the whole range of human activity from the economic base to the heights of ideology. It should be added that Marxist scholars, though well able to pick up the threads of structural methods from abroad as well as from their own Russian school—the so-called Kazan circle at the beginning of the century (who were, broadly speaking, Saussurians)—continue to make censorious (or self-protective) comments about the inherent "idealism" of Western research. The criticism might be said to strike home to the extent to which, say, Naom Chomsky has himself related his work to the search for the "inner form" of language, in which so typical an idealist thinker as Humboldt believed: and to the extent also to which the criticism is relevant to the admittedly limited sphere within which Professor Chomsky is working. Like many another Marxist critique, it points more clearly to what has been neglected than to what should be achieved, to what may be wrong rather than what will be right. "At a given moment," wrote Marx, "individuals will gain control of this inherited product [the language of civilization] as of other products."[5] What they will do with this control, except continue to exercise it, he made less clear. The notion of man taking rational control of

* Alexander Solzhenitsyn speculates on them in his novel *The First Circle.*

society appears to be a self-evident good in the light of Marx's philosophical assumptions.

The origin of language has been the subject of speculation and myth since the earliest times. The Greek historian Herodotus (*c.* 484–425 B.C.) tells a story of an Egyptian king who ordered two babies to be kept in isolation because he was curious to know what language they would speak spontaneously. The question was formulated also by ancient philosophers—perhaps as early as Pythagoras (*c.* 572–497)—in terms of whether there is a necessary or merely an accidental connection between words and meanings. Heraclitus (*c.* 500) appears to have affirmed some principle of "identity" in this as in so many other ultimately metaphysical questions— leaving, with what is said to have been aristocratic disdain, philosophers both ancient and modern uncertain what he meant. His influence was enormous, and it is probable that he helped to stimulate the interest that was shown throughout the 5th century B.C. (and for many centuries after that) in etymology, the hidden meanings of myth, and the like; much of it rested on explicitly religious beliefs that speech must be of divine origin. There were, of course, also scientific atheists such as Democritus (*c.* 450), who denied this on the grounds that linguistic forms are subject to change and irregularities. The fickle character of the Homeric gods might suggest to us now rather that they *were* responsible for man's imperfect instrument! But the desire of serious thinkers at that time to disentangle a rational ideal of truth from the obscurities of religious myth is well known. Plato tried to rescue what he could of the ancient metaphysics while also deflecting the objections of the new scientists. Thus, he supported Heraclitus's general notion that the structure of language corresponds to human comprehension of things, but he did so by directing all philosophical inquiry into a new path. Cratylus, in the Platonic dialogue bearing his name, is a simple supporter of Heraclitus, and he is opposed by the sceptical Hermogenes. The effect of Socrates' attempt to achieve a compromise is to shift the argument away from the question of whether there is a literal correlation of word-sounds to things, onto the familiar Platonic ground where a more subtle, ideal relationship is sought between objects and ideas. Here the same logical principles are valid for linguistic structure as for the process of thought.

The idea that "the word" must be of divine origin continued to be of interest particularly to theologians up until the 18th century; then it was challenged once again by more scientific minds, who produced rationalistic, but scarcely less speculative, theories about the way in which early men themselves had invented language. Moreover, as the dominance of neo-classical culture waned, the languages of "primary" importance were no longer considered to be exclusively Latin and Greek. The scientific curiosity of the Enlightenment resulted in the collection of data about hundreds of other languages, among them Sanskrit, the ancient (literary) language of India. Classical scholars had never succeeded in establishing satisfactorily the connections between the apparently related languages of Europe. One of the first Sanskrit scholars, William Jones (1746–94), was able to assert that Sanskrit, Greek, Latin, Gothic, and Celtic derived from a common language now no longer in existence. The significance of his discovery was not at first widely appreciated, partly for socio-historical reasons (which will be mentioned presently) and partly for philosophical ones. The philosophical importance of genetic, comparative, and above all historical, methods of study had first to be decided (and not only with regard to language). The major concern of the age remained where it had been for centuries: with the logic of grammar. Perhaps the greatest expression of this concern was the *Grammaire générale et raisonnée*, the result of work by the grammarian-philosophers of Port Royal. Because logic is universal and common to all mankind, their argument ran, the essential structure of all possible languages in the world should obviously be reducible to a single grammatical theory. Philosophical grammars of this kind were in demand all over Europe in their day. James Harris's *Hermes, or a Philosophical Inquiry Concerning Language and Universal Grammar* (1751) went through five editions by 1754, and was translated into German and French.

Broadly speaking, then, the mark originally made by Plato on the subject of language (as part of his approach to epistemology as a whole) may be said to have been almost indelible. The question of its origin was irrelevant to the question of the logic of language. The lines of this distinction became blurred again only in the heyday of metaphysical speculation that developed toward the close of the 18th century in Germany. From that romantic age onward, various attempts have been made to recast the basic assumptions and logic of Plato's model of the mind's situation in the world. This model is commonly interpreted as meaning that the universe itself constitutes not a unity but a duality, in which appearance must be distinguished from reality, and things from concepts. Christianity naturally tended to reinforce a doctrine that taught that the relationship of a human word to timeless and unchanging truth can at best be symbolic, i.e. understood in a quite different way from that in which mere factual information is acquired. (Divine revelation could then, of course, be regarded as giving to men just this symbolic "best"—the most that, in their earthly circumstances, they could expect.) The validity of this model came to be challenged in practice by the desire of scientists not merely to contemplate truth as on a distant, ideal shore, but to seize and act upon it. And inevitably the model came to be challenged also in theory by thinkers who reacted in ever more romantic, and ultimately irrational-istic, ways to the revolutionary aspirations of the age of reason. Marxism has claimed to be the chief heir to the scientific materialism of the En-lightenment; and in looking forward to a total possession by the mind of its environment, it posits not only a logical unity of language and thought, but a dialectical process of *rapprochement* to unite reality and mental reflection. At the same time, however, a quite different conception of the unity of being has haunted the modern European mind, filling it no less with feelings of alienation in the present, but pointing not forward but backward to the distant past, to pre-Socratic metaphysics and myth, for an understanding of the problem. This has involved rejection of the Platonic-Christian structure of values and renewed speculation on the primal acts of human consciousness, and thus on the origin and function of language.

At the opposite ideological extreme from the Marxist attack on formal-ism, therefore, we may refer to a defence of one of the first poets to be obviously obsessed with the sources and process of verbal creation: Heidegger's praise of the poetry of Hölderlin. No poet has more passion-ately identified the secret of poetic language with the secret of civilization; and for Hölderlin the ideal civilization was that of ancient Greece. Heidegger says of him what Charles Williams said of Hölderlin's exact contemporary, Wordsworth—that essentially his work is "poetry writing poetry"; and the same could be said of many romantic poets.* For, whatever social reasons may be adduced for the self-consciousness of the moderns, their inwardness has often led them to identify in various ways the mystery of words with the mystery of existence, and to blur the boundary between self and world. Thus, Hölderlin writes of the gift of language with a kind of mystic awe:

> To man, godlike, has been given higher power to command and
> to accomplish, and therefore has language, most dangerous of
> possessions, been given to man, so that creating, destroying, and
> perishing, and returning to the ever-living, to the mistress and

---

* See, in this context, Volume IV, "Leopardi, Hölderlin, and the Post-Revolutionary Crisis." The question of phil-Hellenism is introduced in the concluding chapter of this volume.

> mother, he may affirm what he is—that he has inherited, learned
> from thee, thy most divine possession, all-preserving love.[6]

Hölderlin's "mistress and mother" is the fertile womb not only of love but of all being, of which nature is the outward manifestation and poetry the authoritative voice. His ultimate symbol of that "return" was Empedocles casting himself into Mount Etna, and his own path led toward madness. To appreciate Hölderlin's view of language, we need only compare it with that of a typical rationalist such as Locke. Locke's explanation of the power of words (in the *Essay Concerning Human Understanding*) is all in terms of "common use" and "the common sense of that country [which] applies them." And this clearly social explanation is followed by many 18th-century writers: by Hume, for instance, who likewise declares that "languages are gradually establish'd by human conventions."[7] The doom of such enlightened theories of language is always to prove in the end more attractive to pedants than to poets. How many grammarians, school-masters, and clerics of that and almost every other age have busied themselves with defining rules for the "correct" use of words! For if, as they reassured themselves by learned references to Aristotle, Horace, and Quintilian, the meaning of words is determined "only by institution . . . that is, convention or agreement,"[8] then it is but a short step from the convention that Locke and Hume supposed to be freely established, to the establishment of actual institutions, academies, and the like, to regulate the use of language.* Such academies were a prominent feature of neo-classical culture throughout Europe.

Some further points may be mentioned in connection with Hölderlin's attitude to language and the philosophical significance that this had for Heidegger. First, Hölderlin was a student friend of Hegel's, in whose mind idealist metaphysics were to fuse with a form of historical generalization in a way that has since been of enormous consequence for European civilization; Heidegger's own philosophy also owes much to Hegel. Second, Hölderlin grew up under the influence of a national poetic revival that encouraged mystical notions both about what poetry is and about what a nation is. Third, this atmosphere, which prevailed not only in Germany but also in Scandinavia and induced a sense of Nordic culture to rival the heritage of classical antiquity, led to an interest in "non-classical" philology: in the origins and structure of Europe's national languages and also in their long-neglected literature, especially their primitive ballads and sagas. More important still, it led to a new concep-

---

* The political and social importance of the desire to regulate language is discussed also in
Volume II, "The Romance Languages."

tion of philology, which had for centuries been based on the grammar and etymology of Greek and Latin. To call the foundation of modern philology by such men as Rask and Grimm, Bopp and Schleicher, "romantic" would perhaps be misleading, but a number of facts about them are suggestive. They were all Germans or Danes. They conceived of language as a kind of organism—Grimm had a great amateur interest in botany—whose growth they expected to follow an ideal pattern of evolution. They looked not only to the past but also to the East for the source from which all European culture had grown, thereby going beyond the primacy of classical antiquity. (Rasmus Kristian Rask actually travelled to India; the influence of the East on the imagination of many writers of the romantic generation in Germany was considerable; others besides philologists regarded Europe as part of a larger culture, which they often called *Indo-Germanic* and half believed to be global; Hölderlin, for instance, hails the light that shone on ancient Greece as belonging to "Asia"; and Schopenhauer finds the primal model of mankind's spiritual experience, with which he explains the kinship of all art and religion, in Hindu mysticism.) Finally, they sought the secret of language through the study neither of social conventions nor of classical grammar, but of sounds and their morphology. Grimm associated his famous "law," which may be considered typical of the way 19th-century scholars explained the genealogy of the Indo-European language in terms of sound-shifts, with the psychology of his nation, the progressive desire for liberty found among the Germans: "When quiet and morality returned, the sounds remained constant, and it may be reckoned as evidence of the superior gentleness and moderation of the Gothic, Saxon, and Scandinavian tribes that they contented themselves with the first sound-shift, while the wilder force of the High Germans was impelled to the second one."[9]

This kind of romantic philology scarcely survived into the 20th century (except as a schoolroom exercise). On the one hand it was defeated by what Otto Jespersen used to call "the many-sidedness of linguistic life," its simple inconsistencies and arbitrariness, and on the other hand it was replaced by some of the more rigorous efforts at a science of linguistics that have already been mentioned. A metaphysical interest in the creative function of language has been preserved mainly by existentialist philosophers—and also, of course, by creative writers themselves. Thus, Nietzsche, for instance, shares Hölderlin's belief in the mysterious power of words, together with his conviction that this power declined at some early period of Greek culture. Heidegger similarly speculates on whether the Western mind has not repeatedly misunderstood its relationship to reality for over 2000 years. It has done this, apparently, because its sense of language led it to separate itself from being, thus inducing feelings of spiritual exile or alienation, but also reducing the external world to the status of a mere object. The original meanings of Greek words,[10] he believes, were rich in intuitions of the one, physical-metaphysical process of life. These intuitions he finds "intact" in the (fragmentary) writings that survive from the period before Socrates and Plato. His interpretation of this period springs from a belief, which Nietzsche once formulated: "There must have been a time when man's religious, aesthetic, and moral perceptions were at one."[11] Since that time, civilization has been the story of a progressive division of man's spirit against its whole and living self; in the process there has been much gain in knowledge, but in the outcome a loss of felt value in the world.* This is not to say that division, dialectic, indeed conflict, do not lie in the nature of existence; but Western man has misunderstood—so existentialists generally argue—the meaning of this situation. Heidegger quotes Heraclitus:

> Conflict is for all [that exists] the creator that causes it to emerge, and also the dominant preserver. For it makes some to appear as gods, others as men; it creates some as slaves, others as free men. (Fragment 53)

Our conventional thought process, arising from our notion of language, makes us think that the mind "merely assaults something that is already there." In fact, words, no less than deeds, "project and develop what had hitherto been unheard of, unsaid, and unthought. The battle is then sustained by the creators, poets, thinkers, statesmen. Against the overwhelming chaos they set the barrier of their work, and in their work they capture the world thus opened up. . . . This world-building is history in the authentic sense."[12]

The direction of Heidegger's thought is paradoxical—to say nothing of its obscurities—because it tries to develop systematically the insight that language does not have a systematic relationship to reality, but rather a creative (or, as he would say, a "revelatory") one. The nuances of his interpretation of what language "does" are further dependent upon his use of German, of which he claims that it parallels Greek "in regard to its possibilities for thought, [being] at once the most powerful and most

---

* The greater concreteness of Greek and Latin, which both Nietzsche and Heidegger admire and appeal to in order to correct what they consider a disastrous Western tendency to believe in abstractions, is discussed in less tendentious terms in the two chapters on the Greek and Latin languages.

spiritual of languages."* Thus, whereas the English-Latin word "revelatory" suggests merely taking a veil away from what is already there, Heidegger employs a range of German words (such as *offenbaren, entbergen, entschliessen*) in ways that give them frequently almost untranslatable connotations. The discussion here (in Chapter 12) of the revelatory element in Virgil's *Aeneid*, which shows what epic struggle is needed to achieve —in the sense of to make *and* reveal—Rome's hidden destiny, may be referred to in support of Heidegger's thesis. It is, in fact, generally with regard to poetry that Heidegger's own otherwise fragmentary philosophy may be of interest to the student of literature.

Heidegger's merit is to focus attention on the so-called existential involvement of language with "what is there." Neither logic nor science enables us to realize fully what the world is; but living and literature reveal this to us through the medium of words. "For this reason," Heidegger declares, "the misuse of language in idle talk, in slogans and phrases, destroys our authentic relation to things." And for the same reason he believes that only philosophy and poetry can restore it. He would re-awaken the true passion of the philologist, who should surely love words as a philosopher loves wisdom, and not "mechanically dissect language and set down rules. . . . Language and linguistics have been caught fast in these rigid forms, as in a steel net." European ways of thinking have been too much influenced by those early reflections of Greek philosophers upon the (Greek) language: for instance, upon Plato's differentiation (in the *Sophist*) of the basic components of a sentence into noun and verb, and of Aristotle's further analysis of sentences (in the *De interpretatione* and *Prior Analytics*) in a way that sets apart mere rhetoric or poetry from the logic of true propositions. Harmless and self-evident though it may now appear, Aristotle's observation that "is" and "exists" do not mean the same thing ("Homer is a poet" does not mean "Homer exists") points toward value judgments on which our civilization has—insecurely, in Heidegger's view—rested ever since. The effect has been to introduce into our sense of reality a distinction between the mere facts of existence and more or less "true" statements about existence. Central to Aristotle's theory of language is a theory of judgment or predication. For him, even verbs are predicative in function. Thus, the verb *to be* (on which all predication relies) acquires a logical value that subordinates all substances, qualities, and even actions to itself. It is the primacy of this rational test of "what truly is the case" that has falsely disintegrated, isolated, and

* The question of the character of German is taken up again in Volume IV, "The Development of German Classical Style."

tried to pin down as scientific information a whole universe of essential truths—as distinct from the oneness of existential being, of life as lived by human beings in an indissoluble unity of creative consciousness and created fact.

One of the recurrent topics in these volumes will be the way in which knowledge relates to existence, science to literature, and education to grammar—the art, that is, of rhetoric and the study of the "normative" classics of Greek and Latin. Doubtless at some periods the "classical ideal" in literature and philosophy has seemed, to humanists gazing wistfully back across the centuries, more like a secure norm and less like a creative struggle than in fact it was. Beneath that cultural mirage, in which few people nowadays believe, there lie and have always lain the gritty and immediate problems of men's perennial struggle to achieve civilization. The politics of daily life are still swayed by crude affirmations and denials, and Plato already recognized the practical urgency of the problem they present, tackling it again and again in his dialogues. The problem has also remained associated with the name of Plato's enemies, with "sophistry," and this should always remind us of the social importance of the debate that focussed philosophical attention on the way in which language is used. There is a Marxist argument that also holds—needless to say, for different reasons from those advanced by existentialists—that philosophy became deflected from its true path in Plato's day.[13] The fact that the philosopher in ancient Greece could take it for granted that the basic necessities of existence should be provided, or at least cheaply subsidized, by slave labour allowed him to turn his mind away from real problems of production and distribution to purely speculative "science"— arcane discussions about the nature of being and existence. Yet the relationship of the necessary to the existential, of science to history, of truth to words, has been experienced again most keenly in the communist world of the 20th century. A poignant comment on the ideal of language as an instrument of scientific control is given in Solzhenitsyn's novel *The First Circle*: there, linguistic research is seen contributing its part to the technology of tyranny, while the "higher" reality that is embodied in individual experience, and that only imaginative language can interpret for us, is once again vindicated.

In conclusion, it is appropriate to recall how the subject of mythology has been taken up again in recent times with renewed intellectual serious-ness. It had received considerable stimulus from the philological work of the 19th century, which it then helped (along with linguistics) to oust from the centre of interest. For the "science" of mythology offers common ground to social anthropology, psychology, philology, and indirectly also to the critical appreciation of literature. Part of the importance of mythology for literary studies is (and always has been) due simply to its recurrent use by writers throughout the centuries; even in such a sceptical age as the present, poets have felt the need to refashion a literary mythology (for reasons that will be discussed in the Preface to Volume VI). Part of its usefulness for literary analysis, however, has been discovered by critics who have been influenced by the philosophy of Ernst Cassirer (1874–1945).[14] He has shown how mythology can shed light on the way in which the mind originally "conceives" reality—in the sense of giving birth to the primary images, and gradually more distinct concepts, that constitute the world as we know it. The myth-making imagination functions, he believes, in the same manner as the word-making imagination. "We have," he writes, "to pursue the ways of myth and language . . . back to the point from which these two divergent lines emanate. . . . [The] same form of mental conception is operative in both. It is the form which one may denote as metaphorical thinking."[15]

In some respects Cassirer's investigation of language parallels Heidegger's more grandiose attempts at a new metaphysical comprehension of being, but it has several distinct advantages. It is easier to understand because Cassirer confines himself to analysing the available structures of language, without trying to go beyond them to formulate the character of being by means of new verbal forms. Cassirer does not, moreover, reject the progressive rationalization and abstraction that more refined grammar, and hence more logical thought, have *achieved*. He admits that "if language is to grow into a vehicle of thought, an expression of concepts and judgments, this evaluation can be achieved only at the price of forgoing the wealth and fullness of immediate experience." But he maintains that through poetry we continue to have access to the original power that resides in language, its "mythic power of insight" into the immediate personal relationship of self to world. This is not to say that more abstract forms of insight are invalid, or that the creative basis of our personal relationship to the world could ever again be expanded into a systematic or social one: such "systems" could only be magical ones, as in primitive times when societies were based on superstitious codes rather than on rational ideals. Cassirer's recognition of the *limitations* of metaphorical thinking is quite as important as his attack on the Platonic division of the world into two—a division that he also sees as ultimately responsible for the modern sceptical view of facts as "real" and values as merely "imagined." Cassirer's philosophy constitutes, in fact, a true critique of language, inasmuch as it distinguishes between the necessarily different functions and evolutionary stages of language, and thereby provides a non-sceptical basis for assessing its truth content in any given context.

As a result, Cassirer avoids the obscure, irrationalistic tendency of Heidegger's thinking, which may be glimpsed even in brief quotation given above, where it is implied that "creators, poets, thinkers, statesmen" exist in the same category and that their work follows the same creative principle. The political implications of applying a single concept, such as that of "conflict" (which Heidegger, like Nietzsche, derived from Heraclitus), to the activities equally of poets and of politicians, are potentially disastrous.* Language is certainly the medium of man's civilized life, but it cannot alone provide "creative" mastery over the fate of society (whatever prayer, or poetry, or private philosophical incantations may do for the individual). In this connection, too, we may add that, despite Cassirer's avowed debt to German idealist philosophy, his idealism is by no means nakedly exposed to Marxist criticism, in that he does take account of the interaction between social and linguistic forms:

> Only what is related in some way to the focal point of willing and doing, only what proves to be essential to the whole scheme of life and activity, is selected from the uniform flux of sense impressions, and is "noticed" in the midst of them—that is to say, receives a special linguistic accent, a name.[16]

Cassirer's position may be described as an intermediary one, capable of mediating between philosophies based upon the logic of concepts and philosophies based upon the science of things. He thus situates language "in the middle," the medium through which concrete experience moves toward abstract conceptions, and is named according to its place in this process. There can be no sense in pronouncing one end of this process to be more "real" than the other; but, equally, we should not conclude, from the fact that value pronouncements of this kind are nonsensical, that there are no values "in reality." Value is realized through the fullest grasp of the general and the particular, that mysterious fusion that is the mark of greatness in literature. Civilized society likewise seeks to combine general welfare with the good of the individual—not neglecting either end of this value scale, nor arbitrarily equating them. Literature is thus a

* It is notorious that Heidegger at first did not recognize the character of Nazi politics, whereas Cassirer did, and emigrated in 1933.

mirror of society, in the sense that it provides not a literal record but an ideal standard of what is true.

The parallel between language and mythology to which Cassirer has pointed means that each ultimately arises from a pre-rational basis in immediate experience. Their existential origin thus remains inscrutable to rational explanation. This manner of conceiving "existence" has been widely considered in the present age as a sign of nihilism, despite the manifest inspiration that "existentialists" of various sorts have found in this awareness. A man is not a disembodied mind; he exists through a body, which will die. He may conclude that no reason can be found for this—which is to say, in the fact that he is there at all, or in the fact that the world is there at all. But in thinking thus, he has become aware of a power of rational comprehension in himself. He has made what appears to be the simplest, but is surely the most sophisticated and extreme, pronouncement about what he judges to be reasonable. He is acknowledging not one thing but two: his being there and his awareness of his being there. Neither thing alone defines his being; both together do. Both together explain man's power of speech, his distinctive attribute, his *logos*, which Greek philosophy interpreted as leading to an ideal logic of being, but which St John associated with a divinely creative power beyond human reckoning. The different social and historical circumstances underlying the Hellenic and the Judaeo-Christian ways of thinking are discussed in another chapter; and in later volumes the always changing circumstances of man's confrontation with the irrational will be stressed. These circumstances influence the costume, the plot, the language of the confrontation, but not the dramatic act itself, which follows as man obeys the command *gnothi seauton*—know thyself. The famous inscription at Delphi is sometimes invoked in support of an optimistic rationalism, as though mankind might overcome all irrational failings through knowledge. Indeed, that should be the direction of civilized striving. The Greeks may have intended to symbolize this enlightened direction when they reconsecrated the temple at Delphi, which tradition associated with Gaia, the goddess of earth, to Apollo, the sun god. But the condition of achieving enlightenment was seen by Sophocles as remaining still inescapably tragic; and even the ironic intelligence of Socrates found that what the Delphic oracle meant in declaring him the wisest man was that he could be certain only that he did not know—and that in professing such a certainty he was condemned to die. There was no way in which the meaning of his words could be loaded with value for all time other than through the "reason" for his death. Again, it may sometimes seem as though the import of the Jewish divine command—"Be still and know that I am God"—contains a more forthright promise of salvation from outside. But in the outcome the Christian (and the Jewish) drama was to prove no less tragic. "Being still and knowing" turned out to mean being innocently crucified for the sins of man's irrational nature. What, if not this, had happened to Oedipus? What else can happen to any man?

The ultimately non-rational basis of language does not, then, simply disqualify the efforts of reason. It should not suggest either that anything is permissible or that truth is an unfounded concept. The parallel between language and mythology is revealing in that it shows in each case how the mind originally becomes self-aware: and what it becomes aware of is "the other," the thing unlike itself, which is given immediately in the deeply anonymous intuitions of the imagination and which reason must then make sense of as best it can. Modern psychology continues to assert the presence, within even the most rational individual, of a core of pre-personal, barely individualized, irrational being. Not only can he not lose this part of himself; his very mind will become impotent if he cuts himself off from it. With what else should he work, what other "reason" should he have to speak? But equally, the irrational thing itself cannot tell him what to say. In order to come to terms with it, he must create the terms himself, in response to his encounters with his environment. This matters to him in proportion to the force and quality of his desire, and thus he makes a sign for it. A word is in the first place a mark of interest, signifying neither the desire itself nor the thing desired, but that which exists in between, the beginning of a civilized relationship, *quod inter est.* Let the first sound, the verbal or other signs, be fortuitous; man will refine them, as he has refined his other instruments. They are the tools with which he arranges and joins together and instructs himself about the world, and constructs a civilized place (*civitas*), such as the Romans built to the point where it meant a city, but less civilized peoples seem to have known as nothing more than a settlement or house (if the Gothic word *heiva* is "the same" as the Latin word *civis*). The refinement of words and the gradual structuring of language is not fortuitous, therefore, any more than is the refinement and structuring of other instruments for dealing with the world. The root of the words "instrument," "instruct," "construct," is the same (*struo*, I join). There is, however, a paradox in the character of man's instruments for dealing with the world, a two-sidedness inseparable from their function of go-betweens: they are both modelled according to what it is possible to make of the world, and they themselves make possible the joining of things together as regards both the instruction of the mind with words and the construction of material things themselves. To ask whether formulations in language are true is like asking whether a given instrument is the right one. It is relatively easy to judge whether it is altogether the wrong one, and even to define the limits of its competence; but "the" truth is a question of what *could* be done with the world, what life *could* be, not a matter of what the facts unchangeably are.

The study of literature finds here its justification: it is the study of a possible use of words, of the possibilities of living. With words, the imagination is free to explore many more possibilities than can ever be the case with a given set of concrete things. Only madmen will ignore the difference between these two different realms of possibility; poets have been likened to madmen because they appear to ignore it (and so have magicians—and saints). Certainly, in earlier ages men did experiment rather freely with imaginative possibility in actual fact, and sometimes the results were barbarous and cruel. The origin of many myths has been sought in the theory that they are survivals of savage practices and rituals. The question remains, however, as to what the function was of these imaginative experiments, and it is still a very relevant question for a student of literature, because poets continue to explore the possibilities of words, even if modern civilization prides itself on no longer putting poetry into practice, i.e. confusing magic with science. (It could be argued, incidentally, that in fact ritual sacrifices are still made for mythological causes, and that this dilemma can never be avoided; in order to become conscious of any value in the world, men evidently need a myth, and myths spur them to actions, to try to possess their vision in reality.) But assuming that we now know better how to deal with the actual world, why should we devote serious attention to matters of fiction, or indeed to any non-scientific use of language? The question arises no less with regard to the novels of Dickens and Dostoyevsky than with regard to the myths of Homer and Hesiod. By approaching the phenomenon of language from a functional standpoint, we may come to understand afresh its justification in a way that complements, rather than conflicts with, that of science, and that provides a link between the myths of the various epochs of literature.

In general terms, myths may be said to describe the origin of the world, in both a cosmic and a local sense; they tell how the universe came into being and how a particular society acquired its habits and rules. This latter aspect of myth is closely tied up with ancestor worship and passes over from stories about more or less supernatural beings to stories about more or less historical persons. The typical impulse of more civilized (rationally self-conscious) minds, who for some reason, good or bad, have thought they understood better the nature of things and of history, has been to assume generally that myths represent a confused, disguised, or in some other respect false, account of actual facts. This is to regard myth as standing for something else—the truth—about which it is possible to speak more plainly and accurately. As we might expect, we find Plato putting such an allegorical interpretation into the mouth of Socrates (in the *Cratylus*), although probably none too seriously, for elsewhere he makes Socrates say that he finds "such interpretations rather an artificial and tedious business" (in the *Phaedrus*). And indeed they are self-defeating, for they are themselves responsible for reducing mythological notions to mere mumbo-jumbo at the same time as they purport to redeem their "true" meaning. Of course, this attitude toward pagan myth suited Christian thinkers, though they did not invent it. Cicero, Aristotle, Euhemerus, and many other thinkers of antiquity regarded myth as science or history or social legislation in disguise—"to persuade the many, and to be used in support of law."[17] What else were intelligent men to think, when confronted with the irrational heritage of their culture?

Fundamentally, the attitude toward myth remained the same right up to modern times. For Herbert Spencer and Max Müller in the 19th century, myth was still to be explained as a form of misconception (different though their theories are as to *why* men ever misconceived).[18] The analysis presented in 1900 by J. G. Frazer[19] is scarcely different in its essential method—which is to explain mythological rites and stories as a magical way of understanding and controlling the "spirits" of vegetation— and neither are Robert Graves' introductory remarks to the effect that "a large part of Greek myth is politico-religious history,"[20] i.e. connected with the struggles between patriarchal and matriarchal forms of society, and the desire to promote fertility and hence the welfare of a king- or queendom. Stories that cannot be explained in this realistic way Graves declares not to be true myths at all. Again, it is a strange mode of defence— like defending only those parts of Shakespeare that have a basis in history. What remains unexplained by theories such as these is the reason for our being interested now in such ancient history, especially when it is fancifully misrepresented. However, Graves' own interest in myth is evidently inspired as much by genuine poetic passion as by curiosity for mere information. Doubtless the accumulated details of knowledge about what "really" lay behind ancient myths are in large measure true; but the truth of their permanent interest to mankind, if they have one—and this attraction for the poetic imagination in every age suggests that they do have one—must be of a different order. The only solution to this problem is to accept that myth represents a form of truth *that cannot be known in any other way.* Other historical circumstances, like other social conventions, may furnish the imagination with variant materials; this provenance no more explains the meaning of the finished product than the biography of a poet explains the meaning of his poetry for other people, or the social provenance of language the vaster comprehension of the world it is capable of creating. Research into the pseudo-scientific or otherwise superstitious function of myth can only make us turn away from it to more rational ways of ordering our affairs. Does it have any other function that could make us want to look at it again?

The answer must surely be that myth, like language, does have more than one function. We should not be surprised to discover that it does not simply communicate the facts. It is not mere facts, after all, that are doing the communicating, but human beings; and their *sense* of fact lies at the origin of all utterance. The demands of practical existence make men subject the quantitative aspect of things to various norms, which enable them to agree about what the case is. Whether their assessment is correct they may judge by their success in handling the task before them. But in applying themselves to even the most practical tasks, they discover there qualitative questions of a quite different order: how is success to be measured, why are these tasks imposed, to what kind of higher rules are all human rules subject, and who or what ultimately determines them? Myths are stories about these puzzling problems; they retain their interest because they make vivid to the imagination what a qualitative, as opposed to a quantitative question is like. They tell us how the world was created, what powers rule it, why men must behave in certain ways, and why they must die. The illusion to which Western civilization has been prone again and again since the earliest days of Greek science is to believe that truly scientific understanding of the quantitative aspects of existence will show that such qualitative questions are unfounded and unnecessary— "misunderstandings in the use of language," as philosophers in England have again recently been tempted to assume. Commenting on a current form of this illusion during the 16th century, Montaigne put his finger precisely on the difference between the two kinds of question: "You do not die because you are ill, you die because you are a man."[21] No doubt primitive societies did not adequately distinguish between quantitative and qualitative questions, between stories and history, between myth and science, between religion and politics. No doubt, the assumption common to most mythologies (including, in a sense, the Judaeo-Christian one), that death is not natural, but a violation of some ideal order, and thus inextricably bound up with violence, is not a helpful view for welfare politics or medical research. No doubt, poets and critics and philosophers whose imagination is drawn toward periods in history or forms of society in which heroic, mythological, religious attitudes to death seem to predominate are in danger of being bad counsellors in public affairs. But the 20th century is no less in danger of succumbing to the primitive illusion of not recognizing that there *are* two questions, a qualitative and a quantitative one, when it wishes for purely rationalistic, scientific counsellors. The barbarism of the earliest ages in which myth predominated shows a startling similarity to the barbarism that threatens modern society. Indeed, in the crude suffering that barbarism inflicts on the individual, the "mistake" is always the same: the two-sidedness of man's nature has not been recognized.

Myth is important, then, because it reminds us of the two-sidedness of life, the deep and tragic division of the world, the qualitative character of existence that quantitative formulations cannot replace but can only ignore. Not least among its functions is to tell symbolic stories about the qualitative aspect of language itself, which is surely the very last thing that language can measure and is more likely to lose sight of throughout all its range of works. What happens when man tries to possess that spiritual quality—which myths describe as the food of gods or some other divine property? He is cast out of Paradise like Adam, or made to suffer like Tantalus. In order to illustrate further the function of myth, we may say (to take another example) that a scientific explanation of combustion does not tell us what it *means* that man should be able to make and use fire, i.e. one of the basic processes of nature; but the myth of Prometheus may bring home to us something of that meaning. On the other hand, the myth of Sisyphus, which was to symbolize for thousands of years the doom of man's cunning and striving spirit, can scarcely have helped the people of Corinth to make the best practical use of the spring Peirene, which Sisyphus is said to have provided for them.

We should also observe that in both these examples the form of the stories varies greatly. Hesiod's version of the Prometheus myth (in the *Theogony*) shows that man ultimately suffered more than he gained by stealing from the gods. Aeschylus, however (in the trilogy of plays devoted to the subject), makes that heavenly fire the source of all civilization and Prometheus the spiritual animator of the human race. The spring at Peirene was "explained" by stories involving quite different agents: it was said to have been struck by the hoof of Pegasus, and so became associated (as the myth grew and changed) with the Muses. These variations or

71

changes of shape in the myths about one "thing" are typical of the way in which the qualitative imagination works. The expression of quality in terms of shape, of narrative, of mythic cult, and of poetic form is never literal (even if superstitious people mistake it for such); it is symbolic. Language itself functions in this symbolic and creative way, in that there is no single, exact linguistic form in which any "thing" has to be said. Language mediates between the totality of all things and the particularized perception of individual human beings. From this confrontation language, myth, and all men's articulate works spring; from the confrontation of the universe that remains and the individual who does not.

The mythopoeic imagination may be seen, then, as giving articulate shape to a range of qualities, from the primary or titanic presence of the elements, through the heroism and pathos of mortal struggles with the gods, to a more realistic account of human doings, in which meaning is controlled in terms of metaphor, allegory, and moral principle; finally it passes beyond into extremes of fanciful invention. Its range parallels the process of language, and hence of thought, from the darkest, barely verbal intuitions, which press themselves upon the mind with more force than rational sense, to the most elaborate working out of vision into words, where infinite freedom of fancy may be achieved—but at the risk of seeming to be no longer quite serious about the world. A part of this range appears already in the oldest authors. Hesiod tells of the origin of the world in his *Theogony*, a work dating back to the early 7th century B.C., and if its crude stories about successive dynasties of gods have any meaning for us today, it must surely be because they are a mythological way of picturing a mystery that we may still experience: our sense that the world is really "one," even though it consists of parts, and above all of individuals, who are brought into existence only to be destroyed again.*
We can, of course, seek additional explanations, of a social or psychological kind, for these Greek cosmogonic myths: for instance, the fact that Cronos (who was victorious in the first dynastic struggle) was the youngest son, whereas Zeus (who was victorious in the second) was the eldest, may reflect a social change in the customs of primogeniture; or the fact that

---

* It was once a commonplace of etymological studies to note the connection between words meaning "whole" and words expressing some ideal value, e.g. "hale" (Eng.), *heil* (Ger.), deriving from Indo-European *qoilos*, which supposedly gave the Slavonic root *tsel-* ("whole" in Russian, "healthy" in Old Slavonic) and the Greek *kalos* (beautiful, good). Similar intuitive associations have been discovered between, e.g., "entire," *intero* (Italian), in+*tag* (*tangere*, Latin,) untouched; or, "total," *totus* (Latin), *touto* (Oscian), *thyda* (Gothic), from some root signifying the togetherness of a people or state. A. O. Lovejoy once remarked rather ironically on man's recurrent obsession with the thought that all things are one (*The Reason, the Understanding, and Time*), but Jung accepted it as the key to psychic health.

the avengers (the *Erinnyes*) sprang from the fallen blood, when Uranus was castrated by his son, may be related to Freud's attempt to explain guilt as rooted in the killing of a primal father. Such theories about details do not have to be proved correct in order to persuade the imagination that the presences identified by such myths are real, and that the order in which they "rule" represents a scale of values: beginning with the un-individuated vastness of Earth and Sky, followed by a more distinct race of still gigantic powers, and ending with the personalized relations of Zeus, who may be known in fairly well-established provinces, such as sea and harvest and home. We do not have to accept that there is any literal truth in such stories in order to see what value is being established by man's increasingly articulate relationship to the facts of his existence. He has distinguished its essential qualities.

Hesiod's more famous poem, *Works and Days*, reaches far toward the other end of the imaginative scale, including much practical advice on the art of living peacefully and productively, and fabricating the first known fable in Greek literature ("The hawk and the nightingale"). But the quality that unifies this account of the way man works, and the days and seasons most propitious to his toil, is the background of myth, the mysterious origin of man's situation in the world, with which his language, like all other rules of civilized existence, tries to come to terms. For "what man needs, the gods have hidden from him; else the work of a day would suffice for a year—and he would live without doing anything more." Hesiod goes on to "explain" this situation by telling again the story of Prometheus. Modern civilization now studies more technologically useful explanations, and so it should; but the quality of the human predicament remains unchanged, whether in the poverty-stricken or in the leisure-stricken parts of the globe, and so it must remain, because the necessities of work and time exist prior to mankind's efforts to regulate them. Between the cosmogonic and the didactic writings of Hesiod, we may locate the kind of myth developed by Homer. This weaves some undoubtedly *real* event, the history of a national war, together with *stories* of the presence of gods among men. No greater claim can be made for the truth of language: only religious writing makes such claims, and for centuries the Greeks recognized this unique quality in Homer's poems. Again, by the standard of later definitions of truth—whether Platonic, or Christian, or scientific (they are all equally inappropriate)—we no longer "believe" Homer's myths. We no longer believe that history, let alone the gods, can "be" like that. Yet have the essential qualities of man's struggle changed? What, after all, are the essential qualities that

73

Homer's poem makes visible to us? The self-defeating victory of violence; the self-effacing cunning of persistence. The *Iliad* and the *Odyssey* tell a tale about the symbolism of names, about the manner in which Achilles and Odysseus are heroic—one because he will admit no slight upon his name, no obstacle to his will; the other because he will never lose sight of his goal, no matter how much he must hide or how long he must endure. It is through the contest of human individuality with fate that the meaning of a name is born, and the quality of a life symbolized.

The extensive naming of heroes in ancient epic is likely to puzzle or bore a modern reader. The act of naming has doubtless lost much of its ritual significance, along with most other echoes of particular meaning that many names probably had for their Greek or Roman heroes. Some were associated with places, some with actions, some with families or peoples, some with things. Together they made up the mythological history of ancient civilization, and their value was symbolic; it rested on that vaster store of ordinary words, the common language by which a nation identifies and preserves itself. For a name acquires its spiritual value from the fact that it has the quality of endurance that the bearer manifestly lacks, be this a person, an object, or an event. Should we conclude, then, that there is a realm of enduring qualities, as distinct from things? This is not a conclusion toward which either language or literature points (though mystical philosophers are prone to do so). The paradox of language is that it appears to confer immortality upon things, but can only reveal this spiritual reality through clinging to words, and thus to the world of things. The pagan gods have been contrasted with the Judaeo-Christian one, in that they were always given a local habitation and a name.[22] They were the gods of this or that place or action or family, conceived in a manner congenial to the poetic imagination, whereas Yahweh remained invisible. It should be added, however, that Yahweh's reality was made known no less locally in the history of his chosen people, and finally embodied in the sufferings of one man. No more complete fusion of word and reality could be imagined than that claimed by the Christian faith, which promises immortality to all men in the man-god's name. The speaking of that name is said to make a new reality, to save from death: not as poetry had done, but in truth. Upon this claim to have replaced the fictions of the ancients by a word that really transfigures the world, really embodies the secret by which mere food is transubstantiated into spirit, really incarnates the presence of God, Christianity was to sweep aside the mythology and literature of Greece and Rome.

References

1. LEO SPITZER, *Linguistics and Literary History* (New York 1962), p. 8.
2. See Lévi-Strauss's articles on structural analysis in *Word* (New York 1945) and more recently in *Signes* (Paris 1960).
3. See especially FERDINAND DE SAUSSURE, *Cours de linguistique générale* (Paris 1960).
4. WILHELM VON HUMBOLDT, *Über die Kawisprache auf der Insel Java* (1836–40).
5. KARL MARX, *Die deutsche Ideologie* (Berlin 1932), p. 405.
6. FRIEDRICH HÖLDERLIN, *Sämtliche Werke*, ed. by N. V. Hellingrath (Munich and Leipzig 1913–23), Vol. IV, p. 246.
7. *A Treatise of Human Nature* (1739).
8. JAMES MONBODDO, *The Origin and Progress of Language* (1773–92).
9. JACOB GRIMM, *Geschichte der deutschen Sprache* (1818).
10. See especially M. HEIDEGGER, *Introduction to Metaphysics*, trans. by R. Mannheim (paperback: New York 1961); *Nietzsche* (Pfullingen 1961).
11. *Nietzsche*, Musarion-Ausgabe, Vol. XVI (Munich 1922), p. 235.
12. HEIDEGGER, *Introduction to Metaphysics*, p. 51. Other short quotations are also taken from this translation.
13. See, for instance, B. FARRINGTON, *Greek Science* (Harmondsworth 1944).
14. See especially his *Philosophy of Symbolic Forms*, trans. by Susanne K. Langer (New York 1953–7). Susanne K. Langer is his best-known disciple writing in English (see her *Philosophy in a New Key* [New York 1955]); but many critics, such as Northrop Frye, might be thought of as working along similar lines.
15. ERNST CASSIRER, *Language and Myth*, trans. by Susanne K. Langer (New York 1953), p. 84.
16. *ibid.*, p. 38.
17. Aristotle, *Metaphysics* XI, 8, 19.
18. See HERBERT SPENCER, *Principles of Sociology* (1876–96); MAX MÜLLER, *Lectures on Language* (1864).
19. J. G. FRAZER, *The Golden Bough* (London 1911–36).
20. ROBERT GRAVES, *The Greek Myths*, 2 vols. (paperback: London 1955); but see also his *The White Goddess* (London 1952) and *The Golden Fleece* (London 1944).
21. *Essais*, Book III, Ch. 13.
22. See the discussion of this point in ERICH AUERBACH, *Mimesis*, trans. by W. Trask (Princeton 1953).

CHAPTER 3

Non-Classical Languages of the Mediterranean Region

G. Devoto[*]

Man has been living in Europe for over half a million years, though not continuously, because the ice ages caused notable intermissions in human settlements. He developed speech probably between the Magdalenian age, dating from about 200,000 years ago in the areas not covered by ice,[1] and the emergence of Cro-Magnon man 12,000 years ago. The earliest stratum of speech in Europe was brought by settlers who came back after each ice age through three main routes, the first of which went from North Africa through Spain and France, the second from the Balkans, and the third from north of the Black Sea.[2] Remains of this first stratum can be found in four areas, Greece, Italy, Gaul, and Spain; they are uniformly non-Indo-European. An article by Antoine Meillet[3] in 1908 first drew attention to some Greek and Latin words whose similarity cannot be accounted for through a common framework of normal Indo-European phonetic laws—notably words for flowers, trees, and fruit unfamiliar to later invaders of the Mediterranean.[†] There followed attempts to trace pre-Indo-European nouns through neo-Latin dialects spoken in secluded regions,[‡] and investigation of the significance of impressive similarities between the place-names of Mediterranean regions far removed from each other. The widely spread occurrence of certain river-names[§] suggests not migrants or colonizations but a common original Mediterranean stratum,

---

[*] Former Professor of Linguistics and former President of Istituto di Studi Etruschi, Florence.

[†] E.g. Gk. *kypárissos* and Lat. *cupressus* (cypress); Gk. *leirion* and Lat. *lilium* (lily); Gk. *sykon* and Lat. *ficus* (fig); Gk. *oinos* and Lat. *vinum* (wine).

[‡] E.g. *camox* (chamois), *ilex* (holm-oak), *larix* (larch), which are Latin names of non-Indo-European origin.[4]

[§] E.g. Arno, Tanagro, Amato. Cf. also town names such as Pisa, Sessa (Aurunca), Mazzara (in Sicily).[5]

evidence for which has also been found in certain stems* (which have been called "Mediterranean relics"[6]) in Romance languages. In general, initial evidence for this basic linguistic stratum is inferred from (i) the difficulty of establishing an Indo-European etymology for certain words and (ii) the occurrence of these words over a wide area, extending from Biscay through Central Europe to the Caucasus and, through a parallel sweep, from Spain through North Africa to the Near East. The term "Nostratic"[7] has been suggested to indicate this basic stratum, so immense and so remote from us.†

Above the basic stratum two more have been inferred, gravitating respectively northward and southward. The former, extending from the Pyrenees to the Caucasus, is called Basque-Caucasian or, less specifically, palaeo-European.‡[9] The latter has been variously called Euro-African,[15] Ibero-African,[16] Afro-Libyan, and even Indo-Mediterranean. Each of these large areas may be subdivided into lesser areas, often distinct but sometimes overlapping. Prehistoric Sardinia, it has been argued, is not linguistically uniform;[17] the north shows Ligurian and Gallic connections through derivational suffixes§ and the south shows Ibero-African connections through place-names. || Other lesser areas within the Mediterranean world[19] include the Ligurian—the land-belt that goes from the Pyrenees through Southern Gaul to the Po basin, which has some characteristic suffixes¶—and, south of this, spreading eastward toward the Aegean Sea, the Tyrrhenian area, where the Etruscan linguistic tradition (see below) has deep roots.** Area boundaries, however, may overlap in

---

* E.g. *barga* (hut), *zata* (paw).

† As a characteristic example, one may cite the stem *ausa* (source, spring), attested in Tuscany (with its Etruscan plural ending) in the Latin name of the River Serchio, Auser; and also in Northern Italy (Liguria, Venetia), in south-central Italy, in Gaul and Ireland in the west, in the Rhineland in the north, and even in Libya and Arabia.[8]

‡ In it are represented root-words such as *magiusta* (strawberries), attested from the Pyrenees through Northern Italy to the Caucasus;[10] or roots surviving in Basque *čoko* (angle), and Georgian *čoka* (knee-joint);[11] in Basque *kukur* (comb), and Caucasian *kuk* (summit, point);[12] in Basque *arri* (stone), and Sumerian *har* (millstone). The root *alba* is attested in pre-Celtic Gaul,[13] in Italy, and in the name of the Albanoi, a Caucasian people. A palaeo-European connection, illustrated by TOVAR[14] (who uses the term Euro-Asiatic), is Basque *ezker* (left hand), spreading as far as the Finno-Ugrian area.

§ Such as those in the place names (Orot)elli, and (Bos)incu.

|| (Itt)iri, (Is)ili, formed in a similar way to African Gilgili or Iberian (Bilb)ili.[18]

¶ E.g. the suffix *-asco* (found also in Basque),[20] appearing in Giubiasco (Tessin) and Carasco (east of Genoa); the suffix *-inko*, found in the Ligurian name of the River Po, Bodincus, and also in Corsica; and the suffix *-allo*, *-ello*, as in the north-west Italian place-names Varallo, Vercelli, Rapallo.

** Among its notable characteristics are the plural ending *-ar* and the derivational suffix *-en(n)a*, as in the Etruscan word *tular* (boundary stones), and the modern place-names Bolsena and Ravenna.

the Ligurian-Tyrrhenian areas as they do in Sardinia, so that one finds Ligurian forms* in Tuscany and Etruscan forms in Liguria.†

In eastern Italy, we distinguish the Rheto-Euganean area in the north from the Picenian in the centre and south.‡ The difference between the western and eastern sides of the Italian peninsula shows particularly in the difference between the Etruscan language and the language of the stele of Lemnos in the Aegean Sea (see below). In Sicily, too, there is an assortment of types, though the island is substantially Tyrrhenian. The Elymi are linked by some scholars with Asia Minor; others believe the Elymi were responsible for a number of place-names linking western Sicily not with the Aegean or Tyrrhenian Italy but directly with Liguria.§

Geographical distribution, then, is a significant factor in the recognition of pre-Indo-European relics. But phonetic elements are, of course, also important in such recognition: there are interesting differences between the Indo-European vowel system and the Mediterranean system. ‖ With regard to consonants, there are differences¶ between eastern and western areas of the Mediterranean world, the boundary line between the two running through the Po valley. The lexical approach is also helpful in the reconstruction of the Mediterranean heritage: there is the evidence provided by nouns attested in Latin, Greek nouns connected mostly with social life, names inferred from ancient place-names,

---

* E.g. Capalle, Montefioralle.

† E.g.-*ar* plurals followed by a second neo-Latin plural ending in -*i*, as in Bav-ar-i, Chiav-ar-i. Also in originally Ligurian territory one finds -*enna* forms, e.g. Chiavenna, the name of a river near Piacenza and of a town in the Central Alps.

‡ The derivational suffix -*te* is found in Venetia, e.g. in Ates-te (today Este), and further south in Rieti (Lat. Tea-te) and Chieti (Lat. Teaite).

§ E.g. the ancient names of Eryx, Segesta, Entella, corresponding to the Ligurian place-names Lerici, Segesta (now Sestri), and Entella (a river).[21]

‖ Unlike the Indo-European vowel system, where *E* and *O* alternate as basic vowels, *A* as full vowel, and sonants vocalized as *I* or *U*, the Mediterranean system has *A* as basic vowel, *O* and *U* tending to merge into *U*, and *E* liable to change both into *A* through *Ä* and into *I*.[22] Interesting evidence of the mobility of *E* are the pairs, Lat. *menta*/Gk. *minthe* (mint), and Lat. *citrus*/Gk. *kedros* (cedar or citrus), both leading back to a Mediterranean stem with -*E*-. Other pairs, such as Barge and Bergamo, suggests *Ä* as the intermediate stage of the sound-shift *A* > *E*.

¶ In the west, voiced and unvoiced consonants are distinguished; in the east, voiceless consonants tend to predominate. The western (Ligurian) name of the River Po is Bodincus, with voiced consonants in the first two syllables; its Latin name, mediated by a Mediterranean stratum, is Padus, with one unvoiced and one voiced consonant. The town name derived from it is Patavium, with two unvoiced consonants. Similarly the Ligurian names Barge and Bergamo, with two voiced consonants, contrast with Parga in Tuscany and Pergamum in Asia Minor, both beginning with an unvoiced consonant. The well-known lenition of intervocalic Romance consonants appears obviously connected with this state of things. Its supposed Celtic origin is contradicted by its appearance in Sardinia, a region never overrun by Celts.[23]

nouns surviving in modern dialects, and nouns inferred from modern place-names.*

Pre-Indo-European Strata

Pre-Greek languages extinct since time immemorial are mentioned in ancient traditions. Herodotus (I, 57) mentions Creston in Thrace and Plakia and Skylake in the Propontis as places where such languages were spoken. Thucydides (IV, 6, 4) mentions "bilingual barbarians" living in the region around Mount Athos. Finally, Plato (*Cratylus* 409 DE) speaks of many Greek words as being of foreign origin—that is, taken from extinct peoples to whom the Greeks had been subject in ancient times.

The first signs of an alphabet more or less closely connected with Egyptian hieroglyphs are found in Crete. At first some of them, such as the star or the *bipennis* (two-edged hatchet), function as religious symbols. Hieroglyphic writing, however, soon develops during the middle Minoan period (*c.* 2300–1600 B.C.) into a pictographic script in which Arthur Evans nearly a century ago identified 135 different signs. At the end of this period, pictography is replaced by a linear script.[24] Evidence of these pre-Greek languages is shown by a number of relics and inscriptions.† The most characteristic, if not the most ancient, document is the stele of Lemnos (7th century B.C.), discovered in 1885. It contains on both sides an inscription of about 200 letters, on the order of which there is no general agreement among scholars. The script reminds one of the ancient Phrygian inscriptions of the same period. Linguistically, on the

---

* Nouns attested in Latin; e.g. *casa* (hut or cabin); *glarea* (gravel); *malva* (mallow); *talpa* (mole)—all related to nature and everyday life.

Greek nouns connected mostly with social life: e.g. *basileus* and *anax* (king); *tyrannos* (lord); *brabeus* (moderator); *philos* (friend); but also with nature: *ampelos* (vine); *élaion* (oil); *tryge* (vintage); *biblos* (papyrus); *leon* (lion); *sphex* (wasp).

Names inferred from ancient place-names: *alba* (stone), through Alpes; *ausa* (source) through Latin Auser (now the River Serchio).

Nouns surviving in modern dialects: *baita* (mountain cabin); *malga* (Alpine pastures); *lanca, palta,* and *brata,* denoting stagnating branches of a river and local words for mud.

Nouns inferred from modern place-names: *balma* (rock ledge used as a shelter); *klava* (alluvium, e.g. Chiav[ari]); *barga* (hut, cabin; cf. Barge, etc.).

† A small number of hieroglyphs appear on the Phaistos disc, discovered by PERNIER.[25] FRIEDRICH[26] published some "Eteo-Cretan" inscriptions of Praisos (6th–4th century B.C.) written in the Greek alphabet but in an unknown language representing a previous linguistic phase. More evidence is given by the so-called "Eteo-Cypriot" inscriptions, of which two were discovered in 1910 and 10 more between 1910 and 1924, written in the same syllabic script as the Greek inscriptions of Cyprus, but also in an unknown language. One bilingual inscription belonging to the second half of the 4th century B.C. is of no help, because the Greek text is not a translation but a summary.[27]

other hand, it appears related to a well-documented language, Etruscan*[28] (see below).

Transitional Strata

Besides these clearly non-Indo-European remnants, there are also faint traces of a "peri-Indo-European belt."[30] The most characteristic example is the word *Tindaridae* (descendants of Tindaros).† A large number of tablets written in a syllabic script called "Linear A," not much different from the well-known "Linear B" (see below), date from as early as the 17th century B.C.[32] Scholars have attempted to interpret and simultaneously to classify them, but there has been no agreement.‡ But even if the gap between the Linear A and B languages is for the time being insuperable, it can be said that Linear A was used until the late Minoan period (*c.* 1600–1100 B.C.). It was at first concurrent with Linear B and only later replaced by it.

Non-Classical Indo-European Languages

Was Greek the first Indo-European language of Greece? Some scholars believe in an earlier strain, which they term "Pelasgian," from the name

---

* It has been suggested that the vowel-consonant ratio is greater than in Etruscan, but this argument does not appear valid—the same imbalance appeared gradually in Etruscan, becoming established only in the Roman period. As in Etruscan, there are no voiced consonants. *O*, apparently the only velar vowel, means *U*. There are obvious similarities in the endings of words: Lemnos *-z, -eiz, -zi, -ai, -aith, -ale, -ial;* Etr. *-s, -eis, -si, -ai, -aith, -ale, -ial.* From a lexical point of view the series *ziazi, maraz, aviz, zivai, zeronai, morinail, arai,* and the formula *aviz sialchviz* compare well with Etr. *zia, mar, avils, zivas, zeri, murinasie, Aras,* and *avils . . . sealchlsc.* These similarities should not be explained by supposing an Etruscan stopover in Lemnos during their alleged journey to Italy, but by considering them as a linguistic remnant that resisted obliteration by subsequent Indo-European strata.[29] This does not exclude the possibility that, in this particular case, the Lemnos "Tyrrhenians" came from the nearby Asian coast only at the beginning of the 7th century B.C.

† Believed by KRETSCHMER[31] to be evidence of a first archaic branch of the Indo-European languages (*protoindogermanische Schicht*). It seems more reasonable to consider it as evidence not of a language but of isolated Indo-European elements, taken in this instance from the root *din* (light, day) and deformed by contact with a still Mediterranean world. Similar elements may be found in Etruscan *Tin-ia* (Jupiter), and *tiv* (moon).

‡ PERUZZI's interpretation[33] leans heavily on Linear B. Totally different methods were tried by GORDON, who still insisted on possible Semitic comparisons,[34] and by R. Kamm, who resorted to Indo-Iranian affinities. It seems advisable, however, not to stray too far from the Cretan area, in which case GEORGIEV's ideas[35] may be useful, even if it is perhaps premature to define Linear A texts as written in Luvian. PALMER's views[36] seem more judicious; I favour an even more cautious position. The prejudice against the survival of any pre-Indo-European remnants in the Aegean area has in my opinion nothing to commend itself, especially when we take into account the very early date (4000 B.C.) of the first settlements in Crete.

Within the field of Linear A developments the problem of the Hagia Triada inscriptions remains to be solved; these, according to GEORGIEV,[37] belong to a different language, unconnected with that of the Linear B inscriptions (i.e. Greek).

of a tribe scattered in Crete, Thessaly, and other places, in whom the later Greeks recognized the aborigines of their country. These scholars are surely right to recognize the fact that many Greek words lack a clear Indo-European etymology, even if their denial that Aegean (i.e. pre-Indo-European Mediterranean) elements could have survived in Greek seems arbitrary.* Although the evidence may not justify the theory of an organic pre-Greek language, it establishes the fact that isolated Indo-European non-Greek elements were accepted by the Greek world as a result of the impact of post-Greek (*not* pre-Greek) civilization. It therefore seems advisable to give up the "Pelasgian" concept, and to separate these intervening elements into two groups: the former and more ancient is accompanied by consonantal shift, and must therefore be connected with Phrygian-Armenian traditions;[40] the latter, more recent, is to be linked with Illyrian[41] traditions.† Illyria was the general name for the area east of the Adriatic and extending at this early period northward to the Danube: the Romans called the Danube provinces Illyricum. Illyrian elements later came into Greek with the Dorian invasions.[42] Some stopped farther north, giving rise to the Macedonian language, characterized, for example, by a type *kebala* compared to Ionic-Attic *kephale* (head).

The "Thracian" linguistic tradition begins east of Macedonia, on the north-eastern border of the Greek area. Its only organic document is the Ezerovo inscription,[43] discovered in 1912, and consisting of about 10 words written in 5th-century Greek-Ionic script. Beyond this, all our knowledge of Thracian is based on glosses and proper- and place-names diligently collected by the Bulgarian scholar D. Dečev.‡[44]

Pre-Classical Indo-European Traditions

The discovery by Ventris and Chadwick that the language called by scholars "Linear B" was in fact a form of Greek revolutionized our

---

* The chief proponents of this theory are GEORGIEV[38] and WINDEKENS.[39]

† Examples from the first group show: (a) *P* changing to aspirate *PH* as in *aleipho* coexisting with *lipes, aphnos* compared to Skr. *apnas*, and *elphos-bútyron* to *elpos-elaion;* (b) *K* changing to aspirate *KH*: cf. *takhys* to Skr. *takus*, or *akhne* to Goth. *ahana*; (c) guttural changing to sibilant: cf. *sitos* to Germ. *Weizen* (from *kweit-*), or *soma* to Swed. *ham*. Examples from the second group show: (a) voiced aspirate consonants losing their aspiration: cf. Hes. *aidossa* to *aithusa*, *aldaino* to *althaino*, *baskein-legein* to *phaskein*, *arbakis oligakis* to Lat. *orbus* deriving from *rbho-*; (b) *o* changing to *a*, as in *ambon* compared with *omph(alos)*; (c) persistence of initial *S-*, e.g. *sys* beside *hys*, *selinon* beside *helinos*, *selma* beside Hes. *helmata*.

‡ Some essential characteristics of Thracian are: fluctuations between *E* and *A*, e.g. Germizera/Germisara: *e > i*, e.g. *zilas* (wine) from a basis *ghela*; syllabic division of the type *o-wyo* and not (as in Baltic) *ou-yo*; development of the diphthongs *EU, AU* into *E, A*; *N* sonant changing to *A* (as in Greek and Sanskrit), but *R* sonant changing to *UR* (as in the Germanic area), as in *burd* (ford); assibilation of guttural consonants, e.g., *Berz(ovia) < berg*; possible assibilation of labio-velar consonants, e.g. Zermisera beside Germizera.

knowledge of the non-Greek part of the Greek language. Two points, however, should be noted here. The first is that the Greek linguistic tradition did not develop in a straightforward way by branching out from a single original, but went through alternate stages of synthesis and fragmentation. A first synthetic stage (Common Greek I), as early as the first half of the second millennium B.C., was brought about by the merging of several Indo-European streams. It was followed by a split between the tradition that led to the Mycenaean Greek of the Linear B variety, and the missing link with the later Ionic-Attic tradition. A new process of amalgamation in the 11th century B.C. caused the Dorian-Illyrian tradition to be absorbed into the Greek stream (Common Greek II). The second point concerns the Mediterranean influences accepted by Greek phonetics alone or in common with other Indo-European languages.*

ITALY

Non-Classical Non-Indo-European Languages

The inscription in Punic—the semitic language of the Phoenician colonists who founded Carthage—that was discovered in 1964 at Pyrgi near Civitavecchia is the first in our series of non-Indo-European linguistic relics in ancient Italy. It is also the easiest to place in its historical context, because it commemorates the dedication of a temple to the goddess Astarte by Tiberius Veliana, tyrant of Caere, at the beginning of the 5th century B.C. It is about 10 lines long, paralleled by two similar but slightly longer Etruscan texts. Obviously it does not show that there was a Punic-speaking area in Central Italy at the time, only that there were important links between Carthage and Etruria.[45]

Greater importance must be assigned to the inscription found at Sciri, near Caltagirone (Sicily), and published by Francesco Ribezzo in 1933. It is thought by some to represent the language of the Sicanians, a tribe of African origin, whom the ancients (e.g. Thucydides) supposed to have come from Spain, and whom Virgil associates (wrongly) with the Pelasgians and Auruncans as the first inhabitants of Italy (*Aeneid* VII, 795; VIII, 328; XI, 327). It is likely that the island of Sicily was called Sicania (the name is in Homer's *Odyssey*, XXIV, 307) before the Sicels drove out the Sicans. Written in the 6th century B.C., the Sicanian inscription consists of 58 letters in a Greek alphabet similar to the early one used

---

* E.g. the change $u > \ddot{u}$, the vocalic prothesis before r- (and occasionally other sonants); $ti > si$; the weakening of S, Y, and W.

in Syracuse.*[46] Also of the 6th century B.C. is the famous inscription of Capestrano, discovered in 1934. It contains about 40 signs without gaps between words.† The nature and significance of the Novilara inscription, discovered in 1889, are doubtful.[49] It appears on a block of sandstone on which a five-spoked wheel is carved, and consists of about 40 words spread over 12 lines.‡ No amount of study and research has so far brought anyone near its interpretation. One of its puzzling features is its profound difference from neighbouring Etruscan, not only because of its morphology and vocabulary but also because of the independent use of *o* and *u*, and the presence of voiced consonants in a script of Etruscan origin.

In northern Italy, precisely in the area between the Trento–South Tyrol region and the pre-Alpine mountains stretching from Lake Garda to Padua, about 70 so-called Raetic inscriptions have been found. Though of only moderate antiquity, they are too unlike Etruscan—with which the Roman historians associated the Raeti, a wild tribe according to Horace, though Virgil praises their wine (*Georgics* II, 95)—to be considered relics of the North-Etruscan stratum pushed northward from the Po valley by the Gallic invasion of the 5th century B.C. Their alphabets belong, however, to the North-Etruscan type and have been classified into the two varieties of Bolzano and Sondrio.§ The text of the *lituus* (augur's wand) found at Collalbo, near Bolzano,[52] is clearly Etruscan, and brings us to the chief problem of pre-Indo-European settlements in Italy as represented by the Etruscan language.

The origin of the Etruscans is mysterious: Herodotus gives a circumstantial account of their being colonists driven from Lydia by a famine, and after much dispute modern scholarship tends now to agree at least

---

* According to RIBEZZO, the inscription belongs to a time when Sicily had already felt the impact of the Indo-European tradition. Other scholars, such as PISANI,[47] consider it as evidence of the Indo-European language of the Siculi. In fact the inscription is still Mediterranean: words such as *nendas, tebeg, pra arei, pagesti, kealte, inrube,* hardly lend themselves to an Indo-European interpretation. Its meaning, as given by Ribezzo, is "Nenda Purene destroyed in war the citadel of the town of Burena, conquering five territories."

† RADKE[48] grouped the signs as follows: *Ma Kaprih K. oram opsu Tr Minis R akinebihi pomp . . . II.* Of 11 words thus identified, 6 are supposed to be personal nouns, 2 numerals, *oram* is said to be a pronoun, *opsu* a verb, and *akinebihi* the name of a public office. Radke's Indo-European-based interpretation seems premature, even if some Indo-European influences cannot be ruled out.

‡ The first two read as follows: *mimniś erút gaares'tadés//rotnem uvlin parten úś.*

§ They have been published by WHATMOUGH and PISANI.[50] The most important inscriptions are the situla of Caslir (Val di Cembra, Trento), Inscr. no. 215, of 60 letters; the bronze spatula from Padua, no. 244, of about 30 letters; and the Verona sword, no. 247, of about 40. The Etruscan origin of their alphabet shows through the lack of signs representing voiced consonants and the vowel *O*, and the fluctuations in the use of unvoiced and aspirated unvoiced consonants. Characteristic forms of the type *trinaXe, tinaXe,*[51] are reminiscent of Etruscan perfects.

that they came from Asia Minor. In the 6th century B.C. they dominated one third of Italy, but they vanished altogether under the attacks of the Greeks, the Romans, and the Gauls, probably because their organization in 12 great cities that were federated only for religious purposes made it difficult for them to resist invasion. They have left statuary, metalwork, and painting of great beauty, bearing witness to a luxurious civilization, to a love of music, dancing, and horse-racing, and to a strong belief in life after death. The Romans learned the interpretation of omens from them, and they have fascinated many writers, notably D. H. Lawrence. Nevertheless they have left no literature, and their language is still not fully understood, although of all the records of non-classical languages in the whole of Europe, none is as rich and significant as the body of Etruscan inscriptions. There are about 10,000 of them, but only a handful contain more than 30 words. A few are bilingual, and a few dozen isolated glosses: they are still being collected and published in the *Corpus inscriptionum etruscarum* begun in 1890. Their scripts are not wholly homogeneous, but they derive from West-Greek models, and are therefore perfectly legible.* Ever since classical times the Etruscans and their language have been objects of interest and study. Dionysius of Halicarnassus realized that the Etruscan language was different from all others.[54] The Emperor Claudius had many literary records collected in a book that has since been lost. In more recent times Thomas Dempster, an English scholar of the 17th century, revived Etruscan studies: his work *De Etruria regali* was not published until the 18th century.[55] Luigi Lanzi[56] (in the late 18th century) and Karl Ottfried Müller[57] (in 1828) took up the loose threads left respectively by Italian and German antiquaries.

The first problem was whether Etruscan had Italic origins (all modern scholars now believe it did not).† There are undeniable

---

* Some signs, such as *B, D, O,* and the sibilant *samech*, became supernumerary; at a later stage (4th to 1st century B.C.) *K, Q,* and *X* sibilant were also dropped. From the signs actually used one can infer a phonetic system consisting of four vowels, *A, E, I, U; V* semivowel; the aspirate *H*; six stops, *C, T, P,* and their aspirate equivalents; the labio-dental *F*; three sibilants, *S* interdental, *S* palatal, and *Z*: two laterals, *L, R*; and two nasals, *M, N*. This system has been accepted, apart from a few minor changes, for about a century.[53]

Some of the principal relics are: the text of the Zagreb mummy, a linen book, containing 530 lexical items; the Capua file, preserving 62 lines of writing with about 300 legible words; the Perugia cippus CIE 4538, containing 46 lines and 130 words; the leaden tablet of Magliano, CIE 5237, containing about 70 words; the Pulena inscription (from Tarquinia, CIE 5430), containing about 60; and a similar number of words written on the two plates found at Pyrgi with the Punic inscription quoted above.

† Corssen, Lattes, and Nogara chose the former hypothesis; Deecke and Skutsch and all modern scholars accept the latter. GOLDMANN,[58] and to a lesser extent VETTER,[59] tried to identify alleged Indo-European characters in Etruscan. In 1925 KRETSCHMER[60] introduced a third hypothesis, with his theory of the *protoindogermanische Schicht* or "proto-Indo-European" stratum,[61] which, in

Indo-European elements in Etruscan, but they do not prove relationship.*

The basic meanings, or at least the semantic field, of some Etruscan words have been outlined in three stages, the first using etymological methods,† the second using the quite different "combinational" methods,‡ and the third combining both.§ Besides the phonetic characteristics that may be inferred from the evolution of alphabets, attention should be drawn to three fundamental points of Etruscan linguistic structures. In the phonetic field one notices the increasing influence of stress, weakening unstressed vowels.‖ In morphology one sees the progressive establishment of declension, the spreading of the process of morphological change,[71] and, from the initial absence of a distinguishing mark of masculine and feminine gender, one begins to notice traces of grammatical gender. With regard to vocabulary, a list of words is given at the end of this chapter.

The Etruscan language raises countless historical and cultural questions. When Etruria began to import works made by Greek artists and craftsmen, its vocabulary began to accept several Greek words, beginning with the names connected with the myths represented by those works, and the nouns connected with the materials traded.¶ The prestige of Etruscan civilization, at its height in the 6th century B.C., encouraged and built up

my opinion (see above), should be transferred from the historical to the geographical plane, as "peri-Indo-European" stratum. Thus the words *Tinia* (Jupiter) and *tiv* (moon) should be considered as early developments of the Indo-European root *di(n)* (light), drastically implanted into, and deformed by, the Etruscan world.[62]

* *Lautni* (=*libertus*) comes from the proto-Latin tradition (see below); *etera* (outsider, foreigner) from Oscan-Umbrian (see below); *aisar* (gods) from the proto-Villanovan tradition (see below); *-umno-*, e.g. in Vertumno,[63] again from proto-Latin. The following words are also worth noting even if their process of development cannot be reconstructed: *turce* (he/she gave), from the Indo-European root *do* extended with an *R*, as in Gk. *doron*, with the perfect suffix *-ce*; *-c* < Indo-Eur. *KwE*, *ta* < Lat. *(is)tod*, *mi* < Lat. *me*; locative case marker *-th* < Indo-Eur. *dhi*, lost in Latin; finally there is the elaboration of a declension system, with a yet imprecise correspondence between notional cases and identifiable case-markers.[64]

† Etymological methods compared Etruscan first with each Italic language, later also with Armenian (Bugge), Basque and Caucasian (Thomsen), Finno-Ugrian (Martha), even Dravidian (Konow), and more recently Greek (COLI)[65] and Hittite (GEORGIEV).[66]

‡ Vetter and Pallottino are the chief representatives here; they disregarded external similarities with other languages and tried to establish the meaning of words through internal "historico-cultural" comparisons within the contexts in which they habitually recur.

§ The two previous methods were combined and applied to an area larger than that studied by the "combinational" methods, but smaller than the field of etymological research. The new technique, known as "bilingual," again uses comparisons between Etruscan and another language, in search not so much of identical etymologies as of structural correspondences between the texts of those two languages. Its forerunner was GOLDMANN.[67] It has been successfully applied in recent years by OLZSCHA and especially PFIFFIG.[68] Both structural and bilingual methods have influenced my approach to the interpretation of the Iguvine Tablets.[69]

‖ As is shown by Gk. *Klytaimestra* > Etr. *Cluthumustha* > *Clutmsta*.[70]

¶ E.g. Achmemrun < Gk. *Agamemnon*; *Telmun* < Gk. *Telamon*; *phersu* < Gk. *prosopon*.[72]

cultural life, and favoured the spreading of words such as *populus, par, spurius,* and formulae such as the first name (noun) followed by family name (adjective),[73] e.g. Marcus (noun) Tullius (adjective).

An interesting problem is why Etruscan did not survive, because the conquering Romans did not deliberately set out to destroy Etruscan language and culture. Nevertheless the two cultures did not mix. In its last stages the Etruscan language took refuge not in the lower classes, as usually happens, but in the upper classes, surviving as the language of a by then closed and exclusive aristocracy. This explains why the Latin tradition was better preserved in Etruria, where it remained unmixed, than in Latium, where it mingled with Sabine and Campanian traditions. The hypothesis of a connection between the aspiration found in North Tuscan dialects and the Etruscan substratum is based on a statistical datum: there are many more Etruscan than Latin inscriptions in central and southern Tuscany, whereas the opposite is true in the north, which leads one to believe that the two linguistic traditions must have mingled only in this region.[74]

Non-Classical Indo-European Strata Remote from Latin

In the current epigraphical terminology "Lepontic" is the language of about 70 inscriptions (studied by J. Whatmough[75] and V. Pisani[76]), originating from the territory between the rivers Toce and Adda and connected with the area typical of the ancient tribe of the Lepontii[77] and the present Val Leventina in the Tessin (Switzerland). The notion of Lepontic may justifiably be extended to postulate an Indo-European tradition unconnected with either Gallic or Italic influences because of the evidence provided by names and place-names recorded in the triangular area between Genoa, Piacenza, and Parma.*[78] The fact that these two areas are not adjacent but show a few common linguistic characteristics warrants the hypothesis that a wedge was driven between them by the Celtic invasion at the beginning of the 5th century B.C. Because the name of "Ligurian" has been given to the pre-Indo-European stratum in this region, the need arises in this connection for the artificial term "Lepontic." The Lepontic area may be further extended by the study of place-names.†

* These records appear in two Latin inscriptions, the *Sententia minuciorum* of 117 B.C. (CIL I 284) and the *Tabula alimentaria* of Veleia belonging to the age of Trajanus (CIL XI 1147).

† Lat. *Genua* (Genoa), naming the site at the bottom of a well-delimited gulf, can hardly be unconnected with Lat. *Genava* (Geneva), naming the point where the waters of Lake Leman flow again into the Rhône. One of the estates mentioned in the Tabula of Veleia is called Genavia. The common base is *genu* (knee-joint), by analogy with the coastline bending into a gulf. Another

The notion of Lepontic is as much limited as the notion of Illyrian is vague and exaggerated, not only in ancient Italy. It has only recently been reduced to a reasonable scope. It should conventionally be given a negative definition, to indicate the remains of the Indo-European tribes that did not leave their original abode after the Celts began to spread westward, the Germans and the Balts northward, and the Slavs eastward. (Pliny mentions a story to the effect that the Lepontii were followers of Hercules who got left behind in the Alps when their limbs froze.) Just east of the Illyrians, the Thracians (see above) also belong to these "middle" Indo-Europeans.[80] One should resist the tendency to give the notion of Illyrian a positive definition through the records of place-names and other names, which show mostly not Illyrian but pre-Indo-European features.[81] This does not preclude the existence in Italy of links across the Adriatic, which are necessarily posited by Italy's ascendancy in Umbria, Venetia, and the proto-Latin area. But these are nevertheless undifferentiated Indo-European links, which cannot be defined simply as Illyrian.* Things change, however, when one enters Apulia. The general name of Iapygi and the particular ones of Dauni, Peucetii, and Messapii correspond approximately to the general notion of Apulia and its three historical provinces of Foggia, Bari, and Lecce. Ancient Greek writers often called the whole of this area "the land of the Iapygi," a people whom they regarded, of course, as barbarians. Taken as a whole they represent an Indo-European stratum superimposed upon the proto-Latin stratum from, say, the 9th to the 8th century B.C.† Within this

instance taken from toponymy is Bormio, a town in the Central Alps, and Bormida, the name of a river flowing through Piedmont and Liguria. The stem *bormo-* is certainly the same as in Irish *gorm* and Lat. *formus*, but the phonetic treatment of the voiced aspirate labio-velar consonant is different from both the Italic and the Celtic tradition. Similarly the dative-ablative plural *debelis* in the Veleian Tabula originates from a root DHEGwH, from which also derives, but in a different form, Lat. *foveo*. The same treatment of voiced aspirated consonants shows in the name of *fundus Roudelius* (the corresponding modern name is Rudella). The Latin name of the river flowing into the sea just west of Genoa is Porcobera, consisting of an element *porca* (sod) and a stem *bero-* equivalent to Lat. *fero*. This could show Gallic influence but for the fact that the Gauls never occupied Val Polcevera and in any case their language would not have allowed an initial *P-*. A near-Germanic treatment of the vocalized nasal *on* shows in *vico Blondelia* from the same Tabula, proving the existence of a stem **blunda* that was formerly thought only Germanic, introduced during the late years of the Empire to indicate the reddish brown colour of horses; whereas it now appears to have been present much earlier, presumably to indicate reddish soil. A Lepontic stem seems to have spread also toward central Italy, reappearing in Lat. *bitumen*, deriving from a root *bitu* found in Lepontic toponymy: *Bittelus*, now Bettola (Piacenza), and *Bettonianus* presupposing Betunia, now Bedonia (Parma).[79]

* Festus's saying, *Paeligni ex Illyrico orti* (248 L), implies a geographic, not an ethnic, origin, as many were tempted to believe.[82]

† The settlement of the Dauni may have been affected by some proto-Latin influences, because Lat. *Fauni* is a word distinguished from *Dauni* only by the different treatment of the initial voiced aspirate, turning to a fricative in Latin, losing its aspiration among the Dauni.

group, definable as Illyrian, the Messapic tradition surviving in the Salento (i.e. the Lecce area) is the richest in linguistic records. The name also occurs most frequently in the work of Greek historians, poets, and playwrights, who knew the Messapioi as the native inhabitants of Boeotia, Crete, and the islands of Tarentum. The Messapic language[83] is attested in more than 300 inscriptions written between the 6th and the 1st century B.C. Its Illyrian characteristics are very pronounced, owing to the impact of other eastern Indo-European currents (e.g. Thraco-Phrygian).* This language, as attested by its records, has distant links with Albanian.†

Non-Classical Indo-European Strata Related to Latin

One of the first streams of Indo-European contributing to the formation of Latin flows from the Venetic tradition.‡ There are 270 Venetic inscriptions, including 119 from Este, 15 from Adria, 19 from Padua, 73 from Cadore, and 23 from the Gailthal beyond the Carnic Alps in Austria. They date from the 6th to the 2nd century B.C., the beginning of the Roman age, the Veneti having been finally put down by Julius Caesar. The inscriptions are written in an alphabet derived from Etruscan, with all the difficulties arising from its adaptation to a different phonetic system.§

---

* They include $\overset{\circ}{O} > A$, voiced aspirate consonants losing their aspirations, and assibilation of guttural consonants.

† This is the view of RIBEZZO.[84] An interesting morphological characteristic is the genitive singular ending -*ihi*. Its alphabet is connected with the Greek alphabet used in Tarentum, apart from a few variants illustrated by PARLANGÈLI. Words are not distinguished from one another. The sign *O*, less used because of the $\overset{\circ}{O} > A$ change mentioned earlier, came nearer the *U* value and ended by replacing the Greek sign *Υ*. Parlangèli divides the inscriptions into four phases: archaic, classical, later, and final. Here are a few interesting words: *argora* (*panaes*) (silver assayer), probably the name of a public office connected with Gk. *argyro*-; *Barzidihi*, proper name from the root *bhergh* (inscription no. 277); *berada* and similar words from the root *bher* (279); *bilia*, cf. Lat. *filia* (280); *blavit* (he offered), from the root *bhlau*; *deranthoa*, Gk. *gerusia*, according to HAAS;[85] *dehatan*, verbal adjective connected with the root *dheigh*, to mould (300), *deivas* (god) (302 ff.); *hazavathi* (he pours) (314) from the root *gheu*; *kalatoras* (320), cf. Lat. *calator*; *klaohi* (323) imperative, from the root *kleu* (to listen); *kos*, interrogative pronoun; *pido*, from a root *do* with the prefix (*e*)*pi* (350); *zatotthebis*, dative-ablative plural connected with the Indo-European stem *teuta*,[86] -*thi* (to be), probably connected with Gk. *eti*. (370); *veinan* (380) from *sweino*-, his/hers; *venas*, probably analogous to Lat. *Venus* (380); *zaras*, connected with the root *gher* (384); *Zi*, perhaps connected with *Zeus* (386); finally the name Brendon, related to Brundisium (396 ff.).

‡ Our knowledge of Venetic is now epitomized in an important work by PELLEGRINI and PROSDOCIMI.[87]

§ Voiced consonants, for which Etruscan lacked appropriate signs, are represented by the Etruscan signs for spirates, *CH*, *PH*, and *Z* for *G*, *B*, and *D* respectively. There are three signs for sibilants: *S'* and *Š* are often confused but always distinguished from *S*. It appears that the first two were transliterated into Latin as *SS*, e.g., *sselboisselboi* (Belluno No. 1). The sign that once was read as *H* is today interpreted as *I*: the name of a goddess is Reitia and not Rehtia.[88] The labial element of labio-velar consonants, or of comparable series, is significantly reinforced as represented by the spellings *kvidor* (Cadore 64) or *ekvon* (Este 71). The importance of Venetic

The Venetic vocabulary consists of about 150 words.* An appendix of the Venetic world is represented by the Camunian inscriptions, showing the Indo-Europeanization of an originally Euganean population. They date from 350 to 70 B.C.† The Venetic area as a whole is important because of its links with a great communication network. In ancient times cultural and linguistic influences flowed southward from Venetia to Latium (one of the Latium tribes was called Venetulani). In a more recent period, however, Venetia was the region through which all the currents carrying the runic system of writing northward had necessarily to pass.[91]

The Umbrian people—Pliny's *gens antiquissima Italiae,* whom the ancients believed to have been a single "people" occupying central and northern Italy before the Etruscans—come immediately after the Etruscans in linguistic importance. Certainly their name is an ancient Mediterranean one, but it is used now as a specialized linguistic term to indicate a particular Indo-European tradition,[92] originating on Italian soil on the middle Adriatic coastline corresponding to the provinces of Ascoli Piceno and Teramo, and extending through Gubbio and Rieti as far as the Straits of Messina. In its maximum extension it is called Oscan-Umbrian. Its first record is given by the so-called "Proto-Sabellian" inscription, whose relationship to the Umbrian Iguvine Tablets (see below) remained long unrecognized.[93] A few uncertainties in their reading‡ do not invalidate the relationship clearly shown by the words *petro, puqlo, patere, matere, postin, estas,* whose meanings are sure to be: "four," "son," "father," "mother," "later" (or "second"), and a demonstrative pronoun. Only three show a different historical development from Umbrian.§

phonetics consists in the change from voiced to voiceless aspirates in non-terminal syllables, like Latin but unlike Osco-Umbrian (see below): Ven. *louzerophos* implies an original base *loudherobhos* (dative-ablative plural), *liberis.* Notable morphological characteristics are the pronouns *ego/mego* (cf. Lat. *ego/me,* Goth. *ik/mik*); the sigmatic aorists *donasto* (Lat. *donavit*), *fagsto* (Lat. *fecit*); the so-called injunctives, such as *kvidor* (he paid) or *toler* (he placed); and the dative-ablative plural ending *-bos,* applied also to the declension in *-O*: cf. *louderobos* (Lat. *liberis*).

* Among them are: the archaic *deivos* (gods, acc. pl.); *doto,* athematic aorist from the root *do* (give); *ekvon* (Lat. *equom*); *dono* (Lat. *donum*); *aisu-,* central Indo-European stem, with a religious significance, found also in Etruscan; the well-known stem *teuta* (people); the stem *foug,* deriving from the Indo-European *bheug*; the two names of goddesses *Loudhera* (Lat. *Libera*) and *Reitia* (semantically equivalent to Gk. *Orthia*). An important but less clear root is represented by *iorobos,* perhaps related to Germ. *Jahr.* Among the prepositions *op(i)* corresponds to Latin *ob* and *per* is the same as in Latin.

† They were first described by ALTHEIM,[89] who underlined their Latin characteristics, whereas RADKE[90] wanted to relate them to the Umbrian tradition. In fact the only forms with an Italic flavour—*Sanco, Leima, Ju'vila*—are too few to be assigned to a specific linguistic group.

‡ E.g. Pisani reads as *-F* a sign that RADKE[94] interprets as *-H.*

§ Aspirate consonants have not yet merged into *F*; diphthongs are not yet assimilated (cf. Proto-Sab. *svaipis* and Umbrian *svepir*); noun stems end in *-es* instead of *-os.*[95]

The most important records of Umbrian are found away from the Adriatic coast, on the Tyrrhenian side of the Apennines, at Iguvium (modern Gubbio). A trace of a previous phase, east of the Apennine ridge, is left in the name of the fraternity of the Gubbio priests, called "Brothers of Atiedio," a name still surviving today at Attigio, a village near Fabriano.* The Iguvine Tablets[96] are seven bronze tablets written in two different alphabets, of Etruscan and Latin origin, both partially adapted to Umbrian phonetics. They were found in 1444 and are preserved in Gubbio, in the Palace of the Consuls. They date from a period between the 3rd and 1st century B.C.† and are written in an Indo-European language fairly near to Latin and other ancient Italic languages. Occasionally, though, it seems nearer to Greek and other Indo-European languages than to Latin.‡ Words similar to Greek, because of a common ancestry, may be found near words borrowed from Etruscan.§ With regard to phonetics, Umbrian and the other languages of this group show certain common features. || The Umbrians borrowed from the Etruscans the name formula of individual first name followed by the family name, but they follow the Po valley Etruscans (as opposed to the Etruscans of Tuscany and the Latins) in putting the patronymic before the family

* The original name of this ethnic tradition must have derived from the root *sabh*; its derivatives, however, were not preserved either by the "Proto-Sabellians" or by the Umbrians at Iguvium, but reappear later in history as names of peoples settled farther south, in Abruzzi and Sannio, Sabini, Sabelli, Samnites.

† The Etruscan alphabet distorts Umbrian phonetics because it makes no difference between *O* and *U* and between voiced and unvoiced consonants. This results from a comparison between parallel passages in both scripts, e.g. Tab. VIIb, 6, *Rubine porca trif rofa* (where the Latin alphabet distinguishes between *B* and *P*, *O* and *U*) and Tab. Ib, 28 *Rupinie e tre purka rufra*, both meaning "three red sows." Two new signs were added to the Etruscan script—the first, which we transliterate as *R*, to indicate the rhotacized pronunciation of intervocalic *D*; the second, transliterated as *Ç*, to indicate the palatalized pronunciation of the voiceless guttural before *E* and *I*. The Latin alphabet was also correspondingly adapted by using *RS* and *S'* respectively. Thus Tab. Ia, 15 *Fise saçi* corresponds to Tab. VIb, 3 *Fiso Sansie* (to the God Fisus Sacius).

‡ E.g. *purom-en efurfatu* (let it be taken from the sacrificial table and thrown into the fire), where *purom* is the accusative of the stem *pur* (Gk. *pŷr*, fire) and *efurfatu* is the imperative of a denominative verb from a stem *furfo-* (table), surviving in Germanic languages as *bordo-* (Eng. board) from an Indo-European root *bhordho*.

§ E.g. Tab. Va, 11 ff., *esunes-ku vepurus . . . prehubia* (with the sacrificial words...let him prepare), where *vepurus* is the dative-ablative plural from the same stem as Gk. *wepos* (word), and *esunes-ku* shows the postposition *co(m)* with the dative-ablative plural of a stem borrowed from Etr. *aisuna*.

|| E.g. a common treatment of aspirated consonants, whatever their position in the word: *DH* and *BH* always give *F*, whereas in Latin *F* appears only at the beginning of a word (except, of course, in compounds). The following characteristics are exclusively Umbrian: palatalization of *K* and *G* before *E* and *I*; the development of *Ū* into *Ü* and *I* obviously through an intermediate phase *ü*; rhotacism of *S* also in terminal position, as in gen. plur. *-arum* < *-asom* and dat.-abl. plur. *plener* (Lat. *plenis*).

name: "Titus (son) of Cajus Fulonius" instead of "Titus Fulonius (son) of Cajus."

Several tribes detached themselves from the Umbrians. Starting from the Rieti plateau they may be grouped as follows: the Sabines westward, reaching the outskirts of Rome; several Sabellian branches eastward; farther eastward still, the Samnites. Only isolated words are left of the Sabine language, despite their enormous fame in legend, literature, and history. (The rape of the Sabine women is legendary, but the Sabine ruler Numa Pompilius has greater claim to historicity.) The Sabine impact on Rome may be divided into two phases: proto-Sabine, corresponding to the town's foundation and settlement, and Sabine *stricto sensu*, culminating in the first century of the Roman Republic.[97] The Romans established supremacy over the Sabines by their victory of 449 B.C. and granted them full Roman citizenship after 268 until 89 B.C.

The most ancient record of Oscan-Umbrian influence in Latium is the *Fibula prenestina* (7th century B.C.), showing the unmistakable characteristics of the dative singular in *-oi* (*Numasioi*) and the reduplicated perfect *fhefhaked*, contrasting with Arch. Lat. *feced*, deriving from an Indo-European aorist.

The Sabellian records are not homogeneous. Bottiglioni[98] collected two Vestinian (Nos. 119–20), one Marrucinian (121), ten Paelignian (122–31), and four Marsian inscriptions (132–5). These consist mostly of a few words, apart from the Marrucinian bronze tablet from Rapino (12 lines) and the Paelignian inscriptions from Herentas (7 lines).*

The Tablet of Velletri, of the 3rd century B.C., is the only record we have of the Volscian language, which was spoken by another of the most famous tribes in literature. (They were famous for their warlike character, as Virgil's *Aeneid* shows; Shakespeare likened them to "an eagle in a dovecọte" in *Coriolanus*.) Although the Volscian tablet is only four lines long and comes from a southern location, it is possible to classify it as belonging to the Umbrian, and not to the Sabellian, group: in fact the name formula has the patronymic before the family name, like Umbrian and unlike Latin; guttural consonants are palatalized and diphthongs are assimilated.

Unlike other Italian languages, Oscan is notable for the breadth of its territory and for the unity it gave to practically the whole of southern

---

* The comparison between Marrucinian *totai* (Umbr. *tote*) or Paelignian *coisatens* (Lat. *cura-*) and Marsian (*marts*)*es* (instead of *-ois*) shows the passage between the earlier phase, preserving the diphthongs, and the later assimilation.

Italy from the 4th century B.C. There are over 200 Oscan inscriptions.*
Oscan language is in general more conservative than Umbrian: it keeps
diphthongs and guttural consonants intact, independent of the following
vowel. It uses two alphabets, one of Etruscan-Campanian origin, the other
Latin. There are a few instances in which the Greek alphabet is used.†

Indo-European Traditions not yet Classical

The linguistic tradition from which Latin originated has been called
proto-Latin. The distinction between non-classical proto-Latin and
classical Latin is determined not by abstract criteria but by the elementary
and concrete fact of intelligibility. For a language to be "classical" means
that its linguistic tradition has been so established and fixed as to be
easily handed down from generation to generation. In comparison with
Greek, Latin becomes classical at a later stage in history (not before the
4th century B.C.). This it reached after passing through two distinct
phases: in the first, the proto-Latin tradition became increasingly
specialized (in other words, impoverished); in the second phase, it was
enriched by new traditions or had to adapt itself to them.

The first phase of such a development should be related to the Matera
culture, where a linguistic and cultural influx from beyond the Adriatic
established itself from about 1600 B.C. The term "proto-Latin" conventionally defines its linguistic significance.[102] This culture spread westward
over the whole of southern Italy, where it established itself more or less
firmly, to be overcome eventually by further currents. This happened
rather early in Apulia through the Illyrian influx mentioned above.
Immediately west of Apulia the proto-Latin stratum was represented by
the Oenotrians, who held their ground (without, however, leaving
linguistic records) until the 5th century B.C., when they were replaced by
the Lucanians. The proto-Latin stratum reached southward from Lucania

---

* The most important are: the Tabula of Agnone (Molise) of the 4th century B.C. containing
a 48-line list of gods and goddesses;[99] the Abella cippus (Campania) dealing in 58 lines with
the establishment of a temple to Hercules, on the boundary line between the Nola and Abella
territories; the *Tabula bantine*, from Bantia (in Lucania, north of Potenza), of 39 lines plus an
additional fragment discovered in 1966—a law text; and the Curse of Pacius Clovatius, of 13
lines, from Capua. The bulk of minor inscriptions comes from Capua. Finally one should mention the Mamertine inscriptions from Messina[100] and the inscription from Adrano in Sicily.

† In the Etruscan-type alphabet a vowel *I'* is introduced between *I* and *E* to indicate a very
closed *E* or a particularly open *I*. This important innovation is one of the first signs of the distinction between the degrees of vocalic opening characteristic of vulgar Latin.[101] There is also a
vowel *U'* used to indicate the difference between *O* and *U* reflected by the Etruscan alphabet.
Also in the lexicon Oscan shows interesting cases of independence from the Latin tradition,
e.g. the stem *feihos*, identical with Gk. *teikhos* (wall), from a root *dheighos*, which has no Latin
derivation.

through Bruttium as far as Sicily, where it left a few imprints in the Sicel language. There are three inscriptions relevant to this point. The first is the *Guttus Centuripae* (today Centorbi),[103] the interpretation of which is by no means clear.*

North and west of the Oenotrian territory one finds the Opii. Unlike the Oenotrian, of which no linguistic records have been found, the Opician language left some traces, surviving the advent of the Samnitic superstratum (see above), that have been investigated with great acumen by F. Ribezzo.†

North of the Opician territory there is the Ausonian region and farther north the Latin territory, which is not at all uniform. (In literature, the name "Ausonia" is used to mean Italy, by Virgil, for instance, and by many a European poet after him. It is a Graecized form of Aurunci, the Latin name of the tribe living between Liris and Volturnus.) North of Rome one finds a proto-Latin remnant, the Faliscan territory, subject to both Sabine and Etruscan influences. (Many ancient writers refer to them simply as *populus Etruriae*.) The source of our knowledge of Faliscan is the work of G. Giacomelli,[105] who edited about 150 important inscriptions, found between CIE 8000 and 8600 (some, however, are Etruscan). They are written in the archaic Latin alphabet, except *F*, which has a different shape. Their spelling, partly influenced by Etruscan, uses Z for *S* and *T* for *D*, and occasionally *U* for *O* and *K* for *G* (e.g. *eko*, Lat. *ego*).‡

There are no direct records of Latin dialects outside Faliscan, but certainly there must have been numerous variations.§ Because of the small

---

* The word *nunus*, obviously identical with Lat. *nonus*, shows no connection with the Oscan-Umbrian tradition (which would have produced *novio-*) and establishes the inscription as proto-Latin. The glosses evidence an important proto-Latin phonetic character. The form *aitne* (as it appears in Greek transliteration) seems obviously related to the Indo-European root *aidh* (burn), which suggests the change *DH > T*. This allows one to infer a difference between proto-Latin and Latin (where *aedes* appears with a *D*), and to explain the presence in Latin of an adjective, *rutilus*, or a place-name, Liternum, as relics of a proto-Latin tradition going back to earlier root forms *rudh*, *ludh*. A similar case is *litra*, as opposed to Lat. *libra*. Other interesting glosses, attributed to Sicilian, are *unkia*, *moiton*, *kybiton*, *obolos*, respectively Lat. *uncia*, *mutuum*, *cubitus*, *obolus*.[104]

† One of these traces may be *hipid* for *habuit*, with the voiceless *p* replacing an ancient voiced aspirate.

‡ Archaic Faliscan forms, not necessarily due to proto-Latin influence, are: *neven* (Lat. *novem*), *peparai* (Lat. *peperi*), *eti* (Lat. *et*), *-osio* (genitive singular ending, Lat. *-i*). The lexicon shows an interesting word, *lecet* (he/she lies), cf. Gk. *lekhetai*. In common with Latin *OU > OI*, e.g. *lei(firta)*, Lat. *libertas*. Unlike Latin, *DJE > JE*, e.g. *foied*, Lat. *hodie*. The presence of *F* in place of an internal voiced consonant felt as an ancient aspirate is an important Sabine influence, e.g. *loifirta* (v. Lat. *libertas*); *carefo* and *pipafo* are proto-Latin futures (not found in the Oscan-Umbrian area) subjected to Sabine phonetic influences.

§ In Lanuvium the voiced aspirate labio-velar developed into *B*, and not *G* as in Rome, e.g. *nebrundines*.

size of the Latin area, one is not surprised to find dialectal elements (besides the Tyrrhenian remnants already mentioned) within the Latin language.* The small area of Rome is therefore at the root of the classical tradition in Italy. It remains small even if one takes the whole "Latin" territory to include the Pontine region occupied by the Volsci in the 5th century B.C. The extreme geographical contraction was paralleled by a period of socio-political isolation. During this period Roman Latin underwent such radical changes as to make it incomprehensible to outsiders in slightly more than a century.†[106]

Only after this period of turbulent development does it become legitimate to speak of classical Latin. The corresponding date in political history may be fixed at 338 B.C., when, after the dissolution of the Latin alliance, Rome's political horizons widened and it therefore became necessary to stabilize the language.‡

GAUL

Because of the vigour and energy of its tradition, the question of how Latin came to conquer new frontiers must be considered in a different way from that of the spread of Greek. Latin moved through Gaul and Iberia, superimposing itself over functioning languages that survived only partly and for a few centuries. Only the Germanic languages stood firm, but their tradition, as recorded, belongs to an age that was no longer classical.

When Gaul was subdued by the Romans in the 1st century B.C., it had been Celtic for centuries.[107] A Gallic literature must have existed, but being unwritten, it eventually disappeared. There are only limited linguistic records, less than 100 inscriptions, glosses of ancient authors, place-names surviving in the Gallo-Roman tradition, several names recognizably Gallic but attested only in the Roman age.

The most important inscriptions are: the Coligny calendar (Ain) in the Lyons museum, containing the names of the months; the Rom inscription (Deux-Sèvres), consisting of 23 lines on both sides of a bronze tablet of the 3rd to 4th century A.D.; the bilingual inscriptions in the choir of Notre-Dame in Paris, containing proper names; and 36 graffiti from Graufesenque (Aveyron) with the series of ordinal numerals. Three Gallic inscriptions have been found in Italy, at Zignago (La Spezia),

---

* E.g. *bos* instead of *vos; *lupus* instead of *lucus; *forfex* instead of *forbex.

† E.g. the drastic simplification of consonantal groups making *iouxmenta* > *iumenta* and *louksna* > *luna*; the introduction of an internal vowel-shift whereby the compounds of *facio* become *efficio, effectus* (*A* changing in open syllable to *I*, in closed syllable to *E*).

‡ See Ch. 5, "The Latin Language."

Briona (Novara), and Todi, the last one bilingual. A manuscript contains the Vienna Glossary, of the 5th century A.D., consisting of 18 words. Ten Gallic formulae are included in Marcel de Bordeaux's work, *De medica-mentis liber*. The Gallic language represents the most recent Celtic stratum settled in France.*[108]

The remarkable establishment of Latin is shown by the inscription of Diana at Nîmes; according to St Jerome, however, people in the Trier region spoke a language not much different from that spoken by the Galatians in Asia Minor. That Latin should have become so strongly imbued with the Gallic tradition is due not so much to population factors, as to the fact that in Gaul Latin was always the language of the ruling classes. This helps to explain why the Gallic pronunciation of Latin, instead of being despised as a provincial form of speech, was considered worthy of imitation.[110]

IBERIA

In Iberia, too, pre-classical linguistic strata may be classified as pre-Indo-European or Indo-European. Within the former group one should distinguish between Basque, a language spoken today and certainly spoken in ancient times, of which there is no direct ancient record, and the bulk of records technically, though not geographically, classifiable as "Iberian." This pre-Indo-European stratum was followed by non-classical but already Indo-European linguistic traditions, not exclusively Celtic. There is no agreement among scholars about the relationship between the Basques and the Iberi.†

* Gallic records usually agree not with the Gaelic but with Britannic tradition, which develops labio-velar into labial consonants (e.g. the numbers 4 and 5, *petor*, *pempe*) and nasal sonants into *AN* (not *EN*). There are, however, traces of earlier "Gaelic" conditions, as in the name of the river Sequana[109] with the labio-velar *Q* not transformed into *P*. It is interesting to compare the Graufesenque ordinals with Gaelic and Welsh forms:

1st	cintuxos	cetnae	cyntaf
2nd	alios	aile	eil
3rd	tritos	triss	trydyd
4th	petuarios	cethramad	petwyryd
5th	pinpetos	coiced	pymhet
6th	svexos	seissed	chwechet
7th	sextametos	sechtmad	seithvet
8th	oxtumetos	ochtmad	wythvet

† In the 19th century, under the influence of HUEBNER[111] and SCHUCHARDT,[112] scholars maintained that the two languages had a common origin or were practically identical. In the 20th century, however, on the authority of VINSON[113] and GOMEZ MORENO,[114] the opinion has prevailed that they are distinct; this view has been accepted, at least on its general lines, also by TOVAR.[115] The hypothesis that the pre-Indo-European elements in Iberia were stratified might lead to an intermediate view, which is already reflected in some of TOVAR's statements:[116] e.g. the relation-

There are over 100 inscriptions generically called "Iberian." The longest, with 342 signs, was found at La Serreta (Alicante), followed by the Pujol inscription (Valencia) with 155. The Iberian lexicon that survives contains just under 1000 words.[117] Some of them have reached us in isolated glosses, many others were engraved on coins. Their chronology extends from the 4th century B.C. to the Augustan age. Within the corpus of these inscriptions there are two subclasses that show important differences, according to scholars such as Tovar,[118] or just slight dissimilarities, according to Gomez Moreno.[119] In fact, the mere examination of their scripts allows one to separate them into a Turdetan-Andalusian variety (south-western) and one from Hispanis Citerior (eastern), with extreme points at La Granjuela westward and Enserune in French territory northeastward. The south-western group includes about 20 published inscriptions from the Portuguese region of Algarve, and from Alcala del Rio near Seville. The distinction is basically that the western script is alphabetic, whereas the script of the other group is prevalently syllabic. Tovar's considered deductions may be thus summarized. The first onset of oriental influences must have taken place near the mouth of the Guadalquivir, at the time Cadiz was founded (about 1000 B.C.). The famous kingdom of Tartessus (the Biblical Tarshish) constituted in this area was the starting point of the first types of alphabet, inspired by Cretan or Cypriot models, that spread all over eastern Spain; at a later time a Greek type of alphabet became established in the extreme south-western area, comparatively secluded from the rest of Spain, although open to the major proto-historic trade routes.*

North and west of the "Iberian" band there are Indo-European remains commonly called "Celtiberian." In addition to these, Tovar[121] felt the need to identify a further group, which he simply calls "Western." There may be a need for a more sophisticated classification. These records consist of a few inscriptions, isolated words, and proper names. They are scanty: the Luzaga bronze tablet contains 24 words, the inscription of Penalba de Villastar only 18. A first group of records shows not only a

---

ship of Lat. Iberus (the name of the river Ebro) with Basque *ibar* (valley) and *ibai* (river); or the lack in both languages of initial *F* or *R*; or the change from *LD* to *LL*. In Tovar's terminology, they may be due to "proto-historical connexions."

* An interesting analogy between the inscription of Alcala del Rio and the eastern Mediterranean is given by the form *zeronaith*, found also in the Etruscan inscription of Lemnos (see above). Among the inflexional elements recognized by SCHUCHARDT,[120] the following are worth mentioning: a type of nominative singular without suffix; a genitive singular ending in a nasal consonant; a genitive plural ending in -*cen*(-*scen*) with some variations; an accusative singular ending in -*k*; an instrumental or ablative singular in -*s* with some variations; and a dative singular in -*i* or -*e*.

few Celtic characteristics but also features typical of the more ancient Celtic stratum ("Gaelic").* A second Celtic stratum, no longer Gaelic but "Britannic,"† belonged to a group of newcomers (corresponding to the Hallstatt culture) who bypassed the previous settlements to occupy an area farther west. Tribal structure appears to be replaced by a social organization in "centuries," establishing itself in Galicia and central Portugal.‡ A third stratum, corresponding to La Tène culture, bears pre-Celtic phonetic features.§

Notes on Etruscan Vocabulary

From the religious vocabulary: *ais* (god); *aisar* (gods); *fler* (offer); *sacni* (sacred place or action); *mul* (to dedicate); *tur* (to donate); *trutnvt* (augur); *nets'vis* (haruspex); *cletram* (trolley for offerings). From the funeral vocabulary: *thaura* (tomb); *cela* (cell); *mutna* (sarcophagus); *lupu* (to die); *hinthia* (soul, shadow); *phersu* (mask). Words related to society: *lautn* (family); *lautni* (freedman); *etera* (outsider, inferior); *par* (equal, i.e. having full citizen's rights; opposite to *etera*); *lauchume* ([Lat. *lucumo*] lucumon); *lucairce* (former lucumon); *zilc* (praetor); *maru* (maron: a magistrate); *cepen* (priest); *macstrevc* (master); *spur* (town); *tuthi* (state); *mechl* (nation); *rasna* (Etruria); *tular* (boundaries); *rumach* (Roman); *frontac* (Ferentine); *naper* (measure of length). From the domestic vocabulary: *vinum* (wine); *verse* (fire); *cape* (container); *pruchum* (jar); *sren* (figure). Words related to time: *tin* (day); *thesan* (morning); *tivr* (month); *avil* (year); *ril* (aged [. . . years]); *acale* (June); *celi* (September). Some Etruscan words of this kind survive in Latin: *velcitanus* (March); *traneus* (July); *ermius* (August). Names of animals: *andas* (eagle); *arakos* (sparrowhawk); *arimos* (monkey); *capu* (hawk); *damnos* (horse); *thevru* (bull). A few verbs: *am* (to be); *aval* (to live); *zich* (to write‖). Finally, two examples of inscriptions:

* This stratum preserves labio-velar consonants without labializing them. In the field of toponymy the features typical of this stratum are present in the second element, *-briga*, spreading westward, however, only as far as (*Coim*)*bra*. A characteristic of this first stratum is the family name in the genitive plural found from Saragossa and Teruel to Burgos and the Asturias. The archaeological equivalent of this first stratum may be the urn-fields culture.

† Shown by the labialization of the type *petranios*, from Lamas de Moledo in Portugal.

‡ Their toponymy shows endings in *-dunum*.

§ The syncope of internal vowels,[122] unknown to Celtiberians; the labialization of voiced aspirate labio-velars as from *Baedoro* (attested in CIL II 325) from a root *GwHAID*;[123] initial P preserved as in *paramo-* (plateau) show a condition similar to Lepontine in Northern Italy,[124] a stratum that also bypassed Celtiberian settlements. A characteristic feature of this region is the first instance of lenition, a phonetic process destined to spread vigorously through Spain, France, and Northern Italy, which cannot be considered of Celtic origin because it is widely attested in Sardinia, and must therefore be seen as peculiar to pre-Indo-European Spain.

‖ See M. PALLOTTINO, *Etruscologia*, 3rd edn (Milan 1955), p. 361 ff.

Partunus Vel Velthurus Stalnal-c Ramthas clan avils lupu XXIIX.
(CIE 5424)
(Partunu Vel, son of Velthur and Stalnei Ramtha, died aged 28.)

Arnth Churcles Larthal clan Pevthial zilc parchis amce marunu
spurana cepen tenu avils machs semphalchls lupu.
(Fabretti CII 2070)
(Arnth Churclo, son of Larth and Pevthi, was praetor of the freedmen, acted as priest of the town marons, died aged 75.)

References

1. See OBERMEIER, "Diluvialchronologie," in EBERT, *Reallexikon der Vorgeschichte*, Vol. III (Berlin 1925), pp. 403 ff.
2. EICKSTEDT, *Historia mundi*, Vol. I (Berne 1952), pp. 118 ff.
3. *Mémoires de la Société de Linguistique de Paris*, Vol. 15 (1908), pp. 161 ff.
4. *Bulletin de dialectologie romane* 3 (Brussels 1912), pp. 1–18, 63–86.
5. F. RIBEZZO, *Rivista indo-greco-italica* 4 (Naples 1920), pp. 83 ff., 221 ff.
6. TAGLIAVINI, *Zeitschrift für romanische Philologie* 46 (Halle 1926), pp. 27–54.
7. G. DEVOTO, *Scritti minori* II (Florence 1967), p. 29.
8. *ibid.*, p. 48.
9. B. GEROLA, *Studi etruschi* 16 (1942), p. 350.
10. J. HUBSCHMID, *Mediterrane substrate* (Berne 1960), p. 27; *Thesaurus praeromanicus* II (Berne 1965), p. 60.
11. BOUDA, *Boletin de la Societad vascongada de amigos del pais*, XII, p. 247; HUBSCHMID *op. cit.*, p. 32.
12. DEVOTO, *op. cit.*, p. 29.
13. V. BERTOLDI, *Colonizzazioni* (Naples 1950), pp. 146 ff.
14. A. TOVAR, *The Ancient Languages of Spain and Portugal* (New York 1961), p. 116.
15. *ibid.*, p. 115.
16. V. BERTOLDI, *Zeitschrift für romanische Philologie* 57 (Halle 1937), pp. 137–69; V. PISANI, *Scritti in onore di A. Trombetti* (Milan 1938), pp. 199–213.
17. B. TERRACINI, *Osservazioni sugli strati piu antichi della Toponomastics sarda*, 2nd edn (Reggio Emilia 1929).
18. DEVOTO, *op. cit.*, pp. 20 ff.
19. G. DEVOTO, *Storia della lingua di Roma*, 2nd edn (Bologna 1944), pp. 43–50.
20. TOVAR, *op. cit.*, p. 117.
21. DEVOTO, *Scritti minori* II, pp. 20 ff.
22. *ibid.*, p. 21.
23. TOVAR, *op. cit.*, p. 115.
24. J. SUNDWALL in EBERT, *op. cit.*, Vol. VII (Berlin 1924), pp. 95 ff.
25. Published by its discoverer in *Ausonia* 3 (1908), pp. 255 ff.; in Pauly-Wissowa, *Realenzyklopädie*, Vol. XI, col. 1811.

26. J. FRIEDRICH, *Kleinasiatische Sprachdenkmäler* (Berlin 1932), pp. 147 ff.

27. Pauly-Wissowa, *op. cit.*, Vol. XII (1924), pp. 88ff.; FRIEDRICH, *op. cit.*, pp. 49–52.

28. W. BRANDENSTEIN in Pauly-Wissowa, *op. cit.*, Vol. VIIa (1948), col. 1921–38; cf. FRIEDRICH, *op. cit.*, pp. 143 ff. M. PALLOTTINO, *Etruscologia*, 3rd edn (Milan 1955), pp. 73 ff.

29. G. DEVOTO, *Gli antichi italici*, 3rd edn (Florence 1967), pp. 54 ff., 58 f., and 80 f.

30. DEVOTO, *Scritti minori* II, pp. 79 ff.

31. *Glotta* 14 (1925), pp. 300 ff.

32. W. C. BRICE, *Inscriptions in the Minoan Linear Script of Class A* (Oxford 1961).

33. *Le iscrizioni minoiche* (Florence 1960); cf. R. MERIGGI, *Primi elementi di minoico A* (Salamanca 1956).

34. C. H. GORDON, *Evidence for the Minoan Language* (London 1966); J. C. GREENFIELD, *Journal of Biblical Literature*, 86 (London 1967), pp. 241–4.

35. VL. GEORGIEV, *Atti e memorie del I Congresso internazionale di micenologia* (Rome 1967), pp. 184 f.

36. LEONARD R. PALMER, *Atti e memorie del I Congresso internazionale di micenologia* (Rome 1967), pp. 329–42.

37. GEORGIEV, *op. cit.*, pp. 192–4.

38. See the numerous works by VL. GEORGIEV, including *Träger der kretisch-mykenischen Kultur* (Sofia 1937), and *Vorgriechische Sprachwissenschaft* (Sofia 1941).

39. A. VAN WINDEKENS, *Le pélasgique. Essai sur une langue indoeuropéenne préhellénique* (Louvain 1952).

40. See G. DEVOTO, *Scritti minori* I (Florence 1958), p. 67.

41. G. DEVOTO, *Origini indeuropee* (Florence 1962), pp. 398 ff.

42. See A. VON BLUMENTHAL, *Hesych-Studien* (Stuttgart 1952).

43. See FRIEDRICH, *op. cit.*, pp. 148 f.

44. D. DEČEV, *Charakteristik der thrakischen Sprache* (Sofia 1952).

45. DEVOTO, *Scritti minori* II, pp. 200 ff., including a bibliography.

46. *Rivista indo-greco-italica* 17 (Naples 1933), pp. 197–211.

47. V. PISANI (ed.), *Le lingue dell' Italia antica oltre il latino*, 2nd edn (Turin 1964), Inscr. no. 128.

48. Pauly-Wissowa, *op. cit.*, Suppl. IX, col. 1779; PISANI *op. cit.*, pp. 225 ff.

49. G. GIACOMELLI and G. CAMPOREALE, *I Piceni e la civiltà etrusco-italica* (Florence 1959), pp. 93–104; PISANI *op. cit.*, Inscr. no. 66; CONWAY-WHATMOUGH, *The Prae-italic Dialects* II (Cambridge, Mass. 1933), Inscr. no. 343.

50. PISANI, *op. cit.*, pp. 317 ff.; CONWAY-WHATMOUGH, *op. cit.*, Inscr. nos. 188–254.

51. PISANI, *op. cit.*, pp. 318 and 323.

52. C. BATTISTI, *Studi etruschi* 18 (Florence 1944), pp. 199 ff.; 19 (Florence 1946–7), pp. 249 ff.

53. The best compendium of information on the Etruscan language is to be found in PALLOTTINO, *op. cit.*

54. *Roman Antiquities* 30, p. 2.

55. Florence 1923.

56. L. LANZI, *Saggio di lingua etrusca e altre antiche d'Italia* (1st edn 1789; 2nd edn [posthumous] 1824).

57. K. O. MÜLLER, *Die Etrusker*, 1st edn (Breslau 1828); 2nd edn (W. Deecke, ed., Stuttgart 1877).

58. E. GOLDMANN, *Beiträge zur Lehre vom indogermanischen Charakter der etruskischen Sprache* I (Heidelberg 1929).

59. E. VETTER, *Etruskische Wortdeutungen* (Vienna 1937).

60. *Glotta* 14 (1925), pp. 300 ff.

61. E. PULGRAM, *The Tongues of Italy* (Cambridge, Mass, 1958), pp. 192–3, translates Kretschmer's term as "Pre-Proto-Indo-European stratum."

62. DEVOTO, *Scritti minori* I, pp. 63–9.

63. DEVOTO, *Scritti minori* II, pp. 185 ff.

64. *ibid.*, pp. 79–87.

65. U. COLI, *Saggio di lingua etrusca* (Florence 1947); *Nuovo saggio di lingua etrusca* (Florence 1966).

66. VL. GEORGIEV, *Die sprachliche Zugehörigkeit der Etrusker* (Sofia 1943).

67. GOLDMANN, *op. cit.*, e.g. the tables, pp. 12, 13.

68. PALLOTTINO, *op. cit.*, pp. 311 f., 334; K. OLZSCHA, "Interpretation der Agramer Mumienbinde," *Klio-Beiheft* 40 (1939), p. 218; A. PFIFFIG, *Studien zu der Agramer Mumienbinde* (Vienna 1963).

69. G. DEVOTO, *Tabulae iguvinae* (1st edn Rome 1937; 3rd edn 1962); cf. *Scritti minori* II, pp. 254 ff., 289 f.

70. DEVOTO, *Scritti minori* II, pp. 99 f.

71. PALLOTTINO, *op. cit.*, pp. 345 f. Cf. DEVOTO, *ibid.*, pp. 83–5.

72. DEVOTO, *ibid.*, pp. 97, 119.

73. DEVOTO, *Storia della lingua di Roma*, pp. 78 ff.

74. G. DEVOTO, *Italia dialettale* (Gubbio 1968).

75. CONWAY-WHATMOUGH, *op. cit.*, Vol. III, Inscr. no. 255 ff.

76. PISANI, *op. cit.*, pp. 281 ff.

77. FLUSS-PHILIPP in Pauly-Wissowa, *op. cit.*, Vol. XII, col. 2067 ff.

78. B. TERRACINI, *Sezione Goidanich* 20 (Rome 1926), p. 125.

79. G. DEVOTO, *Scritti minori* II, pp. 332 f.

80. DEVOTO, *Origini indeuropee*, pp. 395–402.

81. G. DEVOTO, *Studi etruschi* 11 (1937), pp. 263–9.

82. DEVOTO, *Gli antichi italici*, p. 110.

83. O. PARLANGÈLI, *Studi messapici* (Milan 1960). The numbers in the text refer to the pages of this book. See also O. HAAS, *Messapische Studien* (Vienna 1962).

84. F. RIBEZZO, "L'originaria area etno-linguistica dell'albanese," *Rivista d'Albania* 2 (1941), pp. 129.

85. HAAS, *op. cit.*, p. 212.
86. *ibid.*, p. 221.
87. G. B. PELLEGRINI and A. PROSDOCIMI, *La lingua venetica*, (Padua 1967).
88. *ibid.*, p. 16. The inscriptions are numbered as in this edition.
89. F. ALTHEIM, *Vom Ursprung der Runen* (Frankfurt-am-Main 1939).
90. In Pauly-Wissowa, *op. cit.*, Suppl. IX, col. 1764.
91. ALTHEIM, *op. cit.*, pp. 36 ff.
92. DEVOTO, *Scritti minori* II, pp. 217 ff.
93. A. VON BLUMENTHAL, *Indogermanische Forschungen* 47 (1929), pp. 48–72; V. PISANI *I piceni e la civiltà etrusco-italica* (Florence 1959), pp. 75–92; PISANI, *Le lingue dell' Italia antica oltre il latino*, pp. 225ff.
94. PISANI, *ibid.*, p. 226; G. RADKE in Pauly-Wissowa, *op. cit.*, col.1770.
95. RADKE, *op. cit.*, col. 1780.
96. See DEVOTO, *Tabulae iguvinae*, 3rd edn.
97. DEVOTO, *Storia della lingua di Roma*, pp. 77–88.
98. G. BOTTIGLIONI, *Manuale dei dialetti italici* (Bologna 1954).
99. DEVOTO, *Studi etruschi* 35 (1967), pp. 179–97.
100. O. PARLANGÈLI, "Le iscrizioni osche di Messina," *Bollettino del centro di studi filologici e linguistici siciliani* 4 (Palermo 1956), pp. 28 ff.
101. G. DEVOTO, *Profilo di storia linguistica italiana*, 4th edn (Florence 1964), pp. 12 ff.
102. DEVOTO, *Storia della lingua di Roma*, pp. 54 ff.; *Scritti minori* II, pp. 317 ff.
103. CONWAY-WHATMOUGH, *op. cit.*, Inscr. no. 578.
104. DEVOTO, *Origini indeuropee*, pp. 383 ff.
105. G. GIACOMELLI, *La lingua falisca* (Florence 1962).
106. DEVOTO, *Scritti minori* II, pp. 169 ff.
107. POKORNY, *Keltologie* (Berne 1953); DEVOTO, *op. cit.*, I, pp. 169 ff.
108. DEVOTO, *ibid.*, pp. 186 ff.
109. *ibid.*, p. 173.
110. DEVOTO, *Profilo di storia linguistica italiana*, p. 13.
111. E. HUEBNER, *Monumenta linguae ibericae* (Berlin 1893).
112. H. SCHUCHARDT, *Die iberische Deklination* (Vienna 1907).
113. J. VINSON, *Revista internacional de Estudios Vascos* I (1907), pp. 441 ff.
114. M. GOMEZ MORENO, *Miscelaneas . . . I* (Madrid 1949).
115. TOVAR, *op. cit.*, pp. 3–31.
116. *ibid.*, p. 64.
117. *ibid.*, p. 61.
118. *ibid.*, p. 40.
119. M. GOMEZ MORENO, *op. cit.*, pp. 260 ff.
120. SCHUCHARDT, *op. cit.*
121. TOVAR, *op. cit.*, pp. 91–111.
122. *ibid.*, p. 95.
123. *ibid.*, p. 100.
124. In agreement with M. LEJEUNE, *Celtiberica* (Salamanca 1955), p. 131. Cf. DEVOTO, *Scritti minori* II, pp. 324 ff.

CHAPTER 4

The Greek Language

D. M. Jones*

The Greek language is known from written records covering more than three millennia. From the 8th to the 4th century B.C. it was the vehicle of the earliest literature of Europe, a literature of great originality and aesthetic value, which expressed—among other things—an intellectual and rational culture of a new order. In the following centuries it was a medium for works of scholarship, history, science, and philosophy, and for the dissemination of Christianity. The techniques of expression developed by Greek writers have influenced, both directly and through Latin, all the languages of Europe and a large number in other parts of the world. The aim of this chapter is to give an account of the history and characteristic features of Greek for those whose concern is chiefly with the works composed in it, and whose knowledge of those works may be derived in part or wholly from translations. The terminology of comparative and historical grammar and of modern descriptive linguistics will as far as possible be avoided, and examples of the language will be given in transliteration.

Our knowledge of ancient Greek is derived from sources of three kinds. First in extent and importance are the manuscripts that contain the bulk of surviving Greek literature. These are mostly copies made during the Byzantine period, 1000 years or more after the date of composition, and bear the traces of scribal tradition as well as changes that the language underwent during the period. They are therefore not altogether trustworthy witnesses to the original linguistic form of the works they contain. The picture they give is nevertheless on the whole a fair one, and their errors can be corrected from other evidence. Secondly there are the papyri recovered in Egypt, most of which belong to the Hellenistic and Roman periods. The literary papyri, mostly fragmentary, contain works already known from manuscripts and others not preserved elsewhere; they too are

* Professor of Classics, Westfield College, University of London.

separated, often by several centuries, from the time of composition. The official and private documents, written by persons of diverse social positions and degrees of education, are indispensable evidence for the history of the language in the post-classical period. The third source consists of inscriptions, both public (comprising laws, decrees, resolutions of various kinds, inventories, and records) and personal (including particularly dedications and epitaphs, names and short texts on pottery, and *defixiones*—imprecations inscribed for magical purposes on lead tablets). All these, like the non-literary papyri, have for the linguist the merit of being contemporary records; but even so they may not always represent the latest developments of current speech. To inscriptions we owe almost all our knowledge of dialects other than Attic and Ionic.

In the latter half of the second millennium B.C. the Greeks of the Mycenaean period took over and adapted to their language a syllabary consisting of signs for vowels and for each combination of consonant plus vowel; a related syllabary continued in use in Cyprus throughout the classical period for writing the Cypriot dialect. Following the downfall of the Mycenaean states writing appears to have been discontinued or at least severely restricted; when written records begin again, toward the end of the 8th century B.C., we find the Greeks using an adaptation of an early Semitic alphabet, into which they had introduced the important innovation of representing vowels as well as consonants. The Greek alphabet existed in a number of local variants, of which the Ionic was finally adopted by all Greek states, no doubt chiefly because of its more precise indication of vowel length and vowel quality. This alphabet, in a later cursive form and with the addition of marks to indicate aspiration and accentuation, is now used for written and printed Greek of all periods from Homer to the present day.

Of the individual sounds of ancient Greek, and of its general acoustic effect, we have only an approximate idea, derived from study of its orthography and from statements of grammarians in late antiquity. The Greeks, unlike the ancient Sanskrit grammarians, did not develop an adequate technique and terminology for phonetic description. Nevertheless, the pronunciation is known in broad outline, and has some importance for the appreciation of Greek literature. In particular, the rhythm of the word and sentence had a role not only in the structure of metre but also in rhetorical prose. This rhythm was determined not by the distribution of syllables with stronger and weaker stress, but by the sequence of long and short syllables; ancient Greek had an accentual system, but this is described by grammarians purely in terms of pitch and intonation, and although some surviving fragments of Greek vocal music take account of it in the melody, it was not used to constitute metrical structure. The current style of reading Greek verse by stress rather than by length is unlikely to convey much of its original effect on the ear.*

Greek is an Indo-European language, of the same origin as almost all European and many Asiatic languages. The date of its introduction into Greece is a matter of controversy; thanks to Michael Ventris's decipherment of the Linear B syllabic script in 1952, it is at least certain that Greek was the administrative language of the chief centres of Mycenaean Greece and Crete by the 13th century B.C., or even by the 15th, according to the more widely held view of the dating of the Linear B tablets found at Knossos. The documents of Mycenaean Greek, incised on clay tablets, consist of administrative records—inventories of stores and livestock, lists of personnel, registers of land-holdings, dues and payments in kind, and the like. If the Mycenaean Greeks used their script for documents of any other kind, no trace of them remains; no inscriptions on stone or metal have been found, and if they had a written literature they did not, like the Mesopotamian and Anatolian peoples, commit it to clay tablets, but to some perishable material. The contribution of the Linear B tablets to knowledge of the early history of the language is severely limited by the lack of diversity in their subject-matter and the gross inadequacy of the syllabic script for noting the sounds of Greek; even so, they contain much of interest. They show, for instance, that Mycenaean Greek had affinities especially with the southern and eastern dialects of later times, the Arcado-Cyprian and Attic-Ionic groups, rather than with the northern and western Doric dialects that later occupied much of the area in which Mycenaean had been used. Except to the scholar, however, perhaps the most interesting aspect of the language of these tablets is a general one. The sites from which they have been recovered are widely dispersed—Knossos in Crete, Pylos and Mycenae in western and eastern Peloponnesus, Thebes in central Greece—yet their language is highly uniform, with few and uncertain traces of the dialect differences that may be supposed to have existed over so extensive an area. It may be that the administrative language of the Mycenaean centres was the first example of the tendency to form common languages that culminated in the Hellenistic period; the uniformity of the language reflects a high degree of cultural and political cohesion, together with well-developed

* A theory of stress in Greek appears in w. s. ALLEN, *Vox Graeca: a Guide to the Pronunciation of Classical Greek* (Cambridge 1968), pp. 120–4.

conditions of communication and trade. Echoes of this unity remain in later literature, for example in the catalogue of ships and the overlordship of Agamemnon in the *Iliad*, in Telemachus's journey from Pylos to Sparta in the *Odyssey*, in the ship intercepted by Apollo on its voyage from Knossos to "sandy Pylos" in the Homeric *Hymn to Apollo*.

The energy and enterprise of the Mycenaean peoples not only implanted their language over a wide area of central and southern Greece, but also carried it overseas to Crete and eastward through the islands of the south Aegean to Cyprus. This was the first phase in a process of expansion that was to be of great importance for the destiny of the Greek language. Toward the end of the second millennium B.C. the Mycenaean powers were overthrown and their speech was overlaid almost everywhere by other forms of Greek. A second wave of expansion carried other varieties of the language—Aeolian, Ionian, and Dorian—to the islands of the central and northern Aegean and the west coast of Asia Minor, which henceforth form, together with Greece proper, the central homeland of Greek. A third wave, in which Ionians and Dorians participated, began in the middle of the 8th century B.C. and continued for some two centuries at its most intense level, establishing Greek along the coasts of southern Italy and Sicily and sporadically on the south coast of what is now France, on the north coast of Africa at Cyrene, and on the coasts of the Sea of Marmara, the Bosporus, and the Black Sea. The cities to which this movement gave rise were independent states, but they tended to retain ceremonial and sentimental ties with their founder cities, and participated in the pan-Hellenic festivals of mainland Greece. Their populations were not dispersed over wide land-masses; they remained concentrated along the coasts and in constant touch with one another by the sea routes that carried their trade. This intercourse maintained their cultural and linguistic character against assimilation into that of the non-Greek peoples of the hinterland. The Greek language had not yet reached its territorial limits, however; its fourth phase of extension in the wake of Alexander's conquests will be the subject of a later section.

Greek, like almost all ancient and not a few modern Indo-European languages, was highly inflected. The inflexions serve not only to express various referential meanings such as person, number, and tense (the predominant function of inflexion in many languages, including modern English), but also as exponents of syntactical structure, a function for which English and many languages use mainly word order and auxiliary words. This inflexional character gives a greater compactness and conciseness to the sentence by concentrating much of the formal structure, as well as the semantic content, in the individual word. A short example from Aeschylus may be contrasted with an English version:

> nun d' eutukhes genoit' apallage ponon
> euangelou phanentos orphnaiou puros[1]

> (and now [nun d'] may there come about [genoit'] a fortunate release [eutukhes apallage] from suffering [ponon] when there appears [phanentos] the beacon [puros] bringing good tidings [euangelou] in the darkness [orphnaiou].)

In the course of its preliterate development Greek had considerably reduced the inflexion of nouns, but it retained the full richness of the Indo-European verbal system and in certain respects increased it, particularly by completing the provision of infinitive and participle for each tense of the verb. These forms permit a great number of syntactical transformations. For example, in the passage quoted above, *phanentos* is a participle of the aorist tense; used in the genitive case with *puros* as its subject it conveys a relation of time and cause; it would be equally possible to convey this in Greek, as in English, by a clause with a finite verb. Thus Greek writers had available to them a considerable number of more or less equivalent syntactical constructions, which they fully developed in the interests of stylistic variety and harmony. If Latin and later European literatures show in varying degrees a similar use of language, it is largely because Greek is the ultimate model. Here, as elsewhere, it is appropriate to distinguish the resources of a language from the use made of them: the writers of Sanskrit, for example, operating with a language very similar in structure to Greek, succeeded only in reducing its use to a high degree of predictable monotony.

The basic vocabulary of Greek consisted of words retained from Indo-European or borrowed from languages with which the Greeks came into contact in the Mediterranean region. As their culture developed, this stock was augmented and adapted by procedures internal to the language rather than by the adoption of words or models of word-formation from foreign sources. The chief expedients used are semantic extension and specialization, derivation by suffixes, and composition. The first of these can be illustrated from the terminology of Athenian judicial procedure, which includes, in addition to special terms, a number of general words used with specialized meaning: *dike* (justice; case, law-suit); *graphe* (writing; indictment); *diokein* (pursue; prosecute); *pheúgein* (flee; be a defendant); *hairein* (take; convict). Derivation by suffixes is a procedure common to all Indo-European and many other languages. In Greek the commoner suffixes tend to form systematic structures, such as the set *-sis*, *-ma*, *-tos*, *-tikos*, *-tes*: for example, from *poiein* (make, compose poetry) are derived *poiesis* (act of making, poetical composition); *poiema* (thing made, poem); *poietos* (made, makeable); *poietikos* (capable of making, poetical); *poietes* (maker, poet). Moreover, adjectives and participles, generally preceded by the definite article, can be used as nouns: *he poietike* (the art of poetry); *to dikaion* (the just, justice); *to on* (the existent, the real), in addition to the derived noun *ousia* (existence, reality).

Composition, the grammatical union of two (sometimes more) words, is also an Indo-European procedure. Its great development in Greek is, however, an independent phenomenon; the proliferation of compounds in Germanic and Slavonic languages is held to be due in the first instance almost entirely to the model of Greek as the language of Christianity. Of the various types of compound the most important is that in which the word as a whole has adjectival function, for example *polu-pous* (many-foot), which means not many feet but many-footed; such adjectives may also be used as nouns denoting an object so characterized, in this case octopus, polyp. Compounds, of which the number in Greek is enormous, seem to have been less numerous in the spoken language; their main fields are poetic, technical, and intellectual, and they provide the majority of personal names: *Phil-ippos* (devoted to horses). A great number have been borrowed into modern languages and others are still formed from Greek components, for example "helicopter" from *helix* (screw) and *pteron* (wing). Also numerous and important are the verbal compounds, consisting of a verb preceded by a preposition, which, as in Latin and a number of modern languages, provide a great range of primary and derived meanings.

To illustrate these procedures and the plasticity that they give to the lexical material of Greek, let us take the primary verb *legein* and the corresponding noun *logos*, which are related by an Indo-European vowel alternation. Formed from *legein* (gather, count, say, speak) are the noun *lexis* (speech, diction, style), adjective *lektos* (spoken, selected); various prepositional compounds such as *dia-legesthai* (converse), with its derivatives *dialektos* (manner of speaking, dialect, language), *diolexis* (discussion, debate), *dialektikos* (conversational, dialectical), with noun *dialektike* (dialectic); *ek-legein* (pick out, select), with adjective *eklektikos* (selective, eclectic); *kata-legein* (select, enrol, enlist); the corresponding nouns formed from *logos* are *dia-logos* (dialogue), *ek-loge* (choice, selection), *kata-logos* (list, register, catalogue). Also formed from *logos* with its many meanings—e.g. speech, statement, argument, explanation, account, value, principle, rule, reason, correspondence, proportion, ratio, narrative, tale, tradition, and so on—are adjectives *logios, logimos, ellogimos* (of account, authoritative), *logikos* (rational, logical), with noun *logike* (logic); compounds formed with negative prefix include *a-logos* (irrational, speechless, unaccounted for), with noun *a-logia* and verb *a-logein*; the derived verb *logizesthai* (count, reckon, calculate, consider), from which arise numerous forms: *logismos* (reasoning, calculation), *logistes* (accountant), *logisterion* (accountant's office), *logistikos* (capable of reasoning, rational), with contrary forms *a-logistos* (irrational, thoughtless), noun *a-logistia*, verb *a-logistein*. Among numerous other compounds are *logo-poios* and *logo-graphos* (prose-writer, historian, professional speech-writer), each with its derived verb and noun, from *poiein* (make) and *graphein* (write) respectively; *astro-logos* (astronomer) from *astron* (star), with derivatives *astro-logein* (study the stars, be an astronomer), *astro-logia* (astronomy), *astro-logikos* (astronomical).

This array of vocabulary is but a selection from the host of derivatives, compounds, and derivatives of compounds to which this word-pair gave rise, serving the various needs of current speech, poetry, and technical language. The originality and diversity of Greek intellectual culture was matched by a linguistic inventiveness that Roman writers envied and, with some diffidence, sought to imitate. Cicero calls the Stoic Zeno "a discoverer even more of new words than of new ideas," and records an innovation of his own: "I have therefore introduced '*qualitates*' for what the Greeks call '*poiotetas*'; this Greek word is itself not a popular but a philosophical term."

One of the most important features of Greek, in contrast with Latin and many other ancient and modern languages, is its possession of the definite article *ho*, with its various forms for case, number, and gender. Originally a demonstrative pronoun, the article has a number of functions: it particularizes a thing or concept as an individual or as belonging to a class; it is used not only with nouns but with adjectives and participles, with adverbs and prepositional phrases, with infinitives and infinitival expressions, and even with some types of clause; and by organizing word-groups it helps to articulate the structure of the sentence. For example, "those who administered the city at that time" may be expressed in Greek "*hoi kat' ekeinon ton khronon ten polin dioikountes*" (the at that time the city administering); "to consider licence democracy" is distinguished in Greek from its converse, "to consider democracy licence," not by the order of words but by the omission of the definite article from the noun in the predicate. Of particular importance is the classifying function: *hoi dikaioi* (the just) usually denotes the just as a class, rather than a particular group of just persons.

Inflexion, not word-order, indicates the grammatical structure of a Greek sentence. This does not mean that the order of words is indifferent or undetermined. Within certain types of collocation the sequence is relatively fixed: "to the city" cannot be anything but "*eis ten polin.*" The overall order of the sentence is determined by considerations of clarity and stylistic balance; any part can be placed in a position of special prominence, as (for example) in modern Russian. Beginnings of sentences and sense-groups are usually marked by particles—short indeclinable words that serve to express the logical connection of a statement with what precedes it and sometimes its implications for the general sequence of thought. The dictionary translations of these particles are often too explicit and lacking in subtlety ("for," "at least," "indeed," "on the one hand," etc.), but a parallel by which their role can be to some extent appreciated is perhaps the unemphatic use of such German words as *doch* and *mal*. To judge from texts that reflect spoken language, such as the plays of Menander, they were not obligatory in conversation, but in the developed literary style, especially that of prose, the connection of every sentence with the preceding one is marked by one or more particles, except in a few cases under well-defined conditions.

Greek has a number of varieties, dialectal and social. Of the dialects, few were used for written literature. The others are known mainly or solely from inscriptions, a few short passages in Athenian comedy and other works in Attic, and information, chiefly vocabulary, gleaned from grammarians. The dialects fall into groups, but the interrelation of these groups cannot be determined with certainty, because the material is insufficient for the kind of dialectological survey applicable to modern spoken languages. Certain innovations, some already attested in Mycenaean (such as the change of *t* to *s* before *i*, e.g., *didosi*, he gives, for *didoti*), mark off two groups. The first, consisting of the widely separated Arcadian, Cypriot, and Pamphylian, has particular affinities with the administrative language of the Mycenaean states; the second is constituted by Attic and the various Ionic dialects of Asia Minor and the Aegean islands. Both Attic and Ionic were destined to be the vehicles of an important literature; but the former, until the rise of Athens in the 5th century B.C., was the speech of a relatively introvert community with a mainly agricultural economy, and retained a number of conservative features, especially the use of the dual number, whereas Ionic, the language of a people active from an early period in commerce and colonization, was among the most innovatory dialects. The Doric or West Greek dialects, together with the closely similar North-west Greek, represent the speech of those Greek peoples who had remained outside the Mycenaean culture and whose southward movement was associated with its end. The Dorians too had been, and a number of their communities remained, enterprising and expansionist; their dialects accordingly present diverse patterns of conservation and innovation, together with traces of the dialects they supplanted. The Aeolic group, comprising the Lesbian of the island of Lesbos and a few cities on the adjacent coast of Asia Minor, and the Thessalian and Boeotian dialects of northern and central Greece, shows features in common with Doric on the one hand and Arcado-Cyprian and Attic-Ionic on the other, and clearly forms some kind of link between them; but the linguistic and historical affinities of Aeolic remain among the difficult problems of Greek dialectology. In Lesbos it achieved literary status with an accomplished and influential tradition of lyric poetry.

From the earliest inscriptions until the 4th century B.C. and later, each state used its own official dialect in public and for the most part in private documents. The official language of a state was not necessarily identical with its local spoken dialect. The Ionian cities of Asia Minor, with their close religious, cultural, and commercial relations, shared a common official Ionic, although Herodotus tells us that they differed among themselves in dialect.[2] The cities of Boeotia, which formed a political union under the leadership of Thebes, similarly used an identical language in their inscriptions, whereas in Thessaly, with its looser and more intermittent political groupings, the inscriptions reflect a number of local variants. Two general aspects of official language deserve mention. The first is the care shown by certain states for the standard of their official documents. The Boeotian inscriptions show that their orthography was methodically revised on several occasions to bring it into line with changes of pronunciation. Athenian inscriptions maintain a generally consistent standard of language and spelling, including a few features not found in current spoken and literary Attic: for example, the ending *-esi*, in contrast with current *-ais*, for the plural of the second declension is used until 420 B.C., from which date the current form appears exclusively; both the consistency of usage and the suddenness and completeness of the change suggest some degree of official control. At the opposite pole are the Spartan documents, the spelling of which, to judge from its inconsistency, seems to have depended on individual choice. The other point concerns style and diction. Official Greek has, naturally, its technical words and turns of phrase, but in general it is close to current language and free from jargon and over-elaborate phraseology; without being naive or gauche, it makes its meaning clear in a vocabulary that is either that of ordinary life or easily understood from it. For instance, the constitutional laws of Chios[3] (about 600 B.C.) contain the following provision: "A session of the public council shall be held on pain of fine for non-attendance . . . for the transaction of public business including all suits due on appeal for the month." A word-for-word translation would be: "Let the public council assemble subject to fine . . . to deal with both the other (matters) of the people and all suits as-many-as become on appeal during the month." In this there are two technical terms, the adjectives *epithoios* (subject to fine) and *ĕkkletoi* (on appeal), from the verb *ek-kalein* (call out, appeal to higher authority). The rest is expressed in the plainest everyday language. Similarly in a law of Halicarnassus[4] of the mid-5th century the clause "any attempt to subvert this law or any proposal for its annulment . . ." is expressed "if anyone seeks to confuse this law or puts forward a vote for this law not to be. . . ." This closeness of one form of written language to ordinary speech is an important aspect of the Greek linguistic situation.

In the case of documents to which more than one state was party, copies appear to have been drawn up in the language of each, because treaties are always in the official dialect of the state in which the copy was found. It may be assumed that envoys used their own dialect in addressing the magistrates and assemblies of another state. Clearly the dialects were mutually intelligible at the official level; how far they were so in private communications can only be conjectured, and may have depended on the opportunities an individual had for hearing speakers from other states. Such opportunities were not lacking to the citizen of an important city such as Athens in the latter part of the 5th century B.C.; he would hear other dialects on the lips of visiting merchants and the considerable non-Athenian population of the city, as well as from foreigners with business before the Council and Assembly or in the law-courts. Socrates is represented by Plato as asking the court to make allowance for his unfamiliarity with the forensic style of speaking, "just as, if I were really a foreigner, you would of course forgive me for using the dialect and manner of speech in which I had been reared."[5] In his comedy *The Acharnians*, Aristophanes introduced characters speaking Megarian and Boeotian, and in his *Lysistrata* several Spartans using the Laconian dialect; presumably, because what they say is essential to the dialogue, his audience understood them, and were able to appreciate an amusing misunderstanding, when the Athenian Dicaeopolis takes the Megarian *diapinames* (we are starving—in Attic, *diapeinomen*)—for Attic *diapinomen* (we are drinking).[6] Only intense commercial, diplomatic, and cultural exchange accounts for the fact that the dialects, instead of diverging into mutually incomprehensible forms of speech, maintained and even increased their resemblance to one another, and were felt to be forms of one language. Political fragmentation and frequent inter-state hostilities did not outweigh the constant contact that the Greek cities maintained at both public and private levels, and the common features of their religion (including the pan-Hellenic oracles and festivals), political institutions, art, and literature. From an early date a distinction was made between *barbaroi*, those who, regardless of their level of civilization, spoke other languages, and *Hellenes*, the Greeks, whose language reflected both their diversity and their basic unity of character.

Of the social varieties of Greek the scant evidence provides only a sketchy picture. Greek literature, even drama, makes only a restrained use of linguistic realism. In Aeschylus's *Choephori*, Orestes' old nurse recalls the trouble he gave her as a baby. Her sentiments and interests are those of her calling, but her expression of them has no resemblance to the language of a Mrs Gummidge and little to that of Juliet's nurse, when she calls the baby's cries of discomfort that rouse her from her bed *nuktiplangton orthion keleumaton* (night-roaming—i.e. causing to roam by night—shrill commands),[7] in which the first word is a typical poetic compound and the second an adjective characteristic of epic and tragic verse. There is nevertheless evidence of differences between colloquial and literary language. Reference has already been made to Herodotus's statement that dialect differences existed between the Ionian cities of Asia Minor; he must have had in mind the spoken dialects, because no such differences are reflected either in the official language or in literary Ionic. For Athens too there is testimony: an anonymous writer in the late 5th century B.C. (generally known as the Old Oligarch) makes the following comment: "(the Athenians) through hearing every dialect have taken this from one and that from another; the other Greeks use their own dialects, as they do their own ways of life and fashions; but the Athenians use a dialect mingled of elements from all the Greeks and non-Greeks."[8] This, if intended as descriptive of literary Attic, would be gross exaggeration. We have some examples of uneducated speech. Touches of vulgarity in Old Comedy, introduced more for humorous effect than for realism, show something of its vocabulary; explanatory legends on Athenian vase-paintings reveal divergences from standard grammar and spelling, though such evidence is sporadic and perhaps partly due to non-Athenian craftsmen. Departures from normal written standards are found also in the *defixiones*. The scurrilous verse of Hipponax shows that the lowest level of speech in the Ionian cities contained non-Greek as well as Greek words. Such details reveal the existence of vulgar speech and some of its features, but they do not suffice for a full linguistic description. It is possible to form a rather clearer picture of educated Athenian speech, because it is obviously represented in much of Plato's dialogues and in New Comedy. Its colloquial character resides not in formal differences of pronunciation and grammar, but in those features that arise naturally in the conversational situation—a vocabulary copious and varied enough, but in general free from poetical or technical elements; the use of shorter and less elaborately constructed sentences, and of incomplete sentences and phrases the full meaning of which depends on the context of the conversation; frequent indication of the speaker's attitude; and appeals to the interest of the listener by means of questions, interjections, and particles.

The majority of literatures have owed their original impulse and much of their development to external influence. Greek literature, apart from some possibility of eastern influence on the beginnings of its epic tradition, was one of the few primary literatures of the world, in the sense of being an autonomous creation. Its development from the 7th century B.C. onward is associated with some, though not all, of the chief centres of initiative in the economic and political fields: Aeolic-speaking Lesbos, with its important city Mytilene, the Ionian cities, Athens, and the mixed but predominantly Doric-speaking communities of Sicily. Greek literature, wherever produced, became the property of Greeks everywhere; even communities whose contribution was meagre or non-existent could play a part as patrons. In view of the dialectal divisions of Greek, this combination of regional production and universal dissemination of literary works is of the greatest relevance to the character of the language in which they were written. Moreover, during the formative and classical periods of their literature the intellectual activity of the Greeks, at least in the centres of literary importance, was not subject to hierarchical or ideological authority, and so their language is not the rigid idiom of a priestly, bureaucratic, or learned caste, but one of great range, variety, and flexibility, providing for individual experiment and the development of personal styles.

Greek poetry includes a number of genres, and to each belongs its variety of language. One characteristic is common to almost all, namely some degree of artificiality. This remark does not necessarily apply to style and content: most classical Greek poetry is marked by a natural directness of expression and sincerity of feeling, and is capable of a high degree of realism in picturesque description, in narration of incidents, and in delineation of character and motive. However, most varieties of verse language are artificial in the sense of diverging in grammar and vocabulary from current usage. Such divergence is in general unacceptable in modern English poetry, and one of the most difficult tasks in translating Greek poetry into English is to give a fair impression simultaneously of its linguistic character and of its qualities of expression. This artificiality has its origin in the language of epic verse. It is generally agreed that the language of epic was developed during a centuries-long tradition of oral composition, beginning at least as early as the Mycenaean period, and that down to the emergence of the *Iliad* and the *Odyssey* at the end of the 8th century B.C., it had undergone a process of accretion, adaptation, and modernization at the hands of successive poet-reciters. Hence the language of epic, as it appears in the Homeric poems, presents an amalgam of older and later forms, together with poetic innovations motivated by metrical needs. Its vocabulary contains a high proportion of words no longer current or found only in remoter dialects such as Cypriot—the so-called *glottai* that seemed to Aristotle[9] the most characteristic feature of epic diction; even the meagre evidence of the Linear B tablets is enough to permit the inference that many or most of these were current in Mycenaean Greek. The final phase of the oral epic tradition belonged to Ionia, and its language assumed the form of an archaic Ionic mingled with non-Ionic, chiefly Aeolic, elements; by a natural association of linguistic with literary form this language was accepted as alone appropriate to verse in the heroic metre, the hexameter, and in the closely related elegiac metre. The dissemination of epic verse to other parts of the Greek world carried this language with it; the Boeotian Hesiod used it for his didactic, personal, and moralizing poetry with a few variations, some of which may reflect his local dialect. Elegy in the epic language was written not only by Ionian poets but also by the 7th-century Spartan Tyrtaeus and some half a century later by the Athenian statesman Solon.

In Ionia the 7th-century elegists made some concessions to contemporary dialect by admitting current forms and avoiding to a considerable extent the non-Ionic component, whereas their successors reverted in both respects to Homeric usage. The elegiac metre was also used for short funerary and other epigrams, in local dialect but so heavily under epic influence as to be virtually transposed epic: thus in an example from Sparta the expression *manin opid(d)omenos* is simply a Laconian version of the epic formula *menin opizomenos* (dreading the wrath).

The language of epic prefigures those of the other genres. It was artificial, in the sense defined; it was universally accepted and continued in use through the classical and post-classical periods as the appropriate language for verse written in certain metres; but at the same time it was not rigidly prescribed and incapable of variation. Moreover, just as early epic provided a model of poetic composition to which all other genres are heavily indebted, so its language deeply influenced theirs. It provided a stock of vocabulary and patterns of vocabulary formation already imbued, by association, with poetic quality, and its composite grammar supplied a number of metrically convenient and poetically charged variants.

The language of choral lyric, composed for performance at religious and other festivals, closely resembles that of epic in vocabulary and in much of its phonetic and inflexional character, but at the same time includes a number of features in common with the Doric dialects. This Doric colouring does not reflect the speech of any particular locality; the specifically Laconian elements in the *Partheneia* ("Maiden-song") of the 7th-century Spartan poet Alcman may be due to subsequent editing. Various hypotheses have been put forward to account for this mixture: that it is a generalized Doric developed under strong epic influence; that it is epic adapted to the speech of Dorian audiences; more recently, that it continues the language of a lost Mycenaean lyric, the apparently Doric features being explained as due to a different dialect base in Mycenaean Greek. However that may be, the language of choral lyric represents another common form of literary Greek, although admitting considerable variation. In the work of the early 6th-century poets Stesichorus and Ibycus (both Sicilians), the Doric, or apparently Doric, element is less marked than in that of Pindar, the greatest exponent of the genre, whose native Boeotian had many features in common with Doric; whereas in that of Simonides and Bacchylides (both Ionians) the non-epic element amounts to no more than a few conventional features. In this form it appears also in the choral parts of Attic tragedy.

Two poetic genres—the monodic (solo) lyric of Lesbos and Ionia, and verse written in iambic and trochaic metres, of which the tradition stemmed from Ionia—differ from those already mentioned in being composed in the dialect of the poet, and in being less elaborate in style. The use of native dialect is appropriate to verse forms the subject-matter of which includes the expression of personal feeling, as in lyric, and comment (often satirical) on personal experiences, contemporary affairs, and the human situation generally, as in iambo-trochaic verse. Epic influence tends to be confined to particular contexts, for example adaptations of Homeric expressions and themes, and invocations of gods; at the opposite pole, iambic verse, but not lyric, admits occasional vulgarisms. Varieties of iambic and trochaic metre were also adopted for the dialogue of Attic tragedy and comedy.

Athenian tragedy was a concomitant of the city's rapid rise to power and prosperity in the 5th century B.C. It was a form of mass entertainment, but with an intellectual as well as a popular appeal; its plots are derived almost wholly from epic and legendary material, but this is handled with freedom by the poets, who explore its possibilities for the expression of general human problems in terms of contemporary experience and attitudes of thought. The language of tragic dialogue is therefore close to normal Attic in form and basic vocabulary, yet sufficiently removed from it and sufficiently stylized to be the vehicle of poetry. Like early Attic prose, in contrast to the spoken and official languages, it uses *-ss-* rather than the native *-tt-* (which was perhaps felt to be a provincialism) in such words as *thalassa* (sea), *prassein* (act, do), and the peculiarly strict Attic use of the dual number is relaxed; it introduces variations of vocabulary, such as simple verbs for compound (*thneiskein*, die, for current *apo-thneiskein*), and alternative formations, such as *ekhthos* (hatred) for *ekhthra*, *stephos* (wreath) for *stephanos*, *naubates* (sailor) for *naútes*), together with synonyms and paraphrases to replace ordinary words, and a limited number of epic, Ionic, and even Doric words. The language of tragic dialogue is moreover not static; it reflects changing fashion and the development of the current language. Of all forms of Greek poetic language, that of tragic dialogue is perhaps the most supple and versatile.

The language of Old Comedy is basically current educated Attic, but corresponding to the range of topics it has a protean power of assuming the character of any grade or style of language. On the one hand are the elements of popular and vulgar speech, such as *oud' an stribilikinx* (not a bit), *tuntlazein* (to grub about); on the other hand are words invented to serve the purpose of parody or humour, such as *phrontisterion* (thought-shop, thinkery), and monstrous compounds such as *gliskhrantilogexepitriptos* (pettifogging) from *gliskhros* (sticky), *antilogos* (contrary, disputatious), and *epitriptos* (rogue). Within a century the Old Comedy of satire and phantasy had, in consequence of social and political changes, given way to New Comedy, with its realistic treatment of character and its plots of private intrigue and situation; this is written in elegant contemporary Attic, adapted—by a delicate range of shades between the more colloquial and the more literary—to the variety of characters and moods presented.

The first region to have a prose literature was Ionia. Although the dialect is clearly Ionic, its character is difficult to assess, partly owing to the fragmentary preservation of writings earlier than the latter part of the 5th century B.C., partly because the textual tradition and the work of later editors have introduced many changes of detail in dialect forms. It seems likely, however, that the Ionians had a single literary language, as they had a single official one. The fact that the prose tradition appears later than that of verse has given rise to a view, already held by some writers of antiquity, that prose had its origin in verse. Greek had its fables, handed down under the name of Aesop; that these were in prose is clear from the fact that Socrates is represented by Plato as occupied during his last days in versifying some of them.[10] Secondly, although epic verse and elegy were used for works of a partly didactic and expository character, metre and language were so closely connected that one can hardly conceive such a procedure as that described (for instance) by Strabo, when he speaks of the earlier prose writers as "having removed the metrical form while preserving the other poetic features." It is true that some of the early philosophers who used Ionic prose adopted epic words and used metaphor and simile in a way that may seem to us poetic, but this practice may signify no more than an attempt to extend the means of expression and to produce a style commensurate with the nature of the subject. The language of the early prose chroniclers is stated by more than one critic to have been simple and in pure dialect, in contrast with that of Herodotus, which is described as "variegated," "blended," "poetic," "most Homeric of all." The poetical element in Ionian prose appears therefore not as a survival from verse but as a deliberate embellishment. At the same time the original characteristics of Ionian prose continued in the more scientific kinds of writing: the medical treatises of the Hippocratic school are written in pure Ionic dialect and in a plain style; the case records preserved among them perhaps exemplify one of the earliest types of non-literary (technical) prose.

The prestige of Ionian culture was such that Ionic was used as a written dialect also by non-Ionians, such as the medical writers of the Doric-speaking islands Cos and Cnidos, and the historians Antiochus of Syracuse and Hellanicus of Lesbos in the late 5th century B.C. The use of Ionic by a Syracusan historian is the more remarkable because there existed already in the culturally and commercially advanced states of Sicily a tradition of Doric prose, of which little survives; the most important works composed in it, the mathematical treatises of Archimedes, belong to a later period, when it had become little more than a formally Doricized variety of common Greek.

The second half of the 5th century saw the beginnings of prose literature in Athens. The basis of Attic prose is the same educated spoken Attic heard in the language of comedy. Its earliest writers, especially Thucydides, made some concessions to the usage of Ionic and the majority of dialects by using -*ss*-, -*rs*-, in such words as *thalassa* (sea), *tharsos* (courage— Attic *thalatta, tharros*); some Ionic influence is perceptible in the epideictic or "display" oratory of the early orator Antiphon; but in the main, Attic prose, although stylistically elaborated on lines suggested by such teachers as Gorgias of Leontini and Thrasymachus of Chalcedon (themselves non-Athenians), is based on Attic speech and reflects the changing features of the dialect in the 4th and 3rd centuries B.C. This is natural, because its most characteristic genres are the speech, whether composed for actual delivery or as a pamphlet for written publication, and the philosophical dialogue. The new movement in education associated with the so-called Sophists in the 5th century had brought about a great extension of vocabulary, especially in the sphere of rhetoric and in the moral, political, and psychological fields, which can be detected not only in prose but also in the dialogue of tragedy and comedy, and much of which no doubt became current in educated speech, to judge from occasional parodies in Aristophanes. During the 4th century the conservative character of Attic was becoming less marked, and variations between earlier and later, anomalous and regularized forms appear, especially in the language of the orators.

Apart from its high degree of stylistic maturity, the most conspicuous feature of all Greek writing is its intellectual character. This is not a feature of prose alone; verse, too, is often discursive and logical, quick to grasp the significance of the particular in relation to the universal, and not merely to imply this but to give it overt linguistic expression. Examples are not rare even in Homer. Agamemnon, disciplining unruly troops, reminds them that they are not all commanders, and clinches his words with the general statement *ouk agathon polukoiranie* (not a good thing [is] many in command).[11] In these famous words, repeated by Aristotle in the *Metaphysics* as the final argument for the unity of the divine government of the universe, the compound is used in a way typical of prose; it transposes the syntactical collocation *polloi koiranoi* (many commanders) into a form that marks its detachment from any particular concrete situation; similarly the use of the adjective *agathon* in the neuter, instead of in agreement with the feminine gender of the subject noun, marks its function as not merely descriptive but categorizing.

A language capable of serving as the means of intellectual expression is, in its most important aspects, a deliberate creation, produced by exploitation and extension of resources available in its formal structure of grammar and vocabulary. It is therefore a social and cultural phenomenon, and, no less than the works written in it, an index of the intellectual level of the people who use it. Intellectual expression requires a number of linguistic features that are related in their functioning and usually to some extent combined in their exponents. The first is a grammatical structure that, while providing for stylistic variety, makes it possible for the units of meaning to be placed in a variety of syntactical relations and to be modified in various ways. The principal means by which these operations are carried out in Greek have already been described. The second requirement is a stock of words of wide semantic extension, such as *prattein* (do, act); *gignesthai* (become, come into existence); *paskhein* (undergo, be affected); *ekhein* (have, be in a certain condition); these provide for a common framework of discourse adaptable to particular types of subject matter. A third need is for special and technical terms by which that framework can be applied to the particular subject treated. In English such vocabulary is mostly borrowed or constructed from borrowed elements so that, especially in the case of philosophical and scientific terms, it forms a constituent of the vocabulary initially distinct from that of ordinary discourse. In Greek it is constituted by semantic specialization, or sometime generalization of ordinary current terms, and by derivation from current terms. Modern medical and mathematical terminologies preserve a number of these, such as "cachexia," from Greek *kakhexia*, a transformation of the common expression *kakhos ekhein* (be in a bad condition); "nephritis," from *he nephritis* (*nosos*) (the disease of the kidneys, from *nephros* [kidney]); "hypotenuse," from *he hupoteinousa* (*gramme*) (the line stretching underneath, subtending), participle of the common verb *hupo-teinein*, which has a number of non-mathematical meanings; "isoceles," from *isoskeles* (having equal legs—*isos*, equal, and *skelos*, leg). Current and technical vocabulary form a single corpus in Greek to a degree unknown in most modern languages. In Greek philosophy, at least down to the time of Aristotle, the most striking aspect of the language is its capacity for generalization and the direct relation of its terminology to current speech. For example, the Sophist and rhetorician Gorgias, whose style was famous in antiquity for its use of antithesis and other stylistic ornament, formulates in the following sentence a principle later known as "the right of the strong": *pephuke gar ou to kreisson hupo tou hessonos koluesthai, alla to hesson hupo tou kreissonos arkhesthai kai agesthai, kai to men kreisson hegeisthai, to de hesson hepesthai* (for it is natural, not for the stronger to be restrained by the weaker, but for the weaker to be ruled and led by the stronger, and for the stronger to command, the weaker to follow).[12] The vocabulary of this sentence is both simple and highly general; the use of neuter adjectives as nouns gives no indication of particular context or subject-matter, so that the sentence as a whole can be read as a formula applicable to any pair of terms satisfying the relation *kreisson* (stronger): *hesson* (weaker). Such a language is, of course, no guarantee against the risk of ambiguity, tautology, or even downright nonsense; but it allows general arguments to be stated and developed without the encumbrance of a semantically restricted vocabulary tied to traditional thought-patterns; it is free from over-specialized terminology and easily intelligible to the ordinary educated person. This is especially true of the philosopher Plato. The ordinary Greek might have found it hard to follow Plato's thought, but he would not have found it hard to understand his language.

Factors tending to linguistic unification have already been noted: inter-dialectal communication, the establishment of regional official languages, the diffusion of genre languages. Even by the end of the 6th century B.C. conditions were ripe for more thorough unification, given a favourable sequence of historical developments. The Persian invasion of Greece in 480–479 B.C. called forth an unprecedented unity of purpose and effort on the part of Athens and the Peloponnesian states. This unity did not long survive the withdrawal of the Persian army, and its collapse provided the opportunity for Athens, already the chief naval power, to assume the leadership of those cities, chiefly Ionian, that had been liberated from Persian rule. The league that they formed soon became virtually an Athenian empire; during the 5th century B.C. Athens rose to eminence as the chief cultural centre of Greece, and one of its leading commercial powers. Its foreign population increased; numbers of Ionians became temporary residents while awaiting the settlement of legal business that they were obliged to transact at Athens; and settlements of Athenian citizens, different from the old type of colony in not being independent states, were set up on the Aegean islands and coasts. The extension of the Attic dialect has thus two aspects. As a means of oral communication it spread in the Ionian area owing to Athens' dominant political and commercial position. Attic influence is perceptible in the inscriptions of some Ionian cities before the end of the 5th century, and becomes increasingly marked during the 4th. At the same time the prestige of Athens as a literary and educational centre led to an extended use of Attic as a language of prose; the 4th-century historians Ephorus of Cyme and Theopompus of Chios, both pupils of the Athenian Isocrates, used it for their historical works. The Attic that was now spreading beyond Attica was no rigidly codified language, but a developing form of speech; many of its more recent features coincide with Ionic, and are probably due to Ionic influence. One Athenian writer, Xenophon, used a language so aberrant as not to be regarded as true Attic; this was no doubt partly due to the fact that for most of his life he was an exile, and wrote his chief works in Peloponnesus. His vocabulary shows a considerable mixture of Doric and poetic as well as Ionic words, together with many that became common only in the ensuing Hellenistic period. Other Athenian writers—e.g. Hyperides, Menander, Epicurus—show in varying degrees the changing character of Attic, chiefly in vocabulary but also in some details of inflexion and syntax. The linguistic development of the Attic-Ionic area in the late classical period is therefore a process of assimilation between the dialects, the outcome of which was to be a single form of speech based on Attic, to which Ionic in its final phase made a significant contribution.

At the same time the character of Hellenism was changing. Isocrates, in his *Panegyricus* (*c.* 380 B.C.), noted what was emerging: "It is the achievement of our city that the name of Hellene is no longer considered that of a race but of a way of thought, and that those are called Hellenes who share in our culture rather than those who share our common blood."[13] The Greeks had created a culture capable of universalization, and the language that had come to express it was Attic. Already by the middle of the preceding century, and possibly earlier, a step had been taken that was to be crucial for the future of Greek: the Hellenization of the ruling family and aristocracy of Macedonia, among whom the tragic poet Euripides and the painter Zeuxis found a welcome. Philip of Macedon had not only political astuteness and military power to promote his rise to hegemony of Greece, but also his Hellenic culture. On the basis of Graeco-Macedonian military potential his son Alexander succeeded in 10 years in uniting under his command two worlds—Greece (apart from its western outpost in Italy and Sicily), and the Persian Empire (from the Black Sea to the frontier of Nubia and from the Mediterranean to the borders of India). He thus opened the East to the spread of Greek culture and language; the story of his carrying a text of Homer on his campaigns has even more symbolic than factual significance.

The effect of Alexander's conquests, continued by the kingdoms into which his empire was divided after his death, was to shift the political and cultural centres of the Greek-speaking world away from the old states of Greece. The administration and security of the Hellenistic kingdoms were based on Greek or Graecized bureaucracies and Graeco-Macedonian armies, which provided careers for those whose energies and ambitions could no longer find satisfaction in their native cities. The Hellenistic capitals—Alexandria in Egypt, Antioch in Syria, Pergamum in Mysia—were enabled by the patronage of their rulers to outstrip the old cultural centres. Greek settlements carried Greek language and culture into the interior of non-Greek-speaking territories. In all this area Greek became the universal medium of administration, inter-state relations, business, and culture. Beyond the frontiers of the Hellenistic states, the kings of Nubia and the border kingdoms set up their inscriptions in Greek and no doubt used it as a diplomatic language; so to some extent did Rome, for example in its dealings with Carthage; a series of Roman historians in the 3rd and 2nd centuries B.C. wrote histories of their own state in Greek; and in the time of Augustus, King Juba of Mauretania used Greek for his numerous historical, philological, and other writings.

Within the Hellenistic kingdoms, besides being the administrative and cultural medium, Greek had two roles: as a mother tongue and, for non-Greeks, as a second language. Except in Asia Minor the spread of Greek did not lead to the extinction of other tongues, which continued to be spoken and in a few cases, such as Egyptian, written. It was thus natural that Greek should be used for the dissemination of Christianity, and that eventually the various Christian communities should adopt local languages, Aramaic and Syriac, Egyptian (in its later form known as Coptic), and in the Byzantine period Gothic and Slavonic, into which they also translated the scriptures. In this way a number of new literary languages were constituted on the model of Greek. In the West, Greek influence was no less important, though different in its means of action; the Hellenization of Roman culture and its effect on the Latin language, and consequently on the linguistic development of Europe in general, is a fascinating and far-reaching subject. When Greece and the Hellenistic kingdoms were ultimately absorbed into the Roman Empire, both Latin and Greek were used as administrative languages, and Latin administrative terminology was borrowed into Greek or translated by Greek terms.

The relationship of this Hellenistic Greek with the older Greek dialects deserves mention. The process of inter-dialect assimilation continued, and the official texts of many cities give the impression of being written in a common Greek, in which dialect features are a concession to local speech and an assertion of political identity; occasional faulty adaptations to dialect suggest that their authors habitually spoke and thought in Attic. Some dialect inscriptions incorporate documents in this common Attic; for example, an inscription of Larisa[14] contains the text, in Thessalian, of decrees passed by the city in accordance with instructions given in two letters of Philip V of Macedon, written in 219 and 214 B.C. The letters are given in their original Attic form, and the first also in a local version that is little more than a mechanical adaptation of the original to Thessalian pronunciation and grammar. The same tale is told by the inscriptions of the Aetolian and Achaean leagues, which in the 4th and 3rd centuries B.C. maintained themselves as independent powers; their official languages are forms of West Greek so attenuated as to be merely common Greek with a few formal West Greek features. In one city after another, dialect forms disappear from inscriptions, apart from occasional archaizing revivals as late as the 2nd century A.D., which mean nothing for the history of the language. The spoken dialects in country districts must have been more tenacious; literary references attest the use of Doric in Messenia and elsewhere as late as the 2nd century A.D.; but gradually they must have sunk to the status of regional speech, in the same way that over considerable areas of England local dialects have given place to regionally coloured variants of common English. Finally they disappeared, making little or no contribution to the further development of the language, except in Laconia, where the Tsaconian dialect of Modern Greek contains a substantial element derived from old Laconian.

The common Greek of the Hellenistic period is known by the name given to it in antiquity, the Koine—*he koine* (*dialektos*) (the common language). This term is applied, in accordance with the practice of Greek grammarians, both to the spoken form and to the language of post-Aristotelian prose writers, except those of the Atticist school in the 1st and 2nd centuries A.D. The Koine is a continuation of 4th-century Attic, modified by the influence of Ionic and further developed in the new conditions created by Alexander's empire. The Ionic element consists mainly of details of vocabulary. Changes of pronunciation are partly disguised by spelling, which remains as established at the adoption of the Ionic alphabet in Athens at the end of the 5th century B.C., but are betrayed by spelling mistakes, especially in documents written by less-educated persons. A tendency to lose the distinction between long and short vowels may have manifested itself in uneducated speech as early as the 5th century B.C.; it gradually became general and led to a change in the rhythm of the language, which ultimately came to depend on the position of the accent. The loss of the aspirate may have been partly due to the influence of Ionic, from which it had long since disappeared. The use of the dual by Hellenistic writers is an archaism confined to the Atticists. The optative mood, which Greek had continued from Indo-European alongside the subjunctive, survived mainly in formulas of wish, as in the New Testament; the Atticists, in attempting to revive its other uses, reveal its absence from the spoken language by their mistakes. The infinitive was beginning to be rivalled by the construction *hína* (in order that) with the subjunctive, which was eventually to replace it completely; and the distinction between the perfect and aorist tenses was in process of disappearance. To judge especially from some papyri and works of a linguistically popular character, such as the first two Gospels, the spoken Koine was already characterized by the initial stages of developments that were to culminate in Byzantine and Modern Greek.

As a written language the Koine was an idiom of prose; poetry continued to be written in variations of the old genre languages, with such innovations as Theocritus's use of Sicilian Doric in hexameter verse and Callimachus's Doricized epic in elegy. In prose the Koine was used almost exclusively for works of importance in every field. It shows considerable variation from one author to another, however, according to the extent to which they approximate to the norm of classical Attic or to the spoken language. The Atticizing movement reached its extreme expression in the so-called Second Sophistic of the 2nd century A.D., when a rhetorician could make it his boast to have used no word that he had not found in a book,[15] and scholars compiled dictionaries of Attic words to distinguish "Attic" usage from "Hellenic" or "common." Even the language of Christianity came under Atticist influence, to which the duals and optatives (often wrongly used) of Clement of Alexandria bear witness; writers such as Basil and Johannes Chrysostom are, in style as in language, rhetoricians in the Atticist manner.

The polemic of the Atticists and anti-Atticists should not, however, obscure the fact that the written Koine too was tending to become artificial and archaic in relation to the spoken language. No language used as a literary medium can be entirely free from tension between its written and spoken forms. Where there is a fairly high level of general literacy this may cause little difficulty and even pass more or less unnoticed. If the literary form has a long tradition, however, and particularly if it looks back to a classical period of high prestige, it is liable to be trammelled by conservative tendencies that increasingly divorce it from the development of the spoken idiom. Sometimes a breaking point is reached and a new literary language, based on the spoken language, is created, as in the case of Latin and the Romance languages. Greek from the Hellenistic period onward has known this tension to a high degree, but despite the conservatism of the written language on the one hand, and the development and eventual diversification into dialects of the spoken language on the other, the link was never broken; the unity of Greek has been maintained by a series of partial accommodations. The "language question" that has troubled the history of Modern Greek has its roots in the Hellenistic period. It has never been completely solved, but equally it has never reached the breaking point.

References

1. Aeschylus, *Agamemnon* 20–1.
2. Herodotus, *Histories* I, 142.
3. M. N. TOD, *A Selection of Greek Historical Inscriptions*, Vol. I, 2nd edn (Oxford 1946), p. 1.
4. *ibid.*, p. 37.
5. Plato, *Apology* 17d.
6. Aristophanes, *Acharnians* 751–2.
7. Aeschylus, *Choephori* 751.
8. *Constitution of Athens* II, 8.
9. Aristotle, *Rhetoric* III, 1406b; *Art of Poetry* 1459a.
10. Plato, *Phaedo* 60d–61b.
11. *Iliad* II, 204; quoted in Aristotle, *Metaphysics* XII, 1076a.
12. Gorgias, *Praise of Helen* 6.
13. Isocrates, *Panegyricus* 50.
14. *Inscriptiones graecae* IX, ii, 517; C. D. BUCK, *The Greek Dialects* (Chicago 1955), pp. 220–3.
15. Aelius Aristides, *Rhetoric* 2, 6.

Bibliography

J. CHADWICK, *The Decipherment of Linear B*, 2nd edn (Cambridge 1968).
A. DEBRUNNER, *Geschichte der griechischen Sprache*, II: Grundfragen und Grundzüge des nachklassischen Griechisch (Berlin 1954).
O. HOFFMANN, *Geschichte der griechischen Sprache*, I: bis zum Ausgang der klassischen Zeit, 3rd edn, revised by A. Debrunner (Berlin 1953).
A. MEILLET, *Aperçu d'une histoire de la langue grecque*, 6th edn (Paris 1948).
E. SCHWYZER, *Griechische Grammatik*, Vol. I, 3rd edn (Munich 1959), pp. 1–165.

CHAPTER 5

The Latin Language

N. E. Collinge*

No intrinsic qualities are indispensable to a language's being the vehicle of a sophisticated literature, nor to its achieving world-wide use. Once it has become the medium of political or cultural or financial dominance, non-natives will fall over themselves to master its intricacies and inadequacies. Latin had other advantages too. Its phonology, or system of sounds, rested on articulations that were neither particularly complex nor exotic; and while the language was a living idiom, the system was always able to evolve without disruption. The orthography mostly reflected the essential sound oppositions, and had achieved a stable format by the time of Rome's imperial expansion. Hence, alongside the vivid varieties of speech that spawned the Romance descendants,† a standardized form emerged. Its grammar, although complex in terms of selection of subtly different items, was generated by syntactical rules few in number and rarely involving alternatives or ambiguities in meaning. This standard form, despite local predilections for *uerba non trita Romae* (words not common coin at Rome),[1] produced an amazingly homogeneous literature, although among its practitioners an actual Roman was a rarity.[2]

We know the language of the classical Roman civilization from contemporary inscriptions: some official, stilted, and formulaic, others thoroughly informal scratchings of love and hate; we know it also from fragmentary papyrus documents, late in date, on the fringe of the Roman social area and not commonly of literary value. Above all, we know it from the mediaeval manuscripts, a slender and arbitrary lifeline, with the exemplars mostly lost; using the correctives supplied by study of the inscriptions and by the comments of native writers, scholars have from this source produced more or less definitive texts.‡ In these, two things are clear. First, that although linguistic performance normally reflects social

* Professor and Director of the Centre for Linguistic Studies, University of Toronto.
† See Volume II, "The Romance Languages."
‡ See Volume II, "The Survival of Culture."

levels, there are no fixed literary conventions of speech discrimination (although aptness and degrees of high and low style distinguish genres from one another). The wide differences of language that mark the distinct social classes in Sanskrit drama, or the stylized dialectalisms imposed by the different genres in Greek literature, are absent from Latin. Second, no form of Latin literature is entirely native, not even the varied group of documents usually called "satire." The Greeks gave the forms; and in taking them over, the Romans opened their own speech to the topics, allusions, verbiage, and even structures of the Greek vehicle. We shall later consider how Latin, at all levels, reacted to this inescapable kindred culture, so articulate and for the most part so prestigious.

To use traditional terminology, Latin is an inflexional language. Its semantic categories and its word segments are equally easy to analyse and list, but devilish to match: the genitive plural of *puella* is *puellarum*, but where precisely is one to locate the "genitive" and the "plural" element in the ending? Even the location of the stem-boundary (before or after the *a*?) can be in dispute. Rare appearances of "agglutination" do not nullify this diagnosis, despite the formal congruence in semantically opposed bits of, say, *e-uoca-ba-nt-ur* and *de-terre-bi-m-us*.* Equally irrelevant is the isolating tendency of late Latin (*ego amare habeo*) for the future, etc.). It is, in fact, a "word-and-paradigm" language,[3] employing comparatively few "form" words, i.e. isolated items that other languages use to show things such as the tense of the verb. This does not mean that Latin was more efficient as a language. But it does make for the quality sometimes obscurely called "lapidary," which enlarges meaning essentially by means of word order. Take, for example, *Rusticus urbanum murem mus paupere fertur / accepisse cauo, ueterem uetus hospes amicum.*[4] (A country mouse, the tale goes, welcomed in his modest den a city mouse, friends of long standing, host and guest.) Horace here prettily juxtaposes the corroborative words, which tell us that in both cases a mouse is involved, and that their friendship and hospitality are equally long-standing. This juxtapositioning is balanced by another one, which calls attention to the differences in the mice's roles and status (*rusticus urbanum, hospes amicum*). The skill lies in the placing together of grammatical meaning and dictionary meaning. Again, contemporary religious acceptance (even of ruler worship up to a point), the promise of Roman empire and its world-wide domain, its

---

* In each case the prefix modifies the meaning of the stem (*uoco*, I call; *euoco*, I call out, summon; *terreo*, I frighten; *deterreo*, I frighten from, discourage) and the three elements after the stem show respectively the tense (*ba* for imperfect, *bi* for future), the person and number (*nt* for third person plural, *m* for first person plural), and the voice (*ur* for passive, *us* for active).

need for fair administration and the smiling acquiescence of all subject nations—all these Horace can convey in six words: *te minor laetum reget aequus orbem*[5] (accepting your [Jupiter's] divine leadership he [Augustus] will be the just ruler of a happy world).*

Upon these basic features Latin superimposes usages of native "intuitive style," as it were. One such is that pairing of items of balanced meaning known as "dicolon." The device is not limited to contrived antithesis of the Hellenic sort or emotive repetition on the Asiatic pattern, though Latin has plenty of the *terra marique* and *abi abi* types. Where Sanskrit fuses couples into compounds (*ajāvayas*, goats and sheep; *kṛtākṛtam*, the done and the not done; even *vayaṃvayam*," our very selves), Latin leaves the items separate, sometimes not even coupled at all. An early republican epitaph offers the compliment *fortis . . . sapiensque*, and about three centuries later Suetonius glosses the Sabine name Nero as *fortis ac strenuus*.[6] Epithets of this kind link themselves two by two throughout the classical period, 12 examples appearing in Horace's *Epistles* alone. The uncoupled type *reppulit propulit* (pushed back and forth), *lepida hilara* (charming and gay), decreases in frequency outside legal or religious formulae, but in its heyday it makes the most of that lively sense of the sound of a word, particularly its initial syllable, that the Italians certainly did share, along with early word-initial stress: *labitur liquitur* (glides and flows), *dant danunt* (give and

---

* The aspects of the Latin language that are involved here can perhaps be simplified by seeing what happens when one tries to turn these sentences into English. The opposition between the country mouse and the city mouse cannot be expressed in English by the position and order of the words, because in English position and order are needed to make the grammar clear, and we have to lay out the sentence in such a way as to indicate grammatical structure by word order and not, as in Latin, by case-ending. Literally translated, the Latin sentence reads: "Country (nominative) city (accusative) mouse (accusative) mouse (nominative) in modest, it is said, received in den old (accusative) old (nominative) host (nominative) guest (accusative)." The meaning can, of course, be communicated in English prose (as in the text above) but the poetic interest of the line cannot. Doubtless this is true of the difference between prosaic and poetic statements of the "same" thing in any language; Latin poetry itself differs from Latin prose. The particular advantages enjoyed by Latin, and here exploited by Horace, lie in its being not dependent on words such as "a" and "in," and in its being able to put the major semantic markers in patterned juxtaposition.

In the second quotation from Horace, we see how Latin can go from word to word, expressing the facets of a situation with an economy for which English knows no equivalent. In *laetum reget aequus orbem*, the placing of *laetum* first is a common device (hyperbaton, or inversion of the "natural" order), which might be imitated in English thus: "Happy the realm he will rule, just dealer—yes, the earth." We have used, however, eleven words instead of four, and have still lost the force of the final placing of *orbem* because English demands that some noun be made to follow "happy." The Latin *laetum* does not tell us what is to be made so happy by the rule of the virtually divine Augustus, whose presence is established by and as *aequus*—a word that is an adjective, but has the concreteness also of a noun ("the just and honourable man"), and the adverbial effect here of qualifying the way Augustus rules. The juxtaposition of *aequus* and *orbem* matches the virtue of the ruler against the hitherto undisclosed magnitude of all that is happy in his rule—"yes, the earth."

donate), *ui uiolentia* (by force and violence), *seruitutem seruire* (have the status of slave), or with copula *satis superque* (enough and more than enough), *armis animisque* (by arms and courage), *lance et licio* (with dish and loin-cloth—a legal term connected with the Roman rules about house search).

Natural extension then obscures the idiom: Plautus's *algor error pauor* (chill, loss of way, fright) or Cato's citation of *prohibessis defendas auerruncesque* (restrain, repel, avert) foreshadows alike the laconic *ueni uidi uici* and the architectural

> Quid pater Ismario, quid mater profuit Orpheo?
>   carmine quid uictas obstupuisse feras?[7]
>
> (What good did his father, what good did his mother do Ismarian Orpheus? What did it avail that the beasts had been bent by song dumbfounded to his will?)

This is the "tricolon" with parts of increasing length, a figure familiar from many sources.[8] Familiar, too, is the redundant enumeration that leads to Ennius's *maerentes flentes lacrumantes commiserantes* (grieving, weeping, shedding tears, bewailing) or *neue inde nauis incohandi exordium coepisset*[9] (the "start to commence to begin" way of speaking, so dear to our childhood). Just why Latin is so markedly devoted to this pleonasm is less easy to say. It is not a matter of subtle philosophical distinctions (typical of the Greek Sophists) or of antithesis (typical of the Greeks generally), but rather the lawyer's reluctance to leave loopholes plus the priest's awareness of the aura cast by alliteration. So we find phrases such as *posidere fruique* (possess and enjoy), *posidere habereque* (have and hold), *inprobus intestabilis* (in legal error and disqualified), *dolo sciens* (with guile and malice), and in poetic Romanized philosophy *inane uacansque* (emptiness and void), or *speciem ac formam* (shape and form).[10] There is poetic padding in Virgil's

> omnia praecepi atque animo mecum ante peregi[11]
>
> (all this I have already envisaged and already rehearsed in my mind).

But this (like his, and others', tricola and tetracola and pentacola and so forth) is less to the point than emotional, but not stylized, utterances such as

> quia *me meamque rem*, quod in te uno fuit,
> tuis *scelestis, falsidicis* fallaciis
> *delacerauisti deartuauistique* opes.
> confecisti omnis *res ac rationes* meas.[12]
>
> (because me and my interest, as far as you could unaided, with your villainous and misleading deceits you have torn and dismembered my possessions; you've ruined my property and my plans.)

Likewise, Cicero's phrase for "perfection" is *absolutio perfectioque* and for "trickery" is *fraudes atque fallaciae* or *fucus ac fallaciae*.

From structures, let us get back to bricks. For Indo-European speakers the minimum unit of sound in language, at least of intuitively recognized significant segments, is the phoneme. This distinctive unit has long been credited with a psychological reality. (There are perhaps "prosodic" languages, in which the sounds that distinguish meanings are carried, in over-lapping fashion, over long stretches of the utterance. But Latin is not of their number; clues such as regular vowel harmony are not to be seen in it.) The phoneme is a good yardstick, therefore, to measure the viability and elasticity of the idiom. This is all the more so because the spelling reflects the phonemes fairly efficiently. In the early period the phoneme inventory totals 27 (if one counts vowel length as a single separate item), or 31 (if long and short vowels count individually). By Cicero's time the tally was 31 or 36.[13] The range can be from 13 (Hawaiian) to 84, although the latter figure (Ubykh) is extreme, and around 45 (Chipewyan in Athabascan) is a safer citation. What matters is the distribution; this depends partly on the ratio of those phonemes that habitually occupy an articulatory peak to those that occur in the troughs or transitions between peaks of inherent sonority (see Allen[13]). This is the ratio of vowels to consonants, which we intuitively accept. It normally lies between $1 : 1\frac{1}{11}$ (Bella Coola) and $1 : 1\frac{5}{8}$ (8 : 13) (Finnish, ignoring diphthongs) or $1 : 1\frac{3}{5}$ (5 : 8) (Hawaiian). Early Latin has $1 : 2\frac{2}{3}$ (6 : 16), Ciceronian Latin $1 : 3\frac{1}{6}$ (6 : 19), if we discount diphthongs and the length feature. However, if long and short vowels are differentiated, and diphthongs are allowed to function as peaks like simple vowels—as they do in quantitative verse—the proportions become 15 : 16 and 17 : 19 respectively, giving more or less maximal flexibility in the building of vowel and consonant (V and C) sequences. Prodigality recurs in the permitted shapes of syllables. Normal are V, VC, CV, CVC, CCV, $CCVC$ (with some limitations of CC combinations). No sequence of syllables is impossible, but some are rare. Even $V + V + V$ occurs every time a woman is called *Gāĭă*. And for literature two results follow. First, an enormous variety of expressive sound patterns is possible without loss of intelligibility. Second, every type of quantitative verse (that is, of metrical sequences based on the structure of syllables, these being assigned to one or other of two classes, heavy and light) could be imported, however foreign, with no need arising to tailor the language in order to use the borrowed verse-form.[14] This receptivity was, however, not put to the test by the Greek metres that actually were brought in, because the two languages are too similar at this level.

Some scholars are happier without phonemes. They prefer to state the sound segments as items of grammar, and to define them with reference to rules that specify combinations of distinctive features universal to all languages. For them the prodigality of Latin consists in this: it needs but five or six such features, with choice of presence or absence in a given segment, to establish its segment inventory, and it uses 11. To put it crudely, it has more sounds than it needs for its way of establishing significant segments of sound. This gives an efficiency fraction, if we divide the features needed by the features used, of 45–55 per cent, although several languages hover around 50 per cent. There is also a sliding scale of acceptability for sequences of consonants; an adequate grammar, it is said, will account for the fact that English has /brik/† (brick), happens not to have */blik/, but "cannot" have **/bnik/. In Latin there are numerous degrees: *cras*, **clas* (*clam*, *clarus* occur), ***cnas* (*Cn-idus*, etc., only in borrowed names), ****cmas* (-*cm*- medially in borrowings). We arrive at complete rejection finally with the type *****cpas*. The language sets a limit, then, to its freedom of form, but remains elastic enough to welcome exotica aboard.

In grammar (in the sense of morphology and syntax), however, one sees a counterbalance, in the underemployment of distinctive markers. The fact is unmistakable. In the four main noun declensions there are 66 grammatically distinct case + number situations; to express these, only 28 different terminations occur.[15] Many functions are assigned to one form, and several forms have the same function (by the inherited division into "declensions"). The marker -*as* operates in indeclinables (*fas*), nominative singular of various stem types (*uas*, *mas*, *optimas*, or the fossil *paricidas*), accusative plural of *a*-stems (*terras*), as well as the formulaic relic in the genitive singular (*paterfamilias*), to mention only noun forms; add to these the verb forms, second singular present indicative (*amas*), subjunctive (*regas*), and past indicative (*eras*), and the time adverbs (*cras*, *alias*)—and the point is clear enough. To assess the literary value of this economy in forms one must calculate the degree of choice open to a writer at given points in syntactical structures. For literature the moral is that the ends of words are less crucial and more predictable than their beginnings (novel as this idea may seem in Latin) and less listened to: Latin writers reflect this deafness by their very sparing use of end rhyme. Ennius alone presses it hard, and even he employs syllable clusters:

† A letter set off by oblique strokes, e.g., /k/, represents a *phoneme*, or basic theoretical unit of sound in language; a letter in square brackets, e.g., [k], represents a positionally determined pronounced variant, or *allophone*, of the phoneme; a colon,: , after a vowel lengthens it. Syllables preceded by one or more asterisks denote forms that *can* be generated but that do not, acceptably, occur; the more asterisks, the less thinkable the form.

>caelum nitescere, arbores frondescere,
>uites laetificae pampinis pubescere,
>rami bacarum ubertate incuruescere.[16]

>(the sky is bright, the trees in leaf, the cheering vines and their shoots
>move to maturity, the branches bend with the rich olive crop.)

Such also are his often cited verses that play on the disyllable -*ari* and the trisyllable -*arier*. The -*escere* forms beguiled Tertullian four centuries later. Otherwise, rhymes such as Virgil's successive verse endings in -*abat* or -*ebant*, and the so-called "leonine" effect (where the last word of the line rhymes with the one before the caesura) are comparatively uncommon varieties of the general figure known as homoeoteleuton (like-ended), which was by no means common itself. Middle-to-end rhymes in Horace's *Odes* have been shown to be limited to words between which grammatical concord subsists;[17] the device is just another syntactical signpost, to help the reader who is labouring with disturbed word-order in an unfamiliar verse-form. The sound effect is merely a consequence of this. Larger structures of sound are another matter, as indeed with Ennius. Hence the liking for repetitions:

>passer mortuus est meae puellae,
>passer deliciae meae puellae

>(dead is my lady's linnet, my lady's darling linnet)

or

>quam bene, Caune, tuo poteram nurus esse parenti,
>quam bene, Caune, meo poteras gener esse parenti

>(well, Caunus, could I have been your parent's daughter-in-law,
>and well could you have been my parent's son-in-law)

or the ring-structure, of whole words;

>cessas in uota precesque,
>Tros, ait, Aenea, cessas?

>(are you so slow to pray, she cried, Trojan Aeneas, so slow?)

or the precious phrasal intricacies of

>crudelis tu quoque, mater;
>crudelis mater magis an puer improbus ille?
>improbus ille puer; crudelis tu quoque, mater.[18]

>(you too are cruel, mother Venus; or is the mother cruel, and not,
>rather, the boy Cupid unfeeling? Unfeeling the boy; but you too
>are cruel, mother.)

Sound patterns use all parts of words. Horace's *qualem ministrum fulminis alitem* (like to the winged guardian of the thunderbolt), or Virgil's *nec uero* hae sine sorte *da*tae, sine *iudice, sedes* (nor are these resting places assigned without discrimination or arbiter) or *ille uolat* simul *arua fuga* simul *aequora uerrens* (he flies and sweeps in flight at once the fields and the ocean), are harbingers of the mediaeval exploitation:

> hora novissima, tempora pessima sunt, vigilemus:
> ecce minaciter imminet arbiter ille supremus[19]
>
> (the hour is our last, the times at their worst, let us keep watch; see,
> threatening looms the greatest Judge of all)

—only one of the many astonishing refabrications of the now two-millennia-old hexameter.[20]

Literary Latin had a love-hate relationship with Greek. "Let us use our own language and not, like some, ram in Greek words and earn derision," cried Cicero (who Hellenized, in fact, more than most: Shakespeare's Casca makes no unfair comment on him—"he spoke Greek").[21] Latin digested mouthful after mouthful of Hellenic speech-forms. Their linguistic confidence allowed Latin speakers not to worry about distancing their idiom from all that is foreign, but neither did they diffidently let it be swamped by the locutions of influential outsiders. There were sporadic expulsions of the *peregrina insolentia*[22] (foreign affectation), but they had little effect on the evolution of the self-conscious idiom, except where an individual author made a stand. The proportion of all foreign and rare words in the *Aeneid* is less than half that in the comparable poetry of Catullus or Cicero; but this indicates how untypical Virgil is. The Greeks had much to offer at all levels of civilized expression; each Roman period and genre borrowed extensively and in its own way.

A convenient terminology for such loans runs through a scale from "code-switching" by way of "interference" to "integration."[23] The first extreme leaves the model unchanged, a foreign word, usually in a foreign spelling (even Greek letters), and obtrusive: *lyncas* or *hamadryasin*. This is perhaps "code-transfer," for true switching should mean things such as Scaliger's famous *utinam hunc haberemus integrum et amisissemus Lucanum, Statium, Silium Italicum et tous ces garçons-là*." And indeed one may be unsure to what tongue a transfer belongs, as with Cicero's two-word sentence *plane aporo* (I am wholly at a loss).[24] Interference denotes an obtrusive loan that has nevertheless been accepted into the dictionary of the borrowing language: for example, *tmesis* in Latin or in English.

Integration is of two kinds: either some tinkering fits the loan into the systems of its new language (so *scaena* offends no Latin rule of sound or form), or a translation-replacement (a *calque**) is found. Unselfconscious writers and speakers intuitively adopt integration of the former type. The soldiers who brought home the first great importation of Greek words as Sicilian loot, and the unacademic tradesmen who linked the cultures, brought back isolated words, and *kraipale* > *crapula* (drinking session, hangover) sufficiently indicates their sort of semantic motivation. They heard them in terms of Latin phonology and tailored them to fit Latin morphology: *kubernàn* > *gubernare*, *theatron* > *teatrum*, *krepida* > *crepida(m)* (where some suspect Etruscan mediation).

Yet the receptivity of Latin blurs the distinction between interference and integration. The inventory already has voiceless stops and a pure breath phoneme; hence the new aspirates in *machina* (machine), *charta* (page), *thermipolium* (hot drinks bar), etc., once properly heard, can fit snugly. There is symmetrical space available in the disposition of vowels in the Latin system: so /y/ [ɨ] can be accommodated, as in *cyathus* (measure), *hyacinthus* (name of flower—lily?), where *uaccinium* is the equivalent non-Greek item, perhaps a Mediterranean substrate form, the initial *w*- of which some Greek dialects made into a vowel. The borrowed /z/ replaced the native voiced sibilant conveyed by the old sixth letter of the alphabet, which had long been replaced by length, /:/, or /r/, by sound-shift. Thereafter /z/ could sometimes partner /s/ as /b/ did /p/ and so forth. The need to suppose co-existing systems, to handle the fact that some items are arbitrarily restricted to certain positions and the range of variants differs in those positions, may be a difficulty removed by handy imports. No special device is any longer required for /f/—which occurs nowhere but in first place in a word, when it reflects what is directly inherited into Latin—as soon as Italic loans have supplied its medial occurrences (*rufus, uafer, inferus*). Roman dislike of the sound persisted: "barely human," Quintilian calls it,[25] whereas he loves *z*. Other loans caused sequences such as -*tm*- to shift along the scale of acceptability.

Deviant grammatical forms remain unstable. "Greek declension" is tolerated for names and some nouns (*Aenean, Daren* or *Dareta, tigridis*); but the dative -*dryasin* is an affectation of Propertius, and Ennius's "Homeric" genitive *Mettoeoque Fufetioeo* is not repeated. Borrowed syntax is hardier. Greek nominative constructions—*phaselus . . . ait fuisse nauium celerrimus* (this pinnace claims it was the swiftest of all ships) or *sensit*

* A *calque* is a "translation-loan" word or a word-for-word translation from the idiom of one language into another: e.g. "that goes without saying" is calqued on French *ça va sans dire*.

medios delapsus in hostis[26] (he realized he had fallen into his enemies' midst)—catch the breath in poetry. But Latin has enough remnants of the Indo-European "middle" voice of the verb for the so-called "Greek accusative" to pass for a native locution: *purgor bilem* (I purge my wrath) → *crinis religata* (having tied-back hair) → *concussa mentem* (stricken in mind), and even with an active verb → *tremis ossa* (you tremble in your bones).[27] Students of grammar are still at pains to contest to what extent these several structures are non-Latin.[28]

Lexical borrowing may be controlled by blending native with foreign: *tyrsi-ger* (bearer of the Dionysiac wand) and so on. Interference is lost in the total integration of "calquing," and only the use of, say, *grauis* as the term for *absence* of word-accent hints at the fact that it was borrowed from the Greek pitch system. Plautus's *exhibere negotium* (cause trouble) is from the Greek idiom *pragmata parekhein*; Horace calls a beauty *publica cura*, aping Alcman's name *Astymeloisa*, the people's darling (and his phrase *melema damoi*);[29] and Latin authors commonly replace Greek compound adjectives by a phrase—*Memphin carentem . . . niue* for *tan akheimanton . . . Memphin*.[30] Use of calques shows understanding of the complexities of one's own language combined with some approximation to an intuitive grasp of the foreign source. Latin usage is interesting. Lucretius is anxious not to allow unfamiliarity of linguistic form to hamper men's appreciation of a saving creed; he complains more than once of *patrii sermonis egestas* (the poverty of his native idiom). Cicero, claiming only to offer Latinized philosophy, has no qualms of this kind; his *uerba tantum adfero, quibus abundo* (I contribute only words, and I've plenty of them)[31] may be relevant.[32] Yet on occasions deliberate distancing is an attractive proposition. Lucretius's scorn of men's preoccupation with sex reveals itself in the Hellenisms he quotes (like other writers before and after him) from the deluded lips of code-switching lovers:

> nigra *melichrus* est, immunda et fetida *acosmos*,
> caesia *Palladium*, neruosa et lignea *dorcas*,
> paruula, pumilio, *chariton mia*, tota merum sal,
> magna atque immanis *cataplexis* plenaque honoris . . .[33]

> (a swarthy girl is *peau de miel*, a filthy one *déshabillée*, with green eyes she's *une petite Minerve*, all sinews and woodenness makes her *une faune*; if she's undersized *voici une des Grâces* with all the wit in the world, and a great hefty wench is *miracle de ville* and honoured for it . . .).

In other specialist vocabularies native neologism and foreign loan share the load. Quintilian handles rhetoric with *adumbrare, inuersio, transumptio*, and so on alongside Greek *antonomasia, amphibolia, periphrasis*, much as

Christian writers let *mediator, paganus, redemptor* rub shoulders with Greek *diaconus, paracletus, presbyter,* or with Hebraisms such as *gehenna, mammon(a), pascha.* Greek floods into Latin at all registers, starting with the Twelve Tables, the early law code. Other loans have limited domains; and many Italicisms or Celticisms, tied to commonplace objects—*popina* (pub); *lupus* (wolf); *tesca* (wasteland); *alauda* (lark); *r(a)eda* (wagon)—penetrate literature from the bottom up, so to speak. Even so, it is arresting to find that so apparently Roman a word as *poena* (penalty) is a Greek loan, or that a Sabine origin is strongly claimed for *dirus* (spine-chilling), which Quintilian thought an epithet suitable beyond compare in Horace's pen-picture of Rome's nightmare, Hannibal.[34] But Latin has its own key words that never fail to unlock emotional sluices: *rex* (tyrant) and *heres* (heir) to give you a public and a private shudder; *priscus* (bygone) and *maiores* (forefathers) to evoke "the spirit of '76"; *otium* (leisure) and *pellicere* (entice away) to bring out the puritan in you.

Latin is a contradictory language. For one thing, it is not systematic. A false impression of homogeneity is given by the purifying zeal of "analogists" such as Caesar, and by the pruning of rank growth by Cicero and influential mid-classical authorities. There were areas of vacillation, naturally enough: so *parsi* or *peperci, nixus* or *nisus, tertium* or *tertio* (as English has "dreamed" or "dreamt," and rivals for the negative past form of "he dares"). For Varro and others this fluidity was more noticeable in derivation, the so-called *declinatio uoluntaria* (optional formation). Style and register for the moment set aside, preferences can mark individual authors. Caesar rejects *quamquam* for *etsi,* and Lucretius prizes the more precious *momen* over *momentum* (much as Leopardi will have *speme* and not *speranza*). Or they mark periods, as when *offensiuncula* has yet to yield place to *offendiculum.* Or they indicate mere arbitrariness, like the permanent exalting of *seruitus* over *seruitudo.* The rules of "tense sequence" in mixed-mood sentences are still today inculcated as some salutary graven law; but a commentator has with justice translated a Tacitean sentence into a Livian and a Ciceronian version, and all differ in their verb forms.[35] It is this sort of thing, rather than the gap between literary and popular language, that makes Quintilian agree that speaking Latin is one thing and speaking grammatically quite another. An example of the tug-of-war, and of a typically Roman compromise solution, is afforded by the syntax of gerundives like *utendus* in literary Latin, which did not allow them to be used in so completely transitive a manner as was usual in common speech. The regular rule generates a gerundive with full adjectival properties only from sentences that have a finite verb plus an accusative object. With *uti* (which takes the ablative) and similar verbs the rule is half relaxed. It may be applied to produce the attributive-predicative gerundive, but will not let the form be actually predicated: therefore **ea sunt utenda* will not do, but *ea quae utenda acceperis . . . iubet reddere Hesiodus* (Hesiod recommends returning the things you have borrowed)[36] is an honest sentence. In fact, *dare utendum aliquid* is standard Latin for "to lend." So English lets "few" be an apparent singular in "a few," but not in "*few drinks vodka."

Nor is Latin always logical. Where English appears to spread or misplace its tense-markers ("I who could-have-been consul" = *was* able to *be* consul), Latin is punctilious: *consul esse qui potui . . . .*[37] Where English is careless over "only"—which verb does "only" qualify in "You only know how to promise" or "He only does it to annoy"?—Latin is more careful: *ea pacisci modo scis* (you only to promise know how),[38] *modo* as usual qualifying what precedes it. Yet the awkwardness of "I'll get my own dinner, thank you" (which implies not "I'll not get *your* dinner" but "nobody else shall get *my* dinner for me") has a Latin parallel. The converse shift occurs in *quid enim est negoti continere eos quibus praesis, si te ipse contineas* (it's easy to control those under you, if you control yourself),[39] where *ipse* appears for the expected *ipsum* in a typical and repeated idiom.

And Latin is not always discriminating. In the citation above, *ea quae utenda acceperis*, the perfect stem in *acceperis* marks the sense of completion and result; it acknowledges the time-lag that must occur between borrowing and being in a state of possession and ability to give back. Such subtleties are common. Yet oblique speech, so frequent in historians' reports and in their assessments of contemporary attitudes to the recorded events, obscures many of these crucial nuances. A hypothetical future event can be marked off from one that is reasonably predictable by differences in the mood of the verb in direct speech, but in indirect speech the difference can get lost. A future infinitive (or future participle) construction cannot measure probabilities. (Thus, we are left quite in the dark about Octavia's marital prospects by Poppaea's reported outburst: *at si desperent uxorem Neronis fore Octauiam, illi maritum daturos*, that if her supporters despaired of Octavia's remaining Nero's wife, they would find her another husband—but did Poppaea say "they would" or "they will"?[40]). The "historic infinitive," of which whole batteries are used in descriptive sequences of rapid and overlapping events (actions on the battlefield, or the many-faceted picture in those verses of Ennius on the trees of summer), represents not, as is sometimes suggested, so headlong a progress that one cannot waste time conjugating, but a deliberate suspension of the precise relating of grammatical categories to situational features. It is like the verblessness that has been noticed in the first page and a half of *Bleak House*, contributing to "an oppressive simultaneity, a timeless continuum."[41] And indeed the ambiguities to which Latin is prone may also be used deliberately for literary effect, as when Plautus plays on the indicative and imperative senses of *obloquere* (insult).[42] The most famous exploitation of ambivalent syntax is the oracular *aio te, Aeacida, Romanos uincere posse* (I tell you, Pyrrhus, that you the Romans can conquer),[43] where the duality has been transferred bodily from the Greek.

Whether speech is cardinally a matter of biological disposition or of behavioural pattern is at present in dispute; that biology and behaviour conspire to set language in social situation is obvious. Historical linguists have generally paid little attention to sociological approaches to language, the results of which have hitherto been meagre. Certainly, the social dimension is there. And if an everyday Latin word for "defender" (*uindex*) derives from the asserting of legal rights of control, or when the present participle of the verb "to be" exists only in the meaning of "guilty" (*sons*), one senses the abiding Roman ambience of court and case and statute. But on the whole the non-phenomena bulk largest where Latin is concerned. It is again a reflection of linguistic confidence. At no stage were special forms evolved or structures preferred for addressing those in authority, nor was grammatical account taken of social ranking or proximity (whereas Malay has 10 social levels of the pronoun, and Korean is credited with 27 modal forms permutating comparative rank with scale of deference). Latin developed technical jargon for law and religion, but no other special features apart from the addiction to assonance that we have seen. There are no deliberate avoidances, as of forms associated with a nationally feared or hated speech-group. To be sure, the politically astute were prepared to adopt the usage of the under-privileged; so P. Claudius Pulcher amended his *nomen* to Clodius, accepting the popular monophthongization that is usually submerged in our data but at times betrays itself (and can lead to over-anxious hypercorrection: so the original *o* maintained in *explodere* is replaced by the more "respectable" *au* in *plaudere*, etc.).

Varro has attracted notice by his contention[44] that analogically created forms such as *equabus*, which recover the gender difference obscured in some case forms by sound mergers (*equis* can mean either "by stallions" or "by mares"), show a calculated marking of distinctions crucial to the speaker's everyday life. The sex of a domestic creature is obviously an important matter. Varro cites the non-existence of *corua—coruus* means both a male and a female rook—as an example of a distinction that was too trivial to be needed. Still, the absence of *seruabus* (by female slaves), etc., undercuts the evidence of such forms as *deabus* (by goddesses), and the word for dog and bitch is the same (*canis*).[45] The traces of pragmatism are slight.

Glimpses of primitive closeness to the soil, on the other hand, are widespread in all natural idioms. Industrial metaphors such as "on tenterhooks" are grossly outnumbered in English by rural clichés of the type "counting one's chickens." Virgil's epic contains only one image from technology (the use of hydraulic cement).[46] That Latin started as a peasants' tongue is trite. Our interest is caught, not by the referential widening of the milking word *promulgare*, or of the technical irrigation term *deriuare* (draw water from the sluices at the head of a parched field), or by the thresher's act of crushing corn with a studded sledge that gives us *tribulatio*; intriguing rather are signs of holding on to the concrete and the definite, even of deliberately edging toward it. *Laetus*, applied to crops and beasts, is "healthy" or "productive"; the derived *laetare* (though early evidence is lacking) and *laetamen*—far from following the generalized sense of "happy," as does *laetari* (and *laetare* here and there)—simply signify "to manure" and "muck." A verb's lexical meaning may be nominalized and made abstract by the formant -(*t*)*io*(*n*-), as in *affectio*, *defensio*, etc.; but the practical action, or its visible result, commonly re-asserts itself: *legio* (a legion); *oratio* (a speech); *rogatio* (a bill)—cf. English "building," "helping." That this is a popular tendency can be argued from Plautus's object accusative with *aditio*, *notio*. Again, the elder Pliny's phrase *deus est mortali iuuare mortalem* (it is god-like for one mortal to help another) and Virgil's *refulsit alma parens confessa deam* (bright gleamed his gentle mother, revealing her divinity) are interesting because they use the concrete *deus*, *dea* (god) to signify "divine nature." *Deitas* is neither extant nor wanted in classical Latin, any more than *auitas* (the fact of being a grandfather), when Statius writes *confessus auum*.[47]

A sign of Latin's addiction to the definite has been seen in the so-called *ab urbe condita* construction, in which what is in most European languages a noun clause or abstract phrase—"the city's foundation"—is expressed in Latin by a straight noun joined with an adjective, commonly participial: "the city founded." Thus, *Lentulus et Cethegus deprehensi* stands for "the expo*sure of* Lentulus and Cethegus," and *ante solem exorientem* for "before sun*rise*."[48] Virgil exploits and explains the Latin working of the direct situation-to-grammar relation when to Aeneas, shocked by Priam's merciless butchering at Pyrrhus's hands,

> subiit deserta Creusa
> et direpta domus.[49]

(Creusa left alone, and his own house despoiled, came to mind.)

The Latin presents this not as a mere thought that Creusa had been left alone, nor as a possibility that disaster might have overtaken his home. Creusa in visible distress and danger, and his house as if already pillaged, stand up in picture clarity in his mind, as his father's image has just done (*subiit cari genitoris imago*) and as Creusa's own ghost shortly will. In effect, the distinction between abstract and concrete that we have been discussing is not readily available to a Latin speaker.[50] The concrete use is no fossil, embedded in epic formula. It lives and spreads in the gerundival sector, for instance: the classical era normally prefers *urbs condenda* to *condendum urbem* for "the founding of Rome." Livy can write *ab urbe oppugnanda Poenum absterruere conspecta moenia* (the sight of the walls frightened [Hannibal] out of any notion of storming the city). The immediacy of the idiom (*absterruere . . . moenia*, the walls . . . frightened) is clearly a prime source of personifying metaphor, as in *cum mea domus . . . deflagrationem urbi . . . minaretur* (when my house threatened the city with conflagration).[51]

This is not entirely a Latin speciality. Greek has the same thing, and Thucydides especially; the bones of it may be in some common source. "After Solon's departure" is *meta Solona oikhomenon*, and a Euripidean hero can complain *Aias m' adelphos oles' en Troiai thanon* (what ruined me was my brother Ajax's death at Troy).[52] But in Greek it remains largely a prose usage with no syntactical extension.[53] Besides, easily visualized notions of frequent occurrence soon make the apparently abstract acceptable: *aduentus* for "arrival" is normal. Important ideological words, such as *uirtus* or *dignitas* or *grauitas*, were so clearly received that a Roman could practically draw pictures of them. One reaches with no great surprise Tacitus's *dum inter Vespasianum ac Vitellium proeliis legionum, captiuitatibus urbium, deditionibus cohortium iudicatur* (while legionary battles, seizures of cities, and surrenders of units were deciding the issue between Vespasian and Vitellius).[54] Simple statement of the palpable was admittedly sometimes set aside, rather self-consciously, in favour of abstractions, already in Cicero's time (106–43 B.C.): for example, *fontium gelidas perennitates* (icy eternities of springs), where the meaning is just that the springs are cool and do not dry up; or *exardescit beneuolentiae magnitudo* (a plenitude of goodwill kindles), where goodwill is simply meant to be warm and large.[55]

And this tendency toward affectation was pronounced enough for Catullus (*c.* 84–*c.* 54 B.C.), when he wanted to produce an impression of mental directness, to use by contrast a much-admired concatenation of verbal action:

> odi et amo. quare id faciam, fortasse requiris.
>   nescio, sed fieri sentio et excrucior.[56]

> (I hate as I love. Perhaps you wonder why I do it. I don't know, but
> I feel it happening and I'm tortured by it.)

Here eight verbs, seven of them finite, crowd the distich with never a noun, even an objective one, in sight.

It is customary to speak of "registers" in a language, and to distinguish "field," "mode," "tenor," or similar dimensions, and to assign a text to its proper place, before judging its impact. The terms that scholars have devised for discussing Latin texts have included normal versus technical, neutral versus expressive, formal versus familiar, and native versus foreign. Yet the genre, the context, and the author's personal predilections impose permutations that make boundaries hard to define and misleading to use.[57] Normal, familiar, native Latin, whether neutral or expressive, is unknown to us (except for tiny pieces). "The strong current of living speech disappears under the ice-crust of literature and only on occasions becomes fleetingly visible to us through the odd accidental crack."[58] The author of the treatise *Rhetorica ad Herennium* cities an extended example of low-class speech of the late Republic, including things such as *ecce tibi iste de trauerso, heus, inquit* . . . (see, this chap all of a sudden says "Hey you!" . . .). Before that there were odd colloquialisms inset in the highly stylized farrago of the comedians: *hau uidi magis* (what a tale!); *tam gratiast* (no, thanks); *si frugist usque admutilabit probe* (if he's on the ball he'll really take him to the cleaners).[59] Later come the Pompeii graffiti. These scraps show at least that it would be wrong to suppose that a written language is always in some way an artificial one. Though they are only scraps, they provide a point of contrast to the elliptical, Hellenizing mode of intellectual conversation that we find in Cicero's letters, or to the impure "realism" of Petronius's novel, the *Satyricon* (1st century A.D.).

Early Latin often sired a popular form that vanished to reappear after centuries of purist suppression. The verb used by the comedians for "to talk" (*fabulari*) returned in Spanish *hablar*; their, and Cato's, use of *quando* came back with French *quand*, Italian *quando*. The purist canon was essential if the exuberant inaccuracies of a largely immigrant population (*inquinate loquentes*, or murky speech) and the differing *sermo urbanus* of Rome and Padua, and indeed Cordoba, were not to tear apart a small literature in which the meagreness of what was universally binding was offset by an intricate interplay of motifs and expressions, between author and author. It was a restrictive canon. It eliminated free variants, e.g. in morphology, where *ipsum* won over *eumpse* and *eumpsum*, and in syntax, where *num*, not *si*, had to introduce indirect questions. It allowed only the infinitive construction for reported speech, although *quod*, *quia*, or *ut* clauses were available; and it disallowed the infinitive of purpose. It fought the inflationary tendency to replace small words by more corpulent ones (*uadit*, *manducat*, *oricula*, for *it*, *est*, *auris*). Diminutives such as *pauxillisper* and *maiusculus* were frowned out of use. Conversely, it insisted on the full rigours of a complex set of paradigms, where vulgar speech had long set itself to remove the "second conjugation" of verbs and to reduce the "fourth declension" of nouns; and it kept anomalies such as the group of "middle" verbs governing the ablative, which the *corona sordidior* (Seneca's phrase for the "man in the street") wanted to make simply transitive. It would have no truck with the popular craze for certain forms, such as the *-bo* future that had seeped into the "third" and "fourth" conjugations.

The result was a standardization of idiom that made it possible to see and measure artistic achievement. Classical Latin in the widest sense begins with the legal texts that may have been formulated in the 5th century B.C., although the Twelve Tables are known only as conflated from quotations in later periods.[60] The real start for us is in the mid-3rd century B.C., with fragments from the literary gropings of Livius Andronicus and the epigraphic testimony of the Scipio family epitaphs (although the occasion for these was probably much earlier than their actual composition; they are arguably less ancient than two Italic-influenced notices protecting sacred precincts). The end of the classical language may be marked by Charlemagne's official recognition of the vernaculars in A.D. 813, but it had only lain in state for many a year. Its general sameness within that span renders somewhat esoteric the conventional division into "early" (*c.* 240–*c.* 80 B.C., that is, Livius to Cicero's debut), "classical" *stricto sensu* (*c.* 80 B.C.–A.D. 14, that is, to the death of Augustus), and "silver" (A.D. 14–180, or whenever Apuleius died). There is some justice in the view that Latin itself has little history, even though its prehistory (the process of its forming) may have been long and complicated, like the post-history of its fragmenting.* The Romans piously preserved archaic

* See Volume II, "The Romance Languages."

texts such as the *carmen Aruale* or the *carmen Saliare*, but these can have been no more intelligible to classical Romans than the Duenos bowl inscription or the *lapis niger* (probably of the 6th century). The *leges regiae*, on the other hand, are so readable that they cannot reflect the Latin of the ancient kings (pre-509 B.C.); for Polybius was at sea, and so were the Romans of his day (*c.* 140 B.C.), in deciphering a treaty text attributed to 509 B.C. If the idiom of Cicero's age, as compared with that of the preceding century, could with exaggeration be termed *prope totus mutatus sermo* (a speech-form nearly 100 per cent different),[61] the preliterary epoch must have been one of revolution indeed, not only politically but also linguistically. Thereafter Latin mopped and tidied up. New furniture was introduced and the old shifted around; but the house was built by 300 B.C.

A terse review of those authors who were conscious of their language, or whose expressive weight carried the literary world with it, will show how the framework was moulded and modified. The prosaists make an unpolished start in the 2nd century, if the prose version given by Lactantius (a Christian rhetorician, *c.* A.D. 300) of Ennius's translation (*c.* 200 B.C.) of Euhemerus (*c.* 310 B.C.) is a safe point of departure. Religious and legal formulae, in early and late, credible and suspect citations, prepare us for simple and repetitive sentence shapes garnished with native assonance—*rem tene uerba sequentur* (take care of the sense). Audus Gellius reports Cato as crying:

> quis hanc contumeliam, quis hoc imperium, quis hanc seruitutem ferre potest? nemo hoc rex ausus est facere. eane fieri bonis, bono genere gnatis, boni consultis? ubi societas, ubi fides maiorum?[62]

> (Who can bear this insult, this tyranny, this slavery? No king has dared to act so. Is this to happen to good men, sons of a good stock, men of good counsel? Where is our solidarity with our allies, where is our loyalty to our forefathers?)

From Cato (234–149 B.C.) via Gaius Gracchus (153–121 B.C.) to Varro (116–27 B.C.) runs a mixed vein of semi-technical, semi-expressive, semi-formal, and even partly foreign diction. If two features can summarize the period's progress, they are the evolving technique of not shifting the sentence subject every time action passes to another initiator, and the reduction of the role of low-tension elements such as the pronouns *is* and *hic*. Sallust (86–*c.* 34 B.C.) is hailed as *uerborum nouator* (a coiner of words), though how new his "innovations" are is unclear: he is reputed to have had a tame philologist to hunt down archaisms for him![63] His style has a certain breathlessness, in keeping with its still abundant variations in the forms of words.

The purist reaction is stronger in none than in Caesar, famous for his bigotry on points of analogy (for instance, where verbs have been careless enough not to keep their nasal infix throughout, like *nancisci-nactus*) and for his ascetic horror of the unusual: *ut tanquam scopulum sic fugias inauditum atque insolens uerbum* (as for a new, unusual word—avoid it as you would a reef),[64] although, as has been pointed out, he does not there scorn the dicolon. His, and Lucius Crassus's, fastidiousness (*elegantia*) won the praise of Cicero, whose own language has many registers: epistolary, technical, poetic, and oratorical. The paradox is that the less prescriptive Cicero became the exemplar of classicism. The reason is partly the sheer bulk and breadth of Cicero's writing and speaking, partly the increasing intellectual regard for what was fitting. In his attempt to give to sophisticated content a coherent and intelligible container, Cicero asserts a by no means Draconian regularity. The grammatical permissiveness prevailing earlier explains why he has to recommend using the right case, tense, gender, and number before thinking about articulation and delivery.[65] In fact, he still experimented, and the increased flexibility in the use of participles has been taken as an index of his evolutionary influence on the language.

There is something of a watershed about Livy (59 B.C.–A.D. 17). Much that had been condemned became, with him, accepted and the silver age was on its way. Provincialism fought for its limited foothold, but the criticism made by the Roman politician and *littérateur* Asinus Pollio (76 B.C.–*c.* A.D. 5) of *patauinitas* ("Paduism")[66] shows how uncompromising the metropolitan canon had become. Yet the formal inventories and structures were barely amended; and what now happened had, in other guises, happened before. For example, flexibility in the participles recurs in Livy (and thereafter), but as a weakening of the exigencies of tense: so *seruum . . . caesum medio egerat circo*[67] in the sense "he had driven through mid-circus a slave who was *at the same time* being flayed," or *post paucos dies rediit, multis . . . donis . . . donatus*[68] meaning "he returned after a day or two, receiving *thereafter* many gifts."

The subsequent historians, and Seneca (4 B.C.–A.D. 65) as a prose moralist, fill the books of modern analysts with their idiosyncrasies of stylistic choice; but only Tacitus (*c.* A.D. 55–*c.* 115) really remoulds the shape of Latin prose. He extends the semantic and colligational ranges of the genitive case and the infinitive. These are commonplaces with the poets, and Tacitus is almost a second Virgil in his power of expression.

K

Now the abstract noun does move to greater prominence; and by a deliberate perversity, sense and grammar are frequently set at odds, as are the customary choices between an adjective and a defining genitive.[69] Formal prose is being ever more distanced from the familiar; and the 2nd century A.D. sees a stampede that way. The cost is the jettisoning of simple purism. Apuleius (*c.* A.D. 123–*c.* 180) indulges his taste for the florid by digging up words long since dead (*prosapia, domuitio, famigerabilis*), as well as by having recourse to grandly elaborate expressions. Fronto's *elocutio nouella* (novel style) gives the lie to its own epithet, being neither diminutive nor novel, as long as it can unearth rusty items of early republican speech.[70]

The poets need not be sundered from the prose artists. Admittedly, there was a tendency among writers (before Seneca, anyway) to specialize in one craft or the other; Cicero's poems or Varro's Menippean satires scarcely constitute exceptions. But, except in word-order and density of Graecism, and of course in type of rhythmic pattern, Latin poetry is basically written in the same language as Latin prose. Individual adventures in sensibility are another thing, and produce distinctive style as much in prose as in poetry. The only "language" peculiar to a genre seems to be found in early epic and tragedy. This is because of their lumbering attempts to build, largely on a Greek base, something solidly impressive (hence, among other things, the *-as* genitive singular in Livius, Naevius, and Ennius). These are the grand genres. In Martial's catalogue[71] the scale of "elevation" runs from epic through tragedy, lyric, satire, and elegy, down to epigram (although the value of the list is reduced by the absence of comedy, pastoral, and didactic and iambic poetry). Pacuvius's line *Nerei repandirostrum incuruiceruicum pecus* (Nereus's snub-snouted, crook-necked flock)[72] is both Greek-inspired and grand; so were the crowd of high-flown compounds, adventitious to Latin but in no way formally difficult for the language, such as *arquitenens* (bow-bearing), *odorisequus* (scent-following), *sonipes* (noisy-footed), *flammifer* (flame-bearing). Some influence is, then, wielded by the exigencies of the genre (except perhaps in the case of satire), by the preferences of individuals (commonly related to the requirements of the task each has been set or has set himself), or by the collective artistic vision of a côterie, whether deliberate (as with the *poetae noui*) or tacit (as with the Augustan poets around Maecenas).

If the earliest poets can be dubbed, as Livius and Ennius were in particular, *semigraeci*,[73] it is all the more tantalizing that we have nothing remaining of the convivial homespun ballads, celebrating folk heroes,

that seem to have enlivened early Roman dinner parties, a native equivalent of the Greek *scolia*.[74] Where we do have a sizable body of data, namely
in the comedians, the plays are of the derivative type called *palliatae*,
and contain Hellenic furniture: the plots, characters, scenes, culture,
dress, money, and basic law are all Greek. Much is Roman, in a patchy
way—above all, the jokes. But the language of Plautus and Terence is
much further from contemporary Roman speech than is that of, say,
Gilbert's operettas from the language spoken in 19th-century England. It
is a rich, stylized, and immensely clever artefact.[75] The Greek element
often marks the lower orders and the Roman scorn for Greeklings shows
itself (despite the convention that forces "in Latin" to be rendered by
barbare). There are loans: *danista* (money-lender), *machaera* (dagger),
palaestra (gymnasium); and there are mock Greek forms: *nai tan Prainesten*
(by Praineste), etc., where the oaths are really taken in the name of
Italian towns—inspired by the ambiguous *nai tan Koran* (*Kora* being both
Persephone and a town of the Volsci); and there are calques, such as
auribus teneo lupum based on *ton oton ekho ton lykon* (I have the wolf by the
ears) or *ipsissimus* on Aristophanes' *autotatos* (his very self).[76] But the native
component is highly spiced, too, with repetitions—"I beg you" can be
clamo postulo obsecro oro ploro atque imploro fidem (I call on, claim, beseech,
pray for, cry for, and implore your good faith)—and with assonances:

> laudem lucrum ludum iocum festiuitatem ferias
> pompam penum potationes saturitatem gaudium[77]
>
> (praise and gain and play and jest and parties and holidays and
> dinner courses and food and drinks and fullness and fun).

There are flowery periphrases such as *caerulei campi* (the sky-blue plains)
or *uiae caerulae* (the sky-blue roads) for "the sea"; comic formations such
as *exclusissimus* (shut-outest lover), and *patrue patruissime* (uncliest uncle);
and comic compounds such as *pultiphagus* (porridge-eating), and *denti-
frangibula* (tooth-crackers—meaning fists). There is tragic parody:
Plautus's *o Troia o patria o Pergamum o Priame* outdoes Ennius's *o pater o
patria o Priami domus* (o father, o fatherland, o house of Priam).[78] Yet in
comes also the phraseology of Roman lawyers: despite the Greek context,
the formula of claim *hunc* (*scil.* "*uidulum*") *meum esse dico* (I claim this
[trunk] as mine), and the legal commonplace *mare . . . commune* (the sea is
common property) give the key to what seems otherwise a mere tug-of-war
by two slaves over lost and found property. There quickly follows *fero . . .
condicionem* (I offer terms) and *ibo ad arbitrum* (I'll go before a judge), and
uin, qui in hac uilla habitat, eiius arbitratu fieri? (do you agree to abide by the

decision of whoever lives in this homestead?)—which in its order of clauses mocks lawyers' verbal structures of the type *quem agrum eos uendere . . . licet, is ager uectigal nei siet* (a piece of land for available sale is not to be taxable).[79]

In the 1st century B.C., Lucretius and the *poetae noui* (Valerius Cato's school: Calvus, Ticidas, Cinna, Cornificius, Furius Bibaculus, and Catullus) display in a somewhat counterpoised fashion the influence of individual and of group. Lucretius latinizes Epicurus into an idiom of still-wavering morphology and syntax; but his vehicle is well supplied with alliteration and dicola and expressive fullness, and neologisms join hands with archaic turns of phrase. The new poets, however, quarrelled not only with long poems and crude workmanship, but with any language that lacked polish and point. Yet their goal of artistic sophistication (*doctrina*) was not a simple one. In search of sharpness they would admit the provincial—the north Italian *basium* (kiss) supplants *sauium* and *osculum* in less elevated poetry and the Romance vernaculars—and the coarse (*uerpa, futuere, pedicare,* etc.). In search of polish, they stopped the optional elision of word-final *-s* after a short vowel and before a consonantal onset; and they promoted the Hellenistic poetic figure of postponing sentence connectives.[80] This curious foot-in-both-camps technique allowed Catullus to write an epic provided it was tiny (poem 64, like Callimachus's *Hecale*), and personal lyrics of any length (poem 68, as against all the short poems). In language it meant a fusing of several registers and fields so that they can be extricated, if at all, only on a poem-by-poem basis.

Virgil and Horace are of linguistic interest all the time. On the one hand they exploit and extend the verbal resources of Latin by using historical vestiges such as *olle* (for *ille*) or the genitive in *-ai*, the long vowel tense formant in *tondebat hyacinthi*, and the free-standing adverb role of what had by their time become preverbs and prepositions (as in oddities such as *extremos inter euntem*, among the runners at the rear). But on the other hand—and more noteworthy—is the way Virgil especially underlines the overall one-ness of Latin. The Emperor Augustus had no love for obsolete or abstruse words (*exoletae et reconditae uoces*); but he probably inspired the attack—by his army commander, of all people—on the poet's new affectation that lay in the building of a poetic vocabulary out of everyday words. The trick was not merely tasteless, it was said, but sly as well.[81] Virgil's imagery may be allowed some general elevation; but at the level of words he espouses the commonplace and is ready for the colloquial where the colloquial is apt: *hoc habet* (got him); *ecce tibi* (there now, see); *hoc illud . . . fuit?* (this was it, then?)—an expression that lives in French *oui*.[82] His linguistic depth, like Horace's (particularly in the *Odes*), is to be appreciated in what the latter named *iunctura*, the unfamiliar setting of familiar words.[83] This process makes the unpoetic poetic. It shows up the ingenuousness of our predisposition to set poetry and prose firmly apart and to tie onto items labels such as "unpoetic." A subtle and wary tread is needed, especially in a dead language; for "tired," *fessus* always seems loftier than *lassus*, but the frontier is ill-drawn. In Horace, *Odes* II, 11, 21, we find the word *scortum* (whore); nobody can say, by other than Olympian pronouncement, whether the so-called "laws" of the genre permit this term or not.

These great Augustans remake the poetic language by evocative handling of a surprisingly normal Latin; they also help their own age to mark out afresh the boundaries of literary types and categories. There is nothing else quite like Horace's *Epodes*, for instance. Satire was always being redefined. It was never wholly Roman, despite the common claim; too much of the Hellenistic diatribe and even of Old Comedy had helped to form it for the hope to make it *tota nostra* to be other than a patriotic dream. The language of the first Roman satirist, Lucilius (*c.* 168–*c.* 102 B.C.) is often heavily Graecized, but of itself it rarely apes—except to mock—the clumsy grandeurs of early epic and tragedy (the curiously high rank given to satire in Martial's later listing seems to mistake the register). The native habits of alliterative repetition and coupling are its base. Lucilius, of course, was a Roman gentleman, and it may be that Horace later gave satire not only an autobiographical and literary-critical slant but also an admixture of scabrous verbiage, in order to bring it home more forcibly to the common man. Persius (A.D. 34–62) leans heavily on Horace, and again the coarseness is there, though less in mere choice of words. It is in Juvenal (A.D. *c.* 60–*c.* 130), however, the greatest Roman satirist, that language is cleansed most notably, despite his journalistic touch and his claim to effervescent indignation against vice and crime. As a critic has remarked,[84] *meio* and *mingo* are as far as he will go.

The late epicists are not remarkable for what they do to Latin, as the late prosaists and the Christian enthusiasts are. Rhetorical intensity forges brand-new rhythms and accents and rhymes, a new eagerness to toy with what is, to be sure, a new language; now begins mediaeval Latin, which has its own story. The classical analyst must halt and look back, like any paganist, now that *Roma più non trionfa*.

References

1. Cicero, *Brutus* 46, 171.
2. Gnaeus Naevius, possibly; unless one who has "Campanian cheek" must be born in Campania (Aulus Gellius I, 24, 2). Although the family of the Annaei, which produced the two Senecas, was thoroughly Spanish, the epicist Lucan came to Rome as an infant. E. FRAENKEL, *Horace* (Oxford 1967), p. 4, allows no important literary figure to be a Roman.
3. See R. H. ROBINS, *Trans. of the Philological Society* (1959), pp. 116 ff.
4. Horace, *Satires* II, 6, 80 f.
5. Horace, *Odes* I, 12, 57.
6. *Corpus inscriptionum latinarum* I (2), 7, 2; Suetonius, *Tiberius* 1, 2.
7. Ovid, *Amores* III, 9, 21 f.
8. L. P. WILKINSON, *Golden Latin Artistry* (Cambridge 1963), p. 176, has some entertaining examples at various registers, including "Dubo... Dubon... Dubonnet." Cicero, *Tusculanae disputationes* V, 6, 15,dem onstrates the diminuendo form: *si idem paupertatem ignominiam infamiam timet, si debilitatem caecitatem, si denique seruitutem...*, where the inset elements are themselves tricolic, dicolic, monocolic. Wilkinson also notes (p. 175) the dualities of "to acknowledge and confess our manifold sins and wickednesses."
9. Ennius, trag. frag. 255 f. in E. H. WARMINGTON, *Remains of Old Latin*, 4 vols. (London 1935–40).
10. *Corp. inscr. lat.* I (2), 584, 24; 614, 6; *Twelve Tables* 8, 6; *Leges regiae* 3; Lucretius 1, 334; 4, 52.
11. Virgil, *Aeneid* VI, 105.
12. Plautus, *Captivi* 670–3.
13. The items are: (early) /a, ā, e, ē, i, ī, o, ō, u, ū (*ou*), ẹ̄ (*ei, e*); ae (*ae, ai*), au, oe (*oe, oi*), ui; t, d, p, b, k (*k, c*), g (without separate marking at first); r, l, m, n, j (*i*), w (*u*); s, f, h, q (*qu*) /; (classical) /a, ā, e, ē, i, ī, o, ō, u, ū, y, ȳ; ae, au, oe, ui, eu; t, th, d, p, ph, b, k (*c*), kh (*ch*), g; r, l, m, n, j (*i*), w (*u*); s, f, h, q (*qu*)/. The tally varies if other views prevail, e.g. as to the phonetic status of [ŋ] and aspirated consonants; two historically distinct values for *qu* (/k + w/ and /kʷ/) seem to have fused, and only oppositions such as *quis-cis*, *qui-ui* are relevant. Diphthongized contiguous vowels in *ne + uter*, *se + u* are counted in one classical phoneme /eu/; ad hoc contractions (*dẹinde, prọ̄ut*) are ignored. On /ẹ̄/, see W. S. ALLEN, *Vox Latina* (Cambridge 1965), pp. 53 ff.
14. A particular verse-form made particular words inadmissible, as *magnitudo, aestuosus, increpare* in dactylic hexameters; hence *maximitas* (Lucretius), *aestifer* (Cicero *et al.*), *increpitare* (Virgil *et al.*). The point is that these incidental awkwardnesses could at once be remedied, even by readily naturalizing a Graecism such as *Scīpĭăd-* for *Scīpĭŏn-* (Lucilius *et al.*). In the 3rd plural perfect active the inherited *-ēre* gave

the metrical values -◡ and (elided) -; -*ĕrunt* (<-*is-ont*) provided ◡-. The hybrid form -*ērunt* added - -; but the poets are shy of it, even if it is the accepted form at colon ends in Cicero, and it probably seemed odd to those whose everday use was -*ĕrunt*. (So D. W. PYE, *Transactions of the Philological Society* [1963], pp. 1 ff., esp. p. 22.)

15. The case + number signals are calculated without the vocative or locative as separate categories, although their forms are included by coincidence in the 28 cited. The dative-ablative plural counts formally as one case, already fused in proto-Indo-European. The purely graphic difference between -*ibus* and -*ubus* is honoured. The vacillating fifth declension is omitted.

16. Ennius, trag. frag. 157–9; cf. 92 f., 106–8 in WARMINGTON, *op. cit.*

17. See O. SKUTSCH, *Bulletin of the Institute of Classical Studies* 11 (London 1964), pp. 73 ff.; *Proceedings of the Classical Association* 62 (1965), pp. 26 f. ("Concord" includes linked nouns in the same case. Non-conforming -*us* and -*um* are exceptional; the only real adverse case is *Odes* III, 23, 13.) End rhyme in successive hexameters at *Ars poetica* 99 f. seems inadvertent. The "leonine" end-to-middle rhyme (cf. Ovid, *Ars amatoria* 1, 59) becomes a commonplace only in mediaeval poetry.

18. Catullus, 3, 3 f.; Ovid, *Metamorphoses* 9, 488 f.; Virgil, *Aen.* VI, 51 f.; *Eclogues* VIII, 48 ff.

19. Horace, *Odes* IV, 4, 1; Virgil, *Aen.* VI, 431; *Georgics* III, 201; Bernard of Morlas's hexameter poem.

20. The mediaeval Latin poet was working with stress-based quantity, which reduced his store of separate sound entities but increased his rhyming items. Accent, juncture, intonation, verse-beat—and, in prose, breath unit (cf. Cicero, *Orator* 62, 211, and 66, 222 f.)—are essential elements in the sound texture of Latin. Things such as vowel elision between words (cf. Cicero, *Orat.* 44, 150, and 45, 152) can be understood only if word-boundary signals are properly known; and all poetic sound-play rests on such complexities. The whole field is one of battling theories.

21. Cicero, *De officiis* I, 31, 111; Shakespeare, *Julius Caesar* I, 2.

22. Cicero, *De oratore* III, 12, 44.

23. See E. HAUGEN, *Proceedings of the Eighth International Congress of Linguists* (1958), pp. 777 f.

24. Cicero, *Ad Atticum* IX, 10, 7.

25. Quintilian XII, 10, 29; cf. Cicero, *Orat.* 49, 163.

26. Catullas 4, 1 f.; Virgil, *Aen.* II, 377.

27. Horace, *Ars poet.* 302; *Odes* IV, 11, 5; Virgil, *Aen.* XII, 468; Horace, *Satires* II, 7, 57; cf. Lucretius 3, 489.

28. So, most recently, E. ADELAIDE HAHN, *Transactions of the American Philological Association* 91 (1960), pp. 221 ff.

29. Horace, *Odes* II, 8, 8; Alcman in *Oxyrhyncus papyri* 2387, 3, 4, 13, and 14.

30. Horace, *Odes* III, 26, 10; BRUNO SNELL (ed.), *Bacchylides carmina cum*

fragmentis (Teubner: Leipzig 1949), frag. 30, 1; see L. R. PALMER, *The Latin Language* (London 1954), p. 103.

31. Lucretius 1, 832; 3, 260; Cicero, *Ad Att.* XII, 52, 3.

32. This opposition of views is as traditionally interpreted. However, D. R. SHACKLETON BAILEY, *Towards a Text of Cicero: Ad Atticum* (Cambridge 1960), pp. 61 f., points out that we do not really know what Cicero meant by the phrase.

33. Lucretius 4, 1160–3; cf. Lucilius, frag. 567 ff. in WARMINGTON, *op.cit.*; Juvenal 3, 66 ff.; Martial 10, 68.

34. Cf. Servius auctus on Virgil, *Aen.* III, 235; Quintilian VIII, 2, 9.

35. M. ANDREWES, *Classical Review*, new series I (1951), pp. 144, 145 (footnote 1).

36. Cicero, *De off.* I, 15, 48.

37. Cicero, *De republica* I, 6, 10.

38. Plautus, *Pseudolus* 226.

39. Cicero, *Ad Quintum fratrem* I, 1, 7.

40. Tacitus, *Annals* XIV, 61, 7.

41. R. QUIRK, *Charles Dickens and Appropriate Language* (Durham 1959), p. 9.

42. E.g. D. N. LEVIN, *Classical Philology* 54 (1959), pp. 109 ff.; K. QUINN, *AUMLA* (Australian Universities Lang. and Lit. Assoc.) 14 (1960), pp. 36 ff.; M. W. EDWARDS, *Transactions of the American Philological Assoc.* 92 (1961), pp. 128 ff. Cf. *Rhetorica ad Herennium* II, 11, 16; IV, 14, 21; Quintilian VIII, 2, 16.

43. Cicero, *De divinatione* II, 56, 116.

44. Varro, *De lingua latina* 9, 56.

45. Early Latin nom. sing. *canes* (fem.), on the model of *indoles*, etc., is not used as a sex-distinguishing device, nor so spoken of by Varro, who cites it (*De ling. lat.* 7, 32).

46. Virgil, *Aen.* IX, 710 ff.; see M. COFFEY, *Bulletin of the Institute of Classical Studies* 8 (1961), pp. 69 f.

47. Pliny the Elder, *Natural History* II, 5, 18; Virgil, *Aen.* II, 590 f.; Statius, *Thebais* 2, 122.

48. Sallust, *Catilinae coniuratio* 48, 4; Plautus, *Bacchides* 424.

49. Virgil, *Aen.* II, 562 f.

50. That is, on the basis of B. L. Whorf's notion, namely that the organization of a speaker's language conditions his manner of thought and powers of discrimination.

51. Livy XXIII, 1, 10; Cicero, *Pro Plancio* 40, 95.

52. Herodotus 1, 34; Euripides, *Helen* 94.

53. Also, the impact in Greek is of an unusual trope, as in English. A better translation of the Euripidean verse is "It was my brother Ajax finished me, killing himself at Troy like that." On the construction in Latin, see further E. LAUGHTON, *The Participle in Cicero* (Oxford 1964), pp. 84 ff.

54. Tacitus, *Historiae* III, 70, 2.

55. Cicero, *De natura deorum* II, 39, 98; *De amicitia* 9, 29.

56. Catullus 85.

57. See J. COUSIN, *Evolution et structure de la langue latine* (Paris 1944), p. 122 (for Latin); M. GREGORY, *Journal of Linguistics* 3 (1967), pp. 177 ff. (for the terminology). Ancient distinctions may be found in *Rhet. ad Herenn.* IV, 8, 11; Cicero, *De optimo genere oratorum* 1, 2; Aulus Gellius VI, 14, 1.

58. F. SKUTSCH, *Die lateinische Sprache*, 3rd edn (Leipzig and Berlin 1912), p. 539.

59. *Rhet. ad Herenn.* IV, 10, 14; Plautus, *Capt.* 561; *Menaechmi* 387; *Capt.* 269.

60. The Twelve Tables may reflect in content a 5th-century legal code, but they are built up for us out of late citations. In language they are complex. There are echoes of "Indo-European structures" (cf. C. WATKINS, *Harvard Studies in Classical Philology* 71 [Cambridge, Mass. 1966], p. 116) and of Greek (cf. PALMER, *op. cit.*, pp. 64, 119).

61. Polybius III, 22, 3; Quintilian VIII, 3, 26.

62. Cato in Aulus Gellius X, 3, 14.

63. Quintilian I, 6, 39; Asinius Pollio in Suetonius, *De grammaticis* 10.

64. In Aulus Gellius I, 10, 4.

65. Cicero, *De orat.* III, 11, 40.

66. Quintilian I, 5, 56; VIII, 1, 3; cf. P. G. WALSH, *Livy: His Historical Aims and Methods* (Cambridge 1961), pp. 267 ff.

67. Livy II, 36, 1.

68. Livy XXV, 25, 13.

69. See PALMER, *op. cit.*, p. 143, for examples such as "citizens' war" (for "civil war") and "Vesta's virgins" (for "Vestal virgins"), and Tacitus, *Annals* I, ed. by N. P. Miller (London 1959), pp. 14 ff., for good examples of non-congruent sense and grammar.

70. From what was said above about Latin receptivity, it follows that, in spite of the theory of E. NORDEN, *Die antike Kunstprosa*, 5th edn (Darmstadt 1958), Vol. II, pp. 608 f., the obscurities of Fronto, Tertullian, and others of similar style are not the result of Graecizing.

71. Martial 12, 94.

72. Pacuvius, trag. frag. 352 in WARMINGTON, *op. cit.*

73. Suetonius, *De gramm.* 1

74. See Cicero, *Brut.* 19, 75; *Tusc.* IV, 2, 3; Varro in Nonius Marcellus, frag. 107, ed. by W. M. Lindsay (1903). Also cf. A. MOMIGLIANO, *Journal of Roman Studies* 47 (1957), pp. 104 ff.

75. See PALMER, *op. cit.*, p. 88, and H. HAPP, *Glotta* 45 (1967), pp. 60 ff.

76. Plautus, *Capt.* 880–3; Terence, *Phormio* 506; Plautus, *Trinummus* 988; cf. Aristophanes, *Plutus* 83.

77. Caecilius, frag. 202 in WARMINGTON, *op. cit.*; Plautus, *Capt.* 770 f.

78. Plautus, *Trin.* 834; *Rudens* 268; *Men.* 698; *Poenulus* 1197; *Mostellaria* 828; *Bacch.* 596, 933; Ennius, trag. frag. 101 in WARMINGTON, *op. cit.*

79. Plautus, *Rud.* 938–1044; *Sententia Minuciorum* in *Corp. inscr. lat.* I (2), 584, 6 f.

80. Cf. Cicero, *Orat.* 48, 161 (but note Catullus 116, 8). Also cf.

J. MAROUZEAU, *L'ordre des mots dans la phrase latine* (Paris 1953), Vol. III, pp. 73 ff.

81. On this *cacozelia*, see Suetonius, *Augustus* 86; *Vergili uita Donatiana* 180–3; Quintilian VIII, 3, 56 f. Also, for a new idea, J. J. H. SAVAGE, *Transactions of the American Philological Association* 91 (1960), pp. 370 ff. On the register of Virgil and Horace, note the judgment of L. P. WILKINSON, *Classical Quarterly*, new series IX (1959), pp. 191 f.: "both poets do use ordinary words to a marked degree" and they "represent a reaction . . . against the tendency of their immediate predecessors . . . to enrich their language with words unfamiliar to the plain man."

82. Virgil, *Aen.* XII, 296; 3, 477; 4, 675.

83. N. E. COLLINGE, *The Structure of Horace's Odes* (London 1961), pp. 19 ff.

84. G. HIGHET, *Juvenal the Satirist* (Oxford 1954), p. 295.

CHAPTER 6

Homer: the Meaning of an Oral Tradition

G. S. Kirk[*]

The Mycenaean Empire had sunk into final decay by about 1120 B.C.
The next two centuries were a period of isolation and decline; but during
those years many Greeks, especially Ionians from Athens and elsewhere in
Attica, joined the movements across the Aegean that led to the Hellenization of the Asia Minor coast and the foundation of the important settlements of Ionia and Aeolis. By the 8th century B.C. Greece was already
through her "Dark Age," and had re-emerged as a strong and individual
force in the world of the eastern and central Mediterranean; colonization
proliferated north-eastward into the Black Sea, and westward to Sicily
and southern Italy. It was at this time that "Homer" was active in Ionia.
His is a name to which we can attach almost no plausible and meaningful
biography, beyond that its bearer is held to have composed both the
Iliad and the *Odyssey*. He was primarily, at least, an *aoidos*, a singer; the
age of real literacy was still to come. Archilochus, working about 650 B.C.,
is the first author of whom we can be sure that he wrote his poems down,
and, more important, that he composed them with the help of writing—
whatever use he may have made of the old, traditional, oral techniques.

From this time forward, Greece became again what it had been to a
slight extent in the last centuries of the Mycenaean Empire, the possessor
of a literate culture. Even now the kind and degree of literacy was strictly
limited. Even at the time of the greatest flowering of Greek literature,
in the 5th and 4th centuries B.C., the era of Pindar, the tragedians, and
Plato, the ability to read and write was far from universal, and the uses
made of that ability, by many who possessed it, were circumscribed.
Most slaves, of course, were illiterate; but so were many free-born

* Professor of Classics, University of Bristol.

155

citizens—small farmers and farm-workers and the urban proletariat. This was the case in Attica, and literacy was almost certainly less widespread in most other regions of the Greek world. A comparison with Elizabethan England might not be too misleading for the sheer scope of literacy; but it would certainly be so for its implications in depth, because for archaic Greece the age of total illiteracy, of oral poetry and word-of-mouth tradition, still lay close behind.

It lay close behind in chronological terms; in addition the *Iliad* and *Odyssey* provided each new generation with a direct bridge into the past. It can hardly be coincidence that the greatest triumph of the oral tradition coincided so closely with the end of the oral era. Some have believed that it was precisely the availability of new writing techniques that enabled the great poems to be created out of traditional and preliterate materials. It is certainly a problem how and why the normal range of oral narrative poems (which, on the evidence of comparison with other oral cultures, as well as of the two singers described in the *Odyssey*, is unlikely to have exceeded what could be absorbed at a sitting) was suddenly and so brilliantly transcended. The concept of a monumental epic seems to imply a fully literate culture; it seems to call for a reading audience and developed book-production. Yet this cannot have been so: the production of complete and accurate texts of Homer was slow, and not for several generations was anything like an official text produced for the purposes of rhapsodic contests in the Panathenaea, the festival held every four years at Athens. There was no reading public in the full sense for a further couple of hundred years at least; the poems of Homer (or large portions of them) were learnt by heart by boys at school, and the texts owned by cultivated Athenians in the 5th century B.C. were *aide-mémoires* rather than versions to be continuously studied.

It is possible, on the other hand, that some lesser use of the new technique of writing *was* the determining factor in the ability to compose such long and complex poems out of pre-existing and much shorter oral songs. Many critics, mindful of the huge gap in quality as well as quantity that separates Homer from any other purely oral singer ever known, feel that this is so. The question is difficult, and part of the difficulty is technical. *In essence* the poems belong to an oral culture, whether or not their monumental form owes something to the main poet's ability to compose with the help of writing. And to an important extent their further transmission was oral too; these were works that continued to be known, erratically and incompletely perhaps, "by heart." Yet, once produced, the great poems must have had a stifling effect on their shorter and simpler, more typically oral, predecessors. Their propagation throughout the Hellenic world, beyond Ionia where they probably were composed, was rapid. The memory of earlier songs seems to have been all but obliterated; and one suspects that the *Iliad* and the *Odyssey* contributed just as much as did the rise of literate forms of poetry to the obsolescence of the old narrative tradition. If this is so, their appearance so soon before the transition from an age of illiteracy to one of partial literacy seems less strange. At the same time the aristocratic way of life reflected in the great poems, one that had to some extent supported the singers and their craft (though my own view is that the heroic epic had flourished equally strongly in informal popular gatherings), was being replaced: by mercantile oligarchies in many of the settlements of Ionia during the 7th century B.C., and by more or less enlightened tyrannies in other of these settlements and in some of the most powerful cities of the mainland. Soon the *demos*—in Homer merely the nameless mass of dependants and upholders, in peace or war, of the great families—gained full rights of assembly and voting. This happened most notably at Athens during the course of the 6th century B.C. The *polis*, or city-state, emerged as the main focus of loyalties that had earlier been directed toward persons and families, toward feudal archetypes that still reflected some of the glow of the heroic world of Homer.

Why this emphasis on the oral nature of the *Iliad* and the *Odyssey*, and on the state of literacy or illiteracy of the world into which they emerged? The answer is that orality is no mere incidental detail, an accident to be emphasized just for the sake of the unusual. It is of crucial importance for the understanding of the poems as poetry, as works of literature in the broader sense, and as vast and erratic forces in the cultural history of the ancient world. The Greeks themselves were unable to see literature as something apart: in its large-scale forms (epic or tragedy or the great histories of Herodotus or Thucydides) it was a moral and didactic exercise as well as art. The *Iliad* and the *Odyssey*, in addition, were documents about the national past—almost the only ones that survived. It is just possible that Homer himself, and the generation for which he sang, did not see them in this light; but almost all subsequent generations certainly did so, and the modern reader who judges the *Iliad* simply as a great drama of warfare, or as a poem about the dilemma of a great hero, is missing something of the flavour it possessed for the contemporaries of Peisistratus or Pericles or Plato. Within the poems, he will be liable to miss much more if he ignores the oral background out of which they grew.

The language of Homer was never spoken by any man. It is an artificial, poetical construction containing elements, both of vocabulary and of phraseology, that originated at different dates over a period of at least 200 and perhaps as much as 500 years. Some parts of it are highly conventional, and consist of fixed or formular phrases, each designed to express a particular idea within the limits of a particular rhythmical impulse. The famous fixed epithets—goodly Odysseus, king of men Agamemnon, black ship, well-built hall, windy Troy, and so on—are merely the most prominent aspect of a highly developed *system* of formular language that allowed the unlettered singer to develop a poem of a length and complexity far beyond the range of one who selects each word anew and for itself alone. Precisely how far the formular system extended, and where it merges with the symbolic and repetitive aspect of all language, remain subjects for disagreement; but the need for illiterate poetry of any length to be formular in essence is confirmed by the study both of Homer himself and of surviving oral traditions in Yugoslavia, southern Russia, Cyprus, and Crete. Moreover, of these traditions the least complex and the poorest in expression are also the least formular, while the best have the richest formular systems. This is important, because it confirms the suggestion that formularity increases, rather than inhibits, the powers of the oral singer. It thus reverses a basic rule of classical literate creation— that the repeated use of fixed or conventional language (except in special formal or hieratic circumstances) is incompatible with true originality and true poetical or literary power. In this respect, as in others, the oral poet behaves quite differently from the literate poet, because he accepts without question a groundwork of traditionally perfected phraseology, and indeed of traditional theme-structures, and makes his own individual contribution above and beyond that level.[1]

In the final result the language itself, conventional though many of its elements are, acquires a special and quite original poetic quality. I take as an example the first mention of Penelope in the *Odyssey*, because it also describes an *aodios* (Phemius, the regular singer in Odysseus's house in Ithaca) at work:

> Τοῖσι δ' ἀοιδὸς ἄειδε περικλυτός, οἱ δὲ σιωπῇ
> ἥατ' ἀκούοντες. ὁ δ' Ἀχαίων νοστον ἄειδε
> λυγρόν, ὃν ἐκ Τροίης ἐπετείλατο Παλλὰς Ἀθήνη.
> του δ' ὑπερωιόθεν φρεσὶ συνθετο θέσπιν ἀοιδὴν
> κούρη Ἰκαρίοιο, περίφρων Πηνελόπεια.
> κλίμακα δ' ὑψηλὴν κατεβήσετο οἷο δόμοιο,
> οὐκ οἴη, ἅμα τῇ γε καὶ ἀμφίπολοι δύ' ἕποντο.
>
> (*Odyssey* I, 325–31)

(For them [the suitors] the famed singer was singing, and they in silence
sat listening; and he was singing the return of the Achaeans,

the dreadful return, which Pallas Athene ordained for them from
  the land of Troy.
His inspired song did she, from the upper storey, apprehend in her
  heart,
the daughter of Icarius, thoughtful Penelope;
and she descended the tall stair of her house,
not alone, since with her two servants followed.)

The language in this simple but touching passage is almost entirely formular, made up of phrases that occur elsewhere in the *Iliad* or the *Odyssey*, in some cases repeatedly. Thus not only the famed singer and his inspired (or divine) song, not only Pallas Athene and thoughtful Penelope and the tall stair and the two servants who followed, but also the sitting in silence, the return of the Achaeans, the apprehending in her heart, and the words for listening, singing, and descending (in those positions in the verse), are all standard in the language of Homer. So, too, are devices such as the cumulation of "dreadful," at the beginning of the following verse, upon the idea of "return," which transforms a neutral or even friendly concept into something sinister, by an apparent after-thought; or the addition of the whole verse about Penelope's servants, an almost automatic conferment of dignity, applied in the same words elsewhere to Helen and again to Penelope herself, always as she ascends or descends these evocative stairs. The words, the phrases, the rhythms, are familiar, but the style of the passage as a whole is relaxed, effortless, and faintly muted, rather than stale, redundant, or mechanical. The familiar words and phrases and rhythmical cola, acquired from the singers of older generations and refined of needless excrescence or pointless variant, are cast up anew, sometimes in fresh combinations that are almost indistinguishable from the old simply because they are equally natural. And yet there is a quite individual poetical gain in this ability to re-create traditional language, something beyond the negative virtue of reproducing a perfected phraseology without loss. For each of these accustomed phrases, as it is dropped into the listener's consciousness, is clustered with an aura of the heroic past, ennobled rather than staled by its archaic associations, and thick with echoes of other contexts, other heroines, other actions in other islands, under the impulse of other but still familiar gods.

The diction of Homer was archaic and yet constantly renewed, and that accounts for the existence side by side of terms and linguistic forms from the Mycenaean dialect of the Achaean heroes, from the contemporary world of Homer himself, and from many anonymous generations between. The importation of language from Homer's own time, or that of the generation that immediately preceded him, is quantitatively slight, and its effects are mainly superficial—or rather they cannot often be detected in the welter of language that is not identifiably formular and traditional. Yet it is significant that the language of the similes, which are especially frequent and form a conspicuous element of style in the *Iliad*, is not only often untraditional—which might be expected from their unheroic subject-matter—but is often demonstrably late within the time-range of the oral tradition. I believe that the elaboration and careful placing of many of the developed similes must be due to the monumental composer himself, and cannot either be a random procedure (or anything like it) or be derived from the older and shorter poems upon which Homer drew, and many of which he must have worked, as episodes, into the texture of his monumental version.[2]

Iliad XVI, 257 ff., for instance, is a crucial point in the development of the poem: Patroclus is at last allowed by Achilles to fight—he leads the Myrmidons into battle and saves the Achaean ships, but at the eventual cost of his own life, which moves Achilles to avenge his death on Hector. The moment when the troops first appear is one of special emphasis. The mere sight of them, and of Patroclus, casts the Trojans into confusion (278 ff.), and so draws Patroclus across the plain to his death. The device used to mark their appearance is a rather surprising simile; one that compares them, not to lions or wild boars or other heroic beasts, but to something less obvious:

αὐτίκα δὲ σφήκεσσιν ἐοικότες ἐξεχέοντο
εἰνοδίοις, οὓς παῖδες ἐριδμαίνωσιν ἔθοντες,
αἰεὶ κερτομέοντες, ὁδῷ ἔπι οἰκί᾽ ἔχοντας,
νηπίαχοι. ξυνὸν δὲ κακὸν πολέεσσι τιθεῖσι.
τοὺς δ᾽ εἴ περ παρά τίς τε κιὼν ἄνθρωπος ὁδίτης
κινήσῃ ἀέκων, οἱ δ᾽ ἄλκιμον ἦτορ ἔχοντες
πρόσσω πᾶς πέτεται καὶ ἀμύνει οἷσι τέκεσσι.
τῶν τότε Μυρμιδόνες κραδίην καὶ θυμὸν ἔχοντες
ἐκ νηῶν ἐχέοντο. . . .   (*Iliad* XVI, 259–67)

(Straightway they poured forth *like wasps*
by the roadside, which boys habitually provoke,
always taunting them—wasps which have their homes by the road;
thoughtless boys; they make a common evil for many people.
Those wasps, if some traveller going by
unwittingly disturbs them, summon up all their defensive spirit
and each one of them flies forth and fights in defence of his offspring.
With heart and spirit like theirs the Myrmidons
poured them from among the ships.)

The wasps make an apt, even a powerful, comparison, because they are wildly aggressive, insensible to danger, and very frightening, especially when they swarm. They are not heroic in their ordinary associations, but the poet draws them half-humorously into the heroic context by the standard martial phrase about "all their defensive spirit." Their swarming, the compact and terrifying mass of them, is suggested in an oblique and rather sinister way by the vague and aphoristic language of verse 262: "a common evil for many people." At the same time their individuality is brought out by a strikingly anthropomorphic touch (reinforced by the "homes" or "houses" of 261), which establishes a counterpoint to the massed and anonymous heroes: the wasps are fighting, not for the "heroic" ideals that are the most obvious driving force of Homeric warriors, but for their children. This artifice, only apparently naive, makes the wasps seem human at the same time as the Myrmidons are seen as partly animal; it arouses our sympathy for them as they respond so violently to trivial but powerful threats. If the image of the wasps were less than piquant and pathetic in itself, it would seem absurd. As things are, it is neatly placed in a context that it illuminates more brilliantly and subtly than a more explicit and heroic image could. Moreover the simile is indispensable here, for otherwise the march-out of the Myrmidons would be inadequately stressed—particularly as Patroclus's brief address to them, at 269–74, is concerned with the conflict of honour between Achilles and Agamemnon rather than with the terror and magnificence of the actual moment. It is no casual afterthought, and its deliberate collocation of heroic and unheroic suggests imperiously that it does not belong, in its present developed form at least, to the archaic tradition. It is, quite simply, Homeric.

Now the similes not only deal, often enough, with subjects remote from the heroic world—with wasps' nests, and small boys beating donkeys, and flies clustering around the milk-pail, and men arguing over the boundaries of their fields, and women staining ivory—but also do so in a way that reveals a quite distinct and unheroic view of life and action. Thus, if my conjecture is right, and many of these similes *were* due to Homer in the 8th century B.C., then it must be accepted that the main composer of the *Iliad* (and probably that of the *Odyssey*, too) was prepared on occasion to alter the whole heroic colouring of the epic tradition that he had inherited. It is reasonable to expect that every generation, in a long tradition of oral heroic poetry, would tend to leave its own mark on the ethos of the poems; we know, from the comparative study of the oral epic in Yugoslavia and elsewhere, that no singer reproduces a song exactly as he has received it from his elders. Yet this special argument from the language and values of the similes goes a good way further.

The question to be asked at this point—and it is one that tends to be

debated in excessively schematic terms in current Homeric scholarship—
is how far the total Homeric picture of the late Achaean age, and of the
lives and thoughts of Homer's heroes of the Trojan War and its aftermath,
is artificial and illusory. That it is not a completely full and accurate
report of the realities of late Bronze Age Greece goes without saying; we
are, after all, dealing with poems, and poems about events that lay a very
long time in the past, and we must expect some degree of distortion and
omission. And yet many scholars have been eager to argue—especially,
curiously enough, since the decipherment of the Linear B tablets—that the
Homeric poems do give, in all essentials, a more or less accurate picture
of life in the Mycenaean era. There may be additions and interpolations;
the description of Alcinous's mythical land of Phaeacia in the sixth and
following books of the *Odyssey* may remind one of Ionian towns in the 8th
century B.C. rather than of Achaean domains in the 13th or 12th; but
broadly speaking, according to this view, the *Iliad* and the *Odyssey* can
be used as a counterpart to the tablets in the effort to reconstruct the
historical realities of the Achaean Empire at the time of the historical
war against Troy. Against this view other critics have argued that the
social and institutional structures of the poems are really quite different
from those suggested by the tablets, and indeed that the poems are permeated by ideas, values, and institutions, alien to those of the Mycenaean
world, that were derived from the conditions of the subsequent Dark Age.[3]

The facts of the linguistic tradition, and the special argument from the
similes, have shown that the chances of obtaining consistent and accurate
Mycenaean information, with little important interference from later
generations, are exceedingly remote. Admittedly the *Iliad*, because it
describes a nationally organized military expedition, is easier to associate
with the late Mycenaean era than with the period of disintegration that
followed; its concentration on a military subject makes the preservation
of a heroic standpoint more natural. With the *Odyssey*, which explores
several of the facets of post-war existence, the discrepancies are more
obvious, particularly because a direct comparison can be made with the
glimpses of historical palace-states in the tablets from Pylos and Knossos.
Little of the extraordinary cult-ridden and accountancy-dominated
society of the tablets is conveyed in the relaxed and informal palace
scenes of the *Odyssey*, in Ithaca, Pylos, Sparta, or the imaginary world of
Phaeacia. Whether or not this almost country-house atmosphere would
have been possible in the last generations of a rapidly collapsing imperial
system is a matter of opinion; but the absence from the *Odyssey* of elaborate
divine offerings and of a highly organized scribal system for the central

control of commodities (and the absence from the tablets of divination and singers) is symptomatic of the poem's historical ambiguity. Either it includes many elements and values derived from a later age, or it has distorted the original Mycenaean material through later misunderstanding, or both. Rather than embark on yet another attempt to strike a precisely formulated balance between the more concrete Mycenaean and non-Mycenaean details of the Homeric poems, I prefer to draw attention to some implications of the earlier phase of the oral tradition itself, and to concentrate not on such extraneous matters as shield or helmets, furniture or house-plans, or even social organization, but rather on what can loosely be called the Homeric system of values and its relation to the attitudes of the Heroic Age.

It is now more than half a century since W. P. Ker and H. M. Chadwick evolved the concept of a Heroic Age: the age of a special kind of militaristic and aristocratic society, whose leaders are bound by a rigid code of personal honour and self-esteem and by the glorification of physical prowess and personal possessions.[4] The 13th century B.C. in Greece (the period most clearly suggested by the Homeric poems) has consistently been treated as one of the chief exemplars of such an age, with Homer as its chief recorder. Yet the strict formulation of such a culture—its crystallization into a type free from ambiguity and confusion—has been shown to be the work not so much of the culture itself, or of its contemporary observers, as of a subsequent period of decline, conquest, migration, or drastic political and social change.[5]

In such circumstances a kind of nostalgia ensures the simplification and exaltation of a vanished epoch of apparent glory and success. This tendency is confirmed, in the history of the epic tradition in Greece, by the diverse (and only slightly Mycenaean) characteristics of the poetical language.

Some important consequences follow. If the formulation of the Achaean heroic age were to turn out to be largely the work of a post-Mycenaean tradition, intent upon distilling, out of the partial and confused impressions of informal reminiscence, an obsolete aristocratic and militaristic ethos, then complications of that ethos, excrescences or faults in an otherwise straightforward model, are likely to be due primarily to complexities in the attitude of the original formulators of the tradition, and, at a much later stage, of the monumental composer, Homer. Inconsistencies in the character and attitudes of the Achaeans themselves, and accidental conflations in the development of the oral tradition, are likely to be additional but quite secondary causes.

Such complications in the heroic ethos are to be found in the *Odyssey* more than in the *Iliad*. In a martial poem about an Achaean expeditionary force abroad, engaged in the last and greatest of all heroic enterprises of the Achaean world, the opportunities for non-heroic responses are relatively slight. Achilles in the ninth book rejects Agamemnon's envoys with unusually introspective passion; but when he questions the need for risking his life in day after day of bloody fighting, it is because he does not consider it worth risking for *Agamemnon*, who has engaged him in war on behalf of Helen and then arbitrarily deprived him of his own Briseis.[6] This is logic and heroic pique, not pacifism. Even the sixth book, which shows Hector momentarily tender with his wife and child, is not really unheroic: what makes him persist in fighting, even though it will mean Andromache's enslavement, is the determination not to be thought *kakos* (a coward) and to win *kleos* (glory) for himself and his father.[7] Hector is, indeed, uniquely prone to question his own motives and to think of what others will say—but this is a refinement, not an abandonment, of the heroic sense of *time* (honour). Thus the grief that Andromache's capture would cause him is largely stimulated by the thought of what people will say about *Hector's wife* being reduced to such circumstances: his own honour is at least as important as his compassion.[8] Less understandable in terms of normal heroic standards is the gentleness of Hector toward Helen, and of Patroclus toward Briseis.[9] These are real idiosyncrasies, but they are easily acceptable because the relationships involved are only incidental. Achilles' temporary compassion for Priam, come to beg for the return of his son's body in Book XXIV, is more unnerving; but then Achilles sees his own father in Priam, and in any case he rapidly suppresses the unheroic emotion and threatens a renewal of anger, the proper heroic reaction to an enemy.[10] Now, we cannot be sure whether actual Achaean noblemen were capable of pity and tenderness even in the midst of war—presumably some of them were; but that is an academic question, because what is happening here is that the *subsequent poetical tradition* has allowed these occasional flashes of humanity to illuminate the severer architecture of the heroic soul.

With the similes, on the other hand, it is Homer himself (or at least someone at a relatively very late stage of the tradition) who has introduced a new outlook; and the same is probably true of the scenes of peaceful life wrought by Hephaestus on Achilles' new shield in Book XVIII: the careful argument about a case of manslaughter, the king sitting rejoicing in his fields as the harvesters cut the sheaves, the simple rustic scenes, and the singing and dancing. These intrusions are morally and aesthetically permissible: they do not break the heroic mood that must predominate before Troy, because they are formally enclosed in similes or in a digression about armour. From within these enclosed scenes, shafts of heroic reference can be discharged (intentionally or not) without any serious disturbance of tone, but so as to produce a confrontation in miniature of two separate ways of life. In the harvesting scene just mentioned, for example, the heroic attitude momentarily re-asserts itself at XVIII, 556–60, where, as the king watches and the young men clutch their armfuls of sheaves, two separate alfresco meals are being prepared: the one a humble lunch of barley-meal, appropriately prepared by women for the workers, and the other an anomalous heroic banquet consisting of a great ox slaughtered by heralds under an oak-tree, presumably for the now ambivalent king.

In the *Odyssey* the effect is similar in quality but different in means; for this poem is set not in the typical heroic milieu of battle but against the equivocal and more varied background of a Greece to which some, but not all, of the heroes return from the ruins of Troy. That a true Achaean king, or even a true heroic king, could have travelled far and wide in search of poison for his arrows, or could have had a father who dressed, behaved, and lived like a peasant, seems inconceivable; yet this is what is suggested in the poem.[12] Odysseus's wanderings on the way home to Ithaca take him beyond the known world of men (and any attempt to plot them on a map is a waste of ingenuity); yet even in these unusual circumstances of phantasy and terror, where we do not look for conventional reactions, there are certain events and attitudes that stand out as startlingly alien to the whole concept of a heroic ethos. The formal boastfulness of the Achaean warrior has become, with Odysseus and the Cyclops (for example), the braggartry of a picaresque eccentric:[13] Odysseus's account of meeting his former companions in the underworld is not so much that of a warrior as of a gentle moralist;[14] and in his deep desire to leave the goddesses Calypso and Circe for the homelier mortal virtues of Penelope he is the type not of the hero (who generally sets availability above sentiment), but of the prudent antithesis to those unfortunates of Greek mythology who, like Peleus or Tithonus, suffered physical alliance with creatures who do not grow old. The land of the Phaeacians is a curious mixture of fairy-tale and, perhaps, the neatness of a new colony in the 8th century B.C.; its young men, who delight in music, ball-games, dancing, and hot baths, and King Alcinous, who is ready to confess that they are quite hopeless at the rougher contests of physical prowess, belong to an age and an ideology quite apart from those of the conquerors of

Troy.[15] Nausicaa, it is true, finds none of the Phaeacians attractive as a bridegroom, and hankers for the more rugged Odysseus;[16] but merely by being put in this situation, and by the almost refined delicacy with which he wards off her admiration, Odysseus is denying the heroic mentality—or rather, and more significantly, he is showing how it *can* be adapted (though in the process it is subtly transformed) to alien circumstances. At the beginning of his acquaintance with this young girl, when he has crawled out of his thicket by the sea-shore, caked in salt, rushing among her maidens with only a branch to hide his nakedness, battered and impetuous as a mountain lion, he flatters her with soft words, likens her to a tall palm-tree he has seen on his travels, and ends with a reference to her future husband and a little homily on the joys of harmonious marriage: "For nothing is better than this, when a man and a woman dwell together in their house with their thoughts in harmony, much grief to their enemies, but joy to well-wishers; but they know it best of all."[17] *We* find this affecting, and so no doubt did the poem's ancient audiences; but in its implied glorification of the quiet as opposed to the competitive virtues it is quite unheroic.[18] The theme of "harm your enemies, help your friends" we may regard as typically Hellenic; but it is unique in Homer, for the very good reason that such a sentiment is normally taken for granted, and does not require or allow of explicit expression, in a true heroic ambience. It was only when the heroic view of life had lost its power, had become permeated by other and more complex and humane attitudes, that it became necessary for poets such as Theognis and Aeschylus (and Homer before them, in this one exceptional statement), to re-assert openly the old basis of the heroic creed against the incompatible requirements of philosophical introspection or an integrated society.

The real Achaean princes lie almost entirely beyond our reach. We can excavate their graves, measure their bones, put their metalwork in museums, even reconstruct a little of their methods of warfare, agriculture, accountancy, and religious cult; but themselves we cannot re-create. Agamemnon and Achilles are not real people, except in an ideal or Platonic sense: the complex human archetypes that inhabit these names are a product of the subtle embroidery of generations of epic singers, especially of Homer. The heroic attitudes had been made larger than life, and gradually they were tempered by subtleties and contradictions that in any other kind of epic tradition would not have been stated or even observed. It is largely this blend of magnificence with fallibility that makes the characters of Homer less stereotyped and ultimately much more interesting than those of the Teutonic or even the Nordic heroic epics (which embody other Heroic Ages), and renders the Greek poems more than a massive reiteration of the glories of manliness in war or the satisfactions of overcoming danger to regain hearth and home. Moreover the tempering of the heroic attitudes did not diminish their heroic effects. Paradoxically it increased them, by extending their range to situations and experiences outside the usual epic ambience. With the Teutonic epic, at least, nothing of the sort happened—largely because the distillation of the past was not so pure a process, but became infected by partial literacy and, more decisively, by Christianity, a cult whose attitudes cannot be combined with the heroic except at the cost of sentimentality.

It is the oral nature of the Homeric poems that gives them some of their most striking qualities, both in their means of expression (the formular language) and in their social, moral, and psychological tone. Moreover the societies that the poems describe, part real and part imaginary as they are, were themselves dominated by the idea of tradition, by singers and a heroic *geste* as the main form of static diversion. And even after the monumental composition of the poems, even in the 7th, 6th, 5th, and 4th centuries B.C., it is on the infra-literate levels that they continued to exercise their most persistent impression—both among illiterates, that is, and among that great majority of literates for whom an author was to be recited or listened to, rather than carefully read in private. Unfortunately these levels can only rarely be perceived beneath the surface of the new literate tradition. We can learn something of the part the *Iliad* and the *Odyssey* continued to play in Greek culture by literary "asides" and by the fact that so many of the literary papyri recovered from Hellenic settlements such as Oxyrhyncus, in the Graeco-Roman Egypt of the 2nd century A.D., were copies of Homer. Homer at that time (and not only because of his predominance as a school text) was better known than the tragedians, or Demosthenes, or Plato and Aristole, or even the urbane and more contemporary figure of Menander. I only wish we could gauge with reasonable accuracy the response to Homer, generation by generation and region by region, through the climactic centuries of Greek culture; for in the process we should learn much more than is now known about the configuration of the Greek mind.

In the immediately post-oral period, and in the new forms of elegiac, iambic, and lyric poetry, the heroic attitudes are often ignored as irrelevant; but often, too, they are subjected to implicit criticism or inconspicuously adapted or amended. Archilochus wrote his poems around the middle of the 7th century B.C., and is the first major literate composer of the Hellenic tradition. Yet the epic phraseology still rings out through his verses, transposed though it often is, with extreme virtuosity, into different metrical patterns. His ideas, as well as his language, combine tradition and novelty; *his* conception of the ideal general is not a Hector or an Agamemnon but closer to an Odysseus, even with a touch of the physical abnormality of the unspeakable Thersites, "the ugliest man who came to Troy"; for Archilochus's general is short, stocky, bandy-legged, but full of heart.[19] Appearance, aristocratic or otherwise, no longer counts for quite so much, though *aprepeia* (unseemliness) and *aidos* (the feeling of shame it arouses) are still important. Thus Tyrtaeus, writing in the martial and conservative atmosphere of Sparta at about the time of Archilochus, adapted a well-known passage of the *Iliad* (XXII, 71–6) to make an impassioned appeal to young warriors to protect their elders, because for an old man to be stripped naked by enemies, to lie wounded and dying, clutching his bleeding genitals, was deeply shameful.[20] Homer had imagined such an event only in special circumstances, as part of Priam's highly emotional vision of the approaching sack of Troy. Tyrtaeus turns it to the purpose of a more explicit profession of the responsibilities of citizenship and the beauty of youth—even in death—in contrast with the ugliness and pitifulness of old age. This suggests a fresh approach to what is important, what needs stating in life—an approach that nevertheless has to be harmonized with the persisting attitudes of the oral heroic tradition and expressed, where possible, in its language.

By the 5th century B.C. social and political conditions have changed more radically. Now Pindar calls in vain for the restoration of the world of myth and the truly aristocratic excellence that comes by nature and cannot be acquired by political or intellectual manipulation. By his standards even Homer is insufficiently austere, because by over-praising Odysseus he disguised the real responsibility for the death by suicide of the more admirable and less devious Ajax.[21] In this respect Pindar was responding, somewhat idiosyncratically, to the ambiguous epic picture of the military aristocrat. Yet his insistence was more than a personal whim, because he explicitly recognized that Homer's valuation, where it seemed misleading, was unusually dangerous; for (in the words of the seventh *Nemean* ode) "his fictions and soaring skill have something majestic about them; his poetic art leads us astray, beguiling us with stories."[22]

Pindar's influence was restricted both locally and by social class. With the rise of tragedy as a great popular art the influence of poetry became universal once again, as it had been in the heyday of oral heroic song.

Moreover the tragedians revived the mythical world of the old epic tradition. With them, however, the myths constitute the formal background for the exploration of predicaments that generally lay beyond the experience of the Homeric heroes. Questions of punishment and guilt, of differing loyalties and conflicting laws, of the moral status of gods, belong to a new and more introspective world. Yet even here the attitudes of the oral heroic tradition show themselves from time to time— as inadequate in some respects, exemplary in others. Sophocles in his *Ajax* develops still further the Pindaric confrontation between the inflexibility of heroic virtue in Ajax himself and the over-flexibility, amounting to devious unpredictability, of the more modern Odysseus. As a whole, however, the tragedians avoid explicit reference to Homer; and the historians Herodotus and Thucydides, too, name him mainly as an occasional source of antiquarian detail, or, as Pindar does, as the archetype of the persuasive poet. As conscious innovators they would naturally avoid excessive lip-service to a pseudo-historian whom they were out to supplant. Even Aristophanes, who is more conservative as well as more openly didactic, restricts himself to a few Homeric tags and glosses— except for a famous passage in the *Frogs* where he makes Aeschylus say, perhaps a little condescendingly, that Homer's glory depends on his teaching of concrete subjects such as weaponry and tactics.[23] This line of assessment continued into the next century and, through Socrates, into Plato. Throughout these crucial generations there is more than a hint of an intellectual conspiracy—or at least a strong unconscious wish—to downgrade Homer to the level of a purely practical and demotic instructor.

Yet in the end Plato has to treat Homer more seriously. Homer is, after all, regarded by the people as a great teacher; yet what he teaches is immoral, and encourages vanity or excessive emotion or disrespect for the gods. It is really for this reason that Plato proposes to crown the poets with garlands and escort them to the borders of his ideal state: from Homer downward they have represented a tradition of old-fashioned and distorted morality, all the harder to refute because it is expressed not as philosophy but as poetry. This is the true cause of what Plato termed the "ancient quarrel between poetry and philosophy."[24] Even Isocrates, Plato's rival and inferior, has this in common with him; for, although he concedes Homer's paramount place as a teacher, he finds himself at odds with Sophists who spend their time quoting and discussing Homer and Hesiod in a quite unoriginal manner.[25] These unnamed Sophists, the aridity of whose talk one can easily imagine (though Isocrates would not have done much better), presumably found audiences. They are yet another sign of the close grip that the poetry of Homer, conventional and outdated though it in some ways seemed to be, retained on the public imagination, especially at the level of oral and informal discussion.

It seems that from about 450 to about 350 B.C., at least, there was an important but largely unrecorded conflict between different systems of values. The clash was complex and untidy, and not merely between an old-fashioned conservative morality and the sceptical, self-centred, and pragmatic tendencies of the Sophists. The epic tradition operated ambiguously here—not only, as one might expect, on the side of the conservatives. Even apart from the Sophists, life in the developed city-state had become selfish and competitive, and certain of the more obviously "heroic" attitudes, such as an excessive preoccupation with public esteem, were coming into their own once again. Moreover these attitudes were no longer kept in reasonable check by the fear of divine retribution— an idea nascent in the *Iliad* and overtly, if only occasionally, stated in the *Odyssey*.[26] It was thus that the Socratic and Platonic tradition, hostile to Sophists and Homer alike, sought to adduce controls based on an abstract idea of just behaviour and its relation to the human psyche. Meanwhile, beneath the surface, the ordinary man pursued his course, vainly trying to reconcile the traditional and oral configuration of nobility and manhood with such complex factors as the anti-aristocratic bias of democracy, the post-heroic but still archaic and respectable code of "nothing to excess," and the atheism and scepticism of the Sophists and of Euripides. Out of this conflict and these uncertainties, which are indefinite in outline but of enormous importance, the spiritual tradition of Homer, supported as ever by the sheer quality of the poems as well as by their status as national epics, emerged still vigorous if not unscathed.

References

1. The basic work on the formular language of Homer was by MILMAN PARRY, especially in *L'Épithète traditionnelle dans Homère* (Paris 1928); reprinted in A. PARRY (ed.), *The Making of Homeric Verse* (Oxford 1971).
2. G. S. KIRK, *The Songs of Homer* (Cambridge 1962), pp. 202 f. and 345 ff.
3. The two views are represented respectively by T. B. L. WEBSTER, *From Mycenae to Homer* (London 1958; paperback: 1964), *passim*, and by M. I. FINLEY, "Homer and Mycenae: Property and Tenure," *Historia* 6 (1957), pp. 133 ff., reprinted in G. S. KIRK (ed.), *The Language and Background of Homer* (Cambridge 1964), pp. 191 ff.
4. W. P. KER, *Epic and Romance*, 2nd edn (London 1908); and especially H. M. CHADWICK, *The Heroic Age* (Cambridge 1912).

5. C. M. BOWRA, "The Meaning of a Heroic Age" (Earl Grey Memorial Lecture: Newcastle 1957), p. 34; reprinted in KIRK, *The Language and Background of Homer*.
6. *Iliad* IX, 321–7 and 337–43.
7. *ibid.*, VI, 441–6.
8. *ibid.*, VI, 459–65.
9. *ibid.*, XXIV, 767–75; XVII, 204 and 670–2; XIX, 295–300; XXIII, 252.
10. *ibid.*, XXIV, 507–51 and 560–70.
11. *ibid.*, XVIII, 490–508 and 550–72.
12. *Odyssey* I, 260–4 and 189–93; XXIV, 226–31.
13. *ibid.*, IX, 473–555.
14. *ibid.*, XI, 385–567.
15. e.g. *ibid.*, VIII, 246–9.
16. *ibid.*, VI, 283 f. and 244 f.
17. *ibid.*, VI, 127 ff. (quotation: VI, 182–5).
18. For the distinction between quiet and competitive virtues, see A. W. H. ADKINS, *Merit and Responsibility* (Oxford 1960), especially pp. 34 ff.
19. Archilochus, frag. 60 (ed. by E. Diehl), *Oxford Book of Greek Verse* (Oxford 1931), no. 109.
20. Tyrtaeus, frag. 7 (ed. by E. Diehl), *ibid.*, no. 97.
21. Pindar, *Nemean Odes* 7, 20 ff.
22. *ibid.*, 22 f.
23. Aristophanes, *Frogs* 1035 f.
24. Plato, *Republic* III, 398a; cf. X, 606e–7a; X, 607b, 3 ff. On this topic, see E. A. HAVELOCK, *Preface to Plato* (Oxford 1963), Ch. 1 and Ch. 15.
25. Isocrates, *Panathenaicus* 18–9.
26. Especially *Odyssey* XIX, 109–14; and see ADKINS, *op. cit.*, pp. 65 ff.

Bibliography

A. W. H. ADKINS, *Merit and Responsibility* (Oxford 1960), Ch. V.

H. M. CHADWICK, *The Decipherment of Linear B* (Cambridge 1958), Ch. VII.

M. I. FINLEY, *The World of Odysseus* (paperback: London 1967).

G. S. KIRK, *The Songs of Homer* (Cambridge 1962); published, abridged, in paperback as *Homer and the Epic* (Cambridge 1965).

A. LESKY, *A History of Greek Literature*, trans. by J. Willis and C. de Heer (London 1966), Ch. III.

A. B. LORD, *The Singer of Tales* (paperback: Cambridge, Mass. 1965).

D. L. PAGE, *History and the Homeric Iliad* (paperback: Berkeley and Cambridge 1963).

A. PARRY (ed.), *The Making of Homeric Verse*, the collected papers of Milman Parry (Oxford 1971).

W. B. STANFORD, *The Ulysses Theme* (Oxford 1954), Ch. V.

C. H. WHITMAN, *Homer and the Heroic Tradition* (paperback: Cambridge, Mass. 1965), Ch. VI.

CHAPTER 7

The Legend in Greek Tragedy

Richmond Lattimore[*]

With few exceptions, the plots of Athenian tragedy are drawn from heroic legend. This may be defined as what the Greeks themselves believed to be their own history, from the origins of things down to the generation that followed the Trojan War. Within that vast period, however, tragedy—as we may conclude both from 32 extant tragedies and one satyr-play, and from the fragments and titles of lost plays—concentrated particularly on the four or five generations preceding, including, and immediately following that war.[†]

This is the age of the heroes. Hesiod spoke of three previous ages: gold, silver, and bronze.[‡] Then came the heroes, and then for Hesiod's own time we revert to harsh metal and the age of iron. Clearly, there is an overlap here, and the bronze age (of Homer's "bronze-armoured Achaeans" and "brazen spears") and the heroic age ought to be the same,[§] that is, Mycenaean. But Hesiod distinguishes. For him, the iron age was fit subject for his own *Works and Days*, the immediate problems of life in a wretched time; but not for stories told of high adventures. The tragic poets of Athens also avoided the history and local traditions of the iron age, from the great migrations, the rise of the Dorians, the colonizations, down to their own times. Either this taboo was imposed on them, or they imposed it upon themselves. We do not know.[||] But they respected it with remarkable consistency.

---

[*] Professor Emeritus of Greek, Bryn Mawr College, Penn.

[†] Four generations, according to FINLEY, *The World of Odysseus*, p. 19; but Cadmus and his daughters and Danaus are further back than that from Orestes and Neoptolemus. Prometheus, who is not mortal, is still more remote.

[‡] *Works and Days* 106–75.

[§] See FINLEY, *op. cit.*, pp. 17–9.

[||] Generally speaking, the "myths" of lyric poetry through the 5th century B.C. are confined to this period. Pindar, however, does make references to recent events, such as the Battle of Salamis (*Isthmian Odes* V, 48–50); he speaks of the Dorian invasion (*Pythian Odes* I, 61–6; *Isth.* VII, 12–5; Frag. 1, ed. by C. M. Bowra [Oxford 1947]); and he connects the heroes with colonization (*Nemean Odes* XI, 33–7).

Tragedy, then, deals with heroes. The term has many meanings for us, and many implications for tragedy. For one thing, this may perhaps be why we still refer to the leading characters in drama or in drama's successor, the novel, as "heroes" and "heroines." But we begin, not with what we mean by a hero, but with what the Greeks meant by a hero: the minimum definition, that is, as it applies to the story-sources of tragedy.

Here, we see, the term implies a date, at least a *terminus ante quem*. Pindar's usage is clear. Of Adrastus he says:

> I will speak of him and adorn him with glorious honours, the hero
> who as king *at that time* . . . .[1]

Such heroes are set apart from the men of Pindar's day. Aegina produced

> Heroes supreme in battle. This showed in her men also.[2]

These heroes are the legendary Aeacidae, whose standards are still maintained by the Aeginetans of Pindar's day. For heroes are the conventional originators and exemplars, for good, but for evil too: Heracles and Aeacus, but also Aesculapius (who came to grief), Ixion, and Sisyphus.* But although the heroic age had its villainies and villains, there is a quality of greatness about it and them. Thus Hesiod calls them

> The godlike race of hero men, one more righteous and greater; they
> are called demigods, the race before ours on the boundless earth.[3]

Because tragedy draws its material from this age and its legends, this is the tragic world and its population. Here, then, it may be well to point out some special aspects that affect the nature of tragedy itself. The tragic world is remote in time. It is peopled by kings, or at least great lords and ladies, placed in power and position above the general run of mankind. It is an age of great enterprises by which the heroes demonstrate the qualities that make them heroic in the sense in which we generally understand the term. These may involve the vast pan-Achaean groups, drawing in almost every memorable name of their generation: the Calydonian boar hunt, the voyage of the *Argo* and the quest of the golden fleece, the sieges of Thebes and Troy with their aftermaths. But there are also the adventures, labours, and quests of heroes who go mostly alone (although sometimes cast as leaders of armies), such as Perseus, Heracles,

---

* Heracles is characterized as a pioneer of navigation (Pindar, *Nem.* III, 2, 2). Aesculapius, the original healer, presumed to heal the dead, for which he was struck by Jupiter's thunderbolt; Ixion was first to shed family blood treacherously; Sisyphus was the first in legend to return from the dead. This Pindaric usage may even be foreshadowed, anachronistically, in Homer, who (*Iliad* IX, 524–5) makes the (heroic) Phoenix appeal to the example of the great men of the past. This is not Homer's regular usage.

Theseus, and Bellerophon. Heroines prove their beauty and wealth by the noble suitors they attract: such are Helen, Penelope, Atalanta, and many others less familiar to us. The prominence of the distaff side, and the value placed on nobility of blood, help to make the legendary material in part the stories of great houses. The family is of great importance, for good, but also for ill; certain great houses, the line of Pelops in Argos or Mycenae, of Cadmus in Thebes, of Oeneus in Aetolia, display in their histories a varied and startling repertory of heroisms, misunderstandings, and crimes.

One further aspect of this age, as Greek tradition knew it, should be noted. The gods were near. As Hesiod (if it truly is Hesiod) puts it:

> At that time feastings and sessions were held in common by immortal
> gods and mortal men.[4]

This is seen in two chief ways. Heroes were believed to have been helped in battle and achievement by immortal protectors, chiefly goddesses: Heracles, Perseus, Achilles, Odysseus, and Diomedes by Athene; Jason by Hera; Hector by Apollo; Aeneas and Paris by Aphrodite. But we also find many instances where male gods are said to have visited heroines and begotten heroic children upon them. The line of descent is traced back to god and heroine or, less frequently, hero and goddess. Thus, although the child in such cases is born mortal, the terms "demigod" and "godlike" are literally justified; and thus also the gods may become not only the controllers of action but participants in it.

The foregoing brief account of the heroic age, or the world of Attic tragedy, has necessarily implied a sort of vulgate, a pool of tradition on which the poet could and did draw. One must therefore ask, where was and where is this material to be found? Although there seems to be no really adequate treatment of this problem, only the briefest kind of description can be attempted here. First, of course, ther are the surviving Homeric epics, the *Iliad* and the *Odyssey*. Second, there is what is commonly termed the *Epic Cycle*, lost to us except in the form of prose summary and a number of fragments.* In the narrower sense, these poems filled out the areas of the tale of Troy not covered by the *Iliad* and the *Odyssey*. In the wider sense, however, the *Epic Cycle* may be used to denote a great body of early epic, which amounted to a history of the Greek world down to the death of Odysseus.† Third, there is that body

---

* The material is to be found in the Oxford Text of Homer, Vol. 5. For discussion, see LESKY, *A History of Greek Literature*, pp. 79–84.

† See LESKY, *op. cit.*, p. 79.

of heroic poetry, mostly genealogical in type and arranged in order of heroines, that has come down under the name of Hesiod.* Finally, there is the corpus of lyric poetry from the 7th to the 5th centuries that sometimes included heroic narrative.

Although so much of this material is lost, we can reconstruct a considerable amount from later sources: from subsequent poets, Greek and Roman, such as Apollonius of Rhodes, Virgil, Ovid, and the fragmentary Latin tragedy; from *scholia* (notes) that accompany various ancient documents; from compilers of mythological handbooks, such as Apollodorus and Hyginus; and finally, though this is necessarily a circular process, from the tragic poets themselves and the contents of extant plays.

Certainly, they show consciousness of a tradition. Thus, Euripides' chorus, in its eulogy of Alcestis:

> The poets will have much to say of you, bespeaking your fame both
> with the seven-strung lyre of wild tortoise-shell and in lyreless songs.[5]

Sophocles makes his chorus attempt to comfort Antigone, herself a heroine of the heroic age, by examples of older myth;† and there are other such cases of recognition, within the plays, of tragedy's own sources.‡

We may ask exactly what material Aeschylus, Sophocles, and Euripides had, and in what form (written or oral, verse or prose) it was available to them. The question is unanswerable; but we must assume the existence of the tradition.

The tradition was regarded as historical. For the Greeks, the sieges of Thebes and the Trojan war were not fictions, and Achilles, Odysseus, Heracles, and Oedipus were not fictitious characters.§ At the same time, the body of legend permitted considerable variation in important detail. Thebes was attacked by seven champions, but who were the seven? Available lists vary, as they do for Agamemnon's daughters. Where and how did Oedipus die? Who married Hermione? Did Helen go to Troy at all? A dramatist was not bound to follow the same variant from one

---

* The so-called *Eoeae* or *Catalogue of Women*. How extensively this was used by Athenian poets is uncertain. It did, however, describe the sacrifice and deification of Iphigenia, though she is called Iphimede; and it contains the earliest known mention of Electra, daughter of Agamemnon. (See Frag. 23, *Fragmenta Hesiodea*, ed. by R. Merkelbach and M. L. West [Oxford 1967].)

† Sophocles, *Antigone* 944–87.

‡ See, for instance, Aeschylus, *Choephori* 602–38; Euripides, *Medea* 1282–9; *Iphigenia in Aulis* 793–800.

§ Fiction is recognized and identified early. Thus the Muses of Hesiod say (*Theogony* 27–8):
> We know how to tell many lies that resemble the truth; and we also know
> how to tell the truth, when we wish to do so.

Fiction is thus recognized as a form of art, but identified with falsehood. See also Homer, *Odyssey* XIX, 203; Pindar, *Nem.* VII, 20–4; *Olympian Odes* I, 30–4.

play to another. Euripides in his *Electra* and *Helen* adopted the account, derived from Stesichorus and possibly from Hesiod,* that Helen never went to Troy but was represented by an *eidolon* or phantom. In the *Orestes*, however, he has her go to Troy and return to Argos, there to be translated to heaven and immortality. In *The Trojan Women* he ignores such variants. In his *Electra* and *Orestes* Euripides also gives different versions of the ultimate fate of Orestes.

It is thus wrong to insist on the absolute fixity of the legend.† Yet, at the same time, it must be understood that alternative or even new versions move around a number of fixed points, such as the murder of Laius by Oedipus, the defeat of the seven against Thebes, the ten years' siege and capture of Troy, the treachery of Clytemnestra, the murder of Agamemnon, and the vengeance of Orestes.

The nature of tragic plots is necessarily conditioned by the nature of the heroic age in the tradition from which they are drawn. Tragedy's quality is deeply affected by the requirement not to be about contemporary Athens. This works in several ways.

The heroic age was remote in time, and so were its sufferings. The sorrows of Thebes and Troy and of the house of Atreus were tolerable and tolerated; those of the poets' own day were not. In the rare cases where contemporary events were used, the sorrows of distant Persia were tolerable but the sorrows of Miletus were not. Aeschylus and Phrynichus could compete and win by enacting the great pan-Hellenic victory of Salamis, Aeschylus in *The Persians*, and Phrynichus in ⋆*The Phoenician Women*;‡ but Phrynichus was fined for his ⋆*Capture of Miletus*, as Herodotus puts it:

> Because he reminded them of familiar troubles.[6]

Here "familiar troubles" may indicate not only their *own* troubles, but also griefs near and now. Many scholars, reading between the lines, have seen references to contemporary events in various passages of tragedy, or even in whole plays. The best-known instance of this is the reading of *The Trojan Women* in the light of the capture and extermination of Melos. But no overt reference could be made.§

* See, however, DALE, *Euripides: Helen*, Introd., p. xxiii; and WOODBURY, *Phoenix* 21, pp. 159–60.

† This is implied by, for instance, Jean Anouilh in his *Antigone*: "Another thing that she is thinking is this: she is going to die. . . . There is no help for it. When your name is Antigone there is only one part you can play; and she will have to play hers through to the end." (*Collected Plays*, Vol. II [London 1967], p. 179.) See LATTIMORE, *Story Patterns in Greek Tragedy*, pp. 3–5.

‡ The symbol ⋆ before a title, as here, henceforth denotes a lost play.

§ Other examples of possible allusions to contemporary events or people are: Aeschylus, *Agamemnon* 438–55 (the ashes of young men killed in action shipped home from abroad); Euripides,

M

The heroic age was an age of kings. The audience of tragedy was formed by the citizens of democratic Athens; but the tone of tragedy could scarcely be called democratic. Kings walk the stage, although their status, as seen in the context of political forms contemporary with production, remains vague. It is true that the tragic king, particularly in the type of drama that may be called the suppliant play, may consult his people, as in *The Suppliants* of Aeschylus. In Euripides' *Orestes*, the Homeric assembly, attended by the great men of Argos, seems to turn into a rather violent public meeting at which commoners as well as princes speak. In *Oedipus at Colonus*, however, Sophocles makes Polynices explain how his brother thrust him out of Thebes:

> Without besting me in argument, without bringing the matter to ordeal by combat, but by persuading the city.[7]

The contempt shown for such constitutional practices is illuminating.* The type of the Sophoclean king, good or bad, seems in the main to be one who controls his state as if he were the head of a family, or by sheer force of character. In any event, it is the nobles whom the story concerns. As Euripides puts it,

> The stories of the great deserve more grief.[8]

Here is a significant difference between Greek tragedy (and that of Shakespeare and Corneille) and modern plays conceived as tragedy, such as *The Master Builder, The Seagull,* or *Death of a Salesman*.† Euripides anticipated the moderns at least in his concern for people of no particular degree. The common man or woman may be courageous, like the servant prepared to die for the right cause in *Helen*. He may be more virtuous than his betters, like the farmer in *Electra*. Almost always, the humble are faithful. But even in Euripides, tragedies are not the tragedies of these people, who, created at will by the poet, fulfil their minor parts in mere

Electra 1347–8 (the relief fleet sent to Syracuse); Aeschylus, *The Seven Against Thebes* 592–6 (the character of Amphiaraus applied to Aristeides); Euripides, *Orestes* 902–6 (the character of a demagogue applied to Cleophon). These last two interpretations go back to the ancient scholia. Individual references may be doubted or denied, but (for instance) there can be no doubt that the Spartan hero Menelaus suffered, as a tragic character, from anti-Spartan feeling in Athens, particularly in the *Ajax* of Sophocles and the *Andromache* of Euripides.

* Thus Pindar, *Nem.* VIII, 26, speaks of secret ballots as if they were something disreputably underhand—not because Pindar was a Theban aristocrat, but because he was speaking of the heroic age, for which the secret ballot was an anachronistic misfit.

† See ARTHUR MILLER, *Collected Plays* (London 1958), Introd., pp. 31–2. *Romeo and Juliet* is, as *The West Side Story* shows, essentially just the story of a boy and a girl, of whatever station, who would be enemies by heredity but fall in love instead. Shakespeare, however, begins his tragedy with "Two households both alike in *dignity*."

support of the people of high degree, the legendary heroes. The legend implies aristocracy.*

The heroic age was an age of heroines. Fifth-century Athens produced only two women who can properly be called famous today, or even notorious: the shrewish wife of Socrates, and the gifted, Milesian-born mistress-wife of Pericles. It is all the more striking to find tragedy so dominated by women, those heroines so magnificent for good or evil, the Helens, Clytemnestras, and Antigones who could have found no scope for their actions in the Athens where they were perfected and presented (imagine an Athenian Clytemnestra facing, and facing down, the Athenian *ecclesia* or *boule*). Of the 32 extant tragedies, 10 are named after heroines and 7 more after female choruses. Only one extant tragedy, the *Philoctetes* of Sophocles, presents no females.

The heroic age was an age of gods who moved freely among mortals. Fifth-century Athens had not lost belief in the gods or in sacred heroes. Cult and ritual were meticulous; and certainly—as abundantly attested by historians and other prose writers—oracles, the voice of the gods, played an important part in the public as well as the private life of the Greek states.† But Athenians of the time of Sophocles' *Ajax* did not expect Athene *personally* to exalt one of their generals and to cast down another one; and at the time of Euripides' *Ion*, they would not expect Apollo to be identified as the father of such a mysterious infant as Ion is. Athenian contemporary life is reflected rather by new comedy, based on the fortunes of everyday citizens, where the girl is raped by a wild young man (whom she will subsequently marry), not by a god.

Finally, heroic legend is there and fixed, normally unshakeable in its main outlines. The plots are to a very considerable degree not invented (as they are in Old and New Comedy), but given or chosen.‡

The total result of the differences that have been set forth, between the world of tragedy and the world of the tragedians and their audiences, is that tragedy is an interpretation of life, but, to the Athenian, not exactly of his own life. As Lesky puts it: "Tragedy gained . . . by having a type of subject that already lived in the consciousness of the people as a part of their own history, while at the same time it gave a distance and perspective to the matter treated, which is an invariable postulate for the greatness

---

* There are, of course, other considerations besides the nature of aristocratic legend: fairy stories of all lands, composed for peasants and mostly by peasants, are frequently about kings and queens, princes and princesses.

† See, e.g., Herodotus, 7, 139–43; Thucydides, I, 118; VIII, 1.

‡ For exceptions to prove this rule, see Aristotle, *Poetics* IX, 7–8 (1451b).

of any work of art."* Whether or not this last judgment is accepted, we must accept an idealization of life in tragedy, despite flashes of realism and illuminations of eternal truth; a certain artificiality, even, that corresponds to the conventions of actor and chorus, the rigorous metres and poetic language, the claim to speak for divinity, all compelled by the tradition.

But the compulsions of the tradition or legend do not destroy choice or creation. Tragedy does not grow out of epic; it has to be made. The selection within the received legend of materials to be transformed into acted-out drama, the process of that shaping, are acts of creation. If we look for the essentials of the tragic quality, we find it partly in the material itself; partly in choice within the given material; and partly in the economy of the poet, his own arrangement of the actions he has chosen.

On the evidence not only of surviving tragedy but also of the titles and fragments of hundreds of other tragedies, it is possible to analyse further the choice of material. There is, of course, the element of suffering. As Simonides puts it, acknowledging the separate and special character of the heroic age,

> Not even those who lived in the former time, and who were the half-divine sons of the lordly gods, came all the way to old age without toil, wasting, and peril.[9]

Tragedy does not require an unhappy ending, but it does require hardship, and the great heroes suffered much. Homer and Hesiod describe the blissful life of communities under kings forever just and kind.† Such would be the life of Hesiod's golden age, from which tragic stories were not derived, rather than the age of heroes, from which they were derived.‡ Such bliss is uneventful and remains a dream and an ideal, not a story.

Again, the tragic material might be divided, roughly (because there will be overlaps), into several varieties. There were, as we have seen, traditional career-stories of the great, lonely, wandering heroes, giant-killers and achievers of almost impossible tasks, of whom the most notable were Heracles and Theseus. There were the tales of great enterprises, among which the stories of wars and cities, the tales of Troy and Thebes, were especially popular. Last, and most important of all for tragedy, there were the stories of the great families.

Dimensions, order, and the nature of events count. Here is Aristotle:

---

* LESKY, *op. cit.*, p. 228.
† Homer, *Od.* XIX, 107–14; Hesiod, *Works and Days* 225–37.
‡ Hesiod, *Works and Days* 109–19.

> So it seems that all those poets who have composed a Heracleid or
> Theseid, and other such poems, have gone astray.[10]

Aristotle, it is true, is here speaking of epic, not drama; but he credits
Homer, as epic poet, with much of the fine economy that he finds in the
best of tragedy. In a whole tale, the labours of Heracles and Theseus are
far too numerous. They are also too linear and unvaried; and tragedies
detailing them would suffer from the faults of Marlowe's *Tamburlaine*,
which is stately but monotonous.

Tragedy fixes rather on the terrible dealings between Heracles and
members of his family. This is seen in the two extant tragedies in which
Heracles is the main character:* *The Women of Trachis* by Sophocles, and
Heracles (or *Heracles Mad*) by Euripides. Each tragedy is concentrated on
a fixed point in the hero's career. We do not know which play is the
earlier, but whichever dramatist wrote second avoided the episodes and
characters used by his predecessor. Sophocles tells of the very end of
Heracles' career, his destruction through the poisoned shirt of Nessus
given to him as a charm by his wife, Deianira, in the hope of regaining his
love. Euripides tells of the end of the first part of his career. Heracles
returns from the kingdom of Hades just in time to rescue his first wife,
Megara, and their three sons; then he destroys them all in a fit of madness,
and at length goes to Attica with his friend Theseus. Each poet concentrates on one marriage and ignores, rather than denying, the other; but
the point is that for each the tragedy of Heracles is domestic tragedy. In
both plays, the labours that have made Heracles the great man that he is
are related to a subordinate position. In Euripides' play, they form the
substance of one choral ode. Sophocles makes Heracles, in a long speech,
begin to detail them, and then break off.

Theseus appears, though not as a main character, in several extant
plays besides Euripides' *Heracles*, including *Oedipus at Colonus* by Sophocles,
and *Hippolytus* and *The Suppliants* by Euripides. His parts are straight and
uncomplicated. In *Hippolytus* he is the angry father who causes the death
of his son. In *Oedipus at Colonus* and *The Suppliants* he is the just king who
defends the refugees. We know nothing about the *Theseus* of Sophocles,
but something about the *Theseus* of Euripides. It dealt with the Cretan
adventure, and thus, presumably, with Ariadne's betrayal of her father
and Theseus's betrayal of Ariadne. Theseus appeared also in the *Aegeus

---

* Heracles plays supporting parts in the *Prometheus Unbound* of Aeschylus, the *Philoctetes* of
Sophocles (as *deus ex machina*), and the *Alcestis* of Euripides. He appeared also in various lost
tragedies as well as satyr-plays and comedies. According to Aristophanes (*Wasps* 80), "Heracles
withheld from his dinner" was a theme over-employed to the point of tedium in comedy.

of Euripides as the proposed victim of a poison-plot by his trouble-making stepmother, Medea.

When we come to the tale of Troy, the surprising thing is how little use tragedy made of what we call Homer, that is, the *Iliad* and the *Odyssey*. Athenaeus tells us that Aeschylus called his plays "slices from the great feasts of Homer."[11] He seems, despite this, to have contented himself with one trilogy from each epic. The Iliad gave him *★The Myrmidons*, *★The Nereids*, and *★The Phrygians* or *★The Ransoming of Hector* (alternative titles). These seem to have enacted Homer's account quite faithfully from the fight at the ships and the intervention of Patroclus to the ransoming of Hector's body. The *Odyssey* seems to have given him *★The Psychagogi* (The Necromancers or Ghost-Raisers), *★Penelope*, and *★The Ostologi* (The Bone-Gatherers), which presumably exploited the main dramatizable actions. *★Proteus*, the satyr-play for the *Oresteia*, was probably based on the fourth book of the *Odyssey*.

There is no evidence that Sophocles drew any plots directly from the *Iliad*. There is, however, a statement from his anonymous biographer: "He copies the *Odyssey* in many plays."[12] This, like the statement attributed by Athenaeus to Aeschylus, is rather mysterious. We find among his titles only *★Nausicaa* and *★The Phaeacians* that would seem to fit this description. *★The Niptra* or *★Odysseus acanthoplex* (The Washings or Odysseus Stabbed) told of the death of Odysseus at the hands of Telegonus, his son by Circe. It was derived, not from the *Odyssey*, but from the *Telegony*, a part of the *Epic Cycle* attributed to Eugammon.

Euripides based his *Rhesus* on the 10th book of the *Iliad*. Otherwise, except for a satyr-play, *The Cyclops*, based on the 9th book of the *Odyssey*, Euripides seems to have avoided both the epics that we call Homeric.*

When we come to the *Epic Cycle*, the situation is entirely different. Aristotle puts it simply:

> One tragedy, or only two, can be made out of the *Iliad* and *Odyssey* respectively; but many are made from the *Cypria*, and from the *Little Iliad* more than eight.[13]

It has indeed been suggested, and it is barely possible, that the tragic poets of Athens did not distinguish between the *Iliad* and *Odyssey* on the one hand and the cycle on the other, but that the whole tale of Troy was "Homer" to them.† The point is unprovable, and perhaps not essential.

* Both Euripides' authorship of *Rhesus* and Homer's authorship of *Iliad* X have been questioned since ancient times.

† See PEARSON, *Sophocles: Fragments*, p. xxiv. To Plato and Xenophon, however, "Homer" seems to have meant only the *Iliad* and the *Odyssey*. See Xenophon, *Symposium* III, 6. In Plato's *Ion*, all quotations from and references to "Homer" are confined to the *Iliad* and the *Odyssey*.

Viewed not as final works but as dramatic *material*, the poems of the cycle provided far more plots for tragedy than did Homer himself. There are more than 30 titles from the three great tragic poets alone that indicate plays based on the tale of Troy but not on the main stories of the *Iliad* and the *Odyssey*.*

What are the qualities that make this material so rich for tragedy? Full consideration is obviously impossible here, but some points may be indicated. With the *nostoi* (homecomings) of the heroes, heroic saga tends in tragedy to merge into the story of the house of Atreus; and the Trojan war in general tends to be used as a set for tragedy that is not so much political or military as private, domestic, and inward. The Trojan war in Homer is really more of a huge heroic exploit than a regular war (though the 5th century did not always understand this). Only certain plays of Aeschylus, it seems (e.g. the trilogies concerning Achilles and Memnon), were really martial. Other plays exploit general dramatic situations set against the background of the Trojan war. There are variations on the themes of friendship true and false, of loyalty and treachery, in the plays about Philoctetes, Palamedes, and Ajax. We find the individual sacrificed for the group in the stories of Iphigenia, Protesilaus, and Polyxena; and the dangerous child as foundling lost and found in the plays about Alexander. Here again, it seems to be Aristotle who has stated the principle:

> Let us consider what kinds of incidents appear to be terrible or pitiful. Such dealings must take place between friends or enemies or neutrals. If an enemy does it to an enemy, whether he is actually doing it or only intending to, there is nothing pitiable except in the actual suffering, nor is there when neutrals are concerned. But when these harsh dealings take place between friends (i.e. those with close ties either of kinship or of friendship): as when brother kills brother or son kills father or mother kills son or son mother, or is on the point of doing this or something else horrible: that is what is required.[14]

The words *philos* and *philia* cannot be adequately translated by any single-word English equivalents.† The underlying idea is that of a close bond between or among persons. The range is normally from "friendship" to "membership in the family," but *philos* may even indicate, as in "dear hand" (or our "dear life"), "own-ness." The antonym of "friend" is "enemy." When Aristotle first uses the term, contrasting it with

---

* These include the following extant plays: Aeschylus's *Oresteia*; Sophocles' *Ajax, Electra,* and *Philoctetes*; Euripides' *Andromache, Hecuba, The Trojan Women, Electra, Iphigenia in Tauris, Orestes, Iphigenia in Aulis,* and *Helen.*

† The following discussion is deeply indebted to ELSE, *Aristotle's Poetics,* pp. 349–51. For this passage, however, he seems to confine *philia* to blood-relationship.

"enemy," he must mean "friend." When, however, he speaks of "harsh dealings between friends," he goes on to illustrate this by examples of terrible dealings between members of the same *family*. The shift of meaning is probably unconscious. English demands a distinction, but it is all *philia* to Aristotle, who did not have to translate it into English. But at least one principle emerges. The tragic situation is not complete unless the participants are inflicting injuries that contradict close bonds between them.*

This may have some bearing on the choice of material, and provide a reason—perhaps the chief reason (as against mere length or the awkward fact of Homer's vast prestige)—why the *Iliad* and the *Odyssey* were so little used in tragedy. When Achilles kills Hector and Odysseus slaughters the suitors, what is happening but enemies dealing harshly with enemies? This is, in fact, exactly what Homer makes Achilles say:

> Just as there are no truthworthy oaths between men and lions, and
> as wolves and sheep have no accord in their hearts but go on hating
> each other forever, so there can be no friendship between you and
> me, nor any oaths.[15]

In the *Philoctetes* of Sophocles, by contrast, Neoptolemus is harassed not only by his sense of honour but by the friendship that so rapidly and naturally springs up between himself and the man he has undertaken to betray. In *The Seven Against Thebes*, the climax toward which all action is directed is the mutual slaughter of the two brothers, virtually a communal suicide. In the given material, other pairs (six, of course) of notable champions fight fatally, Amphiaraus and Lasthenes† for instance. Since they are mere enemies, their combat is subordinate in this play; it leads to tragedy only through the betrayal of Amphiaraus by his wife Eriphyle, the revenge taken on Eriphyle by their son Alcmaeon, and the whole lurid, bloody, incestuous Alcmaeon saga to follow.

After defining the dramatic hero as a man of high degree, such as Oedipus or Thyestes, who, like them, comes to grief through some terrible error,‡ Aristotle goes on to say, in support of this:

> In the beginning, the poets used up the stories as they came along,
> but now§ the best tragedies are composed about a few households,

---

* Or are about to do so: Aristotle distinctly allows for cases where the intention is not carried out.

† Or, as generally, Melanippus.

‡ This celebrated and difficult passage will not be discussed here. See ELSE, *op. cit.*, pp. 375–99; LATTIMORE, *op. cit.*, pp. 18, 74–5, 79–80. In the main, I follow Else; he seems, however, to be somewhat exclusively concerned with mistaken identity and action in ignorance.

§ I do not know what Aristotle means by "now"; but he can hardly have wished to exclude the great dramatists of the 5th century.

such as those of Alcmaeon, of Oedipus, of Orestes, of Meleager, of Thyestes, of Telephos, and of such others as had the misfortune to do or suffer horrors.[16]

It seems plain from the context that Aristotle is here talking not so much about the tragic character as about the tragic situation. Tragedy is about horrors, and much of the time about family horrors. Thus Bruno Snell asks: "Does not tragedy by its nature rest upon such scenes of excess, upon parricide, the murder of children, the killing of brothers, and incest?"* These we find in the stories of the great houses, as an example of which we may be content to enumerate the gruesome occurrences in the house of Pelops:†

Tantalus cut up his son Pelops, boiled him in a pot, and offered him to the gods at supper. But the gods restored Pelops to life. King Oenomaus had a daughter, Hippodamia, whose marriage he was resolved to prevent. Either he was in love with her himself, or he feared death at the hands of a son-in-law.‡ By means of a deadly ordeal of flight and pursuit, Oenomaus got rid of a large number of suitors. But when Pelops arrived, he and Hippodamia contrived the defeat and death of Oenomaus through the treachery of his charioteer, Myrtilus. Myrtilus was also in love with Hippodamia and was therefore treacherously killed by Pelops.

In some accounts, Hippodamia and her sons Atreus and Thyestes murdered Chrysippus, the son of Pelops by a previous affair. Atreus and Thyestes subsequently quarrelled over the adultery of Aerope, wife of Atreus, with Thyestes; and also over a golden lamb, the symbol of kingship. Thyestes was exiled, but returned. Atreus cut up the sons of Thyestes, cooked them in a pot, and served them to their father, who ate them. Thyestes committed incest with his daughter, Pelopia, either deliberately, in order to produce a son-avenger, or in ignorance of her identity. Their son was Aegisthus, who got his name because, when his mother exposed him, he was suckled by a she-goat. When Aegisthus grew up, he murdered his uncle, Atreus.§

Agamemnon, son of Atreus, killed Tantalus, son of Thyestes, and his

---

* BRUNO SNELL, *The Discovery of the Mind* (Oxford 1953), p. 106.

† This summary account is based mainly on that of Apollodorus, II, 3–15, supplemented by (among other sources) the notes of Frazer. For full detail, see ROBERT, *Die griechische Heldensage*, pp. 206–21, 285–302. For horrible dealings in the other great houses enumerated by Aristotle, see ELSE, *op. cit.*, pp. 391–8.

‡ Or the two motives may have been combined, because if Oenomaus married his daughter, he would be his own son-in-law.

§ *Sic.* The murder of Agamemnon, rather than of his father Atreus, by Aegisthus is a much more widely circulated tradition.

infant son, and seized Clytemnestra, the wife of Tantalus.* He sacrificed his own daughter, or attempted to, in order to insure the success of his expedition against Troy. Clytemnestra committed adultery with Aegisthus and they murdered Agamemnon, whose son, Orestes, murdered both his mother and her lover.†

Though no dramatist seems to have dealt with all this material, it all figured in tragedy, including eight extant plays and a large number of lost ones whose contents can to some extent be reconstructed. It is natural that such a budget of violence and treachery, among people intimately linked, should make the poets speak of the whole house as one doomed and cursed from the time of the original Tantalus, of Oenomaus, or of Myrtilus. The legend gave tragedies of various kinds. Sophocles, in his *Thyestes, seems to have composed a lurid melodrama of a sort more commonly associated with Euripides.‡ But Aeschylus somehow wrought, out of this sickening material, the noblest and most magnificent of all Greek tragic works, the *Oresteia*.

If we consider tragedy from the point of view not of the underlying legendary material but of the extant plays themselves, we shall find this element of *philia* (intimacy or inwardness) predominant or at least vitally present in almost all. Exceptions might be the *Andromache*, *Hecuba*, *Suppliants*, *Trojan Women*, and *Rhesus* of Euripides, and *The Persians* of Aeschylus. Yet although this last play is in the main a public, political, externalized tragedy, it is interesting that in the Queen's dream Europe and Asia (or Greece and Persia), who stand for the conflicting powers of the world's armies, are sisters who quarrel (*The Persians* 185). Frequently, of course, as in Sophocles' *Oedipus tyrannus* or Euripides' *Iphigenia in Aulis*, the public and private issues are intertwined, but it is usually the private crisis that is resolved in the climactic scenes of recognition.

We may conclude the scrutiny of *philia* in tragedy by glancing at two specimens of domestic tragedy: *The Women of Trachis*, by Sophocles, and *Ion*, by Euripides.

The Women of Trachis tells, as we have seen, about the death of Heracles. Heracles won Deianira after a struggle with the river god Achelous, and led her away. Nessus, a centaur, offered to help the couple to cross the River Euenus by ferrying Deianira over, then tried to rape her. Heracles

---

* This is another rare variant, but it is adopted by Euripides, *Iph. Aul.* 1149–52.

† For the end of the story, see PEARSON, *op. cit.*, on the fragments of Sophocles' *Erigone*. Orestes apparently murdered Aletes, son of Aegisthus (and Clytemnestra?), and either attempted to murder, or married, Erigone, daughter of Aegisthus.

‡ But if his lost plays had survived, Sophocles' image would be drastically altered.

mortally wounded him with a poisoned arrow (note the analogies with Pelops, Hippodamia, and Myrtilus). The centaur gave Deianira his shirt stained with his poisoned blood, telling her it was a love-charm. Later, Heracles proposed to bring home a captive princess, Iole, and set her up as a second wife. Deianira sent him the supposed love-charm, which devoured his flesh, causing unquenchable agony. Deianira killed herself after the reproaches of Hyllus, her son; and Hyllus, by his father's orders, married Iole, whom he thought of as his father's destroyer.

Deianira had intended to regain the love of Heracles, not to destroy him; but there was a mark of heredity in what she did. Her father was Oeneus, king of Aetolia, her mother was Althaea, and her brother was Meleager. Meleager was a hero who rivaled Heracles for greatness, but his fate was controlled by a log of wood; when it burned up, he must die. Meleager killed Althaea's two brothers in battle, without knowing who they were. Althaea burned the log and destroyed her son. The story was told in plays by Sophocles and Euripides, and several others, but none has survived.*

Aside from the similarity, in the legend, of the parts played by mother and daughter, the stories are linked by an essential theme: the destruction of a hero, who is virtually indestructible, through one most close and dear to him. *The Women of Trachis* exhibits a whole tissue of interwoven patterns. The hero can be destroyed by no ordinary means, no living creature either human or monstrous, but only by dead Nessus abetted by the hero's own loving wife: after becoming infected with a love-charm stained with his own poison from his own arrows, he perishes at last through flames that have been lit on his own orders, leaving his son to marry his concubine.

Quite another style of domestic tragedy is seen in Euripides' *Ion*. Little is known about the original legend apart from what Euripides tells us in his play. Creusa, princess of Athens, was raped by Apollo. She concealed her pregnancy and exposed the child at the scene of the rape, and when he vanished she thought he was dead. But Apollo caused the infant Ion to be conveyed to Delphi, where the priestess brought him up, carefully concealing the tokens of identity (baby-basket and ornaments). When the

---

* The story in this form was told by Bacchylides in his *Fifth Victory Ode*. Homer had told the story of Meleager quite differently, *Iliad* IX, 529–99. In Hesiod, frag. 25 (*Fragmenta Hesoidea*), Meleager was killed by Apollo. Bacchylides in his ode links Meleager, Heracles, and Deianira. He tells of Heracles' descent to Hades, where he encountered the ghost of Meleager. Meleager told him the story, and Heracles asked if he had a sister, being convinced that such a girl must be the girl for him. Bacchylides also, in frag. 16 (in B. SNELL [ed.], *Bacchylides carmina cum fragmentis* Leipzig 1949]), told the story of Deianira and the shirt of Nessus, as did Hesiod.

play opens, Ion, a very young man, is employed as a temple servant.
Meanwhile, Creusa has married Xuthus, a Thracian prince, but they have
no children. Creusa, and later Xuthus, arrive at Delphi to consult the
oracle about their problem. Apollo, through the oracle, makes Xuthus
believe that Ion is actually his son, begotten in a passing love-affair of
his youth. Creusa, as a conventionally jealous stepmother, tries to poison
the boy; when the plot fails and is discovered, he pursues her with intent
to kill. The situation is saved when the priestess appears from the temple
with the foundling's tokens of identity; the two deadly enemies embrace,
and Ion's lingering doubts about his paternity are dispelled when Athene
descends from heaven to speak for her somewhat embarrassed brother.
She confirms the story and predicts a glorious future for Ion as founder
of the Ionians, the senior branch of all the great tribes of Greece.

The play is intricately and skilfully plotted, and conforms (as we have
seen) to the type of action admired by Aristotle. Scholars, although of
course recognizing that *Ion* is a tragedy in the Greek sense of the term,
still cast about for special terms in which to define it and other plays of
this general type ("tragicomedy," Kitto and Conacher; "*drame romanesque*,"
Grégoire). The legend is an obscure variant of the Erechtheus saga,
about which we should know much more if certain lost plays had survived.
Some invention in plot has been suspected, and this conforms more with
comedy than with tragedy; but Sophocles may well have told the same
story in his *Creusa*. The foundling with his recognition-tokens may suggest
comedy to us, but neither the foundling nor the divinely fathered bastard
is any stranger to heroic legend or to tragedy. What is true is that the action
of drama, in tragedy and in comedy (the New Comedy of Menander, that
is, rather than the Old Comedy of Aristophanes), may run along remarkably similar lines. One small dramatic trope will illustrate this. In *The
Mother-in-Law* by Terence, after Menander, the ravisher seizes a ring from
the girl he ravishes. In *The Arbitrants* by Menander, the girl snatches a ring
from her ravisher. Such rings are of course recognition-tokens, and they
seem characteristic rather of New or romantic comedy than of tragedy.
Yet we are almost forced to believe, in the *Thyestes* of Sophocles, that the
following scene was part of the plot. Thyestes raped his daughter, Pelopia,
She did not recognize him because his head was covered with his cloak,
but she snatched his sword and hid it away, to be an ultimate recognition-
token. In the heroic age, swords were thought of as being commonly
worn; in Menander's day, they were not. We have for this episode only
the account of the compiler, Hyginus (87), but it is generally believed
that it is based on Sophocles' play. A vivid imagination will conjure up a

scene so violent, or even slapstick, as to be almost unbearable as tragedy; but of course it was never enacted, but only recounted by one of the participants.

To return to *Ion*. If it is a genuine tragedy, not some kind of comedy, what makes it so? One set of factors must be the tragic occasion, the actors, costume, language, and metres. It is a tragedy because Euripides and all the Athenians say so. But it is a tragedy also by certain rigid formal rules of subject. Tragedy is about gods and kingly heroes. Apollo in *Ion* may resemble the wild young man of comedy, but he *is* a god. He can violate girls, but he cannot marry them. Creusa is princess of Athens, Ion is the future king and ancestral hero of the Ionians, and Xuthus, though an alien, is also a great dynastic hero of the heroic age. Theophrastus, the pupil of Aristotle, defined tragedy as "a catastrophe of heroic fortune."[17] He apparently also defined comedy as "an unimperilled sequence of private doings."[18] Comedy concerns *philia*, but it is about private (one might say "bourgeois") people; tragedy is about heroes from the legendary heroic age.* Comedy is not about matters of life and death, or horrors; but tragedy is.

To conclude. Two main aspects of Greek tragedy have been emphasized in this chapter: the origin of the action in heroic legend, and the nature of that action, particularly its violence and inwardness. Many issues that absorb the attention of scholars have here been left out or scanted: for example, fate and divine ordinance, the hero as cult hero, the moralities and moralizations, the poetry and rhetoric, the tragic character, the heroic temper, the mind and beliefs of Aeschylus, Sophocles, and Euripides, and, possibly most important of all (though all are important), the dramatic economy, the order, arrangement, and timing that make these poets the master dramatists they are. The chapter will thus be found to be one-sided. But it may be useful to have shown that the genius of the Athenian tragic poets was so fully realized because it found, in the heritage of tradition, material that, although often horrible, contained such rich potentiality for dramatic exploitation.

---

* There could be heroic or mythological comedy, such as *Amphitryon*, which we have in the version of Plautus after an unknown Greek original. But here, in the prologue, Mercury calls the play a tragedy before amending the term to tragicomedy; for it cannot be comedy when kings and gods appear (Plautus, *Amphitryon* 50–61).

References

1. Pindar, *Nemean Odes* IX, 9–11.
2. Pindar, *Pythian Odes* VIII, 27–8.
3. Hesiod, *Works and Days* 158–60.
4. Hesiod, frag. 1, 6–7 in *Fragmenta Hesiodea*, ed. by R. Merkelbach and M. L. West (Oxford 1967): but Hesiod's authorship is generally doubted.
5. Euripides, *Alcestis* 445–7.
6. Herodotus, VI, 21, 2.
7. Sophocles, *Oedipus at Colonus* 1296–8.
8. Euripides, *Hippolytus* 1465–6; cf. *Helen* 1678–9.
9. Simonides, 7, in *Anthologia lyrica graeca*, ed. by E. Diehl (Leipzig 1924).
10. Aristotle, *Poetics* VIII, 2 (1451a).
11. Athenaeus, VIII, 347e. The context shows that Aeschylus meant he helped himself to the centre cuts, the choice parts of the great roasts.
12. *Vita of Sophocles* 20.
13. Aristotle, *Poet.* XXIII, 7 (1459b).
14. *ibid.*, XIV, 6–9 (1453b).
15. Homer, *Iliad* XXII, 262–6.
16. Aristotle, *Poet.* XIII, 7 (1453a).
17. Quoted by Diomedes, in *Grammatici latini*, ed. by H. Keil (Leipzig 1857), p. 487.
18. *ibid.*, p. 488 (but without naming Theophrastus).

Bibliography

W. S. BARRETT, *Euripides: Hippolytus* (Oxford 1964).

D. J. CONACHER, *Euripidean Drama* (Toronto 1967).

A. M. DALE, *Euripides: Alcestis* (Oxford 1954); *Euripides: Helen* (Oxford 1967).

J. D. DENNISTON, *Euripides: Electra* (Oxford 1937).

J. D. DENNISTON and D. L. PAGE, *Aeschylus: Agamemnon* (Oxford 1957).

E. R. DODDS, *Euripides: Bacchae* (Oxford 1944).

G. E. ELSE, *Aristotle's Poetics* (Cambridge, Mass. 1957).

M. I. FINLEY, *The World of Odysseus* (paperback: London 1967).

E. FRAENKEL, *Aeschylus: Agamemnon*, 2nd edn (Oxford 1962).

J. G. FRAZER, *Apollodorus* (London and Cambridge, Mass. 1921).

ROBERT GRAVES, *The Greek Myths*, 2 vols. (paperback: London 1955).

H. D. F. KITTO, *Greek Tragedy* (paperback: New York 1950).

R. LATTIMORE, *The Poetry of Greek Tragedy* (Baltimore and Oxford 1958); *Story Patterns in Greek Tragedy* (London and Ann Arbor 1964).

A. LESKY, *Greek Tragedy*, trans. by H. A. Frankfort (London and New York 1965); *A History of Greek Literature*, trans. by J. Willis and C. de Heer (London and New York 1966).

D. L. PAGE, *Euripides: Medea* (Oxford 1938).

A. C. PEARSON, *Sophocles: Fragments* (Cambridge 1917).

M. PLATNAUER, *Euripides: Iphigenia in Tauris* (Oxford 1938).

M. POHLENZ, *Die griechische Tragödie*, 2nd edn (Göttingen 1954).

C. ROBERT, *Die griechische Heldensage* (Berlin 1921).

H. J. ROSE, *A Handbook of Greek Mythology*, 6th edn (London 1960).

W. SCHMID, *Geschichte der griechische Literatur* (Munich 1929–48).

T. B. L. WEBSTER, *An Introduction to Sophocles* (Oxford 1936); *The Tragedies of Euripides* (London 1967).

C. H. WHITMAN, *Sophocles* (Cambridge, Mass. 1951).

L. E. WOODBURY, *Phoenix* 21 (London 1967), pp. 159–60.

CHAPTER 8

Greek Comedy

K. J. Dover[*]

Comedies, like tragedies, were performed at Athens at two festivals of Dionysus: the City Dionysia and the Lenaia. Like tragedies, too, they were produced in competition for a prize, but each poet submitted only one comedy on each occasion. Comedies were first officially recognized as part of the City Dionysia in 486 B.C. and of the Lenaia c. 445. New plays continued to be written until at least 125, though revivals had begun before 300, and after 200 there were many years in which (as we see from the fragmentary records of the festivals) no comedies were performed. We hear in the mid-4th century[1] of comedies at a third festival, the Rural Dionysia, but we do not know when this began or how long it lasted.

We possess 11 complete plays by Aristophanes—only one quarter of his work, but well distributed in time, for they include the *Acharnians* (425) and *Wealth*[†] (388), and we know that his first play was produced in 427 and his last in 387 or 386. We possess also a complete play, *Dyskolos* (316), by Menander (341–290), and mutilated but substantial fragments of a few other of his plays.[‡] Aristophanes and Menander were regarded by posterity as the pre-eminent poets of the Old and New Comedy respectively. We have the names of more than 150 other poets, and the titles of some 1500 plays, but for the content of this imposing mass of drama we depend on a few fragments of ancient texts and several thousand quotations in Hellenistic and early Byzantine authors; most of the quotations are single words or phrases explained in lexica, but some (especially those in Athenaeus [early 3rd century A.D.]) run to 20 lines or more. Much can also be learnt about New Comedy indirectly through

---

[*] Professor of Greek, University of St Andrews.

[†] This play is more commonly called *Plutus*, a Latinization of *Ploutos* (wealth).

[‡] *Dyskolos* is known from a manuscript of c. A.D. 300, first published in 1958. Apart from a large number of short quotations from Menander in ancient authors, most of our knowledge of his work comes from fragments discovered and published during the last 60 years; more fragments await publication at the present time.

the Latin adaptations of it by Terence and (with less certainty, because of his blending of Greek and Roman elements) by Plautus.

An Athenian who had seen Aristophanes' *Wealth* in his boyhood could have seen Menander's *Dyskolos* in his eighties. If he had been a regular spectator at the dramatic festivals he would have known a secret that is almost completely hidden from us: the precise succession of changes by which Old Comedy was transformed into New Comedy. The term "Middle Comedy," used by Hellenistic scholars, is not helpful to us, because it lacks positive content, and the very numerous quotations available from plays of the period 380–320 throw virtually no light on the plot-types and dramatic structure of that period. When we come out of the dark, we are in a world for which Aristophanes has hardly prepared us; we can make very few generalizations that are valid for both Old and New Comedy.

Origins

Speculation about the origin of comedy is as old as the 4th century B.C., and in modern times it has been given a new lease of life by the use of inference from vase-paintings. Aristotle's theory was that both tragedy and comedy evolved from elements that had long existed in Attic festivals of Dionysus: tragedy from differentiation between leader and chorus in the choral dithyramb, comedy from a similar differentiation in the songs that accompanied the procession of the giant phallus.[2] The theory was methodologically intelligent, because most Greek art-forms evolved within the framework of occasions (simultaneously religious, ceremonial, and festive) in which the community participated, but we should not assume that Aristotle, writing 150 years after the incorporation of comedy in the City Dionysia, had empirical evidence that would impress us. The typical dress of the comic actor in Aristophanic comedy included a very large artificial phallus and padding of the paunch and buttocks, and creatures possessing these and similar characteristics appear in vase-paintings among satyrs (demons or goblins) associated with Dionysus and with phallic processions. But there is an important gap that Aristotle's theory has to jump: the actors in Aristophanic comedy are not playing the part of supernatural creatures, but of human beings, and however fantastic the development of the plot may be, its starting-point is always a contemporary human predicament.

Aristotle had to contend with a rival theory propagated by the native historians of Megara, the Doric-speaking neighbour of Athens at the gateway to Peloponnesus. The Megarian arguments, as Aristotle gives them, are poor: one is a specious etymology, the other a claim that Epicharmus was earlier than Attic comedy and came from Sicilian Megara, a colony of mainland Megara.[3] Epicharmus certainly wrote plays (it would be pedantic to refuse them this name and to speak of "humorous dialogues"), but such evidence as we have places him as late as *c.* 475 and indicates that he was a Syracusan. Mythological burlesque figured largely in his plays, and it is fairly certain that some of them had a part for a chorus; but we have little idea of their scale and structure, and it is possible that Epicharmus's work was not a precursor of Attic Old Comedy but a product of its influence. A quotation from one of the earliest Attic comedies (the text is corrupt, but the context of the quotation shows what its point must have been) makes a derogatory reference to "Megarian comedy,"[4] but this is compatible with the supposition that Megarian culture was influenced by Attic. We hear for the first time in the 3rd century of a certain Susarion as having "invented" comedy *c.* 570[5] (Greek historians of literature tended to ascribe each genre to an individual "inventor"), and in an alleged quotation from Susarion, first known to us from a Byzantine source,[6] he calls himself a Megarian; but the quotation is linguistically implausible.

Aristotle half realized[7] that the historical question at issue was not "Where and when did the first humorous dramatic performances take place?" but "Where, when, and by whom was this art-form raised to a level worth acknowledgment of authorship and transmission in writing?" On present evidence, the most likely answer to the second question is, "At Athens, by Chionides and Magnes, at the beginning of the 5th century B.C." But the first question is worth a brief pursuit, if only to indicate the deficiencies and ambiguities of the evidence.

Some Attic vase-paintings in the 6th century depict rows of men dressed as birds or horses and dancing to the accompaniment of a flute. *Birds* and *Frogs* are among the earliest known titles of Attic comedies, and they persisted until the time of Aristophanes, whose *Wasps* (422), *Birds* (414), and *Frogs* (405) we possess. Depictions of the animal chorus in historical times are known so far only from Attica, but a Mycenaean fresco, on which men wearing asses' heads bear a pole or a rope across their shoulders, takes us back to the middle of the second millennium B.C. Excavation of a sanctuary at Sparta has revealed clay models of grotesquely ugly masks, datable to the early 6th century; was the ugliness meant to be funny, and were masks used dramatically at Sparta at that date? A Corinthian vase of the 7th century depicts what is either a brutally humorous story or the dramatic enactment of such a story; there are arguments for and against both interpretations. Hellenistic writers tell us of festivals, in various parts of the Greek world, that contained some elements akin to ingredients of Old Comedy: disguises, violent buffoonery, ridicule of the audience or of eminent contemporaries. Were these elements of great antiquity and thus "pre-literary," or were they "sub-literary" or "para-literary"? How old is a custom that a Hellenistic writer calls "old"? In general, modern discussion of the origin of comedy has given insufficient weight—perhaps because there is not much that the classical scholar can say about it, although the anthropologist can provide analogies—to the hypothesis that comedy is immeasurably older than tragedy. Its origins may indeed go back to a time when that part of the Indo-European linguistic continuum that eventually was to become Greek would not be recognized as Greek by us.

Although positive theories about the origin of comedy are so heavily laden with doubts and ambiguities, there are at least two firm negatives. First, we cannot argue* from the obscenity of language and action in Old Comedy that the genre must have had its origin in a fertility cult. The Greeks had a sense of occasion and more inhibitions than is sometimes alleged nowadays,† but they did not need the compulsion of religious duty to laugh at dirty jokes. The grossest obscenities are found in the poems of Archilochus (*c.* 650) and Hipponax (*c.* 500), who did not write for recitation at any kind of fertility cult, and the tradition that they established still flourished in the 3rd century, when comedy was much more decorous. Second, it is perilous to argue backward from Aristophanes as if dramatic form had remained unchanged from the early 5th century. He represents the final stage of Old Comedy; in his hands it underwent great changes, and there is no reason why it should not have undergone many changes in the previous 60 years. There is, in fact, evidence to support this supposition in one of the very few substantial fragments of pre-Aristophanic comedy, the *Plutoi* of Cratinus (datable by its allusions to the period 435–430), in which the chorus on its first appearance addresses the audience directly, explains its own nature, and proceeds at once to ridicule of contemporaries—elements that Aristophanes in his earlier plays concentrates in the *parabasis* in the middle of the play (see below), although he reverts in the *Frogs* to something like the technique used by Cratinus in *Plutoi*.

* But many have so argued. My view differs from that expressed in many of the available books on Greek comedy, but not, I think, from that now held by most professional scholars.
† The idea that sexual inhibition suddenly began with St Paul will not survive the most elementary acquaintance with the evidence.

Plot, Structure, and Characters

The type of plot peculiar to Old Comedy is a phantasy that in bare outline resembles a blend of fairy-tales, dreams, and long-winded jokes. It resembles all three in that the poet works by selecting from the normal framework of cause and effect only what suits his purpose, ignoring motives and consequences whenever they would introduce unwelcome complications, and utilizing the supernatural without consistent or systematic transfer of the action to a supernatural plane; and it resembles a dream in so far as we wake up at the end realizing that it is pointless to ask what would have happened if the sequence of events had been prolonged. In the *Birds*, for example, the Athenian Pisetaerus—endowed, like a true Athenian, with the gift of the gab and a restless urge to manipulate other people's lives—persuades the birds to unite in a blockage of heaven and earth, and, after successful negotiation with an embassy from the gods, emerges as the new sovereign of the universe. The metaphors and abstractions of ordinary language can be translated into concrete terms or personified. In the *Acharnians* Dicaeopolis, fed up with war and wanting to make a private peace with the enemy for himself and his family, tastes samples of wine (*spondai*, in the sense "libations") and chooses from among them a peace (*spondai*, in the sense "peace treaty") of the long duration that he wants.* The samples are brought to him by a supernaturally swift messenger who has been entrusted by the gods (why?)† with the task of making peace between Athens and Sparta but has been refused a travel allowance by the authorities at Athens. In *Wealth*, Chremylos finds a blind old man who is Wealth himself (Wealth was proverbially blind, for so many bad men are rich and good men poor), has his sight restored by taking him to the sanctuary of Aesculapius, and thereafter takes him home and becomes wealthy—of course, since he "has Wealth in his house."

Much of the humour in plays of this type is drawn from the creation of analogies to human habits and institutions among animals and gods. This must have been prominent (and some fragments and quotations indicate that it was) in a genre of comedy that was popular from the mid-5th to the mid-4th century: the burlesque treatment of myths about gods and heroes. Apart from the humour of translating mythical events into terms

* Greek states made peace for a specified number of years: they seemed to regard war almost as the natural order.

† Perhaps a Greek would not have asked "Why?" We demand motivation in a plot, but for Greeks divine intervention in issues of war and peace was notoriously arbitrary, and the audience may have accepted such intervention in a comedy as readily as they accepted "the design of Zeus" as necessary to the story of the *Iliad*.

of everyday human life, the comic poet exploited to the full that same right to amplify or alter myth that the tragic poet exploited within narrower limits; on occasion a myth could be turned into satire on contemporary politics, e.g. by making obvious an analogy between Zeus and Pericles.

It is in the realm of plot, however, that we know least about the stages by which New Comedy evolved. In Menander's *Dyskolos* a rich, handsome, and honourable young man, hunting in the foothills of Mt Parnes, falls in love at first sight with the ineffably beautiful and incomparably virtuous daughter of a farmer. The play is about his efforts to establish communication with her pathologically solitary and misanthropic father. Having succeeded by a fortunate accident, he talks round his own father in a few lines of impeccable sentiment, and secures the instant betrothal of his sister (whose opinion is not sought) to the girl's honest and hardworking half-brother. The dowries are settled; no one is left out in the cold; even the old misanthrope is bullied into joining the festivities that celebrate the betrothals. Although this train of events is set in motion by the god Pan, it thereafter remains within the bounds of causal possibility. This is true of Menander as a whole: he deals with human beings in situations that, although tidier, swifter in movement, more symmetrical, and more subject to rare coincidence than life as most of us know it, are none the less human situations. The operative supernatural force is commonly Chance; but, after all, it is chance—whether we explain it mathematically or sacrifice to it as to a goddess—that transforms a complex of events here and there in the vast routine of life into a story worth telling or enacting. The reunion of long-lost relations and the recognition of heiresses abandoned or kidnapped in infancy are common elements in New Comedy, and they are an inheritance not from Old Comedy but from tragedy. Prevalent attitudes to tragedy in the 4th century are shown by the fact that Aristotle in his *Poetics*, written in Menander's boyhood, lays great weight on the theatrical power of the realization by one character of the true identity of another.[8]

In the earlier plays of Aristophanes the chorus is of fundamental importance. Its entrance comes 200 lines or more after the start of the play, and is dramatically exciting and spectacular. In the *Acharnians* it assaults the hero vigorously, and it is touch-and-go whether it can be made to listen to what he has to say; in the *Knights* (424) it bursts into the *orchestra* (literally, "dancing-place") with a song based rhythmically on the cries of charging cavalry. In the *Clouds* (first performed in 423: the version we have was incompletely revised during 420–417) we hear it singing, in the language and rhythms of elevated lyric poetry, before it drifts into sight. The plot is so constructed that in the middle of the play the actors are all off-stage and the chorus addresses the spectators directly. In this part of the play (the *parabasis*), the chorus is half in and half out of its dramatic role. It praises the poet to the detriment of his rivals, and actually functions as his mouthpiece ("I" equals "I, Aristophanes"); then it reverts to speaking and singing in character, but still remains outside the bounds of the story that has been enacted, and addresses us as if it were a group of clouds (or birds, etc.) visiting Athens on the occasion of the festival. After the *Birds*, the parabasis, and indeed the entire relation of the chorus to the plot, undergoes modification. *Lysistrata* (411) has two half-choruses in the first part of the play and in the middle, a combination of the two at the end, and no parabasis; *Women at the Thesmophoria* (411) and the *Frogs* have truncated parabases. In *Women in Assembly* (392) the chorus arrives in ones and twos, and its first utterance in unison is when it leaves the stage, to return 150 lines later; the play has no parabasis. In *Wealth* we feel for the first time that the chorus is not merely extraneous to the plot (and this could be said, with some justification, of the *Frogs*) but has become a conventional encumbrance. The texts of *Women in Assembly* and *Wealth* contain at several points the word *chorou* (literally, "of [the] chorus"), to show that a song—not composed by the dramatist and not necessarily relevant to the play—appeared there as an *entr'acte*. This had become standard practice by the time of Menander, who has a riotous chorus, wholly irrelevant to the plot, appearing four times, dividing the play into five "acts." Reference to its approach is made in the dialogue on its first appearance ("Here comes a gang of drunken young men; we'd better get out of their way"),[9] but not thereafter, and its utterances (presumably up-to-date popular songs) are not included in the dramatic text.

Rupture of dramatic illusion, taken to an extreme in the parabasis, is characteristic of Old Comedy. References to the theatre, to the audience, and to the fact that the action represented is a comedy, abound in the dialogue, in a manner totally alien to tragedy, which preserves dramatic illusion rigidly. Some plays of Aristophanes begin with a soliloquy that, under varying degrees of disguise, conveys information to the audience; but in the *Knights*, *Wasps*, *Peace* (421), and *Birds* he uses a different technique, arousing our interest and curiosity by a lively passage of dialogue and action and then making one of the characters turn to us and explain the situation. We know that this "delayed prologue" was used by Menander in at least two plays, but in *Dyskolos* his technique has its origin rather in Euripidean tragedy: a true prologue, explaining the situation, is spoken by the god Pan, who does not appear in the play itself—just as Euripides' *Hippolytus* and *Hecuba* begin with prologues respectively by Aphrodite and the ghost of Polydoros. The prologue aside, reference to the audience in New Comedy is virtually confined to the last few lines of the play, where one of the characters asks for our approval and applause (a convention sometimes reduced by Terence to "*plaudite!*" as the last word of the play). In Old Comedy the audience is conventionally abused for dishonesty and immorality; so in the *Frogs*, when Dionysus and Xanthias have met after taking separate ways in the underworld, Dionysus says, "Well, did you see the parricides and perjurers" (*sc.* undergoing eternal punishment) "that Heracles told us about?" "Didn't *you*?" asks Xanthias. Dionysus replies: "I certainly did! And"—waving toward the audience—"I can see them now too!"[10] This unsophisticated humour is replaced in New Comedy by a wealth of generalizations—about the mutability of human fortunes, the vices of society, or the defects of human nature—incorporated in persuasive speeches addressed by one character to another.*

The characters who dominate the action and emerge triumphant in the *Acharnians*, *Peace*, and the *Birds* have enough features in common to justify us in speaking of a "comic hero." All three are elderly and reasonably prosperous. They are physically strong, toughened by hard work all their lives, capable of deep drinking, and impressive performers in bed or haystack; through long experience of hand-to-hand fighting they are brave, callous, resilient under misfortune, and quick to violence, but under no illusions about the superiority of peace and comfort to war and privation. They are accustomed to speak their mind and stand no nonsense, impatient of pomp and pretence, and somewhat philistine in their attitude to intellectual or artistic novelty. In so far as they represent the middle-class Athenian citizen (normally a farmer) as he saw himself, they are lifelike, but they are shrewd and resourceful as one would like to be rather than as one is, and successful to a degree that is attained only in the wildest dreams or phantasies. One can recognize in this picture traits of the character assumed by the popular comedian in all ages, including our own; but even the three "heroes" from whom the picture is constructed differ from one another in detail. Dicaeopolis in the *Acharnians* is all out for number one, and refuses his fellow-citizens a share in the private

---

* Until the discovery of the Cairo Codex in 1905, our view of Menander was distorted by the large number of generalizations extracted from his work in antiquity and preserved in anthologies. We now have one complete play and large portions of others, and can see how these generalizations fitted into the dialogue and action.

peace that he has made because they would not talk peace when he thought they should have done; Trygaeus in *Peace* is a man with more of a conscience, whose anxiety from the first is for the Greek world, not for himself alone; Pisetaerus in the *Birds* is a caricature of the Athenian who claims to enjoy nothing better than rural peace and comfortable routine, but in fact cannot resist the exercise of persuasive eloquence in a quest for power.

Strepsiades in the *Clouds* and Bdelycleon in the *Wasps* are comparable with these heroes in the fundamentals of their character and outlook; but Strepsiades is muddle-headed, a moral coward and unstable, and Bdelycleon a youngish man whose moderation and rationality have not yet withered under the blight of advancing years. Neither achieves an unalloyed triumph: Strepsiades takes a violent revenge on Socrates and the Sophists, who have corrupted his son, and Bdelycleon at least succeeds in converting his old father from a fierce passion for serving on juries and condemning every defendant who appears before him; but both of them face a black future at the end of the play—Strepsiades with a son who treats him like dirt, and Bdelycleon with a father whose riotous drunkenness will bankrupt the family in payment of fines and damages. The sausage-seller in the *Knights* emerges as a "hero" only toward the end of the play, rather as a dirty beggar in a fairy-tale is transformed into a prince by a wave of a magic wand; the satirical point of the play (which is not, however, its only point) is that Demos (i.e. *demos*, the Athenian people) can sink no lower in the choice of shameless, uneducated rogues to whom the management of his household (i.e. affairs of state) can be entrusted. The old kinsman of Euripides in *Women at the Thesmophoria* is essentially the funny man to whom things happen (the type of comedian with which we are most familiar nowadays), and a somewhat unexpected happy ending releases him from the humiliations and tribulations that make this play—nowadays comparatively little read and hardly ever performed—a masterpiece of knock-about humour.

Lysistrata in the play that bears her name, and Praxagora in *Women in Assembly*, conform to no type: they are intrinsically humorous—to the original audience, which restricted all political and administrative responsibility to the male sex—because they are women who plan, command, and win.

In *Wealth* Chremylos the master is overshadowed by Carion the slave. This is not the first time that slaves have played a significant part in comedy, for the *Knights*, *Wasps*, and *Peace* all begin with dialogue between

slaves, and Xanthias outwits his master Dionysus in the first half of the
Frogs (if we took the two halves together, we could not talk about a "comic
hero" in *Frogs*), but it is the first time that a slave comes to the fore
throughout the play. The young man in love in *Dyskolos* says: "Why don't
I go and get father's slave Getas? That's what I'll do! He's really hot
stuff—plenty of experience in every kind of problem!"[11] We then find
that Getas, although conspicuous in the scene of broad comedy with
which the play ends, in fact makes no significant contribution to solving
the problem on which the plot hinges. We may suspect that the resourceful
slave to whom the family turns in emergencies—an impudent and vulgar
Jeeves, if that can be imagined—had already become a regular comic
character in the mid-4th century, as he did later in Plautus.

It would, however, be an injustice to Menander to suppose that he
dealt in stock characters, slave or freeman, and bad historical reasoning to
suppose that he was compelled or even encouraged to do so by the fact
that the range of masks used in New Comedy was finite. His plots exclude
the top and the bottom of the scale of power, prominent politicians as
well as hired labourers who are free men in legal status but in little else.
To that extent his characters belong either to the bourgeoisie or, if slaves,
to bourgeois households: and in addition to scenes that involve only
slaves there are many in which master and slave are on the familiar terms
that we should expect to find in ordinary life. Moreover the role of chance,
accident, and coincidence is so large that Menander cannot exploit as
freely as we might wish the determination of events by individual character. Within these limits, however, he was free, and exercised his freedom,
to differentiate between people of identical status in similar predicaments
and to portray idiosyncrasy to the point where (as in some of the *Characters*
described by his contemporary Theophrastus) it treads the boundaries
of insanity.

If stock characters existed in Greek comedy—and I should call A in
Play 1 and B in Play 2 representations of a stock character if they were
such that we could not imagine A, planted in Play 2, reacting differently
from B, or B in Play 1 reacting differently from A—they existed only in
inferior work that has not survived. Aristophanes speaks of "Heracles
cheated of his dinner"[12] and "the old man who hits with his stick anyone
who's there, covering up poor jokes."[13] Heracles—who in Attic folklore
was not quite the same person as the Heracles of epic, tragedy, and cult—
appears in the titles of plays by minor authors (e.g. *Heracles Getting
Married*). As for the old man with the stick, we are not bound to believe
everything Aristophanes says about rival playwrights, whom he deni-

grates recklessly and regularly, but a compromise between his prejudiced opinion and our own *a priori* expectations is permissible.

Production

Most extant comedies require four actors for the speaking parts, and all are constructed to allow an actor time to change costume and to take two or more parts in the same play. The only exception is the opening scene of the *Acharnians*, which needs five actors, but this is the exception that proves the rule, for the fifth actor plays a Persian who utters only one line of pseudo-Persian and one of pidgin Greek. It is always possible for us to allocate the roles within a play in such a way that most of the work is done by only three actors and very little by the fourth; but the fact that we can do this does not prove that the Athenians did it. In addition to the speaking parts, there are (especially in Old Comedy) many dumb parts, taken by "extras," and we have no evidence for any conventional limit on the number of these.

All actors were men (except, possibly, that some of the extras may have been female slaves), and all wore masks. When, as was often the case in Old Comedy, a character in a play represented a living contemporary, a portrait mask was customary; but because grown men did not shave, and no one smoked or wore glasses, and because a mask had to have large apertures for the eyes and mouth, the scope for creative caricature available to the mask-maker was far more limited than the range open to a modern political cartoonist. The evidence for the types of mask used for fictitious characters in Old Comedy is scanty, but it is more plentiful for New Comedy, which employed about 40 stereotypes; as there is some evidence for the origin of stereotypes in the 5th century, it is reasonable to assume that the same mask might be used in many different Aristophanic comedies.

The costume of actors in Old Comedy was grotesque and indecent, whereas in New Comedy they wore ordinary clothes. We do not know at what point in the 4th century the balance tipped in favour of the latter, but the change must clearly be associated with the gradual change in taste that, during the same period, compelled poets to substitute allusion for the coarse language that Old Comedy had used without restraint.*

The standard background set in New Comedy was a façade containing three doors; this is apparent not only from representation in the visual

---

* Aristotle remarks (*Nicomachean Ethics* 1128a, 23) that in his day comedy achieved by *hyponoia* (literally, "thought [lying] under [words]") what in Old Comedy had been achieved by *aiskhrologia* (literally, "speaking what is disgraceful").

arts, but from the prologue of *Dyskolos*: "This farm on my right is inhabited by Cnemon. . . . He's never spoken a word to anyone except to me, Pan; he has to, because he's my neighbour. . . . His wife left him and went to live with her son by her previous marriage, who owns this farm next door. . . . The old man's daughter worships the Nymphs who dwell with me. . . ."[14]—and the action of the play shows that the three doors in a row consistently represent Cnemon's house, the shrine of Pan and the Nymphs, and the house of Cnemon's stepson. In Old Comedy, on the other hand, there was no standard background, for complete changes of scene—from town to country, from one pair of houses to another, from heaven to earth and earth to underworld—are common, and the extent to which any attempt was made in the theatre to show such changes realistically is highly controversial. It has been argued that the background of Old Comedy was never more than a façade containing one door, which served as the point of transition from "indoors" to "out of doors" and was at any given moment imagined by the audience to represent whatever place the words of the play told them to imagine. It has also been argued that Old Comedy freely used temporary and flimsy sets, which would certainly not have presented any serious mechanical or financial problems; and there is some evidence that representational sets had come into use for tragedy by Aristophanes' time. The controversy necessarily turns on imponderables: how much the audience was willing to use its imagination, whether it minded seeing scene-shifters and stage-hands scurrying about in the course of a play, and what was the most comically effective way of enacting certain scenes within the undisputed limitations of the Greek theatre.

So long as the chorus was important to the plot of a play, and much of the action involved close contact between actors and chorus, movement between the near-circular orchestra and the area immediately in front of the façade cannot have been restricted, and if the latter area was higher than the orchestra there must have been access to it by wide and easy steps. New Comedy, by excluding the chorus from the action and confining it to intermezzi, created new conditions and led to the establishment of a true stage in front of the façade.

Politics, Society, and Religion

Old Comedy attacked and ridiculed eminent contemporaries with a zest and virulence to which modern satire vainly aspires, owing to the restraints imposed, mainly by the modern law of libel but also by our sensitivity to the distinction between accident and responsibility. We do not nowadays jeer at a politician for lameness, diseases of the eye, or his mother's adulteries; and the law prevents us from accusing him publicly of running away in a battle, stealing public funds, taking bribes, or prostituting himself to homosexuals. A law of libel existed in Athens, but its application was very limited and it was seldom invoked. Jeers and allegations of the kind described were normal in Old Comedy, and we see from 4th-century oratory that they were normal also in the law courts and the Assembly—a salutary reminder that comedy was not uniquely privileged. We hear from time to time of attempts to restrict by legislation "ridicule of individuals by name" in times of crisis, but we do not know the details or the motives of these attempts. Cleon in 426 prosecuted Aristophanes for ridiculing Athenian magistrates "in the presence of foreigners" (the City Dionysia was a great cultural occasion), but whatever the outcome of the case it was not a significant setback to Aristophanes' career; in the *Knights*, two years later, he represents the household of Demos as bullied by a hateful and dishonest Paphlagonian slave (a very thin disguise for Cleon).

In Aristophanes' time the establishment was radical-democratic; it had been so since before the end of the 6th century, and the final constitutional steps that made this democracy fully effective had been taken in the lifetime of Aristophanes' father, not in his own. Political parties were not lasting alignments determined by social and economic interests, but groupings that changed in composition from one issue to the next; revolution, as in the military crisis of 411 and after military defeat in 405, came from the Right; the majority of its leaders were men who had not been active in politics hitherto, and in each case it was short-lived. When we call Aristophanes "conservative" (as in some respects he was), when we enrol him in "the peace party" (not without some justification), and when we observe that almost everyone conspicuous in politics during his lifetime comes under his lash, we must remember that nothing in his plays carries the implication that Athens would be happier and wiser if the power of political decision was taken out of the hands of the citizen-body as a whole and restricted to the propertied classes. Political satire was for him one aspect of satire on human frailty, and other comic poets of his and the previous generation seem to have ridiculed every individual who attained political influence.

We should not imagine Aristophanes either as a prophet crying woe to his own nation or as an effective manipulator of public opinion. *Peace* was written when majority opinion had already swung in favour of a peace-treaty, and it was performed within a few days of the formal conclusion of the treaty; it is celebration rather than advocacy. There is strong reason to believe that the amnesty and generosity proposed in the *parabasis* of the *Frogs*[15] already had the audience's sympathy, and that the conflicting attitudes to Alcibiades expressed toward the end of the play[16] reflected contemporary division of opinion. The *Knights* won first prize in 424 B.C., but Cleon was none the less elected to a generalship for 424/3. The *Acharnians* presents the argument that it is as sensible to make peace now as it was unnecessary to start fighting in 431; but the presentation is so inextricably interwoven with ludicrous parody of Euripides' *Telephos*, the hero is so ruthlessly sensual and selfish, and the plot so absurdly divorced from cause and effect as we know them, that the message of the play may not have seemed quite the same at the time as it does after 2400 years. We do not know how *Lysistrata* fared; to us it seems a more profound plea for peace than the *Acharnians*, but (unlike the *Acharnians*) it does not carry the implication that peace can be achieved by a purely Athenian initiative, and it may have seemed to the audience to belong so completely to a world of make-believe as to have no bearing at all on practical politics.

Politics declined as a comic subject during the 4th century, but neither suddenly nor completely. Whereas Aristophanes' last two extant plays—*Women in Assembly* and *Wealth*—could be relieved of their strictly political element by a few neat cuts, some other dramatists were still treating political topicalities and personalities as central. Until the victory of Philip II of Macedon at Chaeronia in 338 cast the first long shadow over the future of Athens as a truly free city-state, there were no political reasons why comedy should develop as it did. The reason was probably cultural; by the end of the 5th century, tragedy was being performed and read throughout the Greek world, and comic poets (Aristophanes himself among the first of them) came to realize that there would also be an international public for comedy, once it ceased to be preoccupied with persons and issues of particular interest only to Athenians. Menander's plays were designed for this wider public. Even so, political allusion was not wholly abandoned by his contemporaries: we know, for example, that the historian Timaeus drew from a comedy a scandalous allegation against the Athenian politician Demochares (d. *c.* 275).[17]

The second half of the 5th century was a period of extraordinary intellectual development in the Greek world, particularly at Athens, whose power, cultural status, and wealth attracted intellectuals from elsewhere; there have been few periods of history in which so wide a gulf has opened, within so small a community, between sophisticated theory and primitive tradition. The scientific speculations of Diogenes of Apollonia, for instance, and Socrates' attempts to define value-terms, were as vulnerable to ridicule by the ignorant—and by accomplished comic poets who wrote, in intense competition for prizes, for an ignorant audience—as Darwin was 100 years ago, and as Freud is even to this day; but many factors in 5th-century Athens combined to give ridicule a sharper edge. Many people felt that they lived in continuous, intimate contact with their local gods and heroes, and in spite of their natural antipathy to profession of religious certainty they were capable of being afraid to countenance theories that seemed to lead to neglect of those observances on which the favours of the gods depended. Moreover, some intellectuals professed to teach (for very high fees) techniques that would lead to political influence and power in the community; this meant, in effect, the teaching of political and forensic oratory, and this sharpened not only latent prejudice against wealth but also that kind of mistrust and prejudice that is still reflected in the derogatory use of the word "clever." Aristophanes in the *Clouds* turns Socrates into a composite intellectual, ascribing to him the study of astronomy and zoology, the rejection of traditional religious practices, the analysis of language and metre (a useless pursuit in the eyes of the plain man, then as now), the teaching of rhetoric for fees, and a philosophic indifference (admirable to a few, ludicrous to most) to the good things of life. The play did Socrates no immediate harm; but Plato claimed a generation later that it helped to form the ordinary man's unfavourable impression of Socrates and thus contributed to the latter's condemnation in 399.[18]

The pace of artistic innovation in Aristophanes' day was slower than it had been earlier in the century,* but there was enough change to make possible the exploitation of the average man's reluctance to adjust his tastes to Euripidean tragedy or to new developments in musical virtuosity. We may compare this with 20th-century satire on Stravinsky and Picasso; but, again, Greek comedy has an added dimension, for the belief was widespread that the arts determined the moral character of an audience by direct example. We may well envy a population capable of enjoying a comedy such as the *Frogs*, which is largely concerned with the contrast between two of the giants of European literature, Aeschylus and Euripides; but the terms in which the issue is presented seldom resemble the terms in which we should formulate it ourselves—perhaps they did not resemble

* This conclusion, although contrary to the impression one would get by reading only Aristophanes, is inescapable if one examines all the relevant evidence—sculpture, vase-painting, the theatrical experiments of Aeschylus, and the development of Aristophanic comedy itself.

those in which Aristophanes would discuss tragedy with another poet in a private conversation—and the criticisms that "Aeschylus" directs against "Euripides" do not always stand up to rational scrutiny. The audience had seen most of Euripides' plays and some revivals of Aeschylus; only the oldest could remember Aeschylus himself—a dramatist bolder and more fertile in experiment than Euripides, but destined after his death to become a symbol of the good old days. The fact that Old Comedy is permeated with parody and allusion does not necessarily mean that the mass of Athenians were sensitive literary critics. Sometimes, perhaps, they tolerated literary jokes that were above the heads of most of them; more often, we may suspect that Aristophanes made use of precisely those passages and tags that he knew to be familiar to the majority of his audience.*

One of the paradoxes of Old Comedy is that although it made so much of the conflict between tradition and innovation and ranged itself on the side of tradition (for that, in all ages, is usually the most comfortable position from which to shoot), it also made fun of the gods; in no less than four of Aristophanes' extant plays—*Peace*, the *Birds*, the *Frogs*, and *Wealth*—gods are portrayed in discreditable and undignified situations (in the *Frogs* Dionysus, in whose honour the dramatic festivals were celebrated, shits himself when suddenly frightened).[19] The explanation of this lies in the fact that the Greeks, and especially the Athenians, were nothing if not outspoken. As a soldier and a citizen the Athenian obeyed his generals on the battlefield and his elected magistrates at home, but he enjoyed seeing his generals portrayed as halfwits and his magistrates as thieves. As regards the gods, he combined tolerance of blasphemy on the comic stage with savage punishment of seriously intended sacrilege. It may be that people are most enraged by blasphemy when they most fear a shaking of their own faith; the average Athenian took it for granted, as part of the natural order of things, that his life was ruled by the gods, and as he had always been accustomed (whether he realized it or not) to moulding his gods into conformity with the demands of society, he required them to put up with ridicule in comedy on condition that they received honour and sacrifice on other occasions. But there were limits: Zeus and Hera were fair game, but the comic poet was very chary of anything that might be taken as mockery of the cult of Demeter and Persephone at Eleusis.

Ridicule of philosophy was quite common in 4th-century comedy.

* If today a comedian used the tag "Water, water everywhere . . ." we could safely assume that the audience knew its meaning—but we should not conclude that the audience was familiar with the works of Coleridge.

A long quotation from a play by a certain Epicrates describes how Plato and his students were engaged in discussion of taxonomy and had reached the problem of the pumpkin when "a doctor from Sicily," passing by, farted at them in derision—whereupon Plato set his students the problem of classifying the fart. The passage is remarkable equally for its typically comic philistine view of intellectual activity, for the correct observation that Plato at one stage of his life (as we see from his *Phaedrus* and *Sophist*) was greatly interested in the nature and application of classification, and for its assumption—apparently incorrect, or at least not easily reconcilable with Plato's works as we have them—that this interest extended to zoology and botany. Several plays of the same period caricatured Pythagoreanism, and this was a rewarding subject, for many Pythagoreans at that time were ascetics and their philosophical school was unusual in resembling a religious sect, with unusual taboos and much of the mumbo-jumbo associated with initiation into "mysteries." Another quotation from Epicrates, in which it is suggested that Pythagoreans were ascetics not from high-minded frugality but simply from the poverty that is the natural result of abstention from useful work, strikes just the same note as Aristophanes' ridicule of Socrates in the *Clouds*. Yet however similar the words and the jokes, the relation between the play and the audience was different. When the *Clouds* was written, science, philosophy, and rhetoric* were genuine novelties, and their conflict with tradition was sharp and deep; no one on either side of the conflict, no matter how tolerant or how disposed temperamentally to see the funny side of everything, could deny its reality. In the mid-4th century, Athens was a different place; people looked back admiringly to the valour and discipline of their ancestors, but they could no longer see the world through their ancestors' eyes. Constitutional democracy was absolutely secure from oligarchic revolution, and imperial ambitions were cramped by factors outside Athenian control; hence internal and international politics were played (if that is the right word to use of a game so deadly for so many) according to rule. What is more important for the understanding of New Comedy, the seeds of science and philosophy, sown in the 5th century, had germinated everywhere. Criticism of the philosophical disposition could not strike down to a deeper level than, say, nostalgic criticism of literacy in an essentially literate culture, and the philosophical ascetic had no more prominent a place among a wide range of eccentrics than the bookworm and the absent-minded professor have today.

* By "rhetoric" I mean the technical study, not the practice, of oratory.

Sicily and South Italy

From the middle of the 5th to the end of the 4th century, Greek literature was so dominated by Athens that we are always in danger of forgetting that the literature of the 3rd century, in which Alexandria and the southern Aegean dominated, was neither a complete innovation nor a simple product of Athenian influence, but had other traditions to draw upon. As already remarked, Epicharmus wrote comedies in Sicily in the early 5th century; later in the century, Sophron, another Sicilian, wrote *mimes* (humerous dialogues) that must be reckoned among the influences on two poets of the 3rd century, Theocritus (who was born a Syracusan) and Herondas (whose nationality is uncertain). These *mimes*, like the poems of Theocritus and Herondas, were meant for the reader, not for the stage. But from the mid-4th century onward a series of vases painted in southern Italy depicts grotesquely humorous scenes in which the characters, who have enormous genitals and features resembling comic masks (though sometimes wearing expressions appropriate to the moment of action), move on or up to a low platform. Some of these scenes are burlesque versions of myths. At the beginning of the 3rd century a certain Rhinthon (almost certainly a Syracusan, but associated also with Tarentum, in southern Italy, where perhaps he worked) wrote what were called *hilarotragoidiai* (literally, cheerful tragedies), performed, according to an epigram by a contemporary, by tragic *phlyakes*—a word peculiar to southern Italy and probably meaning "buffoons" or "comedians." It appears from these data that Rhinthon gave literary status to a type of comedy that flourished in this region throughout the 4th century and remained popular there when Athenian poets had abandoned mythological burlesque as material for comedy. The contribution of this local genre to the early development of Latin comedy and farce was distinct from the more lasting contribution made directly by Attic New Comedy.

References

1. Aeschines 1, 157.
2. Aristotle, *Poetics* 1449^a, 10 f.
3. *ibid.*, 1448^a, 29 ff.
4. Ecphantides, quoted by Aspasius (2nd century A.D.) in a commentary on Aristotle's *Nicomachean Ethics*.
5. In the Parian Marble (3rd century B.C.), an anonymous chronicle inscribed on stone.
6. Johannes Tzetzes (12th century A.D.), who used, indirectly, some ancient sources that did not survive into the late Middle Ages.

7. *Poetics* 1449[b], 1 ff.
8. *ibid.*, 1452[a], 29 ff.; 1453[b], 27 ff.; 1454[b], 19 ff.
9. Menander, *Dyskolos* 230 ff.
10. Aristophanes, *Frogs* 274 ff.
11. Menander, *op. cit.*, 181 ff.
12. Aristophanes, *Wasps* 60; cf. *Peace* 741.
13. Aristophanes, *Clouds* 541 ff.
14. *Dyskolos* 5 ff.
15. *Frogs* 686 ff.
16. *ibid.*, 1422 ff.
17. Polybius XII, 13.
18. Plato, *Apology* 18D; 19BC.
19. *Frogs* 307 f.; 479 ff.

Bibliography

Owing to the rate at which our knowledge of Menander is growing, there is no comprehensive and up-to-date book on New Comedy or on the history of Greek comedy as a whole. KATHERINE LEVER, *The Art of Greek Comedy* (London 1956), has good insights but some errors. GILBERT NORWOOD, *Greek Comedy* (London 1931), has a high concentration of factual data but idiosyncratic aesthetic judgments. *Entretiens de la Fondation Hardt*, Vol. XVI (Vandoeuvres 1970), is a valuable collection of papers on aspects of Menander.

There are many books on Aristophanes. GILBERT MURRAY, *Aristophanes* (Oxford 1933), is brief and lucid; but Murray was even less at one with Aristophanes than he realized, and he found some of the characteristic qualities of the comic poets hard to understand. C. F. RUSSO, *Aristofane autore di teatre* (Florence 1962), and P. HÄNDEL, *Formen und Darstellungsweisen in der aristophanischen Komödie* (Heidelberg 1963), contain detailed discussions of dramatic technique; Russo is more concerned with theatrical effect, Händel with literary form. CEDRIC H. WHITMAN, *Aristophanes and the Comic Hero* (Cambridge, Mass. 1964), explores the ethos of Aristophanic comedy and its relation to the circumstances and attitudes of its time. Both Whitman's and Russo's books are marred by some inaccuracy in details, and Whitman attributes to Aristophanes concepts and judgments that may be only the product of our own literary categories and historical hindsight. H.-J. NEWIGER, *Metapher und Allegorie: Studien zu Aristophanes* (Munich 1957), is the most perceptive and rewarding of recent attempts to define the essence of Aristophanic comedy; J. TAILLARDAT, *Les images d'Aristophane*, 2nd edn (Paris 1965), is the best study of Aristophanes' vocabulary. V. EHRENBERG, *The People of Aristophanes*, 2nd edn (Oxford 1951), a collection of data on Athenian society, makes full use of Old Comedy but, almost unavoidably, does not allow enough for comic convention and exaggeration. W. SÜSS, *Aristophanes und die Nachwelt* (Leipzig 1911), is an admirable account of Aristophanes' influence on European literature.

On the origins of comedy T. B. L. Webster's thorough revision of
A. W. PICKARD-CAMBRIDGE, *Dithyramb, Tragedy, and Comedy* (Oxford 1962),
is indispensable. L. BREITHOLZ, *Die derische Farce im griechischen Mutterland*
(Stockholm 1960), is very thorough, but the author's scepticism sometimes overreaches itself.

T. B. L. WEBSTER, *Studies in Later Greek Comedy* (Manchester 1953), and
Studies in Menander, 2nd edn (Manchester 1960: the 1st edition was
written before the discovery of *Dyskolos*), offer reconstructions and
interpretations of lost plays and a characterization of 4th-century comedy
(including New Comedy) in general.

The best account (copiously illustrated) of the southern Italian vase-
paintings depicting comic performances is in M. BIEBER, *The History of the
Greek and Roman Theater*, 2nd edn (Princeton 1961), Ch. X.

CHAPTER 9

Roman Drama

Gordon Williams*

Our knowledge of dramatic activity in ancient Rome is very patchy. Plays were continually being written and produced during the century and a half following the first recorded performance in 240 B.C., but of all these plays, both tragedies and comedies, only 20 comedies of Plautus (with large fragments of a 21st) and six comedies of Terence have survived. Apart from these, there are only fragments, mostly very brief, quoted by later authors (mainly grammarians, to illustrate obsolete words and meanings). For almost two centuries of dramatic activity, then, the only complete plays to have survived were written by two dramatists who were writing within about 30 years of one another at about the mid-point of the period. Furthermore, both dramatists were writers of comedy. The earliest preserved tragedy comes from the middle of the 1st century A.D., 300 years after dramatic productions began at Rome. This is a serious loss, because tragedies seem to have been produced at Rome almost as often as comedies; yet, if a historian were to judge from the evidence of the surviving comedies, he would be inclined to imagine an atmosphere in Rome conducive to the production of farcical comedy and, on the whole, inimical to tragedy.

This judgment would be quite wrong, but the situation that accommodated these divergent tastes in drama cannot be reconstructed with any certainty in the absence of anything more than meagre fragments of tragedy. Nevertheless, something like a coherent picture of dramatic activity during the early period can be built up by analysis of the life and works—where anything is known of them—of a number of individual writers. After the early period, very little is known of dramatic activity until the tragedies of the younger Seneca, written about the middle of the 1st century A.D. It will be best, therefore, to give an outline sketch of the period 240–80 B.C., followed by a more detailed consideration of the

* Professor of Humanity, University of St Andrews.

work of Plautus and Terence; after that, a brief account of the period from 100 B.C. to A.D. 60 will be given, and finally a survey of the dramatic writing of Seneca. Any attempt to give a synchronistic analysis of dramatic activity as a social phenomenon at Rome would be vitiated by the nature of the evidence.

Production

The general supervision of dramatic performances at Rome was in the hands of minor magistrates, the *curule aediles* who bought plays and authorized their performance. The production was mounted by an actor-manager and a small troupe of no more than six actors, all male, who acted the speaking parts. The status of actors is unclear; some were slaves, but there is enough evidence to show that others were freemen. The actor-manger could be a person of some consequence, such as Ambivius Turpio, an attractive character who produced the plays of Caecilius and then of Terence, and for whom Terence wrote the prologues to his plays. In general, stage-management at Rome was modelled on the practice of Greek New Comedy. Curiously enough, our evidence leaves the question of masks uncertain: some evidence suggests that until after the death of Terence actors altered their appearance merely by the use of make-up; other evidence puts the use of masks much further back in time—and this seems more likely.

The stage was a raised platform with a back wall on which the façades of three houses were represented; the house-doors seem never to have been used to reveal action within—hence the fixed convention, Greek and Roman, of making a character direct his words backward toward a doorway when setting the scene of the action; the action itself took place outside on the stage. There may have been purely notional alley-ways between the houses, in which characters could lurk in hiding or escape, but this would have been a convention, unspokenly agreed by audience and dramatist. The exits and entrances were at each side of the stage: conventionally, the entrance or exit at stage-right was to or from the centre of the town (the market-place), and that at stage-left to or from country-side or harbour. We do not know what other visual aids were given to spectators; but they would scarcely have been needed, for Greek dramatists had built up over the centuries a sophisticated technique of writing speeches in such a way that all necessary information was contained in what was actually spoken.

It is clear that the Roman audience consisted of the whole of society, from slaves to senators, and that most members of any audience had been trained from early childhood to be theatrical spectators. Dramatists could afford to take liberties, providing only that they held their audiences' attention.

Drama at Rome from 240 to 80 B.C.

Plays were a regular entertainment at the public festivals of Rome—the *ludi romani*, *ludi plebeii* (first instituted probably in the late 3rd century B.C.), *ludi apollinares* (instituted in 212 B.C.), and *ludi megalenses* (instituted in 204 B.C.). Some form of dramatic entertainment is reported to have been a feature of the *ludi romani* since 364 B.C., but nothing is known about this, and the first reported performance of a true play is one by Livius Andronicus in 240 B.C. (Cicero, *Brutus* 72).

Livius Andronicus is reported by Accius—the first scholar of these poets, and himself a playwright—to have come from Tarentum (southern Italy); his name suggests that he was a slave and then a freedman of the family of the Livii. If so, the likeliest possibility is that he was taken prisoner when Rome captured Tarentum in 272 B.C. His place of origin is very important, because Plato (*Laws* I, 637) reports that the people of Tarentum were passionately devoted to the theatre, and so Livius would have brought not only a knowledge of Greek drama to Rome, but also the technical skills of dramatic production that had been built up over centuries under the influence of the Theatre of Dionysus at Athens. Livius was still alive in 207 B.C. (Livy, XXVII, 37, 7) but was dead by 200 B.C.; he had a long and distinguished career in Rome and, in recognition of his poetical services in composing ritual lyrics, the temple of Minerva on the Aventine was set aside as a place where writers and actors could meet.

Unfortunately very little is known of his dramatic writing, but some important details emerge that show him to have been the founder and legislator of Roman drama. In complete defiance of Greek tradition, he used the same structure of iambic line for the dialogue both of comedy and of tragedy; all later writers followed him, and the result was a far less sharp stylistic distinction between the two genres. The other fundamental practice that he established is inferred with great probability from a fragment of his *Equos troianus*: this is in cretic metre but seems to come from a speech of Sinon. If so, Livius, like later dramatists, probably dispensed with the Greek chorus as such, and instead converted sections of trimeter monologue into lyric *cantica*—that is, into musical arias for solo performance. This practice was then transferred to comedy: the Romans seem to have enjoyed virtuoso performances by accomplished singers as much as they disliked choral performances on the 5th-century Athenian pattern. Only eight titles of tragedies by Livius Andronicus are now known, and they suggest that he favoured Sophocles and Euripides as his models; but our knowledge of his comedies is almost nil.

Cnaeus Naevius was of Italic stock and came from the neighbourhood of Capua—a region that offered him equally close contact with Roman colonies and Greek cities. By 235 B.C. he was active on the Roman stage. He was a man of fiery temperament, and he tried to take part in political activity by criticizing members of Rome's leading families from the stage. His most indiscreet attack was on the aristocratic family of the Metelli. The details are obscure, but he seems to have been imprisoned about 204 B.C., then went into exile and died at Utica about 201 B.C. Rome was not a police-state, but the world of the stage could not be brought into collision with the real world of politics.

Only very meagre fragments of Naevius's tragedies remain, but there is one important fragment from the *Danae* that reports the disgrace of Danae, yet is written as a bacchiac tetrameter. This must mean that Naevius, like Livius Andronicus, took a passage of trimeter monologue from the Greek play and turned it into a lyric *canticum* (dispensing with the chorus as the musical element). Some 28 titles of comedies are known and there are several interesting fragments: one especially, from the *Tarentilla*, depicts a girl flirting in a circle of young men, and gives a sense of great vigour and liveliness. Other fragments indicate that Naevius, like Plautus, blended Greek and Roman elements, and they make clear a considerable linguistic community between him and Plautus—which can only mean that Plautus was deeply indebted to him.

Naevius took one very interesting step in a new direction: he wrote tragedies based on Roman historical and mythical material, and known titles of his plays refer to the legend of Romulus and—from his own time—to the single combat of Marcellus against the Gallic chief at Clastidium in 223 B.C. This was a remarkable innovation, and the reasons for its later failure will be considered below. It is clear from the fragments and from the ancient evidence that Naevius was an original dramatist of great vigour and inventiveness, but probably as impetuous and hasty in his writing as he was in his life.

Quintus Ennius's literary activities were even more varied than those of Naevius. Ennius was a Hellenistic scholar-poet after the manner of Callimachus, and there was hardly a literary genre on which he did not set his mark. He was born in 239 B.C. and was probably a younger contemporary of Plautus; they were both writing plays for the Roman stage about the same time, but, whereas Plautus died about 184 B.C., Ennius lived on till 169 B.C. Ennius was born at Rudiae in Calabria and says himself that he had three hearts: one Greek, one Oscan, and one Roman. It is odd, in view of his literary talent, that he should have written in Latin rather than Greek. It must be that, despite appearances from our point of view, Rome's position in the Mediterranean looked likely to become dominant—even to a young man who, at the age of 21, saw Hannibal invade and ravage Italy almost at will.

It is a very curious fact that, although his older contemporary Plautus did what Greeks had always done, and concentrated on a single dramatic genre, Ennius wrote both comedies and tragedies. It must be reckoned an aspect of his Hellenistic versatility that his comedies were clearly inferior to those of Plautus, because only four (separate) lines from them have been preserved. His tragedies, on the other hand, were very successful; they aroused the admiration of Cicero more than a century later, and it is to this fact that we owe the preservation of significant fragments. Here it is at last possible to make meaningful comparisons with Greek originals. Titles of 20 tragedies are known and 12 of these are Euripidean. The *Medea* of Ennius is extant in a number of fragments scattered throughout the play and these may be compared with the corresponding passages of Euripides. The opening of Ennius's play has survived and here he takes seven lines to represent five and a half of Greek—but of these only three and a half are actually represented in the sense of the Latin. The simple, vivid style of Euripides, enlivened by occasional metaphors, was converted by Ennius into a solemn, even bombastic, exposition, in which the sound of the words predominates over their sense by means of alliteration and assonance. The misery of the nurse, which Euripides was anxious to convey, disappears in artificial word-play and rhetoric. The result is impressive where Euripides is more natural.

A few lines have been preserved of the speech of Medea (214 ff.) when she addresses the women of Corinth. This is sufficient to show that Ennius, like Livius Andronicus and Naevius, turned passages of Greek trimeter monologue into polymetric *cantica*. Here the effect of such a change can be gauged. Euripides composed a highly sophistic speech for Medea in which, by drawing a series of fine distinctions, she explains how it is right for her to come out and put her case in public. The fine points all disappear in Ennius, and Medea comes out, addresses the women of Corinth in high-flown and solemn style, and then launches into a lecture on patriotism, simple in conception but impressive and weighty in language. The subtlety of thought in which Euripides delighted could not possibly be conveyed in the style of *cantica*, where interest and attention are concentrated on the sound and verbal effects.

It is also clear from the fragments that Ennius, more appropriately, converted into a *canticum* the great speech in which Medea, about to murder her children, addresses her heart, urging firmness in her terrible purpose, and speaks a last farewell to her children. It is difficult to gauge the extent to which Ennius's alterations to Euripides were due to the influence of the different audience and the Roman milieu: certainly the patriotic motifs and the simplification of mythology may confidently be attributed to this.

It is apparent from a comparison with his other works that Ennius, who was perfectly at home in the world of Hellenistic Greek literature, designed his plays to fit a series of conventions that had been established on the Roman stage, the effect of which was to create something of a stereotyped style and method of "translation." Within these limits, however, even the relatively meagre fragments show that Ennius imposed his own imaginative range and energy on his material, reshaping the Greek schemes into a turbulent flow of impressionistic ideas. This is clear, for instance, in the lines that "translate" Aeschylus's *Eumenides* 905 ff. Whereas Aeschylus established an orderly arrangement of the blessings promised to Attica into those of land, then sea, then air, Ennius totally abandoned this framework in favour of a richly sensuous and earthy impression of nature and the processes of growth.

Like Naevius, Ennius wrote tragedies based on Roman history and mythology; a fragment of his *Sabinae*, on the rape of the Sabine women, is particularly interesting because it shows him using in this play of his own creation a motif from Euripides' *Phoenissae* 571 ff. Ennius—and, no doubt, Naevius before him—set a pattern for Roman literary activity: Roman poets learned to achieve an originality of their own, in spite of the enormous range and achievement of Greek writers, precisely by adapting Greek material and ideas to their own purposes.

The next great dramatist known to us followed Plautus in confining his literary activity to comedy. He was Caecilius Statius, who came to Rome (probably as a slave) from the Milan region about 223 B.C. and died in 168 B.C. He was highly regarded by ancient critics for his plots and his emotional power, and one critic ranked him greatest of all comic poets. Titles of 42 plays are known, and of these at least 16 seem to have been adapted from plays of Menander. It is not easy, however, to get much of an idea of his writing from the meagre fragments, with the exception of one series. Aulus Gellius, writing his *Noctes atticae* (a record of scholarly and artistic discussions) in the 2nd century A.D., recalls how he and some friends happened one day to be reading the *Necklace* of Caecilius and were enjoying it greatly; then they happened to look at the play by Menander on which Caecilius's play was based, and were astonished to discover how much better the Greek play was. To substantiate this judgment, Gellius quotes three passages of Caecilius side by side with the original Greek. In general the comparison shows Caecilius to have substituted power and vigour for the delicate subtlety of Menander, but one of the passages is particularly interesting. Gellius quotes 16 lines of a trimeter monologue in which Menander made a husband complain of his wife's actions and then of her appearance and unattractiveness; it is a lively and amusing speech, full of the pithy proverbial phrases for which Menander was famous. Caecilius, following the practice of his predecessors, turned this into a polymetric *canticum*; he discarded the logical progression of ideas—even the wife's action (essential to the plot) is described later and then only allusively—in favour of a turbulent flow of bombastic and extravagant language. This is funny but coarse, and it is pitched in far too high a key to catch the delicate changes of tone that Menander achieves. It is farce, whereas Menander is mannered comedy. But there is no doubt that the nature of the Roman comedy was fundamentally different—a fact made sufficiently clear by the turning of such a key speech in the drama into an aria.

The nature and explanation of this difference are complex and obscure, because most of the relevant evidence has been lost. But one basic factor must have been social. The world of Greek New Comedy was a prosperous middle-class world, its values dictated by characteristic bourgeois attitudes to the profit motive and a morality based on a rather stereotyped view of humanity. Constant generalizations on a high philosophical level, expressing a high-minded outlook on life, are characteristic of Menander, and won him fame in the ancient world. The world of Roman comedy, on the other hand, is a world of widely separated classes in society and an audience that spanned the whole citizen-body from the greatest aristocrats to the slaves. It is a world on holiday, with slave actors imitating Roman magistrates and comparing their own exploits to the deeds of Roman army commanders. Yet there are moments of high seriousness, and this same audience also sat appreciatively through Roman adaptations of Greek tragedy set in the far-off world of Hellenic mythology. Whereas Menander might be said to have moved comedy in the direction of Euripidean tragedy, so that the purely comic element was muted, Roman comedy moved to the opposite extreme and regarded the production of a comedy as an opportunity for play-acting that found its ideal in a blend of farce and comic opera, with interpolations of a more serious kind. Statistically, the Roman audience was probably far less sophisticated than that of Menander, with a strong sense of patriotism and a love of its own institutions.

The conclusion that drama was mainly escapist entertainment in early Rome seems unavoidable. There was probably nothing in it of social comment, still less of political reflection, and the world to which it admitted the audience for the period of the play was a strange phantasy-world with occasional elements of the real Roman world that achieved humour by the very unexpectedness of their appearance and the strangeness of their setting.

This impression is reinforced by another consideration. All the writers who have been mentioned have been non-Roman, and some of them came to Rome as slaves. The poets of New Comedy in Athens were of a different kind—if our meagre knowledge of them allows the generalization. Menander, for instance, was an Athenian citizen of thoroughly respectable social status; his standing in the community is indicated by the fact that he was a close friend of Demetrius of Phalerum, who ruled Athens in the period 317–307 B.C. The stage, for Menander, was a place where he represented life more or less as he knew it—idealized and stereotyped, no doubt, but with plots that were not so fantastic as to be inconceivable as abstracts from reality. This can never have been true for the Roman dramatists already mentioned, who set their plots in a world of imagination. Furthermore, whereas Menander's plays were purely literary products, Roman dramatists used (and often misused) music as an integral element in their plays: Caecilius, in the *Plocium*, constructed great arias without regard for the dramatic dislocation that they caused. It is no accident that Caecilius's successor, Terence, dispensed with this practice altogether: as we shall see, he was interested in a more accurate interpretation of the dramatic coherence and subtleties of the Greek plays.

The work of Terence seems, by contrast, to have given new impetus to the production of comedies set in Rome or Italy, parallel to Naevius's and Ennius's tragedies on themes from Roman history and mythology. This led to the creation of two closely related dramatic forms, neither of which flourished for long. The *fabula togata* was a comedy on the pattern of Greek New Comedy, but was set in an Italian town. The names of three writers of the genre are known—Titinius, L. Afranius, and T. Quinctius Atta (who died in 77 B.C.)—but scarcely anything of value can be known about their work from the fragments that have survived. The dramatic motifs seem also to have come from Greek New Comedy, and it looks as if the poets may have gone back beyond Terence to the older practice of introducing arias (*cantica*) into comedies. The other genre was the *fabula atellana*, named after the town of Atella in Campania and so, it is likely, based on a native comedy. It certainly seems to have incorporated native comic types—clown and glutton and old man—but when it became a literary genre it, too, borrowed motifs from Greek New Comedy. It was on a lower, coarser level than the *togata* but its obscenities did not ensure it a longer life. The names of two playwrights are known— L. Pomponius Bononiensis and Novius—but again, the poverty of fragments tell us little that is significant. It is not unjustifiable, however, to see in it the beginning of the end of public performances of literary drama at Rome.

As Plautus had been the first dramatist at Rome to confine himself to comedy, so Marcus Pacuvius was the first to devote himself to tragedy alone. He is said to have been a nephew of Ennius's; he was born in 220 B.C. and died about 130 B.C. Only 13 titles of his plays are known, and this may reflect a small output, in spite of his long life. Only his *Antiopa* suggests an original by Euripides (who had been the favourite Greek dramatist with Roman writers); several other titles suggest originals by Sophocles and by post-Euripidean writers. From the fragments it looks as if he treated the Greek originals with some freedom, using the technique that Plautus and Terence applied to comedies, and combining elements from several plays. His style was highly idiosyncratic: he revelled in bold neologisms, and was famed for his extravagant use of compound adjectives (a formation, on the whole, as alien to Latin as it was suited to Greek).

A more important tragedian was Lucius Accius, born in 170 B.C.; he was a friend of Pacuvius's, and they both produced plays at the same games (Pacuvius aged 80 and Accius aged 30). He lived till at least 80 B.C. His was a many-sided genius, reminiscent of, but narrower in range than, that of Ennius. But it was as a tragedian that he was most admired; indeed, in the general view of the 1st century A.D., he was the greatest of all Roman tragedians. Forty-six titles of Accius's plays are known and most of those recognizable were probably based on originals by Euripides. His style was more sober and more impressive than that of Pacuvius, whose eccentricities he avoided. In many ways his style is reminiscent of that of Ennius, but he is more fluent; he was as interested in sonority of diction, but was probably less easily deflected than Ennius from achieving a concomitant precision of expression. He was a great favourite with Cicero (who knew him) and is often quoted by him. Like Ennius, he wrote original tragedies on themes from Roman history (a *Brutus* and a *Decius* are known). But he was the last real tragedian in Rome; with him, tragedy virtually died as a literary genre to be performed on the stage.

Plautus

Almost nothing is known about the life of Rome's greatest comic playwright. Only two plays can be dated: *Stichus* in 200 B.C., and *Pseudolus* in 191. He is said to have died in 184 B.C. and he was certainly already writing plays by 209. He is said to have been born at Sarsina in the Umbrian hill-country, but this (and other details) may be extrapolation by later scholars from his plays. Some of his plays were based on originals by Menander (*Aulularia, Bacchides, Cistellaria, Stichus*, and perhaps others), some on originals by Philemon (*Mercator, Mostellaria*, and *Trinummus*), and two on originals by Diphilus (*Casina* and *Rudens*). Plautus wrote very many more comedies than the 21 that have survived, but it is hard to guess the total because his fame has caused the plays of other writers to be attributed to him. The impress of his own personality on all that he wrote is clear in the fact that, although his plays are based on originals by all the greatest Greek writers of New Comedy, it is difficult to differentiate with much conviction between plays based on different Greek writers' works. What he took from Greek sources, like all the great Roman writers, he melted down to make into something quite new of his own.

The plots of Plautine comedy are typical of Greek New Comedy and they well illustrate not only the variety of situation invented by the Greek poets but also the universality of Plautus's interest. The plot of the *Captivi*— in which a slave takes his master's place to enable him to escape while the slave loyally stays to face the consequences—is serious and, in its own way, has strong elements of tragedy; the *Casina* is an uproarious farce in which an old man, anticipating the sweets of a self-legislated *droit de seigneur*, is circumvented by his wife, who substitutes a male slave for the bride. Most of the plays are set in Athens, but (to name a few exceptions) *Rudens* has a romantic setting on the sea-coast of Cyrene, *Poenulus* is set in Calydon, and *Curculio* is set in Epidaurus. Most have a love interest at the centre: if the girl is a courtesan, the plot hinges on attempts to obtain the necessary money to buy her; if she is a free girl, she probably appears at first to be a courtesan, but will turn out to be the long-lost daughter of a respectable family, and her recognition as such will enable the young man to marry her. Old men are the enemies of lovers, who are eagerly helped by their slaves; old women are the wives of hen-pecked old men, whose enjoyments they are determined to hinder.

In short, the plays were founded on a series of characters whose general patterns of activity were an agreed convention, but within that broad framework the dramatist showed his skill by giving fresh shape to the characters in response to the different situations of different plays. Menander and other Greek writers of New Comedy held up a mirror to life, but that life was an artistic abstraction from reality, and their skill was concentrated on subtly representing the motives and responses of human beings in more or less conventional situations. The phantasy of the situations did not inhibit the dramatist from exploring and expressing the whole range of human emotions. What this means fundamentally is that the interest of the play does not depend on any immediate and material relationship to reality: elements of reality are used in the construction of the situations—law, custom, scenery, religion, local characteristics, and so on—but the plots are the construction of phantasy and imagination.

Plautus seized eagerly on this basic lack of relationship to reality. It was already greatly multiplied for him simply by placing a Greek situation on the Roman stage, and he expanded it further by giving free rein to a boisterously creative imagination. The world in which his comedies are set is purely imaginary: the action may ostensibly be set in Athens, but Greek and Roman elements are so blended together that the world of the drama is not that of Athens or Rome, or anywhere else that can be geographically or ethnically located, but a world in which anything may happen that seems relevant to the dramatist.

The result is to increase the element of farce and to reduce the intellectual analysis of human behaviour. The characters become larger than life, especially the characters whom Plautus most loves—the slaves. Endless phantasies of slave punishment mingle with the presentation of slave-exploits as the deeds of Roman army-commanders. The Greek dramatists kept their slaves within proper bounds, but slaves dominate the comedies of Plautus so that interest and attention become concentrated on them. And they repay our interest. There is Pseudolus, for instance, who, when not reflecting movingly on life and destiny, prepares grandiose plans for action that are invariably rendered useless; there is Tranio, in the *Mostellaria*, a complete opportunist who lets trouble come right up to him before he devises an impromptu escape, with the result that his own great net of intrigue closes more and more tightly around him. The tremendous, bombastic character of Pseudolus would completely dominate the play named after him, were it not for another, equally low-life creation, the pimp Ballio, a perfect monster of evil—a man whom audiences loved to hate. Both characters are basically Greek, but that basis is totally overlaid with Roman colouring, and no doubt part of the essential comedy of the situations for Roman audiences lay in the very contrast with a reality in which such characters were lowest of the low and were controlled by the strictest discipline.

This re-working of plays by Plautus—and particularly the addition of Roman colour—had a curious result, which it is plausible to regard as something approaching a principle of method. A straight translator is not faced with the problem of maintaining the close coherence of a complex plot because this has already been done by the writer of the original. But Plautus re-worked each scene, recreating it after his own conception of it. The result is that a Plautine drama appears to the reader to be a series of scenes, each of which has been regarded as a unit, and in the process the coherence of the plot as a whole has been disregarded.

The *Pseudolus* is a good example of the method. The play opens with a scene that the Greek dramatist modelled on the opening of Euripides' *Iphigenia in Aulis*: a young man is weeping over a letter that he has received from his girl. She is one of the girls owned by the pimp Ballio, and he has arranged to sell her to a Macedonian soldier who has made a down-payment on her; only the remainder of the price needs to be paid for her to be lost for ever to the young man. The slave Pseudolus reads the letter and makes extravagant promises to find sufficient money to get the girl for his young master. A pleasant imaginary picture is created of the girl, devoted to the young man and desperately anxious for him to find her purchase-price. But in the next scene the pimp comes out of his house, reviews his slaves, and gives orders for the celebration of his birthday; then he reviews his girls, and a most appalling scene is created of a Roman brothel, where the girls are treated as slaves and threatened with revolting punishment unless they extort acceptable gifts from the various types of clients in whom they each specialize. The last girl in the series is the young man's girl, Phoenicium, and she too is presented as a slave and prostitute, trying—like a Roman slave—to scrape together enough money to buy her freedom. The picture is worlds apart from the romantic impression created in the first scene, and there is no mention of the Macedonian soldier.

In the third scene, the young man confronts the pimp and begs for more time to find the girl's purchase-price. The comedy of this scene depends on the fact that the young man has no knowledge of the bargain with the Macedonian soldier, in spite of the letter in the first scene. Here Plautus has been concerned to build Ballio up into a most unscrupulous monster; to achieve this, he has invented a contract, on a Roman model, whereby the young man is to buy the girl from the pimp—a contract that the pimp repudiates by revealing the bargain with the Macedonian soldier. The whole moral basis of the scene depends both on the young man's ignorance of the bargain and on the Roman nature of the contract that he made with Ballio.[1] This makes nonsense if it is set side by side with the first scene, where the bargain with the Macedonian soldier was on the normal Greek pattern; but Plautus has ignored these inconsistencies in the interest of producing a scene that would make the strongest possible impression on a purely Roman sense of morality.

There are many similar situations in his plays, which show clearly that he was content to think in terms of one scene at a time, and there are a number of reasons why he successfully created a play that reveals such flaws to a careful reader. In the *Pseudolus* the two scenes are divided by the tremendous scene of Ballio reviewing his household; this makes such a gulf that inconsistencies are swallowed up in its imaginative power. Here a further consideration needs to be weighed, which is difficult to calculate. This second scene is a *canticum*: that is, Plautus has taken a brief speech by Ballio (probably merely spoken back through the open door of his house), in which he set the scene, revealed his character, and made plain the motive for his action, and he has turned this into a great aria, many times the length of the original speech and composed in lyrical metres. Thus the first scene was spoken, without music, in a style that represented ordinary conversation; but Ballio emerges on to the stage and sings the second scene as an aria. This musical factor—absent from the Greek play —must have had the effect of breaking the continuity of purely dramatic action. Finally, Plautus conceived a new unity of his own, which is not a unity of plot but a unity of character. In the *Pseudolus* he built Pseudolus and Ballio into such enormous characters that they totally dominate the play, and all the changes and incoherences that he introduced into the plot were directed to this end. What he has done, therefore, is to create a new unity, which centres on the participation of Ballio or Pseudolus or both in every scene. This is not a unity that a reader finds entirely satisfactory, but it is very impressive on the stage. The inconsistencies are probably grosser in *Pseudolus* than in any other surviving play by Plautus, and yet this play is one of his finest. But the same procedure of treating each scene as a unity could be demonstrated in many of his other plays.

Plautus revelled in the imaginative freedom that he created for himself, and his joy in it is as great in his forms of expression as in the dramatic details. A Plautine play has three formal elements: one is the dialogue in *senarii,* the metre that most closely represents the level of ordinary factual conversation or prose. Another is dialogue written in longer metres (mainly trochaic *septenarii* and iambic *octonarii*); these were accompanied by music, but the relationship between words and music is unknown. The stylistic level of these scenes was higher, the forms of expression more ornate and emotional, the whole manner of expression more poetic. Finally there are the *cantica,* which were sung as great solo performances: here all resources of language are used to create the maximum impression on hearers. It is typical of Plautus that even in the first element, the dialogue in senarii, he could never write for long before raising the stylistic level and importing effects that, strictly speaking, should be reserved for other metres. But his riotous imagination could not restrain itself, particularly when his favourite low-life characters were speaking, and so they burst out, in the midst of a scene intended to advance the dramatic action, in ways that retard it but that add greatly—if crudely— to the effervescent liveliness of his comic spirit.

Terence

He was born in North Africa, perhaps about 190 B.C., and probably died before he was 30 years old. He must have come as a slave to Rome and he became the freedman of a senator, Terentius Lucanus, whose name— as usual—he adopted. In his short life he wrote six plays, all of which have survived, and this was probably his total literary output. They all seem to have been performed in the years 166–160 B.C., and they all have a distinct character of their own that marks them as totally different from any plays by Plautus.

A striking difference can be seen immediately in the prologues. Half the extant plays of Plautus have prologues that explain the course of the action, and in particular make clear where one character is posing as another, or where a character who appears to be a certain type of person (e.g. a courtesan) will turn out to be something quite different. Most of Plautus's prologues also contain an appeal to the audience to be quiet and to pay attention (a few prologues contain only this sort of appeal). Five of his plays have no prologue at all. All Terence's plays, however, have prologues, but they are quite different from those of Plautus: they are all concerned with literary questions, and with defences of his own procedure in adapting Greek plays. They contain requests for a fair and unprejudiced hearing, but no expository material whatever. The style of these prologues is in contrast to the general style of the dramas—

bombastic and highly wrought, using all the devices of rhetoric to create an impression: that is, they are conceived as formal public speeches, and this is consonant with the fact that they were spoken by Terence's producer, Ambivius Turpio. Two conclusions can be drawn from the nature of these prologues. The first is that Terence was addressing them to the particular section of his audience that would take an educated interest in literary problems. In other words, the nature of such public entertainment had changed quite considerably since the time of Plautus, who addressed himself to a widely differentiated audience of the whole people. No doubt, Terence wished as large a section of the people as possible to enjoy his plays, but his ideal listeners were educated, with literary interests. His *Hecyra* had to be put on three times, because its audience deserted it twice —first to a rope-dancer and a boxer, and then to a gladiatorial combat.

The second conclusion is that the prologue was entirely divorced from the dramatic action; this meant that his plays proper plunged instantly into the action. All Greek plays of the New Comedy that have their openings preserved have prologues expository of the action, and there is no reason to suppose that Greek writers ever dispensed with this feature. Consequently Terence, who concentrated on Menander (four of his plays are Menandrian and the other two are by Apollodorus of Carystus, an imitator of Menander), deliberately dispensed with the prologue and inserted the necessary expository material in the opening scenes. His motive becomes clear when set beside other features. He had an aversion to monologue and in *Andria*, for instance, he converted the monologue that formed the first scene in Menander's play into a dialogue; he similarly created a dialogue out of the great scene in *Eunuchus* (539 ff.) where the young man, who has raped the girl he loves, explains how he did it. Terence's motive here must be a feeling that monologue on the stage is artificial, because alien to real life. He also avoided rupturing dramatic illusion by declining to address spectators during the action (a hallmark of Plautus), and by considerable restraint in his use of theatrical devices such as asides or comments by a "hidden" actor. He never used *cantica* or other opera-type scenes (such as Plautus's lengthy meeting- and greeting-scenes between slaves). His dramatic style, too, is far closer to real everyday conversation than Plautus's: it is much the richer in exclamations, interjections, interruptions, ellipses, and so on. Side by side with this interest in achieving a particular kind of realism went a fanatical interest in preserving the Greek milieu: whereas Plautus creates a phantasy world, blended from Greek and Roman elements alike, Terence presents the Greek world free of Roman taint, even in scenes where he uses his own invention (for instance, the extra character introduced into *Eunuchus* 539 ff. is a young Greek on Athenian military service, arranging a Greek type of bottle-party). Clearly his plays were intended for a more sophisticated audience than Plautus had in mind.

A final characteristic may be mentioned that also coheres closely with all that has been said. Terence was hardly ever content to adapt a single Greek play straight: almost invariably he combined elements from several plays. For instance, in his *Andria* he blended in scenes from the *Perinthia* of Menander; to the *Eunuchus* he added the characters of the boastful soldier and the parasite from the *Colax* of Menander; to the *Adelphi* of Menander he added a scene from the *Synapothnescontes* of Diphilus. The result is always a considerable complication of the plots, but it was achieved with such skill that there is still little agreement among scholars on the limits of the material from different plays. In this delight in thematic complication, Terence anticipated a literary motif that was to become powerful in Augustan poetry; it is one more indication that he was aiming at something different from the kind of popular entertainments of Plautus and his predecessors.

Roman Drama from Accius to Seneca

It has already been seen that the attempts to create native Roman drama, in the sense of using Roman and Italian material to compose purely Roman tragedies and comedies, were comparatively short-lived. There were probably a number of reasons for this. The most general reason also explains the sharp decline of drama in Rome throughout the 2nd century B.C., so that it practically ceased as a literary activity with the death of Accius. In the course of that century an ever-widening cleavage grew between popular entertainment and literary activity: the latter moved progressively into the ways of Hellenistic Greek poets, becoming more and more sophisticated, while the former diverged into spectacles of all sorts, from circuses to obscene mimes. It therefore became less and less easy for a writer to span the two fields. The *curule aediles* could not afford to put on unpopular shows (the price was too high in terms of political ambition), and so poets moved away in search of other audiences and more discriminating patrons. But the failure of native drama, as opposed to that derived from Greek drama, needs explanation. One explanation is that the Greek setting provided imaginative freedom and inspiration to create new combinations, whereas the setting in Rome or Italy had an inhibiting effect because reality kept breaking through and imposing restrictions on the imagination. This imaginative freedom evoked by Greek settings was to be transferred to more sophisticated poetic forms and was later thoroughly explored by Augustan poets.

There is evidence that the plays of Plautus were revived in the generation after his death; and revivals of plays by early dramatists—especially those of Plautus and Ennius—seem to have been almost the only drama produced in Rome during the age of Cicero. Plays had to compete, less and less successfully, for stage time with mimes, farces, and spectacles of every sort. There is no evidence of plays being written for the stage during this period, and even the *Thyestes* of Varius, which may have been put on at the games in celebration of the Battle of Actium, may well not have been written for stage performance in the first place. Augustus tried to revive the practice of producing plays on the stage, but these plays seem to have been revivals of those of the early dramatists. Ovid wrote a tragedy called *Medea*; but as he makes an explicit statement that he never wrote anything for the stage,[2] this play must have been written as a work of literature to be read (perhaps publicly, as a play-reading). A few plays were still written, some for performances (e.g. by P. Pomponius Secundus, consul in A.D. 44), but not many. Ovid gives a depressing picture of the standard of works produced on the Roman stage in his day.[3] Sometimes poetical works (such as Ovid's *Amores* or even Virgil's *Eclogues*) were used as a kind of libretto for dances on the stage, and these, together with mime and pantomime—none of it of the least worth as drama—occupied the stage in the brief intervals between dancing and spectacles till Nero's time. Sometimes dramatic scenes of violence were produced on the stage, with condemned men cast as the victims so that their execution should not be wasted but give pleasure to their fellow-men. The love of drama had long since died in the Roman people.

Seneca

Lucius Annaeus Seneca was one of a series of brilliant writers who came to Rome from Spain during the 1st century of the Empire. He was born at Corduba at the beginning of the century, rose to eminence under Nero, and committed suicide in A.D. 65 when he came under suspicion of being involved in the conspiracy of Piso. One of the tragedies handed down under his name, the *Octavia*, was not written by him (he is, in fact, one of the characters in it), and is the only surviving example of the drama that sought material in Roman history. The nine surviving tragedies by Seneca all deal with the Greek myths that were the material of Aeschylus, Sophocles, and Euripides. They were probably written as literary pieces, not to be performed as dramas but to be recited with all the histrionics of rhetoric in which the age so conspicuously specialized. They are extremely flamboyant and melodramatic compositions that linger with loving detail over physical horrors: for instance, at the end of *Hippolytus* Theseus is represented as trying to fit together the various bits into which his son's body has been torn by the chariot crash. Horrors such as Heracles clubbing his wife and children to death or Medea murdering her children are represented as actually happening while they are described. The decencies and distance of report by messenger have been abandoned. The plays, in fact, show no sense of the living theatre and stage; they are masterpieces of the rhetorician's art. It is worth defining this a little more closely, for the word "rhetoric" covers a range of meanings and implications. Basically, rhetoric is a good thing: the art by which men express their ideas in the best possible form. But communication is a dynamic relationship between two poles: ideas, and audience. This relationship may become unbalanced in two ways. If there is excess of concentration on the ideas, the result may be obscurity or at any rate an impairment of the impact that the ideas ought to make on the audience. If, on the other hand, there is excessive concentration on the audience, then the ideas may become subordinated to the effect that the writer or speaker wishes to produce on his audience; in that case, the ideas become no more than part of, or even the servants of, the form of expression.

This was the basic vice in the intellectual climate of the 1st century A.D. The pressure of ideas was low, partly because the growing curbs on political freedom inhibited the natural expression of ideas that arose from the contemporary situation; this meant that ideas were sought in the past, especially in the sphere of the mythological and fantastic. But there was also a new professionalism in literature that made a virtue out of interesting and startling sophisticated audiences. Here Seneca's tragedies belong. He took Greek tragedies, relying mainly on Euripides, and found new ways of surprising his expert audience or readers. His *Oedipus* is not completely unrecognizable as the great drama of Sophocles; but where, for instance, the Greek poet allowed the horrible truth to dawn slowly first on Jocasta, then on Oedipus, Seneca invented a long necromantic scene in which the ghost of Laius appears, with much attendant hocus-pocus, to reveal the secret. In Seneca's *Agamemnon*, the prologue is spoken by the ghost of Thyestes who gradually realizes that the sun is refusing to rise in his odious presence and gracefully withdraws so that day may dawn. In his *Medea* and his *Heracles* what is most striking is that the warm human element that Euripides portrayed in those two strange creatures is omitted by Seneca; he is interested in exploring their inhumanity, because that supplies a readier ground for melodramatic sensationalism. All these characters are given clever and memorable epigrams to speak, even at the most inappropriate moments: for instance, in the *Thyestes*, the hero, invited by Atreus, his brother, to recognize his children who have been served up cooked, on plates, says "I recognize my brother" (i.e. "I see his hand in this"). The poet's mind is concentrated on the effect that he can produce by his clever manipulation of words.

In his tragedies, Seneca gives the impression of writing in a social and intellectual vacuum, and this is surprising for two reasons. First, in his philosophical works (among which are to be numbered the *Epistles to Lucilius*) he shows himself capable of responding to real human problems, however stereotyped the philosophical Stoicism of his response and however abstract or artificial the problems. Yet he has no capacity for realizing the figures in his dramas as human characters: a man such as Heracles becomes a cardboard figure of conventional Stoicism. The second reason, however, is more significant. Tacitus, in his *Dialogue*, represented Maternus as composing tragedies with names such as *Cato* or *Thyestes*, which showed a dangerous relevance to the contemporary political situation. Such themes, far-off though they were, provided an opportunity for comment on political situations such as tyranny or kingship or democracy. There is nothing of this political relevance in the plays of Seneca. An ingenious man could find quotations in Seneca that could, set in the right context, supply rhetorical material for political invective, but no dramatic situation in Seneca draws the reader inevitably to reflect on the contemporary political situation. We need not conclude that Seneca was a coward. It is far more likely that he saw his function as a dramatic poet to entertain a highly sophisticated audience with a constantly arresting verbal symphony, in which the ideas were simply the indispensable basic matter: the instruments, as it were, without significance in themselves. The dignity and nobility of his Stoicism—which often found expression in the philosophical works, and which found expression, however futile and miscalculated, in the martyrdom of more than a few friends and contemporaries—simply cannot find a foothold in the fantastic, de-humanized situations that he devised so carefully in his tragedies. The situations are manipulated in the interest of providing certain types of verbal pattern: the ideas are the slaves of the form of expression.

It cannot be denied that Seneca had great literary skill: many ideas are memorably expressed, and real poetry is to be found here and there. But it is sad that these are the sole surviving representatives of Roman tragedy. As such, they have gained attention and admiration that they little deserve. Their greatest interest lies in the influence they exercised on the growth of European drama from the 16th century onward.[4] But Rome had known much better in the 2nd century B.C., when love of the theatre was an important element in the national life, and when dramatists came from outside Rome to enrich the Roman stage with a blend of cultures—Greek, Roman, and Italian. In that century, drama served a recognized and definable social purpose of public entertainment, and it was presented to a society trained from youth to enjoy the theatre; it was a challenge and an inspiration to dramatists to experiment. And they did so until literature went one way and the public's idea of entertainment went another.

References

1. For a discussion of the detailed structure of *Pseudolus*, and especially of the relationship between the Greek and Roman laws of sale, see G. WILLIAMS, *Hermes* 84 (Wiesbaden 1957), pp. 424–55.
2. *Tristia* V, 7, 27.
3. *ibid.*, II, 497–520.
4. On this aspect of Seneca, see F. L. LUCAS, *Seneca and Elizabethan Tragedy* (Cambridge 1922).

Bibliography

W. BEARE, *The Roman Stage*, 3rd edn (London 1964).

M. BIEBER, *The History of the Greek and Roman Theater*, 2nd edn (Princeton 1961).

H. E. BUTLER, *Post-Augustan Poetry from Seneca to Juvenal* (Oxford 1909).

G. E. DUCKWORTH, *The Nature of Roman Comedy* (Princeton 1952).

E. FRAENKEL, *Elementi plautini in Plauto* (Florence 1960). This translation of an original German edition of 1922 contains valuable new addenda.

E. HAFFTER, "Terenz und seine kunstlerische Eigenart," *Museum Helveticum* 10 (1953), pp. 1–20 and 73–102.

G. W. LEFFINGWELL, *Social and Private Life at Rome in the Time of Plautus and Terence* (New York 1918).

F. LEO, *Geschichte der romischen Literatur: I. Die archaische Literatur* (Berlin 1913), still much the best account of early Roman poetry.

E. SEGAL, *Roman Laughter: the Comedy of Plautus* (London 1968).

E. H. WARMINGTON, *Fragments of Old Latin*, Vols. I, II, and III (London 1935–40), a good presentation of the fragments of the early dramatists, with translations.

CHAPTER 10

Ancient Satire

J. P. Sullivan[*]

Satire as a recognizable literary genre in its own right was first developed by the Romans, and Quintilian's boast, *satura quidem tota nostra est* (satire at least is a wholly Roman achievement),[1] is not without foundation. Whatever the primitive origins and foreign influences, there was early established in Roman literature a broad, multifarious genre called *satura*, one important strain of which usurped the name as its prerogative, even in classical times. It was this strain, or historical refinement, of the broader poetic form that gradually became the paradigm of "satire" (in our sense), although even then it retained some topics and elements of technique from earlier stages of its development. For the modern reader, then, many poetic compositions called *satura* by the Romans are not "satire," except in a purely historical sense, although because the form had a fairly long history one should not lay down too rigid or exclusive a definition. By the time of Horace, and even more so for Persius and Juvenal, *satura* meant primarily artistic denigration of a moralizing or aesthetic kind, but the literary models then extant allowed the introduction of much else, such as autobiographical reflection and literary discussion.

Horace complains:

> sunt quibus in satura videar nimis acer et ultra legem tendere opus.[2]

> (there are those to whom I seem too harsh in my satire and strain my work beyond legitimate limits.)

Juvenal insists that, such is the wicked nature of the times, *difficile est saturam non scribere* (it is difficult not to write satire): for him *satura* is what it means to us, and he does not bother to qualify the word. And although Horace included in his two books of satires (to which he gave the title *Sermones*) poems that are hardly satirical in our sense, both Persius and Juvenal wrote little else.

[*] Faculty Professor of Arts and Letters, State University of New York at Buffalo.

The origins of the word "*satura*" are disputed. The ancient views stated by Diomedes and perhaps going back ultimately to Varro in the 1st century B.C. suggest several derivations: from *satyr*, because of the ridiculous and obscene content of the genre; from the *lanx satura*, the full plate of mixed fruit offered to the gods; from a stuffing of all kinds of things, which was also called *satura*; or from the so-called *lex satura*, an omnibus law containing unrelated provisions. The Etruscan word *satir* (to speak) has also been invoked to explain it.* Livy tells us of a dramatic *satura*;[3] this was supposedly a stage in the development of Roman drama, although Livy may be trying to provide a parallel in Latin literary history to the primitive satyr-play from which, in Aristotle's account, Attic drama partly derived. This *satura* is described as a medley of songs, music, and mime; but, even if it existed, it would have had very little influence on the development of the literary genre, for Horace's claim that Lucilius owed a very considerable debt to Attic Old Comedy refers to the extreme freedom of Lucilius's personal, social, and political attacks rather than to his form.[4]

Whatever the etymology, Quintus Ennius (239–169 B.C.) was described by Horace as the "first originator" of the broader, miscellaneous *satura*, which is absent from Greek literature;[5] and the characteristically Roman achievement that had such great influence later is the direct descendant of this. Ennius published four (or possibly six) books of miscellaneous poems, which he probably called *Saturae*. The extant fragments make it clear that the collections were very much of a medley in both form and content. Not only were they written in a variety of metres, but their content varied from beast fables, moralizing pieces, and autobiographical sketches to truly satirical poems in which the poet describes and mocks gluttons, busybodies, and parasites. Despite this mixture of true satire and other subjects and themes that found a place in Lucilius's and Horace's satires, the grammarian Diomedes (the source of our limited information about the early development of *satura*) is careful to distinguish the work of Ennius and his nephew Pacuvius (who imitated him) from that of their successors. He describes *satura* as follows:

> satura dicitur carmen apud Romanos nunc quidem maledicum et ad carpenda hominum vitia archaeae comoediae charactere compositum, quale scripserunt Lucilius et Horatius et Persius, sed olim carmen quod ex variis poematibus constabat · satura vocabatur, quale scripserunt Pacuvius et Ennius.

* For a full discussion of the question, see VAN ROOY, *Studies in Classical Satire and Related Literary Theory*, pp. 1–29.

(*Satura* is the name of a poetic form among the Romans. Nowadays, certainly, it is defamatory and written to criticize human vices, after the manner of Old Comedy; examples are the writings of Lucilius, Horace, and Persius. But at one time *satura* was the name given to a poetic composition consisting of miscellaneous poems, such as Pacuvius and Ennius wrote.)

Gaius Lucilius (*c.* 168–102 B.C.) is therefore the most important figure in the history of verse satire, and Horace rightly describes him as its true founder (*inventor*).[6] Although his work has come to us in a very fragmentary form,* we know that he was extremely popular in the classical period and continued to be admired and imitated by the great classical satirists. It was Lucilius, with his biting personal and general attacks on prominent figures and contemporary vices, who gave *satura* its predominantly satiric note and ultimately its modern connotation—so much so that his successors, living in very different social and political conditions, were hard put to it to match his achievements; indeed, they never really succeeded, even though they respected and aspired to the standards of free speech that he had set. It should be said in defence of his successors, however, that Lucilius was more fortunate in his political and social circumstances. The struggle for political power and influence in the later Republic between small groups of aristocratic families allowed more literary freedom for the writer—or at any rate for the writer of some social standing—than did the autocracy of the principate. However disguised the realities of power may have been then, both Horace and Juvenal were aware of them. Lucilius was not only a man of good position and ample means; he also enjoyed the patronage (and no doubt the protection) of the younger Scipio Africanus.

There were, it is true, other elements in Lucilius's *saturae*—discussions of literature, personal reflections about his own life and philosophy, descriptions of journeys, and so on—that would continue to find a place in Horace's compositions, yet it was due to Lucilius's most characteristic writing that the range and connotation of *satura* became progressively narrower as time went on.

Another important influence that Lucilius had on Roman satire was that, although initially he used other metres, his exclusive use of the hexameter in his powerful second volume made this metre the obvious one for the satirists who followed him.

Before we look more closely at Lucilius's literary achievement and

---

* Of the 30 books, published in three successive volumes with the title *Saturae*, we have less than 1300 lines extant. See F. MARX, *C. Lucili carminum reliquiae* (Leipzig 1904, 1905), or, more recently, W. KRENKEL, *Lucilius Satiren* (Berlin 1970).

influence—the beginning of Roman satire as we think of it—it is well to emphasize that Quintilian's boast refers only to a recognizable literary form: the particular qualities, aims, and techniques that make Latin satire what it is in modern eyes were not necessarily original to Latin literature; they could, after all, be carried over into other literary genres and—not surprisingly, given the nature of the *genus irritabile vatum* (the excitable race of poets)—they were to be found elsewhere in earlier writing. Satire as a literary mode was not invented by the Romans; they merely gave it a local habitation and a name.

Greek Satirical Writing

The satiric spirit, in our sense, had had a long history in Greece. Its first obvious manifestation is in the anonymous *Margites* (*c.* 700 B.C.), a poem that described, in pseudo-Homeric hexameters interspersed with iambics, the ludicrous adventures of an ancient Simple Simon, who was reluctant, for instance, to perform his conjugal duties for fear of his mother-in-law. This lost work seems to have combined literary parody (a favourite weapon of later satirists) with satire directed against a type of personality. From the extant fragments it is difficult to decide whether the literary or the social impulse is the more prominent.

The case is different with Archilochus of Paros (*fl.* 648 B.C.), the first great Greek satirist, who wrote in bitter and amusing iambics of his personal troubles and sufferings in a world where traditional values were, if not breaking up, at least changing for the worse. His *Iambi*, like much Roman satire, are topical, self-expressive, and unconventional, a radical departure from the impersonality of Homeric epic. His attacks on Lycambes, who broke the engagement of his daughter Neobule to the poet, were famous, and he may be seen as the founder of personal satire. His normative standards are at the mercy of his personal grievances, and his satirical methods include direct insult, sarcastic ridicule, and mocking description, all to become standard equipment of the satirist. Horace was later to imitate him in the youthful *Epodes*, but his social and political situation was so different that Archilochus's personal directness was impossible: insignificant or non-existent persons were Horace's targets, and most of the poems, although remarkable for their technique, were exercises in obscenity, factitious abuse, or forced historical parallels, rather than poems rooted in any deeply felt social or personal reality.

This iambic satire of Ionia continued in the writings of Semonides of Samos (*fl.* 600 B.C.) and Hipponax of Ephesus (*fl.* 540); their work also reveals a sense of personal grievance in a world of change that has disappointed and enraged them. In Semonides we find one of the earliest attacks on that favourite target of the satirist—the monstrous regiment of women. The work of Hipponax was characterized by a brutal realism, which was later to make him popular and influential in Alexandrian literary circles when older poetic forms were revived.

Xenophanes of Colophon (*c.* 500 B.C.) was the first theological satirist, continuing the satiric tradition of Ionia, but expressing the newer Ionian rationalism that lies at the root of Western philosophy. In his *Silloi*, written in hexameters interspersed with iambics, he ridicules the anthropomorphic tendencies of the religion of Homer and Hesiod; and in his elegies he attacks the luxurious lives of the Colophonians of Lydia, the Pythagorean belief in transmigration, and the absurdly high prestige enjoyed by athletes. Some of the targets of satirists are clearly perennial.

For Horace, as we have mentioned, the spiritual precursors of Roman satire, as it had so far developed with Lucilius, were the playwrights of Attic Old Comedy: Eupolis, Cratinus, Aristophanes, and others.[7] Aristophanes (*c.* 450–385 B.C.) was the greatest of these, and his surviving plays may be taken as representative of both Old and Middle Comedy. The phantasy and sheer comic invention of his work did not blunt the savagery of his attacks (with the weapons of ridicule, irony, parody, and obscenity) on contemporary political, literary, and social figures; he attacked demagogues, Sophists, and poets. Essentially he was a middle-class conservative, sympathetic toward the farmers oppressed by the Peloponnesian War (in the *Acharnians* and the *Knights*), and opposed to what he regarded as the literary, philosophical, and moral decadence of such playwrights as Agathon and Euripides, and such philosophers as Socrates and the Sophists (*Women at the Thesmophoria* and the *Clouds*). So swingeing were his personal attacks on named or thinly disguised individuals that there was even a political attempt to silence him—one of the many incidents in the long history of literary repression.

Aristophanes' professed aim, as stated in the parabasis of the *Frogs*, was to blend seriousness and humour. This was to become the aim of many later Greek and Roman satirists; it may be seen in the *spoudogeloion* of the Cynic diatribe, although the humour was to become more witty and sardonic, as a concern for language began to predominate over the humour of situation. But it became and remained a hallmark of literary satire.

The *Knights*, produced in 424 B.C. at the Lenaia and winner in that contest, shows Aristophanes at his satiric peak. The play is a sort of allegory, which represents the sovereign people of Athens as Demos, a respectable old householder. Demosthenes and Nicias, two prominent Athenian generals of the time, are his slaves, along with Paphlagon, a thin disguise for the notorious demagogue Cleon, who is the principal target of Aristophanes' attack. Paphlagon has wormed his way into his master's confidence by various underhand means. Tired of his bullying and blackmailing, the other two set out to look for someone to drive him from his position of power. An oracle guides them to a sausage-seller, and the main action of the play consists of the great contest between him and Cleon: this slanging-match ends in an appeal to Demos, in effect the people of Athens, in the assembly. The mock battle has always been a favourite setting with satirists—one thinks of Swift's *Battle of the Books*—and Aristophanes deploys caricature, parody, comic abuse, and obscene jokes in his successful attempt to pillory Cleon's vulgarity, venality, and demagogy.

Naturally the possibility of such direct satire and invective depended upon the liberal and self-confident attitudes of the democratic society of 5th-century Athens, where great freedom was allowed and taken if such freedom could be shown to be in the interests of the Athenian people. Once these social and political conditions passed away, as they did after Athens' defeat by Sparta in 404 B.C., personal attacks and political criticism had to be muted into social strictures of a less offensive kind. Hence the less aggressive social criticism of Middle Comedy. Aristophanes' last two plays turned to broader themes, such as the attack on the capricious distribution of riches in *Wealth*, produced in 388 B.C. Even the religious origins of comedy's bawdiness and general licence could not protect the playwrights in the changed political milieu. Nevertheless, for Horace it was the original freedom with which Aristophanes had attacked the prominent figures of his heyday that made him seem the model for the equally outspoken Lucilius. As is usual in literary history, the purely artistic aspects of Aristophanes—his phantasy and sheer comic invention—were somewhat overlooked in Horace's account.

The torch of dramatic satire was to be carried on; not, however, in the amusing but limited stereotypes of New Comedy, which were subject to the social and political conditions that had changed Attic drama in the first place, but in the realistic mimes of Sophron of Syracuse and his successors, Epicharmus, Herondas, Theocritus, and others. Sophron flourished in the early 5th century and he may indeed have influenced Attic Old Comedy. But he and his successors did not deal with political issues, concentrating instead on the realistic and sardonic depiction of social types, although there are signs of an interest in humorous mythology and amateur philosophy. The dialogue form and the realistic content of the Hellenistic mime writers were to have a considerable influence on the methods of the Roman satirists.

Indeed, in spite of Horace's claim to see in Lucilius the spiritual descendant of 5th-century comedy, the Hellenistic age was of the utmost importance in various ways for the literary development of Roman satire. It was from the occasional writings of this period, for instance, that it derived its strong philosophical and moral bias. The devotion to the small city-state, to the *polis*, that had characterized the 5th and 4th centuries, had waned with the decay of that political system. Traditional civic and religious loyalties had succumbed both to the supranational allegiances demanded by the imperialism of Alexander and his successors, the *Diadochi*, and to the shifting partisanship encouraged in such a period of political transition and instability. Belief in the gods of the city-state yielded to a belief in Fortune; the spirit of patriotic self-sacrifice was supplanted by a desire for personal security and material prosperity. Greek morality, however, had no obvious basis in Greek religion: spiritual regeneration, as envisaged by the few idealist reformers who spring up in most ages, would come through philosophy of one sort or another. Some philosophers therefore substituted cosmopolitanism or self-sufficiency for the broken ties of the small state; others rejected man's dependence on Fortune for his happiness and preached a contempt for conventional aims, the cultivation of inward virtue, or the pursuit of tranquillity in quiet, everyday pleasures.

The Cynic philosophers and other philosophical sects of the 3rd and 2nd centuries B.C. aimed to detach men from their material possessions and their immoral obsessions, and in their criticism of the ways of the world they were far from disdaining the help of formal and informal literature.[8] The greatest of the Cynics, Diogenes of Sinope, wrote some tragedies, and his pupil Crates of Thebes produced parodies and a number of short satirical poems (called *paignia*) on Cynic themes. About this time, and for the same purposes, Phoenix of Colophon revived the Ionic tradition of Hipponax, and we find in his extant choliambic fragments attacks on gluttony and on the perversity of the rich. Cercidas of Megalopolis selected similar targets, but different metres, for his satire. Perhaps more famous than either of these was Timon of Phlius (*c.* 320–230 B.C.); Timon's thinking was influenced by the sceptical philosopher Pyrrho of Elis, whose quest for inner tranquillity by conquering all false beliefs and useless attempts to achieve knowledge had much in common with the Cynic philosophy. Timon's most influential writings were his satirical poems in the manner of Xenophanes, which he also called *Silloi*. These parodied Homeric verses and consisted largely of abuse of the different philosophies of the time. Here we see the establishing of such motifs as a battle between the philosophers and a journey to the underworld.

The most important literary vehicle of the sect, for our purposes, was the homily (the so-called *diatribe*),* which was essentially a hortatory sermon enlivened by quotations, parody, allegory, imaginary dialogue, anecdotes, and (above all) witty ridicule of human folly: all these devices in various degrees were to play a part in the developed Roman satire. The *diatribe* was no doubt preferred to the more structured literary forms because of its capacity to incorporate the themes and traditional wisdom of the poorer classes, whose way of life struck the reformers as being closer to the simplicity of nature than the bourgeois culture the reformers were attacking. The writer mainly associated with this genre was Bion the Borysthenite (*fl.* 320 B.C.), whose homilies were mostly directed against the various human passions and prejudices. Horace acknowledges his debt to him when he describes his own pointed satires as *bionei sermones*[9] (*causeries* in the style of Bion, rather than sermons). The tone aimed at in such pieces was a mixture of humour and seriousness: this was the famous *spoudogeloion*, more familiar to us in Horace's phrase *ridentem dicere verum* (speaking the truth with a smile). Unfortunately little of these influential works survives, although we can get some idea of the genre from the more copious fragments of the later Cynic writer Teles. His onslaught on modern sophistication in favour of an idealized primitive naturalness recurs in Roman satire, although there is more than a tinge of irony in its presentation in Juvenal's sixth satire.

The myth of the golden age or the golden landscape, a time or place of natural abundance and pastoral simplicity, exercised over these thinkers the same fascination that it had for the more socially or politically minded poets of Alexandrian and Augustan circles. But whereas these poets were looking back wistfully to an age free of social complexity and guilt, the ragged philosophers of the *diatribe* were reacting more straightforwardly, though anarchically, to the loss of individual freedom and ideals, to the materialistic decadence and corruption of the great urban centres, and to the cultural banality of the Hellenistic age, whose highest artistic manifestation, it will be remembered, was the New Comedy of Menander with its middle-class aspirations to wealth and social station or, later, the etiolated private poetry of Callimachus and his near contemporaries.

A further and more important development of this style of writing was

* The grammarian Hermogenes defines the *diatribe* as "the moral exposition of some brief topic."

the work of Menippus of Gadara (*fl.* 275 B.C.). In his hands the brief philosophical sermon became a more ambitious literary form. The earlier *diatribes* had doubtless included verse quotations and parodies, but Menippus gave his name to a satiric genre that alternated consistently and deliberately between prose and verse. These *saturae menippeae* were to be taken over into Latin literature as a separate art-form by Cicero's friend Varro, and, as we shall see, it developed alongside, but separate from, the classical hexameter satire. Its finest achievements were to come in the Neronian age with Seneca and Petronius.

In Greek, however, Menippus's true descendant was the talented and witty satirist Lucian of Samatosa (born *c.* A.D. 120), who, however, reverted to prose narrative and dialogue. Lucian was a sceptic and a rationalist, and he brought a light and mocking touch to such traditional subjects for satire as the unhappiness of riches and power, the vagaries of the philosophical schools, and religious fakery. Phantasy, literary allusion, and irony perhaps predominate over any truly satiric impulse, so that he lacks, for instance, the cutting edge of Swift, whom in other ways he resembles. His parody of travellers' tales in the *True History*, therefore, has none of the genuine satirical depths of *Gulliver's Travels*.

There are those who would deny both Menippus and Lucian their claim to be satirists, on the grounds that their work is purely negative and written mainly for amusement. But it must be stressed, before turning to Roman satire proper, that satire is a *literary* genre, and whatever light it throws upon contemporary life or whatever the moral lessons it inculcates, its aim is art; and although the great satirists achieve an intimate fusion of morality and literature, what makes them satirists *per se* is not successful sermonizing, but their mastery of what is often regarded suspiciously as an impure form straddling life and literature. This is of great importance for the evaluation of Juvenal.

Lucilius

The complicated origins of the concept of satire and the diverse Greek influences on its development cannot hide the essential truth of Quintilian's claim. And because it was Lucilius who impressed its most characteristic stamp on the form, he deserves closer attention than the meagre extant fragments of his work seem to warrant. His range of subjects was wide, and there is little doubt that it was through him that many of the Greek influences, particularly those of the Hellenistic period, became grist for the Roman satiric mill. Apart from his personal onslaught on corrupt personalities of the time and the vices of the society around him, we find in the fragments evidence of literary discussions, autobiographical reports, epistolary exercises, descriptions of journeys and dinner parties, and much else. Such topics continue to find a place in Horace's experiments in the basic form. But it seems clear that Lucilius's most striking contribution to literature was his truly satirical writing, whether we define this in terms of the topics (or targets) he chose or of his tone. And so for Horace *satura* came to mean just that Lucilian contribution. He himself was careful to describe his *saturae* as *Sermones* or *Epistulae*, partly because they contained more than satire. Indeed, between the early and the late work, Horace moved further and further from this aspect of the Lucilian *oeuvre* to the more overshadowed biographical writing that the form also lent itself to.

In spite of his genius and his popularity with later classical readers, Lucilius clearly had grave artistic faults, as Horace was not slow to point out. His output was large and correspondingly hasty: Horace describes his style as *lutulentus* (muddy), and it must be admitted that the longest fragment we have illustrates his prolixity; there is a dull clumsiness about his technique that is very different from the variety and polish Horace shows in his handling of the satiric hexameter:

> virtus, Albine, est pretium persolvere verum
> quis in versamur, quis vivimus rebus potesse,
> virtus est homini scire id quod quaeque habeat res,
> virtus scire homini rectum, utile quid sit, honestum,
> quae bona, quae mala item, quid inutile, turpe, inhonestum;
> virtus quaerendae finem re scire modumque,
> virtus divitiis pretium persolvere posse,
> virtus id dare quod re ipsa debetur honori;
> hostem esse atque inimicum hominum morumque malorum,
> contra defensorem hominum morumque bonorum,
> hos magni facere, his bene velle, his vivere amicum;
> commoda praeterea patriai prima putare,
> deinde parentum, tertia iam postremaque nostra.[10]

(Virtue, Albinus, is the ability to pay our true debts in our financial and social dealings: virtue is the knowledge of what each thing entails for a man; virtue is the knowledge of what is right, advantageous, and honest for a man, what is good and, similarly, what is bad, what is disadvantageous, base, dishonest; virtue is the knowledge of the limit and proper measure for acquiring wealth; virtue is the ability to give riches their due; virtue is giving what is truly owed to honour; to be an enemy and hostile to bad men and bad morals, and, on the other hand, to be the protector of good men and good morals, valuing these highly, wishing them well, and living on friendly terms with them; besides this, it consists in putting the good of our country first, then our parents, then, third and last, our own.)

Unlike the self-sufficient anarchists who had pioneered the *diatribe*, Lucilius saw culture as a robust and hard-won discipline that was to enlarge the sympathy and understanding of the leaders of the state. Like his contemporaries Laelius, Panaetius, Polybius, and Terence, he wrote not for the masses, who were politically unimportant, or for the learned, but for the active, pragmatic members of the Roman governing class, who led the armies and governed in the Senate. Chiefly he wrote for, and in defence of, the Scipionic circle, a literary and philosophical coterie with a programme of moderate social and political reform.

Neither the literary devices he took over from his Hellenistic models nor his own careless haste prevented Lucilius from producing a vivid and scarifying picture of the social life of contemporary Rome with an inflexible honesty that Persius and Juvenal were to look back on wistfully.* The realism of Lucilius and the down-to-earth style in which it was embodied sprang from the new philosophical insistence in his circle on free speech and the truth—the principle Polybius also embodied in his Roman history. In the candour of the Cynic *diatribe* and the licence of Old Comedy, Lucilius recognized the free informal style that might fittingly express his ideal of *humanitas*. Terence's purer, but still plain, style was based on a similar supposition. Protected by his social standing and his friendship with Scipio, Lucilius's realism found one of its main outlets in personal confession, autobiography, and the frank reaction to society around him. Similar elements were to be found in the work of Bion, Crates, and Menippus, but the interest of the Scipionic circle in the biographical memoirs of the Socratic writers such as Xenophon encouraged this form of composition, as did the growth of that most characteristic form of Roman literary genius, the epistle, whether as personal correspondence or as a minor literary genre. The Romans were at last becoming self-conscious, and under the stimulus of their growing contact with Greek letters and philosophy they were examining their home-grown ideals and traditional way of life, and reflecting on the defects of their society and on the individual's place within it.

Lucilius, then, set an example of social realism that was to be a mark of, or at least an ideal for, Latin satire in the future. It was from this that the other manifestations of satirical realism sprang; hence the occasionally offensive sexual descriptions, the frequent cynicism about human motives, as well as the graphic picture of their times, left by satirists such as

---

* Persius's first satire opens with an allusion to Lucilius, and envisages the consequent necessity of having to do without popular acclaim; Juvenal (*Sat.* I, 165 ff.) contrasts the dangers of his own literary ambience with Lucilius's freedom.

Juvenal. Naturally the form could, and did, absorb all manner of literary techniques: mock mythology, epic parody, historical anecdote, and popular fable. But the satiric tradition tried hard to be down-to-earth; in Juvenal's words:

> quidquid agunt homines, votum, timor, ira, voluptas,
> gaudia, discursus, nostri farrago libelli est.[11]

> (Whatever mankind does, its prayers, its fears, its rages, its pleasures,
> its joys, its scurryings—this is the hodgepodge of our book.)

Similarly, Lucilius's colloquial manner, or at least his avoidance of a strictly poetic diction, was taken as a starting point for the admittedly different linguistic developments of his successors. Both the subject-matter and the language offered a contrast with the subject-matter and language of the loftier poetic genres such as epic and lyric. Horace was to achieve a subtle and artistic impression of ordinary conversation: a *sermo pedestris* for which he modestly disclaimed any relation to true poetry. Persius elaborated a highly individual, almost clotted, style, which, although heavily dependent on colloquial language, recalled Lucilius in its fondness for striking out-of-the-way phrases and images and rare idiomatic usages. Juvenal was to add to the flexible medium of colloquial language an epigrammatic terseness and a declamatory range that derived from the growing importance of rhetoric in education and in literature. But all of them allowed into their verse the bluntness, the obscenity, and the colloquialisms of everyday speech.

Although the inheritors of the tradition fulfilled the *artistic* possibilities of Latin satire, it might be argued that their work shows a lack of range and spontaneity by comparison with Lucilius. Even their imitation of his casual structure imperfectly concealed their greater attention to intellectual structure. (Juvenal is perhaps an exception, but he composes by the paragraph, as it were, and within this unit his tactics are far more refined than those of Lucilius.) The blend of humour and seriousness (*spoudogeloion*), or the mixture of wit and moralizing that passes for it, remains the characteristic note each strives for, but the wealth of pure poetic play seems to have diminished. The later satirists are less interested in unpretentious impromptu composition (the *schedium Lucilianae humilitatis*, as Petronius terms it), in parody, in extensive character depiction, or in the free use of Greek literature. And the symposium theme, autobiographical anecdote, and beast fables are used with greater restraint, and always subordinated to the "satiric" purpose.

Horace's Sermons and Epistles

Although a few unimportant names have come down to us from the intervening period—Sevius Nicanor, Varro of Atax, Lucius Abuccius, Pompeius Laenas, Valerius Cato, and even Cicero's friend Trebonius—as writers of ineffectual or ephemeral satires in prose and verse, Q. Horatius Flaccus (65–8 B.C.) was essentially Lucilius's literary heir in the development of Roman satire. His modest claim for second place in tradition (*Sermones* I, 10, 46 ff.) is certainly justified; it also explains perhaps the critical ambivalence he shows toward his great predecessor.

As the son of a freedman and an active supporter of the losing side in the republican fight against Antony and Octavian, Horace may have been driven by his lowly circumstances into poetry as the only means of advancement open to him (*Epistles* II, 2, 50 f.), but his early choice of satire—so unlikely a genre for someone as unprotected as he was then—can be explained only by the challenge he saw in Lucilius's relatively unpolished products. The Augustan age was the period in which the major verse-forms and metres were refined and standardized, and in Horace's satires the hexametric satire of Lucilius, notwithstanding the cavillings of the contemporary admirers of antiquity and archaic poetry, achieved a standard of polish and unassuming art that would have been impossible earlier. Horace's aims are implicit in his defence of his criticism against Lucilius's admirers:

> Nempe incomposito dixi pede currere versus
> Lucili. quis tam Lucili fautor inepte est
> ut non hoc fateatur? at idem quod sale multo
> urbem defricuit, charta laudatur eadem.
> nec tamen hoc tribuens dederim quoque cetera: nam sic
> et Laberi mimos ut pulchra poemata mirer.
> ergo non satis est risu diducere rictum
> auditoris: et est quaedam tamen hic quoque virtus:
> est brevitate opus, ut currat sententia, neu se
> impediat verbis lassas onerantibus auris;
> et sermone opus est modo tristi, saepe iocoso,
> defendente vicem modo rhetoris atque poetae,
> interdum urbani, parcentis viribus atque
> extenuantis eas consulto. ridiculum acri
> fortius et melius magnas plerumque secat res.[12]

(Certainly, I did say that Lucilius's verses flow with an uncertain rhythm. Who is so silly an admirer of Lucilius that he doesn't admit this? But on the same page he is praised for rubbing plenty of witty salt into the city's skin. But while granting him this, I would not allow him all the other qualities as well. For then I should have to admire Laberius's mimes as beautiful compositions. So it is not enough to make your audience grin with amusement—although there is

some virtue in this too. You need brevity, so that the thought flows
freely and doesn't tie itself up with verbiage that overloads and tires
the listener's ear. You need also a style that is sometimes grave,
sometimes gay, playing the part now of the orator and the poet, now
of the man of culture, who does not exert all his powers and
deliberately spreads them thin. Matters of moment are usually
dissected better and more effectively by humour than by anger.)

It is clear from this passage that Horace saw his success in terms of
language, rhythm, and (above all) tone; it was not a question of any
deep moral philosophy or the sharpness of his social criticism. And it must
be stressed that his situation, even under the protection of Augustus and
Maecenas, was very different from that of Lucilius. He was open to personal criticisms and was exposed to a guilt-ridden and suspicious
atmosphere of which Lucilius never dreamed. Consequently, unlike
Lucilius, Horace rarely attacked identifiable persons, and then only if they
were dead or insignificant. Horace's aim was to develop the artistic potentialities of the genre, even while narrowing its range and diminishing
somewhat its realism, just as Persius and Juvenal were to narrow its
range even more, while developing its potentialities in other ways.

Horace's two books of *Sermons*, published around 34 and 30 B.C.
respectively, give an adequate idea of his achievements in the genre
(although much of the later two books of *Epistles* must be classed as satire
also). The first three pieces of Book I are "homilies" (the Hellenistic
diatribes), good-humoured and witty sermons in verse. The first attacks
the vanity of human wishes, whereby envy and discontent prevent men
enjoying what they have. The second takes human inconsistency as its
theme, and ends with a long and scabrous discussion of the dangers of
adultery. The opening of the third satire paints a satiric portrait of the
recently dead Tigellius, which shades into a discussion of censoriousness
in general and the absurdity of the Stoic paradox that all vices are
equal.

It is clear from these three satires that Horace was aiming at an
apparently conversational structure that ranged at will through social
observation, character depiction, and informal philosophizing: obscenity,
autobiographical reminiscences, and topical references were naturally not
excluded. His intention was to bring the *sermo*, the reflective chat, to a
high degree of artistic perfection. The language is deliberately, but
artistically, colloquial; Horace refined not only the metre but also the
crude, vigorous, but unselective language of Lucilius, ridding it of its
roughness and monotony, its Greek admixture, and its rustic vocabulary;
and, while retaining the apparent informality, he tightened the essential

structure. Pope's Horatian epistles approach closer than any other English writing to the tone that Horace aimed at in Latin.

Just as Augustus found Rome brick and left it marble, so the favoured poets of the Augustan circle were determined, or were encouraged, to build a poetic monument to the spirit of the new age. The harsher rhythms and language of the older poets was to be replaced by artistic polish, urbanity, and control—qualities that suited the complex political and social New Order that Augustus had instituted. In the proclamation of this New Order, in the organization of opinion, the poets—thanks to Maecenas and to the emperor himself—were to play a significant role. And this search for "what the age demanded" extended also to satire. Horace's self-consciousness about this is to be seen in the fourth satire of the first book, the satirist's *apologia pro opere suo*; the theme, in a stylized form, became almost *de rigueur* for later practitioners of the genre. Horace's defence is that his satires do not profess to be poetry and are not motivated by malice. They are a continuation of his father's practice of giving him moral advice by pointing to everyday examples of what was to be avoided in one's own life. It is difficult to see in this reply to possible critics— or anywhere else in the satires, for that matter—that Horace gave any real grounds for complaint as a harsh social critic. His defensive posture is in fact as much a literary pose as is the later satirist's pretence of helpless indignation.

Further inspection of these two early books gives a fair idea of the range of Horace's satire: there is the famous Journey to Brundisium (*Sat.* I, 5), a challenging imitation of a similar, but longer and more diffuse, travel piece by Lucilius. The autobiographical element in Roman satire is represented by a long personal memoir addressed to Maecenas (I, 6), which sketches the poet's education, advancement, and attitudes to life: the target of the satire is that great vice of the Republic, personal ambition. The famous Encounter with the Bore (I, 9) shows Horace's art at its best, with its economy, irony, and firm control of such devices as dialogue and epic parody. Literary criticism (essentially a defence of Horace's own way of writing) is represented in the last satire of the first book, which, as we have seen, discusses the literary merits of Lucilius, and replies to those who protested against Horace's earlier criticism of his predecessor.

Literary criticism and apologies for satire continue to recur, notably in *Sermons* II, 1, in *Epistles* I, 19, and in the specifically literary epistles of Book II, although here we are getting closer to the formal treatise in verse, and away from the more casual treatment of literary topics in true satire. Moral homilies—the essential core of Roman satire, whatever the level of seriousness—are of course the best-represented. These generally take one or more vices or virtues or ethical precepts (Stoic or Epicurean), and discuss or illustrate them either in straight soliloquy or by imaginary dialogues between the poet and some real or invented interlocutor. The traditional devices of Hellenistic *diatribe* are used much as Lucilius used them: the beast fable, for example the story of the town mouse and the country mouse (*Serm.* II, 6, 79 ff.)*; the mythological setting, as in the dialogue between Ulysses and Tiresias on legacy-hunting (*Serm.* II, 5); instructive anecdotes; and so on. Many of the satiric themes were, or were to become, standard topics: Horace's satiric description of a dinner (*Serm.* II, 8), for instance, was to be followed by Petronius in Trimalchio's feast (*Satyricon* 26, 7 ff.) and by Juvenal (*Sat.* XI).

Horace's contribution was not to sharpen the savagely satiric note of Lucilius but, on the contrary, to take the edge off it. His subject-matter retained something of Lucilius's variety—that is, he kept the genuinely satirical themes down to a reasonable proportion of his total output, whereas Persius and Juvenal concentrated almost entirely on this more promising field. Horace brought to perfection the style and language of satire: his careful but seemingly artless construction and his control over his material are concealed by apparently casual and effortless drifting conversation or soliloquy; he sacrificed the fire and exuberance of Lucilius for compactness, elegance, and ironic wit. Persius caught his wry and almost gentle manner when he wrote:

> omne vafer vitium ridenti Flaccus amico
> tangit et admissus circum praecordia ludit,
> callidus excusso populum suspendere naso.[13]

> (The sly Horace manages to probe every fault while making his friend laugh; he wins admission and plays about the innermost feelings, with his knowledgeable talent for tossing up his nose and catching the public on it.)

Persius

Aulus Persius Flaccus (A.D. 34–62) exemplifies the "serious" satirist among the Roman writers in the genre, but his achievement, like Horace's, is essentially a *literary* achievement. His great contemporary (and later) popularity is due to this rather than to his derivative Stoic preaching (although his moral norms are the most consistent of all the satirists).

---

* Such popular Hellenistic sub-genres could be developed in their own right, with moralistic, if not satirical, aims: Augustus's freedman Phaedrus produced a famous collection of fables, as had Aesop earlier.

His targets and satiric themes are standard ones: he attacks hypocrisy and the wickedness of man's prayers to heaven in *Satires* II; laziness and moral inconsistency in *Satires* III (which in spite of its abrupt and difficult structure is perhaps the best of the six); the desire for popular acclaim in *Satires* IV. His positive teaching is strongly Stoic: self-knowledge (*Sat.* IV); true freedom—that is, freedom from base passions (*Satire* V); and the proper use of money (*Sat.* VI). Like Horace, he uses imaginary dialogue (Socrates and Alcibiades in *Satires* IV), parody, illustrations from everyday life, and autobiographical reminiscence, most notably in his heartfelt tribute to his Greek philosopher friend, Annaeus Cornutus (*Sat.* V):

> cum primum pavido custos mihi purpura cessit
> bullaque subcinctis Laribus donata pependit,
> cum blandi comites totaque impune Subura
> permisit sparsisse oculos iam candidus umbo,
> cumque iter ambiguum est et vitae nescius error
> diducit trepidas ramosa in compita mentes,
> me tibi supposui. teneros tu suscipis annos
> Socratico, Cornute, sinu. tum fallere sollers
> adposita intortos extendit regula mores
> et premitur ratione animus vincique laborat
> artificemque tuo ducit sub pollice vultum.
> tecum enim longos memini consumere soles
> et tecum primas epulis decerpere noctes.
> unum opus et requiem pariter disponimus ambo
> atque verecunda laxamus seria mensa.[14]

(When first the guardianship of the purple-edged dress of boyhood ceased to awe me, and my protective amulet was hung up as an offering to the household gods in their old-fashioned dress; when my youthful friends were pleasant, and the now-white folds of my grown-up robes allowed me to cast my eyes at will all over downtown Rome; just when life's path was uncertain, and youth's inexperienced wanderings led the trembling heart to the point where the road branches, I put myself in your care: you gathered my tender years to your Socratic bosom, Cornutus; and then your rule, with its deceptive wisdom, straightened the moral twists it detected; my spirit was moulded by reason; it struggled to be conquered and took on plastic features under your thumb. I well remember how I used up long summer suns with you, and with you plucked the early flowers of the night for feasting. We two have one work in common and have one and the same time for rest, and we unbend from serious matters at our modest table.)

Such elements, however individual in their handling, however convincing in their obvious sincerity, are part of the tradition developed by Lucilius and Horace. Similarly, occasional touches of deliberate coarseness and crudity, even of obscenity, pay tribute to the realistic strain in this tradition. Persius, however, goes beyond Horace (or perhaps back to Lucilius) in the apparently haphazard and abrupt development of his chosen themes, switching so rapidly from brisk dialogue to rhetorical soliloquy or quotation that he leaves the reader rather breathless. Hence springs the difficulty, in the opening of *Satires* I, of allocating the proper lines to the two speakers.

Nevertheless Persius's unique and compressed style was responsible for his influence and popularity. Although its linguistic complexity makes it somewhat alien to modern taste, which is fostered almost exclusively on the Augustan classics, Persius's manner was largely responsible, for instance, for the deliberate crabbedness and compactness of such English satirists as Donne and Oldham.

This first satire illustrates his place in the tradition, his literary aims, and his style. He opens with a quotation from Lucilius, which is of a piece with his frequent reminiscences of that poet and also of Horace. This and his complimentary references later in the same poem to both of these writers and to the giants of Attic Old Comedy (lines 114 ff.) identify his poetic allegiance. His savage criticism of contemporary writing, with its mythological and derivative subjects, its facile fluency and metrical preciosity, and his condemnation of the contemporary taste for archaism— a taste Horace also had complained of (*Ep.* II, 1, 23 ff.)—indicate his firm allegiance to genuinely poetic themes and to a modern individual style. This style he seems to have painfully and slowly forged, moving away from the careful conversational tone of Horace to an idiom that better represented the fluctuations and abruptness of the inner monologue or the passionate engaged dialogue that Horace's more leisurely and sympathetic poetic persona had avoided. Persius seems to be restoring to satire Lucilius's vigorous and engaged passion, while preserving, indeed developing still further, Horace's economy and compactness of language. This combination of power and compactness is to be seen also in his tight, complex, and highly allusive imagery, of which a typical example is:

> quo didicisse, nisi hoc fermentum et quae semel intus
> innata est rupto iecore exierit caprificus?[15]

> (What is the use of one's learning, unless this fermenting yeast and
> the sterile fig-tree, when once it has taken root within, bursts the liver
> and comes out?)

The related images of learning fermenting inside the student and learning like a fig-tree that bursts through the stones about it are curiously vivid and very different from the generally sedate metaphors of Latin poetry.

The style is an amalgam of careful allusion to his satiric predecessors, parody of contemporary style, a basis of earthy language, and highly individual metaphor and description—all with a minimum of conjunctions, transitional phrases, or qualifications. And it succeeded in uniting, as no other satirist did, Lucilius's power and linguistic freedom with Horace's brevity and economy. His work, as he himself claims (*Sat.* I, 125), is *aliquid decoctius*, something rather more boiled down and concentrated than the flaccid and musical inanities of contemporary verse. It is this claim, rather than the concomitant pose of disdaining danger in the interests of social reform, that is the key to Persius's achievement. Persius's morality, however genuine, is at the service of his art rather than the other way round. He was against bad writing even more than he was against the decadence of the Neronian age. And given the dangerous situation of the satirist and the lampoonist under the sensitive and tyrannical rule of Nero, perhaps this was just as well.*

Menippean Satire

Menippean satire, that strange *mélange* of prose interspersed with different kinds of verse, had been invented in Hellenistic times and was introduced into Latin literature by the erudite Marcus Terentius Varro (116–27 B.C.). We can get a reasonable idea of its naturalized form from many extant fragments. It had many of the characteristics of the Cynic *diatribe*, and so had much in common with Latin satire proper. It was its literary *form*, rather than its themes, targets, or dramatic techniques, that distinguished it from its more popular, and perhaps more artistic, counterpart. Varro is said to have produced about 150 books of these satires, each book presumably containing a short and separate piece. Following the lead of Menippus, Varro seems to have directed a humorous, but nonetheless serious, attack on the various forms man's folly takes, and he ridiculed both social conventions and philosophical systems. According to Cicero (*Academica* I, 18), Varro imitated—rather than translated—Menippus, and this is obvious from the fragments, some of which deal with topical Roman subjects, such as the First Triumvirate; nevertheless it is clear from their titles that they show a not unexpected preoccupation with Greek mythological and philosophical themes. Many take as their starting point some Latin or Greek proverb, but tragic and epic parody is also common (e.g. *Oedipothyestes* and *Ajax stramenticius*). An imaginary

* There is little reason to believe the story that Persius's first satire was slightly doctored to avoid possible offence to Nero, but exile was a frequent punishment for literature offensive to the regime.

circumnavigation (*Periplous*) forms the framework of a long satire on philosophical systems, and the popular Rip-Van-Winkle story is the plot of the *Sexagesis*. The style—unsurprisingly, in view of its Hellenistic origins —is colloquial and full of quotations, and admits a large number of Greek words and phrases.

The literary renaissance of the Neronian period saw a revival of the form. Shortly after the death of the Emperor Claudius in A.D. 54, the younger Seneca, who had reason to dislike that emperor because of his long exile in Corsica, composed a malicious lampoon, the *Apocolocyntosis divi Claudii*, a highly personal satire on Claudius's physical and mental disabilities, that also incorporates lavish praise for the new emperor, Nero. The prose style is very colloquial, and the different verses interspersed are in a variety of metres, with not a little stress on the parody of epic language. The whole work is itself a parody of the conventional deification of an emperor, and the title is best translated as the *Deification of Claudius the Clod*.* The work describes Claudius's death and progress to Heaven, where his candidacy for admission to the company of the gods is debated in the Olympian council, and (on the urging of the deified Augustus) is refused. Claudius is then taken to Hades, where he is greeted angrily by his countless victims and, as an inveterate gambler, is condemned to play dice with a bottomless cup, and made the slave of his former freedman. Most of the traditional charges against Claudius are raked up: his mumbling, his uncouth physique, his fondness for pedantry and litigation, his careless cruelty, his subjection to his freedmen, and his liberal distribution of the citizenship. The work, which shows some signs of hasty composition, was no doubt written to establish good will toward the youthful Nero: its topicality allows little doubt but that it was a squib circulated for political motives in the last months of A.D. 54.

Perhaps more important than the piece itself—which seems to depart little from Varro's precedent—is its value as evidence that the Menippean form was still viable, whether for ephemeral pampleteering or for more ambitious purposes in the hands of a superior writer. And indeed the culmination of this literary form is undoubtedly one of the most interesting works that has come down to us from classical antiquity—the *Satyricon* of Titus Petronius, the *elegantiae arbiter* at Nero's court, whose life is so elaborately described by Tacitus:

---

* The title has usually been taken as meaning, literally, *The Pumpkinification of the Divine Claudius*, playing on the allusion to the deification (*apotheosis*) accorded most emperors after their death. The lack of any mention of a gourd or pumpkin in the work has led some to deny its Senecan authorship. In fact, Claudius is already a pumpkinhead himself, and the satire plays with the notion of deifying such an idiot.

nam illi dies per somnum, nox officiis et oblectamentis vitae transi-
gebatur; utque alios industria, ita hunc ignavia ad famam protulerat,
habebaturque non ganeo et profligator, ut plerique sua haurientium,
sed erudito luxu. ac dicta factaque eius quanto solutiora et quandam
sui neglegentiam praeferentia, tanto gratius in speciem simplicitatis
accipiebantur. proconsul tamen Bithyniae et mox consul vigentem
se ac parem negotiis ostendit. dein revolutus ad vitia seu vitiorum
imitatione inter paucos familiarium Neroni adsumptus est, elegantiae
arbiter, dum nihil amoenum et molle adfluentia putat, nisi quod ei
Petronius adprobavisset.[16]

(He was a man who spent his days sleeping and his nights working or
enjoying himself. Industry is the usual foundation of success, but
with him it was idleness. Unlike most people who throw away their
money in dissipation, he was not regarded as an extravagant sensua-
list, but as one who made luxury a fine art. His conversation and his
way of life were unconventional, with a certain air of nonchalance,
and they charmed people all the more by seeming so unstudied. Yet
as proconsul in Bithynia and then as consul, he showed himself active
and equal to his duties. His subsequent return to his old habits,
whether this was real or apparent, led to his admission to the small
circle of Nero's intimates, where he became the Arbiter of Elegance.
In the end Nero's jaded appetite regarded nothing as enjoyable or
refined unless Petronius had given his sanction to it.)

From A.D. 59 onward, Nero had around him a cultured literary circle
that composed, criticized its members' poems, and listened to philosophical
discussion. There can be little doubt but that the *Satyricon* was composed
for the amusement of this coterie, whose members could be expected to
appreciate its subtle contemporary allusions and parody.

Petronius was all that Seneca was not: an Epicurean in literature and
in life, a classicist in literary taste, and an Atticist in style. For the real or
assumed vehemence of most Latin satirists and contemporary moralists,
he substituted broad humour, verbal wit, and ironic observation. His
satiric norm was simply good taste. It is not surprising that many scholars
have detected in his work philosophical parodies of Seneca, as well as
poetic criticism of his nephew Lucan's *Pharsalia*;* such a literary feud no
doubt had political implications, once Seneca was forced to retire from
his influential position at Nero's court in A.D. 62.

The *Satyricon* represents a stretching of the usually brief Menippean
form to the size of a long novel—there seem to have been 16 or 20 books,

---

* For the parody, see (for instance) *Satyricon* Ch. 71, 1–4; 88; 100, 1–3; and 115; the criticism
of Lucan and a pastiche of the *Pharsalia* are in Ch. 118 ff. It is possible that Seneca was counter-
attacking Petronius with a vicious criticism of Epicureanism and Roman dandyism in his
Epistulae morales CXXII–IV (written about A.D. 64–5).

of which about two and a half survive in extensive fragments. The basic plot is once again a parody. The wrath of Poseidon against Odysseus in Homer's epic is kept constantly before us as we follow the misadventures of the mendicant hero, or anti-hero, Encolpius, pursued by the anger of the great sexual deity Priapus. Encolpius joins up at intervals with other characters as disreputable as himself: Ascyltos (an aggressive homosexual), Eumolpus (a hypocritical poet), and the young and fickle Giton. But this parodic plot is merely the tree to which are grafted a number of amusing or literary episodes essentially unconnected with it, and these have much in common with traditional Roman satire. For example, Trimalchio's feast (*Satyricon* 26, 7 ff.) is a long and elaborate satire on the vulgar and pretentious freedman Trimalchio, in the popular setting of a dinner party. Here his character, his friends, and his milieu are examined with a novelistic observation almost unique in Latin literature. In other sections of the work the satire is directed at the aggressive libidinous woman, in the persons of Quartilla, Tryphaena, and (above all) Circe (*Satyricon* 126 ff.). Another traditional target of the Roman satirist, legacy-hunting, makes its appearance, as it does in the satires of Horace and Juvenal.

From a sociological point of view, there can be little doubt but that the sexual emphasis in the *Satyricon*, although sanctioned by the Roman satiric tradition, was aimed at the Neronian smart set, the leader of which, the emperor himself, at one period enjoyed anonymous excursions into the seamier parts of Rome as much as any 18th-century Mohock in London.[17] Such a combination of literary culture and *nostalgie de la boue* has not been uncommon in other periods, as J. K. Huysmans' *A rebours* and Wilde's *Portrait of Dorian Gray* will witness. But Petronius offers a literary defence of his work that stands up squarely for the long-honoured principle of realism. Life as it is constitutes a proper subject for art. And in essence this was to be Martial's defence for his scabrous epigrams, and also the justification for Juvenal's artistic apotheosis of similar material (amid all the rhetorical accretions) in his famous 3rd, 6th, 9th and 10th satires. The setting of Petronius's *credo* is mildly obscene, but the irony of the setting does not detract from its artistic message, for Petronius is always ironical:

> quid me constricta spectatis fronte Catones,
>   damnatisque novae simplicitatis opus?
> sermonis puri non tristis gratia ridet,
>   quodque facit populus, candida lingua refert.
> nam quid concubitus, Veneris quis gaudia nescit?

> quis vetat in tepido membra calere toro?
> ipse pater veri doctos Epicurus amare
>   iussit, et hoc vitam dixit habere telos.

A paraphrase, more helpful here than a translation, would run like this:

> The work you are now hearing no doubt provokes the usual raised
> eyebrows from the more censorious members of society, who believe,
> in accordance with Stoic principles and literary theories, that a work
> of art should be instructive and moral, not least in the narrowest
> sense of that term. Such critics will condemn this work, which is a
> reaction against our present styles of writing and old-fashioned
> puritanism, and has its own literary and stylistic intentions. Its pure
> latinity has but one end: to charm you, not to instruct you. My
> subject is human behaviour, and the narrative is realistic and honest.
> No one is unaware of the important and pleasant part sex plays in
> ordinary life. Does anyone take a moral stand against harmless and
> natural sexual enjoyment? As an Epicurean, I could even invoke
> philosophical principles in its defence, not least Epicurus's doctrines
> about its supreme importance.

Notwithstanding his claims to describe life as it is—the realist's impossible
ideal—Petronius brought to satire the acute, although apparently
detached, empathy of the novelist. And it is for this reason that his work,
which belongs to the minor Menippean tradition of satire on human types
and follies, is regarded by many as a precursor of the picaresque novel in
European literature. His portrait of Trimalchio, like Cervantes' portrait
of Don Quixote, began as satire and ended in a great comic creation. Above
all, its topicality was subordinated to its literary invention, humorous
observation, and wit; this battered fragment was not to find its like until
the 20th century produced Joyce's *Ulysses*, which also used Homer's
Odyssey as an imaginative springboard.

The Menippean *mélange* of prose and verse continued to be used, notably
by Macrobius, Martianus Capella, and Boethius in his *De consolatione
philosophiae*, but their intentions were no longer satirical and so are
not relevant to this survey.

Juvenal

Between Persius and the last great writer of satire in Latin literature we
hear only a few names such as Turnus and Manlius Vopiscus, and little
or nothing survives of their actual writing. But there can be small doubt
that Decimus Junius Juvenalis (*c.* A.D. 60–140) was, in certain ways,
the culmination of the tradition and the writer who most affected its
prestige and changed its associations in the eyes of later generations.

Juvenal's 16 hexameter satires (totalling approximately 4000 lines)

255

differ in one important respect from the work of his predecessors: although he adopted as his persona the mask of an indignant and disgusted observer who cannot help attacking what he sees around him, he gave very little information about himself; despite the late lives and a few ancient references, we know almost nothing about him. He seems to have been connected with Aquinum, a small town near Monte Cassino; he was the son or adopted heir of a freedman; there is some evidence for his rhetorical training, a military career, some personal knowledge of Britain and Egypt, and perhaps a period of exile during the reign of Domitian. But any certainty in these matters is impossible. His five books of satires seem to have been published at intervals after A.D. 100, the death of Domitian in 96 being the prelude to an era of greater freedom of speech under Trajan and his successors. The first book (*Sat.* I–V) refers to the year A.D. 100; the second (*Sat.* VI) refers to the period between A.D. 114 and 116; the opening of the third book (*Sat.* VII–IX) has a reference to Hadrian's accession in A.D. 116; and the fifth book (*Sat.* XIII–XVI) alludes to the year A.D. 127. His writing therefore extends over a period of almost 30 years and there is a corresponding change in style.

The opening satire of Book I sets out Juvenal's programme. His intention is to write satire in the style of Horace and Lucilius—satire in the now established sense of biting attacks on the vices of the age; the decadence of the times forces the sensitive author into satire and turns him away from the stale mythological themes that were clearly as popular with poets in Juvenal's day as they had been in Persius's. But just as Horace had been warned by Trebatius of the dangers of writing personal satire, so Juvenal, following Persius's example, introduces an imaginary inter-locutor who also warns the poet against it: Juvenal therefore announces his decision to write about characters who are now dead. A poor-spirited attitude for a would-be reformer, one might think, far removed from the frank invective of Lucilius; but, as we have seen, satirists from Horace onward are working in a literary form; they are not writing, in any serious sense, sermons or tracts for the times.

Horace had refined Lucilius's style and language, and his few assaults on named contemporaries did not add up to much. It is of course true that Roman life did not encourage literary freedom of this sort in either the Republic or the Empire, but much greater liberties might have been risked by a truly indignant satirist. To put the great Roman satirists in their proper perspective, one has to see that the essential impulse behind their poetry is literary and artistic, even though their subject matter is often morals and contemporary life. It is this that accounts for Horace's criticism of Lucilius's writing, for the contempt in Persius for a large audience (odd if his real aim was moral reform), and also for Juvenal's choice of such bizarre topics as cannibalism (*Sat.* XV) and his selection of satirical targets from history —a rather ineffectual way, one would imagine, of curing the evils of a sick society.

This is not to say that Juvenal does not give us vivid, though distorted, glimpses of Roman society, or that his prejudices and passions have no influence on his work. His pictures of the sorry plight of poor clients, humble guests at rich tables, and struggling writers have the brushmarks of authenticity and inner knowledge, and his xenophobia is Roman enough to be convincing. Similarly, it would be a mistake to assume because his attack on the monstrous regiment of women in *Satire* VI is too high-pitched and prurient to allay the reader's doubts of his moral sincerity, that *all* the moral norms invoked throughout the satires are therefore perfunctory or assumed. What must be realized is that the moral and realistic material of his writing is subordinate to his artistic intentions, which were, essentially, to superimpose on the informal, down-to-earth, conversational structure of hexameter satire all the resources and techniques of the declaimer; to substitute for the subtle humour of Horace and the tortuous, allusive word-play of Persius the forensic verbal wit of the rhetorician, the characteristic pointed style of Silver Age Latin, which may be seen—if not always admired—both in Lucan's historical epic and in the *Annals* of Juvenal's great contemporary, Tacitus.

Our own ideas of what satire should be make us resist this conclusion. Our preoccupation with the ethical or reforming elements of satire leads us to expect moral coherence and positive programmes, to distrust— somewhat, at least—heightened language and the techniques of hyperbole and wit. Hence the critical unease of some discussions of Roman satire, and of Juvenal in particular. It seems as though it would have taken a revolution—or a pogrom—to cure the ills of Roman society in the first two centuries of the Empire. But Juvenal is no radical, and no Christian either. He is not discontented with a social order based on slavery and land tenure: he merely wishes that ex-slaves were kept in their proper place and that the aristocratic land owners would do as well by him and his fellows as their ancestors supposedly did by their clients. Juvenal, like Martial, was writing for this small educated class, and consequently it was the presuppositions of this class (of which he was, at least by inclination and nature, a member) that moulded his attitudes and tempered his criticism. At no point in the development of Roman satire did there exist the freedom enjoyed by the poets of Old Comedy or by radical novelists in modern democracies. Either one was protected by powerful friends, as was Lucilius, or one limited one's material to generalities, invented personages, or people and vices of no account; it was the art that mattered. Juvenal indeed shows the effects not only of a lack of political freedom but also of a lack of intellectual freedom. But, as if in compensation, he became a master of the Latin language.

Juvenal's programme, then, is to be interpreted not as the writing of contemporary satire under the guise of attacking great examples of vice in the past, but as the exploration of the new possibilities of the satiric genre. The realism and occasional obscenity of Roman satire is supplemented now by historical examples such as the Fall of Sejanus (*Sat*. X, 56 ff.) and the career of Hannibal (*Sat*. X, 146 ff.), but also by themes from the rhetorical handbooks (*Sat*. X, 306), and the two are not always distinguishable. Juvenal's achievement was to wring from both their full literary potential.

These contentions may be supported by a brief glance at Juvenal's third satire, on the evils of life in Rome, which was so neatly and easily imitated in *London* by Samuel Johnson (who insisted that a man who was tired of London was tired of life). In this satire everything is seen from the viewpoint of the client, the poor hanger-on of some noble house, who despises alike the upstart foreigners, the decadent and irresponsible scions of the nobility, and the whole mercantile and venal atmosphere of the Roman capital. But there is no *serious* social criticism, no revolutionary ardour or philosophical resignation in the piece, beyond a conventional longing for the quiet life, with a modest sufficiency, in the country. Indeed what serious critique of the crime rate in Rome could be extracted from such apostrophes as

> qua fornace graves, qua non incude catenae?
> maximus in vinclis ferri modus, ut timeas ne
> vomer deficiat, ne marra et sarcula desint.[18]

> (In what furnace, on what anvil, is there no heavy weight of chains?
> The largest proportion of iron goes into the production of fetters, so
> that you fear that there will be a shortage of ploughshares, a scarcity
> of hoes and mattocks.)

Elsewhere the exaggeration, often achieved by means of sonorous epic parody, is matched by equally effective deflation. In the 10th satire, for instance, on the vanity of human wishes, there occurs the dramatic description of the fall of Sejanus, a set piece imaginatively adapted in Ben Jonson's play of that name:

> . . . descendunt statuae restemque sequuntur,
> ipsas deinde rotas bigarum inpacta securis
> caedit et inmeritis franguntur crura caballis.
> iam strident ignes, iam follibus atque caminis
> ardet adoratum populo caput et crepat ingens
> Seianus, deinde ex facie toto orbe secunda
> fiunt urceoli, pelves, sartago, matellae.[19]

> (. . . the statues topple and follow the rope, then the axe forcefully
> smites the very wheels of the chariots and the legs of the inoffensive
> nags are smashed to pieces. Now the foundry fires hiss, now the head
> adored by the populace glows from the bellows in the furnaces, and
> mighty Sejanus cracks; then from the face that was second in all the
> world there comes—jugs, basins, saucepans, and chamberpots.)

This passage, however (and many passages like it), also illustrates
Juvenal's other great strength, not the least of the weapons in the orator's
armoury: close and compelling description, often based on the exigencies
and impressions of everyday life in Rome. And it is this, perhaps, that
affects the modern reader most, once he has suppressed his doubts about
the factual distortion and the incoherent moral sensibility revealed in most
of the satires. Juvenal's unit is the paragraph, whence the cinematic shifts
from one subject to another even within the same satire. Almost every
satire provides a choice of these powerful vignettes: the pushing freedmen
and the legacy hunters of *Satire* I; the hypocritical homosexual philosophers of *Satire* II; the unlucky victim of a Roman street accident sitting
on the banks of the Styx without a penny for his crossing; the hungry
mice gnawing at the rolls of Greek poetry in a poor man's garret; the
portraits of the adulteress and the bluestocking, of the virtuous but
intolerable Cornelia and the vicious, and equally intolerable, Messalina
in the satire on women; the miserable careers of famous men and the
misfortunes of beauty in *Satire* X. But what is perhaps under-appreciated
is the enormous care Juvenal exercises in his control of the sonorities of
the hexameter, in his choice of the *mot juste* or the poetic allusion, and in
his rhetorical climaxes.

To see Juvenal in this light—as a "supreme manipulator of the Latin
language," in the words of one critic[20]—is to cut through the problems
that might be posed by Juvenal's eclectic moral attitudes. He has been
accused at various times of loving the vices he castigates; of confounding
minor peccadilloes with major sins, particularly in his censure of women;
and of exaggeration and unreality in his depiction of the life of his times.
Such criticisms become irrelevant, if we approach him not primarily as a
moralist but as a writer and stylist with Dickensian powers of observation
and description and something of Pope's polish, concision, and wit. In

fact, even the familiar epigrams, so long treated as detachable gems to be wrenched from their setting, will be found to have additional, sometimes ironic, point in their satiric context, where they may be appreciated as poetry rather than as texts for speechday declamations.

Later Satirists

Juvenal's satires marked the climax and the effectual end of the Roman satiric tradition. With him the satire of indignation, or feigned indignation, became the hallmark of the Roman achievement. The few diffuse traces of the genre thereafter are disappointing. The Christian convert Tertullian (A.D. 150–230) waxes furious and satirical in such works as the *De cultu feminarum*, the *De pallio*, and the *Apologeticum*, and he was followed in this polemical mode by many of the Christian Fathers, such as Arnobius, Ambrose, and Jerome. But in spite of their literary vigour, these specifically Christian productions scarcely conform to the artistic requirements and principles of Latin satire. Other writers, however, whatever their religious affiliations, seem to belong to the Latin literary mainstream: D. Magnus Ausonius (A.D. 310–95), Rutilius Namatianus (*fl.* A.D. 416), and Apollinaris Sidonius (A.D. 430–80) all show flashes of the satiric spirit in certain passages of their works and in their epigrams. (The satiric epigram continued to flourish, of course, in both Latin and Greek.) More ambitious attempts are to be seen in such anonymous, and disappointing, productions as the *Carmen contra paganos* (*c.* A.D. 394) and the near-contemporary *Carmen ad senatorem*. But the only pretender to the claim of being the last of the Roman satirists is Claudian (Claudius Claudianus, *c.* A.D. 374–404), whose two long hexameter satires, the *In Rufinum* and the *In Eutropium*, although directed chiefly at certain ministers of the court of the Emperor Arcadius, do show something of the generalizing power and literary culture of Lucilius and Juvenal.

The satire in these two poems is, of course, personal (and sometimes confusingly mixed with eulogy of the great Vandal general, Stilicho), but Claudian does manage to set his vitriolic denunciations in a traditional framework of epic burlesque, and he lightens his elaborate personal descriptions with literary allusions and some of the motifs of earlier Roman satire, such as the tribunal of the underworld before which Rufinus's victims drag their persecutor. And perhaps it is fitting that purely personal satire that names names and is clearly prompted by individual spleen—or, more likely in this case, friendly association with a powerful person—should make its reappearance at the end, as it had done at the true beginning, of Latin satire.

References

1. *Institutio oratoria* X, 1, 93.
2. Horace, *Sermons* II, 1, 1–2.
3. Livy, 7, 2.
4. Horace, *Serm.* I, 4, 1 ff.
5. *ibid.*, X, 66: *rudis et Graecis intacti carminis auctor* (the founder of a primitive poetic form not touched by the Greeks).
6. *ibid.*, X, 48.
7. *ibid.*, IV, 1–2.
8. For the history and literature of the sect, see D. R. DUDLEY, *A History of Cynicism* (London 1937).
9. Horace, *Epistles* II, 2, 60.
10. E. H. WARMINGTON (ed. and trans.), *Remains of Old Latin* (London 1935–40), Vol. III, 1196–1208.
11. Juvenal, *Satires* I, 85–6.
12. Horace, *Serm.* I, 10, 1–15.
13. Persius, *Satires* I, 116–8.
14. *ibid.*, V, 30–44.
15. *ibid.*, I, 24–5.
16. Tacitus, *Annals* 16–18.
17. See, for instance, Suetonius, *Nero* 26; Tacitus, *Annals* 13, 25; Dio, LXI, 8, 1.
18. Juvenal, *Sat.* III, 309–11.
19. *ibid.*, X, 58 ff.
20. H. A. MASON, "Is Juvenal a Classic?" in *Critical Essays on Roman Literature: Satire* (London 1963), p. 176.

Bibliography

A. P. BALL, *The Satire of Seneca on the Apotheosis of Claudius* (New York 1902).

A. CAMERON, *Claudian: Poetry and Propaganda at the Court of Honorius* (Oxford 1970).

D. R. DUDLEY, *A History of Cynicism, from Diogenes to the Sixth Century A.D.* (London 1937).

J. W. DUFF, *Roman Satire: its Outlook on Social Life* (Cambridge 1937).

V. EHRENBERG, *The People of Aristophanes: a Sociology of Old Comedy* (Oxford 1951).

G. C. FISKE, *Lucilius and Horace: a Study in the Classical Theory of Imitation* (Madison 1920).

E. FRAENKEL, *Horace* (Oxford 1957).

G. HIGHET, *Juvenal the Satirist* (Oxford 1954).

U. KNOCKE, *Die römische Satire*, 2nd edn (Göttingen 1957).

W. KRENKEL (ed.), *Römische Satire* (Rostock 1966).

C. A. VAN ROOY, *Studies in Classical Satire and Related Literary Theory* (New York 1965).

W. J. N. RUDD, *The Satires of Horace* (Cambridge 1967).

J. P. SULLIVAN (ed.), *Critical Essays on Roman Literature: Satire* (London 1963), including essays on Horace by W. S. Anderson, on Juvenal by H. A. Mason, and on Persius by R. G. M. Nisbet; *The Satyricon of Petronius: a Literary Study* (London 1968).

F. VILLENEUVE, *Essai sur Perse* (Paris 1918).

A. H. WESTON, *Latin Satirical Writing Subsequent to Juvenal* (Lancaster, Penn. 1915).

C. H. WHITMAN, *Aristophanes and the Comic Hero* (Cambridge, Mass. 1964).

C. WITKE, *Latin Satire: the Structure of Persuasion* (Leiden 1970).

CHAPTER II

Literature and Society in Augustan Rome

Gordon Williams[*]

Historical explanation opens up an infinite regression before the investigator: where can he stop? What happened to the Roman Commonwealth between 133 B.C. and 27 B.C. was a social and political revolution. Power had been concentrated in the hands of a closed and highly conservative oligarchy: *nobilis* was applied to a man if a member of his family had held the highest office of state, the Consulship. From time to time newcomers broke into the circle, but, like Cicero, they were usually persuaded into a well-meaning (and self-interested) acquiescence in the traditional values of the oligarchy. This whole system was gradually (often violently) eroded during the century that preceded Augustus's "Restoration of the Republic" in 27 B.C. If a single paradigm case can be picked out, it might be the action of the senate (the council of the oligarchy) in 77 B.C. After years of civil war Sulla had finally come out on top in 82 B.C., had liquidated much of the opposition, and had been made dictator; he used the office to introduce a series of reforms designed to restore and consolidate the authority of the senate and to prevent anyone else doing what he had done. But in 77 B.C., faced with the rebellion of Lepidus in Italy and then of Sertorius in Spain, the senate conferred on Pompey first an extraordinary propraetorian, then a proconsular, command. Sulla's constitution lay in ruins, and the way was again wide open for ambitious men to bid for supreme power.

In the years that followed, the old oligarchy was virtually wiped out in a series of such attempts—by death in battle or in proscriptions, by failure to leave male heirs, or, not least, by the healing hand of time that produces sons who know not the ways of their fathers. Liberty disappeared

* Professor of Humanity, University of St Andrews.

with the "Restoration of the Republic," but in this sense liberty was "that licence that fools call freedom,"* and the freedom that it had guaranteed had come to be the freedom to conduct civil wars for personal *dignitas* and ambition. Power was now concentrated in the hands of one man, Augustus, and he surrounded himself with a new class of men drawn from unknown families, while he also revived and collected around himself members of the old nobility, reconciled of necessity. The traditional system of clientship, whereby families of the old oligarchy had created support for themselves from among lower orders of society, was replaced by a single centre of power from which lines of influence radiated outward. The effect of this—and of other factors too—was to create a wider political and social unit comprehending all Italy, and not just Rome.

Liberty went, but security and order came: political ambition was blunted, but patriotism and nationalism gained a new and wider significance: law took the place of licence and even the principate was founded on the laws. For the great majority of citizens, loss was, for a time, far outweighed by gain. Augustus began as Octavian, the latest and most successful of the opportunist party leaders, but he became the central institution of the new Roman state; in the process naked ambitions were satisfied, yet Rome also began to prosper economically, socially, and militarily, so that it soon became plausible to see the glories of the past not only renewed in the present but even surpassed. The views that can be taken of a complex historical situation are as many as the positions on which an observer can take his stand: so it is—and was at the time—with Augustus's seizure of power or restoration of the Republic or foundation of the imperial monarchy. To a few he was a usurping tyrant, but a majority must have been satisfied to give up privileges that, in the main, benefitted a few at the expense of the many. Or, to put it a different way, the end of civil war was a benefit of such magnitude that, for most people, it impeded their capacity to foresee the development of a political organization that was to become an instrument of tyrannical exploitation.

Poetry and Society

Poetry in Rome started abruptly, by all accounts, with the performance of a play (probably a tragedy) by Livius Andronicus in 240 B.C. During the century that followed, plays—both tragedies and comedies—were produced at the major Roman festivals for public entertainment. Minor magistrates, the *curule aediles*, were in charge of these entertainments, and

---

* Tacitus's description (*Dialogue on Orators*, 40, 6), which he attributes to Maternus, of the *libertas* of Cicero's age.

purchased plays for performance. The playwrights were socially inferior: of the early dramatists only Ennius attained—late in life—Roman citizenship, and Livius Andronicus (and perhaps Terence also) started life in Rome as a slave. They had to watch their step, and refrain from expressing opinions unwelcome to authority. A tradition is preserved that Naevius, an Italian from Campania, went so far as to attack the family of the Metelli from the stage, was imprisoned for a time, and died in exile. The incident is evidence of a powerful class system in Rome and of the patronage exercised by great families; it does not mean that Rome was in any sense a police state, for Plautus could make a joke about the incident at the very time it happened (*Miles gloriosus* 209–12). In their dramatic activity, then, these poets were the paid servants of society and performed a clearly defined task. But they did more than this. Livius Andronicus, for instance, translated the *Odyssey* of Homer into Latin; or, rather (because the act of "translation," which these early poets called *vortere*, was far from being literal), he wrote a Latin poem that was based on the *Odyssey*. Naevius wrote an epic poem on the Punic Wars, and Ennius wrote an epic on the history of Rome, which he called *Annales*. In these works the poets were indeed writing in Rome for men who spoke Latin, but they felt themselves to belong to the cosmopolitan Hellenistic community of Greek poets whose technique and style they imitated. The antithesis between the two aspects of their activity can be expressed by saying that their dramatic writing was intended for public entertainment of the community as a whole, whereas their epic poetry was serious and directed to a reading public educated in Greek—and especially Hellenistic—literature.

This dichotomy continued throughout the 2nd century B.C., with the gap between the two activities growing wider and wider as popular entertainment became less literary and the interest in poetry more sophisticated. But poets too were social inferiors, dependent on the patronage of Rome's leading families. Aristocratic gentlemen did not write poetry or plays; if they felt any impulse to literature it was to write technical works in prose on agriculture or history or law.

Toward the end of the 2nd century B.C., a new poetic genre established itself. It began with Gaius Lucilius, member of a wealthy land-owning family on the borders of Campania. He was a friend of Scipio and mixed on equal terms with the greatest men in Rome. He wrote what he termed *Satires*, but this was a form of literature unknown before in Greek or Latin (the *Satires* of Ennius and Pacuvius being quite different). Their peculiarity lay in their autobiographical character—not in the sense that they were "confessional," but that they were simply the direct expression of the individual Gaius Lucilius (*c.* 180–*c.* 102 B.C.). The basic assumption of his poetry was that everything that happened to Gaius Lucilius—what he saw, ate, felt, thought, and his views on all this—could be made the subject-matter of poetry and would hold the attention of readers. It is an attitude suggestive of remarkable self-esteem. It makes a sharp break with the past but also makes a bridge to the future. For it was on the same assumption that Catullus—and presumably all the friends and contemporaries who were associated with him, but who are little more than names to us—composed the personal poetry that constitutes most of his output. Catullus (*c.* 84–*c.* 54 B.C.) writes about himself and his world from a directly autobiographical point of view, with uninhibited immediacy of self-expression. In this respect he contrasts sharply with contemporaries such as Cicero and Lucretius, although all three were probably not much below Lucilius in social standing. But here a further distinction needs to be made. To Cicero and Lucretius the function of poetry was indeed to give pleasure, but it was only a part of its function; the other part was to improve, to offer instruction (particularly moral instruction), and especially to give serious treatment to serious events—most of all, to events of Roman history. In this attitude they were continuing the work of poets such as Ennius; and, in spite of his autobiographical approach, it is clear that Lucilius's view of poetry was serious—he often put forward opinions and ideas that were intended to be taken seriously. But Catullus and his friends were much nearer the view of poetry held by such great Hellenistic Greek poets as Callimachus, and in poem 36 Catullus sneered at poems with the title *Annales* on Roman history. He scarcely mentions anything to do with Rome, her history, or her politics other than with a sense of disgust. His viewpoint is consistently autobiographical and it is the powerful passions of hate, contempt, and love that find expression in his poetry.

We do not know when Catullus died—perhaps about 54 B.C.; at any rate it is not more than 10 years later that Virgil's earliest *Eclogues* are to be dated, but already these belong recognizably to Augustan poetry and the contrast with Catullus could scarcely be greater. The most striking feature of Augustan poetry is the depth of its political commitment. In this respect it is entirely novel, because, whereas earlier poets had celebrated the history of Rome and even great recent events, Augustan poets treated also the immediate, living issues of contemporary politics. The transition from the personal and irresponsible poetry of Catullus to the seriousness of the Augustans is concealed in the decade or so that saw the triumph and fall of Julius Caesar and the rise of Octavian; it is extremely obscure. Modern analogies suggest that these poets were purchased propagandists, but the suggestion should be rejected. Socially, Augustan poets were comparable with their predecessors: Propertius, Tibullus, and Ovid had estates in Italy, like Catullus; so, too, had Virgil, although he may have been less wealthy. Horace, with his insistent claim to be a freedman's son, seems different at first sight, but there was enough money to arrange for him to be schooled in Rome and then to go to the University at Athens. One feature that they all had in common (except Ovid, who was too young) was to have lost their estates in the civil wars. This certainly provided a lever for patronage, but only Horace seems to have fought on the "wrong" side (and he was, as he says in *Odes* III, 14, 27, "hot-headed with youth"); the others suffered simply because their lands were designated as settlement areas for veterans—a decree that Propertius's family resisted by force of arms (I, 21 and 22). But this patronage is no more than a minor, accidental factor in the poetic situation; the major factors lie elsewhere and the significant facts are the high quality of Augustan political poetry and the variety of political viewpoints that find expression in it. If the factor of patronage is over-emphasized, the most important consideration is obscured: what the régime of Augustus brought to an end was essentially the destructive struggling for power of the upper classes among themselves. None of these poets could feel any self-interest in such struggles, and sides were taken in the civil wars for reasons in which ideology played little part (Horace, for instance, was caught at an impressionable age by the high-minded, aristocratic Brutus in the hot-house atmosphere of Athens). A practical solution to end civil war was needed, and Octavian's success provided pragmatic justification: no pressure was required to make poets celebrate it, once they came to see such subject-matter as poetic.

A new concept of what a poet was grew up, and the Augustans found a word for it—*vates*, which a century earlier had been confined to meaning something like "fortune-teller." The Augustans resurrected this word to express their concept of a poet who spoke as a prophet with an insight that came to him as inspiration. Here a double distinction needs to be made. First, the contrast with Catullus is most extreme if he is compared with Virgil or with Horace in his *Odes*—genres of poetry that are not comparable without extensive qualification. It is more reasonable to set the writings of Propertius, Tibullus, and Ovid beside the poems of Catullus; but even here the contrast is remarkable, for the Roman political world, taken seriously at face value even when specifically rejected, is a powerful ingredient in their material. A second distinction is then apparent in the poetry of Horace: political poetry is virtually confined to his *Odes* (and, to some extent, his *Epodes*), and is more or less absent from his *Satires* and *Epistles*. There is a well-established tradition to explain this. In the poetry of Lucilius it is the individual Gaius Lucilius who speaks, and in most of Catullus's poems it is Gaius Valerius Catullus. But in the non-dramatic poetry of Ennius it is not Quintus Ennius, the individual who has been given Roman citizenship, who speaks: it is Ennius in his capacity as poet, speaking with an authority that comes from his poetic powers, not from his status as an individual citizen. So it was with Lucretius (and Cicero), and so too with Virgil: the function of being a poet created its own peculiar status and authority. It is in this persona as *vates* that Horace speaks in his *Odes*: but in his autobiographical *Satires* and *Epistles*, based on the tradition founded by Lucilius, it is Quintus Horatius Flaccus, son of a freedman, who speaks. It was a sure poetic instinct that confined serious political statement to poems that spoke with an authority that did not depend on the status of an ordinary individual citizen.

The elegiac love-poets, Propertius, Tibullus, and Ovid, occupy an intermediate position, for, despite their ostensibly autobiographical mode of composition, their themes have a strong element of poetic tradition that lifts them above an immediate expression of their own personalities, in the style of Catullus, and in Book IV Propertius comes near to the persona of Virgil or of Horace in his *Odes*. All this does not explain the difference between Catullus and the Augustans, but it does show how a different conception of the poet in action underlay the treatment of political themes.

Here another distinction needs to be introduced, which concerns the audience addressed by Roman poets—not as a range of readers objectively identified and classified, but as the subjective conception of the poet as he wrote. In their dramatic writing the earliest poets addressed the people of Rome in all their heterogeneous variety, and occasional patriotic references show how the common emotions of such a crowd could be touched. In their poetry, however, although they wrote in Latin, there is a strong sense that they felt themselves to be addressing the cosmopolitan Hellenistic world of the Mediterranean, whose common, unifying culture was Greek—and in this respect it is worth remembering that a very large part of Italy and Sicily was bilingual. These poets are the voice of Rome speaking in the accents of Hellenistic Greeks.

In this field—as in every other—Lucilius was an innovator: he too was steeped in Greek culture and was well versed in the stylistic subtleties of Alexandria, but he instinctively thought of his audience as Roman males like himself and of his own class. Only such a limited audience could grasp and appreciate the gossip, tone, and ideals of the small privileged class that forms the greater part of Lucilius's subject-matter. The same applies to the majority of Catullus's poems, except that he addressed not only Romans in the narrow sense but also provincials from northern Italy, and especially Verona. Here it may be worth recalling that "publishing" was not a stable concept in the ancient world: poems would first circulate separately among a small limited audience—the group of individuals to whom they were primarily addressed. But by the time Catullus had collected his poems for general publication, he had come to hope for a wider audience, and he had eyes on the future as well as the present. In poem 1 he hopes that posterity will value his poems, and of course posterity cannot be identified so precisely as a contemporary audience. Yet there is little trace of that wider concept of his audience in Catullus. Lucretius, on the other hand, thinks of himself as addressing the same audience as Ennius, "who won bright fame throughout the tribes of Italian men" (I, 117 ff.), and, in spite of this mention of Italy and of many illustrations taken from Roman life, his audience is made no more precise than that of Ennius. Cicero is even more cosmopolitan than Lucretius. But here too the change comes with Augustan poets, most of whom are conscious of addressing men of all Italy: their verses are full of the names of Italian towns and precise descriptions of the Italian countryside, and there is a constant evocation of an ideal life set not in Rome but in distant country districts of Italy. This feeling for Italy reflects the new sense of the unity of Rome with Italy that comes into being with the principate of Augustus, the first concrete example of which is the oath of allegiance taken by all Italy in 32 B.C. But even beyond this there is a sense in some Augustan poets (notably in Horace's *Odes* II, 20) that the Roman Empire itself is a unity that includes, or soon will include, the whole known world, and that, ultimately, the poet may count as his audience. A poet must have a confident sense of the wide relevance of his themes to think in this way. This conception of their audience is yet another sign of the high seriousness with which Augustan poets viewed their status as writers who could include the world of politics among their subject-matter—not just the past of Rome, as some of their predecessors had done, but its future and, indeed, its destiny.

Characteristics of Poetic Composition

General features that strike the reader of Augustan poetry include its variety, its sophistication, and the readiness of poets to demand imaginative co-operation from the reader and to create depth by leaving much unsaid. In these and other ways they were original, and in what follows some of the main characteristics of their handling of poetic forms will be analysed.

(i) *The Technique of Dramatic Monologue*

This is a convenient description, but it is a potentially misleading one because occasionally more than one person speaks. Essentially it consists of composing a poem that implies a complex setting, in such a way that nothing is said directly about the setting, which must be imaginatively constructed by the reader himself from odd clues casually let fall in the course of the poem. Usually the poem needs to be read in full before the setting can be fully grasped: it is a technique of gradual and unobtrusive revelation. An important example is Horace's *Odes* I, 28. The poem opens with someone addressing the tomb of the great mathematician and philosopher Archytas: he is dead and all his genius could not save him from that fate; in the same way great men before him died and are in the Underworld, even Pythagoras. (Here the reader must remember that Archytas was a Pythagorean, and believed that the soul is immortal and goes through many incarnations on earth.) But Pythagoras was wrong, although Archytas thinks him an ultimate authority; the speaker goes on to assert that there is only one road to death, which all must take. Surprise and tension are building up in the first 20 lines of the poem, for how can the speaker so flatly contradict these great authorities? The next few lines reveal the essential fact: the speaker knows the truth for the best of reasons—he too is dead, a sailor drowned at sea and washed on shore near the tomb of Archytas. The dead man now turns to address a passing sailor and asks for the ritual burial of three handfuls of dust; the last 16 lines contain this address and threaten the sailor with a similar fate if he fails in his humanitarian obligation. It is a powerful and mysterious composition that gains enormously from the partial and gradual revelation of the setting.

Very similar in the demands it makes on the reader is the moving poem of Propertius (I, 21) written about a kinsman who escaped the siege of Perusia in 40 B.C., but fell in with bandits in the lonely mountains and was killed by them. The literary background to both poems seems to be the technique of epigram, particularly sepulchral epigram, where brevity is of the essence and the setting must be established with extreme economy; but both poems represent the upgrading of epigram to a major literary form, to which there is no parallel in surviving Greek literature. The technique had been used earlier by Catullus. In poem 62 he composed an amoebaean song to be sung by choirs of boys and girls alternately. The occasion is a wedding but the setting and the surrounding ceremonies have to be inferred from unobtrusive hints in the course of the song. (Other examples of this technique in Catullus are poems 42 and 61.) But the technique was taken over by the Augustan poets and widely used by them with great skill. It is, of course, not a technique that has any application to purely narrative poetry, and so it is rare in Virgil's works, except (for instance) in the second half of the 8th *Eclogue*, which is based on *Idyll* II of Theocritus: a girl tries by magic to bring her lover back to her, and the reader must infer the circumstances and her lack of success from her monologue.

Horace seldom uses the technique in his earliest work, the *Epodes*, but does so frequently in the *Odes*. For instance, in *Odes* I, 27, the poet arrives at a drinking-party. His friends are drunk and fighting among themselves but the poet quells the disorder and lectures them on their behaviour. They press him to have a drink and he agrees, on one condition: one of the young men present must confess the name of the girl he loves. The young man is confused, stammers, and blushes, but, reassured by the poet's sympathy, finally lets the name drop. The poet is absolutely horrified and the poem ends with his expressions of desperation. It is a short poem of 24 Alcaic lines; yet none of this dramatic action is described; it must all be inferred by the reader, who has only the poet's monologue to guide him. A different use of the technique can be seen in *Odes* III, 9, where the poet and a girl speak—or sing—alternate stanzas in a six-stanza poem; the artificiality of the form is perfectly devised to carry the sort of apparent simplicity that characterizes a Mozartian duet, and only in the changing, deepening tone and the faintest outline of a self-portrait at the end does reality break through. Nothing specific is said in the poem: the reader constructs a setting for himself.

Different again is *Odes* III, 12, where the girl Neobule must be addressing herself in the second person singular—a fact that Horace has concealed, whereas in the poem of Alcaeus (of which a few fragments are preserved), the model for Horace's ode, it is clear from the beginning that a woman is speaking, and she speaks of (not to) herself and in the first person. Horace used basically the same technique in his *Epistles*; here he invented a form of poetic composition in which there is room for the interplay of the writer's and subject's characters, a brilliant kaleidoscope of tonal alterations and a connection of thought that depends solely on the conversational quicksilver of the writer's mind. The exact circumstances in which the letter is supposed to be written are important and must be inferred by the reader in the same way as in the odes mentioned above. For instance, in *Epistles* I, 13, Horace writes to Vinnius Asina instructing him how to deliver a copy of *Odes* I–III to Augustus: the reader must infer from the poem that Vinnius has collected the copy and is actually on his journey as Horace writes with over-anxious and amusing instructions. Yet the dramatic situation is never so complex and difficult in the *Epistles* as it usually is in the *Odes*—which is another way of saying that the poetic intensity of the *Epistles* is less.

The technique is also used by the elegiac love-poets, each in accordance with his own mode of composition. Propertius has a very characteristic way of conceiving a love-poem: he imagines himself in a particular situation *vis-à-vis* Cynthia and then writes a dramatic speech for himself that gives expression to all the feelings appropriate to that situation. In I, 8, lines 1–26 are an impassioned speech to Cynthia, who is apparently on the point of going off to Illyria with some unspecified man: the poet's thoughts explore the situation in anger and self-pity. Then lines 27–46 are a lyrical expression of joy in which the poet speaks of Cynthia in the third person. For this reason the poem is usually divided into two by modern editors; but, just as the reader must infer the situation between Propertius and Cynthia from what the poet says to her, so he must understand a pause after line 26, during which Cynthia agrees not to go after all, so motivating the poet's joy at his victory.

A more complex example of dramatic movement that takes place outside the poem and must be inferred by the reader is II, 28 (usually divided into three elegies). In lines 1–34 the girl is very ill, and the poet speculates on possible causes and comforts her in the face of death. In 35–58 the poet explains that various magical remedies have failed: so there has been a pause between 34 and 35 in which the reader must imagine desperate efforts of all sorts (indicated by the present tenses in 35–8) to save the girl. The poet then instructs the girl how to give thanks in due form to the gods: so between 58 and 59 there has been another pause, after the poet's solemn prayers, during which the girl has begun to recover. This poem is boldly experimental and dramatic. Simpler is III, 23, in which the poet laments the loss of his writing tablets; the reader only gradually realizes that the poet sent them with an amorous proposal to a girl and is acutely worried because he does not know whether they were genuinely lost and perhaps had the answer "Yes" on them. The girl is not named in this poem, but the reader cannot fail to think that Cynthia is intended, and therefore the loss of the writing tablets is given a symbolic significance in a poem so close to the two that record a final break with Cynthia (III, 24 and 25).

A different type of poem but a similar impulse to suggest mystery is represented by I, 16: there a house door speaks and complains of the infamous behaviour of the lady-owner. What especially hurts the door is the nightly complaining of one particular lover, and most of the poem is taken up by the door's report of the lover's speech (17–44). The lover happens to be a poet, as appears from a casual remark (41). No names are mentioned, but no reader can help fitting the poem into the context of Propertius's love-affair with Cynthia, to which it is an admirably oblique approach and opens up an entirely unexpected point of view. The reader's imagination is teased by the situation suggested.

Tibullus's mode of expression is quite different: whereas Propertius expresses himself in a vigorous, dramatic presentation of his feelings, Tibullus's love-poems happen entirely in his own mind in the form of an interior monologue, a gentle, musing reflection. He, too, avoids any direct explanation of an external situation. For instance, poem I, 2 opens with a command (to a slave, presumably) to pour wine for him because he cannot sleep; he then visualizes his girl's door, the guardian set by her husband; he tells her how to slip out, and imagines himself wandering through the city at night; he remembers his dealings with a witch (helpful in erotic problems); he cannot understand a husband going away, and visualizes pastoral life with her; he reflects on the uselessness of wealth— it does not help one to sleep—and wonders how he can have offended Venus. The reader realizes at the end of the poem that he has been listening to the desperate phantasies of a man trying to drown his sorrows in drink. It is this dramatic and highly original setting that gives the poem its unity. Most of Tibullus's poems—especially those concerned with Delia—have this form: for instance, I, 3 is composed around the fevered thoughts that flit through his mind when he has been left behind, ill on Corcyra (Corfu), by Messalla's staff as they were all on their way east. Much of the force of this and similar poems comes from the half-realized setting that the reader gathers from unobtrusive clues scattered apparently at random.

Ovid's mode of expression is different again: he is like the comedian on stage who involves himself in all sorts of dramatic situations, with or without the presence of other characters, but whose main interest lies in the impact that he himself can make on his audience. He is an adept at the game; with many an aside and wink, many a feigned sigh, and an endless flow of brilliant epigram, he arouses the audience's interest and prurient expectation. Seriousness is what he most lacks, and consequently the carefully built up and gradually revealed situation is a technique he finds time-wasting, but occasionally he uses it with brilliance, as in III, 2, when he finds himself at the races with a girl. He has no interest in horse-races but only in getting the girl into bed; most of the poem is taken up with his wonderful flow of attentive and interested patter to the girl (1–82) and two final lines record his ultimate success. But in the monologue the whole sense of being at the chariot-races in the Circus Maximus is perfectly conveyed to the reader, as is also the impression of the audience all around and Ovid's own amorous capering: it is a *tour de force* by a poet using the technique of dramatic monologue—developed by other Augustan poets—to entirely frivolous ends.

(ii) *Thematic Complexity*

By this is meant not a merely accidental density of subject-matter but a deliberate technique of complicating and interweaving a multiplicity of themes as a poetic principle in itself. The technique has its origin in the practice of Greek Hellenistic poets, for it provided a poetically interesting way of giving new life to the staple material of Greek poetry, the myths. One easily recognized form that this took is what is now called the *epyllion* (miniature epic): here the technique was to set one story inside another, and a favourite way of connecting the two stories was to make a work of art the vehicle of the interior story. For instance, in the *Europe* of Moschus, the girl carries a basket decorated with the story of Io: the interior story is both brief (44–61) and clearly relevant to the situation of Europe. When Catullus came to use the same principle of composition, however, he set the story of Ariadne, abandoned by Theseus, inside the wedding of Peleus and Thetis, to which it was connected by being embroidered on one of the wedding-presents, a quilt. But the extent of the interior story in Catullus is enormous (50–264, the poem being of 408 lines) and its relevance to the surrounding marriage is small (consisting in the fact that over to one side of the picture Dionysus is approaching Ariadne, already in love with her: but Catullus reduces this episode to a very minor incident in his treatment). This greatly increases the complexity of the poem and allows a whole series of tonal echoes and contrasts between the two stories, which are thus put on a level footing.

Nothing like it can be found in extant Greek poetry, and it certainly inspired Virgil's treatment of the story of Aristaeus at the end of *Georgics* IV; the Aristaeus episode extends from line 315 to line 558 and within it is the story of Orpheus and Eurydice (453–527). Virgil follows Catullus in achieving tonal echoes and contrasts between the finally happy main story and the tragedy of the interior episode; but his linkage of the two stories—by making Proteus, to whom Aristaeus goes for help, tell the quite unexpected story of Eurydice (which, in fact, turns out later to be relevant)—is both original and more convincing than the looser device of Catullus.

In other ways, too, Catullus inspired later poets to develop thematic complexity into a poetic principle. Here poem 68 was especially influential. Poem 65 is a poetic letter to Hortensius, sending poem 66 to him and apologizing for its inadequacy. In poem 68, however, Catullus puts the real poem (41–148) inside a verse letter (1–40, 149–60) that is written in a more colloquial style and strongly contrasts with the high poetic level of the interior poem. The two parts of the whole poem are linked by mention of the same themes (for instance, the help and hospitality that Manius gave to Catullus and his girl) but also by a remarkable, almost word-for-word, repetition of a passage on his grief at his brother's death (20–4 and 92–6). In the interior poem this passage comes in the centre, and this is achieved by a deliberately complex manipulation of themes:

> 41–66: Catullus's gratitude to Allius.
> 67–72: Allius's loan of a house in which Catullus could meet his girl.
> 73–86: Her love was like Laodamia's for Protesilaus.
> 87–90: Protesilaus went to his death at Troy.
> 91–100: At Troy, Catullus's brother died.
> 101–104: All Greece went to fight at Troy.
> 105–130: Laodamia's love for her husband.
> 131–148: Catullus's love for his girl.

This is certainly an artificial and symmetrical arrangement of ideas; what is even clearer is that the thematic complexity is deliberate—the poem is an experiment that makes this feature an end in itself. The complexity is not confined to ideas, however, but represents also a constant change of emotional tone between the poles of lyrical joy and grief. It is a most impressive poem, in which rich effects of imagery arise from utter simplicity of language; there is nothing merely ornamental. It would have been surprising if later poets had not emulated it. The 10th *Eclogue* of Virgil looks as if it was inspired by Catullus's pattern: here 1–8 and 70–77 are an address to the Muses about Gallus, and 9–69 is a poem about Gallus's unhappy love (with 31–69 a monologue by Gallus himself), and these two elements are linked by thematic echoes (as in Catullus) and by the overall relationship, such that (as in Catullus) 9–69 is the poem that 1–8 asks for and 70–77 gives thanks for. A remoter analogy is elegy IV, 1, of Propertius: this divides into two (sometimes wrongly regarded by editors as separate elegies), for 1–70 is Propertius's declaration of poetic themes and 71–150 is the answer of Horus, an astrologer. The two parts are linked by various thematic echoes, but especially by the almost verbal repetition by Horus (121–6) of Propertius's account of his birthplace (63–6), as Catullus repeated the theme of his grief in poem 68. This is clearly a poem where the poet has enjoyed deliberately courting the danger of having his poem fall apart and has made its unity rely on an intricate literary counterpoint.

Close to Catullus, at least in the feature of ring-composition, is Tibullus, II, 5, which opens and closes with a prayer to Apollo, but in between, the thematic complexity, held together by inspired leaps of thought, is clear from the many efforts by editors to tame it into more sober logic by cuts and transpositions. These later poets are more skilful than the pioneering Catullus in making the connection of ideas seem the inevitable consequence of an interaction of emotion and thought in a mind open to the impact of random but relevant impressions.

This technique has a valuable poetic function in creating a sense that the poet begins to write not quite knowing where he is going and that inspiration turns him in unforeseen directions. Horace is expert at exploiting this technique so that the reader is aware of a teasing sense of the relatedness of themes long before he fully grasps the purpose of relating them. This is partly due to a complicating of the thematic material in the sense that more themes are introduced into a given poetic form: for instance, in *Odes* I, 28, two types of sepulchral epigram are combined, together with their appropriate themes, into one poem; the way in which both Catullus and Horace develop epigram into a major poetic form is an example of this technique in action. But it is also partly due to a refinement of the connections of thought, so that it becomes more and more subtle in step with the thematic complication.

This can be applied to narrative as well as to reflective poetry. Examples of its application to narrative are the way Horace treats the myth of Europa in *Odes* III, 27, or of Regulus in III, 5; and the strange 6th *Eclogue* of Virgil is an example of a poem constructed from a whole series of mythical stories told in different ways and in different degrees of detail.

In these and many other poems, the artificial juxtaposition of different elements of thematic material, which characterizes Catullus's procedure in poems such as 36 or 68, has been converted into a technique of transition that calls for more and more complex interweaving of material. This technique reaches its highest point in Augustan poets such as Virgil, Horace, and Propertius; its corollary is that it requires even greater subtlety of response in the reader, and this is further evidence that, however they themselves conceived their audience, their poetry can have been properly appreciated by only quite a small circle of highly educated readers.*

(iii) *The Poet's World of Imagination*

The early dramatists, when they freely adapted Greek plays for production on the Roman stage, hit almost by accident on a poetically fertile idea. The Greek plays that Plautus used were set in Greek cities, the characters were Greeks, and the action reflected a Greek way of life and Greek attitudes. Plautus transferred these to the Roman stage, preserving the Greek characters and milieu in general but mixing in details from a purely Roman way of life, as suited him. The result was to create on the stage a world of imagination that belonged neither to Greece nor to Rome, but was an amalgam of both with no immediate connection with real life. This liberated the poet's imagination and enabled him to create effects that were not restricted by any reference to an immediate reality.

It is arguable that the failure of Roman poets to create a native drama was due to the severely limiting effect imposed by the need to set the action in a strictly Roman context. At any rate, all such attempts were short-lived, but the loss of so much poetry of the 2nd and early 1st centuries B.C. makes it impossible to reconstruct a detailed case history. What is clear is that Catullus used the technique in his two marriage hymns (poems 61 and 62), in both of which—but especially in the latter—the poet made use, as suited him, of a blend of ceremonial elements from both Greek and Roman marriages, making it impossible to refer the poems directly to ceremonies in either culture; both poems are set in a situation that is a construction of the poet's imagination. But here, too, it was the Augustan poets who most fully and imaginatively exploited the potentialities of the technique, and they adapted it in different ways to suit the requirements of each poetic genre.

The boldest and most original use of the technique is also the earliest known to us—that of Virgil in his *Eclogues*. This took the ancient world by

---

* Virgil's *Aeneid* was, of course, addressed to a large audience, but we cannot tell how fully it was appreciated by general readers.

surprise, as is evident from the number of quite false allegorical interpretations that were produced—and have continued to be produced down to the present day. It is clear to a reader that much more is meant by these poems than is comprehended by a simple statement of what the words say. Virgil's model was the pastoral poetry of Theocritus, which presents a highly poetical picture of an ideal world inhabited by singing shepherds and shepherdesses, into which no crude reality from the outside world intrudes: such unhappiness as there is, is the unhappiness of unrequited love, portrayed by a delicate and sensitive poetic talent, but remotely, in a setting that might as well be mythological.

At first sight it looks as if Virgil simply took over this apparatus. But then some curious features appear. The shepherds and goatherds of Theocritus may, or may not, have been free men; he only once suggests that they were slaves, and this is in a passage of coarse joking in *Idyll* V. The social situation in Theocritus is so simple that his characters are never imagined in relation to a social hierarchy. In the first three *Eclogues*, however, Virgil makes clear the servile status of his shepherds: it is a basic element in the dramatic situation. The 2nd *Eclogue* is perfectly framed between midday and nightfall, and consists mainly of the song of Corydon, unhappily in love with Alexis, who seems to be the town-slave of the master of both of them, Iollas. The remoteness of the town, and the hopelessness of the situation with Iollas in control of Alexis, are of the essence of a servile relationship conceived in Roman terms. The characters are Greek in outward appearance, yet Corydon, a slave, boasts that he has 1000 lambs pasturing on the mountains of Sicily (21); he has also seen his reflection in the sea and found himself handsome (25–7). Virgil knew that it is impossible to see one's reflection in the sea (although there are commentators who assert either that he did not realize this or that it is possible). This detail and the boast about the lambs are taken from Theocritus's portrait of the Cyclops Polyphemus in *Idyll* XI—a giant is naturally different from ordinary men. But the borrowing is not a foolish mistake on Virgil's part; it illustrates yet another dimension to be taken into account. Not only is the world of his poetic imagination an amalgam of Greek and Roman, but he treats Greek literature as a source of details that will be recognized by his readers and will also be referable by them to their original context. So these details in the song of Corydon underline the hopeless phantasy world in which the slave's mind moves.

There is another difference from Theocritus. This *Eclogue* is based on *Idylls* III and XI of Theocritus, in both of which the love portrayed is heterosexual. Greek poets used both homosexual and heterosexual love as poetic material; but in Rome there was legislation that regulated homo-sexual behaviour, which was, in any case, generally condemned. Yet Virgil has substituted homosexual love in this *Eclogue*. Why? Partly it may have been his desire to avoid following specific poems of Theocritus too closely; but far more important is the tendency of homosexual love to find expression in inward-looking, solipsistic attitudes that perfectly suit the remote sad phantasies of Corydon.

This *Eclogue* is a perfect example of the way in which Roman poets could make more real and concrete the important features of a human situation just because the general setting could be treated as imaginary and not referable to any particular reality in the outside world. The principle is well illustrated by the 1st *Eclogue*, where the ideal life of Theocritean shepherds is invaded by the realities of land confiscation—the normal method by which Romans pensioned off veteran troops. Here one of the shepherds has been evicted and is making his way into exile; the other has succeeded in a petition to exempt his land from confiscation. Virgil uses the social reality of slavery effectively: the status of the evicted Meliboeus does not matter, because he has lost everything, but no doubt he is conceived of as having bought his freedom. The situation of Tityrus is dramatic: he has only just, late in life, bought his freedom. This has involved a journey to Rome, and Virgil gives a most original and unexpected view of the great distant city from the point of view of these disregarded nobodies, eking out a livelihood far away, and knowing only their tiny local market-town (19 ff.). On the visit to Rome, Tityrus met a young man who gave an oracular response to his petition; the other shepherd interprets the response as meaning that Tityrus is confirmed in tenure of his land. This remote allegorical introduction of Octavian is delicately handled so that it does not disrupt the bucolic situation, but suggests the far-off realities of arbitrary power without making explicit a confrontation between a Theocritean shepherd, who is also a Roman slave, and the ruler of the Roman world in the West. The insistence on the servile status brings to life the plight of uncertain tenure of one who has no legal rights.

This *Eclogue*—and the 9th *Eclogue*, which is also based on the land-confiscations of 41 B.C.—has depths of meaning that recede behind the ideal situation and resist any simple prose paraphrase: the imaginative world of the poet remains a poetic unity that only violence can turn into an allegory. This is true also of the 4th *Eclogue*, which for mediaeval and later Europe supported the view that Virgil was a Christian before his time. The "messianic" *Eclogue* celebrates the consulship of Pollio in

40 B.C. in terms of a child who will be conceived in that year; in sympathy with the child's growth the golden age will return to earth, and Virgil gives a detailed portrait of its features. The poet looks forward to the time after the child's birth as a time of great poetic inspiration. Here the traditional portrait of the ideal age is used, like the bucolic scene in the 1st and 2nd *Eclogues*, as a setting that will accommodate in a mysterious and suggestive, but quite concrete, way certain realities of the period in Rome. One such was the peace concluded at Brundisium between Antony and Octavian, an event of universal rejoicing because it seemed to bring a conclusive end to civil war (which underlies several references to "sin" in this eclogue), and so, although war would not end immediately, the wars to come would be national crusades against common enemies such as the Parthians (34–6). Even the child whose identity seems such a mystery is a reality; he is a mystery because commentators are interested only in the identity of his father. Virgil has concealed this; but he has given the child an ancestry and connections that make him a member of the Julian family. He has also, by a series of literary references to Catullus's poem 64, suggested a marriage in the background; but he has equally made use of an ambiguity that exactly suits the political situation. There were two relevant marriages in the period: Octavian, a Julian, married Scribonia, and Antony married Octavia, a Julian. Either marriage would produce the required child. This is a perfectly devised and concrete representation of an ambiguity that was the essence of the real contemporary situation, set inside a purely conceptual and ideal structure.

The *Eclogues* are unique; later imitators failed to grasp their essence and produced only a charade of Dresden-china shepherds and shepherdesses, without depth or seriousness. But the intricate technique that Virgil used in them was not suited to longer poetic forms, and when he came to write the *Georgics* he used the blend of Greek and Roman in a different way. This may seem a strange thing to say of a poem whose subject is Italian agriculture, and that gives an impression of a deeply Italian patriotism. The intellectual range and depth of the *Georgics* and its emotional richness of effect become apparent if it is compared with its Hellenistic models, such as the didactic poems of Nicander or even of Aratus, for in them an encyclopaedic knowledge of a technical subject is skilfully expounded in dactylic hexameters. In the *Georgics*, however, the technical subject-matter of agriculture is set within a deeply realized Italian framework and the poem ranges freely over Italy. But Italy itself is set within a world that, as a geographical entity, embraces all known and mythical lands, and, as a literary concept, evokes echoes from earlier poets and writers, both Greek and Roman. When Virgil, following Aratus and Varro of Atax, describes birds playing in the waves as a storm-sign (*Georgics* I, 383–7), he mentions the water-meadows of the Cayster and Asia Minor, not only opening out the geographical horizons—so that the reader's mind takes in the concept of far-off places as well as of the mud-flats at Ostia—but also recalling a famous simile of Homer about the Greek hosts pouring out in front of Troy (*Iliad* II, 459–65). And in the splendid passage where he describes the excellence of Italy (a passage that recalls, in its own way, John of Gaunt's speech in Shakespeare's *Richard II*), he reaches Italy by way of Persia and India, then swerves away through Bactria, India, Panchaia, and Colchis, before coming back finally to Italy (*Georgics* II, 136 ff.).

The effect of Virgil's application of the technique in the *Georgics* is not, as in other poems and poets already examined, to create a world of imagination, but to create a world in which geographical, historical, and literary extensions are treated as equivalents: the result, however, is something like that in other poems—to give the Italian reality that lies at its core an intenser poetic life of its own that is quite different from straight factual statement. Virgil makes a similar use of the technique in the *Aeneid*: here Roman history is set inside a world where myth, heroic legend, and history meet on equal terms, and the whole of the known world—especially that of the Mediterranean—is treated as a single unity, as it was in Virgil's lifetime, but hardly before. The effect is seen most readily in Book VI, where the Greek Underworld, as established by Homer in *Odyssey* XI, is adapted and transformed by a Platonic process to accommodate the great heroes of Rome's history down to Virgil's own time. Here, as in the *Georgics*, the various modes of apprehension—historical, religious, literary, mythical—are all subordinated coherently to a unity that is a creation of the poetic imagination, and one cannot sensibly be used to contradict another.

Horace uses the technique in a great variety of ways in the *Odes*. In fact, this work demonstrates that, although the technique began as a means of blending Greek and Roman elements into an imaginative unity, it really provided Roman poets with a far more general method of composing a poem: it showed them how to create an imaginative setting for the central idea on which their poetic inspiration was, for the moment, concentrated. For instance, in *Odes* III, 14, the first three stanzas show the poet ordering arrangements for celebrating the triumphant return of Augustus from Spain in 24 B.C. A central, linking stanza reveals the poet's private feelings of joy and relief. The final three stanzas show the poet arranging a private party, but the wine is curiously specified: instead of saying that he would like an old vintage, he asks for a cask "that remembers the Marsic war," one that escaped—if any did—the marauding Spartacus. Then he is oddly casual about the girl he wants invited: "if the hateful doorkeeper makes trouble, just come away"—but he adds that he would not have been so peaceable "when he was hot with youth in the consulship of Plancus." Of course, he can mean—and does partly—"hot with love and anger," but the consulship of Plancus was in 42 B.C. and in that year Horace, hot with Republican talk of liberty, was bold enough to fight against Octavian and Antony at Philippi. And it can now be seen that the wine recalls two of the worst years for Rome in the previous century: the Italic war of 90 B.C. and the terrifying slave-war of 73 B.C. The poet's task of ordering public celebration in the first part of the poem, and his private party in the latter, are both imaginary settings created for the purpose of expressing joy at the return of Augustus in 24 B.C., seen against the grim background of the past from which Rome had escaped under his leadership.

This is a complex poem; but a simple blend of Greek and Roman into an imaginary world is provided by *Odes* III, 12, where Neobule's young man, Hebrus of Lipara, is excellent at games, especially swimming—in the Tiber. A special case of this technique is shown, for instance, by *Odes* I, 12, and III, 4: in both, the framework of ideas is provided by odes of Pindar, and III, 4 is basically unintelligible unless the reader understands the poem's relationship to the 1st *Pythian Ode* of Pindar, because this has enabled Horace to imply far more than he has said. In this poem the myth of the giants who tried to assault the heavens is a sort of political parable, but the clue to its function must be sought in Pindar. Yet the poem is far from being a mere riddle: it is a powerful and imaginative expression of political ideas and the emotions they precipitate, and it acquires depth and mystery from this unobtrusive literary setting based on Pindar.

In his *Epistles* Horace made a different use of the technique: he could not do otherwise, because *ex hypothesi* these works were Roman in setting and intimately autobiographical in mode. For instance, in *Epistles* I, 7, he writes to Maecenas, who is supposed to have reproached him for being away from Rome longer than he had promised. This *Epistle* is normally interpreted as a serious warning by Horace that he values his independence highly and is willing to return Maecenas's gifts rather than have it infringed. This is not only implausible on historical grounds, however, but also fails to assess the *Epistle* as a poem: on this account it might as well have been written in prose. It is more likely that Horace has chosen for his poetical purposes to represent his relationship with Maecenas as of a certain type that Greek philosophers used to exemplify the problems of freedom and independence. It is essentially a relationship regarded as a sort of contract in which the smaller man accepts gifts from the greater and provides services in return. It is an amusing way to treat his relationship with Maecenas and creates opportunities for a series of brilliant anecdotes that take up two thirds of the poem. The serious reality that lies behind it and inspires it is twofold: a friendship with a great man who can be addressed in this way, and that ideal of the quiet, self-sufficient life that inspired some of Horace's finest poetry.

Similarly, *Epistles* I, 19, is often interpreted as an angry and disappointed outburst at the poor reception that his *Odes* I–III have received. The general setting of the poem is a portrait of jealous critics who provoke Horace into asserting and explaining his poetic originality. But first, this concept of jealousy is a theme that was used a number of times by Hellenistic Greek poets; it was a becomingly modest way of asserting success, because a man assailed by jealousy must have accomplished something worthy of it. Secondly, as in *Epistles* I, 7, where the idea that Maecenas complained to Horace provides the whole dramatic setting of the poem, so in *Epistles* I, 19, there would be no poem without Horace's jealous critics: the assertion of their existence justifies the poem and they are a pleasing setting to a poem whose serious core is the claim made by Horace to a significant poetic originality that can be compared with that of the Greek poets he most admires.

A final work by Horace may be mentioned in this context; it is really one of the *Epistles*, although it later came to be known as the *Ars poetica*. This is a striking work, lively and varied in tone and original in its approach to literary criticism. The technique Horace used in its composition is similar to that in the *Epistles* in general. He assumes a request from the sons of Piso for a work instructing them how to write poetry; then he takes as his basic material the *Poetics* of Aristotle (perhaps not directly but using a successor to the original work). Aristotle made tragedy— mainly 5th-century Athenian tragedy—the basis of his analysis, with epic treated in less detail, and other types of poetry scarcely mentioned. So Horace talks mainly about 5th-century Athenian tragedy and Homeric epic, but he also makes unheralded excursions into later forms of these genres or into New Comedy, and creates a setting that suggests that these works are being presented to, and judged by, a Roman audience. In this way, at various times he represents himself as practising poet, member of the audience, literary critic, and historian of literature, and contrives unobtrusively to make serious critical points about poetry. But it is a most complex work and nothing in it can be taken for granted or simply at face value; this subtlety is a result of a skilful application of the technique described in this section to an entirely new area of poetic subject-matter. The critical attitudes that Horace expresses in this work only come through obliquely to the reader as a sort of by-product of the poetical activity.

A different application of the technique was made by the elegiac love-poets (mainly Propertius, Tibullus, and Ovid). Their poems—like the *Epistles* of Horace—purport to be autobiographical, but this truth to reality is modified by two factors: they felt free to invent, to suit their imaginative conception of any particular poem, and they made use of a tradition of conventional erotic situations that had been established by Greek poets (though there is no evidence that Greek poets wrote extensive autobiographical poems like Roman love-elegies). And so we find that, although Propertius gives expression to an erotic relationship with a specific mistress whom he calls Cynthia, yet her nature and even her social status varies from poem to poem in accordance with the dramatic situation that he happens to imagine. The result is to allow the poet the greatest possible freedom to imagine a human relationship in all its variety, with an element of convincing subjectivity that presents a different view of the girl—through the poet's eyes—in different situations. This imposes a real unity on a wide diversity of single poems; it enables the reader to sense the changing perceptions of the poet and to exercise an imaginative sympathy of his own. Attempts have often been made to reconstruct the actual course of the love-affair of Propertius with Cynthia: they are absurd and misguided in principle, because the technique of poetic composition, examined in this section, treats reality as merely one element in an amalgam where fact and invention are indistinguishably fused.

(iv) *Form and Convention*

Some features of Augustan poetry derive from a remote past and are easily misinterpreted if they are taken at face value. The earliest Greek poets devised poetic forms suited to the tasks they had to perform. Homer and other epic poets entertained and inspired large audiences by accounts of great deeds from the past history and the mythology of the race. They were the story-tellers of their people, and their poetry had a social function to which its form corresponded. Lyric poets wrote poems for a variety of social occasions: drinking songs, hymns for religious festivals, odes for celebrating the return of victors, and so on. In all cases the form of the poem reflected the real-life occasion for which it was intended. It was easy to see what the poet was supposed to be doing and why. Drama, too, had a form that reflected its nature as a public entertainment. But gradually, with the growth of communities and the unification of the Greek Mediterranean into a great cosmopolitan community, the close link between the poet's activity and the life of his community was weakened, and the connection between poems and the real occasions for which they were written disappeared. A new type of poet came into being: the scholar-librarian at the great library of Alexandria, who wrote to be read and studied by men as learned as he. These poets created the pattern for poetical activity over the following centuries: they took over the poetic forms that had been designed to meet the requirements of occasions in real life, and wrote poems of the same formal patterns but with no real occasions in mind. So they wrote hymns and prayers but with no idea of a real religious ceremony, or drinking-songs but with no party in mind, or epitaphs but with no idea that they should be inscribed on a tomb. The function of the conventional form was to provide poets with a starting-point, almost an excuse, for a poem; the form could contain and give shape to the poet's immediate inspiration. The danger was that poetic activity could become stereotyped and the formal element become a substitute for inspiration. So much of Hellenistic Greek poetry has been lost that certainty is impossible, but it looks as if Hellenistic poets did fall into this trap, and the conclusion is borne out by the lack of evidence of originality in their treatment of form (the *Hymns* of Callimachus excepted).

Roman—and especially Augustan—poets handled the traditional poetic forms with great inventiveness and independence. In his famous poem (2) to Lesbia's sparrow, Catullus reflects on his relationship with Lesbia while appearing to address a hymn to the sparrow; and through this subtle and oblique treatment unmistakably conveys how much more passionately Catullus loves Lesbia than she loves him. In poem 44 the reader will miss the whole point of Catullus's thanks to his country villa for aiding recovery from a bad chill, if he fails to appreciate that the form of address to the villa is a prayer (marked as such by its formal pattern) and that the villa is thereby treated as a deity. Both these poems represent that up-grading of the epigram into a major poetical form that was mentioned above. A puzzling poem by Catullus (34) is written throughout in formal liturgical style as a hymn and prayer to Diana: it is completely Greek in sentiment and detail until the final three lines (22–4), which ask help for the Roman people. Its seriousness—and especially the tone of the request—is unlike the usual frivolity of Catullus when he speaks of Rome as a political entity. This poem provided the model for a hymn by Horace (*Odes* I, 21). A comparison of the two shows the more practised ease of Horace with serious political topics. He addresses the hymn not only—not even primarily—to Diana, but to Apollo, to whom the final request (13–16) is more appropriate; and the request itself is more precisely political, asking help for Rome in her characteristic Augustan form of people and *princeps*, and mentioning as her enemies the Britons and Parthians. The nature of the supposed occasion is made clear by the device of constructing the poem as an instruction by the poet to a choir of boys and girls.

Horace used the prayer form in the construction of many of his odes, but always as a literary device, never with directly religious intention. For instance, the prayer to Mercury (*Odes* I, 10) gains emotional depth as it moves forward through a series of pictures, from the incident of the theft of Apollo's bow, to the embassy of Priam to Achilles, and the climax in the portrait of the Underworld. But the first is a motif from Alcaeus, the second is from Homer's *Iliad*, and the third recalls the scene of *Aeneid* VI. It is a most skilful construction, with a wide range of tonal variations, but its effect is literary, not religious. The form of a prayer gives the poet an excuse to recall the god's feats and creates a unity within which the variety of incidents is comprehended. One of the most famous of Horace's odes (III, 13: *O fons Bandusiae*) is a prayer or hymn addressed to the spring outside his country villa in the Sabine hills. Here a great variety of thematic material is unified in 16 lines. Like many of the odes it is constructed on a circular pattern so that it opens with phrases that describe some aspects of the spring and closes with the perfect evocation of the spring's sound: *unde loquaces/lymphae desiliunt tuae* (from which your chattering waters jump down). Between these, the poet makes clear that he is speaking on 11 October (the day before the Roman festival of Fontinalia, when flowers were thrown into fountains) and claims that this spring is worthy to be treated like Roman fountains. He then makes a surprising diversion into a promise of a blood-sacrifice (a young goat), which enables him to evoke the pathos of the small creature's death, and to picture the red blood staining the chill waters. The second half of the poem seems to represent that part of a prayer that listed the virtues of the god, but the final virtue attributed to the spring is that it will rank among the famous poetic fountains of the Hellenistic world because Horace has described its features.

This great variety of themes achieves a unity by virtue of the recognizable hymnic form that the poet has used, with its traditional features.

Similarly, in *Odes* III, 18, Horace describes a country festival under the guise of addressing a hymn to the god Faunus. In *Odes* III, 21, he creates a brilliant parody of a prayer, addressed to a bottle of wine that will be used to entertain the great M. Valerius Messalla Corvinus. But this poem makes use also of another formal device that Horace treated in a great variety of ways: the concept of a party that is described or prescribed, or to which someone is being invited. As with hymn or prayer, the concept of a party supplies an occasion or excuse for a poem and thus imposes a unity on a variety of themes.

Horace used this device among his earlier *Epodes*: for instance, *Epodes* 9 is really a celebration of Augustus's victory at Actium in 31 B.C., but the form of the poem is an address to Maecenas prescribing and describing a celebratory feast in which they both take part. The value of this form to Horace was that it enabled him to establish an intimacy of address with a great man that was both free from obsequious flattery and capable of expansion to include a wide range of theme and tone. Particularly impressive is the great fabric of *Odes* III, 29. This ode opens with the suggestion of an invitation to Maecenas; there follows a contrast between the busy, urban life of Rome and the quiet joy of the countryside, elaborated with the names of remote Sabine regions and a portrait of the shepherd at peace by a river bank (5–24). Then the political preoccupations of Maecenas are suggested and the poet's thoughts move out to reflect on the uncertainty of the future (25–32): in a magnificent simile, this is compared with the Tiber, at one time a quiet stream, at another a suddenly turbulent river in destructive flood (33–41). Here the poet's thoughts again turn to philosophical reflections on the necessity of enjoying the present (on which alone a man may count), and the poem ends with a striking statement of the poet's own ideal of an independent life, undisturbed by the vagaries of Fortune or by ambitions for wealth (49–64). The poem starts from the idea of a party and steadily moves out from this to reflections on the human condition in general. Many of Horace's odes that make use of this form are extremely skilful constructions in the technique of dramatic monologue, and require the reader to construct the situation for himself from unobtrusive clues: striking examples of this are *Odes* III, 8 and 19.

Horace also uses this form in *Epistles* I, 5, to invite the aristocratic lawyer Manlius Torquatus to celebrate Augustus's birthday with him. The poem is light-hearted and amusing, with occasional touches of seriousness, and establishes a personally intimate tone with Torquatus that reflects the difference in literary genre between the *Epistles* and the *Odes*. It is worth remarking here that the *Epistles* represent a particular case of the phenomenon described in this section. In fact, they represent a quite remarkable feat in Latin literature, comparable only with Lucilius's invention of his form of satire: they represent the invention of a new literary form, almost a new genre of literature. Each epistle supplies both the occasion and the form of a poem and requires the reader to deduce for himself the characters involved and the situation that has given rise to any particular letter.

Finally, we should mention a poetic form that often gives rise to misinterpretation. It is generally accepted that Augustus was anxious to see an epic poem written in Latin to deal with his own great deeds and the achievements of his principate. The evidence for this is that all Augustan poets in their own ways write poems regretting their inability to write an epic poem about Augustus: if only they could, for he is such a worthy subject! But if a patron could be so importunate as to elicit such a response, surely he could have exerted pressure a little more vigorously to elicit the response he desired? A clue to the reasons for the reticence and apparent modesty of these poets is in the famous prologue to *Aitia* (written two centuries before) in which Callimachus described how Apollo appeared to him and told him to keep his Muse thin, to prefer the voice of the cicada to the braying of an ass, to guide his chariot on byways and not on the main highroads. Callimachus was asserting with polemical vigour his contempt for the writing of epic poetry and his own intention to pursue more original, and finer, forms of poetic composition.

All the Augustan poets who wrote poems regretting their inability to tackle epic modelled themselves on this famous passage of Callimachus, but with a very significant innovation. As an orator might use the figure *praeteritio* ("I forbear to mention this, that, and the other thing") in such a way that he contrived to say what he said he would omit, so these poets, in dwelling on the excellence of Augustus, converted the theme of Callimachus into a method of praising the achievements of the *princeps* under the guise of explaining their own inability to do justice to those achievements. This curious piece of literary history epitomizes the outstanding novelty of Augustan poetry.

Poetry and Politics

Augustan poetry is, above all, politically engaged, and nothing marks it off more sharply—not only from Catullus and his contemporaries, but also from Hellenistic Greek poetry in general—than this involvement in the realities of politics. It is worth considering some of the ways in which political themes were treated in poetry, for not only did this face poets with difficult problems but poets in different genres had to find different solutions.

The earliest treatment of contemporary political themes in Roman poetry is in the *Eclogues* of Virgil. But it is a unique treatment precisely suited to the conceptual pastoral world in which the poems are set. Into the idyllic existence portrayed by Theocritus have penetrated the land confiscations of 41 B.C. and the misery brought arbitrarily upon individuals. The 9th *Eclogue* portrays the involvement of the mysterious poet Menalcas in these troubles, and the way in which he, like Virgil, tries to bring his poetry to bear on them. But in these poems there is little political evaluation: the evils are arbitrary, and so is escape from them. Political evaluation comes in the 4th *Eclogue*, with its presentation of the peace of Brundisium as a turning-point in Rome's history from which the road leads upward; civil war—though it is never mentioned specifically—is condemned as a sin. In the *Georgics* Virgil presents political issues in a more tangible way. This is done generally throughout the work, in that it treats agriculture not simply as a technical science, but as a way of life that is morally superior to the sham values and ambitions of urban existence. This point of view reaches a climax at the centre of the work (Book II, 458–540) in a superb passage where the emotional tone rises to comprehend an ideal way of life, that of a kind of gentleman farmer, which is regarded as the highest point of human culture reached by past ages. But Virgil also airs specific political ideas, notably at the end of Book I, after he describes how the heavenly bodies can be used as weather-signs and to fix the time of year. He speaks last about the sun and then moves on (466 ff.) to describe the portents that came after the murder of Julius Caesar and the civil war that followed. Finally (489–514), he treats Octavian (not named but represented by the figure of a *juvenis*) as the saviour of the Roman world whom they cannot afford to lose. The whole work ends with a picture of Caesar subduing the disaffected peoples on the eastern border of the empire while Virgil spends his time ignobly at peace, concentrating on his studies (IV, 559–66). Throughout, Virgil succeeds in presenting the activity of farming in the historical context of a troubled contemporary world: the reader never loses sight for long of political issues and the past miseries of Italy.

The greatest of Augustan poetical works, the *Aeneid*, is permeated with a sense of the contemporary world. This is done with great originality and an extraordinary consistency of poetic vision. The poem begins in the years after Troy's fall, some 1100 years before Virgil's own time, and tells the story of the founding of Rome from that point of view. But every now

T

and then, the curtain of history parts and the reader gets a quite novel view forward over Rome's history, looking at it from the opposite direction to the normal. In a magnificent speech in Book I (257–96) Jupiter surveys the future of Rome down to the time of Augustus; in Book VIII Aeneas is conducted by Evander over the future site of Rome; and in the same book Virgil uses the traditional epic description of a shield to present a visual survey of Rome's history, culminating in the Battle of Actium and Octavian's triumph. In a similar spirit, in Book VI, Aeneas sees the great men of Roman history in the Elysian Fields, as yet unborn into the real world but marked with their future destiny.

The *Aeneid* is no fairy-tale from Greek mythology, but the work of a man who has reflected deeply and penetratingly on the history of Rome until the whole panorama is a unified vision in his mind. It is an exciting vision of a people's history and one in which the present, in spite of its worries, is the culmination of a past stretching back over 1000 years. This is a specifically Augustan view—a view able, after the consolidation of Augustus's power and the recession of civil strife, to reject the pessimism that had characterized previous historical thinking in favour of a sane, considered optimism. But Augustan attitudes and values come through in many other ways in this great poem, particularly its moral values. For instance, the whole tragedy of Dido depends on the Augustan re-thinking of the institution of marriage and its significance in the life of the community: Dido, in her attitude to her marriage to Sychaeus and to what she considers to be her marriage to Aeneas, is no prehistoric Carthaginian but a noble Augustan woman like the Cornelia whose epitaph Propertius wrote (IV, 11). Deep moral analysis of action—never, of course, made explicitly—is characteristic of the *Aeneid*.

The problems that confronted Horace when he attempted to treat contemporary politics in his lyric poetry were severe. He was writing mainly in a style of personal lyric poetry that required not only that the poems arise from and centre on his own poetic personality but also that he address his poems to individuals who stood in some personal relationship to him. He found various ways around the danger that this approach would trivialize such serious subjects. In *Epodes* XVI, for instance, writing in the satirical style of the early Greek poet Archilochus, he harangues the citizen-body as a whole, almost as if he were himself a magistrate. This was not suitable for the *Odes*. There he sometimes completely avoids a direct address to any individual, for instance, in *Odes* I, 2 and 12 (both of which are more like the odes of Pindar—the latter expressly so—than like those of Sappho or Alcaeus) and in III, 2, 3, 5, and 24. In the Pindaric III, 4, he begins with an address to his Muse; in III, 14, he adopts the Hellenistic role of a herald prescribing celebrations and uses the unique form of address to the populace of Rome: *O plebs*. In III, 6, he addresses his fellow-countrymen by the generalizing singular *Romane*. In III, 1, he addresses the youth of the country. But only in *Odes* IV is he able to use the satisfying device of addressing the head of state directly, as if on behalf of the citizen body as a whole.

The first three books of the *Odes* were probably published by 23 B.C., when the principate of Augustus was only beginning to consolidate itself by victories abroad and legislation at home; but Augustus was still vulnerable, as shown by a number of attempted coups, and also by the rejection in 28 B.C. of the moral legislation to which he attached great importance. It was a time when it was plausible to interpret any opposition to Augustus as a threat to civil peace. This is the theme of most of the political odes in these books, and the possibility of civil war underlies the solemnity of tone. Warnings against opposition are the theme of III, 4, and to some extent of III, 3 (in the form of encouragement to the *princeps* to resist pressure). The sombre tones of III, 6, equate rejection of the moral legislation with disasters to the state and a decadence that is only faintly lightened by celebration of Augustus's programme for rebuilding the temples. In I, 2, civil war is barely over and the poet speculates on divine help—perhaps Mercury is here all the time disguised as Octavian. This emphasizes another difficulty of Horace in this period: how was Augustus to be treated poetically? If Greek models were to be followed, then the relationship of ruler and people would be represented by making him a god. But such an idea was not only repugnant to Romans, it was also untrue of their political organization: the Augustan principate was very different, and seemed very different, from the remote and autocratic Hellenistic monarchy.

In *Odes* I, 2, Horace tries a bold experiment under the inspiration of Virgil's *Georgics* I: its effect is not to make Octavian a god, but to suppose that a god is disguised as Octavian, and the intention is not so much to attribute divine honours to Octavian as to suggest that divine powers are needed if a man is to save Rome from civil war. But Horace confers only a sort of divinity-by-association on Augustus: he mentions him in company with gods—for instance, in I, 12, and III, 5, where he is pictured as the equivalent to Jupiter on earth, holding his power subject to Jupiter's approval. Or he treats him as a military commander or a guardian of the people.

The tone is never panegyrical in *Odes* I–III because the poet succeeds in expressing the anxiety Romans felt in a precariously balanced situation where not mere anarchy but full-scale civil war was the penalty for instability. As the years passed, however, the power of Augustus became firmly established, and he achieved major successes both at home and abroad. By 17 B.C. the Roman world looked a very different place, with growing prosperity, revitalized agriculture, re-established confidence and credit, and an apparently stable situation on most of the imperial boundaries. Horace was invited to compose the official *carmen saeculare* (secular hymn) for the celebrations of 17 B.C., and he probably published *Odes* IV in 13 or 12 B.C. The poetic danger now was of a fat complacency mouthing prosperous commonplaces, unsharpened by the vision that earlier dangers had inspired. The invitation (or command) to Horace to compose the *carmen saeculare* was an official recognition of the new place that Augustan poets claimed for themselves in the life of the community. It was a lyric poem to be performed by choirs of boys and girls; this circumscribed the poet, as did the fact that the performance had to fit into a pattern of religious ceremonies. The choirs address Phoebus and Diana, deities suited to their nature (cf. *Odes* I, 21), but the major part of the poem is really a review of the Augustan achievement (13–60): the moral legislation (which the choir views in its effect over future generations), agricultural prosperity, and peace on the imperial borders, are interspersed with prayers for the future, a poetic picture of Rome's origins, and a prayer that the requests already voiced by Augustus should be answered.

What is remarkable in this passage is the strictly factual way in which the poet has expressed the details of Roman legislation; it is a bold experiment, which has no real precedent in ancient poetry. The poet was forced to mention laws because so much of the Augustan achievement was expressed in legislation, and his solution is striking and successful. His device for concluding this list of achievements is also impressive: he moves out into a series of highly generalizing abstractions (57–60).

Horace used the same basic technique in two odes of Book IV, with appropriate variations. In IV, 5, he addresses Augustus directly and lists the achievements of his rule (17–28) in a series of line-long statements in asyndeton; then his poetic vision broadens to depict an ideal condition of life that had deep emotional attractions for Romans: the farmer peacefully at work in a prosperous and peaceful landscape, far from urban vice and squalor, celebrating the rule of Augustus in his simple way. The ideal quality of the picture insulates the poet from any sense of flattery. In IV, 15, Horace again addresses Augustus directly and lists the achievements of his age (*tua, Caesar, aetas* . . .) in a long sentence, with polysyndeton (5–16), then surveys an Italy now free from the danger of civil war, and the imperial boundaries at peace from surrounding enemies (17–24).

Now the poet's imagination moves out to embrace another ideal picture, set in the future, of Romans engaged in continuous celebration as they recall the glories of their past. In both these poems the poet represents himself simply as one of the people joining in the celebrations, a neat poetical device whereby he shows himself unobtrusively to be speaking for the people as a whole—and not, as in earlier poems of Books I–III, addressing the people as if he were outside, or above, them. This is a device that he had already used in IV, 2, where he subordinates his own poetic personality in an address to Jullis Antonius, nephew of Augustus, alleging that the young man will write a better poem in honour of Augustus, returning from his victories in Germany. He then tells the young man the sort of thing he should say (37–44), and casts himself simply as one of the crowd that will line the triumphal route. This again serves to insulate the poet from any suggestion that he is indulging in flattery.

In *Odes* IV, Horace generally represents Augustus as commander-in-chief of the armies, but in poem 5 he tries a unique experiment: he represents the country as looking for the return of Augustus, as a mother looks for her son who has sailed overseas. It is an attempt to represent the relationship of the *princeps* to the Roman people as a personal one; this is in direct opposition to the relationship that Hellenistic Greek poets pictured when they represented the monarch as a god. The danger is that the poet may slip into a meaningless sentimentality; Horace tries to avoid this by the detailed exposition of Augustus's achievements (17–28), which form the basis of the people's affection. It is hard for a reader to sympathize with this approach if he keeps in mind the ruthless ambition that drove Augustus to seize power: pragmatic justification of success is distasteful. Sympathetic understanding of the poet's intention is needed, and of the difficulties in treating such a subject; Horace is as far from the wretched sycophancy of Hellenistic Greek poets as he is from the exaggerated flatteries of later Roman poets.

Of the elegiac poets only Propertius wrote considerably about politics. Tibullus does not seem to have been gathered into the circle of writers around Maecenas, and Ovid belonged to a later generation, though his first patron was M. Valerius Messalla Corvinus, who had also been the patron of Tibullus. The poems in which Tibullus celebrated his great patron and his patron's son are not overtly political, for they scarcely touch on the great issues of the time. The world of political action enters his poetry in the form of one of the most deeply felt contrasts in human life. Tibullus was a man of action and served with Messalla on a number of his campaigns, for which he was decorated. But his poetry is created out of the tension between active military life and the quiet ideal of a life spent with his girl in the country. It is not political poetry in the sense in which Virgil and Horace wrote it; the Augustan world comes through to the reader of Tibullus in a novel way and from an unexpected point of view, because the poet is all the time trying to reject it and failing.

The contrast with Propertius is great. In Books I–III he, too, rejects the political world. Often he does this in the form of a poem regretting his inability to tackle such great themes: for instance, in II, 10, he hopes that he will be able to write such poetry when he is older. But he makes full use of the "refusal" form to give a concrete sense of the great achievements of Augustus. In some poems, however, he specifically rejects politics and war from his own life: in III, 4, he reflects with enthusiasm on the setting-out of an expedition against Parthia, and pictures the triumphant return, but he himself will be merely in the crowd, or lying in the arms of his girl, or idly surveying the trophies: no Parthian war for him. This is an excellent device for a love-poet, because he thereby achieves a sense of the great importance of such military action while creating a strong impression of sincerity by rejecting it for himself. He thus rises to the great themes of politics without destroying his own character as a love-poet.

When Propertius tries to deal directly with politics in Books I–III (as he does occasionally, II, 16, 37 ff., for instance) he relapses into insincere bombast. His poetry is different in Book IV, and there he deals directly in Elegy 6 with the Battle of Actium and the victory of Augustus; but his poetic style is too mannered to avoid giving the subject an inappropriate effect of artificial prettiness. Much more successful is the great elegy on Cornelia, IV, 11, where, in the form of an epitaph spoken on her own behalf by the dead woman, expression is given to Augustan moral ideals of marriage and the family. This is a powerful and imaginative composition, and it recalls a curious fact. In II, 7, Propertius wrote a short poem recording the joy of Cynthia and himself at the failure of a marriage law. This can refer only to the abortive attempt by Augustus, about 28 B.C., to pass the marriage legislation that, in fact, took him nearly 40 years to complete. It is a surprising sincerity in Propertius that he could express pleasure at the failure of legislation to which Augustus attached so much importance, but it is consonant with the way he expresses himself on political issues in Books I–III.

Yet Augustus may have won in the end. Ovid's Corinna (in the *Amores*) and Propertius's Cynthia are both married, as are most of the women with whom the Augustan poets celebrated their adulterous affairs in elegy. Now, the most novel element in Augustus's moral legislation was the penalty of banishment imposed on a man found guilty of an adulterous relationship with a married woman. It can hardly be a coincidence that, in Propertius's Book IV, written after the first instalment of the legislation was passed in 18 B.C., Cynthia dies and is no longer referred to in the old erotic style; that Ovid insisted that his Corinna was fictitious; and that the Augustan love-elegy ended with the *Amores*. The increasing grip of moral legislation, and the surveillance of poetry by Augustus himself, must have meant the end of such poetry, for it would have been unthinkable to continue the genre in terms of the ready joys of marriage or of commercial transactions with prostitutes; and to have paraded an adulterous relationship with a married woman would now have been too dangerous. Ovid does not write seriously about love, nor does he write seriously about politics; nor, in his would-be epic poem, *Metamorphoses*, does he achieve anything outside the artificial field of Greek mythology: the blending of Greek and Roman elements into an imaginative unity seems beyond him. His exile to Tomis, in southern Russia, marks a new political control of literature that confines it, over the next century, either to the safe artificiality of Greek legend or to ingenious flattery of the reigning emperor. Augustan poetry marks a high point in Rome's literature, and perhaps its very success in involving itself in contemporary politics made inevitable its own downfall under the increasing demands of authority, which had itself learnt from the poets a taste for the sweets of literary support.

Bibliography

A. Y. CAMPBELL, *Horace: a New Interpretation* (London 1924).

D. R. DUDLEY (ed.), *Lucretius* (London 1965).

E. FRAENKEL, *Horace* (Oxford 1957).

F. G. KENYON, *Books and Readers in Ancient Greece and Rome*, 2nd edn (Oxford 1951).

H. LAST, "The Social Policy of Augustus," *The Cambridge Ancient History*, Vol. X (Cambridge 1934).

G. LUCK, *The Latin Love Elegy* (London 1959).

BROOKS OTIS, *Virgil* (Oxford 1963); *Ovid as an Epic Poet* (Cambridge 1966).

K. QUINN, *The Catullan Revolution* (Melbourne 1959); *Latin Explorations* (London 1963); *Virgil's "Aeneid"* (London 1968).

H. J. ROSE, *The Eclogues of Virgil* (Berkeley 1942).

N. RUDD, *The Satires of Horace* (Cambridge 1966).

R. SYME, *The Roman Revolution* (Oxford 1939); *Sallust* (Berkeley 1964).

D. WEST, *Reading Horace* (Edinburgh 1967).

A. L. WHEELER, *Catullus and the Traditions of Ancient Poetry* (Berkeley 1934).

L. P. WILKINSON, *Horace and his Lyric Poetry* (Cambridge 1945); *Ovid Recalled* (Cambridge 1953); *Golden Latin Artistry* (Cambridge 1963).

G. WILLIAMS, *Tradition and Originality in Roman Poetry* (Oxford 1968); *The Third Book of Horace's Odes* (Oxford 1969); *The Nature of Roman Poetry* (OPUS 49: Oxford 1970).

Translations in Paperback

Catullus, trans. by P. Whigham (London 1966).

Horace, trans. by J. Michie (London 1966).

Ovid's Amores, trans. by A. G. Lee (London 1968).

Propertius, trans. by A. E. Watts (London 1966).

Virgil, trans. by C. Day Lewis (London 1966).

CHAPTER 12

Virgil's "Aeneid"

Stephen Medcalf*

> What obligation was strong enough to induce Virgil—whose spirit was so gentle, so delicately strung, so bent on the pleasures of the country—to expend so great labour, over so long a period, upon a thoroughly alien and unsatisfying task?[1]

John Keble, who asked this question about the making of the *Aeneid* in his Oxford lectures on poetry of 1832–41, gave the traditional answer: the wish of Augustus and Virgil's gratitude to him. Because we know certainly of Augustus's interest in the progress of Virgil's poem, and have evidence of pressure put on other poets of Virgil's circle to write such a work, it is an answer with something to be said for it.[2] But we must at least add to it as motives two problems with which Virgil is plainly so concerned in his poem that we might suppose him to be obsessed by them: first, to create a foundation myth that would be for Augustan Rome what the *Iliad* and the *Odyssey* were for Greece—a standard of culture, literature, religion, and behaviour; and second, in so doing to revitalize the ancient epic tradition. The poets who, like Apollonius Rhodius, had attacked this second problem before him, had not been markedly successful in making the epic modern: their best achievement had been the *epyllion* (little epic), a short passage from epic sources given an emotional treatment suited to contemporary tastes.

The result is in some sense necessarily artificial, as Augustan Rome itself was: part of Virgil's achievement lay in making this artificiality itself a delicate means of self-expression, epitomized in his use of metre. Here what one might call an "imperial" metre was already in existence, the use of the quantitative metre of the conquered but superior Greek culture, in a language naturally fitted for an accentual metre (as the Saturnian, the old Latin metre, probably had been). The problem here was how to combine quantity and stress: whether to allow them to coincide,

* Lecturer in English, University of Sussex.

long syllable with stress, or to try to counterpoint them. Virgil's solution, following the experiments of writers such as Ennius, Lucretius, and Catullus, was generally speaking to allow coincidence at the beginning and end of a line, with counterpoint in the middle:

Arma virumque cano, Troiae qui primus ab oris[3]

No more musical metre has ever been devised, nor one with greater possibility of delicate special effects. But it was the metre of a special class, in a special relation to the Empire. The vulgar continued to sing by stress; and as the imperial culture declined, stressed metre prospered again. The artificial Graeco-Latin culture, beautiful though it was, decayed: mediaeval Latin verse is accentual.

Now, the sense of active control in this counterpoint is an essential part of the enjoyment of Virgil's music. It is apparent also in the diction, which has what Owen Barfield calls an "architectural" quality, appreciated "when one takes delight, not only in what is said and in the way it is said, but in a sense of difficulties overcome—of an obstreperous medium having been masterfully subdued."[4] This is apparent even in the syntax and semantics of single lines, such as

> sunt lacrimae rerum et mentem mortalia tangunt.
>
> (Tears exist for the way things happen and mortality touches the heart.)

The great lines of Homer are by contrast like this one (on Helen):

> In face she is strangely like an immortal goddess.[5]

But they are even less translatable. As Barfield points out, Homer trusts the medium he is using, the language of Greek epic, more straightforwardly than Virgil can trust Latin. His diction is not packed in the way of the *Aeneid*: his words give no sense of deliberateness in their fitting together; his descriptions and similes have an unembarrassed speed very unlike the complexities of Virgil.

The contrast is between the less sophisticated—but for that reason more direct, single, and active—movement of Homer and Virgil's more sophisticated, more self-consciously controlled, more reflective motion. All this is certainly characteristic of Virgil and of Augustan culture, a culture of control with an ethic (which we shall discuss presently) of self-restraint.

But there are two important qualifying characteristics: first, the way in which a romantic and turbulent passion continually wells up in and against Virgil's architectonics. Virgil's world, compared with Homer's, is split: but both halves remain present in a counterpoint of clear inevitability and active passion, apparent alike in the music of the poetry and in the conflicts of the story. Second, the management of this duality by Virgil's self-conscious control gives a sense of individual personality that is altogether absent in Homer.

A sexuality almost painful in its intensity, for example, presses against the marble surface of Book VIII when Venus uses all her powers to persuade Vulcan to forge Aeneas's shield:

> dixerat; et niveis hinc atque hinc diva lacertis
> cunctantem amplexu molli fovet. Ille repente
> accepit solitam flammam; notusque medullas
> intravit calor, et labefacta per ossa cucurrit:
> non secus atque olim, tonitru cum rupta corusco
> ignea rima micans percurrit lumine nimbos.[6]

> (The goddess ceased to speak, and with her snowy arms warmed him from either side in his reluctance with a soft embrace. He quickly caught the flame he knew; the old heat came into his marrow, and ran through his melting bones, just as when a fiery rift smashed open by a thunder clap runs through the clouds, flashing with glittering light.)

We have here, fused in the verse itself, a confrontation that reaches its painful height in the mutual incomprehension of Dido and Aeneas. Here are a man and a woman who might seem made for one another, each the leader of a people in exile, whose likeness to one another Virgil stresses by similes: Dido is compared, when we and Aeneas first see her, to Diana, and Aeneas, when the hunt begins that ends in their fatal love-making, to Diana's brother, Apollo.[7] But they are doomed from the start to mutual wounding because they represent two halves of humanity. Dido can no more understand Aeneas's *pietas*, the duty to his gods that drives him on, than he can understand, until he sees her pyre from the sea, the passion that drives her to kill herself. Most pitifully she recognizes this when she sends her sister Anna to plead with Aeneas, saying:

> solam nam perfidus ille
> te colere, arcanos etiam tibi credere sensus.[8]

> (because it is you alone whom that traitor made a friend, and trusted you even with his secret thoughts).

Anna goes, and we have a passage that contains the reason of the situation:

> talibus orabat, talisque miserrima fletus
> fertque refertque soror. sed nullis ille movetur
> fletibus, aut voces ullas tractabilis audit;

fata obstant. placidasque viri deus obstruit auris,
ac velut annoso validam cum robore quercum
Alpini Boreae nunc hinc nunc flatibus illinc
eruere inter se certant; it stridor, et altae
consternunt terram concusso stipite frondes;
ipsa haeret scopulis, et, quantum vertice ad auras
aetherias, tantum radice in Tartara tendit:
haud secus adsiduis hinc atque hinc vocibus heros
tunditur, et magno persentit pectore curas;
mens immota manet, lacrimae volvuntur inanes.[9]

(So she implored, and such were the tearful pleas her sister carried again and again. But he is not moved by any tearful pleas, nor hears any message in a mood to give in. Fate withstands, and a god blocks up his man's ears that might be kind. And as when north winds from the Alps, from one side and another fight among themselves to overthrow with their blasts an oak mighty with the strength of years, there comes a groan, and as the stem quivers the high leaves strew the ground; but it clings to the rocks and as far as it stretches with its top to the airs of heaven, so far it stretches with its roots into hell: just so the hero is beaten from either side by unceasing messages, and feels throughout his great breast the pain; his mind stands unmoved, the tears roll down pointlessly.)

It has always been questioned, whether in the last line the tears are those of Dido or of Aeneas himself. The simile might suggest that the fallen leaves signify tears, in which case they should be Aeneas's. St Augustine took the line so, and made it his example of the Stoic ideal:

Thus is the mind still fixed, holding steadfastly that no passion (though it insult the soul's weaker parts) can domineer over reason, but reason over them, exercising virtue's sovereignty over them by opposition, not by consent. For such a one does Virgil say Aeneas was, *mens immota manet, lacrimae volvuntur inanes* (his mind stands unmoved, the tears roll down pointlessly).[10]

This is an ethic resting on a belief in an absolute dichotomy in the personality between reason and the emotions. It is the part of reason to control and of the emotions to be controlled; control is the essence of this personal and social code. The doctrine is not confined to Stoicism; the peculiarly Stoic feature lies in driving the dichotomy so far as to allow the will to remain fixed even while the passions rage. Ultimately it rests on the fundamental antitheses that governed most classical thought, and that may have led to its downfall: the antitheses between form and matter, character and circumstance, knowledge and opinion, and so on.[11] The classical cardinal virtues—*fortitudo* (courage), *temperantia* (temperance), *iustitia* (justice), and *prudentia* (wisdom)—are essentially virtues of control. So also are the four virtues ascribed to Augustus in the golden shield dedicated to him by the Senate in 27 B.C. and quoted by him in his *Res Gestae*: "*clupeum virtutis clementiae iustitiae pietatis erga deos patriamque*" (the shield of courage, mercy, justice, and piety toward the gods and the fatherland).[12] The significance of this (especially with its culminating *pietas*) for the character of Aeneas, whose first characteristic is *pietas*, is clear.

Augustine comments on the weaknesses of the Stoic doctrine when he continues:

> there is no need to expound more fully what the Christian scripture teaches on this point of feelings. It subjects the whole mind to God's governance and assistance, and all the passions unto it, in such manner that they are all made to serve the increase of justice. Finally, our doctrine inquires not so much whether one be angry, but wherefore; why he is sad, not whether he be sad; and so of fear. For anger with an offender to reform him; pity upon one afflicted to succour him; fear for one in danger to deliver him—these no man, not mad, can reprehend.[13]

Stoicism, he considers, too easily dismisses the emotions without considering that they too have their ends; and it does not give the whole man an end. Elsewhere he argues that all the four virtues are subsumed in love.[14]

It is characteristic of Virgil that he presses the two sides of his conflict so far that the resolution that Christianity was later to achieve seems almost on the point of bursting through. Thus, it is essential in reading him to realize that the mention of *pietas*, of one side of the antithesis, often implies the tormented passions that are the other side. When Aeneas has killed Mezentius's son Lausus,

> mentem patriae subiit pietatis imago[15]

> (the image of a father's *pietas* comes upon his mind),

and he cries:

> quid pius Aeneas tanta dabit indole dignum?[16]

> (What shall *pious* Aeneas give worthy of such a person?)

There is a sense here of "Aeneas who, in the teeth of all disasters, follows his duty, in spite of all regret and pain": this sense is indeed established when he is first called *pius*, after the wreck in Book I,

> praecipue pius Aeneas nunc acris Oronti,
> nunc Amyci casum gemit.[17]

> (Chiefly *pious* Aeneas mourns the fate now of keen Orontes, now of Amycus.)

We must understand the word *pius* in this sense, when it is used at the crisis of Aeneas's relations with Dido. She has made her heart-rending appeals to him and fainted, and immediately Virgil goes on:

> at pius Aeneas . . .
> multa gemens magnoque animum labefactus amore
> iussa tamen divum exsequitur.[18]
>
> (but *pious* Aeneas . . . much as he mourned, and though his heart was ruining with enormous love, still carried out the commandments of the gods.)

Aeneas is killing one side of himself in favour of the other when he leaves Dido; Virgil, whose Dido carries away most readers' sympathies, rejects neither side.

This is an outcome of his empathy, which is akin to Christian love. Conway[19] has given a picturesque example in miniature from the *Georgics*: the swallows, when they take bee larvae for their brood,

> ore ferunt dulcem nidis immitibus escam[20]
>
> (carry in their beaks sweet food for their pitiless nestlings).

We are given by the epithets (Virgil's usual technique) the feelings of either side: "sweet" for the swallows' view, "pitiless" for the bees'. Brooks Otis[21] has analysed the way in which, in the races in Book V, this technique is used to make us take part with all the contestants in turn.

Now, it is in this that Virgil contrasts most sharply with Homer, and it was with the creation of the subjective style that he revivified epic. For Homer's world is all objective, bathed in what Kinglake[22] called "the strong vertical light" of his poetry. His style is insensitive to a degree that makes insensitivity a virtue.

> And I cannot companion him [my father] as he grows old, since very far from my fatherland I sit in Troy, afflicting you and your children.[23]

The unquestioning acceptance of the harsh conditions of a heroic age is chilling. It goes along with Homer's acceptance of all that happens, pleasant or unpleasant. W. H. Auden wonderfully conveys a sense of the style in his poem "Memorial for the City":

> That is the way things happen; for ever and ever
> Plum blossom falls on the dead, the roar of the waterfall covers
> The cries of the whipped and the sighs of the lovers,
> And the hard bright light composes
> A meaningless moment into an eternal fact
> Which a whistling messenger disappears with into a defile:
> One enjoys glory, one endures shame;
> He may, she must. There is no one to blame.[24]

To a romantic sensibility, this world, devoid of intention or value, will appear appalling: which presumably is why Goethe said "The lesson of the *Iliad* is that on this earth we must enact Hell."[25] And there is evidence that the Augustans felt not very differently; for when Horace comes to reckon up the moral lessons of Homer, he finds them to be such things as these:

> quidquid delirant reges plectuntur Achivi.
> seditione dolis scelere atque libidine et ira
> Iliacos intra muros peccatur et extra.[26]
>
> (However rulers rage, the people suffer. Both within Troy and among the besiegers, sinning goes on with treachery, stratagems, lust, and wrath.)

The only positive model he finds is the endurance of Ulysses. It would seem likely that Virgil shared his feelings. "Aeneas enters the poem wishing he were dead, the only epic hero to do so," as Wendell Claussen says,[27] and this—together with his passive horror at the fall of Troy, and his regret, which we have quoted, at killing Lausus—suggests in Aeneas the sensibility of a civilized man fallen into a barbaric age. Virgil expects a human meaning in time. It may be said of him, as Auden says of everyone who has followed Virgil,

> Our grief is not Greek: As we bury our dead
> We know without knowing there is reason for what we bear,
> That our hurt is not a desertion, that we are to pity
> Neither ourselves nor our city. . . .[28]

We may realize the truth of this if we look more closely at the way Virgil outlines his themes at the beginning of the *Aeneid*. In the first line he announces a different doctrine of inspiration from Homer's. Homer's view of inspiration is objective: both the *Iliad* and the *Odyssey* begin with invocations of the Muse:

> Sing, goddess, the wrath of Achilles, Peleus' son. . . .
>
> Tell me, Muse, of the man of many wiles. . . . .

Virgil, combining the two themes of war and a wandering man, contrasts himself with Homer by asserting his own presence and rule as poet:

> Arma virumque cano[29]
>
> (I sing arms and the man).

It is not until his second paragraph that he asks the Muse to help him. It seems like a mere figure of speech. But Homer probably took the Muse seriously: throughout his poetry moments of inspiration, irruptions of passion, and changes of mind are likely to be described as interferences by deities. Impulses often seem merely successive and discontinuous, much as Shakespeare represents the Greeks and Trojans in *Troilus and Cressida*. But Shakespeare exhibits this with an implied disquiet such as Virgil might have felt; Homer describes even character objectively. Homeric heroes rarely doubt their own intentions. The subjective inwardness of Aeneas's struggle of the will is something different, related to his sense of a divine purpose that must be fulfilled.

Correlatively, so to speak, with this presence of the poet in the poem, Virgil announces the presence of purpose in history: in his second line, in the phrase *fato profugus* (a fugitive by destiny), we have a key word, *fatum*, absent from Homer. Homer has *moira* and *ananke* (doom and necessity); but these are not, like *fatum*, instinct with the sense of a general purpose in history. Once into the *Aeneid*, we may feel a qualm whether, after all, this fate is not mere chance; as when Jupiter, in Book X, announces that he is impartial between Trojan and Italian:

> rex Iuppiter omnibus idem
> fata viam invenient.[30]

(Jupiter is king indifferently over all: the fates will find the way.)

Probably even here, fate, though impersonal, is purposive: but one cannot be quite sure. Moreover, in this second line Aeneas ceases to be *vir* (a hero), and becomes an exile, a refugee—by destiny. Is this pessimistic, implying that fate makes us suffer, or optimistic, that there is a purpose at work in our suffering?

The purpose involved is expressed in the final clause . . . *dum conderet urbem* (till he should build the city). There is a sense here of a suspended period of time quite alien to Homer, and this is confirmed in the next two lines by a further postponement, in the threefold prophecy. For Aeneas is not to found Rome itself: his city is Lavinium; his son's will be Alba Longa; only his remote descendants, three or four centuries hence, will found the true city. Homer scarcely uses suspense, the idea of postponed purpose, even as a narrative technique; his world is without expectation, without purpose, without hope beyond the individual life. His fall of Troy is not distinguished from the fall of any other city, whereas Virgil's is the collapse of an ancient civilization. And Homer has no idea, naturally, of a new civilization to found. Virgil's feeling rather resembles the Jewish: Aeneas, called upon to found a nation, plays the role of an

Abraham, Italy appears like a promised land, and the Romans like the chosen people. Finally, we see that Homer's first sentence closes on an emphatic "Achilles"; Virgil ends with

> altae moenia Romae
>
> (the walls of lofty Rome).

Homer celebrates heroes, who win, or lose, and die; Virgil celebrates the founder of a city. Indeed, it might be truer to say that Virgil celebrates not even the founder, but the city itself. Aeneas is so much *not* an epic hero—so much an ordinary civilized man dropped into the epic age—that the emotional focus normally provided in an epic by its hero seems in the *Aeneid* to be displaced on to Rome itself.

The sense of time that already pervades these seven opening lines, before Virgil invokes the Muse, is bound up with his intention of writing an epic whose real subject is Augustan Rome but whose story is that of Aeneas. Virgil seems deliberately to take his stand in the persona of Aeneas, one thousand years before his own lifetime, from there to look forward. It is as if, trying to make sense of the phantasies that beset a culture dying and being reborn, he can get at the reality of his own century only from a great distance in the past. If this is so, the central episode of the *Aeneid*, Aeneas's descent to the underworld, may provide a symbol for the entire book. He forces his way into the world of the dead to meet his father Anchises and to hear the history of his descendants, encountering on the way his past in the ghosts of Palinurus, Dido, and Deiphobus, who died at Troy.[31] The odd thing here is that it is Anchises—the past—who shows Aeneas, weary of his effort, how to engage the dimly known future. One may suggest that Virgil thought of himself as doing something similar to what he made Aeneas do.

The contrast with Homer may be illustrated further by looking at the difference between the shields of Achilles and of Aeneas.[32] Homer describes with relentless beauty the unchanging events of a world with no historical momentum: marriages, agriculture, battles. Virgil describes the ordered development of Roman history from Romulus to the peace of Augustus. The same difference is implicit in their treatment of similes. Homer's simile is based on one point of resemblance only; and this he forgets in order to develop the thing compared for its own sake, thus helping to build up a sense of the constant presence of a hard, clear, objective world beyond any specific troubles of men. Virgil's similes patiently pursue a developing resemblance. Once again we find Virgil dominated, even stylistically, by a sense of purposive time.

U

To be so dominated necessarily raises questions from which Homer was free. If there is a purpose in time, presumably the suffering of the righteous must be part of it. But then, what divinity can demand that the righteous suffer, and why? Again, this is a characteristically Jewish question, the question of Job. In his first paragraph Virgil implicitly raises the question of Aeneas's sufferings, first with a vague and terrible answer, *vi superum* (by violence of the gods): by divine power itself, all the gods. No, he corrects himself, *saevae memorem Iunonis ob iram* (through the remembering rage of savage Juno): only one devilish god. In the second paragraph he invokes the muse to help him answer the question

> quo numine laeso
> quidve dolens regina deum tot volvere casus
> insignem pietate virum, tot adire labores
> impulerit?[33]
>
> (by what divine majesty offended, by what grief did the queen of the gods drive a man so known for *pietas* through so many perils and labours?)

Virgil sometimes seems to be using his gods as epic machinery, but where *numen* (felt divine majesty) is mentioned, he seems to be deadly serious. This divinity is pursuing a man known for *pietas* (duty)—a word that, as we have said, is commonly associated by Virgil with testing and weariness, and that, when it is used to describe Aeneas's relationship toward his father Anchises, can suggest the love that will descend even to the underworld to seek its object. In fact, it is here almost the righteousness of a Hebrew prophet, of Abraham or Job.

In his next section, Virgil, like the Book of Job, offers a myth to explain the suffering of the righteous. Juno loved Carthage and dreaded the coming power of Rome. Virgil introduces us to huge vistas of space and time:

> urbs antiqua fuit . . . Tiberinaque longe
> ostia. . . .
>
> (There was an ancient city . . . over against Tiber's mouths far off. . . .)

There are vistas into the future, when there will be a race

> tyrias olim quae verteret arces
>
> (that some time will overthrow the Phoenician city)

—at some period, that is, between Aeneas's time and Virgil's. But there are also vistas reaching backward; Juno has already heard of a decree that this will happen, and already, because of the pains of the war at

Troy, the last event of the previous age, she hates Troy. And her wrath goes back into the older days, to Paris's decision against her beauty and to Jupiter's love for her rival, the boy Ganymede.

In the first paragraph, Virgil has solved the two poetic problems with which we began, by fusing his live self with the inert stuff of the old, over-used, objective epic, and by directing his epic toward his own ideal, Rome. At this point he is using something more like the technique of Callimachus and other Alexandrians, or, in Latin, like that of Catullus: he takes a mythological person, and imagines a romantic personality for him or her in the manner of the *epyllion* or miniature epic. Such a solution might seem to trivialize the issue; how far it does so in fact may depend on how far Virgil takes for granted the nature of his gods, even in their pettiness, as part of the universe.

In fact, Virgil abandons this explanation of Aeneas's pains almost immediately for another and stranger notion:

> tantae molis erat Romanam condere gentem[34]

> (there was so great a weight to lift in founding Rome)

as if to imply that so great a thing as Rome must require a great effort to build it. But the exact note is hard to catch. Does the passage culminate with despairing acceptance of the grimness of the world, or with pride in Rome?

The themes of Rome, destiny, suffering, and the gods thus abstractly stated are given concrete embodiment in the first episode of the *Aeneid*. At the end of the prologue Virgil has placed us at a great distance from the events we are to survey, giving us a god's-eye view of them. We focus on the Trojan sailors in the sea as Juno sees them. She descends from heaven: the view is localized on the seas around Sicily, where she persuades Aeolus to raise a storm against the Trojans. We rush down with the winds: and are suddenly placed with Aeneas, shouting out that those who died at Troy were three and four times blessed. The storm is hugely described, bringing us back to the god's-eye view:

> apparent rari nantes in gurgite vasto.[35]

> (A few men swimming emerge in the vast abyss.)

Neptune emerges to calm his sea: Virgil, strikingly, compares him and the waves to a man *pietate gravem ac meritis* (weighty with righteousness and virtues), calming a riot—that is, nature is illustrated by analogy with the human world, a thing rare in Virgil (or indeed in any poetry).

We shift back to the Trojans and the sudden stillness of their landfall, in a bay belonging to the nymphs. Aeneas cheers his crew with the old heroic idea that appears in the *Odyssey* and also in the Old English poem *Deor*: you have suffered worse than this, and it will pass. But he adds the new Virgilian touch: we are destined through all these troubles to reach Latium, where Troy will rise again. Aeneas pretends hope in his face, and forces his unhappiness deep into his heart.

When the Trojans sleep, we once more take the god's-eye view as Jupiter looks down on Africa. Venus appeals to him with the universal accusation against fate: *hic pietatis honos?* (Is this the way doing one's duty is rewarded?) Jupiter, with the smile with which he dispels storms, replies with a fuller account of the purpose of time, to which we shall revert.

This storm passage is thus framed between the two passages that overtly state the poem's intent, and clarifies and embodies that intent in four ways. First, Virgil, by employing the cinema technique of the changing point of view, alternating between the views of gods and men, suggests the theme of man against the universe—the hugeness of his troubles on earth, their littleness in heaven.

Second, he introduces us to Aeneas in two speeches, first as the world-weary, backward-looking ghost of Troy, then as the founder of Rome, forward-looking and infinitely enduring: one is again reminded of the Israelites in the Exodus, or of Abraham.

Third, he establishes the great contrasting themes of storm and calm, and suggests their universality, with Jupiter controlling the winds, and Neptune the waves. The simile comparing Neptune with a man dominating a mob probably suggested the recent pains of Rome. In 54 B.C., Cato— "with his calm and bold demeanour"[36]—had in just such a way silenced a crowd attacking him in resentment of his inquiries into bribery. Cato had already been treated by Sallust as the ideal type of Roman statesman; in a sense, therefore, this simile suggests the Republican inheritance of Augustus's principate, as well as the possibility of a connection between god and man.

Fourth, the episode is framed between two gods, who embody these themes of calm and storm. The *Aeneid* is at times apocalyptic:* we see the world split open to reveal on the one hand Juno, passionate, burning with frustrated love for Carthage, and on the other Jupiter, who replies *vultu, quo coelum tempestatesque serenat* (with the face with which he makes heaven and storms serene); the word *serenat* suggests "mental clarity,

---

* Here and throughout I use "apocalypse" and "apocalyptic" in their older sense of "unveiling the purposes that lie behind the world," without any necessary implication of disaster or ruin.

cheerfulness of soul, and the light of the southern sky."[37] Once again we find the classical dichotomy of controller and controlled in politics, of reason and passion in ethics, but now applied to the universe.

Jupiter, the controller, speaks, and Virgil preserves a careful ambiguity, whether he is declaring his will, which is fate (*neque me sententia vertit*, no thought turns me), or only declaring fate (*longius et volvens fatorum arcana movebo* (I shall further unroll and move the scroll of the secrets of fate). The world has a plan, but whether it is the plan of a person or not, we are not sure.

The destiny of Rome adumbrated at the opening of the *Aeneid* is now elaborated, and the threefold sequence—Lavinium, Alba Longa, Rome— is repeated; but now we have two added notions: first, the promise that Venus will raise Aeneas on high to the stars; second, an extension of history so far into the future that it opens on infinity.

> his ego nec metas rerum nec tempora pono:
> imperium sine fine dedi.
>
> (For them I set no limit or period for their state: I have given them empire without end.)

The two additions suggest something like a Jewish apocalypse. ". . . His name shall be called Wonderful, Counsellor, the Mighty God, the Everlasting Father, the Prince of Peace. Of the increase of his government and peace there shall be no end. . . ."[38]

The apocalyptic element continues. Sour Juno will transfer her love from Carthage to Rome: Virgil picks up the word *fovet* (warm, cherish), which he also used at the announcement of Juno's intention that Carthage should rule the world. With Jupiter she will cherish

> Romanos, rerum dominos, gentemque togatam.[39]
>
> (the Romans, lords of the universe, the people of the toga.)

This line, according to Suetonius, was a favourite with Augustus.[40] It mentioned the toga, the robe associated with ancient Roman gravity and the arts of peace, the wearing of which Augustus encouraged; and it suggests that the Romans will be "lords of things"—the literal meaning of the strangely loaded Latin word *rerum*, which in effect means "of the universe." Aeneas's men after the storm were *fessi rerum* (world weary, weary of their fate):[41] and soon in Book I is to come the line

> sunt lacrimae rerum et mentem mortalia tangunt.[42]
>
> (Tears exist for the way things happen [i.e. for the nature of the world and our fate] and mortality touches the heart.)

The fate of Rome and the fate of the world are involved together.

Virgil shifts for a moment from the linear, Jewish conception of time to a cyclical notion, more common among the Greeks, by suggesting that in Rome Troy will conquer Greece:

> domus Assaraci . . . victis dominabitur Argis[43]
>
> (the house of Assaracus . . . will rule the conquered Greeks.)

This is a view going back to Herodotus, in which East and West, Troy and Greece, Greece and Persia, endlessly alternate. But then the parallel appears again with Isaiah's Prince of Peace: for there is to be not only a race whose destiny opens on infinity, but also a single man—

> imperium oceano, famam qui terminet astris[44]

—a man "who will limit his empire at the ocean, his fame at the stars." This man is probably Augustus, although Servius, the 4th-century commentator, says these lines originally referred to Julius Caesar.[45] Whoever is meant, he will ascend to heaven loaded with the spoils of the East, and will, like Aeneas, receive prayers.

There follows a line that is really metaphysical as well as apocalyptic:

> aspera tum positis mitescent saecula bellis.[46]
>
> (Then, wars laid aside, the sour centuries will begin to ripen.)

The emphatic *aspera* here picks up *aspera Iuno*, the sour Juno of 13 lines earlier, who is to cherish Rome. The demonic, the uncontrolledly passionate element that is part of the very nature of things, "the fibrous infelicity of time,"[47] will become part of the ripe sweet fruit of the new age. This, we may note, is a different conception of passion from that which represents it as merely controlled by reason: here passion itself is to change. But then again, after the return of the figures of the golden age, when we see Vesta, grey-headed faith, and Romulus no longer at civil war with Remus—a striking example of the Roman ability to put gods, abstractions, and heroes on one level of divinity—the vision ends with the normal ideal of law conquering fury. This closing image is tied to a particular historical event: Augustus announcing world peace in 29 B.C. by closing the gates of Janus's temple; these were never closed when there was war, and they had stood open then for more than two centuries. The final intense lines, about Fury raging in chains, probably represent a picture by Apelles presented to the forum by Augustus. Here, finally, the paradox suggested by the comparison of Neptune with Cato—that a god and a Roman citizen could be one—is fulfilled in Augustus.

This opening passage, then, presents us sharply with the problem: Virgil—in the character of Aeneas, the exile seeking through faith a country where his descendants will build the apocalyptic city of Rome—evinced feelings about humanity, fate, and time that, already adumbrated in the Old Testament, were to be crystallized a century later in the Epistle to the Hebrews:

> These all died in faith, not having received the promises, but having seen them afar off, and were persuaded of them, and embraced them, and confessed that they were strangers and pilgrims on the earth. For they that say such things declare plainly that they seek a country. And truly, if they had been mindful of that country from whence they came out, they might have had opportunity to have returned. But now they desire a better country, that is, an heavenly: wherefore God is not ashamed to be called their God: for he hath prepared for them a city.[48]

Here, in the Judaeo-Christian tradition, the historic feeling of the Israelites for the promised land appears to have been transformed into a morality about all human life. And Virgil seems to have created a very similar morality for his mythical hero Aeneas, locating its end-point, however, in historical Rome. Did he borrow the idea from Jewish sources, or was it a product of his personal situation?

Light is shed on this question by considering the 4th *Eclogue*, written for the statesman Pollio, who had just negotiated the Peace of Brundisium in 40 B.C. (that is, at least 10 years before Virgil began serious work on the *Aeneid*). Here the apocalyptic vision of peace is associated with a particular person and with Rome. There is a further strange feature: the man of destiny is a new-born child. The poem strongly resembles Isaiah's prophecy:

> Behold a virgin shall conceive, and bear a son, and shall call his name Immanuel. . . . For before the child shall know to refuse the evil, and choose the good, the land that thou abhorrest shall be forsaken of both her kings. . . . For unto us a child is born. . . . The wolf also shall dwell with the lamb, and the leopard shall lie down with the kid; and the calf and the young lion and the fatling together; and a little child shall lead them. . . . And the sucking child shall play on the hole of the asp . . . for the earth shall be full of the knowledge of the Lord, as the waters cover the sea. . . . The desert shall rejoice, and blossom as the rose. . . .[49]

Compare this with the following passage in the 4th *Eclogue*:

> iam redit et virgo, redeunt Saturnia regna
> iam nova progenies caelo demittitur alto. . . .
> tu modo nascenti puero, quo ferrea primum

> desinet ac toto surget gens aurea mundo,
> casta fave Lucina.
> . . . nec magnos metuent armenta leones:
> ipsa tibi blandos fundent cunabula flores:
> occidet et serpens. . . .
> at simul heroum laudes et facta parentis
> iam legere et quae sit poteris cognoscere virtus
> . . . erunt etiam altera bella
> atque iterum ad Troiam magnus mittetur Achilles. . . .
> aspice convexo nutantem pondere mundum
> terrasque tractusque maris caelumque profundum;
> aspice venturo laetantur ut omnia seaclo.[50]

(Now the virgin [Justice] is returning, and the golden age. Now a new generation is being sent down from heaven. . . . Only, goddess of childbirth, smile on the child being born, under whom the iron race shall first cease, and a golden race spring up through all the world. . . . Nor shall the herds fear the huge lions. Your very cradle will pour out flowers to please you. The serpent shall perish. . . . But as soon as you can read the praises of heroes and your father's deeds and can discern what virtue is . . . there shall be a second warfare and again great Achilles shall be sent to Troy. . . . See the world bowing with its massive dome, the lands and seas and deep heaven. See how all things delight in the age that is to come.)

Virgil, we can scarcely doubt, knew the Book of Isaiah: and it is noteworthy that Isaiah LXV applies this very prophecy to the concrete situation in Jerusalem after the exile, providing a precedent for Virgil's placing his apocalypse of the *Aeneid* in Rome.

The tone of Virgil's prophecy, however, does not quite accord with the august associations of Isaiah and of the *Aeneid* as a whole: it is gentle, perhaps playful at times, and fairy-tale in atmosphere. Isaiah speaks of the stern choice of good and evil: Virgil, of reading the deeds of heroes. The wolf dwells with the lamb in Isaiah: in Virgil the sheep change colour in the fields. In Isaiah, the desert will blossom as the rose: in Virgil, the child's cradle will pour out flowers. Everything is focussed on the child; even the heroes of old times will return when he is old enough to read about them, as if his boyish wishes will control history.

Furthermore, the most natural identification of the child gives him no special importance. The author of a previous chapter maintains that his identity is deliberately left ambiguous.* But it appears to me that only the conflicting interpretations caused by hindsight offer this sense of ambiguity. Virgil announces a poem about woods, but woods worthy of a consul, *consule dignae*: that is, the poem is written for Pollio. He addresses Pollio emphatically:

* See Ch. 11, "Literature and Society in Augustan Rome," p. 280.

> teque adeo decus hoc aevi, te consule, inibit

> (when you, I say, when you are consul this glorious age shall begin)

and underlines it with

> te duce, si qua manent sceleris vestigia nostri
> inrita perpetua solvent formidine terras.

> (under your leadership, any traces that remain of our guilt will
> become void and release the earth from its perpetual dread.)

Two lines later, with no mention of any other man intervening, Virgil says of the child:

> pacatumque reget patriis virtutibus orbem

> (he will rule a world made peaceful by his father's virtues).

Whose can this father possibly be but Pollio? And in fact only one person ever laid claim to being the child: Pollio's son, Asinius Gallus.

The obvious objections—first, that Pollio's son could not be said to be the offspring of the gods, and second, that he was not going to rule the world—have little force if the poem is, as I have said, a tender, sweet, and humorous birthday ode, written after Pollio negotiated the Peace of Brundisium, and announcing that surely this baby, born as a dark age seems to be closing, is going to fulfil all our hopes and be king of the world.

If the poem is of this kind, it conforms to the pattern of the other eclogues: all are set in a land where wishes can be fulfilled, and the harsher aspects of the real world are recognized only mutedly, and adorned in the golden dreamland of Arcadia. This is, however, clearly not the whole truth about the 4th *Eclogue*. One would expect a force of agonized desire in Virgil's hopes for peace in the world of 40 B.C., and this seems borne out in particular by the noble passage beginning

> adgredere o magnos (aderit iam tempus) honores
> cara deum suboles, magnum Iovis incrementum.

> (Enter on your high honours [the hour will soon be here], dear child
> of the gods, great offspring of Jupiter!)

Virgil, I think, has been carried away into fusing a tender poem for a baby with a state poem about the issues of the world and the universe, war and peace, world power and omnipotent gods. The imagery with which he makes the fusion probably comes from Isaiah: but the need to do so, I believe, arises spontaneously, from within his own nature.

If this is true, the fusion seems to bear witness to a wish that the tender and personal side of life, and the side where issues of power and politics are settled, could be one. That this wish was very much present in Virgil we can confirm by returning to the *Aeneid*; for a dominant theme of that poem is the tragedy of the destruction of individual lives (Dido, Camilla, Turnus), which is necessary for the building of world peace and the glory of Rome. And included in this theme are the sufferings of Aeneas: as we have seen, he crushes part of himself in leaving Dido.

Now, at this climactic moment of Dido's desertion, Virgil comes close to evoking the 4th *Eclogue*. Dido's first appeal to Aeneas ends:

> saltem si qua mihi de te suscepta fuisset
> ante fugam suboles, si quis mihi parvulus aula
> luderet Aeneas, qui te tamen ore referret,
> non equidem omnino capta ac deserta viderer.[51]

> (If there were only born to me a child by you before your flight, if there were a little tiny Aeneas to play for me at home, who in spite of everything would bring you back by his face, I should not think myself wholly enslaved and deserted.)

This speech, heart-rending in itself, is given a special poignancy in relation to the rest of the poem by being the only point in the 12 books where the diminutive form of an adjective, the sign of personal affection, is used: *parvulus*. It is a moment, therefore, when the personal breaks out in protest against the divine and the political. But, further, it directly evokes Catullus's hymeneal, where the same diminutive is used in the context of the child's evoking its father's likeness:

> Torquatus volo parvulus
> matris e gremio suae
> porrigens teneras manus
> dulce rideat ad patrem
>   semihiante labello.
> sit suo similis patri. . . .[52]

> (I want a little tiny Torquatus reaching out his soft hands from his mother's breast to laugh sweetly to his father with half-opened mouth. May he be like his father. . . .)

And that scene again is echoed by the 4th *Eclogue's* end:

> incipe, parve puer, risu cognoscere matrem.[53]

> (Begin, little boy, to recognize your mother with a smile.)

Catullus's poem thus forms a bridge, making firm the general resemblance between Virgil's two passages.

The *Aeneid*, then, embodies a terrible tension between the public and the personal, in which the personal seems to be the loser. The potentially tragic conflict between the individual and society has always inspired the literary imagination—as, recently, in Pasternak's *Doctor Zhivago*. This tension Virgil could reconcile only in the dream world of Arcadia, where passion does not fight with reason, power politics is the subject of a nursery rhyme, and an old friend's son can be hailed emperor of the universe.

What is resolved in Arcadia is not merely the dichotomy between politics and persons, but also that between reason and passion, and, ultimately, that between the gods who represent fate and the human beings who endure it. This resolution suggests a paradox well phrased by Chesterton:

> Any agnostic or atheist whose childhood has known a real Christmas has ever afterwards . . . an association in his mind between . . . the idea of a baby and the idea of unknown strength that sustains the stars . . .; for him there will always be some savour of religion about the mere picture of a mother and a baby; some hint of mercy and softening about the mere mention of the dreadful name of God. But the two ideas are not naturally or necessarily combined. They would not be necessarily combined for an ancient Greek or a Chinaman, even for Aristotle or Confucius. . . . In other words, this combination of ideas has emphatically . . . altered human nature. . . . Omnipotence and impotence, or divinity and infancy, do definitely make a sort of epigram which a million repetitions cannot turn into a platitude. It is not unreasonable to call it unique. Bethlehem is emphatically a place where extremes meet.[54]

It was this combination of ideas, this peaceful meeting of extremes, that Virgil longed for, and succeeded in envisaging at least in his dream world. It is not unreasonable, then, to call the 4th *Eclogue* a prophecy of Christ; but we may perhaps guess that the yearning to see an identification of the divine, the political, and the intimately personal was not peculiar to Virgil in the Roman world, but was to play a large part in the spread of Christianity.

There is a final dichotomy involved in this yearning—between tragedy, the important event that happens to important people, and comedy, the trivial lives of the ordinary—that Auerbach has pointed out as normal in Graeco-Roman literature: the dichotomy that is, again, resolved in the Gospels and in Christian literature.[55] Virgil, although he has the Jewish sense of purpose, history, and time, cannot quite achieve the Judaeo-Christian sense of humanity and of the relation of humanity to the ultimate ruler of the universe. His chosen race is not the little and politically insignificant one of biblical thought ("the Lord did not set his love upon you, nor choose you, because ye were more in number than any people; for ye were the fewest of all people: but because the Lord loved you, and because he would keep the oath which he had sworn unto your fathers, hath the Lord brought you out with a mighty hand").[56] Nor is Virgil's Jupiter the God whose bowels are troubled for Ephraim, his dear son.[57]

Virgil's great gods are indeed still Homer's, or worse: they are human primarily in their capriciousness. Some divine appearances in the *Aeneid* seem little more than epic machinery (for example, Aeolus and the winds in Book I). But there are three kinds of epiphany that seem something more: first, the little domestic and state gods, *penatibus et magnis dis*,[58] whom Aeneas is actually carrying to Italy; with them goes the fortune of Troy. They may be classed perhaps with the nymphs of the bay where the Trojans make landfall, and with similar divinities of nature. These seem to have been the most real of gods to the Roman mind: they embody *numen*, all-pervading divine power. Virgil's lines about the Capitoline hill give the feeling:

> hoc nemus, hunc, inquit, frondoso vertice collem,
> quis deus incertum est, habitat deus.[59]
>
> (This grove, he says, this hill with its leafy top, what god we do not know, but certainly some god haunts.)

Seneca quotes these lines in one of his *Epistulae morales*, and comments that if ever you come across a thick secluded grove, or a cave beneath a mountain, or a dark or deep pool, their qualities *fidem tibi numinis faciet* (will give you confidence in a present deity).[60] He, however, uses this notion to show that we have the same feeling in the presence of a good man: a Stoic feeling that Virgil adumbrates in Anchises' speech at the end of Book VI.[61] Here, then, is divinity pervading the universe: a primitive feeling taken up by the Stoics.

The second kind of epiphany is one of breathtaking beauty, when Venus appears: *vera incessu patuit dea*[62] (the true goddess was made known by her motion). It suggests the Epicurean idea of gods who dwell apart, but of whom we have visions that influence us by their sheer beauty. Venus is unlike an Epicurean deity, however, in that here she is actively interested in her son.

Thirdly, we have the gods who are the forces of fate: above all, Jupiter and Juno, personifications of control and passion, whose conflict we have already discussed. These have a horrible epiphany, an apocalypse of demons, at the fall of Troy: behind the shattered masses of masonry, rocks torn from rocks, smoke eddying up mixed with dust, Neptune, Juno, Pallas Athene, and Jupiter himself,

apparent dirae facies inimicaque Troiae
numina magna deum.[63]

(terrible shapes emerge, huge epiphanies of gods, hating Troy.)

Contemplating these *numina*, we may understand why another and most important reason for the spread of Christianity was that it claimed to control demons. Few have felt this sense of malignant chaos behind phenomena for 2000 years—until, perhaps, Hiroshima. Ronald Knox commented: "From the old Roman augurs down to Henri Bergson, we have had the temptation to worship the *numen*, the Life-Force at the back of things. And Hiroshima was its epiphany."[64]

This passage on the fall of Troy is the climax of an indictment against the gods that builds up throughout Book II.[65] Panthus, Apollo's priest, calls Jupiter *ferus* (ferocious).[66] "It is only in an extreme situation," says Servius, "that even a priest rushes to accuse the gods." And now Aeneas himself is carried blindly into a ruinous action,

talibus Othryadae dictis et numine divum[67]

(at Othryades' words and possessed by the gods.)

(We may note the dual causation, a characteristic turn of Virgil's.) In the same action the Trojans go *haud numine nostro*[68] (with a divinity, but not on our side). At a moment of hope Cassandra is seen dragged captive, and Aeneas says

Heu! nihil invitis fas quemquam fidere divis.[69]

(Alas! in nothing may one trust the gods against their will.)

Then Rhipeus falls,

. . . iustissimus unus
qui fuit in Teucris et servantissimus aequi
(dis aliter visum).[70]

(the one most just, most observant of righteousness of all the Trojans:
but the gods do not see things as we do, their will was otherwise.)

(This, perhaps, has the Virgilian ambiguity: Seneca makes the last three words an expression of resigned faith, but it can scarcely be only that.) Finally, Priam is killed before the altar: and Servius comments, "It is shown implicitly that religion profits nothing." After this maleficent epiphany, Book III begins:

Postquam res Asiae Priamique evertere gentem
immeritam visum superis . . .[71]

(After it seemed fit to the gods to overthrow the matter of Asia and
Priam's race, undeservedly . . .).

We are perhaps entitled to ask of any poem of the scope of the *Aeneid* that it give us an answer to the question, "What is the world for?" In Book II we feel how much despair entered into Virgil's ultimate sense of the world; and we do not receive much comfort when we turn to his exposition of the other world in Book VI. It is not the noble *pietas* of Aeneas, confronting even death to see his father, that moves the powers below, but the sinister talisman of the golden bough:

> si te nulla movet tantae pietatis imago
> at ramum hunc . . . agnoscas[72]
>
> (If the appearance of such piety does not move you, know this bough),

says the Sibyl to Charon. The rush of souls to Acheron, thick as leaves at the first autumn frost, seems all melancholy—a mood that mingles with a wish for death: the souls are like birds migrating south, as it were, to a happier place than this world.[73] The Underworld is a confused and ambiguous place: the book closes with a doubt, as Aeneas leaves by the gate of false dreams.[74] Virgil mingles Homeric references with Stoic philosophy, and yet implicitly condemns Stoicism (which approved suicide) by condemning the suicide of those who loathed the light (*lucem perosi*).[75] Conversely, Aeneas wonders at the *lucis miseris tam dira cupido*[76] (the crazy lust for light) of the wretches who wish to be reborn. At the end of the book we have the catalogue of Roman heroes, culminating in Virgil's most convincing claim for Rome:

> tu regere imperio populos, Romane, memento
> (hae tibi erunt artes) pacisque imponere morem
> parcere subiectis et debellare superbos.[77]
>
> (You, Roman, remember to rule the peoples with your empire [these shall be the arts for you], to set law upon peace, to spare the defeated, and war down the proud.)

Here, we might be tempted to say, Virgil, uncertain of his other world, places all his hopes in this world, in Rome: the world exists for Rome. But immediately following, to crown the whole book, we see Marcellus, Augustus's nephew, who is doomed to die young; his untimely death is greeted with the lines:

> . . . manibus date lilia plenis
> purpureos spargam flores animamque nepotis
> his saltem accumulem donis et fungar inani
> munere.[78]
>
> (give lilies with full hands: let me scatter purple flowers and heap over my descendant's ghost at least these gifts and fulfil a pointless ceremony.)

Brooks Otis suggests that the point of the Marcellus episode is to show that "the ordeal of empire is based on sacrifice, especially sacrifice of the young."[79]

> . . . nimium vobis Romana propago
> visa potens, superi, propria haec si dona fuissent.[80]
>
> (you thought the Roman race would be too strong, ye gods, if these gifts were to be our inviolable possession.)

But the melancholy is too strong to let us see this as merely a warning against *hybris* (which is Otis's suggestion); we feel also another indictment of the gods, coupled with a doubt even of the value of empire.

Virgil's sense of life, indeed, seems to be tragic. The most securely happy passage is perhaps the vision of future Rome, which gives a double vision as we walk with Aeneas over its site:

> . . . passimque armenta videbant
> Romanoque Foro et lautis mugire Carinis.[81]
>
> (they saw cattle all about, lowing in the Roman Forum and in gay Carinae.)

We are reminded here of Virgil's great praise of Italy in the *Georgics*.[82] Augustus's stress on Italian patriotism must have been a most welcome item of his policy to Virgil. In the country and in the country gods, he finds peace and beauty: in the prehistoric state of Rome as a quiet village and in the unknown god of the Capitoline grove. It is significant that Virgil chooses as the original inhabitants of Rome the Arcadians, as if he would transfer there the pastoral world of the *Eclogues*. The notion was probably not created by him, though we do not find it before his time: it is also found in Livy, Dionysius of Halicarnassus, and Strabo. Although we may sometimes doubt that Augustus's reign fulfilled for Virgil his prophecy of *Saturnia regna*[83] (the kingdoms of the golden age)—he seemed to like it best from a distance—we can be sure that Italy was for him *Saturnia tellus*[84] (the land of the golden age).

He evokes Saturn's reign during Aeneas's wanderings over Rome in another way. Evander says of the Capitol, together with the Janiculum Hill,

> haec duo praeterea disiectis oppida muris,
> reliquias veterumque vides monimenta virorum.
> hanc Ianus pater, hanc Saturnus condidit arcem;
> Ianiculum huic, illi fuerat Saturnia nomen.[85]
>
> (These two towns besides with walls overthrown, these that you see are the ruins and memorials of men of old. This fort father Janus built, and this Saturn: Janiculum this was called, this Saturnia.)

Once more Virgil evokes a vista both forward and back over many centuries. Rome has been a town in the golden age; now, it is a village of Arcadians; it will, in Virgil's time, again be a city. I wonder if it is hindsight, because cattle have wandered again in a ruined city over Virgil's forum, to see in this, as perhaps in the narrative of the fall of Troy, a doubt in Virgil's mind whether history really had reached its term in Rome?

The second half of the same book has no doubts, describing the shield of Aeneas with its pictures of Rome culminating in Actium, the defeat of the barbaric East by Rome, and Augustus's triumph. Here, if anywhere in the *Aeneid*, the Virgilian duality vanishes: there is no shift of vision to the losing side, and the gods who were demons at Troy become emblems of rationality:

> omnigenumque deum monstra et latrator Anubis
> contra Neptunum et Venerem contraque Minervam
> tela tenent.[86]

> (monstrous gods of every form and barking Anubis carry weapons against Neptune and Venus and against Minerva.)

The end is simply a one-sided military procession, unless we count

> pontem indignatus Araxes[87]

> (the river Araxes unconsenting to his bridge)

as an example of shifted viewpoint.

In style and content alike, this passage justifies Auden's criticism:

> Behind your verse so masterfully made
> We hear the weeping of a Muse betrayed.[88]

If all the *Aeneid* had been like this, John Keble's picture of a gentle Virgil working at an unwelcome task would be just, and we should perhaps conclude that Augustan Rome was distasteful to him. But most of the *Aeneid* is different, and the other evocations of empire have a more excited and personal thrill. We might reflect that, because Virgil died in 19 B.C., he was fortunate enough to live through only the very first years of a new age—a time when it is always possible to hope that all promises are being fulfilled.

We can never be sure whether it is right to see Virgil as a shy, provincial, empathic man in love with the hope of a new age, though burdened by doubt; indeed, how far can we ever judge accurately the sensibility of a past age? The duality in Virgil between law and emotion, reason and sentiment, a modern reader can understand; but the shield of Aeneas in

Book VIII is followed by a passage that appears to go beyond mere military brassiness into very strange perversities of taste, revealing a third Virgil altogether. There is first the artificiality of the passage in which Aeneas's ships, cut in Cybele's sacred groves and now threatened with burning, are transformed into nymphs. We are led to expect a poignant miracle; but Virgil describes it thus:

> delphinumque modo demersis aequora rostris
> ima petunt. hinc virgineae, mirabile monstrum,
> reddunt se totidem facies . . .[89]

> (and like dolphins dipping their beaks into the water they dive into the abyss. From there they come out, wonderful portent, as virgin forms in like number . . .).

The beautiful movements of dolphins and their eerily human quality may be meant to make a transition between ships and maidens. But Virgil chooses to stress neither of these points, but rather the likeness of ships' beaks to dolphins' noses. The comparison is just: but is it not slightly, and deliberately, comic? And does not this comic touch, followed by their immediate appearance as maidens, give a mingling of sensations strongly suggestive of what the 1960s were to call "high camp"? Thereafter we have the episode of Nisus and Euryalus in the Italian camp: apparently intended as a description of a beautiful, wholly committed homosexual relationship ending in Nisus's heroic throwing away of his life in an attempt to save his friend. Once more, we have the suggestion of the horror of Virgil's gods, and of the genuine fear of the ancient Roman of demonic possession, expressed in Virgil's balanced duality:

> dine hunc ardorem mentibus addunt,
> Euryale, an sua cuique deus fit dira cupido?[90]

> (Do the gods put this fire in our hearts, Euryalus: or does everyone's mad desire become his god?)

But the duality vanishes, and the horror mounts. Nisus and Euryalus then conduct a mad massacre of sleeping men, described with the utmost horror, as in this picture of a man stabbed in the chest:

> purpuream vomit ille animam et cum sanguine mixta
> vina refert moriens[91]

> (He belches out his purple life and, dying, brings up wine mixed with blood).

Then follows the nightmarish pursuit of the two through the dark labyrinthine woods, pervaded by a hysterical sense of lostness, and the death of Euryalus, described with a lush abundance of epithet that overgoes its Catullan original, and again seems worthy of the adjective "camp." Whereas Catullus had

> nec meum respectet, ut ante, amorem,
> qui illius culpa cecidit velut prati
> ultimi flos, praetereunte postquam
>   tactus aratro est[92]

> (nor will she think again, as once she did, of my love, which by her fault has fallen like a flower at the extreme edge of a meadow after it is grazed by the plough that passes by),

Virgil gives

> volvitur Euryalus leto, pulchrosque per artus
> it cruor inque umeros cervix conlapsa recumbit:
> purpureus veluti cum flos succisus aratro
> languescit moriens, lassove papavera collo
> demisere caput, pluvia cum forte gravantur.[93]

> (Euryalus rolls over in death, and over his lovely limbs the blood goes, and on his shoulders sinks his drooping neck: as when a purple flower, undercut by the plough, droops in death, or as poppies with weary neck sink down their head, when they are weighted, it happens, by a shower.)

This over-ripe style with its double simile, and its combination of homosexuality and sadism to produce a languorous aesthetic effect, reminds one of the rich, lustrous prose of Baron Corvo. It may be fine; it can even be felt as pathetic; but it is not fine or pathetic in the way of the divided, sensitive Virgil. Nisus dies avenging Euryalus, and Virgil hopes that his verse will preserve for ever the memory of this happy pair (*fortunati ambo*)[94]; yet their acts were mad, murderous, and cruel.

One might pass off the massacre as an expression of the fascinated horror that Virgil feels about the heroic age, which we have already looked at. Yet even then the disgust is over-rich. And the total effect of Book IX does suggest a sick sophistication, again reminiscent of the 1960s. An anti-Virgil seems to me to emerge here, in tune with the nastier side of Augustan Rome—the tasteless marble buildings, and the fights of gladiators and wild beasts in the arena. Virgil wrote in an age that had accepted and institutionalized bestial violence. Part of this passage reminds one of the terrible passage in Augustine's confessions about Alypius, the youth who, loathing gladiatorial shows, was induced to go to one and was overcome by blood-lust; part of it presages the baroque style of later Roman literature;[95] and altogether it shows a kind of sophistication that is not ours—though it might be held, bearing in mind Virgil's normal empathy, sensitivity, and duality, to be more complex than ours. For Virgil is not a poet of whom one can say, as of Shakespeare, that he has many moods. The moods interweave into a whole, and some of the qualities that appear in Book IX permeate, though less obviously, the rest of the *Aeneid*.

Virgil thus remains a figure beyond our grasp, and his relation with the rest of his culture is a complex one. On the whole, one would suppose him unhappy in it. Dante seized on this point in some of his uses of Virgilian themes, most notably when he chooses Rhipeus as one of his just pagans, deemed fit to enter heaven, as if he were saying that, after all, God does see as man sees, and that there is ultimate justice.[96] Again, at a high point of the *Divine Comedy*, when Beatrice is coming and Virgil is about to vanish, Dante evokes two lines of the *Aeneid*. One is Dido's doomed words as her love for Aeneas begins to burn:

> agnosco veteris vestigia flammae.[97]

> (I recognize the tokens of the old flame.)

Dante has the same *conosco i segni dell' antica fiamma*:[98] but this is to greet his happiness. And this underlines the more striking use of Virgil's most melancholy words, with which his vision of the underworld ends, to express Dante's utter joy:

> Manibus o date lilia plenis[99]

> (Give lilies with full hands)

cry the ministers in front of Beatrice. Dante surely implies: where your vision failed in misery, our joy begins; where your individual personalities fell crushed, in our heaven they rise.

Dante makes Virgil return to the underworld in the *Divine Comedy*. Virgil himself had been able to conceive of no other, higher fate than to wander in the Elysian Fields with the wise. The words that Dante puts into Virgil's mouth—

> senza speme vivemo in disio[100]

> (without hope we live in desire)—

do express a strong element in Virgil's feeling about the world he knew.

In social terms, this is only to say that the *Aeneid*, working on traditional culture and trying to transform it, uncovers, and brings near to being transcended, problems that classical and Augustan culture itself eventually resolved by adopting Christianity. Virgil adumbrates in imagination what Pasternak alleged of the historical effect of Christ:

> into this tasteless heap of gold and marble, He came, and from that moment there were neither gods nor peoples, there was only man. . . .[101]

References

1. *Keble's Lectures on Poetry*, trans. by E. K. Francis, Vol. II (Oxford 1912), p. 396.
2. Cf. Macrobius, *Saturnalia* I, 24, 11; Horace, *Odes* II, 12.
3. *Aeneid* I, 1.
4. OWEN BARFIELD, *Poetic Diction*, 2nd edn (London 1952), p. 96.
5. *Aen.* I, 462; *Iliad* III, 158. Cf. W. F. JACKSON KNIGHT, *Roman Vergil*, rev. edn (London 1966), p. 240.
6. *Aen.* VIII, 387–92.
7. *ibid.*, I, 498 ff., and IV, 143 ff.; cf. R. W. B. LEWIS "On Translating the Aeneid," in STEELE COMMAGER, *Virgil: a Collection of Critical Essays* (Englewood Cliffs 1966), pp. 41–52.
8. *Aen.* IV, 421–2.
9. *ibid.*, 437–49.
10. Augustine, *De civitate Dei* IX, 4, trans. by J. Healey, ed. by R. V. G. Tasker, Vol. I (London 1945), p. 257.
11. C. N. COCHRANE, *Christianity and Classical Culture*, rev. edn (Oxford 1944), *passim*.
12. *Res gestae divi Augusti*, ed. by P. A. Brunt and J. M. Moore (Oxford 1967), pp. 35–6; cf. D. EARL, *The Age of Augustus* (London 1968), pl. 38.
13. Augustine, *op. cit.*, pp. 257 ff.
14. Augustine, *De moribus ecclesiae* I, 15, 25; cf. COCHRANE, *op. cit.*, p. 342.
15. *Aen.* X, 824; cf. *Aen.* IV, ed. by R. G. Austin (Oxford 1955), pp. 121 ff.
16. *ibid.*, X, 826.
17. *ibid.*, I, 220–1.
18. *ibid.*, IV, 393–6.
19. R. S. CONWAY, *The Vergilian Age* (New York 1967), pp. 102 f.
20. *Georgics* IV, 17.
21. BROOKS OTIS, *Virgil: a Study in Civilized Poetry* (Oxford 1964), Ch. III.
22. A. W. KINGLAKE, *Eothen* (London 1844), Ch. IV ("Everyman" edn [London 1908], p. 33).
23. *Iliad* XXIV, 540–2.
24. W. H. AUDEN, "Memorial for the City," *Collected Shorter Poems, 1927–1957* (London 1966), p. 289.
25. See C. S. LEWIS, *A Preface to Paradise Lost* (London 1942), p. 30.
26. Horace, *Epistles* I, 2, 14–6.
27. W. CLAUSEN, "An Interpretation of the Aeneid," in COMMAGER, *op. cit.*, p. 77.

28. AUDEN, *op. cit.*, p. 290; cf. LEWIS, *op. cit.*, Ch. V and VI.
29. *Aen.* I, 1.
30. *ibid.*, X, 112–3.
31. Cf. OTIS, *op. cit.*, pp. 278–307.
32. *Iliad* XVIII, 478–608; *Aen.* VIII, 626–728.
33. *Aen.* I, 8–11; cf. V. PÖSCHL, "Basic Themes," in COMMAGER, *op. cit.*, pp. 164–82.
34. *Aen.* I, 33.
35. *ibid.*, 118.
36. Plutarch, *Cato minor*, Ch. XLIV.
37. *Aen.* I, 255; cf. PÖSCHL, *op. cit.*, p. 168.
38. Isaiah IX, 6–7.
39. *Aen.* I, 282.
40. Suetonius, *De vita caesarum, Divus Augustus*, Ch. XL.
41. *Aen.* I, 178.
42. *ibid.*, 462.
43. *ibid.*, 284–5.
44. *ibid.*, 287.
45. Cf. T. FRANK, *Vergil* (Oxford 1922), Ch. VI.
46. *Aen.* I, 291.
47. CHARLES WILLIAMS, *Taliessin Through Logres* (Oxford 1938), p. 81.
48. Hebrews XI, 13–6.
49. Isaiah VII, 14 and 16; IX, 6; XI, 6, 8, and 9; XXXV, 1.
50. *Eclogues* IV, 6–10, 22–4, 26–7, 35–6, and 50–1.
51. *Aen.* IV, 327–30.
52. Catullus, 61, 209–16.
53. *Ecl.* IV, 62.
54. G. K. CHESTERTON, *The Everlasting Man* (London 1925), Part II, Ch. I.
55. ERICH AUERBACH, *Mimesis*, trans. by W. Trask (Princeton 1953), Ch. I and II.
56. Deuteronomy VII, 7–8.
57. Jeremiah XXXI, 20.
58. *Aen.* III, 12.
59. *ibid.*, VIII, 351–2.
60. Seneca, *Epistulae morales* XLI.
61. *Aen.* VI, 724 ff.
62. *ibid.*, I, 405.
63. *ibid.*, II, 622–3.
64. R. A. KNOX, *God and the Atom* (London 1945), p. 14.
65. Cf. *Aen.* II, ed. by R. G. Austin (Oxford 1955), pp. XIX–XX.
66. *Aen.* II, 326.
67. *ibid.*, 336.
68. *ibid.*, 396.
69. *ibid.*, 402.
70. *ibid.*, 426–8; cf. Seneca, *Ep. mor.* XCVIII.
71. *Aen.* III, 1–2.
72. *ibid.*, VI, 405–7.

73. *ibid.*, 309–12.
74. *ibid.*, 898.
75. *ibid.*, 435.
76. *ibid.*, 721.
77. *ibid.*, 851–3.
78. *ibid.*, 883–6.
79. OTIS, *op. cit.*, p. 303.
80. *Aen.* VI, 870–1.
81. *ibid.*, VIII, 360–1.
82. *Georg.* II, 136–76, and 513–40.
83. *Ecl.* IV, 6; cf. *Aen.* VI, 792 f.
84. *Georg.* IV, 173.
85. *Aen.* VIII, 355–8.
86. *ibid.*, 698–700.
87. *ibid.*, 728.
88. W. H. AUDEN, "Secondary Epic," *op. cit.*, pp. 296–7.
89. *Aen.* IX, 119–22.
90. *ibid.*, 184–5.
91. *ibid.*, 349–50.
92. Catullus 11, 21–4.
93. *Aen.* IX, 433–7.
94. *ibid.*, 446.
95. Augustine, *Confessions* VI, 8; cf. AUERBACH, *op. cit.*, Ch. III.
96. Dante, *Paradiso* XX, 68–9.
97. *Aen.* IV, 23.
98. Dante, *Purgatorio* XXX, 48.
99. *ibid.*, 21.
100. Dante, *Inferno* IV, 42.
101. BORIS PASTERNAK, *Doctor Zhivago*, trans. by M. Hayward and M. Harari (London 1958), p. 49.

Bibliography

In addition to the books cited in the References, the following are recommended:

C. G. HARDIE, "Virgil," *Oxford Classical Dictionary*, 2nd edn, ed. by N. G. L. Hammond and H. H. Scullard (Oxford 1970).

J. B. MAYOR, W. W. FOWLER, and R. S. CONWAY, *Virgil's Messianic Eclogue* (London 1907).

BRUNO SNELL, *The Discovery of the Mind* (Oxford 1953).

The best modern translation of the *Aeneid* is probably that by Rolfe Humphries (New York 1951). Also recommended are the following books of the *Aeneid* published by the Clarendon Press (Oxford): Book II, ed. by R. G. Austin (1964); Book III, ed. by R. D. Williams (1962); Book IV, ed. by R. G. Austin (1955); Book V, ed. by R. D. Williams (1960); Book VI, ed. by Sir F. Fletcher (1941).

CHAPTER 13

Classical Greek Oratory

K. J. Dover[*]

From the earliest times the Greeks were connoisseurs of oratory as an art. In Homer the Trojan Antenor describes the impression made by Menelaus and Odysseus when they came as envoys to Troy to demand the return of Helen. Menelaus "spoke fluently, not at great length, but in a clear voice; he was not verbose, nor did he put a word out of place." When Odysseus rose, "he stood with his eyes fixed on the ground, and did not move his sceptre in gesture to and fro, but held it still, like an unskilled man. . . . But when he sent forth from his breast his great voice and words like winter snowflakes, then no man could contend against Odysseus."[1]

The orator needs an audience, and the establishment of democracies in many parts of the Greek world from the 6th century B.C. onward provided him with audiences that it was vital to persuade: assemblies of the whole citizen body that took the final decisions on political issues, and very large juries that represented the sovereign assembly and gave verdicts against which there was normally no appeal. Yet the closeness of the connection between oratory and democracy was greatly exaggerated by Greek writers themselves (particularly if they were anti-democratic in sentiment) in the 4th century B.C. In the passage quoted above, Homer imagines the Greek envoys as speaking to the Trojan king and a handful of elders not in secret session, but in the sight and hearing of as many Trojans as could get near enough.[†] Elsewhere he describes two litigants as arguing their cases not simply before a group of judges upon whom the responsibility for decision rests, but in the presence of a crowd that noisily expresses its allegiance to one side or the other.[2] The litigants regard themselves as speaking at least as much to the crowd as to the judges, and what is at stake is not merely the narrowly defined subject of the lawsuit, but their future standing in the community as speakers—

---

[*] Professor of Greek, University of St Andrews.

[†] In the 5th and 4th centuries B.C., "secret sessions" of the Council or the law courts at Athens were exceptional; when the business was interesting, a crowd could be expected.

formidable or contemptible adversaries, accomplished or clumsy craftsmen with words.* Even in an "oligarchy," a state in which the power of political decision was restricted to a fraction of the citizen body, a speaker would commonly find himself exerting his powers of persuasion on an audience substantially larger than a modern parliament, much more fluid in its allegiances (the modern concept of "party" is hardly applicable to Greek city-states), and much less predictable in its decisions.

Oratory remained an unwritten art-form for at least three centuries after the Greeks had begun to commit poetry to writing, and even for two generations after the first written texts of plays. Pericles (d. 429 B.C.) earned high praise from the comic poet Eupolis: "Whenever he came forward . . . he beat all the other speakers by a length. . . . It seemed that Persuasion was enthroned on his lips, such a spell did he cast; and he was the only speaker who left his sting behind in his hearers."[3] Individual sentences of his were remembered and transmitted, like some of Churchill's in our own day; for example, in a funeral oration he said that the loss of young men in battle was as if "the spring had been taken out of the year."[4] Yet no one was able to read a Periclean speech after its delivery, for no written version existed; the speeches that the historian Thucydides (*c*. 470–395 B.C.) puts into his mouth, however accurate the report of Pericles' matter and argument, are cast in the same condensed, difficult, and idiosyncratic style as the speeches attributed by the same historian to all the speakers, of whatever nationality, whom he introduces into his narrative. It is, incidentally, a measure of the importance of persuasive oratory in Greek history that Thucydides attaches equal weight, in his introductory remarks on the difficulty of finding out the facts of the Peloponnesian War, to "what was said" and "what was done."[5] Although Herodotus (died *c*. 428) makes a clear-cut division between formal speeches and passages of continuous narrative—and his practice was followed by Xenophon (*c*. 430–*c*. 360) and most later historians—he included in his own historical work a high proportion of direct "reporting," from formal speeches to informal conversation, even in describing occasions of such a kind that the possibility of discovering what had actually been said did not exist.†

As a literary genre, Greek oratory begins with the Athenian Antiphon,

---

* SIR ARTHUR GRIMBLE, *A Pattern of Islands* (London 1960), Ch. IV, depicts a preliterate culture (on the Gilbert Islands) in which high value is attached to the quality of a man's performance as a pleader.

† Xenophon, in *The Education of Cyrus*, a piece of historical fiction, presents 6th-century Persians delivering speeches indistinguishable in style from those that he attributes to his own contemporaries in his *Hellenica*.

who was executed in 411 B.C. for complicity in an oligarchic revolution, and his speeches (wherever we have any grounds at all for dating them) are later than 430. From Antiphon onward, Athens dominates in oratory, as in drama, philosophy, and historiography; only two of the famous 4th-century orators, Lysias (*c.* 445–377) and Isaeus (d. *c.* 340), were not of Athenian origin (Lysias's father was a Syracusan, and the family had the status of resident aliens at Athens), and even these two lived and wrote in an Athenian ambience. Isaeus and Isocrates (the latter had a prodigious lifespan, 436–338) bridge the period between the "earlier" and "later" orators. Andocides (b. *c.* 440), a contemporary of Lysias, is classified as an early orator. Demosthenes (384–322 B.C.) was the supreme artist among the later orators; his contemporaries included Lycurgus (d. 324), Hyperides (d. 322), and Aeschines (*c.* 395–*c.* 315); Dinarchus was somewhat younger, and remained active until 290; Demades (d. 319) left no speeches in writing, and his name was attached to some Hellenistic forgeries.

It is remarkable that rhetoric, the theoretical study of the technique of persuasion, and the composition of rhetorical "textbooks," did not result from the practice of putting written speeches into circulation, but actually preceded this practice by a small margin and no doubt stimulated it. The *Tetralogies* ascribed (perhaps wrongly) to Antiphon—sets of speeches composed for both sides of hypothetical homicide cases that raise tricky forensic problems—are no later in date than those speeches of his that relate to actual homicide cases, and may well be earlier. The first rhetoricians about whom 4th-century writers seem to have had any information were (like Lysias) Sicilian Greeks. The Sophists, whose emergence in the third quarter of the 5th century B.C. was one of the most notable events in human history, represented collectively a new kind of self-consciousness, man's scrutiny of his own procedures; the word *sophistes* could still be applied at that time to anyone who practised and taught an artistic or intellectual skill, but its meaning shifted rapidly away from poetry and the visual arts toward those who professed to teach the techniques upon which political success depended. Oratory was the essential technique and associated with it were, on the one hand, formal linguistic studies (definition, which is the beginning of lexicography, and attempts to rationalize usage) and, on the other hand, scrutiny—with a strongly relativistic bias of political and ethical concepts. Athens, as a wealthy and powerful cultural centre, attracted Sophists who were not themselves Athenians, notably Gorgias (*c.* 480–*c.* 390), a Sicilian, who is represented by Plato[6] as accepting classification as *rhetor* (speaker, but in Plato's time acquiring the additional meaning "rhetorician"); Thrasymachus of Chalcedon (born *c.* 460), who is harshly portrayed in Plato's *Republic* I; and Theodorus of Byzantium (born *c.* 445). Once oratory as a literary genre had taken root at Athens, rhetoric too became predominantly Athenian, separated from the indiscriminate academic interests of the Sophists and brought into a much closer relation with oratorical practice.

The Greeks regarded speeches as belonging to three main categories, "epideictic," "deliberative," and "forensic," and since this classification was not invented by a literary critic in Hellenistic times but took shape quite early in the great days of the orators, there is no danger of anachronism if we apply it from the outset in describing their work.

Epideictic speeches formed the least homogeneous category. They had two negative characteristics: they were not designed to move an audience to immediate decision on an issue of detail, and they did not have to contend with argument propounded by opponents on the same footing. They could, however, differ widely in intellectual content and in seriousness. There were occasions, such as state funerals and festivals, at which a speaker was expected to give elegantly artistic voice to the sentiments that the audience already held; this category of speech was known as *panegyric*.* A lecture that propounded a philosophical, religious, or scientific doctrine was also an epideictic speech; acceptance of the argument of such a lecture might in the long run affect the hearer's way of life, but he was not called upon to take an immediate decision, still less to choose between alternatives. Another species of the epideictic genus was what the Greeks called *paignia* (toys). Although resembling speeches in form, these were read aloud, or learned and recited, to small groups, and we should nowadays regard them as essays. Their special characteristic was paradox, expressed in refined and attractive language: the defence of a mythical character traditionally denigrated; the application to a humble object of the forms of praise traditionally reserved for gods, heroes, and athletes; or the justification of a proposition that at first hearing would be rejected as patently absurd.

Deliberative speeches were designed for delivery in a council or assembly that had to take a decision on a question of policy. The majority of extant speeches of this category are the work of Demosthenes, who was not merely politically active but for the last 25 years of his life was among the leading politicians of Athens. A speech of this kind, circulated in

* A panegyric was not always a bromide; at the Olympic Games of 388 B.C., Lysias delivered a highly partisan speech that incited part of the audience to violence.

writing after its delivery, took on a new lease of life as a political pamphlet. It is not surprising, therefore, that many speeches that were never in fact delivered should none the less be issued as pamphlets.* Some of Isocrates' works are of this character; Isocrates was not active in the assembly, but he used the form of the deliberative speech in order to circulate his views on questions of policy.

Forensic speeches—and the majority of extant speeches belong to this category—were written on behalf of litigants. Certain important differences between the structure of Athenian society and the structure of ours must be remembered if the nature of the forensic speech is to be understood, and these differences bring the deliberative and the forensic categories rather closer together than we might have expected: closer, for example, than a budgetary speech in Parliament and a barrister's address to the jury on a claim for damages. In the first place, Athenian juries were very large—often 501, sometimes even larger—and the jury was regarded as a representative committee of the sovereign assembly; the speaker often says "you" to the jury when he means "the Athenian people." Secondly, these large juries received no skilled, professional guidance on points of law; there was no summing-up, and although gross mis-statements on matters of law and history by the prosecutor might be corrected (how effectively, would depend on their nature and subtlety) by the defendant, the defendant's own mis-statements might well be believed by the jury. The absence of a professional judge inevitably encouraged irrelevance, and although both the law and public opinion paid lip-service to the importance of relevance, the rigorous modern concepts of admissible evidence have no ancient counterpart. We find on one occasion Aeschines, in the prosecution of a certain Timarchus, brushing aside the evidence offered in the case and urging the jury to give their verdict in accordance with all the gossip and scandal that they have heard about Timarchus in the years before the case was brought.[7] Furthermore, although Athenian law drew a distinction between a lawsuit (*dike*) brought for harm or loss inflicted on an individual and an indictment (*graphe*) for an offence against the state, the initiative in bringing an indictment lay not with officials of the state but with any citizen who was an enemy of the alleged offender, felt strongly on the subject, or wished to advance his own reputation for patriotism.

* Compare the modern "open letter," a form also used by Isocrates; and SIGMUND FREUD, *New Introductory Lectures on Psycho-Analysis*, trans. by W. J. H. Sprott (London 1933), preserves lecture form meticulously, even though these lectures were not delivered orally or intended for delivery.

Political and administrative failures, errors, and malpractices, which in most modern states would issue in a vote of censure or a polite suggestion to the offender that he might offer his resignation, incurred the severest penalties in Athens. A general whose conduct of a campaign had disappointed the expectations of the assembly might be condemned to death (or flee into exile to escape death) on a charge of treason, and the same fate could befall a politician charged with "giving the state bad advice." If a speaker in the assembly proposed a decree that *prima facie* conflicted with an existing law he could be prosecuted—for what we should be inclined to regard as a procedural oversight—even after his proposal had automatically lapsed with the end of the administrative year. All cases of this kind were tried by juries. The path to political influence and power therefore lay through the prosecution of adversaries and actual or potential rivals, and the condition of survival in politics was mastery of the art of self-defence in court.* This invasion of the forensic field by the political one has a converse that may explain one singular feature of Athenian oratory. Just as a man might indict for a political offence another man who had become his enemy on private grounds, so he might bring, or help an associate to bring, a lawsuit for damages in a private matter against a political rival. The outcome of a lawsuit would change the position of himself and his group on the ladder of influence within the community. We have only fragmentary knowledge of the exceedingly complicated pattern of individual and group associations and allegiances that constituted Athenian politics in the 4th century B.C., and when we find Demosthenes devoting his time and trouble to a lawsuit so trivial that today it would hardly rate more than half a column in a local newspaper, we are entitled to suspect that it was a move in one stage of a political contest in which Demosthenes had at least an indirect interest.

The prosecutor and the defendant each had to speak before the jury in person. This put a man in an unpleasant predicament if he knew that his opponent was a much better speaker, and from this predicament there were two ways of escape. One was to persuade eloquent and experienced kinsmen and friends to speak on his behalf; in such a case, one of these friends might bear the main burden, the litigant confining himself to a brief opening statement. It was essential, however, that a man who spoke on another's behalf should be known beyond doubt as a kinsman or friend. Suspicion that he was hired for his eloquence would create strong prejudice against the litigant for whom he spoke, and it was common form to cast aspersions on the motives of those who spoke on behalf

* See also Ch. 14, "Hellenistic Rhetoric and Roman Oratory."

of one's opponents.* The second way of escape was to consult a man who had gained a reputation for giving good advice to litigants; this consultant might compose a complete speech, which the litigant would learn by heart as an actor learns his part, but obviously a defendant, who could not know with absolute certainty what arguments would be used by his prosecutors, would have to be ready, when his turn came to speak, to choose between some equally rehearsed alternatives, to discard some arguments that might suddenly appear likely to do him more harm than good, and even to improvise a rebuttal of unexpected slanders.

All the known speeches of Isaeus, and all but one of those of Lysias, were composed by them as consultants for delivery by "clients"; the three speeches of Aeschines, on the other hand, were composed by him for his own delivery as prosecutor or defendant; and Demosthenes acted both as consultant and, in his own private and political career, as litigant. We are tacitly invited by tradition (Hellenistic as well as modern) to regard a speech that has been transmitted to us under the name of A, but reveals in its text that the speaker was B, as a complete and accurate written version of a speech composed entirely by A but learned and delivered in court by B. There are, however, some grounds for declining this invitation. The first ground is *a priori*. Some of the speeches ascribed to Demosthenes were delivered by men who were politically experienced; speeches XXII and XXIV (the prosecutions of Androtion and Timocrates) are cases in point, for they were delivered by a certain Diodorus, who emerges from the narrative element in the speeches, despite the unassuming and disinterested personality that he assumes, as already a man of some consequence in the politics of his time. It is difficult to believe that the relation of Diodorus to Demosthenes was simply the relation of actor to author-producer; we should expect him to have ideas of his own and to contribute arguments and even wording in consultation with his eminent associate. There is also empirical evidence to suggest that the written versions of speeches that we possess are not simply records of what was said in court, but have undergone revision. This evidence is derived from two of the only three cases for which we possess speeches representing both sides. Aeschines I is the main speech for the defence against Demosthenes XIX, *On the Corruption of the Embassy* (343 B.C.); and Demosthenes XVIII, *On the Crown*, is the defence against Aeschines III, *Prosecution of Ctesiphon* (330). Aeschines in II, Sections 10 and 86, speaks of Demosthenes as

---

* There was one important exception to the general rule: in certain types of case, especially those in which the State had a financial interest, the assembly might appoint advocates to speak on the side of the prosecutor.

having made charges that are not in fact to be found in Demosthenes XIX, and in Sections 124 and 156 he answers charges (again attributing them specifically to Demosthenes) that are quite different in detail in Demosthenes XIX (Sections 175 and 192 ff.). Demosthenes in XVIII, Sections 95 and 238, refers to Aeschines' use of an argument that is nowhere to be found in Aeschines III. If, therefore, the prosecutors' speeches on these occasions were as we have them, the defendants' speeches were revised for circulation and augmented by rebuttal of allegations made out of court; alternatively, if the defendants' speeches were as we have them, the prosecutors' speeches were revised before circulation; in either case a difference between delivered version and circulated version must be postulated. Moreover Aeschines III, Sections 189, 225, and 228, actually counter humorous analogies drawn by Demosthenes; two of the analogies occur in Demosthenes XVIII, Sections 243 and 319, but the third does not. Either Aeschines gathered from gossip what Demosthenes was going to say (and this is a perfectly real possibility, perhaps reflected in the frequent use of "I understand that he will say . . ." in many speeches), but was mistaken in Section 228, or he inserted all three passages after the case, whereas Demosthenes removed from his own written version the point taken up by Aeschines in Section 228. The evidence of the third pair of opposing speeches is inconclusive; Lysias VI represents part (the first part is lost) of one of the four prosecutors' speeches against Andocides in 399 B.C.; Andocides I, *On the Mysteries*, is the defendant's reply to the whole prosecution.

The limited evidence available thus suggests that there could be a difference between delivered speech and written speech, and there is no evidence to the contrary. If the practice were taken to its logical conclusion, we should expect to possess written speeches that were not delivered at all, and there does seem to be one such. Demosthenes XXI, the *Prosecution of Meidias*, is composed for the most part as if for delivery in 346 B.C. in a case arising out of an offence datable to 348. But there are inconsistencies in the speech: certain elements in it point to a date of composition earlier than the alleged offence; certain others point to a different type of offence; the order in which the case is presented differs from the initial statement of the proposed order; two pairs of alternative presentations of the same argument can be located within the speech; finally, we have some external evidence that Demosthenes' complaint against Meidias was settled out of court.[8] Add to this that Demosthenes and Meidias had been on opposite sides of a feud for 20 years, and it seems almost certain that Demosthenes put into circulation, for a reading public, an amalgam of "might-have-been" speeches against Meidias, bearing in outline a formal resemblance to a single forensic speech. Thus the forensic speech, as well as the deliberative speech, could be a disguise adopted by a political pamphlet, and if we ask, in respect of any one extant forensic speech, whether it is known for certain that the case that it represents actually came into court, we have to admit that we can very rarely say Yes. We seldom have any reason to say No, either; but it is worth mentioning (as a salutary reminder of our ignorance) that even if all extant speeches represent actual cases, we seldom know whether we are reading a winning or a losing speech.

Who actually "published" a speech (i.e. allowed a copy of it to pass out of his possession), and who was regarded at the time as its true author, are questions not easily answered.* Client and consultant alike had a motive for pretending that the speech was the client's own work, for there existed a conventional view (in conflict with the observable facts of life) that an honest man pleading a just cause needed no meretricious skill, and throughout the period when consultancy flourished the pretence that it was dishonest and disgraceful was conventionally maintained and could be used as a stick with which to belabour an opponent. No doubt the introduction of client to consultant, the consent of the latter to give his services, and the form in which he was rewarded, were (like usury) overlaid with euphemism and disguise. At the same time, both client and consultant had a different motive for letting the truth be known and giving the consultant credit for the speech. It was to the advantage of the client to be feared as a man who had at his disposal the help of a skilled orator, who might also be (like Demosthenes) a powerful politician; and it was to the advantage of the consultant to claim as his own a speech that had earned admiration in a society imbued with an aesthetic and intellectual passion for oratory as an art.

This being the case, it is not surprising that the correct ascription of forensic speeches to their authors has always presented a much more difficult problem than the ascription of works in other literary genres. When Callimachus, working at Alexandria in the middle of the 3rd century B.C., compiled a definitive list of all known Greek works, he included 425 speeches under the name of Lysias. In the late 1st century B.C. two literary critics, Caecilius of Cale Acte and Dionysius of Hali-

---

* There did not exist at Athens anything quite like modern publication, i.e. the simultaneous release of large numbers of identical copies. (See Ch. 19, "The Writing and Dissemination of Literature in the Classical World.")

carnassus, reduced this list by roughly half, accepting only 233 speeches as the genuine work of Lysias.[9] Critics who deny authenticity sometimes make themselves unpopular, because many a reader resents the disturbance of his assumptions; but although some of the arguments used by Caecilius and Dionysius are open to objection as circular and subjective, their attack on the Alexandrian list was wholly justified in principle. Callimachus did, after all, ascribe to Demosthenes one speech (LVIII, the *Prosecution of Theocrines*) that contains an attack on Demosthenes,[10] and many to Dinarchus that on simple chronological grounds could not possibly have been written by him.[11] What is even more striking is that, at some time between the death of Isocrates (338) and the death of Aristotle (322), Isocrates' adopted son absolutely denied that Isocrates had ever written any forensic speeches, to which Aristotle retorted that there were "innumerable bundles of Isocrates' forensic speeches in the bookshops."[12] This datum shows that disputes about ascription were not an innovation of Hellenistic literary criticism, but were already sharp and uncompromising in the time of Demosthenes. The modern critic has at his disposal more refined stylometric techniques than were available to Dionysius, but most of the extant speeches are too short for the application of persuasive stylometric tests, and in the present state of our knowledge it is advisable to keep an entirely open mind about the relation between, for instance, the individual Lysias and any speech transmitted to us under his name.*

The problem of ascription is also complicated by one important aspect of oratorical technique. It was desirable that the consultant, using all his technical skill on his client's behalf, should avoid too obvious a discrepancy between the client's own character (as suggested by his voice and bearing, or as known to many of the jury and to some of those who would read the written version of the speech) and the impersonality that results from obsession with form. The speaker conventionally represents himself (except when his political eminence would make this absurd) as a peaceable man forced into litigation by intolerable persecution or by his own patriotic zeal, and as a plain-spoken man who can oppose only unadorned truth to the untrustworthy cleverness of his opponents. He must seem to speak with the force of sincerity. Everyone recognized this; the difficulty was to reconcile it with the Greeks' passion for turning every-

---

* Comparatively few of the speeches ascribed in antiquity to Antiphon, Lysias, and Isaeus survived to the Middle Ages and thus to our own day. Those that survived were selected, in the late Roman period, without reference to the opinions of literary critics and historians on their authenticity; there is thus no correlation, positive or negative, between survival and authenticity.

thing they handled into an art that made both aesthetic and intellectual demands, and the difficulty was most acute during the period 420–390.

Epideictic oratory during that period was marked by linguistic extravagance. Gorgias set the fashion for rhyme, alliteration, and (above all) pairs or series of clauses of identical syntactical structure. The influence of Gorgias is obvious in the *Funeral Speech* of Lysias (392 or 391), although Lysias imposed symmetry on a wider scale and with greater subtlety. This tendency toward large-scale symmetry was developed further in the epideictic speeches and political pamphlets of Isocrates, whose relation to Gorgias is rather like the relation of a well-designed and decorated drawing-room to a book of wallpaper patterns. The extant forensic speeches attributed to Isocrates, all datable to the very beginning of the 4th century B.C., used assonance and symmetry to a degree that was already coming to be felt as inappropriate to the law courts because it suggested too strongly that the litigant had learnt his piece and was trying to divert the jury from the point at issue by an artistic display. (In a way, the speech-writer's problem was not unlike the dramatist's, with the important difference that no one's life or liberty hung upon the portrayal of a character in a play.) Antiphon made use of quasi-philosophical generalization, which is also prominent in the deliberative speeches composed for historical contexts by Thucydides, and (also like Thucydides) he experimented freely with the formation of words.*

It seems to have been Lysias (and for convenience we may bring under his name whatever anonymous writers of the period 400–370 wrote speeches that have been transmitted to us as his) who pruned Athenian forensic oratory of stylistic experiments and made a serious attempt to adjust the style of a speech to the nature of the case and the personality of the speaker. It would be rash to say that this adjustment was always successful, for we do not have independent access to the facts of the case or evidence for the speaker's personality, but we can at least observe that Lysias's language has much common ground with Athenian documents and prose literature of the time and that variations from this norm fall within reasonable limits: for example, XII, the *Prosecution of Eratosthenes*, which was spoken by Lysias himself at a time when he was already well-known as a rhetorician, shows a strong tendency to formal symmetry, and there is evidence that VI, the *Prosecution of Andocides*, which contains an unusually high proportion of poetic words, was spoken by a poet.

* Because we have no Athenian prose literature that antedates the last part of the 5th century, there is room for error in judging a word in Antiphon or Thucydides to be a "neologism" or an "experiment," but their vocabularies contain many words that do not occur in any subsequent prose.

By the middle of the 4th century B.C., as we see from Isocrates and the later works of Plato, prose writers felt themselves under an artistic obligation to adopt some exacting refinements, particularly a preference for certain rhythms (especially at the end of a sentence), the avoidance of runs of short syllables, and the avoidance of juxtaposition of a final with an initial vowel. The peculiar achievement of Demosthenes was to combine an exceptionally rigorous application of these refinements with a greater range of mood and effect than any previous orator. No one else conveys so powerful an impression of spontaneity, e.g. "Now consider what you would like me to speak about first. About the illegality of his proposal? Well then, we'll speak of that first,"[13] or "I want to draw your attention to a quite extraordinary aspect of the law that he's proposed; it occurred to me while I was speaking, a moment ago."[14] This is audacious nonsense, for Demosthenes spent twice as much time on preparing an effect of spontaneity as other orators spent on achieving formal smoothness. But he never lacked audacity; wishing on one occasion to use afresh, with only the smallest verbal changes, material that he had used in another case two years earlier, he prepares the way by saying, "Now I'm going to tell you something that will be entirely new to you—except, perhaps, any of you who may have been at the trials in which Euctemon was involved."[15]

In spite of his virtuosity, Demosthenes is not read today as widely as in the last century, and translators, who are not slow to tackle Plato and the dramatists, ignore orators. One reason for this is that many Greek speeches are unintelligible without some knowledge of the technicalities of Athenian law, and our difficulty is increased when the speaker is actually trying to prevent the jury from seizing the real point at issue. A more general reason, perhaps, is that we are shocked by the malice and irrelevance of the slanders that the speaker heaps upon his opponent, and repelled by the complacency with which he proclaims his own virtues. We may understand Greek oratory better (though we cannot compel ourselves to like it) if we reflect that the speeches represent at a high artistic level a non-literate and pre-literate aspect of Greek life, the rivalry of individuals as subjects for the favour of the community as sovereign. From the "corrupt barons" vilified by Hesiod[16] to the eclipse of the Athenian democracy, it proved impossible in practice, however easy in theory, totally to separate the issue of a man's guilt or innocence in respect of a single act from the larger issue of whether he was a friend or an enemy of the power in whose presence he pleaded his innocence.

References

1. *Iliad* III, 204 ff.
2. *ibid.*, XVIII, 497 ff.
3. Eupolis, frag. 94.
4. Aristotle, *Rhetoric* 1365ª, 32.
5. Thucydides, I, 22.
6. Plato, *Gorgias* 449A.
7. Aeschines, I, 92 f.
8. *ibid.*, III, 52.
9. [Plutarch], *Lives of the Ten Orators* 836A.
10. Dionysius, *On Dinarchus* 10.
11. *ibid.*, 2 f.
12. *ibid.*, *Isocrates* 18.
13. Demosthenes, XXIII, 19.
14. *ibid.*, XXIV, 122.
15. *ibid.*, XXIV, 159.
16. *Works and Days* 37 ff.

Bibliography

F. BLASS, *Die attische Beredsamkeit*, 2nd edn, 4 vols. (Leipzig 1887–98), is the classic work, out of date on some points of detail but not yet replaced by anything comparable in scope, learning, and perspicacity. Among works in English, R. C. JEBB, *The Attic Orators from Antiphon to Isaeos*, 2nd edn, 2 vols. (London 1893), is perhaps the best, although it is overshadowed by the first part of Blass's work and does not compete with the second part. Recent books include G. KENNEDY, *The Art of Persuasion in Greece* (London 1963), which offers a concise, lucid, and accurate survey of the subject, with adequate emphasis on rhetorical theory.

O. NAVARRE, *Essai sur la rhétorique grecque avant Aristote* (Paris 1900), demonstrates that the oratorical techniques that we can observe directly only in the extant works of orators and historians were familiar to the poets and dramatists long before. A. BURCKHARDT, *Spuren der athenischen Volksrede in der alten Komödie* (Basel 1924), uses references and parodies in Aristophanes to show the continuity of oratorical conventions from the late 5th century B.C. to the late 4th.

R. J. BONNER, *Lawyers and Litigants in Ancient Athens* (Chicago 1927), and M. LAVENCY, *Aspects de la logographie judiciaire attique* (Louvain 1964), consider the role of the consultant in Athenian life; the generalizations of both authors should be treated with caution when empirical evidence is lacking. K. J. DOVER, *Lysias and the Corpus Lysiacum* (Berkeley and Los Angeles 1968), deals with ancient and modern aspects of the problems of ascribing speeches to their authors, with special reference to Lysias. W. VOEGELIN, *Die Diabole bei Lysias* (Basel 1943), examines in detail the means by which an early-4th-century speaker contrasted his own character with that of his opponent.

No one interested in the orators should neglect to read the *Gorgias* and *Phaedrus* of Plato and the *Rhetoric* of Aristotle. Plato criticized oratory and rhetoric from his own philosophical position, but his criticism contains elements with which most readers are likely to sympathize, whatever their philosophical and political views. It is important to remember that Aristotle died in the same year (322 B.C.) as Demosthenes and Hyperides: the technical analysis in the *Rhetoric* was contemporaneous with the highest development of the art, whereas Aristotle's *Poetics* was written two generations after the deaths of Euripides and Sophocles.

CHAPTER 14

Hellenistic Rhetoric and Roman Oratory

A. E. Douglas[*]

History and reason alike confirm the ancient view that great oratory, as the ancients understood it, could exist only in a free society. The coincidence of the end of freedom at Athens with the end of great Greek oratory was eventually marked by the critics who established a "canon" of Greek orators, 10 in number, ending chronologically with Demosthenes and his contemporaries. Whatever the achievements of the succeeding Hellenistic age in poetry, history, scholarship, philosophy, and science, little was achieved in oratory. There were laudatory addresses to the great kings; oratory of a kind was doubtless employed by embassies between the semi-autonomous cities, although on one famous occasion Athens sent three philosophers to present her case at Rome, and such a choice was not unusual; there was litigation; and there was also a survival of the Sophistic tradition in the *epideictic* ("display") oratory of numerous itinerant lecturers. But, of all the millions of words thus uttered, little was recorded; and of the fraction of that little that survives, nothing commands more than an antiquarian interest.

Yet paradoxically, just as in Roman Imperial and Byzantine times, the study of the *theory* of oratory (rhetoric) flourished. This seemingly misplaced enthusiasm is often treated as an eccentricity of ancient culture that must simply be regretted or ignored. But, although difficult, it is not impossible to see why rhetoric flourished to the extent of being for centuries the main, sometimes the sole, matter of higher education.

Although it was always closely tied to forensic practice, so that the typical rhetorical treatise was largely concerned with methods of winning court-cases, rhetoric also contained much of wider application. Our best

---

[*] Senior Lecturer in Classics, University of Southampton.

knowledge of what such textbooks were like comes from early Latin derivatives (no earlier example in Greek survives), Cicero's *De inventione* and the anonymous *Rhetorica ad Herennium*. Both follow a Hellenistic division of the whole subject under five headings. The first was *inventio* (discovery of what can be said on a given topic, not imaginative invention).* The others were *dispositio* (arrangement of the material thus discovered), *elocutio* (expression, style), and two categories relevant to the spoken word, *memoria* and *gestus* (memory and delivery). Clearly, the first three headings have their place in all orderly utterance designed to reach an audience. Even though in certain kinds of creative writing the sharp distinction between matter (*inventio*) and form (*elocutio*) cannot be maintained, the ancients—in practice as well as in theory—show an acute sense of the distinctions between genres, and of each genre as having the appropriate style in which it should, to use a favoured ancient image, be "clothed." Their theory makes sense in terms of their own practice.

Further, although the detailed rules under the several headings are often formal and pedantic, we know it to be untrue that only formal pedants were produced by rhetorical training. The rules, like those of a game, are formal, but they are only rules. The student had to play the game, too, in endless practice and, if circumstances allowed and ambition dictated, in real life. Rules that pedants elaborated had to stand the test of practice, as even the handbooks themselves show in their use of *exempla*, or illustrative passages: the *exempla* in *Ad Herennium* and elsewhere show that major political issues were discussed in the schools, and even though the belief that the issues were violent contemporary controversies may be founded on a false dating of *Ad Herennium*, at least real life was not very far away.

Again, the rhetoric course included an elementary introduction to logic, in the discussion of means of proof and refutation, and even to moral philosophy, in the discussion of the exploitation of the characters of those involved in the case (a topic that ancient courts always regarded as relevant) or of the ethical nature of a course of action under consideration. It may seem far-fetched to describe as an introduction to ethics sets of crisp copy-book definitions, such as *Modestia est in animo continens moderatio cupiditatem*[1] (Temperance is mental control that checks our passions); yet they taught something not primarily, if at all, useful in the courts, and

---

* Cicero's work, as its modern name implies, dealt only with this section. With youthful enthusiasm he embarked on a complete treatise on a vast scale but never finished it. In his later writings on the topic (*De oratore*, etc.) he avails himself of the complete system, but in a free and individual way.

it may well be that Latin first developed a vocabulary for, and so the capacity to discuss, this kind of thing, not (as is usually asserted) when Cicero started writing philosophical works in the middle of the 1st century B.C. (although he made many innovations), but around the beginning of that century, when Hellenistic handbooks of rhetoric were first translated or adapted.

Rhetoric as a form of education was largely confined to the upper classes, and it is tempting to inquire how far its precepts reflected or established class attitudes. A distinction must be made that can be shown by considering the only area where the question of class is explicitly treated in Latin texts. Here we find that to praise a man for wealth or birth was an ancient convention; equally one might, the rhetoricians tell us, cast aspersions on him for behaviour unworthy of his origins or for unjustly exploiting his status. (Although the author of *Ad Herennium* shows signs of democratic sympathies and might not be typical, much the same line is taken by Cicero—never a democrat—in the corresponding sections of *De inventione*.[2]) These passages show an underlying assumption that the cases will involve members of the ruling class. The assumption reflects the fact: in Republican Rome the great field for oratory was the big case, forensic in form but political in substance, that was typical of the in-fighting within the ruling class. It also reflects an inherently class-conscious assumption: *noblesse oblige*. But precisely because feud and faction within the ruling class were the field of forensic oratory, there seems little to warrant the idea that class structure—envisaged as a set of monolithic groups in conflict—was affected by rhetorical education. That education merely reflected a situation that rested on the far securer basis of traditional sources of power—birth and wealth—though it could offer the gifted outsider (Cicero is the pre-eminent example) a road to high office and a measure of acceptance within the "establishment."

The Hellenistic contribution in our field is thus in theory, not in practice. In leaving the schoolroom for the law-court and assembly—or, as Cicero would say, the shady colonnade and gymnasium for the heat and dust of battle—we must not forget that the great orator shared a grounding in the discipline of rhetoric with the educated members of his audience, who saw and heard not merely a case being argued but a trained virtuoso in action.

In 46 B.C. Cicero produced a history of Roman oratory, *Brutus*, in which all Romans known as orators, from the beginning of the effective practice of that art at Rome, but with the deliberate exclusion of Cicero's living contemporaries, are named, and many are discussed at length. Yet of all those names, and of Cicero's living contemporaries, only Cicero himself is represented in our surviving record by complete speeches. Further, the particular interests of later writers (in pre-Ciceronian literature, for instance, or in grammatical oddities) have preserved many quotations, often substantial (i.e. up to about 20 lines long), of the elder Cato, C. Gracchus, and a few others; yet of Cicero's great rival Q. Hortensius, and even of Julius Caesar, we have merely a few words. Thus even the scanty record of fragments is chronologically unbalanced.

Yet such tentative conclusions as can be drawn from this limited evidence do nothing to contradict the ancient conviction that Cicero was Rome's supreme orator: the sheer perfection of his technique and the quality of his thought (to which we refer later) made him an outstandingly formidable pleader in all kinds of case, and also the one who had most to offer posterity. Perhaps, then, we should not lament what in any case we can do nothing about—that for us Roman oratory and the oratory of Cicero are virtually synonymous.

In the great crises of his political career, in his attacks on Catiline and Antony, Cicero convinced himself, or tried to, that he was defending Rome—in the one case against physical destruction and massacre, in the other against a perpetuation of the murdered Caesar's tyranny. Whether his convictions and policies were right or wrong, the grounds of his appeals, the issues of life and freedom, are universally intelligible. More revealing is something different, less familiar, yet in a sense more typical: Cicero's defence in court in the year 62 B.C. of P. Sulla.* Conventionally, an introduction to *Pro Sulla* would run something as follows:

"As consul in 63 B.C., Cicero had suppressed the conspiracy of dissolute nobility and other malcontents led by Catiline. Among those allegedly involved was P. Sulla (a distant relation of the dictator L. Sulla), already discredited both by his condemnation for corrupt practices in his successful electoral campaign for the consulship of 65—of which office, with his equally guilty colleague Autronius, he was accordingly deprived—and also by his alleged complicity in the so-called 'First Catilinarian Conspiracy' of 65 B.C. In 62 he was charged with complicity in the conspiracy of 63 by L. Manlius Torquatus, son of the Torquatus who replaced Sulla as consul for 65. On the latter's deposition, Cicero undertook his defence. The speech devotes little time to refuting the charges: it is largely

---

* Though not among the best-known of the 50-odd speeches of Cicero that survive, it has its place in history as the speech to which Robespierre's successful self-defence of 5 November 1792 owed a good deal.

concerned with justifying Cicero's own action in defending a suspected Catilinarian, and with Sulla's whole career. . . ."

This is all right as far as it goes, but it falls short in two ways. First, it implies by silence either that Roman society was no different from our own (which is untrue) or that, if it was different, the task of the orator was not thereby affected (which is likewise untrue). Secondly, the judgments offered in such an introduction and the commentary we may imagine following it will hardly explain how Cicero won his cases—if, that is, his speeches consisted mainly (as modern accounts often imply or assert) of bombast, irrelevance,* and distortion—in short, of nonsense. Clearly the two defects are linked. Cicero won his cases by what may appear to us to be nonsense, because he lived and spoke in a society that accepted his arguments (not, of course, in every detail, but in the methods and fundamental notions involved) as sense. A great advocate sways his audience, and a virtuoso orator can, while on his feet, get away with anything; but Cicero published his speeches, obviously intending to enhance his reputation with an audience allowed some time to reflect.

We must fill in the background by asking (i) who was Cicero? (ii) who composed his audience? (iii) who was Sulla? (iv) who was Torquatus?

Cicero was an important person in Rome, and not only on his merits as an orator: in 62 B.C. he had just been consul, and this consular status, apart from being a striking achievement for a man of modest, though not lowly, origins, made him a notable person, as he remained even in periods of political eclipse. His audience consisted of a large jury drawn from the upper ranks of Roman society, and as many bystanders as could get within earshot: court-proceedings took place in the open air. Sulla may have been disreputable, but he was well connected—a nobleman and a patrician.† Torquatus, likewise, was a noble and a patrician; he was a young man of 27 years of age, and stood in a curious relation to his intended victim. He had prosecuted Sulla in 66, following a practice of the time whereby a rising young politician took as his first step the prosecution (on charges not necessarily well-founded) of a senior politician. As

---

* It is probable that many "irrelevant" passages were added to the speeches for publication. But these were mainly passages of propaganda and homilies of various kinds. We are still left with much, intrinsic to the speeches, that would be both out of order and ineffective in modern courts of law.

† "Nobility" in Cicero's day meant being a member of a family one or more of whose members had held the consulship, and it mattered greatly. Being a patrician in itself mattered little at this date—but enough to be the subject of a gibe in the *Pro Sulla* (Section 23).

a result of his success, in the words of Cicero, *honos ad patrem, insignia honoris ad te delata sunt*[3] (the office of consul passed to your father, the insignia of office to you).

It has only recently been shown[4] that this and some similar passages mean simply what they say: the successful prosecutor acquired the official insignia of the condemned defendant. Precisely what *that* meant is not clear, but Torquatus's second confrontation with Sulla cannot have been other than piquant. Cicero's peculiar speeches were delivered in a peculiar environment.

The general consideration, that cases such as Sulla's involved conflicts at the highest social and political level, may seem too obvious to mention. But although the political implications of such trials are obvious to historians,* the literary consequences are less often appreciated. A speech in an important case was a great public occasion. Cicero in his theoretical writings may, as a successful orator, have exaggerated the significance of, and the acclaim attendant upon, such occasions, but not much. The Ciceronian speech would have made sense only in the context of public concern and excitement that Cicero himself depicts.[5] There is perhaps *no* forensic speech of Cicero's where the only thing at stake was the acquittal of his client.

For his great occasion, his large audience, the Roman orator had, or sought, a style to match both occasion and audience. The ancient critical pre-occupation with "fitness" explains the Ciceronian style. Fitness to audience accounts for such notorious features as repetition in words and structure for clarity and emphasis, for the audience must always know (or think it knows) what is going on. The Ciceronian "period," complex as it is, is heavily signposted (not least by rhythmical means) and rarely ambiguous; and the vocabulary, for both aesthetic and practical reasons, avoids the colloquial, archaic, obscene, poetic, or newly coined. Some of these categories were inappropriate to the dignity of the occasion; others (e.g. the poetic), though dignified, would shock, startle, or otherwise distract the audience. At its best it is so splendid a style that it has been imitated throughout the ages, often in forgetfulness of the fact that it was formed in a particular age to do a particular job.

---

* The fact that the trials *were* political arouses curiously little comment among critics in the Western liberal tradition, who are much more excited on discovering, for instance, that P. Sulla lent Cicero a large sum of money. But is "political justice" less offensive when not associated with totalitarianism? This and other implications for the nature of Roman Republican society cannot be explored here, except to say that the fact that the juries' decisions were *both* a matter of persuasion (not *force majeure*) *and* politically significant gave the great pleader his peculiarly significant role (and, in Cicero's view, his responsibilities).

We speak less readily of bombast if we are aware that to read a Ciceronian speech in solitude and silence is merely to read the score of a work designed for public performance. But because, after all, such a speech differed from epic or tragedy in that a man's fortunes and citizenship—to say nothing of a true verdict—might depend on its "performance," irrelevance and distortion of facts may appear more serious, only partly mitigated in Cicero's case by his habit of employing his craft in defence, not in prosecution.

On one occasion—the trial of Cluentius in 66 B.C.—Cicero admits having baffled the jury with a smoke-screen. In *Pro Sulla* he is aware that an issue he wishes to deal with is of limited relevance, and apologizes (Section 31). He may often have been guilty of distortion of fact, though what Cicero could get away with (that is, how stupid or ill-informed his audience was on any individual occasion) is a question that can be answered only by a subjective estimate of probability. Obviously, Cicero would not have made a habit of delivering and publishing material obnoxious to his public. And so the canons of the relevant and the factual in the Roman law court demand further exploration.

First, in some instances Cicero was exploiting a convention, not creating a precedent. The use in defence or attack of a man's whole life and character, sanctioned by all the theorists, was part of the stock-in-trade of Greek and Roman orators alike, because audiences accepted as relevant the question, "Is my client the sort of man to do this sort of thing?" To avoid this queston and concentrate on the case before the court was a desperate measure.[6] Ancient respect for literary tradition is an element here, too. The topics of invective (lowly origins, gross personal immorality, and so on) were hallowed by tradition, and the ancients evidently enjoyed hearing them repeated.[7]

But, second, there are deeper waters than these. A feature of recent scholarship has been the analysis of the abstractions to which Cicero so often appeals (and for which he is usually the main source)—words such as *dignitas* (social and political standing), *fides* (good faith), *mos maiorum* (tradition). The tendency has been to see in them the weapons of an unscrupulous conservatism, so much humbug and fraud concealing the truth about Roman politics in the interests of the ruling classes. Much has been learnt, but there has been much exaggeration. For, apart from the question whether politicians are ever such uncomplicated rascals, the fact is that the trick (if that is all it was) worked only too well. To repeat, Cicero won most of his cases, and the speeches he won them with make no sense unless he worked within a conventional ideology that had meaning and at least a measure of reality for his audience and himself.

The truth rather is that, in their political aspect, Cicero's speeches are those of the eternal politician. "Politicians," it has recently been observed, "are as trapped by the party cries, phrases, and attitudes as their supporters. In several cases political myths are created and preserved by the most sophisticated and intelligent politicians, to a point that is often startling to a young student of politics."[8] W. J. M. Mackenzie,[9] while noting a certain lack of interest among modern students of politics or language in the way political language actually works, makes points that are as relevant to our understanding of Cicero as to that of any modern politician. He refers to "words like 'equality,' 'democracy,' 'justice,' 'freedom' [the Roman set of values differed in part; the moral is the same] which are often used simply as the waving of a national flag, and yet may . . . be treated as if they should be subject to exact definition within a syllogistic system." Again, "one gets at political arguments only by abstraction; they are imbedded in a structure of symbolism and a structure of sound . . . if one takes out the structure of the argument, one is left with something politically dead"; and "vagueness in certain cases is not a political fallacy but a political instrument. . . . Much political action depends on the effective use of words which are vague, but not meaningless." One might add that political language presents special problems in that the politician's utterances often do not merely describe or forecast, but actually create, situations (as can his silences).

We should be on guard, then, against too naïve a cynicism about political language. It is true that Roman political terminology, however high-sounding, is often associated with a nexus of purely material or political relationships and interests, but it will not yield all its historical or literary secrets to those who habitually write "conceals" or "cloaks" rather than the less colourful "is associated with." Even as a purely historical source, a Ciceronian speech demands an imaginative *literary* feeling for the occasion. For it makes both a historical and a literary difference whether Cicero's resounding terms and periods were no more than bluff and smoke-screen, or (on the contrary) contained for the mind as well as for the ear a resonance genuine for both speaker and hearer. If, as I believe, they did, we are still free to form our own judgments on situation and character; but we must start from the right place.

Pro Sulla exemplifies all our generalizations. The trial was important as both a political and a literary occasion. Cicero's speech employs the

resonant terminology and elevated style we have discussed—though it
is not a monotony of complex periods: Cicero could wield the rapier as
well as the sledge-hammer. It employs the argument from a man's whole
life. It is concerned with far more personalities than Sulla alone and with
far more issues than his guilt, as is clear from the opening sentences, which
provide—with remarkable richness, complexity, and stylistic virtuosity—
keys to all that follows.

> Maxime vellem, iudices, ut P. Sulla et antea dignitatis suae splen-
> dorem obtinere et post calamitatem acceptam modestiae fructum
> aliquem percipere potuisset. Sed quoniam ita tulit casus . . .
>
> (Section 1)

> (My dearest wish, gentlemen of the jury, would have been that
> P. Sulla might in time gone by have been able to preserve the
> distinction due to his rank and, after suffering misfortune, have
> enjoyed some reward for his humility. But by an unkind chance . . .).

This opening is doubly artful, with careful balance of thought and
expression indicating the pathetic contrast between *antea* and *post*, the
brilliant social status before, the *modestia* after the disaster. (*Calamitas*
often refers to condemnation in the courts.)

The second sentence is 12 lines long, yet perfectly controlled in thought
and structure, pivoting at its syntactical centre on a transition from regret
at Sulla's misfortune to the opportunity Cicero now has to show himself,
not—as necessity had made him in the Catiline affair—stern and ruthless,
but mild and merciful. Cicero also finds room for allusions to Sulla's
disgraceful colleague Autronius and indirectly (the name first appears in
the next paragraph) to the prosecutor, Torquatus. The sentence thus
provides the key thoughts of Sulla's "humility" in misfortune (suggestive
of innocence), Autronius's indubitable guilt, the relentless persecution of
Sulla by the family of Torquatus, and Cicero's essential mercy—his
sternness arising only from patriotic necessity. This single sentence gives
the basic constituents of the whole speech, and also reminds us that we
are concerned not only with Sulla but with a whole host of *dramatis
personae*, including (besides those mentioned) the whole people of Rome.

The setting of the scene is completed with the third sentence of the
speech.

> Et quoniam L. Torquatus, meus familiaris ac necessarius, iudices,
> existimavit, si nostram in accusatione sua necessitudinem familiarita-
> temque violasset, aliquid se de auctoritate meae defensionis posse
> detrahere, cum huius periculi propulsatione coniungam defensionem
> offici mei.
>
> (Section 2)

349

(My good friend Torquatus thought that, by doing outrage to our intimate friendship in his speech, he could somewhat diminish the authority of my defence; so at the same time as I repel the threat to Sulla, I shall justify as due the service I am rendering him.)

Some implications of this passage, and of its keywords "friendship," "authority," and "service," will be attended to shortly: enough for the present that the conflict of the two counsel, Cicero and Torquatus, is an important part of the case. We turn from the themes thus stated to their development.

Ancient theory laid down a simple ground-plan for speeches (though it enjoyed complicating it too)—proem, narration of the facts, proofs and refutations, and peroration. But the scheme was not always suitable—for instance, for a defending counsel speaking last of a number of advocates, which was Cicero's situation in *Pro Sulla*—and in any case something more subtle might be needed. The great orator, "like a general with his cavalry, infantry, and light-armed troops, placed each argument in that part of the speech where it would be most effective."[10] In *Pro Sulla*, Cicero, like the orator of an older generation thus described, resembles less an architect building a symmetrical structure than a general forced to campaign simultaneously on several fronts. Hence his constant switches of attention, and his returns to sectors temporarily left quiet.* Only great art could manage the transitions and variations of tone needed to make the method workable: and Cicero had that art. The structure seems odd only if one concentrates on a written analysis of the argument—a most misleading guide to what actually happens in any Ciceronian speech.[11]

By this method Cicero was able twice to introduce the strength of respectable support for Sulla (Sections 3 ff. and 81 ff.), twice to depict the abandonment of the guilty Autronius (Sections 7 ff. and 14 ff.), and several times to justify his own appearance for the defence as revealing his true character as a merciful man: at the outset, again in claiming to be entitled to stand alongside Sulla's respectable supporters (Section 8 ff.), and in a final appeal to the jury—like Cicero, juries had been severe in condemning Catilinarian conspirators and must watch their reputation (Sections 92–3).

Torquatus had in fact exploited a twofold weakness in Cicero's position: first, his tough handling of the Catilinarians had earned Cicero great un-

---

* The method is also used in *Pro Caelio*. It was once, but is no longer, believed that the resulting "repetitions" in that speech were ill-thought-out additions made in preparing the speech for publication—the least likely explanation (it has often been pointed out) for such "clumsiness."

popularity; and second, he was—with apparent inconsistency—defending a Catilinarian. In short, Torquatus had argued, Cicero thought he could get away with anything. Cicero had to efface these prejudices from the minds of the jury, yet he was aware of the danger of irrelevance. As notable as what he says is the ingenuity with which his replies are diffused through and integrated into the whole speech.

The first charge was the easiest to meet. The sympathies of the jury, if not of all the bystanders, were with Cicero, so that Torquatus, after lowering his voice in attacking the Catilinarians, was (according to Cicero) misguided enough to shout out his abuse of the cruelty of their fate for the benefit of the bystanders, as if the jury, too, could not hear that abuse (Section 30 f.). Cicero scores a better point in retorting that his rigorous treatment of the conspirators was necessary, but *a fortiori* proves that he would not defend a man whom he believed guilty of complicity.

To the charge of inconsistency his retort is that he is naturally mild. His ruthlessness was a persona, a mask. As a fact, the ancients found it hard to believe in a fundamental inconsistency of character—if it was possible, it was certainly a bad thing—and it was precisely on these grounds that men's whole life stories were retailed in the courts. This theory receives explicit statement: Sulla's life story is relevant:

> Neque enim potest quisquam nostrum subito fingi neque cuiusquam repente vita mutari aut natura converti.
>
> (Section 69)

> (None of us can be formed in a moment, nor can anyone's way of life suddenly be altered or his character given a new shape.)

So Cicero ends his argument on his own actions ("for the moment") with an appeal to ideas of unity and singleness so powerful in ancient thought generally: "you see me with the patriotic citizens who support Sulla, without inconsistency": in the last resort *simplex officium atque una bonorum est omnium causa* (Section 9; the duty of all good patriots is single and their cause one).

The charge of arrogance, of abusing his *auctoritas*, presented Cicero with a complex problem. Apart from the charge in itself—to which he replied, in effect, "Am I to blame if people believe me?"—Cicero must not forfeit sympathy by being overbearing in his treatment of a much younger opponent. That is why Cicero begins with restraint, accusing "my very good friend" Torquatus merely of trying "to diminish somewhat the authority of my defence." But gradually, and at intervals carefully spaced between other kinds of argument, he grows more indignant and outspoken. It later emerges that Torquatus had accused Cicero of *regnum* (despotism), a far more serious charge—even though obviously not meant literally—than the traditional topics of personal invective. Cicero's retort is vigorous enough, but the climax is reserved for the outburst apropos a suggestion that Cicero had falsified official records:

> Fero ego te, Torquate, iam dudum fero . . .
>
> (Section 45)
>
> (I have been putting up with you for a long time, Torquatus . . .).

"I make allowances for your youth, our friendship . . ." Cicero goes on, "but this is too much." Except once, to make more effective a point about the behaviour of Torquatus's father, Cicero never addresses Torquatus directly after this passage.

This subtle disposition of arguments is clearly skilful advocacy, but the speech contains other recurring and interwoven themes that may justify the claim that it is more than an advocate's *tour de force*, though it is that too. These themes, of a specially Roman kind, reflect Roman social and political life as a network of reciprocal services and obligations, a matter on which recent researches into the relevant vocabulary have thrown much light, but again with a tendency to make a strait jacket out of a useful framework.

Thus it has been recognized that *amicitia* often means not friendship, but political or even financial ties of expediency. *Amicitia* was expressed through *beneficia* (services rendered) and *officia* (the repayment of, or obligation to repay, such services), and cemented by *fides* (good faith). The opposite of *amicitia* was *inimicitiae*, personal or political feuds, often between families, that imposed equivalent obligations to do harm. Torquatus could use family hostility to justify his attacks on Sulla (Section 48).

One would then expect to find a society divided within itself into warring cliques, and use of this model has greatly enhanced our understanding of the period. But Cicero's speech shows that the situation was complicated by two insights (as old as Plato), that "to help one's friends and harm one's enemies" is a poor morality, and that a divided society is a bad society, or, to put it another way, that the interests of society outweigh individual interests and associations.*

That is why Autronius was abandoned in the interests of the *patria* by

---

* These are the main qualifications that arise from *Pro Sulla* itself. In any case, it has been shown that *amicitia* can mean just friendship, which might override political disagreements, and that where it has a political connotation, such political *amicitiae* were too fluctuating and impermanent to provide a complete key to Roman political history of the late Republic.[12]

many on whom he had claims of a lower order, *conlegae, sodales,* and *veteres amici,** and by Cicero himself (Sections 7 and 18). Again, there arises a human obligation to defend not only one's *amici* but others, too, in adversity.† The converse obligation to attack *inimici* can be over-ridden by claims of humanity and mercy. Thus (Cicero reminds the jury) the elder Torquatus showed no resentment toward those who defended Sulla in his first trial: "They did their best to deprive your father of the office of consul," but

> inviolata vestra amicitia, integro officio, vetere exemplo atque instituto optimi cuiusque faciebant.
>
> (Section 49)

> (they did it without violence or outrage to ties of friendship or obligation, and in harmony with ancient practice and the custom of all good men.)

In this sentence only *vestra, atque,* and *faciebant* lack "resonance." So Cicero claims to be exempt from criticism for defending Sulla. "After all," he adds silkily, "*I* do not criticize *you*,"

> te enim existimo tibi statuisse quid faciendum putares et satis idoneum offici tui iudicem potuisse
>
> (Section 80)

> (I imagine you set your own course of action and are a perfectly adequate judge of where your obligations lie.)

Only in cynicism can we find grounds for denying that these arguments, as well as others more dubious, aided the success of Cicero's defence of Sulla. At all events we can see why Cicero claimed[13] to be the most philosophical of Roman orators.‡ We may think this an odd boast. But Cicero inhabited a forensic world where the whole proceedings imposed "irrelevance" by their unconcern with mere guilt and innocence. It is not a small thing if Cicero succeeded as an orator not only by subtlety and subterfuge, and an unparalleled mastery of language, but by appealing beyond the social nexus of feud and expediency to the principles, so often

---

* i.e. fellow-members of social and semi-political organizations known as *collegia* and *sodalitates,* and old friends.

† The Roman practice of advocacy originated in the relationship of patron and client (*patronus, cliens*), the client as non-citizen, freedman, etc., being dependent on a patron for the legal defence he was disqualified from making, being technically *infans* (literally, speechless). As advocacy was extended beyond the range of those bound by some formal tie, *patronus* came to mean any defending counsel: but the sense that the *prime* obligation was to those in some way connected, not a merely professional one, survived.

‡ In dealing with the charge of *regnum*, he seizes the chance to define the true *rex* as any man free from slavery to passion, and free in speech and policy (Section 25), a piece of Stoic theory made relevant by the political reference.

z

associated with his name, of *humanitas,* an ideal of what human society ought to be.

The establishment of the rule of emperors soon after his death ensured that Cicero had no successor; one may doubt whether even different conditions would have produced another Cicero. That is why, as Quintilian says,[14] Cicero is—and perhaps would have remained—*non hominis nomen sed eloquentiae* (the name not of a human being but of eloquence itself).

References

1. *Rhetorica ad Herennium* III, 3.
2. *ibid.,* I, 8; *De inventione* I, 22.
3. *Pro Sulla* 50.
4. LILY ROSS TAYLOR, *Party Politics in the Age of Caesar* (Berkeley 1949), pp. 112–6.
5. Especially *Brutus* 199–200.
6. *Rhet. ad Herenn.* II, 5.
7. Cf. R. G. M. Nisbet's edition of Cicero, *In Pisonem* (Oxford 1961), Appendix VI.
8. ROBERT RHODES JAMES in *The Times* (London), 25 November 1967.
9. W. J. M. MACKENZIE, *Politics and Social Science* (Harmondsworth 1967), pp. 286 ff.
10. *Brut.* 139.
11. Cf. CHRISTOFF NEUMEISTER, *Grundsätze der forensischen Rhetorik* (Munich 1964), pp. 99 ff.
12. P. A. BRUNT, "Amicitia in the late Roman Republic," *Proc. Camb. Philol. Soc.,* No. 191 (1965).
13. E.g. *Brut.* 161 and 322.
14. Quintilian, *Institutiones oratoricae* X, 1, 112.

Bibliography

Rhetorica ad Herennium, ed. and trans. by H. Caplan (London and Cambridge, Mass. 1954).

K. L. BÜCHNER, *Cicero: Bestand und Wandel seiner geistigen Welt* (Heidelberg 1964).

M. L. CLARKE, *Rhetoric at Rome* (London 1953).

H. J. HASKELL, *This was Cicero* (New York and London 1942), esp. Ch. I to VI.

J. HELLEGOUARC'H, *Le vocabulaire latin des relations et des partis politiques sous la République* (Paris 1963).

A. D. LEEMAN, *Orationis ratio* (Amsterdam 1963).

CHR. NEUMEISTER, *Grundsätze der forensischen Rhetorik* (Munich 1964).

R. G. M. NISBET, "The Speeches," in *Cicero,* ed. by T. A. Dorey (London 1965).

CHAPTER 15

Religious and Moral Attitudes in Archaic and Classical Greece

K. J. Dover[*]

In this chapter the Persian invasions (490–479 B.C.) are treated as the point of transition from the archaic to the classical period, and the end of the 4th century B.C. as the transition from classical to Hellenistic. Homer's *Iliad* and *Odyssey* and Hesiod's *Theogony* and *Works and Days* are regarded as earlier than 700 B.C. and therefore as the oldest surviving Greek literature.

It is generally agreed that the *Iliad* contains incidents and utterances that are of much earlier date and may imply religious and ethical standpoints alien to most Greeks of the 8th century. Certainly some elements in archaic Greek cults were inherited from the Minoan and Mycenaean cultures of the previous millennium; but cult is only one aspect of religion, and we cannot pretend to know whether a Minoan believed (for example) that the Snake Goddess would punish him if he committed perjury. There are obvious points of resemblance between Homer's gods and those whom we meet in the mythology of Italy, northern Europe, and ancient India (in all of which Indo-European languages were spoken), in Syria and Mesopotamia (which were not Indo-European-speaking), and in Anatolia (which was to some extent linguistically Indo-European but was culturally linked with Syria and Mesopotamia). The resemblances include not only the nature and behaviour of their gods, but also the relations between gods, heroes, men, and monsters. It is impossible to be certain whether we should regard resemblances of this kind as an inheritance from a remote prehistoric era, as the product of diffusion at a less remote era, or as factors arising independently and inevitably from similar cultural and social conditions. The *Theogony*, which narrates the origin of the universe

[*] Professor of Greek, University of St Andrews.

and the genealogy of the gods, also has points of resemblance to comparable narratives in Anatolia, Syria, and Mesopotamia, and in this case occasional striking community of detail makes diffusion through cultural contact a more probable explanation. The evidence on these questions is not our concern here; what matters is the recognition that, however unfamiliar the religion of the Greeks may seem to us now, we are dealing not with something unique but with an unusually well documented species of a large genus: ancient Western and Near Eastern religion.

What was unique in Greek religion was the speed with which it realized its potentialities in the classical period, its fertility of imagination and invention, and its capacity for rational self-criticism. This does not mean that every Greek was either rational or self-critical. The philosophers and scientists were necessarily theologians, in so far as they attempted to explain the nature and working of the universe, and the universe that they inherited was full of gods; in the case of philosophers such as Plato (428–347 B.C.) and Aristotle (384–322) it is difficult to draw a sharp line between metaphysics and theology. Most people, however—whether they are poets, historians, politicians, or peasants—do not devote to the supernatural that degree of connected thought that deserves the name of theology; at different times in their lives, or even simultaneously, they make assumptions and adopt standpoints that, if pursued to a logical conclusion, often prove contradictory.

This much is true of any religion, but the student of Greek religion must remember some further special factors. Because of the extreme political fragmentation of the Greek world, there was no authority able or willing to decide what was orthodox or to enforce general observance of a particular religious practice, as it could be enforced by the Persian kings or, later, by the Roman emperors. The priest who officiated at a Greek religious ceremony had not been trained professionally in a Church that transcended political boundaries; he was a person entitled, by heredity or appointment, to exercise authority within the limits of a single sanctuary or a single local cult. Because no positive creed separated Greek from non-Greek, and because they were not united in acceptance of any single narrative as divinely revealed, most Greeks were agnostic—not in the sense that they had no fear of offending supernatural powers and no hope of securing supernatural aid, but in the sense that their beliefs were fluid and incoherent, adopted or discarded according to the demands of the occasion; they found in a shrug, in a tranquil refusal to press the question, "But is it *true*?" the comfort that other cultures have found in dogma.

An additional complication is that, although the religious beliefs expressed and implied in Homeric epic could justly be called "primitive" by a philosopher contrasting them with the sharp theological speculations of Socrates (470–399 B.C.), they could with equal justice be called "sophisticated" by an anthropologist contrasting them with the religious observances of Socrates' contemporaries. Comparable distinctions could be drawn between tragedy and comedy, or between temple sculpture and many categories of vase-painting. It seems that coexistent art-forms could consistently choose different aspects of religion for description and representation. We shall be true to the nature of the subject if in considering Greek religion we speak only rarely of belief and more often of attitudes, assumptions, and standpoints implicit in cult, myth, intellectual speculation, and social behaviour, and also if we recognize that these attitudes cannot be neatly allocated to places, periods, social and intellectual strata, or individual writers, but are strands running through Greek history, conspicuous at one moment and obscure at another.

During the Hellenistic period we witness the development and dissemination of many attitudes that coalesced with parallel developments in Persia and Palestine to form, for good or ill, major ingredients in Christianity (the novelty of which is sometimes exaggerated by Christians). The seeds of these Hellenistic developments had already begun to germinate before the end of the classical period.

Cult and Observance

In 1932 archaeologists discovered at Menidi, near Athens, a long inscription set up in the 4th century B.C. and containing the words of an oath taken by Athenian youths when they began military training at the age of 18.[1] At the end of the oath comes a list of *histores theoi* (gods invoked as witnesses): "Agraulus, Hestia, Enyo, Enyalius, Ares and Athena Areia, Zeus, Thallo, Auxo, Hegemone, Heracles, boundaries of the fatherland, wheat, barley, vines, olive-trees, fig-trees." Some of these names are immediately familiar to anyone who has read a little Greek poetry in translation. Zeus is ruler of the gods in Homer, and the Labours of Heracles are among the most widely disseminated of Greek myths. But why is the list headed by Agraulus, not by Zeus? Why is there no mention of other powerful deities so prominent in poetry—for example, Poseidon, Hera, and Apollo? Why are Ares and Enyalius both named, when in Homer they are two different names for the same god? Why "Athena Areia" rather than just "Athena"? And why are she and Ares specially coupled? Who are Thallo and Auxo? And what are olive-trees and boundaries doing in a list of gods? The process of answering these questions takes us to the heart of Greek religion, though not to its head.

The last question is the most easily answered. Boundaries and trees are not, in other contexts, "gods," but they can be sworn by, like Zeus or Hera: that is to say, they perform at least one function in the human community's relations with the supernatural world, and it is not necessary that what performs one divine function should perform others as well. A second question is answered by the opening lines of the inscription, which tell us that it was set up by "the priest of Ares and Athena Areia." In other words, the oath stands in a particular relation to a particular cult, and Ares and Athena Areia are jointly the focus of the cult, which consists (like any cult) of a finite, localized sequence or programme of religious acts. Poseidon has no cause for resentment at his omission from this cult, nor Zeus for his subordination in it, because they are the foci of other cults and other localities, each of which has its function in the total religious life of the Athenian people. The same point could be made in respect of any other Greek state. "Hegemone," here apparently an individual goddess, occurs elsewhere as a title of Artemis: "Artemis Hegemone" at Ambracia[2] and at Megalopolis,[3] where there was in addition a cult of "Artemis Ephesia,"[4] just as at Athens "Athena Areia" coexisted with "Athena Polias," "Athena Hephaestia,"[5] and so on. What were different gods in one place might be identified in another, and the processes of identification and differentiation could occur within the same community. The Athenians established in 420 B.C. a sanctuary of Health (a goddess commonly associated in cult with Aesculapius),[6] but they also offered dedications and sacrifices to "Athena Health."[7] Again, if we could ask Aristophanes (*c.* 447–386) whether to him, as to Homer, Ares and Enyalius were alternative names for the same god, he would probably say yes; but he did not equate a prayer to the one with a prayer to the other, as we see from a passage that he wrote in 421: "To Hermes, the Graces, the Seasons, Aphrodite, Desire."—"But not to Ares."—"No!"— "And not to Enyalius, either."—"No!"[8]

As for Thallo and Auxo, no cults devoted to them have so far been discovered, but they are typically Greek in appearing only in a strictly limited locality. The inhabitants of Aegina, an island within sight of the Athenian coastline, worshipped a similar pair, Damia and Auxesia. How far the cult of those two goddesses extended is impossible to determine, for although we can identify them at Epidaurus[9] and Troezen[10] (both on the Peloponnesian coast near Aegina), we then follow a trail of dialect names more or less resembling the two with which we began; there is no point at which we can say that the trail is definitely and finally lost, and there is even a side-trail that leads to identification of Damia and Auxesia with the much more familiar Demeter and Persephone.[11] It would be half the truth (we shall deal with the other half later) to say that, for example, Athena, considered as a supernatural individual with a character and will of her own, is an abstraction from a mass of local cults, or even that she is the concentration of a variety of supernatural functions. If we asked an Athenian, "Do you believe in Athena?" he might assume, unless we had chosen our words very carefully, that we wanted to know, "Do you participate, to the extent and in the ways expected of you by your fellow-citizens, in sacrifices, prayers, dedications, and processions to Athena Polias, Athena Nike, etc.?"

The multiplicity of local divinities and the individual peculiarities of each cult might have led the Greeks to say, when confronted with the strange gods of Egypt and Mesopotamia, "Our gods are concerned with us, the Greeks; other nations are the concern of other gods." In fact, however, the possibilities of identification and differentiation among their own gods led them to say " 'Ammon' is the Egyptian for 'Zeus'," just as they might have said, " 'Pharaoh' is the Egyptian for 'king',"[12] and the unlikeness of the Egyptian cults of Ammon to any Greek cult of Zeus would pose no problem to a Greek, who could have encountered some highly idiosyncratic cults of Zeus on a tour through Crete and the Peloponnese. The Greeks did not say, as some of their Eastern neighbours were inclined to say, "Ours alone are the *true* gods; other nations worship evil spirits"[13] (or "Other nations worship gods who do not exist at all").

Personification

A different aspect of Thallo and Auxo now concerns us. Their names are patently connected with Greek words meaning "flourish" and "increase," and to that extent we may call them personifications of natural processes. The manner in which the Greeks spoke of their deities makes it impossible to define personification precisely. At one extreme, the names of the gods most familiar in widespread cults and poetry are true names, of which the etymology was not apparent to the Greeks* and is not always apparent to philologists. Each of these gods has functions and spheres of activity that are his "concern" or "delight": Zeus is "the cloud-gatherer," the wielder of the thunderbolt, the source of rain; Ares delights in battle and bloodshed; Dionysus showed mankind how to cultivate the vine; and sexual

---

* They made guesses, of course; but etymology is a branch of linguistic history, of which they had no inkling.

desire and its fulfilment are the "gift" of Aphrodite, so that contumacious chastity is offensive to her, just as the teetotaller would be to Dionysus. Poets can even say "Ares" where we should say "war," and (though this is more *recherché*) "Hephaestus" where we should say "fire"; but explicit statements that Zeus is the sky, or that Dionysus is wine,[14] or that Aphrodite is sex belong to an intellectualized strand of religious thought.*

A second category of divinities, of which Thallo and Auxo are examples, have names of obvious etymology, are virtually devoid of personality, and play little or no part in myth. A third category consists of abstractions that a writer may treat indifferently as persons or as things; the English convention by which names of persons begin with capitals but names of things with small letters could not be observed by the Greeks, who used only one series of letters, and choice between "he," "she," and "it" is sometimes a problem for the translator. Examples in this category are Eros ("love" in the sense that it has in our expressions "fall in love" and "be in love"), Panic, Charm, Destruction, Health, Wealth, and Law-abidingness. Personification in literature is matched from the first by personification in the visual arts, but it is not always easy to decide whether we have to deal with the expression of religious belief or with artistic convention—for example, when the chorus in Euripides' *Bacchae* (produced posthumously after 406) expresses its horror at the unrighteous-ness of Pentheus by saying, "Righteousness, venerated among gods, Righteousness, you who fly on golden wing over the earth, do you hear these words of Pentheus?"[15] Not only pervasive phenomena and abstract qualities, but places, winds, springs, mountains, and rivers are personified. Pindar, celebrating in 468 the athletic victory of a Syracusan who traced his ancestry back to Poseidon, contrives to speak of Pitana simultaneously as place and person: "Yoke now my strong mules with all speed. . . . Now the gates of song must be thrown open for them; to Pitana, where the Eurotas flows,† I am come today in good time, who is said to have lain with Poseidon, the son of Cronos, and to have borne a daughter, Euadna. . . ."[16] Pitana and Euadna, and Euadna's child by Apollo, Iamus, were "heroes" and "heroines," also called "half-gods."

The Greeks populated the latter part of the 2nd millennium B.C. with legendary persons who were in many cases the children of mortals by immortals. These were superhuman in stature, strength, and beauty, and

---

* It may well have belonged also to an extremely primitive strand of religion; but this chapter is about the Greeks, not about their Neolithic ancestors.

† Literally "by the way of Eurotas," which leaves open the double status of Eurotas as river and legendary person.

their tombs were the foci of cult in historical times. The precise status of the dead hero in the supernatural order was a matter on which many views were possible, but prayers and sacrifices were offered to him on the assumption that a heroic ghost had the power of intervention in human affairs. He played a part in the life of the ancient Mediterranean similar to that of the Christian saint today. There is at least one important difference—that most noble families traced their ancestry back to a hero and hence to a god or goddess; but there is also an important resemblance— that "canonization" of a contemporary as a hero, with consequent worship after his death or even in his lifetime, was not uncommon. (In Hellenistic times the concept became debased, and the treatment of a dead man as a hero was scarcely more significant than the inscription of a eulogy on his tomb.) The vitality of hero-worship and the absence of a clear-cut division between divine and mortal nature laid a foundation upon which it was comparatively easy in later times to impose the worship of emperors as gods.

Nothing illustrates the fluidity of Greek religious attitudes better than the relation between the words *theos* and *daimon*. Homer on occasion uses *daimones* as synonymous with "the immortals who have their home on Olympus," as when Athena, after intervening in the quarrel between Achilles and Agamemnon, goes up "to join the other *daimones*."[17] But elsewhere he makes Hector threaten Diomedes, "I will give you a *daimon*," i.e. "I will kill you";[18] there *daimon* is equivalent to *ker*, the spirit that flies over the battlefield and bears off to the underworld the soul of the man allotted to it.[19] Hesiod speaks of a multitude of *daimones*, the ghosts of the first ("golden") human species, who act as agents of Zeus and watch over mankind.[20] In lyric and dramatic poetry *theos* and *daimon* are used indifferently to designate a god; when Plato wishes to postulate and characterize a species intermediate between the immortal and the mortal, he gives it the name *daimones*,[21] but in a different argument he adopts an agnostic view of the status of *daimones*.[22] Linguistically the *daimones* of Hesiod and Plato are ancestors of the "demons" of early Christianity, but conceptually they are more akin to angels. The Greeks accepted the existence of mischievous goblins, and did not hesitate to express hatred and fear of their most destructive gods, but they had no Devil, no essentially evil power, and no one but Death himself was implacable.

It would have been pointless to ask a Greek brought up in such an open-ended polytheism, "How many gods are there?" Different enumerations of the family of Zeus as it is portrayed in the *Iliad* would not disagree by much, but the family of Zeus would be—as we have seen—an abstraction from the total supernatural world of the Greeks, among whom it would have been difficult to get a concise and agreed answer to the question, "What is a god?"

Myth

Anyone who likes dogma may perhaps pity the Greeks for wandering in a mist of religious uncertainty, but he should reflect that the obverse of uncertainty was creative imagination. Demotion of a personal god to the status of a force and establishment of a kind of personal relationship with natural phenomena or abstract qualities can, if adequately exploited, give the poet a double register of expression. A similar creativity, from which an element of caprice is seldom wholly absent, characterizes myth. The greater part of serious Greek poetry consists of the narration or dramatic representation of past events that involved gods and heroes, and even where this is not the prime object of the poet, he draws upon myth for illustration and analogy. Portrayal of myth played a major role in the visual arts also. Below the high artistic level of epic, tragedy, and temple sculpture lay other strata of myth, down to the stories told by nurses to infants; we get only occasional glimpses of these lower strata, but their role in forming the average man's concept of, say, Heracles or Orestes must not be forgotten. Because so small a proportion of Greek literature has survived, it is not surprising that we are often at a loss when a poet alludes briefly and enigmatically to a myth that he assumes to be familiar, at least in outline, to his audience. Some myths refer to an exceedingly remote period of the past—for example, the *Theogony* and Aeschylus's tragedy *Prometheus Bound* (c. 457)—but those most favoured by poets and artists concern the age of the heroes: the Trojan War, the family of Oedipus, or the voyage of the Argonauts.

The well-known saying that "Homer was the Bible of the Greeks" must be treated with reserve. It is true that in the classical period ignorance of Homeric epic would have been thought unforgivable in a man who claimed to be educated; it is also true that the Greeks tended to venerate their ancestors, and good poetry of antiquity carried great weight. They treated the poet as a man who owed his skill, and his knowledge of past events not recoverable by any historical technique as yet developed or imagined, to the supernatural operation of the Muses upon his soul. Yet even those least given to criticism of inherited assumptions were aware that different poets gave irreconcilable accounts of the same mythical events, so that, whatever inspiration might be, it could not be a simple communication of truth by the Muses to everyone whom they invested with poetic skill. If several poets told contradictory stories, all but one must necessarily be false; but one could be true, and this was what mattered to the Greek who looked to myth for knowledge of the past and of the gods. Hesiod, in describing how the Muses met him on Mt Helicon and gave him the gift of poetry, makes them say, "We know how to tell many fictions that resemble truth; and we know how—when we wish—to proclaim truth."[23] Contradiction exists from the beginning. In Hesiod, Aphrodite is born from the sea when the genitals of Sky, lopped off by his treacherous son Cronos (the father of Zeus), have fallen earthward;[24] but in Homer, Aphrodite is the daughter of Zeus and Dione.[25] Indeed, the same poet can change his mind: in the *Theogony*, Hesiod makes Strife the child of Night, but in the *Works and Days* he says, "It is not true that only one Strife was generated. There are two in the world. One [i.e. competition] would be praised by anyone who knew her, but the other [i.e. contentiousness] is blameworthy; and they are quite different in spirit."[26]

The earliest scientific speculation about the world's origin was a series of theogonies, resembling Hesiod's in general character but differing in detail from his and from one another. At a time when we might have expected the *Iliad* to have achieved "canonical" status, Stesichorus (6th century B.C.) wrote a poem in which he declared that Helen spent the Trojan War virtuously in Egypt, while a phantom constructed in her likeness by the gods was possessed by Paris in Troy;[27] and this version of the Helen myth was adopted by Euripides in his play *Helen* (412 B.C.). Again, one of the most stable items in the genealogy of the gods is that Artemis was the daughter of Leto; but Aeschylus apparently discarded this and made her a daughter of Demeter.[28] It would be a serious mistake to imagine that an "orthodox" mythology maintained itself intact until intellectual enlightenment in the 5th century B.C. broke down traditional faith and made innovation permissible to the dramatists. Innovation, modification, rejection, and substitution were there from the beginning; mythology in the hands of the poets was a creative art, and this fact was accepted by the pious and the sceptical alike.

There is an important difference here between myth and cult. It was always possible to introduce new cults, and to augment existing cults by adding to the ingredients of a festival (as tragedy and comedy were added to the festivals of Dionysus). Substitution could also occur in the artistic aspects of a festival, as when Euripides in 438 put on *Alcestis*, which is a tragedy in form, in place of the traditional satyr play; but when Cleisthenes, as absolute ruler of Sicyon in the early 6th century, abolished the

363

cult of the hero Adrastus there and distributed its elements between a festival of Dionysus and a new cult of the hero Melanippus,[29] he was acting in a wholly exceptional manner.

The conditions that originally facilitated the creative modification of myth are not difficult to discern: the essential condition was the combination of political fragmentation with a high degree of cultural unity. Each city and tribe of the Greek-speaking peoples had its own myths and its own versions of widespread myths; all or most of these peoples participated in festivals and games that transcended the boundaries of political independence, and at these the singing and recitation of poetry played a significant part. A poet could therefore draw not only on the mythology of his own locality but on the work of poets from other localities, and the audiences were accustomed to his doing so.

The Nature of the Gods

In the course of the 5th century B.C., the motives underlying the continuous modification of myth become increasingly interesting to the student of society, ethics, and theology. As standards of behaviour were modified by experience and self-criticism, the kind of knowledge of the gods that could be extracted from mythology began to be replaced by assurance founded on *a priori* reasoning, and the premise of this reasoning was that divine morality must be acceptable by human standards. No significant part was played in this process by individuals claiming supernatural inspiration or revelation; theology was battered into shape by society, and myths were increasingly rejected because they were incompatible with changing moral and theological standards. One might compare this with the way in which, during the last 150 years, the difficulty in accepting the idea that any creature can deserve eternal punishment at the hands of his creator has led many Christians to ignore, reject, or amplify (on *a priori* grounds) references to Hell in the Gospels.

The philosopher-poet Xenophanes, perhaps before 500 B.C., jettisoned myth wholesale, complaining that "Homer and Hesiod attributed to the gods everything that among men is reproached and blamed—stealing, adultery, and cheating one another."[30] Many myths told of conflicts between the gods, and left these conflicts unresolved. In some of his tragedies Aeschylus modified and augmented these stories to effect a resolution; the idea that he and other Athenians prayed for the same benefits to gods who might be enemies of one another was, one presumes, disquieting. *Prometheus Bound*, which portrays the punishment of Prometheus and his bitter hostility toward Zeus, was linked with a sequel (now lost) in which the enemies were finally reconciled. So in the *Eumenides*, the third and concluding play of the *Oresteia* (458 B.C.), the Furies who have pursued Orestes for the murder of his mother are reconciled to acceptance of his acquittal by an Athenian court by the offer of a sanctuary and cult at Athens; in Stesichorus's earlier treatment of the story, they had simply been kept at bay by the magic bow given by Apollo to Orestes.[31] Pindar, telling the story of Pelops, rejects as unseemly the inherited version of the story, in which the gods ate gluttonously, and invents an alternative that satisfies him morally and aesthetically (it includes the homosexual rape of a human boy by a god, but Pindar regarded the pleasures of sodomy highly and would not have wished to deny them to the gods).[32] Euripides, in *Electra* (*c.* 420) and *Ion* (*c.* 413), forces upon us the intolerable savagery of the myths—in the former by subtly and consistently translating the heroic predicament into terms of life as we know it, and in the latter by emphasizing, through the dialogue and in the plot, the cruelty and selfishness of Apollo. His intention was probably to suggest that such myths must be false, but whatever his intention in these or other plays he has in fact realized the tragic potentialities of the myths with splendid dramatic effect, and it would be perverse to believe that he wrote the *Bacchae*, for example, with nothing better in mind than the dissemination of his theological views.

Xenophanes' harsh judgment was not unreasonable. The modern reader of Homer observes that the disparity of power between men and gods in Homeric myth—the gods live for ever, they move where they wish and in whatever form they wish, they command the elements and can even control the ideas that come into a man's head—is not matched by any dissimilarity of temperament. Homer's gods (and the same is true, with minor modifications, of the gods in all Greek poetry) experience and express fear, grief, anger, jealousy, and lust. They threaten each other with violence, and their threats are not idle: Zeus, annoyed at the nagging of his consort Hera, threatens to lay hands on her, and Hephaestus restrains her by reminding her how Zeus once grasped him by the foot and threw him down to earth from Olympus.[33] Gratitude, obligation, and revenge—the forces that operate in human society—operate also in the relations between gods and in the relations of gods with heroes, humans, and human communities.

This is also one of the fundamental presuppositions of cult at all periods. We sacrifice to the gods just as we give hospitality and entertainment to our friends, and when we are in need we call upon our friends to repay the debt and help us. The demands of the gods, who eat ambrosia and drink nectar, are somewhat less material than those of men (though their demands for attractive mortal women [cf. Gen. VI, 1–4] are conspicuous in mythology); but, like aristocrats or ambitious citizens in any Greek state, they are hungry for *time* (honour, esteem) and resentful of slights. Men honour a god by holding festivals that include not only the sacrifice of animals (which they then eat) but also dancing, singing, poetry, and drama—all that goes to make up the gaiety and brightness of life; the fact that much Greek poetry and all Greek drama were composed originally as an ingredient in religious festivals does not mean that they were listened to with Sunday-best expressions. The average Greek regarded a festival both as an opportunity for eating and drinking more than usual and as an occasion on which he and his community renewed their friendship with the god to whose cult the festival belonged. The purpose of cult is reflected in prayer; at the beginning of the *Iliad* the priest Chryses, angry that the Greeks will not let him ransom his daughter, prays to Apollo: "If ever I thatched a temple to your liking, or if ever I burned for you rich thighbones of bulls and goats, grant me this wish: may the Greeks atone, under your arrows, for my tears!"—and Apollo's arrows (i.e. a plague) strike down the Greeks.[34] So too when Achilles has killed Hector, the greatest of the defenders of Troy, and has maltreated his corpse, some of the gods take pity on Hector, and Apollo in particular reproaches all of them for ingratitude. Hera and Poseidon oppose Apollo, because their hostility toward Troy is still aflame; Hera, employing an argument no superior to what we should expect from a human being in the same circumstances, reminds the gods that Hector was merely the son of mortal parents, whereas Achilles had at least a goddess for a mother ("and you all went to the wedding!"), so that his claims on the gods are greater. Zeus is favourably disposed to Hector: "Hector was dearest to the gods of all the mortals who are in Troy; so he was to me, for he never failed to give me my due. Never did my altar lack the sacrificial banquet, the libation, and the smell of meat."[35] Zeus accordingly sends a divine messenger to tell Achilles that he must give back the body of Hector to the Trojans for burial, and in due course Priam, Hector's father, comes to ransom it. It has been miraculously preserved from decomposition and hungry dogs, and Priam recognizes that this is Hector's reward for "giving gifts at the right times to the immortals."[36]

Both the individual and the community pray for what is not controllable or predictable by man; for health of man, beast, and crops, for success and prosperity, for the right weather at the right time, for the injection of panic or imprudence into one's enemies. It is, however, an observable fact that prayers are not always answered, and any society that regards blight, thunderstorms, and rough seas as the manifestation of divine intervention in the course of events must develop (not necessarily by any process of deliberate, rational thought) a mechanism of protection against disappointment and apparently undeserved disaster.

Part of this mechanism, in the Greek world, was acceptance of the idea that each god was fully a person, possessed of all the irrationality, prejudice, and unpredictability that one recognizes in oneself; and the modern reader of Greek tragedy needs to be reminded that this intense personality, often fundamental to the myth chosen by the dramatist as the basis of his play, may pierce through more sophisticated concepts of divine nature with which the dramatist has overlaid the inherited material. Another kind of defensive mechanism was fatalism. Herodotus (d. *c.* 429 B.C.) represents Solon (who enjoyed in tradition the status of a sage) as saying to the king of Lydia, "In respect of human fortunes, the divine power is entirely given to resentment [*phthoneros*] and to the creation of disorder [*tarakhodes*),"[37] by which he meant that it is the way of the gods to upset human plans and strike down any mortal who achieves an unusual degree of success, power, or prosperity. To a Christian accustomed to expect something better than that from his God, the Solonian dictum is bleak and depressing, but it is not a dictum by which it is impossible, or even difficult, to live; in its frank acknowledgment that men are the subjects of rulers who behave as rulers may be expected to behave, it resembles the attitude of the patient, shrewd labourer toward the baron and his tax-collectors. A ruler does not like a subject who gets "above his station," and the wise subject placates, avoids offence, and makes himself inconspicuous. In another story told by Herodotus, a queen of Cyrene dies of a horrible illness because human beings who take "excessive vengeance," such as she took on her enemies, become objects of resentment (*epiphthonos*) to the gods.[38] *Hybris*—which in Athenian law meant the violent treatment of a fellow-citizen as though he were a slave or a foreigner—in tragedy and didactic poetry usually denotes action that shows disregard for the divine government of the world and for the paltriness of all human power. The Greek's fear of his gods, however, was hardly comparable with the Assyrian's fear of his king. A Greek subject was never servile; the position of a monarch, even in Homeric society, was precarious,* and no Greek

---

* In the *Odyssey* Laertes is father of the absent king Odysseus, but he is old and feeble and no one takes any notice of him. The ghost of Achilles in the *Odyssey* is anxious to know whether his father Peleus, king of the Myrmidons, is still honoured, or is slighted because he is old. Assemblies convened by Agamemnon in the *Iliad* are more like stormy committee meetings than gatherings of obedient subjects to receive a royal fiat.

ruler could expect to be shown more respect in word and bearing than would be shown by decent sons to their father. The Greek lived with his gods as he lived with those above him in authority, speaking his mind to them and about them when he was impelled by his emotions to do so. There were myths in which heroes actually fought the gods (cf. the Mesopotamian hero Gilgamesh), as Aphrodite is wounded and taunted by Diomedes when she has unwisely intervened in the fighting at Troy;[39] and the audience of Aristophanic comedy evidently did not feel it inconsistent to sentence to death men guilty of mutilating statues of Hermes and in the same year to enjoy the grossest ridicule of gods on the comic stage.

One tolerated the gods because one had no choice; but one could go further and make excuses for them. Just as there are limits to the power of mortal rulers, so unexpected storms and other "acts of God" take place against a background of the lunar month, the solar year, the equilibrium of land and sea—a stable order in which the gods could conceivably interfere (there are indeed myths that refer to such interference) but in fact hardly ever do. The existence of this order, the details of which are open to scientific investigation and generalization, gave powerful support to the assumption that there also existed a set of metaphysical laws governing the supernatural world: rules that a god cannot break even when he wishes to repay his debt to a pious mortal. These rules can be extended to the operation of fate, and the interrelation of fate and the gods posed problems that the Greeks either failed to solve satisfactorily or did not try to solve. The traditional personification of the Fates or (increasingly in the 4th century B.C.) Chance hid under a conventional mask a profound difference between these forces and the family of Zeus. At times Zeus may have seemed no more rational than a mortal king, but at least he was not less rational, whereas with the Fates the issue of rationality could not arise; we may ask, even if we cannot answer the question, "Why did Zeus will this?" but the question "Why was this fated?" is meaningless; that is the whole point of fate, chance, and similar concepts. Reflection and response to their own emotional needs produced in different individuals different developments from this starting-point. Aeschylus, in some parts of some plays—for we can hardly ask, "What did Aeschylus believe?" as if there were a single answer to the question—tended to rationalize fate by equating it with the far-seeing will of Zeus.* Whether a painful disease is more easily borne when inflicted by Zeus than when it is due to the blind working of fate depends on the temperament and predilections

---

* This strand is prominent in the *Oresteia*; the opposite is required for treatment of the myth of Prometheus. Cf. the footnote on p. 370.

of the sufferer; but some people undeniably derive comfort from the feeling that their afflictions are imposed by a god who, though inscrutable to mortal intellects, is infinitely good and wise; and a tendency to regard the gods as possessing infinite wisdom and virtue was already gaining ground by Aeschylus's time.

The gain thereafter was rapid. A medical writer (possibly as early as 400 B.C.) declared that epilepsy, popularly believed to be supernaturally inflicted, "is no more 'divine' than other diseases . . . and is no less curable than the others." This is not the comment of a sceptic but of a man of strong religious feeling; the attribution of diseases to gods seems to him blasphemous, and he asserts, "A human body cannot be defiled by a god— what is most corrupt by what is most pure."[40] Even the traditional idea of divine "resentment" was less acceptable in the 4th century. It was rejected explicitly by Plato, who, in introducing a hypothetical account of the creation of the universe by an unnamed divine power, lays down that the creator "was good, and in the good there is never any resentment [*phthonos*] at anything."[41] Plato comes on occasion (this qualification is necessary, for he did not spend the 50 years of his working life in systematic exposition of an unchanged philosophical doctrine) within striking distance of a god who loves the world; but it would have gone against the grain for him or any other Greek to imagine a supremely good and intelligent being loving what does not deserve love—which amounts to saying that philosophers could find no way of accommodating in their metaphysics the phenomenon of love as they must have known it in their ordinary lives. Apart from an occasional flicker of assurance in late-classical drama that gods can feel pity for human suffering without too nice a regard for the merit of the sufferer,* the imaginative accommodation impossible in Platonic philosophy was first made in Christian theology. In the philosophy of the Hellenistic age the continuing process of "depersonalization," which in the classical period had exercised so powerful an effect on myth, resulted in a widening of the gulf between gods and men, and an increasing extrusion of the gods from concern with the accidents of human life.

The Platonic concept of a creator untouched by resentment was not quite as total a revolt against traditional concepts as it might at first sight appear. However vivid the Greeks' awareness that human plans were upset by untoward events—or, to translate from our terminology into theirs, by divine interference—they were also aware of a divine benevolence

---

* The Dioscuri in Euripides, *Electra* 1327 ff., give the explicit assurance that the gods are capable of pity. In *Hippolytus* 1396, Artemis cannot weep for the fate of her favourite Hippolytus because divine law (*themis*) makes tears impossible for a god.

that made it possible for men to learn something of the future through divination, oracles, and even inspiration (but how did one know who was truly
inspired?). Divination and the interpretation of omens were skills handed
down from father to son, like hereditary priesthoods and (till talent ran
dry, as it is apt to do) the arts of poetry and sculpture. Oracles were
sanctuaries at which one might put questions to gods or heroes; in classical
times the oracle of Apollo at Delphi overshadowed all others in prestige
and influence, but there were many others in continuous operation.
Somewhat similar in character were the sanctuaries of Aesculapius at
Epidaurus and Cos, where sufferers from illness or accident might be
miraculously cured, often by following instructions given in a divinely
inspired dream that came to them when they slept a night in the sanctuary. The fact that oracular responses were sometimes ambiguous,
enigmatic, or even disastrous, to those who took the oracle's advice may
make it surprising that so many Greeks—communities as well as individuals—put such faith in them for so long; but we must remember that
one true prophecy carries more weight than a hundred false ones, and
above all that men have no *right* to ask questions of the gods about the
future, any more than Aesculapius had a duty to cure the sick. Thus any
hint of the future that the oracle might give was a favour to be accepted
with gratitude. Similarly the gods were under no obligation to allow
seers to read omens or to inspire the poets with their skill.* The gods as
rulers had two aspects, like human rulers: they could be gracious and
generous or ill-tempered and malicious, and neither their generosity
nor their malice could ever be wholly comprehensible to their subjects.
The general trend of Greek religious thought was to make them comprehensible by postulating their rationality.

We seldom love our rulers, but we can; and although it appeared to an
anonymous Aristotelian that to say "I love Zeus" would be to use the
word "love" (*philein*) senselessly[42]—a view to which Aristotle himself
comes very close[43]—we are not compelled to believe that everyone was
capable of this philosophical detachment, especially at a time when the
gods were conceived in traditionally personal terms. Gratitude for bene-

---

* In general all skills were regarded as gifts of the gods (viticulture, for instance, was the gift
of Dionysus). In *Prometheus Bound* Aeschylus adopts a different view, that Prometheus communicated skills to mankind in defiance of Zeus, who was malevolent toward man; this view has an
ancestor in Hesiod's story (*Works and Days* 42 ff.) that Prometheus gave men fire when Zeus
had hidden it from them. It is important to observe that the Greek dramatist had available to
him not merely myths that differed in detail, but types of myth that implied different views of
the relations between gods and men. The inherent theological difficulties were diminished by
the fact that the gods existed *in time*; friends can fall out and enemies can be reconciled; we
can be angry with someone part of the time and fond of him the other part.

factions, especially when the benefactor had the power to do as he pleased, is easily felt as love, and when Greeks use the affectionate term *philos* in addressing gods it would be perverse to suppose that this is no more than a ritual formula. "Other-worldliness" is not prominent among the Greeks, but a passionate wish to escape from the squalor and pain and frustrations of life by projecting oneself continuously into the company of a deity, dwelling in thought and word on his perfections, cannot have been unknown. Two of Euripides' characters, Ion and Hippolytus, manifest a devotion that contains elements of such a wish.[44]

Justice and Virtue

It is natural that gods should be angry if their own possessions (sanctuaries, statues, and so on) are damaged, their protégés and favourites harmed, the taboos of their cults violated, or they themselves cheated by a perjurer who invokes them as witnesses to the oath that he subsequently breaks. But it is the way of rulers not only to protect and avenge themselves but also to regulate by laws the behaviour of their subjects toward one another. Even in the earliest Greek literature we encounter the idea that a divine sanction lies behind the laws of society. A striking simile in Homer compares the crush of chariots in battle with the storm "on an autumn day when Zeus pours down a flood of water in his anger against men who abuse their power by giving crooked judgments in assembly and drive out justice, paying no heed to the anger of the gods. All their rivers are in flood . . . and the work of men's hands is eaten away."[45] This is crude stuff, and a rationalist might fairly ask whether men are more addicted to injustice in autumn than in summer, pointing out also that rain wets the just and unjust alike. In Hesiod, Zeus is more discriminating. Spirits watch over men constantly, observing their evil deeds;[46] Justice (*Dike*), the daughter of Zeus, complains to her father when she is wronged by men, and Zeus avenges her. It is the law of nature, made by Zeus, that beasts and fishes should devour one another, but that men should settle their differences by litigation.[47]

In the archaic period the link between injustice and perjury was very close; the oath was of primary importance in litigation, and in homicide trials it retained its solemnity and prestige until the end of the 5th century B.C.; for an oath, by its very nature, involves the gods directly. Certain other crimes invested with divine sanctions from the earliest times do not involve gods by any logical necessity, and we have the impression that society was in effect imposing upon the gods the task of deterring by punishment acts—such as the wronging of guests, hosts, or travellers (all subsumed under the Greek term *xenos*) or the violation of a herald's immunity—that society itself regarded as wicked. The general trend was toward the multiplication of divine sanctions as the demands of society increased, and therefore toward identification of the "just" or "honest" man (*dikaios*) with the "pious" man (*eusebes*). "Justice" (*dikaiosune*), as discussed in Plato's *Republic*, embraces much more than the narrowly defined justice of Hesiod's time; it extends to all those aspects of human relations in which the overriding of one man's will by another's is possible.

A good man, in the society depicted by Homer, is above all a fierce fighter, of good physique and handsome appearance, a strong protector, and a valuable ally. When the ghost of Achilles asks after the fortunes of his son Neoptolemus, Odysseus reassures him: "Whenever we took counsel . . . he ran far ahead of the host . . . and slew many men in fierce combat; I could not tell you the names of all those whom he slew. . . ." Achilles' ghost goes away rejoicing at the pre-eminence of his son.[48] "Good" (*agathos*), when applied to adult males, continued to mean "brave" in classical times (not surprisingly, for the very survival of the city-state depended ultimately on the courage and strength of its citizens in battle);* but a more general and sophisticated conception of goodness (*arete*: before Hellenistic times there is no abstract noun formed from the stem *agath-*) had taken shape by the late 5th century. Its definition is plainly implied by words that Thucydides attributes to the Athenian envoys at Melos in 416: "[You cannot expect help from Sparta,] for the Spartans, in their dealings with one another and in observance of their own laws, excel in *arete*, but in dealings with other states . . . they are more conspicuous than any nation known to us for treating what is agreeable as honourable [*kalos*, literally 'beautiful' to sensory perception or contemplation] and what is in their own interest as just."[49] *Arete* here is that sacrifice of pleasure to honour, and of self-interest to justice, that makes a man do his duty—a concept of moral goodness acceptable to most of us but by no means applicable, without rather special definitions of "honour," to the heroes of mythology.

We shall see in the next section the consequences of widening the concept of "justice" while retaining and even enlarging the belief that the gods punish injustice; but before that, let us look briefly at the Athenian law of homicide, which furnishes an interesting illustration of the way in

---

* We should remember this when we are repelled by the totalitarian organization of Plato's ideal state. In his lifetime cities had been razed, their male adults systematically killed, and their women and children sold into slavery, because they had succumbed to powerful neighbours.

which religious ideas and the requirements of society were adjusted to each other. If a murdered man went unavenged, his angry ghost had the power to plague the community, and the gods were his allies. Just as blood stains what it touches, murder metaphorically stains and pollutes those with whom the murderer comes in contact. Too faithful an adherence to this belief would have made war impossible, and few Greeks entertained the idea that war might not be part of the natural order of things; hence those killed in war were held to be appeased if they were given proper burial. Involuntary homicide was regarded as polluting the killer no less than deliberate murder, and it was necessary to send the involuntary killer into exile; later, as the role of intention in morality achieved clearer recognition, an involuntary killer was permitted to return, after a certain minimum interval, with the consent of his victim's kindred. In effect, the community started from the acceptance of an ostensibly supernatural law but adjusted its application on human initiative; the restriction imposed on inconvenient divine sanctions was the counterpart of the assignation of such sanctions to behaviour that it was desirable to suppress.

Reward and Punishment

Hesiod affirmed that Zeus rewards the just man with prosperity and afflicts the unjust.[50] It was, however, as easily observed then as now that some just men suffer hideous misfortune, whereas some villains die, rich and happy, in their beds. These uncomfortable observations could have been reconciled with faith in a system of divine rewards and punishments, either by exaggerating the role of fated events that the gods could not control or by falling back on the idea of an inscrutable yet ultimately benevolent and intelligent divine plan. The Greeks preferred, however, to postulate the deferment of punishment until a later generation. This is implicit in Homer and Hesiod, but is much more clearly formulated by Solon (c. 640–560): "Zeus is not quick to anger, like a mortal man, on every occasion, but he is never unmindful of those whose hearts are sinful, and, come what may, he is revealed in the end; one sinner pays for his sin at once, another later; and while others themselves escape . . . what they have done is paid for by the blameless [*anaitios*, literally 'not being the cause' or 'not incurring a charge'], their children or their descendants in after time."[51] The doctrine is watertight; however the wicked prosper, we can say, "Ah, but their descendants will pay!" and however greatly a virtuous man suffers, we can say, "One of his ancestors must have sinned, for otherwise this suffering would not have befallen him." The mechanism of the curse—a vengeful prayer uttered by the victim of a wrong, granted by the gods, and executed through a chain of disasters in the wrongdoer's family—is of the greatest importance in tragedy, notably in Aeschylus, who thereby imposed a grand design on the myths that concerned the murder of Agamemnon and its antecedents and sequel.

To most of us nowadays it is morally disgusting that one person should be punished for the act of another, whatever their blood-relationship, but the concept of individual responsibility is a sophisticated one and its emergence even in Greece was slow. Both Homer and Hesiod accepted the idea that injustice could bring down divine punishment on the land as a whole;[52] even in the early 4th century B.C. it was still taken for granted that a god might visit a whole city with plague for failure to detect and punish a sacrilegious offender or that he might overwhelm a shipload of passengers if there was one such man among them. Discontent with this lack of discrimination may well have contributed to the development, during the classical period, of new ideas about reward and punishment awaiting the individual after death. In Homer the dead are weak, faded ghosts leading a frustrated existence in a dark Underworld; Achilles, for all his courage on earth, goes to the same place as his meanest underling.[53] A very few receive exceptional treatment: Menelaus is promised that he will not die, but be transported to Elysium because he is married to Helen, the daughter of Zeus by the mortal Leda; he is, as it were, one of the family.[54] Tantalus and Sisyphus suffer eternal torment not for bad behaviour toward their fellow men but for gross offences against the gods as individuals—offences that few would have had the opportunity to commit.[55] In the late archaic period initiation into mysteries designed to secure preferential treatment in the Underworld[56] came into increasing prominence. The cult of Demeter and Kore (better known to us as Persephone) at Eleusis was the most famous cult of this type; but just as Delphi was one among many oracles, so too the Eleusinian Mysteries were one among many mystery cults. Many Greeks underwent initiation; it would be interesting to know why so many did not—a clue to which may lie in the pervasive "agnosticism" of the Greeks in respect of any one particular religious concept.

A consistent tendency in the 5th century was to exaggerate the difference between Elysium (or the "Islands of the Blessed") and the dark Underworld by broadening the qualifications for admission to the former and making the latter more positively unpleasant. By the end of the century the essentials of an antithesis between "heaven" and "hell" had taken shape: a judgment after death, followed by eternal happiness for the good and eternal suffering for the wicked. Plato depicts the aged Cephalus as describing how "when a man comes to realize that he will soon be dead, fear and anxiety come upon him" because he is tormented by the stories, "which he laughed at when he was younger," about judgment after death. Cephalus implies that a man who has made his money by deception and falsehood has reason to fear.[57] Aristophanes in 405 B.C. takes a belief of this kind for granted (though, with characteristic light-heartedness, he inserts a bawdy joke into a list of sins) in referring to "a sea of mud and eternal filth, and lying in it anyone who ever wronged a stranger (*xenos*)—or stole his money back while he was on the job—or thrashed his mother, or hit his father in the face, or perjured himself."[58] He represents the blessed initiates after death not only as having gone through a ritual process but also as having "led a pious life in dealings with strangers [*xenoi*] and private citizens [*idiotai*, ordinary people not protected by power or authority of their own]."[59] Two categories are not mentioned by Aristophanes: the uninitiated but virtuous, and the initiated but wicked. He may imply—but this is uncertain, because he is adopting for dramatic purposes a concept of the after-life different from one he adopted earlier to make a brief humorous point,[60] and we do not know what, if anything, he himself believed—that a virtuous life was a condition that a man must satisfy before initiation, or that initiation helped him to live a virtuous life thereafter. Plato shows himself well aware that a belief in judgment after death (all question of initiation and ritual aside), although salutary in its effects on human behaviour, does not possess the status of demonstrable certainty.[61] Perhaps few Greeks thought it did; but as an assumption it remained of the highest importance, as is clear from the numerous Hellenistic epitaphs expressing the hope or assurance that the dead person will deservedly go to "the place of the pious."

Atheism

The moral and scientific enlightenment that led to the modification or rejection of myths and of popular religious assumptions inevitably tended, in the course of the 5th century, toward the rejection of religion as a whole. It was hardly possible, even in the most enlightened Greek states, to preach atheism and discourage religious observance plainly and openly; in 415 a certain Diagoras of Melos, who was regarded as having so preached, had to flee from Athens with a price on his head; and Socrates was condemned to death in 399 on a charge that included the allegation (rebutted by him) that "he does not believe in the gods in which our nation believes,* but introduces novel supernatural powers."⁶² Yet some intellectuals explained so much of the world in scientific terms that they left little or no room in it for gods, and speculation on the origins of human institutions did not spare the origins of religion.⁶³ The historian Thucydides (*c.* 470–395) exhibits an interest in the scientific explanation of natural phenomena, a contemptuous attitude to oracles, and a determination to treat human history as intelligible in terms of social and psychological laws, that combine to suggest that there was no place for religion in his outlook. It is difficult to estimate how widely, even in the best-educated circles, religion was rejected. Alcibiades and his friends, who parodied the Eleusinian Mysteries for their private entertainment in 415, and the men (whoever they were) who in the same year mutilated the statues of Hermes throughout Athens, obviously cannot have feared divine vengeance. The late 5th century was a period of intellectual exuberance, especially at Athens, and its manifestations included a ruthless moral nihilism (treated very seriously in Plato's *Gorgias* [*c.* 386] and humorously in Aristophanes' *Clouds* [the extant version is partly revised and datable 419–417]) as disagreeable in practice as it was articulate and dextrous in argument. It is possible that a seriously sceptical attitude to religion suffered thereafter through association with nihilism. The memory of the political careers of Alcibiades and Critias remained hateful to many of their fellow citizens, and the reputation of Critias—who, as the leading spirit of the "Thirty Tyrants" imposed on Athens by the victorious Spartans in 404, has demonstrated to fearful effect his contempt for traditional morality and its divine sanctions—was never rehabilitated.

Determinism

Homer's gods put ideas into the minds of men. Agamemnon, forced in the end to apologize to Achilles, excuses himself by saying that he was led into disastrous error by Zeus, who "took away my wits."⁶⁴ In Aeschylus's *Agamemnon* (458 B.C.) the chorus, having described Agamemnon as forced into a situation that left him no choice but to sacrifice his daughter,† immediately thereupon blames him for sacrificing her;⁶⁵ and although the

---

* "Believe in" here translates the Greek *nomizein*, which is derived from *nomos* (usage, custom, law). An unrelated group of verbs corresponds to "trust" or "believe" in a person. *Nomizein* also means "think" in the sense "think that something is true, treat as a datum, assume."

† The translation is in fact controversial. Agamemnon "went under the yoke of necessity," but *edu* can mean either "put on (voluntarily)" or "had put upon him," and *ananke* (necessity) covers not only what is absolutely unavoidable (like a law of nature) but also strong pressure that it is very difficult to resist.

murder of Agamemnon by Clytemnestra is the effect of a curse uttered against his father, Clytemnestra is not commended as the agent of divine vengeance but treated with abhorrence as a murderess.[66] In contrast, the involuntary parricide and incest committed by Oedipus in Sophocles' representation of the story (*c.* 430) were fated, and no action of Oedipus's could have averted them.

Modern critics, in whose conception of the tragic and the dramatic an important role is played by individual responsibility, sometimes find the strand of determinism in Greek poetry repellent, or at least puzzling. Plato and Aristotle set the student of philosophy a comparable puzzle, because although they insist that moral choice is free, the power that they attribute to habituation and their neglect of the possibilities of sudden and radical conversion create a hiatus in their system of thought on the nature of morality.

Detailed discussion of these problems belongs in part to dramatic criticism and in part to philosophy, but some religious considerations may be offered briefly here. Greek determinism is a conglomerate of phenomena of widely differing nature and origin. In a pre-scientific culture it is almost inevitable that moods and ideas that arise in people's minds without conscious decision should be regarded as coming from outside; after all, we still say "he was struck by an idea," as we say "he was struck by lightning," and the Greek Eros still figures as Cupid, equipped with bow and arrows, in popular art. The fate of Oedipus is an exceptional and bizarre exemplification of the general truth that we suffer disaster not of our own making, and unwittingly perform acts that we should not perform if we knew what we were doing; the oracle that foretold Oedipus's fate was not a divine announcement of a decision to punish him for nothing but a divine revelation of the future. Opinions may (and do) differ as to whether suffering incurred by one's own imprudence is more or less tragic than suffering that one can do nothing to avert. We all know that the latter category of tragedy exists, but it is possible to doubt whether the former is always tragic. The fact is that although we have had two millennia longer than the Greeks to think about the problem, and know very much more about psychology and genetics than they did, a man still cannot say with assurance how far a given action of his own or someone else's is determined. Common sense and introspection suffice to tell us that causal determination plays some part in our moral lives, but do not suffice to tell us how large a part; this uncertainty was an ingredient of the Greek experience, as it is of ours, and it is reflected in their literature. Each of us is inclined to think "I have an excuse, but you have none";

it is not surprising that Agamemnon clothes his apology in a long disquisition on the deadly effects of divine interference with one's rational processes, or that Achilles' answer tactfully refrains from comment on this aspect of the matter. Nor is it surprising that Clytemnestra represents herself as the instrument of a divine process, whereas the chorus, although sharing the general theological assumptions that make her plea possible, rejects out of hand her attempt to escape blame. When the gods have decided to punish a man through his descendants, they bring about a situation that sets in motion a sequence destined eventually, by one means or another, to effect the punishment; but that does not mean that every crime that constitutes an item in the sequence is forgivable.

References

1. M. N. TOD, *Greek Historical Inscriptions* (Oxford 1948), Vol. II, p. 204; partly known before from literary sources.
2. Polyaenus, *Strategemata* VIII, 52.
3. Pausanias, VIII, 37, 1.
4. *ibid.*, 30, 6.
5. Hephaestus and "Athena Hephaestia" are named in *Inscriptiones graecae* ii², no. 223 (342 B.C.).
6. *ibid.*, i², no. 293.
7. E.g. *ibid.*, i², no. 395 (5th century B.C.); *ibid.*, ii², no. 334 (*c.* 335 B.C.).
8. *Peace* 456 ff.
9. Herodotus, V, 82 f., tells the story of how the wooden statues of Damia and Auxesia were stolen by the Aeginetans from Epidaurus.
10. Pausanias II, 32, 2.
11. Sophocles (frag. 981 in the edition of Sir Richard Jebb and A. C. Pearson [Cambridge 1917]) called Demeter "*Azesia*," and "*Azosia*" appears as an alternative to "Auxesia" in late inscriptions from Epidaurus.
12. Cf. Herodotus II, 35 ff. on Egyptian religion; and Pindar, *Pythian Odes* IV, 16 (462 B.C.), refers to Libya as the land of "Zeus Ammon."
13. Cf. Xerxes' inscription "H" from Persepolis (R. G. KENT, *Old Persian*, 2nd edn [New Haven 1953], pp. 150 f.).
14. Euripides, *Bacchae* 272 ff. (the seer Tiresias is speaking), on Demeter and Dionysus as the "dry" and the "wet" in human nourishment.
15. *ibid.*, 370 ff.
16. *Olympian Odes* VI, 22 ff.
17. *Iliad* I, 222.
18. *Iliad* VIII, 166.
19. E.g. *Iliad* IX, 411; XII, 326; XXIII, 76.
20. *Works and Days* 121 ff., 252 ff.
21. *Symposium* 202D.
22. *Apology* 27CD.

23. *Theogony* 27 f.
24. *ibid.*, 188 ff.
25. *Iliad* V, 370 ff.
26. *Theog.* 225 f.; *Works and Days* 11 ff.
27. *Poetae melici graeci* (ed. D. L. Page [Oxford 1962]), frag. 192.
28. According to Herodotus, II, 156, 6.
29. Herodotus, V, 67, 3 ff.
30. H. DIELS (ed.), *Die Fragmente der Vorsokratiker*, rev. by W. Kranz, 6th edn (Berlin 1952), Xenophanes, B11.
31. *Poetae melici graeci*, frag. 217.
32. *Olymp.* 1, 25 ff.
33. *Iliad* I, 571 ff.
34. *ibid.*, I, 34 ff.
35. *ibid.*, XXIV, 22 ff.
36. *ibid.*, 405 ff.; cf. XXIII, 184 ff.
37. Herodotus, I, 32, 1.
38. *ibid.*, IV.205.
39. *Iliad* V, 318 ff.
40. [Hippocrates], *On the Sacred Disease* 4 f.
41. *Timaeus* 29E.
42. [Aristotle], *Magna moralia* 1208^b, 30.
43. *Nicomachean Ethics* 1159^a, 4 f.
44. *Ion* 112 ff.; *Hippolytus* 73 ff., 1391 ff.
45. *Iliad* XVI, 384 ff.
46. *Works and Days* 248 ff.
47. *ibid.*, 276 ff.
48. *Odyssey* XI, 505 ff.
49. Thucydides, V, 105, 3.
50. *Works and Days* 280 ff.
51. *Anthologia lyrica graeca* I, Solon, frag. 1, 25 ff.
52. *Works and Days* 240 ff., 260 f.
53. *Od.* XI, 467 ff.
54. *ibid.*, IV, 561 ff.
55. *ibid.*, XI, 582 ff.
56. *Homeric Hymn to Demeter* 480 ff.
57. *Republic* 330D ff.
58. *Frogs* 145 ff.
59. *ibid.*, 454 ff.
60. *Peace* 832 ff.
61. *Phaedo* 114D; cf. *Gorgias* 526D ff.
62. Xenophon, *Memorabilia* I, 1, 1.
63. DIELS, *op. cit.*, Critias, B25.
64. *Iliad* XIV, 86 ff.
65. *Agamemnon* 198 ff.
66. *ibid.*, 1497 ff.; cf. 1468 ff.

Bibliography

The discovery of inscriptions and papyrus fragments of poetry continuously augments the evidence for ancient Greek cult and myth. Important as these discoveries are, they seldom give cause for reappraisal of the now well-established conclusions of scholars in this field.

N. M. P. NILSSON, *Geschichte der griechischen Religion*, 2 vols., 2nd edn (Munich 1955–61), is the best modern work on Greek religion as a whole. One of Nilsson's outstanding merits is his balanced view of the different intellectual and artistic levels of Greek civilization, especially valuable in his treatment of the poets. Other relevant works by this author are *Greek Popular Religion* (New York 1940), published in paperback as *Greek Folk Religion* (New York 1961); *The Mycenaean Origin of Greek Mythology* (Cambridge 1932); *Greek Piety*, trans. by H. J. Rose (Oxford 1948); and *A History of Greek Religion*, trans. by F. J. Fielden (Oxford 1925).

W. K. C. GUTHRIE, *The Greeks and their Gods* (London 1950), is a good general treatment of the subject, but on a smaller scale than Nilsson's. U. VON WILAMOWITZ-MOELLENDORFF, *Der Glaube der Hellenen*, 2 vols. (Berlin 1931–2), is somewhat unsystematic but always stimulating. E. R. DODDS, *The Greeks and the Irrational* (Berkeley and Los Angeles 1951; paperback: Boston 1957), covers a very wide range of Greek religious attitudes.

H. J. ROSE, *A Handbook of Greek Mythology*, 6th edn (London 1960), is a learned and accurate book of reference. A more concise survey of the subject is his *Gods and Heroes of the Greeks* (London 1957). W. K. C. GUTHRIE, *In the Beginning* (London 1957), examines the theogonic and cosmogonic myths, and the transition from myth to early scientific speculation.

H. W. PARKE and D. E. W. WORMELL, *The Delphic Oracle*, 2 vols. (Oxford 1956), is the most comprehensive treatment of the role of Delphi in Greek life. E. ROHDE, *Psyche*, trans. by W. B. Hillis, 8th edn (London 1925), is a classic treatment of Greek ideas about the soul and the afterlife. A. W. H. ADKINS, *Merit and Responsibility* (Oxford 1960), is a readable and stimulating account of Greek attitudes to justice and virtue and their relation to divine sanctions. A. D. NOCK, *Conversion* (Oxford 1933; paperback: 1961), and A. J. FESTUGIÈRE, *Personal Religion Among the Greeks* (Berkeley and Los Angeles 1954), are concerned mainly with Hellenistic religion but include useful observations on the classical period. *Entretiens de la Fondation Hardt*, Vol. I (Geneva 1952), includes interesting contributions on Greek ideas of divinity.

CHAPTER 16

The Social Background of Early Greek Philosophy and Science

G. E. R. Lloyd*

The idea that Thales invented or discovered a new inquiry, "philosophy,"
goes back to Aristotle, as also does the notion that a more or less
continuous development can be traced in certain branches of speculative
thought from Thales onward. Aristotle is our main source of information
about early Greek philosophy, but when he comments on his predecessors,
as he does at length in *Metaphysics* A and elsewhere, it is not in order to
write a history of Greek thought so much as to consider what light they
had thrown on the philosophical and scientific problems (such as that of
causation) that he himself was investigating. In this context he naturally
emphasizes the continuity and homogeneity of pre-Socratic speculation.
He represents many of the first philosophers, particularly the group he
calls the "physicists" (*physikoi* or *physiologoi*), as if their investigations had
the same aims and the same clearly defined subject-matter as his own
physical treatises. Yet the circumstances under which they conducted
their inquiries, and indeed their conceptions of the nature of the inquiries
they were undertaking, were in many respects very different from what
we know about Aristotle and other 4th-century philosophers.

The general history of early Greek cosmological, physical, and ethical
theories can be reconstructed reasonably confidently from the information
in Aristotle and our other sources, the most useful of our later sources
being those that preserve quotations from the original works of the
philosophers themselves. The social background against which philosophy
and science developed among the Greeks raises a series of questions that
are much more difficult to answer, because our earlier and more reliable
sources largely neglect this aspect of their subject. First, what conception

* Fellow and Senior Tutor of King's College, and University Lecturer in Classics, Cambridge.

did the thinkers have of the activity they engaged in? We may choose to represent them as "philosophers" or "scientists," but what view did they themselves have of their inquiries? Second, what economic and political factors were involved in the rise of philosophy and science in Greece, and what, in particular, was the social role of the men who pursued these inquiries? When, for example, did philosophy become a profession in the sense that it provided a livelihood? And third, how were their ideas published or made known? Can we identify the audiences to which philosophical or scientific compositions were addressed, and does the nature of the audience tell us anything important about the nature of the compositions?

Let us begin where our evidence is most solid—that is, with Aristotle at the end of the period under consideration. Here we can answer the first question fairly definitely. Aristotle often discusses the relations between "physics," "mathematics," "first philosophy" (the study of being), "politics," and so on, and he generally draws clear distinctions between these main departments of inquiry, although his classification does not coincide exactly with our own. His conception of the value of philosophy is vividly expressed in *Nicomachean Ethics*, Book X, where he claims that the life of theoretical inquiry is superior to the practical life of the statesman and is supremely happy. We also have a good deal of information about the circumstances under which he worked, and this helps us to answer our other two questions, concerning the social role of the philosopher and the transmission of his ideas. The main events of his life are established, even though many of the details are obscure, and we know that quite apart from whatever private fortune he enjoyed (his father was court physician to King Amyntas of Macedon) he did not lack powerful connections. When he left Athens on Plato's death (347 B.C.) he was invited to go to Assos by Hermeias, the ruler of Atarneus, and he was later engaged by Philip of Macedon to teach the young Alexander. When he returned to Athens in 335 and began to teach in the Lyceum, he evidently had the approval and support of Antipater, Alexander's regent in Athens. When news of Alexander's death (323) reached Athens, Aristotle's position became sufficiently difficult to make him leave Athens for Chalcis, on the west coast of Euboea.

The importance of the Lyceum is obvious. Originally the relation between master and pupils was probably quite informal: it was only under Aristotle's successor, Theophrastus, that the Lyceum acquired extensive property and had (like Plato's Academy) the legal status of a *thiasos*, or religious association. But however informal the school may have been under Aristotle, it enabled him to co-ordinate the work of a number of philosophers and scientists and to begin an unprecedentedly ambitious programme of research in many different subjects, notably biology and the social sciences. The school was also important for more mundane and materialistic reasons. Although we have no direct evidence on the point, we may presume that fees were charged for attending the lectures, as they were in other schools, and in the 3rd century, at least, the pupils were certainly expected to make financial contributions toward the general upkeep of the school. Furthermore, it was for the lectures that Aristotle gave in the Lyceum and elsewhere that most of his extant treatises were prepared, and this has direct bearing on their style and content. Their lack of literary polish is evident: they are often highly compressed, obscure, and repetitious. On the other hand it is worth bearing in mind that several Greek philosophers distrusted the written word and confined their most important doctrines to oral teaching. In Aristotle's case the treatises contain many tentative ideas that served as the basis for discussions in the Lyceum, and he might well have been reluctant to present them to a wider public in the form in which we have them. Above all, the treatises allow us to observe the philosopher at work. His thought has often been described as a fixed, dogmatic system, but this is a gross misrepresentation. It is abundantly clear that he conceived the business of philosophy to lie as much in the defining of problems, the debating of alternative views, and the exploring of difficulties, as in the propounding of solutions. Although not cast in the dialogue form, his treatises at points retain something of the tone of actual philosophical discussions.

We can give a comparatively detailed account of the organization of the Lyceum in the 4th century and of the place it occupied in Greek society. But this account is inapplicable to the earlier pre-Socratics. Philosophy and science as activities conducted in well-established and well-organized institutions were the end-products of long, complex social and intellectual developments. How far can we reconstruct the circumstances under which the men who are considered the founders of philosophy and science actually worked?

A note on Thales will illustrate the magnitude of the problem. It is well known that before Aristotle there is almost no evidence to suggest that Thales engaged in natural philosophy or speculative inquiry of any kind. In popular belief he ranked among the Seven Wise Men, along with Solon, Pittacus, and so on. The exact list varies, but the Seven were in most cases men whose main role in society was as statesmen, law-givers, and constitutional reformers. Their teaching was supposedly expressed, as a general rule, in the form of pithy, oracular statements. Plato (*Protagoras* 343ab) tells us that the maxims "Know thyself" and "Nothing too much," which were inscribed on the temple of Apollo at Delphi, were derived from them. Later writers attribute a set of such statements to Thales, but it is more important to remark that there is good early evidence of his engaging in political activity. Herodotus (I, 170) praises the advice that he says Thales gave to his fellow Ionians, namely to federate and set up a common council. Other stories refer to his success in practical affairs. Herodotus (I, 75) reports how he diverted the River Halys; Plato (*Republic* 600a) says he was responsible for many ingenious inventions (although Plato also has a laugh at his expense when, in the *Theaetetus* [174a], he tells the story of Thales falling down a well while he was looking at the stars); and Aristotle (*Politics* 1259a, 6 ff.) tells how Thales made a fortune by cornering the market in olive-presses. To be sure, we also hear from Herodotus (I, 74) that Thales predicted a total eclipse of the sun to within a year (this would have been the eclipse of 585 B.C.); yet whatever the truth behind this story, it does not allow us to attribute any definite astronomical model to Thales, and even knowledge of eclipses was not a purely theoretical achievement, but had important (if rare) practical applications. None of this proves, or even suggests, that Aristotle's view of Thales as the first natural philosopher is incorrect. But it is important to recognize that Thales impressed his contemporaries and immediate successors not for any remarks about water as an originative substance (whatever these were, they are not mentioned in any extant source before Aristotle), but for his superior skill in a wide range of fields where that skill had practical applications.

Although our testimonies are conflicting, it seems most likely that Thales left nothing in writing and that his teaching was entirely oral. The evidence for Anaximander's and Anaximenes' writings is much more definite. Simplicius (*Physica* 24, 20 f.) comments on the poetical diction of the one quotation from Anaximander that has been preserved, and Diogenes Laertius (II, 2, 3) tells us that Anaximenes used a plain Ionic style. Even so, we must be cautious. Both these thinkers evidently discussed certain cosmological topics. In particular, Anaximander apparently described the development of the world and the origin of living creatures. But it is far from clear how extensive their compositions were; nor indeed can we be certain that their primary purpose was what we should call cosmological. The references to style and the extant fragments themselves prove that both men wrote in prose, and this is in itself quite remarkable, because it makes Anaximander not merely the first philosophical writer, but one of the very first *prose* writers, in Greek literature. But beyond this, on such questions as the relative importance of oral teaching and written text in spreading their ideas, we are reduced to guesswork.

Aristotle was the first to connect the rise of theoretical inquiry with the leisure afforded by affluence (*Metaphysics* A, Ch. 1–2), and certainly Miletus—the home of Thales, Anaximander, and Anaximenes—was the most important and prosperous Greek city in Asia Minor until its destruction by the Persians in 494 B.C. It was famous for its trade, its industries, and especially its colonies (it was said to have founded 90). Moreover, thanks to alliances first with Croesus and then with Cyrus, it retained more political independence during the greater part of the 6th century than most of its Greek neighbours. Internally it was far from enjoying a settled constitution. Herodotus (V, 28) refers to the party strife it suffered, and it was ruled intermittently by tyrants. But these upheavals did not prevent, and may even have done a good deal to encourage, the development of political institutions and political awareness. The growth of a new critical spirit in philosophy in the 6th and 5th centuries may be seen as a counterpart and offshoot of the contemporary development of the habit of free debate and discussion of politics and law throughout the Greek world.

We cannot determine what part either Anaximander or Anaximenes played in the social and political life of Miletus. Important though they are in the early history of philosophy, they are simply not mentioned by any extant source before Aristotle. Anaximander was said to have been responsible for the first Greek map, for which some of the Milesian colonists may have been grateful, and it is reasonable to assume that (like Thales) he took an active part in the affairs of the city. Again, we may infer *some* association between Thales, Anaximander, and Anaximenes, though what form that association took we do not know. Late sources speak of a teacher-pupil relationship in each case, but with their love for cut-and-dried philosophical genealogies the doxographers are notoriously unreliable on such a point, and it would be quite unjustified to infer from their association the existence of a formal school, a prototype Academy or Lyceum. Very likely, speculative inquiry, at this stage, was at most the avocation of a few private citizens.

The next figures who appear in the histories of philosophy—Pythagoras, Xenophanes, Heraclitus, and Parmenides—are all quite different from what we can judge of the three Milesians, and indeed from one another, and the contrasts between them are instructive. Although the evidence for early Pythagoreanism is hazy, we can be reasonably certain about some very important points. (1) Pythagoras was partly, perhaps primarily, a religious and moral leader. One of the few doctrines that can be traced back to Pythagoras himself is the transmigration of souls, and Plato (*Republic* 600b) tells us that he taught his followers a way of life. (2) The Pythagoreans, from early on, formed a distinct group or sect that had a reputation for exclusiveness and secrecy. (3) Pythagorean associations were a political force in several cities in Magna Graecia in the late 6th century B.C. The Cylonian conspiracy at the end of that century was an anti-Pythagorean "counter-revolution" and marks the end of a period during which the Pythagoreans had apparently been a major political influence in western Greece. It is true that the term "Pythagorean" came to be applied to 5th-century thinkers whose association with the sect was quite loose. Nevertheless it is significant that the most prominent and numerous group of philosophers and scientists in the pre-Platonic period was one that had been originally founded—and was still in certain places kept together—at least as much for religious, ethical, or even political motives, as for the purpose of conducting what we should call philosophical and scientific investigations. Furthermore the religious nature of the group influenced the work of its members profoundly. One reason why it is so difficult to establish the individual authorship of early Pythagorean doctrines is that Pythagoras himself was held in such awe, and where the authority of the founder counted for so much, criticism and discussion of his views were slow in developing. Mathematics was considered the key to the secrets of the universe, but mathematical discoveries were, to begin with at least, guarded from outsiders as jealously as were the details of the mystery rites from those who had not been initiated.

Our next philosopher, Xenophanes, belongs as much to the history of lyric poetry as to that of cosmology. True, several of his verses are important for the development of speculative thought, particularly those in which he expresses ideas about god in opposition to the anthropomorphism of Homer and Hesiod. But these fragments were composed by a poet who was as much an entertainer as a philosopher, as we can see from the two complete poems of his that are preserved. One of these (fragment 1) describes a banquet; in the other (frag. 2) Xenophanes claims that his "wisdom" is more valuable to the city than the skill of any athlete, and this poem is especially interesting because it is not as a cosmologist or as a natural scientist that Xenophanes makes this claim, but as a poet and moral leader.

Heraclitus and Parmenides are speculative thinkers of a very different calibre. Heraclitus is the first philosopher from whom we have more than just one or two prose fragments. His reported statements have a very distinctive elliptical style, which justly won him a great reputation for obscurity, but is also undeniably memorable; many of his statements owe their preservation to their very obscurity. If Xenophanes may in some respects be compared with an Anacreon or a Theognis, Heraclitus, like the Wise Men before him, invites comparison with an oracle. Indeed he refers approvingly to the Delphic oracle in one fragment (frag. 93), where he says that Apollo "neither speaks nor conceals but indicates" his meaning. In other ways, too, Heraclitus is exceptional among the early Greek thinkers. Although some of his fragments convey a political message, he apparently refused to take an active part in politics, and expresses his contempt for the common run of his fellow citizens in many of his sayings.

Heraclitus produced a series of oracular pronouncements, and bluntly described his method of approach to the truth (frag. 101) as "I searched myself," a dictum that may echo the Delphic "Know thyself." When we turn to Parmenides, the contrast could hardly be greater, whether we consider the content of his thought, or his style and method. First, he chose verse as his medium. Second, his "Way of Truth" is introduced with a poem in which he describes how he is borne toward the light, how he passes through the gates of the paths of night and day and is greeted by an unnamed goddess who remarks that the road he has travelled is "far from the footsteps of men." Third, the whole of the rest of the poem, both the "Way of Truth" and the "Way of Seeming," is the speech of this goddess. In all this, Parmenides was far from merely following literary convention, but was claiming for his philosophy the status of a revelation. It is striking that the first closely argued discussion of the central philsophical problem of being is in verse, and was composed by a man who considered himself divinely inspired.

We may now pause to take stock of the earlier pre-Socratics. The thinkers I have mentioned are usually considered to form a single fairly continuous "history of early Greek philosophy." From the point of view of their physical and cosmological theories this line of interpretation can largely be justified. At the same time we should recognize how different these thinkers were from one another: different in their *interests*, in the *style* and *medium* they used in communicating their ideas, and in their *attitude toward* and *role in* society. Neither the phrase *peri physeos historia* (inquiry concerning nature) nor the term *philosophia* (philosophy) itself can be dated precisely. Our later sources regularly use the former as the title of early philosophical works, but this evidence is untrustworthy. The term "philosophy" is sometimes said to have been invented by Pythagoras and may have acquired a special sense applied to the Pythagoreans, but it almost certainly had earlier non-technical usages in Ionic Greek. It is not until the later part of the 5th century that we find reliable texts in which these terms are used to refer specifically to "natural philosophy"; and several of the texts in question occur, interestingly enough, not in the philosophers themselves, as one might expect, but in the medical writers, who were often highly critical of the cosmologists and who resisted what they represented as an invasion of medicine by the methods of natural philosophy. So far as the earlier pre-Socratics down to Parmenides are concerned, it is fairly clear that none of them placed himself in any category of "philosopher" or "inquirer concerning nature" that included all the others. It is even uncertain how far any of them saw themselves as part of a single developing investigation, despite the fact that they were often aware of one another's ideas. Thus Xenophanes pokes fun at Pythagoras in one poem (frag. 7), and Heraclitus (frag. 40) criticizes both Pythagoras and Xenophanes. But it is significant that in the fragment in which Heraclitus does this, he lumps the two philosophers together with the poet Hesiod and the geographer Hecataeus: "Much learning does not teach sense; for otherwise it would have taught Hesiod and Pythagoras and again Xenophanes and Hecataeus." The earlier pre-Socratics competed with one another and with others, particularly the poets, for the attention of their fellow-Greeks, but "philosophy" provided as yet no clearly defined role. Besides their interest in cosmology, those whom we know as the first Greek philosophers all had one or more of the further roles of sage, religious teacher, statesman, moralist, and entertainer.

Until after Parmenides there is little evidence of prose works on natural philosophy—indeed, little evidence of prose composition of any sort. During the course of the 5th century, certain major changes take place. First, the sheer quantity of work produced on philosophical, scientific, and technological subjects increases markedly. Second, prose overtakes verse as the dominant medium. And third, alongside the successors of the philosopher-sages of the 6th century, two new kinds of authors appear: professional educators who write on any subject that people will pay them to teach; and (not always clearly distinguished from the former group) professional practitioners who write on technical subjects mostly for other practitioners.

These generalizations must be qualified. Empedocles, for instance, wrote in verse and combined the roles of religious leader, mystic, and prophet with those of physicist and cosmologist. As Parmenides had addressed the goddess at the beginning of his "Way of Truth," so Empedocles, apparently in direct imitation, invoked the Muse in his poem *On Nature* (frag. 3). More interestingly, his other work, the *Purifications*, is (as its title suggests) a religious poem in which he describes the fall, transmigrations, and redemption of the *daimon*. And this begins (frag. 112) with a passage in which Empedocles coolly describes himself as "an immortal god, no longer mortal," and says that people throng to him "asking the path to gain, some desiring oracles, while others seek to hear the word of healing for all kinds of diseases." There is something of the magician in Empedocles, alongside the natural scientist who could produce quite detailed accounts of the physiological processes of respiration and vision.

Yet Empedocles was the last great pre-Socratic cosmologist to write in verse. After Parmenides the usual medium of philosophical writers was prose: this is true of the later Eleatics Zeno and Melissus, of the natural philosophers Anaxagoras, Diogenes of Apollonia, Leucippus, and Democritus, and of the later Pythagoreans Philolaus and Archytas, as well as of a host of lesser cosmologists. And prose is also the usual medium both of the Sophists and of the authors of technical treatises on such subjects as medicine and music.

Although almost all their writings are lost, we know a good deal about the rise of the Sophists, a movement that had far-reaching consequences over the whole field of Greek education as well as specifically in the development of philosophy. Plato (*Protagoras* 349a) tells us that Protagoras of Abdera was the first to demand a fee for teaching virtue. But he was soon followed by many others, the most famous of whom were Gorgias, Hippias, Prodicus, Thrasymachus, Antiphon, and Critias. Some of these specialized in a particular branch or branches of learning: for example, Thrasymachus chiefly taught rhetoric, and Prodicus was mainly known as a philologist. Others, such as Hippias, claimed to be able to teach almost any subject from mathematics and astronomy to mythology. But what all these men had in common, and what marks them out from the earlier generations of philosophers, was that they taught for money and were prepared to travel all over the Greek world to do so.

They acquired and built up their reputations primarily, it seems, by giving public performances at the great pan-Hellenic festivals. Hippias, we are told, went regularly to the festival at Olympia to give exhibition speeches and to answer questions from the crowd that gathered. In some cases we know how much the Sophists charged to attend their courses. Prodicus apparently gave two courses on philology: the beginners' costing 1 drachma (that is, as much as Anaxagoras's treatise *On Nature*), and the advanced costing 50 drachmas. Hippias is said to have earned 20 minae from a visit to a single small town in Sicily, which was about 2000 times the current daily wage for a skilled worker. Even when we allow for some exaggeration in our sources, it is clear that several 5th-century Sophists grew rich from their profession, which continued to be well paid in the 4th century too. For example, Isocrates (*Antidosis* 158 ff.) tells us that he made a considerable fortune as a teacher, although he also indicates (*Against the Sophists* 3 ff.) that there were plenty of minor Sophists in Athens in his day who barely scraped a living from their lectures.

In the late 5th century a new kind of learning began to challenge the old education, which consisted largely of grammar, music and poetry, and gymnastics. Starting with the sons of the richest citizens, who had time and money to spare, the Sophists eventually attracted a wide clientele. Apart from bringing about a general broadening of education, they helped to introduce two other important developments. First, one of the main subjects they professed was rhetoric, and skill in public speaking was becoming increasingly important in many different contexts: in the law-courts, in political assemblies, and on diplomatic missions from one city-state to another. In teaching rhetoric as an art the Sophists undoubtedly helped to make their contemporaries more conscious not only of literary style, but also of the whole question of techniques of persuasion and methods of argument, and thus contributed both directly and indirectly to the development of logic.

Second, the challenge to the old education was seen as a challenge to traditional morality. The new interest in ethics in the late 5th century is associated particularly with Socrates. But he did not bring about this major shift in interest single-handed. It is clear that the Sophists did much to stimulate debate of ethical issues, for example in the controversy between "nature" and "convention." Indeed, had the teaching of Protagoras, Gorgias, and the rest not had an obvious moral significance, Plato would hardly have taken such pains to attack what they said.

Some Sophists were prepared to lecture on a wide range of topics, including technical subjects of which they had little or no practical knowledge. But such subjects (particularly music and medicine) were also taught more professionally, by actual—and to intending—practitioners. The Greeks were careful to distinguish between learning an art for the sake of general education, and learning it in order to practise as a professional. In music, for instance, there was an important difference between learning the lyre as part of one's education as a gentleman, and learning it in order to become a professional lyre-player: the first was allowed and encouraged, the second severely frowned upon, by the higher echelons of society.

By far the most important "technical" subject for the development of science was medicine, and the treatises of the Hippocratic corpus provide excellent examples of the different ways in which this subject was treated. Some works were evidently composed for rhetorical performances by men who were probably not themselves medical practitioners. One such piece is *On Breaths*. Another treatise, *On the Nature of Man*, refers directly to the debates on medicine and other subjects. The writer says (Ch. 1) that the best way to discover how ignorant his opponents are is to attend their discussions. "Given the same debaters in front of the same audience, the same speaker never gains the advantage three times in succession, but now one man wins, now another, now whoever happens to speak most fluently before the crowd." These and other texts prove that medicine was among the subjects on which public debates were held. On such occasions, where the contest was adjudicated either by a lay umpire or by the audience itself, what counted was rhetorical skill, not the technical knowledge that a speaker revealed; and this goes a long way to explaining the superficial quality of the discussion in some of the medical treatises that have survived. On the other hand, the Hippocratic corpus also contains works of a very different kind. The surgical treatises and the collections of case-histories known as the *Epidemics* were written by professional practitioners for their colleagues. These works pay no attention to style. Their aim was simply to convey useful medical knowledge, and this they do most effectively.

Fifth-century writers differ considerably in the extent to which they cultivate literary style. Yet in most cases their works were read aloud, usually before an audience. This is true not only of the exhibition speeches of the Sophists, but also of the cosmological works, whether in prose or in verse, and even of such a sophisticated treatise as Zeno's arguments against the pluralists. The beginning of Plato's *Parmenides* (127a ff.) provides useful evidence on this point, for there we are told that Socrates, having heard that Parmenides and Zeno were in town for the Great Panathenaea, called on Zeno at his lodging to hear him read from the treatises that they had just brought to Athens for the first time. These were definitely written compositions (the term used in Plato is *grammata*) and Zeno interestingly remarks of one piece that no sooner had he composed the work than someone stole it and (as we should say) pirated an edition. But Socrates does not ask to borrow Zeno's book or to read it for himself: he asks Zeno to read it out and they then debate its contents. Even complex philosophical works were more commonly recited and discussed than studied alone and in silence.

The evidence concerning the manufacture and publication of books in the 5th century is poor. Yet by the end of that century it is clear that in Athens one could obtain not only editions of Homer and the poets, but also some highly specialized works. A famous passage in the *Apology* (26d ff.) indicates that Anaxagoras's cosmological treatise could be bought for one drachma at most, from the stalls in the Orchestra. The increasing availability of texts obviously contributed a great deal both to the preservation and to the spread of philosophical and scientific ideas. Although private libraries were still quite rare, certain individuals acquired considerable collections of books. Thus, according to Xenophon (*Recollections* IV, 2, 8 ff.), Euthydemus owned large numbers of medical treatises and works on architecture, mathematics, astronomy, and other subjects, as well as editions of the most famous poets. Such a collection was exceptionally large, but we may presume that the medical schools and the Pythagoreans had their own libraries. Indeed the extant Hippocratic treatises probably derive, in the main, from the library of one 4th-century medical school.

The rise of the Sophists, the growth of such professional groups as the medical schools, and the increasing availability of books, were all important factors in the development of philosophy and science in the 5th and 4th centuries B.C. Yet these changes were far from being always and everywhere approved. Plato's distrust of the written word is well known, and although his own magnificent writings seem to give him the lie, all of them (with the exception of some doubtfully authentic letters) are dialogues purporting to represent actual conversations. Even his favourite word for the activity of the philosopher, *dialektike*, has as its root sense the art of conversation. Again, although several Hippocratic authors emphasize the value and importance of the art of medicine and the difference between the professional practitioner and the layman, doctors were still mere craftsmen, even though in the hierarchy of craftsmen they ranked among the highest. Finally, Aristophanes and Plato were certainly not the only Athenians of their respective generations to disapprove strongly of the profession of paid Sophist.

Despite the hostile reception the Sophists met in some quarters, much of the new learning they taught was taken over into "liberal" education during the course of the 4th century. The era of the great "polymath" Sophists, Protagoras and Hippias, who travelled from city to city gathering pupils as they went, gave way to a period dominated by more stable, and more respectable, schools. Of these the most famous were Isocrates' school of rhetoric and Plato's Academy. Isocrates' school, where the emphasis was laid on useful knowledge, particularly on skill in public speaking, may be considered the direct successor to the 5th-century Sophists. Plato's Academy owed more to the model of the Pythagorean fraternities, and in turn it provided the chief model for Aristotle's Lyceum and for countless other educational institutions. The programme of education Plato prescribes for his statesmen-philosophers in the *Republic* is a long and elaborate one. The student begins as a child with music and gymnastics and proceeds to dialectic, at the age of 30, only after an intensive course in mathematics; a further 20 years pass before the best minds graduate to the highest study of all, the contemplation of the Good. We do not know how closely Plato tried to keep to this scheme in the actual curriculum of the Academy. But we may be sure of two things at least: first, that, unlike Isocrates, Plato placed great emphasis on the role of the mathematical sciences in higher education; and second, that his object was to produce not academic intellectuals, but statesmen-philosophers, men who could and would influence the course of events in their cities and in the Greek world at large.

Much as one might like to represent what we call philosophy and science as the products of a single, continuous development in Greece, the available evidence suggests a very different and far more complex story. We are used to recognizing the variety of political institutions that the Greeks produced—a variety that contrasts strongly with, and was only possible in the absence of, the monolithic authoritarian regimes of the Near Eastern super-powers Egypt and Persia. But equally, and not unconnectedly, the Greeks developed a variety of different conceptions of education. In the 6th and 5th centuries B.C. philosophers and scientists with very different ideas, interests, and ambitions competed with one another, and with the poets and religious leaders, as educators. Even in the 4th century, although competing schools agreed in their claim to teach *philosophia*, what was meant by that term differed from one school to another: it was not only Plato, but also Isocrates, who professed to practise and teach "philosophy." Furthermore, this very variety of competing models of education and philosophy was an important factor, both in making the Greeks more aware of the distinctions between different intellectual disciplines, and in stimulating discussion of fundamental ethical issues. As Plato saw, the question of right education could not be settled except in conjunction with the question of the good life as a whole.

Aristotle's view of philosophy as the product of natural curiosity in a leisured society is helpful as far as it goes. Clearly, it was only because he was comparatively free from anxiety concerning his livelihood that the Greek citizen was able to devote so much of his time and energy to the activities he enjoyed so much—political affairs and the social life of the city-state, including its festivals and entertainments. The economic conditions allowed individuals to engage in theoretical studies without regard to any useful outcome they might have. Moreover the political circumstances in Greece positively favoured the growth of free discussion, so important for the development of philosophy and science. Both logic and ethics may, without too much exaggeration, be said to derive ultimately from the debates of the market places, law courts, and assemblies of the city-state. But the development of science and mathematics required other factors as well, particularly the idea of co-operation in research. Here both the Pythagoreans and the medical schools (in their very different ways) had important contributions to make. But in neither case was the chief motive for these associations any idea of the value of scientific research for its own sake. Religious and political ties helped to keep the Pythagorean groups together, and the medical schools were exclusive associations formed from professional motives, like a mediaeval guild or a modern trade union. Moreover the doctors, like the Pythagoreans, were on occasion secretive about their discoveries.

We noted at the beginning that the first extensive philosophical and scientific investigations were undertaken in the Lyceum. It may now be suggested that the success of the Lyceum was in part the result of its combining the tradition of free discussion with the idea of corporate research that goes back to the Pythagoreans and to the early medical schools. Although the Museum at Alexandria later surpassed even the Lyceum in the range of its researches, the institutions where extensive scientific investigations were carried out were rare throughout antiquity. The ancients lacked the idea that dominates our own society, that scientific research holds the key to material progress. Indeed, although there were many who recognized that civilization had developed in the past, there were few who imagined that it would or could progress much further in the future. The *raison d'être* of the Lyceum and Museum and of the many minor schools modelled on them was not any idea of the usefulness of scientific research, but the ideal of a "liberal" higher education. The

394

physical or the biological sciences were part of philosophy in the widest sense of that term, and with two main exceptions little attention was paid to the possibility of turning scientific discoveries to practical advantage. The first main exception was the application of technology to improving weapons of war—siege engines, catapults, and the like. The second was medicine. Many of the most famous biologists were doctors, who were motivated in their research partly by the desire to improve the treatment of the sick, and sought to apply their knowledge to this end. Yet not even the most famous and successful doctors in antiquity entirely escaped the disdain usually felt for the craftsman. In the Greek scale of values the theorist was always superior to the technologist, and although this ideology did not completely prevent the practical application of scientific discoveries, it certainly inhibited it, and acted as an important barrier to the cross-fertilization of different intellectual disciplines.

Bibliography

H. CHERNISS, *The Riddle of the Early Academy* (Berkeley and Los Angeles 1945).

J. A. DAVISON, "Literature and Literacy in Ancient Greece," *Phoenix* XVI (Toronto 1962), pp. 141–56 and 219–33.

B. FARRINGTON, *Greek Science*, rev. one-volume edn (paperback: London 1961).

W. K. C. GUTHRIE, *A History of Greek Philosophy*, 3 vols. (to date) (Cambridge 1962–9).

F. D. HARVEY, "Literacy in the Athenian Democracy," *Revue des études grecques* LXXIX (Paris 1966), pp. 585–635.

E. A. HAVELOCK, "Pre-Literacy and the Pre-Socratics," *Bulletin of the Institute of Classical Studies* XIII (London 1966), pp. 44–67.

W. JAEGER, *Paideia, the Ideals of Greek Culture*, 3 vols., 3rd edn (Oxford 1946).

F. G. KENYON, *Books and Readers in Ancient Greece and Rome*, 2nd edn (Oxford 1951).

G. E. R. LLOYD, *Early Greek Science, Thales to Aristotle* (London 1970).

H. I. MARROU, *A History of Education in Antiquity*, trans. by G. Lamb (London 1956).

R. PFEIFFER, *History of Classical Scholarship* (Oxford 1968).

L. D. REYNOLDS and N. G. WILSON, *Scribes and Scholars* (Oxford 1968).

E. G. TURNER, "Athenian Books in the Fifth and Fourth Centuries B.C." (inaugural lecture, University College, London, 1951).

CHAPTER 17

The Impact of Philosophy on Graeco-Roman Literature

I. G. Kidd*

One of the most astonishing characteristics of the literature that has survived from the fusion of Greek and Roman civilizations between the 1st century B.C. and the 2nd century A.D. is the pervasive influence and content of contemporary philosophy. Many literary critics ignore it or take it for granted; more philosophers pass hastily from Plato and Aristotle to Plotinus with eyes averted from the intervening desert. And it is true that in this period there was no stimulation from any great philosopher approaching the stature of these figures. Yet it is difficult to think of any other period of literature so imbued with philosophy. Cicero, politician and barrister, when forced to retire from public life, occupied himself not with a Churchillian history of his time nor with an autobiography, but with a long literary series in Latin comprising an encyclopaedia of Greek philosophy *ipsius rei publicae causa*[1] (for the edification of his fellow citizens and his own relief).[2] The Roman emperor Marcus Aurelius, strained by office, refreshed himself in Greek by writing Stoic *Pensées*. One of the great imaginative poems of antiquity was written by Lucretius on the unpromising subject of the atomic physics and hedonism of Epicurus, and was thought by Statius to be on a par with Virgil's writings. Drama becomes philosophy in the hands of Seneca, and so does historical biography with Plutarch. Almost no category of writing, however unlikely—such as medicine (Galen) and geography (Strabo)— escaped the influence of philosophy. All this, of course, was apart from the publications of the professionals, some of whom were incredibly prolific; Chrysippus was credited with more than 700 treatises.[3] This led in turn to a rash of handbooks. At the other extreme, almost all educated writers

* Senior Lecturer in Greek, University of St Andrews.

of the period, however unphilosophically inclined, reveal some slight acquaintance with contemporary philosophical ideas as part of their cultural background.

The philosophy was Greek. It arose mainly from the four great Schools that had become established at Athens by the end of the 4th century B.C. By this time Plato's Academy had been teaching for over 80 years, and the Peripatetic School founded by Aristotle in the Lyceum for over 30 years; but in 306 Epicurus opened his house and garden for his society of friends, and Stoicism began to be taught a few years later by Zeno of Citium in the Painted Stoa. It was the two new Schools, together with the philosophical movement of Cynicism, that were to set their peculiar stamp on the popular conception of philosophy over the next five centuries. Indeed, it could be argued that popular esteem of Academy and Peripatetics in the 1st century B.C. derived not a little from the sceptical reaction of the New Academy under Arcesilaus and Carneades to the new dogmas, followed by the eclectic propaganda of Antiochus of Ascalon. There ought then to be a continuous picture of the invasion of philosophy from the end of the 4th century B.C., but unfortunately this picture is cracked and mutilated by the loss of much of the evidence of the following two centuries. And this is a pity, because part of the missing puzzle seems to be this: although the philosophy is indeed Greek, the unmistakable acceptance of a philosophical background discovered in Graeco-Roman culture does not appear to have been so prominent a feature of Hellenistic education.

A crisis of educational ideals had arisen in the 4th century between Isocrates, who advocated a literary education, and Plato, who argued for a philosophical and scientific base. In practice, in Hellenistic school education there is no doubt but that Isocrates and rhetoric won. The cultural background of Hellenistic literature is primarily literary. This was accentuated by the establishment of the great libraries and literary research centres at Alexandria and Pergamum. Of course many Peripatetics did scientific research at Alexandria, and it would be foolish to think that there was no cross-fertilization between Alexandria and the philosophical Schools in Athens; but the separation remained real and significant. The attitude of the new Schools toward literature did not help. Plato, for all his distrust of literature, had outlined a philosophical rhetoric in *Phaedrus*, and the Peripatetics, following Aristotle and Theophrastus, retained an interest in the classification and analysis of literary forms; so Peripatetic principles of organization and structure based on the nature and function of speeches were not without influence on the theory of rhetoric, and the scholastic casuistry of Hermagoras's rhetorical theories of the 2nd century B.C. has also been linked with Stoic logic. Stoics certainly influenced the development of grammar. But Epicurus rejected the traditional Greek education, sneering at poetry and rhetoric, and for the Stoics rhetoric was subsumed as a minor part of logic, so that truth and validity of argument were held paramount, with formal stress on lucidity and succinctness. Some Cynics were actively anti-literate, preferring to demonstrate their position in action rather than by words.

Such extreme attitudes could scarcely be maintained indefinitely or absolutely, however, for the very good reason that the Schools were evangelical, and so were forced to make contact with their public. So, in the 1st century B.C., the Epicurean Philodemus wrote on rhetoric, and Seneca the Stoic in the following century clearly prided himself on his style. But compromise had no doubt intruded from the very beginning of the period; for example, the pungent popular sermon known as the *diatribe* made headway from the early 3rd century B.C. The finest poetic expression of Stoicism survives in the *Hymn to Zeus* of Zeno's pupil Cleanthes, and the School heads—Carneades, Diogenes, and Critolaus—lectured with great power on the famous "philosophical embassy" to Rome in 155 B.C. But still the major impetus for literature appears to gain strength in the 1st century B.C. Educated Romans such as Cicero were not only trained in rhetoric but were also sent to Athens for courses in philosophy, or to Rhodes to hear Posidonius the Stoic, whom Cicero would not have invited to write up his cherished consulship had he not thoroughly approved of his style. Nevertheless Cicero himself felt the need of prologues justifying his literary metamorphosis of philosophy,[4] mentioning the crabbedness of Chrysippus and the tasteless popularization of Amafinius the Epicurean;[5] and Lucretius admitted that this philosophy required sweetening with the honey of his verses.[6] As popularization increased, the boundaries between philosophy and rhetoric could blur, so that writers could occupy any point on the continuum between the two—for example, Seneca on one side and Dio of Prusa, the Golden-mouthed ("Chrysostomus"), on the other.

One can go further and say that, quite early, philosophy and rhetoric had shown a tendency to overlap. Plato's *Gorgias* shows that the practitioner in one was inclined to claim as its own sphere the area occupied by the other—which was no less, indeed, than the whole sphere of human activity and expression. The philosopher or rhetorician naturally marched on the common territory from his own base: for example, the Stoics could assert that only the good man, *qua* philosopher, was the true orator, whereas Cicero and Quintilian could write that the true orator must be a good man. They did not, however, mean quite the same thing.

After Plato and Aristotle, however, the claims of the philosophical Schools in the social and political sphere underwent a marked change, peculiarly characteristic of the Hellenistic period, that at first tended to widen the gulf again between philosophy and rhetoric, which continued as an accepted education for man of affairs with political ambitions. For the new philosophies appeared to concentrate on the individual rather than on his political activity; or, rather, the conception of the relationship between the individual and his society changed emphasis. It has often been suggested that this reflects a historical change in political society after the conquests of Alexander, and that the individual Greek became disorientated owing to the breakdown of the autonomy of the old Greek city-states. Before then it was in his city-state that the individual found his self-sufficiency; for him it was the matrix of politics, society, education, religion, and art. The cosmic relationship was so close that Plato in the *Republic*, analysing the individual, used the paradigm of the analysis of his state. For Plato and Aristotle all human philosophy was related to the "politics" or social organization or cosmos of the city-state: if the matrix were broken in any one respect, the individual might well have to find new reference points. So it has been argued that Stoicism, Epicureanism, and the Cynics offered a positive response to the new climate of social and moral instability and insecurity, while of the older Schools the Academy (after a period of abstruse mathematical metaphysics) lapsed into scepticism, and the Peripatetics retired into the safer academic problems of scientific research. It is easy to overstress such arguments: neither the history of events nor the history of ideas is so simple. The Greek world did not change overnight; the loosening of the bonds of the city-state civilization was a gradual process, as was the shifting emphasis in the study of philosophy. The old problems remained. Epicurus owed much to Aristotle; Zeno was trained in the older Schools, and derived and incorporated much from them. But the facts of substantive change cannot be dismissed either; one might talk glibly of cause and effect, but it would be careless to ignore the possible social relevance of the Stoa and Epicurus, for therein must have lain much of their appeal. A new era of Greek civilization and culture *did* grow in the Hellenistic period, and it merged eventually with the Graeco-Roman world.

In the new political forms and instability, philosophy abandoned the city-state organism. Although the social form of the city-state continued historically, political power and autonomy had shifted from Athens, the headquarters of the Schools, and this political helplessness may well have been felt by philosophers, particularly as many of them were not Athenian citizens. Two features developed: on the one hand a great diversification of research into academic problems of scientific investigation and of logic, on the other hand a narrowing of human philosophy to the practical ethic of the individual and his personal salvation. Epicureans withdrew from public life. Cynics were positively apolitical and anti-national. Zeno, like Plato, wrote a *Republic*, but his ideal state was a pluralization of his ideal philosopher. Between the individual and his relation to the cosmos there was a political vacuum in which the city-state analogy disappeared. So philosophy, by reducing its claims in this sense, at first widened the gap between itself and rhetoric and affairs.

At the beginning of the 1st century B.C., however, two factors brought the Stoa, at least, back into the political arena. Panaetius, a member of the Scipionic circle, turned his attention to expounding the Stoic conception of social duties, which was thought by Cicero and others to have political importance, and Posidonius perhaps saw in the spread of Roman power the potential of a world state. Stoic cosmic tendencies found expression in a philosophical theory of the brotherhood of man, so prominent in Epictetus and Marcus Aurelius. Certainly, in the 1st century A.D., Stoics were actively connected with politics. And yet it remains true that, despite Seneca and Marcus Aurelius (or, rather, as it was displayed in these men), **Stoicism in itself was not a political force.** The attraction of Stoicism and of other new philosophies remained firmly in the way of life each in its own fashion offered to the individual; and the fact that they continued to arouse interest for several hundred years was due to new doctrines of security that had more practical relevance and application for the individual than for the state.

For illustration we may select a few of the more influential attitudes and ideas, looking for some characteristic phenomena rather than attempting a history either of philosophical details or of literary development. The practical aspect already mentioned was naturally reflected most in the department of ethics and in the way this department tended to over-shadow and influence others, although it had become standard to classify all philosophical activity under the heads of logic, physics (which included metaphysics and theology), and ethics. The *sophia* to which the philosopher was attracted was centred on man's happiness or well-being. As a *bene vivendi disciplina*[7] (training for living well) philosophy shifted from the elevated contemplation of eternal entities, knowledge for its own sake, and the disinterested search for truth, to a concern with practical didactics.

Much intellectual theorizing did indeed remain, but it was more orientated by the conduct of living. Cicero assumes that *omnia philosophiae praecepta referuntur ad vitam*[8] (all maxims of philosophy apply to life). Merely to be theoretically expert in Chrysippus's works was useless.[9] Socrates was the first to bring philosophy from heaven to earth,[10] but Hellenistic ethics completed the process.

Not surprisingly, philosophy was compared with the most practical of contemporary sciences, as the medicine of the soul addressed to a sick society. "The philosopher's lecture room," said Epictetus,[11] "is a hospital." Posidonius thought of man fighting a chronic illness. Epictetus could embark on a sustained metaphor of moral dietetics[12] to an audience no doubt familiar with Epicurus's references to health[13] and Chrysippus's talk of the doctor of the soul;[14] and such an approach appealed to laymen such as Cicero.[15]

It is interesting to pursue the comparison. Like medicine faced by the urgency of disease, Hellenistic ethics at first sight seem dominated by the initial negative drive of releasing men from the endemic disease of mental insecurity. The reward of philosophy was the freedom from fear, distress, lust.[16] Epicurus thought it of the greatest importance to expose the empty agonies of superstition and death. His garden was a haven from the world around him. Lucretius's poem[17] exhibits a deeply personal attempt on the part of a highly imaginative man all too sensitive to the terrors of this world, such as death, pain, and cruelty. "All life" for him "is a struggle in the dark," where men are like children groping for the light. Cynics—the most radical of all—tried to slash themselves free from the tentacles of convention, all ties of family and community, the external and vulnerable values of birth, class, rank, honours, reputation. There was much preoccupation with the uncertain attacks of chance and fortune, the savage game of external circumstances.[18] Stoics were driven in the search for self-sufficiency to free themselves from the inevitable disappointments of all physical and external desires, to discipline themselves to want only what was in their intellectual and spiritual power. But the negative limitations of self-sufficiency might appeal only to the more desperate; corresponding to the positive medical concept of health, the imagination was fired by the ideals of autonomy and independence of spirit canvassed by the new philosophies. Hence it was argued that man's most natural, and therefore perfect, state of health lay in the inner freedom whereby he might attain unassailable peace of mind, in which lay positive happiness and fulfilment. This was a form of humanism derived from an analysis of human nature. And it might be added that whereas the philosophies of Plato and Aristotle were in tendency aristocratic and oligarchic, the new philosophies were much more radical in outlook: they were applicable to man or woman, slave or free.

> To have no fear of anything,
> To want not, is to be a king;
> This is the kingdom every man
> Gives to himself, as each man can.[19]

Cicero's celebrated outburst in praise of philosophy as the *dux vitae* (*Tusculanae disputationes* V, 5) shows that the haven of philosophy was not merely one of refuge.[20]

In practice, philosophy attended to both negative and positive aspects. The world being what it was, philosophers found themselves engaged largely in cures, an activity that spawned appropriate literary genres such as *consolationes*, or the moral correspondence course of Seneca's *Epistulae morales*, or the direct, vivid admonitions of Epictetus's reported *Diatribes*. The core of such plain men's guides to practical conduct lay in the propagation of rules for action, which could simply be issued as a series of maxims, as in Epicurus's *Kyriae doxae*. But the Stoics in particular worked out a complete department of ethics with technical terms for "appropriate acts" classified among the "preferred" or "to-be-rejected" of "the things according to nature." Cicero's *De officiis* shows how a Roman man of affairs reacted to this aspect of Panaetius's work. In the literature of this section the emotions (*pathe*), collectively and singly, occupy a central position. Their eradication (or at least suppression) is advocated by the Stoics through continual training and discipline. Comparison with the athlete is frequent,[21] but above all Heracles became a literary commonplace as the symbol of human achievement through effort in adversity.[22] Another conception of literary importance in this section was that of progression. The Stoic doctrine of duties assumed that most men, although bad owing to the folly of ignorance, were progressing toward virtue and the ideal of happiness. Seneca held that the idea of progress in general was characteristic of Stoicism,[23] and Posidonius based a philosophy of history on this conception. So Stoics took a pessimistic view of the state of the world, but remained optimistic in outlook, a consequence of their attempt to link practice and ideals.

For in the end the holding operation of cures had to give way to the ideal of the complete prevention of sickness, and for this a quite different educative training was held to be necessary, self-imposed and directed by an understanding of the true end for man and its proper method of achievement. This was based on an intellectual dispelling of ignorance through self-knowledge, for which one had to study not only human nature, but also the relation of man to the universe of which he was a part. It was assumed that the ideal was possible, through the capacity of the human mind to achieve and maintain the perfection of its own nature by understanding and discipline. For the Stoics this lay in the autonomy of moral reason. Virtue had absolute value only in the exercise of moral choice; all else in the whole field of human activities in which virtue functioned—including the question of duties and even their attainment—was relegated to a relative value different in kind rather than in degree. So Stoics believed that the sage, armed by virtue, protected himself from the assaults of fortune.[24] Epicureans asserted that *ataraxia* (tranquillity) derived from the exercise of practical wisdom in choosing among pleasures and pains, the immediate experiences of senses and feelings, undistracted by fear and superstition; they sought to free themselves in a communion of friends "from the prison of affairs and politics."[25] Cynics, believing the artificial currency of human standards to be a corruption of their true nature, sought not to devalue these standards (as the Stoics did) but to deface the corrupt coin by continual ascetic practice,[26] honing their physical wants to a minimum in order to realize spiritual independence.

This determined engagement with both practical ethical psychiatry and ideal theories is particularly characteristic of Hellenistic ethics, and accounted for the wideness of its appeal. But the strain between the two poles could break the links and overstress the polarities, so that some Cynic "dog-philosophers" could be both attacked for bestiality by Lucian and exalted to saintliness by Epictetus.[27] Again, Stoics were accused of a black-and-white ideal philosophy of absolute virtue (or absolute vice), or of compromising with their ideals in practice. Some of the many paradoxes raised were real, such as the Stoic admission that although it was in the power of all men by nature to reach the sole autonomy of virtue, the world was full of fools. Yet the insistence on the progression from practice to ideals in this-worldly terms struck home and gained ground. Plato's ideal state and supra-celestial metaphysics remained for many a phantasy divorced from life. But Epicurus's societies of friends based on mutual agreement were a practical demonstration of his principles; and the uncommitted could also admire the wide range of a Posidonius, with his respect for facts and scientific explanation combined with the severity of Stoic ideals. As the sovereignty of reason was rooted in the world of reality, we find Romans such as Cicero advocating the study of Greek philosophy as the theoretical justification for Roman traditional practices.

Much of Hellenistic ethics had a universal appeal akin to that of the modern psychiatrist's couch, but the justification of the ideal ethics lay in the department of physics, which offered a more imaginative attraction. It is true that the new schools were uncompromisingly materialistic. But "physics" tended to become metaphysics couched in physical terms, whereby what was "natural" for man was explained by theories of man's relation to, and part in, the macrocosm of the natural constitution of the universe. As such, one can understand how the atomic theory of Epicurus could appeal to a great poet such as Lucretius, and how Stoic materialism could inspire Cleanthes' fine hymn, or be a source of strength to such disparate characters as those of Epictetus and Marcus Aurelius. For Epicurus, physics supported an ideal of severity and self-sufficiency remote and separate from worldly cares; but the Stoic saw in the *logos* (cosmic reason) a material, rational, creative force for order and good that permeated the whole universe.

In this spiritualization of matter, rationality and value were one, and the well-being of man depended on the divine reason of his soul functioning in harmony with the macrocosm. An influential problem widely debated was that of fate and free will. For Epicurus, experience was not completely determined: whence his idea, in physics, of atomic "swerve"—the capricious motion that causes atomic particles, travelling at equal velocities, to collide. The Stoics, committed both to the determinism of a monistic materialism and to the choice assumed by a prescriptive ethic, sought relief in an extremely sophisticated analysis of causation. They were also at the centre of the debate on the problem of evil and providence, and, through their theories of cosmic coherence, on the problems of divination. All these topics fascinated contemporary lay writers.

Although some aspects of Hellenistic physics appealed to wide human interests left unfulfilled by the formalistic ritualism of contemporary religion, Greek philosophy remained strongly intellectualist, and all the Schools wrote exhaustively on logic, not only as a defence of their systems, but also as the basic structure of their theories. It was logical principles that produced Epicurean atomic physics. Yet this also roused much interest on two main fronts—methodology and the theory of knowledge. These were important not only to scientific writers in the widest sense (such as historians and geographers) but also to practical men of affairs (such as rhetoricians and barristers). Cicero, significantly, began his encyclopaedia of philosophy with logical studies in the *Academica*.[28] One aspect of the Schools debate was between dogmatists (Epicurus and the Stoics) and sceptics (the Middle and New Academy). The latter, in opposition to the confident Stoic assertion of certain apprehension, developed a doctrine of argument from probabilities, and a system of arguing from both sides of a debate, that had strong attractions for the lawyer Cicero. Throughout this period, scepticism maintained a strong salutary influence not only in the Academy but also through an empirical medical school; and in general there is some evidence for the growth of an opinion, voiced by Strabo,[29] that only the philosophically educated man could form judgments—a view expounded by Epictetus[30] and implied by Cicero.[31]

Thus, much philosophy was thought to be relevant to and important for living, and even to be exciting. To be understood by the many it required also to be available and understandable. The simple fact of increased mobility no doubt helped to achieve this. Leading Stoic philosophers came from far-flung states; Epicureans established societies in different cities. The widening horizons swept beyond narrow nationalisms, and philosophy, addressed as it was to the individual, could speak to all, and was in tune with the development toward a universal humanity, the *societas humana* extolled in later Stoicism as the brotherhood of man. But, above all, Cynics, Epicureans, and Stoics were evangelists: "Friendship," said Epicurus, "goes dancing around the world with a call for all of us to wake for the message of supreme happiness."[32] Their message was not just for an intellectual elite, but for all mankind.

There were various methods of popularization. Cynics simply went into the streets to expose the cant of the establishment by action and popular harangue, ranging in style from Diogenes' disciple Crates (the much-loved "door-opener" or poor man's consultant) to the radical mystic Peregrinus (who theatrically burned himself to death before a huge crowd at an Olympic festival, evoking Lucian's biting disgust). A second, more decisive penetration into the Roman world came from the other end of the social and political scale. The philosophers' embassy to Rome in 155 B.C. made an impression; Posidonius was an ambassador in 86 B.C. In the Greek world, princes had occasionally consulted professional philosophers, or found them a place in their entourage. The custom grew in Rome of accepting philosophers as teachers or associates of the great: Panaetius was associated with Scipio and Laelius, Posidonius with Pompey, and Philodemus with L. Calpurnius Piso Caesoninus; Antiochus was a companion of Lucullus; Cicero talks of Diodotus in his establishment; Arius Didymus was a court philosopher of Augustus, and a friend of the patron of the arts Maecenas; Seneca's uneasy tutorship of Nero is notorious; Trajan's consort Plotina had strong Epicurean interests. The culmination, of course, was the assumption of power, in A.D. 161, of Marcus Aurelius, the Stoic emperor.

Between these two extremes of infiltration were many forms of literary popularization: *Ethical Elements*, for example, by Hierocles of Alexandria; compilations of doxographies (Diogenes Laertius), anthologies (Stobaeus), compendia (Aetius), commentaries (Alexander of Aphrodisia); even a 40-yard-long wall hoarding in stone on which Diogenes of Oenoanda advertised to all-comers the benefits of Epicureanism.[33]

Little of this could aspire to the name of literature, and Cicero no doubt had reason to sneer at the literary poverty of the popular tracts of the Epicureans Amafinius and Rabirius, but philosophy had a fundamental influence on some literary genres largely because what had been created as a tool for popular exposition came to be in tune with literary tastes of the time. The most original form was the *diatribe*, a forthright sermon in popular style, gingered with sharp wit and satire, sometimes in the form of fictional dialogue, in which the Cynic Bion of Borysthenes first "tarted up philosophy"[34] in the 3rd century B.C. Horace's *Bionei sermones*[35] explicitly acknowledged their literary significance, as Varro's *Saturae menippeae* acknowledged the form used by Menippus of Gadara. The *diatribe* not only continued as a lively instructional method used by Philodemus, Epictetus, and Dio of Prusa, but developed into a literary genre exemplified by Seneca's *Apocolocyntosis* and by works of Lucian and Petronius. The allied form of the philosophical dialogue—adopted by Cicero and with a continuous literary history from Plato's Socratic dialogues through Aristotle, Dicaearchus, and Heraclides Ponticus—shows a chameleon sensitivity to the fashions of contemporary philosophy. It is pointless to search for the questing dialogues of Plato in Cicero: the latter followed the methodology of the New Academy in the didactic, externalized presentation of both sides of a question and arguing from probability.

Another genre exploited by philosophers and brought to a high literary pitch by Seneca was the epistle: the personal address to an individual is characteristic of Hellenistic ethics. This was also the age of the aphorism in literature, whether in the form of maxims as external rules for conduct (as in Epicurus's *Kyriae doxae*) or as internal admonitions (such as those of Marcus Aurelius), or in the form of anecdotes or of *chreiae* (collections of witty epigrams or quips, usually Cynic or Stoic) that revealed the serious purpose or conduct of their famous authors. Poetry as a didactic form had been traditional from early times in Greek, and it responded again to contemporary demands with variations from the elemental hexameters of

Lucretius and the dignity of Cleanthes' *Hymn*, to the satirical *jeux d'esprit* of Crates, the lampoons of Timon of Phlius, the moralizing choliambics of Phoenix of Colophon on gluttony and the rich, the poetic socialism of Cercidas of Megalopolis, and the astronomical *Phaenomena* of Aratus, to select a few examples of considerable literary as well as philosophical significance.

Not content with the spread of literary forms created or shaped for the occasion, or to which they had a traditional claim, philosophers of this period left a personal mark on established genres, of which drama and historical biography are good examples. The treatment of both is marked by preoccupation with ethical character in action. The Peripatetics in particular were interested (witness Theophrastus's *Characters*) from both a philosophical and a literary point of view; but all the Schools, particularly those engaged with the close relation between individualistic philosophy and type, were attracted by the vivid presentation of famous exemplars. Hence Plutarch's *Lives* are historical only in subject-matter, but ethical in purpose, selection, and form.[36] We can only speculate on the purpose of the reputed tragedies of Diogenes the Cynic and Crates; but Seneca's dramas are Stoic epics on the interaction of human emotions and circumstances, designed to display the ruinous effects of the storms of passion[37] on human beings, and Plutarch wrote the *Life of Demetrius* as a warning to himself and others. The one form actualized mythical figures, the other made myth of history; but the literary purpose of both is the same.

An important factor in the philosophic content of literature during the 1st century B.C. was the strong tendency to eclecticism, encouraged especially by the influential head of the Academy, Antiochus of Ascalon. Eclecticism had, in fact, a long and distinguished ancestry. For example, leading philosophers from all Schools from Aristotle onward wrote special monographs on the emotions. It can be shown that this body of literature interacted to such an extent that eventually any writer, whatever his denomination, began employing a common fund of stock argument, illustration, or example, which became *loci communes* for all literature on the subject. So eclecticism was not simply a feature of writers committed to a philosophical attitude, such as Plutarch (whose *belles-lettres* cover a far wider scope than their modern title *Moralia* would suggest, and range beyond the Academy to which he adhered). On the contrary, educated men, not necessarily committed to any one School, might feel free to back their traditional standards or codes by philosophical theory from various sources, or to employ the stock themes cannibalized from the philosophic and literary debates on a particular topic. Finally, a writer could introduce a philosophical form or attitude for a purely literary purpose. It is reasonable to suppose, for instance, that Horace did not intend the moral maxims addressed to Lollius and Scaeva to be a practical guide to conduct, but was using a fictional poetic form; and Stoic or Epicurean themes discovered in the *Aeneid* are literary devices. It is irrelevant to ask whether Horace or Virgil was an Epicurean or a Stoic. But it seems clear that there was a broad band of philosophical allusion that writers found germane to their subjects, and whose imagery they could depend on to be recognized and understood by their readers.

This audience presumably included all educated men, in the sense defined by Strabo[38] as all who had participated in the general liberal education, including philosophy; and that a liberal education should include philosophy is an assumption demanded by the very purpose of Cicero's philosophical publications. It is true that Strabo said that poetry could draw full houses, whereas philosophy was for the few,[39] and Cicero complained that even legal handbooks had a readier sale.[40] But we must distinguish a much smaller circle of laymen actively interested in reading and discussing philosophy. Cicero implies that the numbers were growing,[41] but the prologues of his own dialogues present his ideal picture of leisured debate: a very few, highly educated Romans in a peaceful villa against a political background. A vivid picture of a comparable society in the Greek world is given by the table talk of Plutarch's friends and relatives in his *Quaestiones convivales*, where the range of reading and erudition is astonishing. The numbers participating in the discussion club on any given occasion were small, but the catalogue of Plutarch's friends preserved in his works runs to about 100.

In the Roman world of the 1st century B.C., if Cicero can be taken as evidence, philosophy and literature were linked partly because they were thought to be the adopted twins of the Greek legacy. Romans regarded themselves as pre-eminent in practical affairs and in their traditional institutions, but admitted that the Greeks surpassed the Romans *doctrina . . . et omni litterarum genere*[42] (in learning . . . and every kind of literature). Cicero considered that his countrymen had already achieved much in the naturalization of the Greek literary genius and forms, and in his attempt likewise to naturalize Greek philosophy he characteristically assumed that to make written learning practical the twins should not be unnaturally separated, indeed should be also united with the Roman expertise in practical affairs.[43] "It is possible for a man to hold right views and yet not be able to express them elegantly; but to commit one's reflections to writing without being able to arrange or elucidate them or in some way charm and attract the reader is the sign of a man who makes extravagant misuse of leisure and writing. . . . For I have always thought the complete philosophy to be that which can speak on the most important problems with a full flow of eloquence."[44] The models to which Cicero refers in this passage are Aristotle and Isocrates,[45] symbolizing the union of philosophy and rhetoric. "Let philosophy be born," he cries,[46] "in Latin literature." But his object in the literary presentation of the whole tradition of Greek philosophy was to perform a practical service for his countrymen.[47]

Modern philosophy is often accused of being confined to the private business of a small circle, who regard their study as a specialist activity, not a doctrine. This was not characteristic of much Greek thought, least of all of Hellenistic philosophy, which offered something to everyone—and everything to some—by the variety of its claims, attitudes, and interests. Like Marxism, it had pretensions to become the intellectual cultural centre of a humanist revolution, and was as much a social phenomenon as a purely intellectual activity. But the security offered was spiritual, not material, which appealed in centuries marked by social turmoil and helplessness, and by scientific and technological advance. Perhaps no other age has held such an arrogant conviction of the possibility of the self-sufficiency of the individual. Yet the "apathy" often linked with this spiritual freedom never had its modern passive connotation. The etymology of the word signifies: not to have something done to you or happen to you through an external agency. Thus mastery of one's self, and thereby of circumstances, required conscious and continual effort on the part of each individual by self-examination of his own nature and structure, the exploration of human conscience, and the resolution of oppositions between ideals and actions.

In practice and in the context of their society, the different doctrines produced every variation from the noble to the ludicrous, and they can easily be attacked in detail by philosophers and sociologists alike; but in their demands on human worth and capacity they were not without dignity. As for the activity of philosophy itself, it was open to anyone who had the means and inclination to pursue it in the Schools. If, outside them, philosophy became diluted to a hortatory propaganda for a way of life, the topics and attitudes were such as to concern and interest cultivated men, and, as such, they entered literature. Literature and philosophy remained distinct in purpose, but in this age, perhaps more than in any other, the material with which both in their own way were engaged was often the same. To a philosopher much of the material now seems to be of only moderate interest, and from a literary point of view the power in the best works of the time does not derive from the philosophical content (as in Aristotle), or from the union of thought and expression at the highest level (as in Plato), but from the revelation of the personal impact of philosophy on individuals. Cicero, Epictetus, Seneca, Plutarch, and Marcus Aurelius reveal this in quite different ways; but an outstanding example is the *docti furor arduus Lucreti*[48] (the sublime frenzy of the learned Lucretius)—it was the heat of a fierce personal passion that fused his philosophy to the disciplined tensions of literary greatness.

References

1. Cicero, *De natura deorum* I, 7.
2. *ibid.*, I, 9; Cicero, *De divinatione* I–VII.
3. Diogenes Laertius, *VII*, 180.
4. e.g. Cicero, *De finibus, init.*
5. Cicero, *Academica* I, 5; *De fin.* IV, 6–7; *Tusculanae disputationes* II, 7; IV, 6–7.
6. Lucretius, *De rerum natura* I, 947.
7. Cicero, *Tusc.* IV, 5.
8. Cicero, *De nat. deor.* I, 7.
9. Epictetus, I, 4, 6.
10. Cicero, *Tusc.* V, 10.
11. Epictetus, III, 23, 30.
12. *ibid.*, III, 21, 1 ff.
13. *Gnomologium vaticanum* 54.
14. *Stoicorum veterum fragmenta* 3, 471.
15. e.g. Cicero, *Tusc.* IV, 62.
16. Cicero, *Tusc.* II, 2.
17. Lucretius, *II*, 54 ff.
18. Fortuna saevo laeta negotio et
    ludum insolentem ludere pertinax
    transmutat incertos honores
    nunc mihi, nunc alii benigna
      (Horace, *Odes* III, 29, 49 ff.)
    (Fortune, rejoicing in her cruel work and obstinately pursuing her high-handed game, changes her fickle favours, and is kind now to me, now to someone else.)
19. Rex est qui metuit nihil
    Rex est qui cupiet nihil
    Hoc regnum sibi quisque dat.
      (Seneca, *Thyestes* 388 ff., trans. by E. F. Watling.)
20. cf. Cicero, *De oratore* I, 9.
21. e.g. Epictetus, I, 4, 13.
22. *ibid.*, I, 6, 32.

23. Seneca, *Epistulae morales* 33, 5 f.
24. Cicero, *Tusc.* V, 2.
25. *Gnom. vat.* 58.
26. Diogenes Laertius, VI, 71; Julian, *Orationes* VII, 208d.
27. Epictetus, III, 22.
28. Cicero, *De div.*, *init.*
29. Strabo, I, 1, 22.
30. Epictetus, I, 7.
31. Cicero, *De officiis* I, 1.
32. *Gnom. vat.* 52.
33. Diogenes Oenoandensis, *Fragmenta*, ed. by C. W. Chilton (Leipzig 1967).
34. Diogenes Laertius, IV, 52.
35. Horace, *Epistles* II, 2, 60.
36. See Plutarch, *Alexander* I, 1–3; *Cimon* II; *Timoleon* I; *Demetrius*, *init.*
37. e.g. Seneca, *Thyestes* 260 ff.
38. Strabo, I, 1, 22.
39. *ibid.*, I, 2, 8.
40. Cicero, *De fin.* I, 12.
41. e.g. Cicero, *Tusc.* IV, 2 and 5.
42. *ibid.*, I, 3.
43. Cicero, *De orat.* III, 61; *De republica* III, 5.
44. Cicero, *Tusc.* I, 6–7.
45. *ibid.*, I, 7.
46. *ibid.*, II, 5.
47. *ibid.*, I, 5.
48. Statius, *Silvae* II, 7, 76.

Bibliography

General References

The outstanding history of Greek literature is by A. LESKY, *Geschichte der griechischen Literatur*, 2nd edn (Berne 1963), trans. into English by J. Willis and C. de Heer (London 1966). It contains up-to-date bibliographies. The fundamental history of Greek philosophy is still E. ZELLER, *Die Philosophie der Griechen* (last edn 1920–23, repr. Hildesheim 1963). The relevant section, "Stoics, Epicureans, and Sceptics," was translated into English by O. J. Reichel (London 1870). G. J. DE VOGEL, *Greek Philosophy*, Vol. 3: *The Hellenistic-Roman Period* (Leiden 1959), presents a convenient selection of texts. Authoritative monographs on all writers of the period are to be found in Pauly-Wissowa, *Realencyclopädie der classischen Altertumwissenschaft* (Stuttgart 1894–). For Latin literature the facts are most conveniently collected by H. J. ROSE, *A Handbook of Latin Literature*, with supplementary bibliography by E. Courtney (London 1966). Interesting discussions are presented in the series *Studies in Latin Literature*, ed. by T. A. Dorey and D. R. Dudley, especially *Cicero* (London 1964) and

Lucretius (London 1965); but see also *Roman Drama* (London 1965) and *Latin Historians* (London 1966). In similar vein: *Critical Essays on Roman Literature: Satire*, ed. by J. P. Sullivan (London 1963).

Background

W. TARN and G. T. GRIFFITH, *Hellenistic Civilization* (London 1966); M. ROSTOVTZEFF, *Social and Economic History of the Hellenistic World* (Oxford 1941); A. H. M. JONES, *The Greek City from Alexander to Justinian* (Oxford 1940); V. EHRENBERG, *The Greek State* (Oxford 1960); E. BADIAN, "The Hellenistic World," in *The Greeks*, ed. by H. Lloyd-Jones (London 1962); E. WILL, *Histoire politique du monde hellénistique* (Nancy 1966–7); P. WENDLAND, *Die hellenistisch-römische Kultur in ihren Beziehungen zu Judentum und Christentum* (Tübingen 1907); H. C. BALDRY, *The Unity of Mankind in Greek Thought* (Cambridge 1965); R. HIRZEL, *Der Dialog* (Leipzig 1895); A. D. NOCK, *Conversion* (Oxford 1933).

Education

H. I. MARROU, *A History of Education in Antiquity*, trans. by G. Lamb (London 1956); M. P. NILSSON, *Die hellenistische Schule* (Munich 1955).

Cynics

Diogenes Laertius, Bk. VI; Dio Chrysostom, *Orationes* 4, 6, 8, 9, 10, 32, and 72; Epictetus, III, 22; Lucian, *Demonax, Peregrinus, Runaways, The Cynic, The Fisher*; Julian, *Orationes* VI and VII; *Teletis reliquiae*, ed. by O. Hense (Tübingen 1909). D. R. DUDLEY, *A History of Cynicism* (London 1937); R. HÖISTAD, *Cynic Hero and Cynic King* (Uppsala 1949); F. SAYRE, *The Greek Cynics* (Baltimore 1948); P. HELM, *Lukian und Menipp* (Leipzig 1906).

Epicureans

Evidence: G. ARRIGHETTI, *Epicuro, Opere* (Turin 1960); C. BAILEY, *Epicurus* (Oxford 1926); H. USENER, *Epicurea* (Leipzig 1887); C. DIANO, *Epicuri ethica* (Florence 1946). English translation: RUSSELL GEER, *Epicurus* (Indianapolis 1964). Lucretius is edited by C. Bailey (Oxford 1947), and Diogenes Oenoandensis by C. W. Chilton (Leipzig 1967). See also Cicero, *De finibus* I and II.

Three recent short introductions: B. FARRINGTON, *The Faith of Epicurus* (London 1967); G. A. PANICHAS, *Epicurus* (New York 1967); P. BOYANCÉ, *Épicure* (Paris 1969).

General: C. BAILEY, *The Greek Atomists and Epicurus* (Oxford 1928); E. BIGNONE, *L'Aristotele perduto e la formazione filosofica di Epicuro* (Florence 1936); N. W. DE WITT, *Epicurus and His Philosophy* (Minneapolis 1954); W. SCHMID, "Epikur," in *Reallexikon für Antike und Christentum*, Vol. 5 (Stuttgart 1961); cols. 681 ff.; R. D. HICKS, *Stoic and Epicurean* (New York 1910); D. J. FURLEY, *Two Studies in the Greek Atomists* (Princeton 1967); A. F. FESTUGIÈRE, *Epicurus and His Gods*, trans. by C. W. Chilton (Oxford

1955); K. KLEVE, "Gnosis Theon," *Symbolae Osloenses* XIX (Oslo 1963); R. PHILIPPSON, "Philodemos," in Pauly-Wissowa, *Realencyclopädie*, Vol. 19 (Stuttgart 1938), cols. 2444 ff.; P. H. DE LACY, *Philodemus: on Methods of Inference. A Study in Ancient Empiricism* (Philadelphia 1941); C. O. BRINK, *Horace on Poetry* (Cambridge 1963); P. BOYANCÉ, *Lucrèce et l'Épicurisme* (Paris 1963).

Stoics

Evidence: *Stoicorum veterum fragmenta*, ed. by H. von Arnim (Leipzig 1903–24): Panaetius, *Fragmenta*, ed. by M. van Straaten, 3rd edn (Leiden 1962). For Posidonius, see K. REINHARDT, "Poseidonios von Apamea," Pauly-Wissowa, *Realencyclopädie*, Vol. 22 (Stuttgart 1953), Part 1, cols. 558 ff.; also published separately; *Posidonius, Vol. 1, The Fragments*, ed. by L. Edelstein and I. G. Kidd (Cambridge 1971). Epictetus is translated by W. A. Oldfather in Loeb Classical Library, which also includes Seneca's *Epistulae morales* and *Tragedies*. Of the latter E. F. Watling has translated *Thyestes*, *Phaedra*, *Trojan Women*, and *Oedipus* for Penguin Classics (London 1966). Marcus Aurelius is edited and translated by A. S. L. Farquharson (Oxford 1944).

General: M. POHLENZ, *Die Stoa*, 2nd edn (Göttingen 1959); J. M. RIST, *Stoic Philosophy* (Cambridge 1969); L. EDELSTEIN, *The Meaning of Stoicism* (Cambridge, Mass. 1966); S. SAMBURSKY, *Physics of the Stoics* (New York 1959); B. MATES, *Stoic Logic* (Berkeley and Los Angeles 1961); A. A. LONG (ed.), *Problems in Stoicism* (London 1971); E. V. ARNOLD, *Roman Stoicism* (Cambridge 1911; repr. London 1958); M. LAFFRANQUE, *Poseidonios d'Apamée* (Paris 1964); A. F. BONHÖFFER, *Epiktet und die Stoa* (Stuttgart 1890); R. D. HICKS, *Stoic and Epicurean* (New York 1910); E. BEVAN, *Stoics and Sceptics* (Oxford 1913).

Peripatos

O. REGENBOGEN, "Theophrastos," Pauly-Wissowa, *Realencyclopädie*, Supplementband 7 (Stuttgart 1940), cols. 1354 ff. F. WEHRLI, *Die Schule des Aristoteles*, Vols. I–X (Basel 1944–59).

Sceptics and the New Academy

The most complete account is to be found in Sextus Empiricus, trans. by R. G. Bury in Loeb Classical Library. In general: V. BROCHARD, *Les Sceptiques grecs* (Paris 1887); A. GOEDECKEMEYER, *Die Geschichte des griechischen Skeptizismus* (Leipzig 1905); M. M. PATRICK, *The Greek Sceptics* (New York 1929); L. ROBIN, *Pyrrhon et le scepticisme grec* (Paris 1944); CHARLOTTE L. STOUGH, *Greek Scepticism: a Study in Epistemology* (Los Angeles 1969); O. GIGON, "Zur Geschichte der sogenannten Neuen Akademie," *Museum Helveticum* 1 (Basel 1944), pp. 62 ff. G. LUCK, *Der Akademiker Antiochos* (Berne 1953); A. WEISCHE, *Cicero und die Neue Akademie* (Münster 1961).

Cicero

Cicero's philosophical works are translated in Loeb Classical Library. The *Academica* are edited by J. S. Reid (London 1885). In general: R. PHILIPP-SON, *M. Tullius Cicero: die philosophische Schriften*, Pauly-Wissowa, *Realencyclopädie*, Vol. 7A (Stuttgart 1939), cols. 1104 ff.; H. A. K. HUNT, *The Humanism of Cicero* (Melbourne 1954); W. SÜSS, *Cicero: eine Einführung in seine philosophischen Schriften* (Wiesbaden 1966); T. W. LEVIN, *The Philosophical Writings of Cicero* (Cambridge 1871). R. HIRZEL, *Untersuchungen zu Ciceros philosophischen Schriften* (Leipzig 1882).

Plutarch

Plutarch is edited and translated in Loeb Classical Library. The most informative monograph is K. ZIEGLER, *Plutarchos von Chaironeia*, Pauly-Wissowa, *Realencyclopädie*, Vol. 21, Part 1 (Stuttgart 1951), cols. 636 ff. (also published separately). See also R. HIRZEL, *Plutarch* (Leipzig 1912); R. H. BARROW, *Plutarch and his Times* (London 1967).

Science

O. NEUGEBAUER, *The Exact Sciences in Antiquity*, 2nd edn (Princeton 1957); S. SAMBURSKY, *The Physical World of the Greeks* (London 1956); B. FARRINGTON, *Greek Science* (London 1953); G. SARTON, *A History of Science*, Vol. II (Cambridge, Mass. 1959).

CHAPTER 18

Theories of Literature and Taste

D. A. Russell*

The reflections that the Greeks and Romans made upon their own literature have many points of connection with the social structures within which they lived and wrote. Most conspicuous in the whole picture are two sets of discussions. One relates literature to morals and concentrates on its educative function: Aristophanes, Plato, and the Stoics are key witnesses. The other treats all writing as directed to convince and persuade: the highest achievements of ancient criticism, in Cicero, Dionysius, Quintilian, and 'Longinus', derive from this line—in other words from rhetoric. It is true that the profoundest and most significant theoretical contribution is not to be found here: Aristotle's conception of poetry as a species of mimesis has little to do with either ethics or rhetoric. Nevertheless, it is from ethics and rhetoric that the main criteria of literary excellence came.

Literary judgments were therefore, on the one hand, a function of the content of ethics, of the recommended qualities of human life. A concept such as that of decorum (*to prepon*) was easily translated from life to letters, from *bios* to *logoi*; there is a strong ethical element in the critical concept of propriety to station and purpose, in the doctrine that some words are, as one might say, "out of court," and even in the refusal to take realistic description of everyday life seriously.†

The Graeco-Roman world enjoyed a fair degree of stability over long periods. The values and traditions of the educated class were rarely challenged. Literature reflected them and preserved them. Moreover, in classical Greece and later in Rome, public activity was more highly prized than the private experience of the individual. Over our whole period, only one sort of "hero" other than a public figure is of any importance: the Hellenistic "hero as philosopher," the man who placed himself

---

* Fellow of St John's College, University of Oxford.

† See especially ERICH AUERBACH, *Mimesis*, trans. by W. Trask (Princeton 1953), Ch. 2.

beyond the range of Fortune's darts. He did indeed affect literary ideals; this is plain, for example, in 'Longinus.' But the dominant ideal is that of the good citizen.

And this is where rhetoric comes in. At first the necessary weapon of political success, it became also an art directed to the production of its own range of intellectual pleasures. In judging ancient literature, the persuasive aim of the writer—not to speak of the actual effect of his performed or recited work on the ear—must always be kept in mind. Changes of style accordingly developed from the need to overcome the resistance of audiences to tricks of which they had become tired. Again and again—in the 4th century B.C., in Hellenistic times, under Augustus, in the period of the Second Sophistic—we see the same sort of conflict develop: an increase in sophistication of wit or language, then a reaction (often thought of in moral terms) toward a purer and more classical manner.

It could be argued that there is no such thing as ancient criticism, because it all falls under ethics or under rhetoric. It is perhaps this that makes the study of the theory, as well as of the literature itself, particularly relevant to a social history of literature. *Logos* and *bios* go together, for *logos* is something central and very important: it is both word and reason, by which the Greeks believed that they civilized the world.

> I should be surprised if there were anything better for men, animals endowed with *logos*, than beautiful and noble *logoi* and every possible variety of them.[1]

What the early Greek poets say about their art and their function in society naturally falls short of anything that could be called theory. Yet it is surprising how many of the ideas and motifs with which the more speculative minds of later periods operated can be traced back to the poets themselves. The most striking instance is in the prologue of Hesiod's *Theogony*. The poem has begun with praise of the Muses. They go about in the night time, invisible to mortal eyes, singing their beautiful songs of the gods. It was they who taught Hesiod, as he tended his sheep on Helicon. They explained their powers to him:

> We know how to tell many lies that resemble the truth; and we also know how to tell the truth when we wish to do so.[2]

They then gave him a staff of bay as a symbol of their favour and "breathed into" him divine song, so that he could tell of things to come and things past.[3] Nor is the poet their only beneficiary; they give eloquence and confidence to the ruler also, and the poetry they inspire has power to comfort men in care and sorrow.[4]

This picture of the inspired shepherd-poet brings to mind parallels in other primitive literatures—Amos and Caedmon, for instance—but there are features of Hesiod's claims to inspiration and knowledge that are of special interest in the Greek setting. The poet is chosen by the Muses as the vehicle of their wisdom; in this he is like the priest or prophet of any other god. When Pindar, two centuries later, calls on the Muse to utter her oracles for him to proclaim, he is expressing the same conception.[5] Neither Pindar nor Hesiod is in anything like a state of ecstasy; that modification of the idea of the poet's inspiration seems to belong to a later period, when orgiastic religion was more familiar and it had perhaps become less easy to see direct divine working in the normal phenomena of life. The early poet believes he has a gift from god that sets him apart and gives him privilege, but leaves his personality intact. Through it, he knows "the past and the future"; and we notice that accurate knowledge of present or past fact is, in this almost non-literate society, at least as wonderful as the power to foretell.

But the Muses do not always tell the truth. The meaning and implications of Hesiod's lines 26–8 have been the subject of a good deal of controversy. The likeliest solution seems to be that Hesiod means that his revelation is a true one, though other poets tell lies. These other poets must be the composers of epic. If this is so, Hesiod takes his place as the first critic to insist on the fictitiousness of Homer. There is an irony in this because later moralists often lumped them together as co-founders of the traditional mythology, with all its coarseness.[6] The interpretation suits another feature of the passage: the fact that it lays stress not so much on the pleasure the Muses bring as on their useful function as givers of comfort and eloquence. In all this, Hesiod is a precursor of many. Rhetoric and poetry are inextricably involved with each other in almost all ancient thinking. The search for a weightier *raison d'être* for poetry than mere entertainment preoccupied both poets and their expounders throughout the whole of antiquity. This road led to allegory: the device of making the Muses tell the truth against their will. Few theorists—though Aristotle is among them—paid serious attention to the truism that poetry gives pleasure.*

Of the other early poets, Pindar[7] alone seems to give some insight into the process of poetic creation, and what he says is essentially a development

---

* But cf. Plato, *Laws* 2, 658E: "I agree with the multitude that music should be judged by pleasure, but not by the pleasure of all and sundry."

of Hesiod's view, though it is far more individually expressed. Pindar wrote not for Boeotian farmers and local magnates, as his countryman Hesiod did, but, in a more opulent world, for lords and princes and cities in all parts of Greece. But he, too, is a prophet of the Muses, to whom he owes his *sophia*, and this is something more than an acquired skill: it is his nature (*phua*); and lesser mortals, like the rivals he often hints at, cannot match it however hard they try. This of course is basically an aristocratic notion: *phua*, like birth and breeding, is something mere success cannot emulate. Again, like Hesiod, Pindar realizes also that the power of poetry to charm and to confer immortality gives it the power to deceive, and that the epic poets sometimes abused their skill, either exaggerating the events they relate or giving morally unacceptable accounts of gods or heroes. "Impossible for me," he says, "to call a blessed god a glutton."[8]

The most striking piece of 5th-century reflection on poetry comes from a different world: the ferment of democratic Athens. Aristophanes' *Frogs* is a testimonial to the quality of Athenian audiences. Ribald, lyrical, and sophisticated, it mirrors an age in which the highest flights of literature were also the popular entertainment of a whole city. In the debate scene (*agon*) of the *Frogs*, Aristophanes makes Euripides and Aeschylus contend for the reward of being brought back to life by Dionysus. In a comic scene, novelty and complexity of thought are not to be expected; they would not amuse the audience. All the more remarkable that there are in this scene a number of ideas, memorably expressed, that are of central importance in all the later development. A moralistic view of poetry is taken for granted: Euripides, unfortunately for his debating position, volunteers the proposition that the duty of the poet is to make men "better," and Aeschylus takes this up in the old sense of military virtue.[9] Again, the whole burden of the debate is a contrast between the lofty manner of Aeschylus and the less grandiloquent style of Euripides—a contrast that anticipates the basic antithesis in the rhetorical doctrine of styles between the grand and the plain. Moreover, Aeschylus's defence of his mountainous language is based on its appropriateness to its subject and its speakers: great thoughts are bound to produce great words, and demigods naturally use bigger language than we do, just as they have grander clothing.[10]

Euripides, continues Aeschylus, offended against this by putting kings in rags to rouse pity. Here is a clear adumbration of that principle of decorum (*to prepon*), at once aesthetic and ethical, that is always of capital importance in Greek criticism.[11] Language, like manners or clothing, must be used in accordance with the properties, and be determined by the status, in some sense, of the speaker. One further point: Aristophanes, speaking perhaps to please his conventionally minded audience, connects changes in musical and poetical technique with the social and moral changes that have made the Athenians no longer the men they were in the days of Marathon. In this, too, he is the precursor of a long line of critics, both Greek and Roman. There are two ways of looking at this attitude. One is to see Aristophanes as a simple, nostalgic clinger to the past. The other, in which there is certainly some truth, is to acknowledge his recognition of a decisive turn in Greek literature and music: the decay of the traditional genres and the loosening of the bond between the *polis* and its poets and musicians. He might, of course, have put forward these ideas without giving evidence of his own judgment and acumen; the evidence of his greatness as a critic, however, is there in the parodies—unsurpassed in Greek—in which the innovations in Euripides' lyrics are hilariously travestied.[12]

As the creative age of classical poetry ended, that of prose began. Systematic speculation about the qualities of prose derives, inevitably, from the teaching of rhetoric. This was a 5th-century development. In Athens and Syracuse, in particular, tyranny and democracy had effaced or greatly weakened established patterns of influence. In such disturbed communities, many more people needed to learn persuasive speech, for their advancement or their security. Tradition says the Sicilians were first in the field with formal instruction on the arrangement of a speech, the "invention"* of suitable arguments, and the projection of a personality acceptable to a given audience. The greatest of these Sicilian teachers was Gorgias of Leontini. His interests went far beyond the practical side of his profession, and he has left us, as part of a declamation in which he sketches possible lines of defence for Helen of Troy, a memorable statement of the power of *logos* in the world (Sections 8–14).[13] It can take away pain and fear, and produce joy or pity. It enables us, too, to feel these emotions in response to the affairs and sufferings of others. It is sorcery and magic. It can sway decision in many fields of activity—in science and philosophy as well as in the assembly and the law courts. In short, it stands to the mind as drugs do to the body, able to destroy and to save. This obviously has as much to do with poetry—"speech *plus* metre" to Gorgias—as with rhetoric. We may fairly see in Gorgias the first extension of the principles of rhetoric to literature in general: a momentous move.

---

* *Inventio*, or *heuresis*, is the discovery of appropriate points to suit the situation; it does not imply fictitious creation.

The first developed criticism of these attitudes that we possess was motivated almost entirely by social and moral considerations. This is not to say that Plato had not, in an aesthetic sense, the capacity to be a great critic. His genius for pastiche and parody proves this of him, as it proved it of his older contemporary, Aristophanes. Brought up as a well-to-do Athenian in the expectation of political influence, and then disillusioned by the breakdown of old patterns of power after the Spartan victory, Plato mounted a private counter-revolution of ideas; and much of this took the form of projected educational reform. He saw how important rhetoric and poetry were in real life, and his massive attempt to diagnose and put into reverse the evil tendencies of the age had therefore to take account of them.

In some early works (*Gorgias, Menexenus*) and in one later one (*Phaedrus*), his target is rhetoric. The central problem is its indifference to moral standards. It is in *Phaedrus*[14] that he makes his constructive contribution. Accepting the view, which Gorgias would have shared, that rhetoric is "soul-guidance" (*psychagogia*), he points out that the prospective orator must therefore both understand what kinds of *logoi* suit particular kinds of people and be able to recognize the phenomena in real life. It is something very like medicine. Aristotle accepted this model, and much of his *Rhetoric* is a filling-out of Plato's schema.

Plato was very concerned about the amorality of rhetoric, but what he says about poetry is in the long run more important (as he himself recognized). Only adults could be persuaded by speeches; poetry was the stuff of education. The poets' claim to inspiration often comes under fire; to Plato, as to Democritus,[15] this really is a sort of madness. Not only can the poet make no claim to knowledge—in this he is no worse off than other unphilosophical experts—but he is peculiarly dependent on irrational and unreliable forces. Moreover, his influence is pernicious; this is the burden of the long educational discussions in the *Republic*[16] and the *Laws*[17] about what is permissible and what is not. The goodness of gods is traduced in the common myths; the weakness of epic heroes is a bad example to the young. Selection and radical expurgation are therefore necessary. Plato's advocacy of censorship and state direction is unqualified by any sense of its dangers. It is bound to shock today, but it is not so clear how far it was calculated to shock contemporaries.

It is in the course of these educational arguments that Plato adumbrates the notion of *mimesis*. Literature, he sees, is in some sense a copy of reality. There is an analogy with painting—an art that the ancients normally thought of as purely representational and also as intrinsically far less serious and dignified than anything involving *logos*. In the first discussion in the *Republic* he does indeed distinguish between "mimesis" as reproduction and the way in which language may be said to "imitate" action; but in the more metaphysical argument in Book X this distinction recedes and we have a curious and unconvincing denunciation of all literature and art as being "a copy of a copy," three removes from the world of reality and the forms.

It is not easy to distinguish in Plato the philosopher's timeless quarrel with poetry from the conservative's quarrel with changing fashions. He was eloquent in the latter cause, and on several themes: disregard of genre distinctions, search for innovation, tasteless audiences. It is his general assumption—owed perhaps to predecessors, especially Pericles' friend Damon of Oa[18]—that the abandonment of rules in poetry or music is both a cause and a symptom of moral decline. Curiously, the innovations he seems to dislike are quite old ones: either his tastes were really very archaic—akin to Pindar's, let us say—or he used past history as a cover for contemporary criticism. *Mousike* used to have definite genres: hymns, dirges, dithyrambs, nomes.[19] New works were judged on their observance of the principles of these genres: the judges were experts, not, "as now," a hissing or applauding mob. "Tasteless lawlessness" was the natural product of composers who "though poetical by nature had no appreciation of the just and lawful rules of the Muses, but were orgiastically inspired and unduly possessed by pleasure." Their theory was that there was no absolute correctness in music, the hearer's pleasure being the only criterion. The result was a "vile theatrocracy of taste," much worse even than a respectable democratic regime. And the decline in music encouraged the disintegration of morals.

How true Plato's observations are of the 4th century is a difficult, perhaps unanswerable, question; but whatever their objective validity, passages like this had great subsequent influence. It is to Plato, even more than to Aristophanes, that we must trace the long line of complaints in which successive generations lamented cultural decline.

This preoccupation with degeneracy, however, is absent from Plato's greatest and most independent pupil. Aristotle, indeed, reveals a new and important concept of development when he traces the stages by which tragedy advanced to its natural maturity. And he is aware that the tragedy of his own day represents no further conquest of the medium. But he is not inclined to preach. Perhaps it is significant that he was not an Athenian and that his father was a doctor—one of a profession that since early times had travelled from city to city, welcomed for their skill wherever they went. Anyway, his commitment to the *polis* can be seen to be of a different nature from Plato's—at least from that of the Plato of *Gorgias* and the *Republic*. He writes as the detached expert on education and government, not as a man passionately concerned to convince his fellow-citizens. Thus, in his discussion of musical education in the *Politics*,[20] he corrects a Platonic attitude by pointing out that, although from the educational point of view some kinds of music are undesirable, and good taste is closely allied to moral virtue, nevertheless even the vulgar need relaxation, and it is proper for them to be given the kind of music appropriate to their nature. The *Poetics* therefore does not judge poetry morally (although in the catharsis doctrine[21] there is an implicit answer to some of Plato's strictures), but explains wherein its proper pleasure lies and how it is best achieved. An artistic, not a moral, standard is also the ground for Aristotle's preference of tragedy over epic, as being more concentrated and having more elements of appeal. Here, again, there is a contrast with Plato's moral order of merit.

With rhetoric, however, the problem was different. This was a practical skill. Excellence in it was measured simply by success, not by any technical correctness. Aristotle took it up with a mixture of irony and seriousness: the tone of the *Rhetoric* reminds one of the exposition of Parkinson's Law. But despite this, and despite its practical presuppositions, the book makes a notable contribution to the development of criticism. What is important from this point of view is mostly in Book III. Here Aristotle, presupposing the *Poetics*, discriminates between poetry and prose. Prose diction has its own virtues—clarity and appropriateness—and the early writers, such as Gorgias, failed to differentiate it sufficiently.[22] Metaphor and other ornaments must therefore be used with restraint. But it is metaphor and the use of the vivid word that produce real distinction—what Aristotle here calls *asteiotes* (urbanity). This is because metaphor is a particularly good way of arousing the pleasure in learning that we are by nature inclined to feel. This intellectual criterion is significant; it reminds us of the strong element of ratiocinative thought in most Greek writing, including poetry, and prepares us for the ingenuities and sophistications of the ages after Aristotle.

In criticism, as in many other departments of thought and literature, the Hellenistic age is known more from the writings of later periods than from its own extant remains. It is clear, however, that the relations between literature and society changed in ways that also affected literary theory. The main social changes themselves are well known. The courts of Alexandria and Pergamum provided new cultural centres that replaced democratic Athens. Hellenized governing classes arose in basically non-Greek areas. In religious and intellectual life, individualism was the mark of the new age; philosophy offered a personal salvation, independent of the life of the *polis*. Three points need particular emphasis here.

(i) Although the Alexandrian poets aimed at originality, it was the kind of originality that consists of giving a new twist to old forms and materials. They worked largely in deliberate imitation of the old genres: they wrote epics never to be recited, plays never to be performed, epigrams never to be inscribed on stone. Style and dialect were archaistic, and they drew on the resources of the growing scholarship of the day in the interests of correctness and subtlety. All this was for the understanding few: the mob that had applauded Sophocles and offended Plato was no longer the literary public. The exhaustive study of the ancient writers, especially Homer, that this sort of imitation demanded gave criticism scholarly and historical perspectives that it had hitherto lacked.

(ii) The long process of the diffusion of Greek culture in non-Greek lands began in Alexandrian times. Language teaching and the study of the great writers—generally in a very elementary way—were among its chief instruments. The result was the rise of a reading public in many different centres. The loss of almost all Hellenistic prose leaves a great gap in our understanding of how this situation worked out. It is not until the 1st century B.C. that we have much direct evidence about stylistic fashions; and we then find a received account of the preceding period that may be very far from the truth. This account speaks of a decline that the archaistic or Atticistic movement has reversed; the decline was due to the corrupting influence of the semi-Hellenized East. We have the story in Cicero:

> Ut semel e Piraeo eloquentia evecta est, omnis peragravit insulas atque ita peregrinata tota Asia est ut se externis oblineret moribus omnemque illam salubritatem Atticae dictionis et quasi sanitatem perderet ac loqui paene dedisceret.[23]

> (Once eloquence had sailed out of Piraeus, she wandered through all the islands and travelled all over Asia to such an extent that she infected herself with foreign ways, lost all the healthiness, as it were, of Attic diction, and almost unlearned natural speech.)

This is, of course, an over-simplification. But we cannot doubt that there were great and exciting changes in style and taste during Hellenistic times. The baroque ornateness of the inscription of Antiochus of Commagene and the nervous staccato of Hegesias[24] testify at least to the development of a virtuosity and ingenuity never completely exorcised by the classicizing and archaizing "renaissance" that followed.

425

(iii) The tradition of philosophical concern with literature passed from Plato and Aristotle to the Hellenistic Stoa and Peripatos. The Peripatetics did little but develop ideas of Theophrastus and Aristotle, but their handbooks had great influence. Most of the technical material in Horace's *Ars poetica* is Peripatetic. It derives from the *Rhetoric* as well as the *Poetics*, concentrates on general principles of unity and propriety, and elaborates the various technical precepts about the use of the chorus, number of actors, length of play, and so on. This is probably a fair indication of the sort of modification that Aristotle's views underwent at the hands of his successors.

The Stoics were the successors of Plato as moralizing critics. Conservers of belief in morals and religion, they attributed to poetry an important didactic function; rather than banish Homer, as Plato did, they allegorized him to fit him for this role.* At the same time they were linguistic theorists, and some (notably Crates of Mallos) made considerable progress in integrating the theory of poetry with grammar and logic. The essence of poetry, as they saw it, was in euphony and metre—the sound-patterns of speech. Beauty (*to kalon*) was a matter of harmony and proportion, in poetry as in the visual arts and in morals. It was this that produced pleasure and emotional effect generally. Poetry was thus a powerful device for influencing character, and must be used for rational and moral ends. Only the wise man could be a good poet.[25]

To judge by the extant works, the great age of Greek and Latin literary criticism covers the two centuries from Cicero to the Antonines. The period covers the Latin golden age; in Greek, too, it was a prolific age (at least in prose), creative and at the same time self-conscious. Not only were there changes in taste, but people reflected on them and planned revolutions. The revival of classical standards under Augustus, the development of rhetorical ingenuity in Flavian times, the archaistic revival under the Antonines—all have the character of conscious literary movements, with their polemics and catch-phrases.

The Romans contributed much: a new language that inevitably modified the sense of the critical terms, mostly of course metaphorical, in the mere process of translation; a sane disinclination to subtle theory; a confident educated society, closely linked with politics and power; and a traditional moral sense that reinforced the moralizing tendencies of the Greek theorists, and gave a new depth to the key concept of decorum.

* The later allegorizing treatises (Cornutus, pseudo-Heraclitus, pseudo-Plutarch) are mainly of Stoic inspiration.

Of the Greek critics of importance, only one is datable: the Augustan Dionysius of Halicarnassus, historian, admirer of all things Roman, painstaking and mechanical critic. 'Demetrius,' whose book *On Style* is mainly of Peripatetic inspiration, has been dated by some scholars in early Hellenistic times, mainly on the ground that his illustrative quotations are concentrated rather surprisingly on 4th-century literature; but his general interests and attitude to the past suggest a later date. The author of *On Sublimity*, much the most original and attractive of these writers, complains of "decline" in the spirit of the 1st century A.D., but the old tradition that he is the 3rd-century scholar-statesman Cassius Longinus is still sometimes defended.[26] If it is right, much of our historical thinking must be re-appraised.

With the Romans we are on firmer historical ground. Cicero wrote about an art of which he was himself the greatest master. Horace makes poetry—or at least *sermones*—out of critical theory and reflection on his own creative experience. The two Senecas provide a lively commentary on the changes of taste in their time; the father's unquestioning pursuit of rhetorical cleverness is tempered in the immensely clever son by uncertainty and disillusionment. In Quintilian, we have the fairest exponent of the rhetorical tradition in its most intelligent and balanced form. Tacitus's *Dialogue* is refreshing for its statement not only of the archaizing position but of the modernistic. Tacitus represents the modernists' case as based on the fact of progress. Rhetorical precepts novel in Cicero's day are now known to every schoolboy. Juries are more sophisticated and quick-witted. Students demand something brief and clever to report to the people at home. Such arguments are rather rare; most extant critical comments are of a more conservative colour.

Two sets of ideas may be said to dominate the critical thinking of all this period.

First, it was an age that looked back at the classical Greek achievement. The genuine creative impulse of Latin literature (as well as that of the contemporary Greek) was channelled by the practice of imitation. This was not always a mechanical business. Dionysius rightly lays emphasis on the spirit as opposed to the letter—on speaking Demosthenically but not in Demosthenes' words.[27] Horace wisely recommends the imitation of life and not merely of books:

> respicere exemplar vitae morumque iubebo
> doctum imitatorem et vivas hinc ducere voces.[28]
>
> (I would have the wise imitator look to the model of life and manners and take his living voice from here.)

Quintilian[29] urges some degree of novelty: without a spirit of enterprise, we should still be eating acorns. 'Longinus' uses the ideas of inspiration and possession to explain the imitator's mental processes:

> Many are possessed by a spirit not their own . . . from the greatness
> of the ancients to the souls of their imitators there flow, as it were,
> effluences from holy caverns . . . .[30]

Indeed, the ancients themselves were thought of as imitating one another: Herodotus was "most Homeric"[31]; Sappho and Alcaeus followed in the footsteps of Archilochus.[32]

None the less, the sense of dependence on the past and decline from its standards was always very strong. It was modified principally by Augustan confidence, Greek as well as Roman. Here was a new peak of performance, a new classical model. Dionysius's discussion is illuminating.[33] His picture of the history of Greek literature—we have already seen something like it, and we find it also in 'Longinus'—is this: the old "philosophical" rhetoric died out about the time of the death of Alexander, and was succeeded by a vulgar and theatrical style associated with the half-Hellenized cities of Asia; now this in turn had died, thanks mainly to the power of Rome and the good taste of her governing class. Among the Romans, Horace is the chief spokesman of the Augustan perspective. For him, the experience of Rome has been quite different from that of Greece. There, the first was the best; in Rome, polish has yet to come, and admiration of Plautus's style and wit is misplaced.[34]

The literary epistles—including the longest and most didactic, the *Ars poetica*—preach a consistent lesson. Poetry must be both formally perfect and morally serious. Classical, not Alexandrian, Greece must be the model. The poet's high mission demands of him the utmost effort in technique. It demands, too, a mind above money-grubbing—and Romans found this hard. These letters are unique among ancient works on poetry as the work of a practising poet, and it is legitimate to see in their message Horace's hopes for his own achievement in the *Odes*. Although he rarely speaks of lyric, but nearly always of the grander genres of epic and drama, the principles of unity, propriety, serious purpose, and meticulous care for verbal felicity are as valid in his own work as anywhere.

Few Roman writers after the Augustans felt they were scaling new peaks. Statius's address to his own epic "not to rival the divine *Aeneid*, but follow at a distance"[35] exemplifies the characteristic attitude. The historian Velleius,[36] who strikes a new note by including sections on literary and cultural history in a general narrative, explains the concentration of excellence in 5th-century Athens and Ciceronian Rome by the stimulus of rivalry or alternatively by the natural law that "what cannot go forward must go back." There are many complaints of decline throughout the 1st century B.C. The younger Seneca's[37] is perhaps the most interesting. His text is *talis oratio qualis vita* (a style is like a life); he illustrates it from the effeminate Maecenas, whose writing reflects his disordered, exhibitionist, spoilt character. Whole generations, he continues, are sometimes affected by this kind of *luxuria* in style, as in food or clothing or any other department of life. This is not just a matter of the imitation of a fashionable mannerism; it is something deep-seated, indicative of moral softness whether in an individual or in a generation.

Seneca lays most emphasis on rhythm and word-order, because these readily display perversity and unnaturalness. It is noticeable how often he (like others of the period) uses language implying lack of virility to castigate affected style. His treatment of archaism is also to be noted: it is, he concludes, a comparatively harmless, though ridiculous, mannerism. He did not, like so many 2nd-century writers, see the revival of archaic form as a road to the recovery of pristine literary and moral virtue. In the main, Seneca's attack is in the tradition of Plato's censure of degenerate music, but set in a context of self-conscious literary movements and fashions.

In the eyes of the next generation, Seneca was himself a modernist; Quintilian[38] found it necessary to warn the young against his *dulcia vitia* and lack of true taste. The complaint, as often, reflects some ingratitude. Much of the subtlety and elegance of the writing of Quintilian and the younger Pliny is due to the generation whose extravagances they deplored, and to Seneca in particular.

Much of the critical situation of the early Empire can thus be explained in terms of attitudes to the past: admiration of the classics, faith in imitation, a running battle between primitivistic* archaism and rhetorical novelty.

The effects of his first set of attitudes, however, were reinforced by another set: the inherited sense of genre, stylistic level, and decorum. As we have seen, it went without saying, even in the time of Aristophanes, that dignity of subject implied dignity of language. The problem of composition thereafter presented itself to the writer as a problem of choosing and maintaining the right tone for the work in hand:

---

* I use this word to recall A. O. LOVEJOY and G. BOAS, *Primitivism and Related Ideas in Antiquity* (Baltimore 1935).

discriptas servare vices operumque colores
cur ego si neques ignoroque poeta salutor?[39]

(If I have neither the capacity nor the knowledge to maintain the
various forms and tones of work, why do they call me a poet?)

Breaches of the rules of genre called forth censure or, in an acknowledged
master, special pleading. The *Odyssey*, for example, presented a problem.
Less grand in theme than the *Iliad*, it had analogues with comedy, and yet
had to be recognized as a great epic. 'Longinus,' in a famous passage,
draws the contrast in detail: the *Odyssey*, to him, is a domestic comedy.[40]
Dionysius justifies his special study of word-arrangement by using it to
explain how the plain, unfigurative language of the scene between
Odysseus and the swineherd, when Telemachus arrives unexpectedly,
achieves its great beauty despite a vocabulary "that any farmer or seaman
or artisan, anyone who took no trouble to speak well, might have found
ready to hand."[41] Later on, Virgil posed a similar problem. Servius's
introductory remarks on *Aeneid* IV are strange to modern taste, and
correspondingly revelatory of ancient taste:

> Est autem paene totus in affectione, licet in fine pathos habeat, ubi
> abscessus Aeneae gignit dolorem. Sane totus in consiliis et subtilita-
> tibus est; nam paene comicus stilus est: nec mirum, ubi de amore
> tractatur.[42]

> (Almost the whole book is concerned with affection, though it has
> strong emotion at the end, where Aeneas' departure produces grief.
> It is indeed wholly occupied with plans and intrigues; for the style
> is almost that of comedy. We should not be surprised at this, where
> the subject is love.)

Within the sphere of prose writing, the principal differentiations were
based on a classification of the styles of oratory. Early writers, including
Aristotle and probably Theophrastus, worked with a theory according to
which there was a grand style, a low style, and a correct mean between
them. The achievement of this mean by Thrasymachus was supposed to
mark the adulthood of Greek prose. Later, the step was taken of trans-
forming this normative scheme into a descriptive one, which listed three
qualitatively distinct styles, each of which had its appropriate use. We
have the doctrine clearly set out in Cicero.[43] There are three *genera
dicendi*. One is grand, serious, energetic, versatile, abundant, emotional,
and may be either rough and unstructured or polished and structured.
Another is delicate and ingenious, "aiming at making things seem plainer
rather than more important," highly refined in a close-textured and
concise way. This genus too may be either unpolished, in deliberate

imitation of the unskilled, or more artificial and tolerant of ornament. Between the two main genera is the third, smooth, even, moderately ornamented, sharing—"or, if we are to be honest, not sharing"—the excellences of both. Isocrates was thought of as the exemplar of this third, intermediate style; Demosthenes and Lysias respectively usually represent the other two.

The scheme was easily extended to other branches of literature. In history, Thucydides and Xenophon are the extremes, Herodotus the intermediate. In tragedy, we have Aeschylus, Euripides, and Sophocles. Moreover, it was possible to isolate and study separately the qualities characteristic of the great authors who represented the genera. From this springs perhaps the main critical achievement of the period—an elaborate body of doctrine about style, that often shows very considerable refinement and discrimination. The critics do not always follow the tripartite division —the "medial genus" is not a very satisfactory concept—but the basic contrast of grandeur and slightness, emotion and mere charm or rational persuasion, is constant. Dionysius operates with a range of qualities (*aretai*) of this kind:

> Under the head of *pleasure* I reckon bloom and charm and euphony and sweetness and persuasiveness and all that kind of thing; under that of *beauty* I reckon magnificence, weightiness, solemnity of language [*semnologia*], distinction [*axioma*], patina [*pinos*] ....[44]

The mysterious characteristic of elevated writing that 'Longinus' calls *hypsos* is an abstraction of this order; so are the *ideai* of Hermogenes. Such qualities involve choice of material as well as of words and rhythms. The provision of recipes for achieving them is characteristic of the whole period. I conclude with a single example, in the hope that it may illuminate the whole way of thinking with which we are concerned.

Dionysius's *semnologia* has a descendant in Hermogenes' *semnotes* (solemnity), an important ingredient of his more general quality of *megethos* (grandeur). Hermogenes' recipe for *semnotes*[45] begins by enumerating suitable solemn ideas: things said of the gods *qua* gods (this limitation excludes undignified myth), facts about the universe and heavenly phenomena, general moral thoughts (e.g. about the nature of law), and ideas concerning the great events of human history. We are then told what method to adopt: direct statement with no suggestion of doubt, allegory, or dark hints. Then comes the appropriate vocabulary: words of grandiose sound, especially those with long A's and O's; metaphor; nouns rather than verbs. Hermogenes concludes with a list of

431

suitable figures, cola, and clausulae. This is a curious mixture of triviality and profundity; behind it lies a close study of Plato and Demosthenes. One thinks naturally of parts of *Timaeus* and *Phaedrus*. Hermogenes' rules should be compared and contrasted with 'Longinus's' far more percipient recipe for his *hypsos*. True, this also is given under headings of the five "sources": bold thought, emotion, figures, vocabulary, rhythm.[46] 'Longinus,' too, is a close observer and analyst of classical texts. But the difference is obvious: to achieve *hypsos* requires a quality of character, a moral effort.[47] And the criteria for diagnosing true *hypsos* are based on its psychological effects. It elevates the mind and makes us feel proud and happy. We never weary of it. Its impact is irresistible, its impression on the memory ineffaceable, its appeal universal.[48] *Semnotes* and *hypsos* are in a way the same thing: a concept of grandeur and dignity that (like "decorum") can be plausibly represented as a transference from the social sphere to the literary one. This "grand style" is the appropriate language of the man of true worth and prestige. But there is of course a great difference: whereas Hermogenes offers purely technical advice, 'Longinus' assimilates his literary aim to a moral ideal, and looks beyond the technique of persuasion to the underlying reactions of the reader. The successes and limitations of classical moral and rhetorical criticism are all here.

References

1. Hermogenes, *De ideis*, ed. by H. Rabe (Leipzig 1913), pp. 214, 217–21. The double sense of *logos* is evident here.
2. Hesiod, *Theogony* 26–8.
3. *ibid.*, 29–32.
4. *ibid.*, 81–103.
5. Pindar, frag. 137, ed. by C. M. Bowra (Oxford 1935).
6. Xenophanes, frag. 11 in *Fragmente der Vorsokratiker*, ed. by H. Diels and W. Kranz, 6th edn (Berlin 1951); cf. Herodotus, II, 53.
7. See C. M. BOWRA, *Pindar* (Oxford 1964), Ch. I.
8. Pindar, *Olympian Odes* I, 52.
9. *Frogs* 1013 ff.
10. *ibid.*, 1058–61.
11. See especially Cicero, *De officiis* I, 93–8, for the moral and aesthetic aspects of "propriety."
12. *Frogs* 1309 ff.
13. See O. IMMISCH (ed.), *Gorgiae Helena* (Berlin 1927).

14. See the translation by R. Hackforth (Cambridge 1952).
15. Democritus, frag. 18, in Diels and Kranz, *op. cit.*; cf. Horace, *Ars poetica* 295 ff.
16. Books II–III and X; discussed, with other Plato texts on these subjects, in P. VICAIRE, *Platon critique littéraire* (Paris 1960).
17. Books II–III.
18. Cf. F. LASSERRE, *Plutarque: "de la musique"* (Olten-Lausanne 1954), pp. 53 ff.
19. *Laws* 3, 700A ff. On these and other "genres," see, e.g., D. A. CAMPBELL, *Greek Lyric Poetry* (London 1967), pp. xiv–xxiv.
20. *Politics* 1341^b, 32 ff.
21. *Poetics* 1449^b, 28. See D. W. LUCAS, *Aristotle's Poetics* (Oxford 1968), pp. 273 ff.
22. *Rhetoric* III.
23. Cicero, *Brutus* 51.
24. Cf. 'Longinus,' 3, 2 (ed. by D. A. Russell [Oxford 1964]).
25. See the passages in H. VON ARNIM, *Stoicorum veterum fragmenta*, Vol. III (Leipzig 1913), p. 164.
26. Most recently by G. LUCK in *Arctos* (Helsinki 1967).
27. [Dionysius], *Ars rhetorica* X, 19.
28. *Ars poet.* 317–8.
29. Quintilian, 10, 2.
30. 'Longinus,' 13, 2 (Oxford 1964).
31. *ibid.*, 13, 2.
32. Horace, *Epistles* I, 19, 28 ff.
33. *De antiquis oratoribus*, preface.
34. *Ars poet.* 270 ff.
35. *Thebaid* 12, 816–7.
36. Velleius, 1, 16–8.
37. *Epistles* 114.
38. Quintilian, 10, 1.
39. *Ars poet.* 86–7.
40. 'Longinus,' 9, 11 ff. (Oxford 1964).
41. *De compositione verborum* 3, ed. by H. Usener and L. Rademacher (Leipzig 1929), pp. 11–2.
42. Servius, ed. by G. Thilo and H. Hagen, Vol. I (Leipzig 1881), p. 459.
43. Cicero, *De oratore* III, 177, 199, and 212; *Orator* 20 ff. and 75 ff.
44. *De comp. verb.* (Leipzig 1929), p. 37.
45. Hermogenes, *op. cit.*, pp. 242 ff.
46. 'Longinus,' 8 (Oxford 1964).
47. *ibid.*, 1.
48. *ibid.*, 7, 3.

Bibliography

C. O. BRINK, *Horace on Poetry: the "Ars Poetica"* (Cambridge 1970), contains a full commentary on the *Ars* and is of great value for the light it sheds on many aspects of the subject.

G. M. A. GRUBE, *The Greek and Roman Critics* (London 1965), is the most balanced descriptive account of this subject.

Oxford Classical Dictionary, 2nd edn, ed. by N. G. L. Hammond and H. H. Scullard (Oxford 1970), *s.v.* "Literary Criticism in Antiquity," contains a good general book list.

D. A. RUSSELL and M. WINTERBOTTOM, *Ancient Literary Criticism* (Oxford 1971), contains translations of many of the principal texts.

CHAPTER 19

The Writing and Dissemination of Literature in the Classical World

C. H. Roberts[*]

The use of writing by Greek-speaking peoples reaches back beyond the events recorded in the earliest literature, and further back still in the civilizations of the Near East. But as yet there is no evidence that Linear B, the earliest form of Greek current both in Crete and on the mainland, was employed for any except practical purposes. It is generally agreed that the composition of the *Iliad* and the *Odyssey*, as we know them, demanded writing; at some point, not later than the 7th century B.C., and in all probability earlier, the words recited by rhapsodes or sung by lyric poets were recorded in writing.

At this time, and for some centuries to come, it would be an anachronism to use the word "book" of such writing; the history of literature, or of the use of writing for literature, is far from coinciding with the history of the book, if by "book" we understand a written copy of an author's work regarded by him not as a tool available to a few but as the principal medium of communication with his audience. The final stage—when the book becomes an independent entity, the multiplication and distribution of which on a large scale is done with the writer's knowledge, if not always with his approval, and is made available for sale (as is the work of authors long dead) by an entrepreneur—is not reached before the Hellenistic period. In Rome of the late Republic and early Empire, the literary scene with its professional authors and scholars, its libraries and book-shops, its publishers and its world-wide distribution of books, is not unlike that of Europe in the 18th century, except for the absence of mechanical means of reproduction.

[*] Fellow of St John's College, University of Oxford.

Between that stage and the earliest recording of oral literature lie several centuries of slow, irregular, and initially unplanned development, a period that includes the formative age of Greek literature. Greek literature, unlike Latin literature, reached its greatest heights without the help of a fully developed book trade. Perhaps because of this, the oral tradition in the classical world never entirely died out. In Rome of the Empire, a new poem was still launched by recitation to a selected audience; all ancient literature was designed to be read aloud, even if the reader was in private, and not till the end of antiquity do we hear of someone reading silently without moving his lips. Near the end of the 2nd century A.D. Lucian can still refer to *hearing* a new historical work,[1] and St Paul can play on the original, still active, meaning of the words "to read" (*anagnorizein*, to know again or recognize);[2] indeed, the ordinary word for "reader" is *akroates* (hearer). All ancient poetry and much prose will lose something vital if the eye merely scans the written words and the ear does not hear them.

Writing was a means of preserving literature long before it became the principal means of disseminating it. In the earliest period, epic lays would be recited and learnt by heart; once the demand for a particular poem was sufficiently great, or once a poet had set a strongly individual stamp on a familiar theme and given all but the final form to it, then we may surmise that, if the art of writing was to hand, the obvious course for him or his successors was to record it in writing. They would nonetheless learn it by heart; but the written copy would serve to train and correct their successors, and to preserve (within limits) the true tradition. At this stage, writing was a tool serving the oral communication of the poem; copies would originally have been written on rolls of skin (to speak of parchment would imply too high a degree of refinement in the material) such as we know the Ionians used when papyrus from Egypt was not available;[3] and it was in Ionia and the islands that literature—epic and lyric poetry—began. To the Greek imagination of later ages leather scrolls had romantic associations, as antique parchments had for Ossian's contemporaries; for writers to whom papyrus had long been familiar they were the recipient of Apollo's prophecies, and on them, or on the equally ancient folded tablets, the gods recorded their judgments.

At this point the written text is an archive, an instrument of continuity and transmission, rather than a book. At the beginning of the 5th century B.C. Heraclitus deposited the manuscript of his apothegms in a temple;[4] temples in Greece, as earlier in Egypt, served as places of record that could be consulted by later generations. The temple of Thespiae in Boeotia conserved a famous text of Homer, and possibly also one of Hesiod. In much the same way "the sons of Hippocrates," or guild of doctors, preserved the treatises ascribed to their founder, probably for strictly professional circulation. The development of lyric, choric, and elegiac poetry in the 7th century B.C. and subsequently must have meant a wider use of written texts; the poet would give copies to his friends, and others would be wanted by soloists, singers, and reciters, and—in the case of choric poetry—for training choirs. Here, then, is public recitation and private distribution of copies; but there is as yet no sign of the book trade. Even in later ages private copies remained as permanent rivals to the professional book trade, and were generally preferred by scholars.[5] A certain snobbery attached to them, reinforced by the absence of copyright and in consequence of a financial interest on the author's part in the circulation of his books; in one of his early works[6] Horace prides himself on the fact that his poems are not advertised or available in book-shops, but only recited, and then under pressure, to a few friends. "Private publication"—a contradiction familiar to modern times—or private copying of manuscripts and the oral tradition are two continuing strands in the history of Greek and Latin books. In the 5th century B.C. the written text reproduced by copying existed side by side with oral dissemination, and by the end of the century was beginning to replace it as a principal means of putting the writer in touch with his public; in the latter part of the 5th and the earlier part of the 4th century B.C. there existed what we might call a mixed economy of reading and reciting, and it was at this time (as near as we can judge) that the trade in books began.

Well before the 5th century ended, books written by Ionians were on sale in Athens; a little later we hear of them being exported to the Black Sea. The trade was still rudimentary, and probably of recent growth. In Aristophanes' parade of hucksters and retailers, the bookseller—who, had he been a sufficiently familiar figure, would have provided an excellent butt—does not feature; elsewhere the way in which Aristophanes pokes fun at the intelligentsia suggests that regular readers or book collectors constituted a small and identifiable class of highbrows.[7] Cloud-cuckoo-land suffered from a plague of books, and the book is the hall mark of the highbrow. Both Socrates and Euripides were known as collectors of books and the latter owned a slave specially trained in the copying of manuscripts. On how small a scale such activity was can be seen from a passage in Xenophon's *Recollections of Socrates*, in which Euthydemus is represented as possessing an unusual collection of the works of poets and Sophists; Socrates is made to comment on the size of his library and, because Euthydemus actually owns a complete Homer, inquires whether he intends to become a professional rhapsode.[8] To this stage of development Chaucer's England might supply a parallel. In 5th-century Athens, reading and writing were part of everyone's education —even of that of Aristophanes' sausage-seller;[9] if a reading, as distinct from a listening, public had been slow in coming into being, the small, intimate society of the city-state with its theatres, its gymnasia, and its lecture halls would have felt the need less. The book trade began as Athens, in her imperial phase, outgrew the city-state. In Greek art of this period we find reading occasionally portrayed; on a 5th-century vase a boy is represented reading the shorter *Hymn to Hermes*, and it may be significant that on a vase dated to the end of the century we find for the first time a bookcase, or cupboard, as distinct from a book box.

That Attic drama was a factor in the change from the book as a tool to the book as a means of general, though irregular, communication is certain. Aristophanes may make fun of the bookish, but—characteristically —he must have been a considerable reader himself. When all allowance is made for what Plato in the next century regarded as memories uncorrupted by the misuse of books,[10] and though only once in the extant plays does Aristophanes refer to a written text (the scene in *The Frogs* when Dionysius is reading Euripides' *Andromeda* aboard ship),[11] the intimate, line-for-line, knowledge of the tragedies he parodies is inconceivable without texts to hand; and for the parodies to make their point, copies must have been available to some, at least, of the audience, though many may have been content with knowledge gained from revivals of the plays. A playwright would have his own final copy written out, either by himself or by a slave under his supervision, on a roll of papyrus from drafts made probably on wax tablets; the prompt copy used for training the cast (and the playwright was normally his own producer, responsible for staging) would have been separate. If the play was a success, not only would friends wish to have copies made, but the stationer who imported papyrus from Egypt might well be interested in selling copies to order, especially perhaps to the overseas visitors who had seen the performances in the theatre of Dionysus. (There is no evidence that in the 5th, or indeed the following, century the stationer or publisher took the financial risk of putting unknown works on the market.) When plays were revived, as we know they were, first at other festivals and later at the Great Dionysia itself, the producer relied on the co-operation of the tragedian or his family, to whom the texts and perhaps the stage properties would be a valuable heirloom. The Athenian state kept its own copies of the plays of the three great tragedians in the archives; very possibly a copy of each play publicly performed had to be deposited. The survival in antiquity of both versions of an originally unsuccessful play (the *Lemnians* of Sophocles, for instance, or the *Clouds* of Aristophanes) is a pointer to the early circulation of texts.

More influential even than the drama may have been the development of prose literature, particularly oratory and popular philosophy. Early philosophers gave public recitations, or employed a rhapsode to give them; prose works were first known generically as "speeches" (*logoi*). But in the middle and later 5th century the Sophists were making a living by their teaching, and the pupils who paid their fees would surely have been interested in acquiring copies, as authentic as possible, of the lectures they had attended, the more so as all the Sophists were peregrinatory professors. The first known case of an author giving a title to a prose work of his own, a firm way of securing identification, is the *Aletheia* (Truth) of Protagoras,[12] and another Sophist, Antiphon, is reputed to have been the first man to write a speech for publication, not primarily to be heard.[13] Beside this we may set the statement[14] that Pericles was the first to *write down* a speech for the law court. Once this was done, circulation among younger orators and politicians, with their reputation to make or unable to be present, would soon follow; supply would come to meet the demand. Plato's suggestion[15] that men of the greatest standing and influence in the cities did not like to record their speeches in writing or leave treatises behind them for fear of being branded with the name of Sophist must be taken with a grain of salt.

The circulation of the works of the great historians is puzzling. Herodotus is said to have recited his history (or part of it) at Olympia, and it may originally have been written with oral publication in mind, on different occasions and in different sections. But a work as intricate, and in a style as involved, as that of Thucydides needed to be available in book form;[16] he tells us that it is intended for the serious student and is not a competitive *pièce d'occasion*; but who these serious students were, and how it circulated to them, we do not know. But we do know that neither Herodotus nor Thucydides divided his works into the books with which we are familiar; this implies that there was no authoritative division of the work by the author, or that, if there was, there was no means of ensuring that it circulated in this form. We may conclude that neither was planned for wide circulation in written form, or that, if it was, the organization of the book trade was still rudimentary.

In the 4th century B.C. the growth of the book as the principal means of communication proceeds apace, and with it, less certainly, that of the book trade. Until the close of the century, references to the trade are still few and far between, and it is likely that it was ill-organized and on a small scale. We are told[17] on the authority of Aristotle that bundles of speeches written for the courts by Isocrates were hawked around by booksellers, perhaps because they admitted of easy adaptation for different occasions; and a pupil of Plato's is reputed[18] to have made a living by travelling in his master's dialogues, though whether it was by reciting them or by selling copies, we do not know. It seems that normally it was the author who arranged the distribution of copies of a new book;[19] and though copies of works already well known could be bought, we do not hear of an entrepreneur arranging to have a manuscript multiplied before it was known to the public by other means. Further, for any book except a play or a speech there was no one moment of publication; books such as the *Republic* would be written, and become known, piecemeal, so that Aristophanes could allude to some of the ideas in it, familiar through discussion and reading aloud, before the work as we know it was complete.

But even this modest advance did not go unchallenged. In the *Phaedrus*,[20] Plato launches an attack on the book as a means of education. Education should be a dialogue between teacher and taught; books corrupt the memory because they become a substitute for it (an echo of a line from a lost play of Euripides), and are mere shadows of the true dialectic. Ideas circulating indiscriminately are liable to misunderstanding and are thus dangerous; the true, as opposed to the bastard, *logos* is something alive, implanted in the soul. Books, however, are useful as entertainment or for reminding man of matters with which he has been familiar; a written *logos* is of real value to the author when he grows old and forgetful. Here, by implication, we get a clear picture of the book as a tool, to be used as a subsidiary to the spoken word. The contrast with his contemporary, the comic poet Anaxandridas, who writes "it is a great pleasure, for a man who has an original idea, to be able to publish it to everyone,"[21] could not be greater.

Plato, like Carlyle preaching the virtues of silence in 35 volumes, was fighting a losing battle. The representative of the future was his contemporary Isocrates. Even Isocrates feels he has to apologize[22] for employing the written rather than the spoken word; but he is the first known author to think of himself primarily as a writer (he was unimpressive as a public speaker), and one of the earliest users of the pamphlet, in the form of a letter, as a means of political propaganda. He consciously looked beyond the bounds of the city-state and wrote to be read throughout the

Greek world. Another writer of the period seems to have taken an interest in the production of books. Prose writers of the 5th and 4th centuries B.C., as we have noticed, were not concerned with the form in which their works circulated. But to the orderly military mind of Xenophon (who could lecture his wife on the precise way in which the pots and pans in her kitchen should be arranged), this was anathema. The divisions of the books of the *Anabasis*, with carefully calculated breaks and prefaces and books of more or less equal length, in all probability are due to the author,[23] and the same may well be true of his *Recollections of Socrates*. But he had no imitators before the following century.

The attitude to books in Athens during the classical age may be illustrated by a comparison with that of the Graeco-Roman world. There, in art and literature, the book is a symbol of wisdom and culture; but in Athens, although the papyrus roll had long been familiar, such a connotation was unthinkable. Even when Euripides described the pleasures of an old age spent in reading, the convention of the writing tablet is maintained,[24] as though the papyrus roll had never been invented—an attitude alluded to by Lucian, six centuries later, in one of whose dialogues Zeus is portrayed as recording all human sins on his tablets.[25] In the *Axiochus*, a dialogue wrongly included in the Platonic corpus but reflecting Platonic attitudes, there is a picture of the earthly paradise: there are dances, concerts, symposia, debates for philosophers, and theatres for poets—but no libraries and no books.[26] Athens, though books could be bought there from at least the middle of the 5th century, was never celebrated, as were Alexandria and Rome, as a centre of the book trade; it is striking that, although the archives of the state were carefully kept, Athens had no public library until it was given one by Ptolemy Philometor, king of Egypt, in association with a gymnasium and temple in his honour, in the 3rd century B.C.

A private library, which was greatly to influence the future of scholarship, was founded in the second half of the 4th century B.C., and its subsequent history demonstrated clearly how inadequate were the existing means of distributing and conserving books. Aristotle is credited by Strabo with being the first to make a collection of books—a real library by the standards of the 4th century B.C.; without it, the work of his school, the Lyceum, would have been impossible. The library was his private property and his own autographs formed the most valuable part of it, in every sense of the word. Autographs (the monetary value of which is being rediscovered by poets today) were the only form of literary property known to antiquity; Pliny the Elder, so his nephew tells us,[27] could have sold the notebooks incorporating his researches to a Spanish scholar for 500,000 nummi. In the state of the book trade in the 4th century, often the only way to get hold of the work of another scholar was to purchase his manuscripts, and this might expose the buyer to the charge of plagiarism, especially if other copies of the purchased work were available for checking. Aristotle is said to have paid 18,000 drachmae for some works of Speusippus, and Plato paid 10,000 drachmae for three books by the Pythagorean philosopher Philolaus. The best safeguard for a philosopher's work seemed to be an institution founded for that purpose, with the added protection that legal succession provided. Aristotle (unlike Plato, whose manuscripts were bequeathed to his nephew Speusippus) left his library to Theophrastus, his successor as head of the Institute. In 287 B.C., 35 years later, Theophrastus died and was succeeded by Neleus, a pupil of both his predecessors. Neleus moved, with the library, to the small town of Scepsis in the Troad (Asia Minor), from which his family had come. Scepsis was close to Assos, a town once presented by a local tyrant to two close friends of Aristotle, and in earlier days, at least, a centre of Peripatetic studies. So far, so good; but at Neleus's death the chain of intellectual succession was broken, and the library, at once the seed and the fruit of the researches of Aristotle and Theophrastus, passed to his physical heirs. They were neither scholars nor philosophers; they allowed no access to the manuscripts, but they were aware of their value.

In the 2nd century B.C., the competition for manuscripts, following on the foundation of the Library of Alexandria and that of its rival at Pergamum, was keen, resulting in increased prices and occasionally in the faking of manuscripts.[28] The Attalids of Pergamum were overlords of Scepsis, and the manuscripts were buried in a cellar to protect them from seizure. Damaged by damp and worms, they were later rescued and sold to Apellicon, a wealthy collector, described as a lover of books rather than a lover of wisdom. He made clean copies, filling in the lacunae with more confidence than judgment. When Sulla conquered Athens in 86 B.C., he chose Apellicon's library as his personal spoils of war. His private librarian, Tyrannion, put the books in order, and under his care a professional scholar indexed the whole, edited the texts, and published an authentic edition. Thus for two centuries Aristotle was represented only by his exoteric works—the now lost dialogues and literary works for general reading—and, not surprisingly, peripatetic studies declined: the corpus that was to be the foundation of western philosophy and science survived only by chance.[29]

Thus even the library attached to a private institution had failed to preserve its books in due order, to make them accessible, or even to protect them from decay and corruption. The accomplishment of these ends on the grand scale was the achievement of Alexandria. In the 4th century B.C., princes and tyrants, following the practice first credibly recorded of Clearchus of Heraclea,[30] had founded libraries as part of their policy as patrons of culture; with their example in mind, but with far more ambitious plans, Ptolemy Soter—the first Greek king of Egypt, one of Alexander's most successful generals, and himself a writer—invited Demetrius of Phalerum, a scholar-statesman and a pupil of Aristotle, to leave Athens and assist him in making the new foundation of Alexandria the centre of Greek civilization. Under him and his son, Ptolemy Philadelphus, two great institutions, distinct but closely connected, rapidly grew to maturity: the Museum, an academy for scholars equivalent to an institute for advanced studies, and the Royal Library, housed in a wing of the palace. With the wealth of Egypt at his disposal, the second Ptolemy invited distinguished scientists and scholars to settle in Alexandria (although philosophy and the drama stayed in the more congenial atmosphere of Athens); his agents were despatched throughout the Greek world to secure manuscripts of all kinds, whether duplicates or not, for the Library.

The Library, the arrangement of which was originally modelled by Demetrius on Aristotle's collection, was invariably placed under the direction of a distinguished scholar; Callimachus, the second director, was famous both as a poet and as the author of the *Pinakes*, the catalogue of the Library. This was a critical bibliographical survey, running to 120 rolls, of all Greek literature; it was divided into 12 sections—6 for poetry, 5 for prose, and 1 for miscellanies and anonymous works. Within each section, each author was listed alphabetically (the section in which he appeared being determined by his principal work) and his genuine works recorded by title (when available) or the initial words, the number of lines in each work being stated as a check on completeness and authenticity. An immense operation of collecting, making inventories, classifying, and collating must have lain behind the catalogue. Incoming manuscripts were divided according to whether they were associated with different cities or with individuals. A later Ptolemy ordered the confiscation of all manuscripts found on vessels docking in Egyptian ports; these were then copied in a scriptorium attached to the Library, and the copies presented to the owners (the original being kept by the Library). The same Ptolemy, Euergetes, borrowed from Athens against a large deposit the state copies of the plays of the three great tragedians, kept them, and sent copies back to Athens. Even if the establishment of a correct text of the great writers of the past had not been a primary object of the foundation of the Library, circumstances alone—in the form of the multiplication of different texts, especially of Homer—would have enforced this task on the scholars of Alexandria. This in turn imposed a degree of selectivity on those engaged in the work; with the Library the concept of classical literature may be said to have been born.

In the 3rd century B.C., the main library (there was a smaller library, possibly intended for more general use, attached to the temple of Sarapis) mustered some 470,000 rolls: by the 1st century B.C. this had grown to 700,000 rolls. Some idea of its extent may be obtained if we recall that the works of Thucydides would be divided into 8 rolls, whereas in the 4th century A.D. the Sophist Libanius could preen himself on possessing a complete Thucydides in a single codex, light enough to be easily carried;[31] and the rolls of the books of Thucydides would be longer than the average. Here we touch on another service of Alexandria to literature. There was no standard length of roll into which all books, or divisions of books, had to fit; but a maximum length of about 35 to 40 feet (the content of the roll varying with the size of the writing and of the margins) does seem to have been established, the norm being slightly shorter. The works of earlier writers, such as Herodotus and Thucydides, were rationally divided with the length of the normal roll in mind, each roll to comprise, as far as possible, a self-contained unit. (The principle of division of the *Iliad* and the *Odyssey* was different, with the result that a roll normally carried more than one book.) It was not long before writers began to construct their works with the roll of conventional length in view; Diodorus explicitly recommends[32] that a unit of writing should be commensurate with the roll, although, as we can see from Polybius, the principle allowed for rolls of varying length; and Galen[33] records that two treatises of Hippocrates, originally a single work, were divided into two because of their length. In Alexandria, too, the epic line was regarded as an "ideal" line or norm and used as a unit of measurement.

There is, however, some evidence that both the idea of a roll as corresponding to a natural unit of a larger work and that of a "normal" line were known in 4th-century Athens in philosophical and rhetorical circles. The historian Ephorus (415–330 B.C.) conceived of each book of his work as being self-contained with a specific theme.[34] Alexandria's contribution lay in organizing and regularizing the production, and in some degree even the writing, of books in a way that set the pattern for the Greek and Roman worlds. The great innovations were the critical catalogue, the establishment of "correct" texts, and the science of bibliography. At the same time the control of the one source of papyrus, which was grown elsewhere than in Egypt but not as a writing material, gave the Ptolemies the opportunity of standardizing and improving manufacture.

Alexandria provided a stimulus to the writing and recording of books in more ways than one; it provided—to put it in modern terms—the first general library, the first university, and the first systematic and organized philological and scientific inquiry. The combined influence of Alexander the Great and Aristotle, mediated by the Ptolemies, established a tradition of cultural patronage that was followed by later princes and generals. Thus other Hellenistic monarchs in the pursuit of culture and the prestige it conferred—notably the Attalids of Pergamum—followed the example of the Ptolemies; but Alexandria was the pace-maker. But besides the demand for books that the Library and the Museum created, the policy pursued by Hellenistic monarchs, above all by the Ptolemies, called for books in great numbers. The Ptolemies' power rested on the Greeks they persuaded to settle in Egypt and on their descendants, who were Hellenists even if they were not purely Greek in blood; for them the provision of schools and gymnasia, and the encouragement of Hellenic culture in general, were vital. The settlers came from all over the Greek world; what unity existed in later Greek civilization was (as Isocrates had foreseen) a unity of culture and based primarily on literature. (A school text on papyrus dating from the 3rd century B.C. illustrates this point neatly: the boys were taught the myths and geography of Greece, not those of the land in which they lived; the list of rivers includes the Eurotas, but not the Nile; and the book ends with extracts from Greek literature.) Even small and remote villages on the desert edge of the Fayûm depression or far up the Nile in Upper Egypt have yielded papyri of Greek—and later a few of Latin—literature, more often of the classics than of contemporary literature. Literacy and reading were widespread in Egypt, probably more so in the 2nd century A.D. than in any other century before the 20th.

Although from the late 4th century B.C. onward we have—thanks to the papyri—specimens of actual books written in Greek, and from the 1st century B.C. of Latin books too (though far less numerous), our knowledge of the book trade and of the author's relations with his publisher and bookseller (when the two were not one and the same) depends on casual information in our literary sources of varying dates. Down to Alexandria a line of development may be traced; after that we may suspect that, even if our sources were much fuller than they are, there would be no

445

great changes to be noted between the 2nd century B.C. and the 2nd (and in some respects the 4th) A.D., for it was not a period of great technical development. Toward the end of the period can be discerned the beginnings of a major technical development that affects the whole later history of books.

Before the invention of printing the publisher had no obvious advantage in speed of production over the private copyist; he might organize a team of skilled slaves, copying either from dictation or by passing "copy" rapidly from one to the other, but the difference between the private copy and the trade copy could never have approached that between manuscript and print. (This helps to explain why on other grounds both Strabo and Galen preferred the authority of the private copy to that of the trade book.) We may guess that in Rome the publisher-bookseller may have had easier access (and on cheaper terms) to the raw material, whether as importer or as wholesaler; we may be sure that as an exporter he would have had means denied to the private individual of distributing his copies to, say, Syria or Britain; but his main advantage over the private copyist, especially where new books were concerned, lay in a close personal relationship with the author. Well-known firms such as the Sosii brothers, who published Horace, or (in the next century) Pollius and Tryphon, who published Martial and Quintilian, earned the confidence of their authors mainly, no doubt, owing to the skill of their copyists and correctors.

The publisher about whom we know most is T. Pomponius Atticus, Cicero's friend and agent, a wealthy man of equestrian rank who also made his mark in politics.[35] He was famous for his texts of the Greek classics, among them Aeschines, Demosthenes, and Plato, and was able to call on the help of distinguished scholars such as Tyrannion and Varro as consultants and correctors. In modern terms, he created an imprint; no doubt the high repute of his elegant and accurate texts of the classics, the *Atticiana*, attracted contemporary authors to him. We find him pressing Cicero to publish, just as, a century later, Quintilian published his *Institutio oratoria* only—he would have us believe—in deference to his publisher's insistence;[36] Cicero in turn emphasized the publisher's responsibility and the need for the most careful attention on his part. These preliminaries over, Cicero made one or two copies by dictation from a draft in a notebook or on tablets; then, presumably after correcting it himself, he sent the manuscript out to his publisher. (In the 4th century A.D. St Gregory of Nyssa first dictated his notes, which were taken down in shorthand; then he reduced the transcribed sheets to an ordered manuscript, and assembled it as a book [*puktion*]; but he was working with a codex, not with a roll.) Atticus now took over; while Cicero retained a master copy on which to make further corrections as necessary, the publisher made his plans for having Cicero's work corrected and transcribed in a large number of copies.

We know little about the size of editions, which must have varied, *mutatis mutandis*, must as it does today; but we hear in one of Pliny's letters[37] of an undistinguished poet publishing an elegy in memory of his son in as many as 1000 copies. Atticus was also responsible for preparing and despatching dedicatory or complimentary copies. Promotion took the form of reading passages aloud to selected guests; on occasion an author's preface may have been separately circulated as a blurb.[38] Then comes the familiar crisis; Cicero finds he has written "Eupolis" when he should have written "Aristophanes," and Atticus has to correct or fudge the whole edition. On another occasion, in the *De republica* the correction clearly arrived too late, as the erroneous form, "Phliuntii" for "Phliasii," persists in our manuscript tradition; presumably it had to await a second edition that has since been lost. (Second editions were not uncommon, and depended then, as now, on the amount and value of the new material they contained; so Martial commends a corrected and enlarged edition of the first seven books of his epigrams.)[39] Another time Cicero prefixed the wrong preface to one of his works, from the stock he kept of ready-made prefaces; this was promptly put right by Atticus. Atticus's publishing was a business and no doubt a successful one; the library, for which he was also famous, may well have served as a bait to prospective authors. This close association of author and publisher secured both the reliability, in point of accuracy and authenticity, otherwise provided only by the scholarly private copy, and the efficient multiplication and distribution of copies. Atticus set an unusually high standard, if we may believe Cicero,[40] and his publishing house was no doubt a model for those of imperial Rome.

Publication followed much the same course then as now. The publisher or bookseller displayed his new books conspicuously and lists of those for sale were written up on the door-posts of the shop. The reception of a new book by the critics was a nerve-wracking affair for the author, and Martial implies[41] that the good opinion of a famous critic of his time, Probus, might be won by the quality of the publisher's production. Earlier, Cicero confirms the low reputation of book-shops, on the ground that both quantity and quality of stock were unsatisfactory.[42] In general, in their attitude toward the commercial aspects of writing, authors then were little different from authors now. Horace complained of his publishers, the Sosii, that they made money while he made a reputation as his books circulated throughout the world.[43] Martial distinguished between Atrectus and Secondus, who (as far as he was concerned) were just booksellers and to whom friends asking for free copies of his books were firmly recommended, and Pollius and later Tryphon, who were his publishers.[44]

We know little about the copying and multiplication of copies in the publisher's office; such literary allusions as we have refer to metropolitan Rome, but the actual copies preserved by the sands of Egypt—although a few may have originated in Alexandria—are mostly local, some even private, productions. Copying would normally be done by slaves; there is some evidence of a *librarius* being paid for his work, however, which would point to the use of freedmen. The "normal" line, i.e. the epic line, was the basis for calculating the scribe's wage. Martial remarks[45] that any faults in the finished copy are the result of the copyist's haste to complete his stint; the corrector should of course have gone over the copies before they were released to the book-shops. In surviving papyri, corrections are usually entered in darker ink, and often, in the Roman period, in a characteristic style of writing, which suggests that correctors may have had some special training. An author, if we may believe Martial,[46] might enhance the value of a presentation copy by making corrections in his own hand.

There were considerable variations in the quality of the papyrus, ranging from the coarse to the almost silken; an average roll would be about 30 feet long, with rather over 100 columns of writing, columns in verse manuscripts being wider than in prose. The height of the roll would be between 8 and 12 inches, the area of writing occupying perhaps three-quarters of the column space. The length of lines (in prose) and the number of lines to a column varied widely, though an average roll would carry between 30 and 40 lines to a column, with about 20 letters to a line. Before the age of the codex, no great effort was made either to justify the line strictly (though line-fillers would occasionally be used) or to maintain a constant number of lines in the column; and even then there were many exceptions to both practices. The influence of reading aloud may be seen in that the rules of word-division at the end of lines were strictly observed.

When the copies had been made, corrected, and checked for completeness, there was still much to be done, at least in the case of fine editions produced in the larger centres. The exterior of the folded roll, or rather its two flatter surfaces, were polished with pumice stone and then soaked in cedar oil—perhaps as a bleaching agent, or perhaps as protection against damp and worms; sometimes they may also have been painted white. Then a jacket (*paenula*, "cloak") of parchment was attached to protect the finer papyrus, and this would be stained red. A roller—or in the case of a long work, two rollers—would be inserted (sometimes physically attached to the papyrus, sometimes not), one or both ends of which would be curled; the rollers were useful both in lifting the book from its shelf or case, and in rewinding after reading. The curled ends or knobs (*cornua*) were painted or decorated. Finally, the parchment would be secured with coloured string. No complete literary roll has survived, and it may be doubted whether provincial Egypt would have indulged in such elaborate productions, but with some surviving papyri the quality of both the material and the writing is very high.

Illustrations were usually confined to texts scarcely intelligible without them—astronomical, mathematical, and botanical works, all of which are represented in the surviving papyri—but the illustration as ornament is not unknown and a fragment in Paris from the 2nd century A.D.[47] has a coloured illustration of a scene in a Greek romance; there is also some evidence for the illustration of popular or children's books. In Rome, with its interest in the individual, it was not uncommon for a portrait of the author to be prefixed as a frontispiece to his work—a tradition that survived in the portraits of evangelists found in early mediaeval manuscripts. The antiquarian Varro, in the 1st century B.C., published a collection of 700 portraits (*imagines*), seven to the page or column; but we may suspect that this was more of an illuminated manuscript, or at most a severely limited edition, than an ordinary book.

While Cicero's correspondence gives us the liveliest picture of an author's relations with his publisher, the clearest account of an editor's duties in preparing a manuscript for publication is to be found in Porphyry's life of his master Plotinus, written at the beginning of the 4th century A.D.[48] As his literary executor, Porphyry was faced with the task of first reducing to order his master's manuscripts. Some, through Plotinus's indifference, were already in circulation under different titles and with different texts; from 54 papyrus rolls, Porphyry brought out a definitive edition in six enneads or groups of nine treatises each. Three enneads made up the first codex, the fourth and fifth made a second, and the sixth ennead occupied a codex by itself. Plotinus, unlike Epictetus, had at least committed his philosophical teachings to writing, but (partly because of his bad eyesight) had never made a fair copy and had never read it over. He wrote (says Porphyry) with no attempt at calligraphy, without even observing the rules of word-division at the ends of lines, and with little care for correct spelling—or, indeed, for anything except nous. (Perhaps because the spoken word took priority, orthography was not second nature even to scholars.) Another admirer of Plotinus, the rhetorician 'Longinus,' had attempted to form a collection of his works; when he had overcome a shortage of scribes in Phoenicia by taking his own scribe, who wrote to dictation, off all other work, he was defeated first by his inability to obtain a complete set of the manuscripts and then by the faulty condition of much of what he had got, another disciple, Amelius, having failed to correct the scribal errors; on this, Porphyry comments that of all copies he would have expected Amelius's to have been as correct as if they had come straight from the very autographs. The book trade does not enter the picture; this may reflect the relationship between a philosopher and his disciples as well as Plotinus's own lack of interest in publication or indeed in giving a final form to his work.

Apart from this fundamental work of re-arranging and correcting manuscripts, Porphyry's work as editor consisted in making a list of chapter headings set out in the order in which the works were written, providing brief summaries of the argument, and writing expository essays on certain passages. His final task, unrealized at the time he was writing the *Life*, was to go through each treatise, punctuating it, and correcting any slips that might have arisen in dictation.

The ordinary book trade, concentrated in Rome, Alexandria, Antioch, and later Constantinople, is taken so much for granted that we hear relatively little about it; in this—as in other areas of ancient life—it is the exceptional, not the everyday, that is the subject of comment. We have glimpses only: Atticus, acting as Cicero's agent, buys libraries and books in Italy and the East;[49] books that are over-produced or unsuccessful in the capital are sold off cheap in the provinces,[50] and for the less well-off there are libraries that lend books for fees.[51] When the gossip-writer Aulus Gellius landed at Brindisi from Greece he found a bookstall on the quay with bundles of books put out for sale; as he mentions only Greek authors, some of them admittedly recondite (such as Aristeas of Proconnesus), the stall may have been the equivalent of an English bookstall at Calais.[52]

The rare-book trade flourished in the early empire; in the case of a manuscript or early copy of the *Annales* of Fabius (a chronicler of the 2nd century B.C.), experts were called in to verify its authenticity and the seller offered to refund if the manuscript was found to be faulty.[53] Autograph manuscripts were in particular demand; the elder Pliny had seen autographs of Cicero, Virgil, and Augustus;[54] Lucian recounts how a collector whose wealth was matched by his ignorance had had foisted on him what purported to be an autograph of Aeschylus,[55] and his contemporary Gellius had seen the manuscript of the second book of the *Aeneid*.[56] Galen refers to manuscripts 300 years old,[57] a tribute to the endurance of the papyrus book in ordinary conditions as well as to ancient bibliophily. In the 1st century A.D. such was the demand for old books—if only because they were alleged to be better written and on papyrus of better quality—that some booksellers would pickle new books in corn to give them the required patina or foxing to deceive the buyer.[58]

To the well-to-do Greek or Roman of the Empire, to whom (we are told) a library was as essential a part of the house as a bathroom, the de luxe edition appealed as much as the autograph or early copy. Books might be written in gold on either papyrus or parchment, probably dyed a darker colour (as some existing mediaeval manuscripts have been); the Jewish Torah was already written in gold in the 2nd century B.C.[59] and the Emperor Maximinus in the 3rd century A.D. is said to have treasured a Homer written in gold on purple vellum.[60] Both the binding and the rollers gave considerable scope for ornamentation and display, as did bookcases.

Scholars and perhaps ordinary readers as well continued to have copies made privately, more often of the classics and of commentaries than of contemporary literature. A private letter has survived from the 1st century A.D. in which we find a circle of scholars in up-country Egypt lending and borrowing rare learned books to fill up gaps in their libraries.[61] Wealthy men were apt to employ their own trained slaves as copyists, and the best copies may well have been those written by professional scribes privately employed. In the 3rd century B.C., Antigonus Gonatas is said to have given the philosopher Zeno, in gratitude for his lectures, a slave who was skilled in copying;[62] such an acquisition, normally a prerogative of the wealthy, would be especially useful for anyone distant from a book-shop. The facility with which private copies could be made, independently of the author and the trade, and the high repute that a good private copy enjoyed, made it difficult for the author to control his own work. A work once published was in effect public property; but as early as the 4th century B.C. we find Plato complaining of work being published against the author's will,[63] and Cicero grumbles to Atticus that a work of his has been pirated before publication.[64] (The employment of a recognized publisher such as Atticus for the authoritative edition would give the author a degree of protection.) In the 3rd century A.D., Origen was able to confute a heretic who had inserted interpolations into a work of Origen's by producing, with some difficulty, the original manuscript;[65] by retaining his own private scribe, a successful author to some extent directed the circulation of his work.

It was not always in the author's interest to publish. A course of lectures on medicine or rhetoric or law might represent the lecturer's source of income in the form of fees paid by pupils; such a reluctance to publish would have its parallel today, even when publication brings royalties as it never did in the ancient world. Galen was unwilling to publish his medical works except in the form of private circulation to friends, because otherwise he would lose control and might suffer in reputation from inadequate or inaccurate texts.[66] Quintilian would have us believe that he was driven to publish by the unauthorized circulation of some of his work by over-enthusiastic students. This could be a real danger, as is shown in Seneca the Elder's concern to protect the great orators of the past.[67]

Whether the author could expect any financial reward from publication (unless he was a dramatist whose plays were publicly produced) may be doubted. It is certain he had no *right* to compensation for his work—a concept quite alien to the ancient world. As Martial remarks, his books may be read but *quid prodest? nescit sacculus iste meus* (what's the good of that? My purse knows nothing about it).[68] True, the firmness with which he directs friends who beg copies of his works to his bookseller might suggest the opposite, but he may merely be concerned for good relations with his publisher. When, in the 4th century B.C., Xenophon remarks that the Sophists circulated their works because they were writing for their own gain, he is probably thinking of the fees that this would attract from pupils.[69] At about the same time, Isocrates won pupils by careful distribution of copies of his speeches.[70] A successful author might be fortunate in his patron, as were Virgil and Horace in Maecenas; the poet Oppian is said to have been given a golden piece by Marcus Aurelius for every line he wrote, receiving a total of 20,000 nomismata,[71] but we may expect some exaggeration either in the number of lines with which he is credited or in the scale of the imperial bounty. Josephus's history of the Jewish wars was approved by its protagonist, the Emperor Titus, who with his own hand put a stamp on it and gave orders for its "publication."[72] If this was a royal recommendation to the trade (comparable perhaps with a dedication in the 18th century), it might have been of considerable benefit to the author; if, as is more probable, it meant that a copy should be placed in the official archives or a public library, it was a gesture that, at a time when patronage flowed most freely from the throne and the patron was the author's best hope of a living, would be of real value to Josephus. Josephus was also, to some degree, his own publisher; he records that, after presenting copies to Vespasian and Titus and other Romans, he sold copies to many Hellenized Jews.[73] Pupils and patron apart, the author's best remaining source of profit was his autographs, which would probably be of more value to his heirs than to him; and there were in addition the indirect rewards that success and reputation bring in any age.

To the author who was not dependent on his writing for a living, and to some extent to all authors, the pursuit of literary immortality (which meant as much to them as it did to European writers of the Renaissance) was a sufficient spur; the writer of light verse thinks of his publisher as the man who will ensure the perpetuity even of his juvenilia.[74] But the importance attached to literature by its readers as well as by its practitioners had certain dangers. Throughout antiquity we hear of books being burnt when they met with the disapproval of the authorities, with consequences more serious to the author under the Empire than in the Republic or in free Athens—if indeed there is any certain instance of this at Athens throughout her history as an independent state; modern scholars discount the stories, surviving only in late authors, of such action being taken against the Sophist Protagoras or the atheist Diagoras of Melos. As autocracy spread its shadow, books and their authors were increasingly liable to punishment, as critics of the Ptolemies in Egypt and later the Stoic opposition to the Julio-Claudian emperors found to their cost. On rather different grounds Augustus instructed the Director of the public library in Rome not to circulate the juvenilia of Julius Caesar,[75] an act of suppression that, as they have not survived, presumably proved successful. The adherents of a religion based on a book, such as Jews or Christians, were obvious targets for this among other forms of persecution, as the Jews learned in their wars against Antiochus IV and later against the Romans, and the Christians above all in Diocletian's attempt to extirpate Christianity and its literature. From time to time the purveyors of works of magic or astrology that might be used (or thought to be used) against the rulers of the state were subject to similar treatment. But the state's interest in literature was not merely negative; its uses as propaganda, in the form of either prose panegyrics or adulatory verse, were not overlooked, although inscriptions and coins were perhaps more satisfactory media for this (the latter especially, because they were both indirect and unavoidable).

Because he read aloud and therefore slowly, the reader was expected to provide for himself most of the helps to understanding that a modern book supplies. In Greek books (elementary school books excepted) there was no word division, perhaps because of the aesthetic appeal of an unbroken column of text; in the earliest Latin manuscripts words were divided, but under Greek influence the practice was dropped in the course of the 1st and 2nd centuries A.D. The paragraph sign may well be as early as the book; this apart, the reader had to provide much of the punctuation for some of the time, and some of it for all of the time. Accents are occasionally found in the pre-Roman period, but even later no papyrus exhibits a complete and consistent system, and this and other aids to the reader are almost confined to the older Greek texts, e.g. the lyric poems or the tragedies, which their successors may have found almost as difficult as we do. The roll itself was not really suited to the reader; back reference when reading, rapid consultation, and checking of references were difficult, if not impossible. There was little point in numbering the columns of the roll; only three instances of numbered rolls are known among the literary papyri, compared with more than a thousand with no numeration, and of these one certainly, and another probably, was copied from a codex. In poetic texts the lines might be numbered by hundreds; this was useful if a commentary (which was always in a separate roll, not, as later, combined with the text) was read side by side with the text. Of a few authors, standard editions were produced for scholars: the commentator Asconius, writing about A.D. 50, assumes the availability, to the limited circle for whom he is writing, of texts in which every 10 lines were marked off, i.e. an edition the copies of which all had lines of the same length; references are given calculated from the beginning, middle, or end of the roll.[76] This was very probably the edition of the speeches edited by Tiro, Cicero's freedman and secretary, referred to by later writers. Such editions would be indispensable for the Roman jurists, and possibly for medical writers; but they were the exception and more easily accommodated in the codex than in the roll. No trace of such a book has survived among the papyri.

The ordinary reader was content with the book-shop copies produced, in the case of popular authors, in very large numbers; at Rome the latest best-seller would be in every hand, every pocket.[77] We have learnt something about the distribution of books in Egypt from excavations; and as Egypt had few Greek cities (in the strict sense) and no Roman colonies, we should expect other provinces—Asia Minor, Spain, or Gaul—to have been even more receptive of classical literature. Martial could expect his books to be read in Britain;[78] and if Martial was read, surely his contemporary Tacitus's account of Agricola's campaigns would have found an audience there too. A book published in Rome, like one published today in London or New York, could reckon on being circulated throughout the civilized world.[79] Martial's picture of his poems being read by a half-frozen centurion on duty on the lower Danube[80] is exaggerated but not absurdly so, as witness the fragments of literary manuscripts (and not only of Homer) found on the site of Karanis, a village on the edge of the Sahara, where Roman veterans constituted the most educated part of the population. If the reader did not wish to buy books, the price of which the publisher could vary at will, public libraries, regarded as an essential service in any self-respecting city, were open to him.

In the late Republic, successful generals might bring a great library to Rome, as Aemilius Paulus's sons brought that of Perseus, king of Macedon,[81] or Sulla that of Apellicon; a generation later Lucullus threw open his library, much of it seized during his successful campaigns in Pontus, to the public. Julius Caesar had assigned to Varro the task of collecting books for a public library, but its completion had to wait until the time of Octavian,[82] when it was established not later than 27 B.C., in the Atrium Libertatis. Augustus himself founded the Palatine Library with separate wings for Greek and Roman literature, an arrangement aped by Trimalchio in Petronius's novel and frequently copied later. Augustus found many imitators; the library founded by Trajan was still extant in the 5th century A.D.,[83] and in the time of Constantine Rome boasted no fewer than 28 public libraries. Rich men would have their private libraries; they were already common in the 2nd century B.C.[84] Vitruvius, writing in the reign of Augustus, assumes a library to every large private house.[85] Cicero had at least three: one of considerable value at Rome, another well-stocked one at Antium, and a third in his villa at Tusculum. That of the poet Persius, an austere Stoic who died in A.D. 62, contained a mere 700 rolls; a contemporary scholar, Epaphroditus of Chaeronea, acquired by purchase a collection of 30,000 rolls.[86]

Libraries, both private and public, were still being founded in the 4th century A.D.; but by then a technical change, symptomatic of a changing attitude to books and literature, and itself in course of time stimulating it, had taken place. The codex or (as far as format goes) the modern book was replacing the roll. It was a Roman invention, developed by substituting for the waxed tablets, common to all antiquity, folded sheets of parchment and later of papyrus. These notebooks (for originally they were no more) were first marketed as books capable of holding texts of some extent in the late 1st century A.D., but appear to have been a commercial failure. The adoption of the new form about the same time by the Christian Church, whatever the reason may have been, provided what was probably the most important single factor in its success, even though initially the influence of Christian literature on secular writing would initially have been slight, because in its early days it was copied and circulated by the communities, not through the book trade. The employment of the new format for sub-literary or technical works, above all for the work of jurists (to whom the ease of reference it offered was of great importance) and of medical writers from the 2nd century A.D. onward, contributed powerfully to its ultimate triumph.

The codex was easy to consult, to carry, to conceal; it was also appropriate to an age that was increasingly more interested in conserving the literature and scholarship of the past than in adding to it, and—in the fields of religion and law—in establishing a canon of received and authoritative learning and commenting on it. The concept of a codex as an authoritative collection, later enshrined in the Codes of Theodosius and Justinian, is first encountered in two legal encyclopaedias compiled at the end of the 3rd century A.D.; the advantages of a format where page and line reference could be given are obvious. In literature the desire for completeness could be met by the codex; Porphyry's edition in codex form of his master's works is a parallel in the pagan field to the often-quoted story in St Jerome[87] of how the damaged rolls in the library of Pamphilus's research institution at Caesarea were transferred onto parchment codices. Libanius's pride in his one-volume Thucydides ("light enough to be carried") has been mentioned; it is worth remembering that the selection of seven plays by each of the three Attic tragedians was made about the same time, and that each selection would have filled a codex. A little later Sidonius Apollinaris has his scribe copy out the Heptateuch in one codex, and the Prophets in a second;[88] each might well have taken 10 rolls.

This change is accompanied by significant changes in vocabulary; *speakers* and *listeners* (used commonly throughout antiquity of authors and their audience) disappear and only *writers* and *readers* (and readers who read silently) are left. The idea of the book as a tool or help to other means of communication has finally gone; in literature, word and book become more nearly coterminous, and the book is both the means of communication and the source of authority.

References

1. *De historia conscribenda* 5.
2. 2 Corinthians III, 3.
3. Herodotus, V, 58, 3.

4. Diogenes Laertius, IX, 6.
5. Strabo, XIII, 54; Cicero, *Ad Quintum fratrem* III, 4 and 5; Fronto, *Epistles* I, 17.
6. *Satires* I, 4, 71.
7. See J. D. DENNISTON, *Classical Quarterly* XXI (London), p. 117.
8. *Recollections* IV, 2, 1 and 8–10.
9. *Equites* 189.
10. *Phaedrus* 274 ff.
11. *Ranae* 52 ff.
12. Plato, *Theaetetus* 161c.
13. Clement of Alexandria, *Stromata* I, 16, 79.
14. Suidas, ed. by A. Adler (Leipzig 1929–38), IV, p. 100, *s.v.* Pericles.
15. *Phaed.* 257d.
16. Thucydides, I, 22.
17. Dionysius of Halicarnassus, *Isocrates* 18; *ibid.*
18. T. KOCK, *Comicorum atticorum fragmenta*, III (Leipzig 1888), no. 269.
19. Isocrates, *Antidosis* 193; *Panathenaicus* 233.
20. *Phaed.* 275 ff.
21. A. MEINEKE, *Frag. com. graec.*, Vol. III (Berlin 1839–57), p. 196.
22. *Ad Philippum* 11.
23. C. HOËG, *Miscellanea Giovanni Mercati* IV (Vatican 1946), pp. 1 ff.
24. Frag. 369.
25. *De Mercede conductis* 12.
26. 371c-d.
27. Pliny the Younger, *Epistles* III, 5, 17.
28. Galen, ed. by C. G. Kühn (Leipzig 1821–33), XV, pp. 105 and 109.
29. For the fortunes of Aristotle's library, see W. JAEGER, *Aristotle: Fundamentals of the History of his Development* (Oxford 1948).
30. F. JACOBY, *Die Fragmente der griechischen Historiker*, Vol. III B (Leiden, 1950), p. 337.
31. *Orationes et declamationes* I, 148.
32. Polybius XVI, *init.*
33. Galen, *op. cit.*, XVIII, 2, p. 323.
34. Diodorus, V, 1, 4.
35. On Atticus's publishing activities and his relations with Cicero, see Pauly-Wissowa, *Realencyclopädie*, Vol. 2, cols. 2237 ff.; suppl. vol. VIII, cols. 517 ff. (with refs.).
36. *Institutio oratoria, prooem.*
37. *Epistles* IV, 7, 2.
38. Polybius, III, 1–3.
39. Martial, X, 2, 1–4.
40. Cf. *Ad Atticum* XIII, 12, 2; 22, 3.
41. Martial, III, 2, 12.
42. Cicero, *Ad Quint. frat.* III, 4, 5; 5–6, 6.
43. Horace, *Ars poetica* 345–6.
44. Martial, I, 113 and 117; IV, 72.
45. Martial, II, 8.

46. Martial, VII, 17, 7; VII, 11.
47. Paris Bibl. Nat. MS. Suppl. gr. 1294: reproduced in K. WEITZMANN, *Ancient Book Illumination* (Cambridge, Mass. 1959), pl. LI.
48. *Plotini vita* 8.
49. *Ad Att.* I, 7, 1; II, 4, 1; VIII, 11, 7; XII, 6, 2; XIII, 8.
50. A. Gellius, *Noctes atticae* IX, 4, 3–5.
51. Diogenes Laertius, III, 39; Gellius, *op. cit.*, XVIII, 3, 11.
52. Gellius, *op. cit.*, IX, 4, 1.
53. *ibid.*, V, 4, 2.
54. *Naturalis historiae* XIII, 82–3.
55. *Adversus indoctum* 99–101.
56. Gellius, *op. cit.*, II, 3.
57. Galen, *op. cit.*, XVIII, 2, p. 630.
58. Dio Chrysostomus, *Oratio* XXI, 12.
59. *Letter of Aristeas* 176.
60. Scriptores historiae Augustae, *Vita Maximinorum Duorum* 30, 4.
61. *Oxyrhynchus papyri*, ed. by E. Lobel, C. H. Roberts, and E. P. Wegener (1941), XVIII, 2192.
62. Diogenes Laertius, VII, 36.
63. Plato, *Parmenides* 128 d7–e1.
64. *Ad Att.* XIII, 21, 5; 22, 2–3.
65. Migne, *Patrologia graeca* XVII, col. 625.
66. *Inst. orat., prooem.* 7–8.
67. Seneca, *Controversiae* I, 11.
68. Martial, XI, 3, 1–6.
69. *Recollections* I, 6, 13.
70. *Panath.* 233.
71. Suidas, *op. cit.*, III, p. 547.
72. Josephus, *Vita* 363.
73. *Contra Apionem* I, 9, 51.
74. Martial, I, 113.
75. Suetonius, *Vita C. Julii* 56, 7.
76. T. BIRT, *Das antike Buchwesen* (Berlin 1882), p. 175; K. OHLY, *Stichometrische Untersuchungen* (Leipzig 1928), p. 111.
77. Martial, VI, 60, 1–2.
78. Martial, XI, 3–5.
79. Pliny the Younger, *op. cit.*, II, 10, 2.
80. Martial, XI, 3, 5.
81. Plutarch, *Vitae* (Aemilius Paulus) 28, 11.
82. Gellius, *op. cit.*, III, 10, 17.
83. Sidonius Apollinaris, *Epistles* IX, 16, 3.
84. Polybius, XII, 27, 4–5.
85. Vitruvius, VI, 4, 1.
86. Suidas, *op. cit.*, II, p. 334.
87. Jerome, *Epistles* 34 (14).
88. Sidonius Apollinaris, *op. cit.*, V, 15, 1.

Bibliography

C. H. ROBERTS, "The Codex," *Proceedings of the British Academy* XL (1954), pp. 169–204.

W. SCHUBART, *Das Buch bei den Griechen und Römern*, 2nd edn (Berlin 1921).

E. G. TURNER, *Athenian Books in the Fifth and Fourth Centuries B.C.* (London 1952); *Greek Manuscripts of the Ancient World* (Oxford 1971).

C. WENDEL, *Die griechische-römische Buchbeschreibung verglichen mit der des vorderen Orients* (Halle 1949).

H. WIDMANN, "Herstellung und Vertrieb des Buches in der griechisch-römischen Welt," *Archiv für Geschichte des Buchwesens*, VIII (1967), cols. 545–640.

CHAPTER 20

The Two Cities
Christian and Pagan Literary Styles in Rome

C. E. Chaffin*

In a letter addressed to Pope Damasus in A.D. 383, St Jerome interprets the husks that the swine ate in the parable of the Prodigal Son as *daemonum cibus* (the food of demons).

> The demons' food means songs of poets, pagan wisdom, the rhetors' wordy display. These things delight all men with their beauty and, as they captivate the ears with the sweet modulation of their flowing lines, so they penetrate the soul and master the body's heart.[1]

It would be hard to find an assessment of classical literature that was at once so appreciative and so damning. "They give their readers nothing but noise; there is no food of truth and righteousness to be found there."[2] *Daemonum cibus*: a world of images is conjured up—pigs that delight in mud and ordure, the idols and sacrifices of the pagans, the unclean spirits that entered the Gadarene swine, Pharaoh and the Egyptian host (Satan and his demons) drowning in the Red Sea. Jerome looks back from the promised land of the Church, fiercely repudiating the Devil's kingdom.

The tone is personal, but the sentiment commonplace. Among the Latin Fathers the other world of pagan culture is frequently dismissed in this way. By means of such contrasts as Egypt and the Promised Land, the Devil's realm and Christ's, Athens and Jerusalem, Hellenism and the Gospel, the Christian teachers (and some pagans too) splendidly simplified the moral structure of their world. We, too, in our approach to the period

* Lecturer in Classical and Mediaeval Studies, University of Sussex.

and its sources may conveniently adopt similar schematic terms: it was an age of ideological conflict, when politics meant coercion, when Christianity was divided by schism and controversy, when the Church clashed with the state, and when literature was distorted by propaganda. It was an age dominated by the moral conflict of the two cities.

Jerome's viewpoint is a useful one. The growth of the Church with its distinctive culture entailed not only change but disruption. Coherent and balanced though Roman civilization might seem, the world of Rome contained deep fissures and fragile compromises. One might say of it, that it embodied not two but many worlds. Between the Latin and Greek spheres there was some rivalry and a progressive failure in communication. Some non-classical languages (Celtic, Berber, Coptic, Syriac) survived on the periphery (indeed were perhaps reviving, at least among the uneducated) and regionalism was sometimes marked.* There were certain broad groupings and oppositions in society—town and country, rich and poor, soldier and civilian, educated and uneducated, *honestior* and *humilior*.[3] There was also a complicated hierarchical gradation into competing groups, which simultaneously represented a hierarchy of social values.[4] The Church sometimes accepted this order, and sometimes disrupted it. There was little that it failed to influence.

Yet one must not talk too glibly of two cultures, Christian and pagan. Although the distinction is real, the boundaries are far from clear. The concept of the two cities is more useful, because it is within a framework of polemic that this tendency toward cultural division can best be discussed.

The Christian sermon highlights the oppositions and contacts in a peculiarly instructive way; it also permits a very exact assessment of the extent to which the Church created something new in Roman culture. This essay is deliberately restricted to Latin literature, and principally to that of Italy in the late 4th century A.D. It will examine, first, the traditional literary attitudes current in this epoch; second, the origins of a new, Christian attitude; third, the debate on the problem among Christians of the period; and finally, the relationship between this debate and surviving examples of contemporary sermon style.

The new development of sermon style is a valuable illustration of the transformation that literary Latin had to undergo if it was to survive the crisis. The old literary order had seemed eternal, but it inhabited a fragile world dependent on an ailing educational system that the social and economic weakening of the Empire was steadily eroding.

* For a further discussion of this question, see Vol. II, "The Romance Languages."

In the traditional world three pairs of opposites were omnipresent: wealth and poverty, education and ignorance, high degree and low. The pursuit of virtue, which was equivalent to the pursuit of philosophy,[5] entailed erudition and leisure, and consequently the possession of a substantial private income. *Humilitas, parvitas, pusillitas, vilitas, paupertas, rusticitas,* and *ignorantia* were all perjoratives and came close to being synonyms.

The literary upper level of this world abounded in select groups of men of letters, amateur and professional. The correspondence of senators such as Symmachus, Ausonius, and Paulinus of Nola is full of their social and literary small-talk. The *Saturnalia* of Macrobius (written early in the 5th century, but set in 383 or 384) recreates the debates of the most famous of these groups. The subject is Virgil, and the discussions probe deep into myth and ritual, ancient history and philology, and all kinds of esoteric lore. Some passages are deeply imbued with pagan religious feeling. Many of the guests were pagans, in fact, and some were implicated in the pagan reaction of 393–4; but there was nothing essentially pagan about such groups.[6] Roman etiquette of the time preferred to overlook religious differences, and paid more attention to faults of upbringing, birth, and style.

Correspondence brought the small group into contact with a larger circle. A ceremonious politeness regulated the content of letters and debate. Letters were exchanged like visiting cards, and small men wrote to great ones (as humble men wrote to Jerome, Paulinus, and Augustine) merely for the favour of acknowledgment.

The group consisted typically of two sorts of person: the professional and the amateur litterateur, the teacher and the pupil; but they tended also to be, respectively, *curialis* and aristocrat, client and patron.[7] The group depicted in Macrobius's *Saturnalia* includes the *grammaticus* Servius (who was to write the great commentary on Virgil), a Greek *rhetor*, two philosophers, and a professor of medicine. The amateurs, including Symmachus, Praetextatus, Flavianus, and four of the Caeionii Albini, were as erudite as the professionals, and some were distinguished as editors and translators of classical texts into Latin and Greek.[8] One sees the same erudite amateurism in the little group of ascetic pioneers— principally leading female members of the Albini—whom Jerome was instructing in another house in Rome at this very time.

These men were the professional and amateur sustainers of the classical tradition. Their world prided itself on the mastery of great texts and the accumulation of obscure knowledge. Virgil and the authors of his age were regarded as literary models of unsurpassable excellence, and new work was admired only in so far as it approached the old. It was the world of the epitome and the cento. Yet it was not altogether sterile. There was a vogue for biting satire, congenial to the taste of a élitist and cynical age. Some of the textual scholarship is of permanent importance. But too much of the verse is soul-less dexterity, and too much of the prose is baroque rhetoric in which the newest image is a cliché 20 times re-used.

The professional élite of this literary world were the *grammatici* and *rhetores*, the expounders of texts and teachers of rhetoric, *ex officio* grammarians and philosophers. Such, for example, were Servius; Jerome's master Aelius Donatus, whose *Ars grammatica* became a standard school book during the Middle Ages; the celebrated convert Marius Victorinus; and Augustine himself, who in A.D. 384 secured from Symmachus, by a little string-pulling, the chair of rhetoric at Milan. The accumulated detritus of 1000 years of Roman history was their professional stock-in-trade, and they had a strong vested interest in its preservation. The state, too, shared this interest, and under its patronage men such as Ausonius, professor of rhetoric at Burdigala (Bordeaux), rose to dizzy heights. All men who hoped for social success followed their teaching, studying to acquire the most polished rhetorical style, the greatest elegance of form, and the most perfect facility in literary allusion. Jerome also, and indeed all the major Christian Latin writers, were steeped in the cultural values of this world, which they affected to despise.[9]

The educated man of the 4th century wrote, so far as he was able, the Latin of Cicero. The literary language had changed, it is true: there had been modifications in syntax and grammar, a progressive change from quantitative to accentual *clausula* (the closing cadence of a sentence). There were also new fashions in rhetoric that stemmed from the influence of the 2nd-century *rhetor* Fronto (creator of the *eloquentia novella*) and his school. When we see Augustine consciously breaking away from this fashion and returning to Cicero, he gives the appearance of innovating; but his "innovation" was quite acceptable to his contemporaries.

The case is different with the language of the Bible and with the language of the people. Properly, this point involves a discussion of Vulgar Latin, a large problem that lies beyond the scope of this essay. Roughly speaking, the situation may be described as follows:[10] even under the Republic, literary Latin was an artificial language, with marked differences from speech. To reconstruct spoken Latin, especially the speech of the uneducated, is not possible. By definition it could not be recorded in writing, because it would immediately have been contaminated by literary form. But there is evidence enough to measure its development, side by side with literary Latin. Being uncontrolled by the *grammatici*, it changed more rapidly than the written tongue. By the late 4th century the gap was wide: so wide, some think, that a bishop preaching in literary Latin might not have been readily understood by an ordinary congregation. Doubtless this view is exaggerated, but the distance between official oratory and popular speech was certainly great.

At some time in the second half of the 2nd century, the Greek Bible of the Christians was translated into Latin, probably in Africa, where more of the congregations were exclusively Latin-speaking than those of Rome.[11] The translator (and there may have been more than one) was not well-educated, and he rendered the sacred text into Latin as best he could, word for word. But the Greek he followed was itself a crude, at times nonsensical, version of the Hebrew: the syntax of this Greek Old Testament was still virtually Semitic. The "Old Latin" Bible (or *Vetus latina*) was consequently heavily contaminated with Vulgarisms,[12] and with transliterations or neologisms from the Greek, such as *episcopus*, *ecclesia*, and *baptizare*. And its word-order showed the influence of the Hebrew language.

Such writing repelled the educated members of society, Christian and pagan alike. Cicero had spoken for them all when he wrote (of contemporary religious writers):

> I forbear to read what affords no pleasure. Inasmuch, therefore, as by their own showing they do not trouble how they express themselves, I do not see why they should be read except in the circle of those who hold the same views and read their books to one another.[13]

In the 3rd century A.D., Bishop Cyprian of Carthage, who wrote in a respectable rhetorical style, earned the epithet "Coprianus" (one who smells of the dung heap) by his practice of quoting the Bible. Jerome, a highly educated man, was anticipating a similar reaction when he wrote in 394 to the newly converted senator Paulinus:

> I would not have you put off, in the Holy Scriptures, by the simplicity and one might say worthlessness of the language. It may have been the failure of the translators, or it may have been deliberate, but they were published in a form which gives easy instruction to an assembly of the ignorant, in which the same statement is heard one way by the educated and another way by the uneducated.[14]

Jerome's apology excuses the fault; it does not deny it. And it is evident that for the literate Christian public—as distinct from the clergy—the

Bible was a book that was not commonly read. Ambrose, who was still a layman at the time of his election as bishop of Milan in 374, came of an eminent and very devout family. But he was completely ignorant of the scriptures when he was elected, and confessed as much to his congregation. When Augustine, whose mother was a Christian, first tried to read the Bible when he was a student at Carthage university, he was repelled by its simple style, which fell so far short by comparison with Cicero.[15] Indeed, according to Jerome, many of the professional monastic teachers in Rome at this time, who preached sermons smooth with *clausulae* to admiring groups of disciples, never looked in the scriptures.[16]

The situation was very different, however, for the ordinary Christian congregations, the *contiones rusticae*. The Bible was their one authority. They heard long passages read or chanted every Sunday, and knew enough of it by heart to riot against the bishop when a new (and better) version was read in church, as we learn from one of Jerome's letters (*Epistles* 104). From this milieu came popular works heavily influenced by Vulgar Latin, and written, if they have any models at all, in the style of the Old Latin Bible. Such are the early Latin Martyr Acts, which were also read aloud in church. Here in embryo is a new literature, a new language, a new public, and a new professional élite without any respect for polite letters.[17]

A new technical vocabulary emerged, including words such as *confiteri* (to confess), *orare* (to pray), *paganus* (pagan), and *refrigerium* (spiritual refreshment). We find a distinctive form of Latin in the writings of the Christian community (except when they are deliberately couched in the classical style), which differs both from the literary and from the vulgar language. This new idiom began to influence even literature of the traditional type.

Before the period that we are examining, no conscious *doctrine* regarding Christian style had emerged within the Church, but the elements of a distinct attitude in the matter were present. Because classical literature was pagan in origin and in content, to quote from it was dangerously close to committing idolatry. Because the Apostle Paul commanded simplicity in dress, the use of an ornate style was akin to vanity. Because Christian wisdom was heavenly and incomprehensible to the world, it was doubtful whether the Christian had any use for worldly knowledge—indeed, whether he needed to read books at all.

In the 4th century, under the conditions of political establishment for the Church and mass conversion, Christian literature began to develop on a large scale. Christian Latin appeared before a wider public, and older forms were adapted for Christian needs. The literature that was produced can be classified under two heads: that which came from the old school, as was clear from its vocabulary, syntax, rhetoric, and the authors it cited; and that which was written in some form of Christian Latin or was otherwise influenced by the new style. In the former may be placed letter writing, poetry, apologetic, polemic, and much theology, along with orations and some translation. In the latter we find most hagiography and similar work, hymnography (a new genre, partly influenced by the psalter), sermon and catechesis, and much translation. We may also include liturgy here.

At once an important distinction appears. Works in the first category were written for an educated public, those in the second for a mass audience; the former were written for private study or for reading before a select audience, the latter were meant to be delivered in loud tones to large assemblies in basilicas. It is not derogatory to describe either the former as self-consciously literary or the latter as utilitarian.

While Symmachus and his circle were exploring the intricacies of Virgil, Augustine, out of curiosity, was going to hear Ambrose preach:

> I listened with attention while he preached to the congregation, not with a proper object, but as it were to examine his ability as a preacher and to learn whether his eloquence agreed with report, or was greater or lesser than was said. I attended closely to his words, but was uninterested in the subject matter and contemptuous; while the beauty of his speech delighted me.[18]

Here Augustine, newly appointed professor of rhetoric in Milan, appears as a representative of the old world, listening curiously and attentively to a representative of the new. His preference for form and neglect of content shows his traditional taste, but he is prepared to recognize "beauty of speech" in something well removed from conventional rhetoric. It was a discovery that set the *rhetor* thinking about his own trade, and would lead him to produce, 40 years later, a complete re-thinking of the traditional theory of rhetoric.

Intellectually, Augustine was of course far more flexible and imaginative than most of his contemporaries. The confrontation of two worlds that he experienced took place for every Christian intellectual; if he were a sensitive man, the encounter could be very painful. Such a man was faced with a clash of imperatives, and in the 4th century Latin Christians found various solutions. Some simply boasted of their ignorance of secular literature: thus, the fanatic Lucifer of Cagliari declares: "We, however, are born with all we need for speech; we have no knowledge whatsoever of pagan literature."[19] Tyrannius Rufinus, an educated man with a good style, is equally firm:

> We disregard all irony and hypocritical evasion, which is hateful to God; and though we shall make our reply in unadorned language and artless speech, we presume to hope, not without cause, that our readers will pardon our ignorance.[20]

He explicitly contrasts his own style with Jerome's, and points out in detail the latter's fondness for classical quotation. He himself never quotes a secular author, save for the one line he lifts from Jerome and turns against him. Clerics such as Chromatius of Aquileia and Maximus of Turin, both educated men, seem equally well able to do without secular literature. Maximus, writing a commentary on the words *tunica de superiore contexta* (John XIX, 23), makes his reasoning clear:

> As for his garment that was not stitched together, we can recognize that it was his heavenly wisdom, because [it was not stitched together] but was woven wholly from above. For our wisdom, human wisdom that is, is stitched together; for it is stitched up when we put children to school, hand them to *grammatici*, instruct them with teachers of philosophy, that they may obtain a wisdom which was not present in them. But the wisdom of the Lord is not stitched up, not sought out. . . .[21]

Other writers, however, who were among the greatest of their age, both as saints and as men of intellect, found it more difficult to be consistent. Such was the case with Paulinus of Nola, for instance, son of a wealthy Roman administrator in Gaul, and educated by Ausonius at Bordeaux; such was the case also with Ambrose and Augustine. All of them quote from classical authors, Ambrose and Paulinus acknowledging their source with an embarrassed apology, Augustine generally suppressing his author's name, and using some vague formula of introduction such as *sicut ait quidem* (as, for example, someone says) or *ut ille dixit* (as a certain person says).

The Christian writer, then, was confronted with two opposed sets of values, and he had to find a *modus vivendi*. For many the solution was simple, as we have seen: Lucifer and Rufinus state an obvious orthodox truth, and they speak for many more for whom the classical tradition meant little. The smooth preachers who Jerome describes as never looking at the Scriptures were adopting the opposite solution with equal ease. In between lie those who were sensitive to both imperatives. Ambrose and Paulinus managed to avoid thinking too hard about the problem;

Jerome and Augustine experienced a deeper, more personal, crisis and found a more personal solution.

What Jerome says is of particular interest. He understands the problem well, being a polished stylist and a most intelligent and erudite man. Because he is a complicated, sensitive individual, he is quite unable to reach a consistent solution. He is also important because of the vast influence that he exerted by his revision of the Old Latin Bible.[22]

The forthright rejection of the classical tradition (implied by our opening quotation) was too facile for Jerome to follow in practice; his mind was too sensitive to adopt a simple rule of *rusticana simplicitas*. He is no more fond of clumsy speech than Cicero was, and treats the affectation of it as humbug:

> I do not mean to criticise the uneducated speech of the ordinary Christian. . . . I have always had a respect not for ignorant verbosity, but for holy simplicity; my only point is that one who claims to imitate the apostles in his speech must first imitate them in his way of life.[23]

The occasion here is a sarcastic onslaught of Rufinus, but the attitude is the fruit of lifelong habit—and the habit was not one of strictly religious perfection. In *Epistles* 22 of A.D. 384 Jerome recalls an incident of the early 370s,[24] when he went on pilgrimage to Antioch and found he could not bear to be without his library:

> So I, like a wretch, used to fast before reading Cicero. I kept frequent, night-long vigils, wept tears . . . and afterwards took Plautus in my hands. If I returned to myself and began to read a prophet, the uneducated language made me shudder.[25]

In the following Lent Jerome became ill and, when the fever was at its height and his life despaired of, fell into a trance:

> I was dragged before the Judge's Tribunal. Such was the light and so great the brightness of those that stood round that I fell to the ground and did not dare look up. I was asked my condition in life: "I am a Christian," I replied. "You lie," said he who sat there, "you are a Ciceronian; 'where your treasure is, there your heart is also.' "[26]

The reason for Jerome's guilty conscience may be seen from the language and style of his *Life of Paul the Hermit*, written while he was in the East. Certainly, at the time when he wrote *Epistles* 22, he identified the study of the pagan classics with the cult of idols, and after the dreadful dream he solemnly swore never to touch a pagan author again: "Lord, if ever I read worldly literature again, I shall have denied you." And whatever may be said of the previous period, it was an oath that at the time of writing he meant to keep. After the letter, his references to classical authors were for a time confined to reminiscence and he conscientiously avoided quoting them. In the preface to the third volume of his commentary on Galatians (*c.* 390) Jerome claims that he has kept the oath, a claim that seems well founded.

But from the time of the commentary onward we begin to find again an increase in the number of classical quotations, as Jerome later acknowledged. He has begun to read again, and has even extended his range. The preface betrays striking equivocation. Jerome evidently feels that he needs refreshment. By 393 he is positively parading his classical erudition, some of it quite spurious. He cannot deny Rufinus's allegations (in 401) about his continuing involvement in secular authors, and he is reduced in the end to admitting the charge and explaining away the vow (What are oaths taken in dreams?). We cannot possibly accept his assertion that he quoted only from memory. And the volume of quotation continues undiminished in his literary works, right up to the end.

On the other hand, Jerome does succeed in excluding not merely quotation but also rhetorical style from his biblical commentaries and sermons, even while writing letters and polemic redolent of the rhetorical school. One statement must serve:

> For we do not repeat phrases in the fashion of orators, nor pile up
> words and arouse hearers and readers to praise us with our rhetoric;
> we direct our efforts to elucidating to men passages that are obscure,
> especially those in a foreign language.[27]

It is clear that, during his early monastic period, Jerome yielded to the strong prejudices current in the Christian world. But the pull of his classical background was strong; and when at length the inner conflict grew too much for him, he resorted to hypocritical excuses. He was unable, because of his training, to recognize the role of *rusticana simplicitas* as literature, and therefore could not make any theoretical contribution to solving the problem. But this did not prevent him from making one important practical contribution. Although he succeeded only in making his sermon style flat, he developed a style of translation for his work on the Bible that represented an important advance in the development of a "biblical Latin."[28]*

---

* For a discussion of a similar problem in relation to Renaissance humanism, see Vol. III, "Humanism and Language."

Jerome's actual statements on the subject are contradictory. He insists
that a good translation should be not only accurate but also idiomatic—
that is, in a polished style; he has in theory no respect for clumsy literal
versions, even if they are hallowed by tradition. But when approaching
the Bible, he is inhibited from making drastic alterations by the enormous
respect prevalent for the old translation, especially the version of the
Gospels. Moreover, in the name of literary simplicity, the ideal he had
adopted for his biblical work in general, he eschews any pretension to
style in a conventional sense. For this reason his revision of the New
Testament keeps very close to the old version (or versions). But with the
Old Testament his knowledge of Hebrew leads him to reject the Greek
("Septuagint") translation on which the Old Latin had been based, and
he is compelled to make a completely new translation. The style he adopts
is not as flat as one would expect from his principles. He uses the old
version as a model, and handles vocabulary and style with remarkable
sensitivity and skill.

Augustine was equally a master of style. He faced the implications of
the problem with more originality and honesty than Jerome. In the course
of a long, industrious, fatiguing career as a Catholic presbyter and bishop
(391–430), he wrote (or dictated) vast numbers of works. During this
period he was continually developing and experimenting with style, and
reflecting on the problem of the nature of a Christian culture. The fourth
book of his *De doctrina christiana*, a practical education programme for
Christians, written *c.* 427, sets out his mature thought on the subject,
especially on the value of pagan rhetoric for the Christian, and on the
literary goals to be pursued by the Church.

There has been some dispute over interpretation. It has been argued
that Augustine, after criticizing the excesses of contemporary rhetorical
practice, put forward a reactionary solution: that there should be a return
to the classical rhetorical technique of Cicero, with the traditional rules
and classification.[29] But, it was alleged, this was for Augustine a paper
exercise. His own practice as a preacher was better represented in his
De catechizandis rudibus (a primer of elementary Christian instruction),
both in the recommendations made and in the sample discourses provided.
If this was the case, then Augustine set no rule beyond the principle of
adaptation to one's audience, and his basic model for preaching was the
Stoic-Cynic *diatribe*. But this interpretation is now generally rejected.[30]
The theory put forward in the *De doctrina christiana* is not conservative but
revolutionary; and it certainly corresponds to Augustine's practice.
Cicero is merely invoked.

Augustine's first argument dismisses the prejudice current among Christians. Pagan rhetoric is a powerful instrument of persuasion. The Christian preacher must therefore be in a position to use it if necessary, though knowledge of what to say is even more important—*eloquentia* is useful but not indispensable. Contrary to the traditional view, Augustine claims, Scripture contains many examples of rhetoric. A Christian can acquire a satisfactory training by studying these, together with good Christian models such as Cyprian and Ambrose, without going through the traditional schools. To be especially schooled in rhetoric is not essential and should not be urged on Christian intellectuals. Common sense is a better guide than rules.

We notice, first, that this approach to pagan rhetoric is at once critical and fair; this is because the starting point is objective and utilitarian. Augustine approaches the question: "What is its moral status?" by asking, "What is it used for?" His answer is that when it is used for its own sake, and treated as an end in itself, it is bad; the superficial pursuit of eloquent speech is dangerous for the Christian. Augustine singles out a passage of Cyprian as an example of the lush Asianism that is to be avoided:

> "Seek we this seat: the neighbouring solitude grants a place of withdrawal; and there the wandering stems of vines in pendant clusters twine about the reedy scaffold, making a vine-branch summer house with leafy roof." This is all said with the most marvellous profusion of luxuriant eloquence, but the quite excessive abundance is unpleasant.[31]

Eloquentia is good when used with discrimination, when it achieves clarity and plainness, and serves a good end. It will be seen that Augustine has rejected both the traditional (and contemporary) secular teaching and also the Christian reply.

Next, Augustine takes up the traditional categories and turns them on their heads. The division into three orders is quoted, the *grande*, the *temperatum*, and the *submissum*—i.e. lofty, moderate, and lowly style, or impassioned, ornamented, and plain. Cicero had joined each variety of rhetoric to an appropriate subject-matter on the basis of an implied moral value judgment; low style was to be used for lowly themes, and so on. For the Church this would not do. No theme could be lowly, for all mattered. And Augustine adopts a classification of his own: *submissum* for didactic speech, i.e. simple instruction as in the *De catechizandis rudibus*; *temperatum*, where one wishes to correct the audience, assigning praise and blame; and *grande*, when the intention is to produce deep emotion. In practice, this classification proves rather too neat: it is hard to classify

Augustine's individual sermons. He seems to use the different styles according to the mood of the moment, as indeed he would recommend. In general, however, his critique of the traditional categories is most fruitful.

Augustine's approach parts company with the traditional rules that stemmed from the orators and schools of the late Republic. He can appreciate the eloquence of the Bible, and imitate it with profit. The final guide, for him, is one's own good sense. He even comes near to jettisoning grammar. In defence of a clumsy piece of literal translation, he says:

> "Bloods" is not Latin; but it is plural in the Greek, and the translator preferred to put it so in Latin, and to speak ungrammatically, in order to make the true meaning plain for uneducated hearers. . . . And I tell you, let us not be frightened of the canes of the *grammatici*; the important thing is that we should grasp a truth that is firm and more certain.[32]

Augustine seems to have aspired to a new kind of eloquence, an *eloquentia christiana*, that is basically distinct from traditional rhetoric, though free to draw on it, and that owes as much or more to the Bible and the language of the people. (Whether his scheme was a practical one for teaching purposes is a different question. At this time the Church was in no way equipped to act as an educational institution.)

We have noticed that the Fathers varied in their approach to the problem, and that the best-educated ones—Ambrose, Augustine, Jerome —came nearest to finding a solution for it. Obviously, their personal upbringing and social background are most important in this connection. Before considering other variations in Latin style that were produced in one pre-eminently Christian genre, namely the sermon, we must look briefly at the social origins of those who preached them.

If we take northern Italy in the Theodosian epoch as a test case, we find that the bishops fall into three groups: grandees, foreigners, and local men. In the first group we have Ambrose of Milan and Petronius of Bologna: scions of great Roman senatorial families, expensively educated, launched on top-level civil-service careers, and falling into the episcopate almost by accident. There are quite a few foreigners, from other parts of Italy and from abroad. The successors of Ambrose come from Rome, Bordeaux, and Mesopotamia; Zeno of Verona is thought to have been an African, and Filaster of Brescia equally alien; Eusebius of Vercelli was certainly a Sardinian, although he came by way of Rome. Such men formed part of that flock of wandering clergy and monks that had come to infest the roads of the empire, rootless men, many of them vagabonds and virtually "self-ordained." Their command of the local tongue was, naturally, not always very good.

The bulk of the clergy, however, appears to have been locally born: such were Gaudentius of Brescia, Heliodorus of Altino, Gaudentius of Novara (who came from nearby Ivrea), Maximus of Turin (who came from a more eastern town), Sabinus of Piacenza and Felix of Bologna (both from Milan), and so on. Sometimes we discover a clerical dynasty, and we have to remember that marriage was not a bar to ordination. The senior clergy were expected not to live with their wives, but it is not clear whether this rule was very generally observed. Low standards among the clergy were a problem in all parts of Italy—owing particularly to the huge expansion of numbers in the 4th century—and even the most active metropolitans could not achieve much outside their immediate area of influence.

The bishops whom we have to deal with were probably not very typical. Their sermons were preserved because they were worth preserving. It is evident in several cases that they were men of more than usual ability who had been chosen to work in difficult areas. Even among them we notice one, Vigilius of Trent, who proves quite incompetent when he tries to write in the rhetorical style. There may have been many who found preaching difficult, and who resorted to expedients such as borrowing other men's sermons. The publication and circulation of sermon collections helped to meet this need.

The senior clergy, above all the bishops, probably came most commonly from the "curial" class—the section of the local gentry that the imperial government obliged to perform many of the functions of local government. A career in the Church offered a chance of escape, although the government did its best to prevent this. Such families were *ex officio* endowed with land, and endeavoured to send their sons to university, with a view to their possible advancement to better positions. They were automatically leaders of local society, second only to the great senatorial families and high officials of the district (who frequently took no interest in local life).

Bishops from this background preserved close ties with local society and shared local patriotism. Their writings show familiarity with the details of local life and speech—at least in the towns—and sometimes betray resentment of the great. How many of them were well educated we have no means of knowing, but it is unlikely that the bishops' contempt for the rhetoric of highly cultivated men was solely a matter of Christian prejudice; it was also influenced by attitudes surviving from the time of persecution.

There were two sorts of public for a bishop's sermons: a small inner ring of monks, pious ladies, consecrated virgins, senior clergy, cultivated local gentry, and other enthusiasts in the congregation; and a large outer mass who came simply because it was the custom, and of whom many were chiefly anxious to avoid the social stigma of not attending. The bishop's style would vary a great deal according to the public he was addressing. Ambrose underlines the importance of not preaching solely to the best-educated in the congregation. The difference in the character of the congregations in Brescia and in Turin must explain some of the differences between Gaudentius's style of preaching and that of Maximus. Particularly striking, in this connection, is the division of Zeno of Verona's sermons into two groups, one elaborate in style, the other very simple; probably they correspond to two audiences.

The Latin sermon of the 4th century has a long prehistory, much of it untraceable. Its deepest roots lie in the Aramaic synagogue address (Luke iv, 16–22), and others in the Stoic-Cynic *diatribe*, the obvious vehicle for Greek evangelists. The Greek philosophical sects of the Stoics and Cynics had developed the technique of spreading their doctrines by means of a popular sermon (*diatribe*, or *declamatio*) preached in the market place, not unlike the modern evangelist or Hyde Park Corner politician. This involved them in important departures from formal rhetoric: first, they adopted a basically informal approach, suited to the audience of the moment, and were ready to adjust to changes in mood. The *diatribe* began carefully but developed in a very casual fashion and might even break off abruptly; the style was consequently unmethodical and slapdash, with strings of short phrases. Second, it involved some dialogue with the audience, including debate with a fictitious (or real) onlooker, and humorous sallies at someone's expense. The rhetorical devices were suited to this approach, including puns and alliteration and bizarre play on words, the quotation of proverbs, the use of paradox, and unexpected, ingenious remarks on serious subjects. It was lively, highly coloured, unexpected, and designed to entertain a popular audience. Several Latin authors acquainted with Stoicism discuss the method, including Cicero in *Paradoxa stoicorum*. (For examples, see Seneca's *Epistulae morales*.)

Unfortunately, there are no examples in Latin of Christian sermons in the *declamatio* style before the 4th century. Previous writers, such as Tertullian and Cyprian (conventionally educated men), write a correct, rhetorical Latin—heavily influenced by the baroque style popularized by Fronto and Apuleius—even in their semi-popular pamphlets. It is therefore not possible to know what Latin sermon style was like before the 4th century. The influence of the *diatribe* then becomes clear, however, besides other influences that we have already discussed and may now summarize. On the one hand, there is the peculiar Latin syntax and vocabulary of the first Bible translation (the *Vetus latina*), together with the realistic style of the *Passiones*; on the other hand, there is the influence of the rhetorical schools, which provided not merely the apparatus of traditional oratory, but also the methods of quotation and allusion (paraphrase), the art of mastering a text and interpreting it, and the techniques of allegory. The latter had originally been developed for handling myth, and formed part of advanced studies in Virgil; they developed alongside, and reinforced, the biblical tradition of typological interpretation.

By this date, too, an elaborate terminology had developed. There were three standard terms in Latin for preaching: *tractatus*, *sermo*, and *praedicatio*.[33] *Tractatus* tended to signify exegetic exposition of scripture (there is also a strong didactic sense, and the term is also used of preaching in general); *sermo* referred to the sermon proper, of all kinds including catechetical; and *praedicatio* signified preaching with a strong pastoral sense, and sometimes with particular connotations of power and responsibility. These distinctions are important, because they show a fine awareness of the significance of style. We have already noted Augustine's stylistic criteria (together with the fact that his genius transcends his own rules). But we find a similar concern for style in a less-able (though not negligible) preacher, Maximus of Turin. He divides preaching into two categories, *consolatio* and *increpatio*. *Consolatio* is to be pleasant in tone, and is concerned with doctrinal exposition of the scriptures and gentle exhortation. Its intention is to foster faith. The mood is formal, and the sermons are carefully prepared and relatively ornate in their use of rhetorical devices. It is clear that Maximus regarded them as rewards to his congregation for good conduct. In *increpatio*, by contrast, the prevailing tone is severe reproof; the preacher's mood is sober, earnest, and visibly angry. The theme is frequently the Last Judgment, and the object urgent: practical reform in such matters as idolatry, avarice, and unchastity. There is little use here of rhetorical ornament and scriptural quotation, explicit or allusive; instead there are bitter, sarcastic sallies, often as funny as they are frightening.

Maximus illustrates a further characteristic of the preachers of his generation: their heavy sense of responsibility. The bishop preaches unwillingly, under divine compulsion. His word is weighted with irresistible power, and his judgment is the judgment of God.

For they say: "How harshly and bitterly the bishop preached!", not knowing that the clergy speak more from compulsion than volition . . . we impress dread on others, while we fear for our own salvation.[34]

His aim is inescapable confrontation with the divine judgment:

For the gospel does not preach in vain, the apostle does not cry to no purpose, the clergy do not speak without a reason. Into whoever's ears the holy voice should come, either they will be blessed for believing, or guilty of resistance.[35]

Altogether we may define four different styles of preaching. There are those who preach in a purely literary style; those who preach in an oral style with a literary basis; those who preach in an oral style with a popular basis; and those who preach in a style that is completely unadorned. Among the first are such as Gaudentius of Brescia and Zeno (and sometimes Ambrose); among the second, Ambrose, Chromatius, and Maximus; among the third, Augustine; and the chief representative of the fourth style is Jerome. In many ways the oral element of style is the most interesting, because it is a new technique, still developing in this milieu, and because it brings one nearest to the living thoughts of the preacher and his audience.

The oral style of the north-Italian preachers may be defined as the style that a literary man would use when he was speaking extempore, intending to persuade and instruct a popular gathering.[36] The *De sacramentis* appears to be an unofficial shorthand record of a series of six catechetical sermons delivered by Ambrose in Milan Cathedral at Easter, *c.* A.D. 390. It will be convenient to set out the elements of the style employed in tabular form:

STRUCTURE: Loose and rambling, with a tendency to digress and to develop arguments ad hoc, and a consequent loss of order and balance.

SERMOCINATIO: A prominent element of dialogue (question and answer); direct address ("you see"; "remember"; "look!"); personal assertion (such as "I think"), coupled with adverbs such as "obviously"; exhortations, demands, commands ("let us . . .!"); personal comments on the audience, and expressions of personal feeling (anger, grief, weakness).

PARATAXIS: Speaking in series of short sentences, clauses, and phrases, juxtaposed but not grammatically connected; *anacoloutha* (sentences with grammatical structure broken); nominal construction (sequences of noun phrases without verbs); sequences of clauses with verbs at the beginning; parentheses and digressions; indirect statement with

477

conjunction and subordinate verb in preference to accusative and infinitive.

PARALLELISM AND RHYME: A particular emphasis on antithetic parallelism in sentence structure; antistrophe; repetition of words and phrases; alliteration and assonance; *homoeoteleuton* and rhyme; use of rhythmic rather than accentual *clausulae*.

IMAGERY: The use of vivid imagery, with homely comparisons and striking illustrations.

Certain elements correspond to the *diatribe* style: *sermocinatio* (debate with a fictitious interlocutor—an interesting parallel is found in Augustine's *Soliloquies*); a strongly personal style, with humorous sallies (disapproved of by Ambrose but used by Maximus); an extremely loose sentence structure; use of many devices in the "rhyme" category—assonance and word play, repetition, use of popular proverbs and slogans; and a readiness even to break off the discourse if the audience was inattentive. Repetition is worth remarking; it is a feature of the times. Trained claques chant at the races and in the theatre (often for the benefit of officials); senators chant slogans in the *curia*, and the urban prefect relays them to the throne. Angry Christians chant in the Roman churches when their candidate has been deposed in a disputed papal election; congregations chant a half-verse as an antiphon throughout the psalm, responding to the deacon.

Both Maximus and Chromatius come close to the style of Ambrose's *De sacramentis*, though they are several degrees more formal. Their sermons are written consistently in the dialogue style, with many interrogations. Chromatius's favourite is *Vis scire*, e.g. *Vis scire qualis speciosa porta sit? Audi David in psalmo dicentem . . . (Hom.* 1, 62) (Do you want to know how beautiful the gate is? Listen to what David says in the psalm . . .). Compare Ambrose's: *Quare? Dicam, accipe* or *Quomodo? Accipe.* Maximus's questions are more strictly rhetorical, but compare the formula: *Quae sententia quem intellectum habeat, diligentius intendamus!* (*Serm.* 86, 41) (Let us understand more accurately how this expression should be interpreted.) Both use direct address frequently. Both like to make a transition by way of subjective assertion. Maximus especially uses (or rather over-uses) *plane*, and is equally fond of *puto, arbitror,* and *dixerim*. An example from *Sermons* 54, lines 42–9, will illustrate the whole technique. I have italicized the key words:

> *Videamus* igitur *quis* ille tantus sit, qui discipulis proponitur imitandus!
> *Non* hunc *arbitror* esse de plebe *non* de publico. . . . *Non, inquam,* hunc
> de publico esse *arbitror, sed* de caelo. Ipse est *enim* de caelo puer, *de*

quo dicit Eseias propheta. . . . Ipse *plane* puer est, *qui* sicut innocens cum malediceretur . . .

(Let us see therefore who may be great enough to be held up to disciples as worthy of imitation. I don't think he is one of the common people, nor is he one of the populace. . . . I say that I don't think he is of the people, but of heaven. For he is the very child of heaven of whom the prophet Isaiah speaks. . . . He is clearly the same child who, like an innocent when he was reviled . . .).

By this means the preacher keeps the whole discussion on the familiar, personal level, never slipping into the didactic. Chromatius is less successful. He is much more methodical than Maximus, and if he should accidentally stray, he conscientiously returns with an apology: *redeamus ad ordinem.*

In all these respects both are near to Ambrose, though Maximus is the closer. Yet neither is delivering true extempore *sermocinatio.* (The nature of Maximus's quotations makes careful drafting certain.) One searches Chromatius in vain for the broken, paratactic structure of Ambrose's *De sacramentis.* And in Maximus it appears only in actual quotations from popular speech. Compare *Sermons* 71, 28:

They say in the summer months: "The day is long, the sun is very hot; we cannot stand the thirst, we need drink to refresh ourselves"; but in winter time: "It's freezing, the frosts are dreadful; we cannot bear the cold, we must have food to warm ourselves."

Other points confirm this difference. Anacoluthon is rare; sentences with the verb in the initial position are infrequent. Maximus again comes nearest in a quotation (*Serm.* 42–21–28): *Hodie audivimus episcopum . . ., rem utilem praedicavit, debemus. . . . Prosecutus etiam . . . requiramus . . .! Admonuit etiam. . . .* (Today we heard the bishop . . ., he preached on a useful topic, we ought. . . . And he continued . . . let us seek! . . . He also reminded us. . . .) Both authors use short parentheses, but rarely so as to break the flow; both use repetition, but of selected words and phrases, not of whole sentences. Chromatius, *Hom.* 3, 83–90, is a typical example of skilful construction, with *Petrus, esurire* (to hunger for), *cibum salutis* (the food of salvation) appearing on every line for nine lines consecutively, with a variation each time.

The paratactic style, with its juxtaposition of short, parallel sentences, lends itself to the traditional rhetorical range of parallel and rhyming devices, although the looseness is unsuitable for the more elaborate forms. Ambrose makes a very marked use of antithetic parallelism, but there are few elaborate arrangements. The other two both draft with more care and use a wider range, but the tendency toward rhyme is definitely more pronounced in Maximus than in Chromatius; the latter is altogether more restrained in his use of ornament.

It is in the use of imagery and illustration that the distinctive personality of the bishop emerges most clearly. For Ambrose, we may consider this passage in *De sacramentis*, the comparison of the reborn Christian with the fish:

> The tempest rages in the sea, the hurricanes shriek, but the fish swims, and is not drowned, because its nature is to swim. So this world is a sea for you. It has its various floods, mighty waves, fierce tempests. Be you too a fish, that the world's wave may not drown you.[37]

For humour one may look to Maximus. He is really very angry in Sermon 30, and indignation makes him wonderfully sarcastic. There had been a total eclipse of the moon, and the locals, very alarmed, had let out a great clamour in order to preserve it from enchanters' spells. Maximus smiled—no doubt wryly—when he heard this, marvelling that "pious" Christians should think of aiding God:

> Indeed it does you credit, this concern for the deity which you display, that your aid may make him able to rule heaven. But if you want to do this properly, you ought to keep watch all night and every night. How often, do you think, has the moon suffered attacks while you were asleep, and yet not fallen from heaven?[38]

Augustine's sermons are probably the best known of all the Latin Fathers', and there is no need to examine them in detail here. (In any case it would be difficult to improve on Erich Auerbach's essay, "Sermo Humilis.") But we may note again the features that have already been found in the oral style of the North Italian preachers: *sermocinatio* with many questions and imperatives; choppy paratactic structure with a volley of short clauses and phrases strung together with *et . . . et*; frequent parentheses and interruptions; extensive use of the analytic construction in indirect statement; antithetic parallelism, antistrophe, assonance, alliteration, homoeoteleuton, rhyme, and word-play; exuberant familiarity, ad hoc response to possible criticisms, interruptions to reprove the audience, requests for silence, patience, etc.; remarks on the time of day; and so on.

The texts are, of course, uncorrected shorthand versions, like the *De sacramentis*, and this explains why the resemblances are so close. But there are important differences too. Augustine's rhetoric flies higher, due to his

North African training. But he uses rhyme and repetition more, and makes plays on words that Ambrose would have disdained; he also adopts in places a biblical form of syntax, and brings in numerous and exotic images. It has been suggested that these features are not only biblical, but popular,[39] and that in his use of rhyme and word-play Augustine was borrowing from popular speech. At all events, he created a distinctive personal style that draws skilfully both on popular sources and on the *sermo humilis* of scripture; and a style, too, that was appreciated by his congregations and by the preachers who came after him.

This study commenced with a quotation from Jerome's *Epistles* 21; we return to him now at the close. At a later point in the argument he recommends that Christians should treat the pagan heritage as Israelites were commanded to treat the beautiful Gentile woman they wished to marry (Deut. xxi, 10–31), shaving her head bare and paring her nails. Subsequently he changed his mind about the bearing of the passage on pagan literature, but his attitude to preaching stayed the same:

> When you speak in church, do not arouse applause but groaning. . . .
> I would not have you be an orator, a stormy speaker and a man of
> eloquence, but a man informed in doctrine and most learned in the
> mysteries of your God.[40]

Jerome was true to his precept. The sermon *De die epiphaniorum* gives a clear illustration. There is no attempt at dialogue, apart from the occasional rhetorical *quid*? There is no personal intrusion with *puto*, *plane*, and so on, to break the formality. There is no alliteration or similar device to give colour and character. Above all there is no illustration. The effect is lucid and scholarly, but cold and unattractive. It is a literary man's attempt to compose in an oral style without any ornament at all.

Jerome was convinced that the biblical model enjoined absolute plainness, *rusticana simplicitas*. We have seen that Augustine reached a different conclusion. What is remarkable is the fact that Jerome, with his greatly superior linguistic ability and the undoubted appreciation of biblical style that he showed as a translator, failed to reach a similar understanding and continued to echo the prejudice of the ignorant, as in *Epistles* 53, 10. Was he as blind as he makes out? It is hard to believe. There is a suspicious resemblance to his equivocation about the use of the pagan classics.

What we have been examining was not, in the authors' intention, literature. Much of it survived only because other men wished to preserve it (sometimes to the preachers' annoyance[41]). The authors themselves, if they chose to publish, revised more or less drastically, and a comparison of the *De sacramentis* and the *De mysteriis* (the "written-up" version of the original sermons), or of Chromatius's homilies and the *Tractatus in Matthaeum*, can give useful indications of what the Christian Fathers regarded as acceptable and unacceptable style in literature. But the circulation of revised and unrevised versions had interesting consequences. Ambrose composed for the moment; Maximus, who imitated his style, undoubtedly made careful written drafts and kept them after he had preached.[42] In due course they became the basis of published editions of his sermons. Oral style was already beginning to turn into written style. But this development had happened long before in the schools of rhetoric. The classical declamations were written for publication. And that is precisely what Ambrose was doing when he revised his sermons according to the conventions of the rhetorical style; he was showing himself to be not so much an orator—for his spoken style was different—as a writer who knew how to compose oratory.[43]

The phenomenon has modern parallels: business records, published interviews, and the transcripts of courts of inquiry, criminal trials, and teach-ins are examples of literature-by-default—a genre that is proliferating as techniques of recording improve. We mentioned at the beginning "a very exact assessment of the extent to which the Church created something new in Roman culture." And we have seen something both of the technique of inquiry and of the answer. The Church had indeed achieved something new, though Augustine was unique among his contemporaries in his conscious realization of this. Ambrose, when he began to preach, instinctively relaxed the rules of oratory. Augustine, the professor of rhetoric, listened and admired; and having admired, he learned, reflected, and went further. The *Confessions* is a kind of first-fruits of this initiative. The pagan schools had reached their term; the *eloquentia christiana* had only begun.

References

1. Jerome, *Epistles* 21, 13 (A.D. 383): *Lettres*, ed. by J. Labourt, Vol. I (Paris 1949), p. 93.
2. *ibid.*
3. A social classification conferring legal privileges on the upper classes. These included exemption from torture when undergoing judicial examination.

4. On the complications of this world, see R. MACMULLEN, *Enemies of the Roman Order* (Harvard 1967), pp. 182 f., 197 ff., and 203.

5. Cf. A. D. NOCK, *Conversion* (Oxford 1953), pp. 174 f. and 178 f.

6. Compare the philosophic circle directed by the recent convert Augustine at Cassiciacum in A.D. 386 and that of the Christian philosopher statesman Manlius Theodorus in Milan, uncovered by Pierre Courcelle. These should be distinguished from the more professional ascetic groups formed around Chromatius at Aquileia *c.* 370–5 and around Jerome in Rome *c.* 383–5.

7. The *curialis* belongs to that part of the gentry that was burdened with onerous and inalienable responsibilities in municipal government. The English J.P. in the late 18th century is a very loose parallel.

8. On the date, setting, and personnel of the *Saturnalia*, see A. CAMERON, "The Date and Identity of Macrobius," *Journal of Roman Studies*, LVI (London 1966), pp. 25–38. Cf. COURCELLE, p. 4 ff.

9. See Jerome, *Apologia adversus libros Rufini*, I, p. 30 f. (*Patrologia latina* 23), discussed in HAGENDAHL, *Latin Fathers*, pp. 182 and 327 f.

10. See the discussion in LÖFSTEDT, especially Ch. 2.

11. See G. BARDY, *La question des langues dans l'église ancienne*, I (Paris 1948), pp. 94–110 and 160 f. Cf. MOHRMANN, *Liturgical Latin*, pp. 50 ff. Greek remained the liturgical language of the Roman Church until the mid-4th century.

12. Cf. VÄÄNÄNEN, pp. 241 f. and 265.

13. Cicero, *Tusculanae disputationes*, II, 3, 7, ed. and trans. by J. E. King (Harvard 1960), pp. 152 f.

14. Jerome, *Ep.* 53, 10 (A.D. 394): *Lettres*, ed. by J. Labourt, Vol. III (Paris 1953), p. 23.

15. See Augustine, *Confessions*, III, 5, 9; trans. by R. S. Pine-Coffin (London 1961), p. 60.

16. See Jerome, *Ep.* 53, 7: *Lettres*, ed. by J. Labourt, Vol. III (Paris 1953), p. 15.

17. On the Latinity of the clergy of Rome and Carthage in A.D. 250, see W. H. C. FREND, *Martyrdom and Persecution in the Early Church* (Oxford 1965), p. 411; and cf. Cyprian, *Epistles* 30.

18. Augustine, *Conf.*, V, 14, 24 (*c.* 400), ed. by A. C. Vega, *Obras de San Agustin*, Vol. II (Madrid 1963), p. 209. For a discussion of Augustine's slow shift toward Christian Latin after his conversion, see MOHRMANN, "Comment saint Augustin . . .," p. 387. Cf. HAGENDAHL, *Augustine and the Latin Classics*, Pt 2, p. 557.

19. Lucifer Calaritanus, *Moriendum esse pro Dei Filio*, XI (*c.* 360): *Corpus scriptorum ecclesiasticorum latinorum*, Vol. XIV (Vienna 1886), p. 306 (quoted in HAGENDAHL, "Methods of Citation . . .," p. 115 f.).

20. Tyrannius Rufinus, *Apologia in Hieronymum*, I, 2 (*Patrologia latina* 21, 542 b).

21. Maximum Taurinensis, *Sermons* 29, 103–10 (*c.* 399), ed. by A. Mutzenbecher, *Corpus christianorum* (Turnhout 1962), Vol. XXIII.

22. The work begins in A.D. 384 when Jerome is commissioned by Pope

Damasus to revise the Psalter and the Gospels; it is concluded some 20 years later, with the publication of the last Old Testament versions; the writing of *Commentaries* takes Jerome the rest of his life.

23. Jerome, *Ep.* 57, 12 (*c.* 395–6): *Lettres*, ed. by J. Labourt, Vol. III (Paris 1953), pp. 72 f.

24. Probably toward the end of A.D. 374.

25. Jerome, *Ep.* 22, 30 (384): *Lettres*, ed. by J. Labourt, Vol. I (Paris 1949), p. 144.

26. *ibid.*, p. 145.

27. Augustine, *De doctrina christiana*, IV, 14, 31 (*c.* 426): G. COMBES and J. FARGES, *Le magistère chrétien* (Paris 1949), p. 474. Jerome cites Cyprian, *Ep.* I (*Ad donatum*).

28. On the style of this translation, see MOHRMANN, "The New Latin Psalter, its Diction and Style," *Études sur le latin des chrétiens*, Vol. II (Rome 1961), pp. 109–32. The correspondence between Augustine and Jerome on the principles of translation reveals the differences in their outlook. For an instructive comparison between this correspondence and the debates of the Reformation period, see W. SCHWARZ, *Principles and Problems of Biblical Translation. Some Reformation Controversies and their Background* (Cambridge 1955), pp. 26–44. (I am grateful to Professor Daiches for this reference.)

29. See COMEAU, *passim*, esp. pp. 22 and 45; cf. FINAERT, pp. 97 f.

30. See MARROU, Ch. 6. Cf. MOHRMANN, "St. Augustine and the Eloquentia," "Augustin predicateur," and "Die altchristliche Sondersprache"; also AUERBACH, Ch. 1, and HAGENDAHL, *Augustine and the Latin Classics*, Pt 2, pp. 566–8.

31. See ref. 27.

32. Augustine, *Tractatus in Iohannem*, II, 14 (*c.* 408–16) (*Patrologia latina* 35 [1394–5], taken from COMEAU, p. 11).

33. See BARDY; also MOHRMANN, "Praedicare-Tractare-Sermo."

34. Maximus Taurinensis, *Sermo* 92, 5–12; cf. ref. 21.

35. *ibid.*, 71, 25–9.

36. For the material in this discussion of the *De sacramentis*, see LAZZATI, and MOHRMANN, "Le style oral du De Sacramentis . . ."; on Chromatius, see the introduction to LEMARIÉ; on Maximus of Turin, see MUTZENBECHER, "Bestimmung der echten Sermones. . . ." It should be noted that although the *De sacramentis* is probably a reliable guide to the style of Ambrose's catechetical sermons, there is no satisfactory way of checking the style of his other sermons, apart from the formal orations.

37. Ambrose, *De sacramentis*, III, 1, 3 (*c.* 390): ed. by O. Faller, *Corp. script. eccl. lat.*, LXXIII (Vienna 1955), p. 39.

38. Maximus, *Sermons* 30, 30–5 (A.D. 401).

39. MOHRMANN, "The Confessions as a Literary Work of Art," p. 376. LÖFSTEDT points out that the sermons remain very artificial, when compared with popular speech, and suggests that the whole argument

for a peculiar Christian language, separate from secular Latin, has been exaggerated.

40. Jerome, *Ep.* 52, 8 (A.D. 394): *Lettres*, ed. by J. Labourt, Vol. II (Paris 1951), p. 183.
41. Cf. Gaudentius of Brescia, *Praefatio ad benivolum* (*Patrologia latina* 20, 831b–832a). Thus the stenographer in the church, like the stenographer at the martyr's trial, is a key figure in the process.
42. Cf. MUTZENBECHER, "Bestimmung der echten Sermones . . .," p. 208, and ref. 34.
43. See LAZZATI, p. 33.

Bibliography

ERICH AUERBACH, "Sermo Humilis," *Literary Language and Its Public in Late Latin Antiquity and in the Middle Ages* (London 1965), pp. 27–66.

GUSTAVE BARDY, "Tractare-Tractatus," *Recherches de science religieuse* XXXIII (Paris 1946), pp. 211–35.

B. BOTTE, *Ambroise de Milan, Des Sacrements, Des Mystères*, 2nd edn, Sources Chrétiennes, XXIX (Paris 1961).

P. R. L. BROWN, *Augustine of Hippo: a Biography* (London 1967), esp. Ch. 22–4.

MAURICE COMEAU, *La rhétorique de saint Augustin d'après les Tractatus in Ioannem* (Paris 1930).

PIERRE COURCELLE, *Les Lettres grecques en occident de Macrobe à Cassiodore* (Paris 1948).

M. D. DIEDERICH, *Virgil in the Works of Saint Ambrose*, CUA Patristic Studies, 29 (Washington 1931).

ROY J. FERRARI, "Saint Augustine's Method of Composing and Delivering Sermons," *American Journal of Philology* XLIII (1922), pp. 97–123 and 193–219.

J. FINAERT, *Saint Augustin rhéteur*, Collection d'études latines, série scientifique, XVIII (Paris 1939).

HARALD HAGENDAHL, "Methods of Citation in Post-Classical Latin Prose," *Eranos*, XLVI (Uppsala 1947), pp. 114–28;
Latin Fathers and the Classics, a Study on the Apologists, Jerome, and other Christian Writers, Studia Graeca et Latina Gothoburgensia, VI (Gothenburg 1958);
Augustine and the Latin Classics, Studia Graeca et Latina Gothoburgensia XX (Gothenburg 1967).

GIUSEPPE LAZZATI, "L'autenticità del 'De sacramentis' e la valutazione letteraria delle opere di S. Ambrogio," *Aevum* XXIX (Milan 1955), pp. 17–48.

JEAN LECLERCQ, "Prédication et rhétorique au temps de saint Augustin," *Revue Bénédictine* LVII (Maredsous 1947), pp. 117–31;
"Sermons de l'école de saint Augustin," *ibid.* LIX (1949), pp. 100–13.

J. LEMARIÉ, "Homélies inédites de saint Chromace d'Aquilee," *Revue Bénédictine* LXXII (1962), pp. 210–77, esp. pp. 209–18.

EINAR LÖFSTEDT, *Late Latin*, Instituttet for Sammlignende Kulturforskning, Serie A: Forlesninger, XXV (Oslo 1959).

HENRI-IRÉNEÉ MARROU, *Saint Augustin et la fin de la culture antique*, 4th edn (Paris 1958), esp. pp. 505–54.

CHRISTINE MOHRMANN, "Die altchristliche Sondersprache in den Sermones des hl. Augustin," *Latinitas Christianorum Primaeva* III (Nijmegen 1932), esp. pp. 16 ff;
"Le latin commun et le latin des chrétiens," *Vigiliae Christianae* I (Amsterdam 1947), pp. 1–12;
"Les origines de la latinité chrétienne à Rome," *ibid*. III (1949), pp. 67–106 and 163–83;
"Le style oral du 'De Sacramentis' de saint Ambroise," *ibid*. VI (1952), pp. 168–77;
Liturgical Latin: its Origins and Character (Washington 1957);
"Saint Augustine and the Eloquentia," *Études sur le latin des chrétiens*, I (Rome 1958), pp. 351–70;
"The Confessions as a Literary Work of Art," *ibid*., pp. 371–81;
"Comment saint Augustin s'est familiarisé avec le latin des chrétiens," *ibid*., pp. 383–9;
"Augustin prédicateur," *ibid*., pp. 391–402;
"Praedicare-Tractare-Sermo," *ibid*., II (1961), pp. 63–72.

ALMUT MUTZENBECHER, "Bestimmung der echten Sermones des Maximus Taurinensis," *Sacris Erudiri* XII (Steenbrugge 1961), pp. 197–293, esp. pp. 202–13.

A. OLTRAMARE, *Les origines de la diatribe romaine* (Lausanne 1926).

VEIKO VÄÄNÄNEN, *Introduction au latin vulgaire*, Bibliothèque française et romane, série A: manuels et études linguistiques, 6, 2nd edn (Paris 1967).

ANDRÉ WILMART, "Un sermon africain sur les noces de Cana, passé sous le nom de saint Augustin," *Revue Bénédictine* XLII (Maredsous 1930), pp. 5–18;
"Le prologue du sermon africain sur les noces de Cana," *ibid*. XLIII (1931), pp. 24 ff. and 160–4.

CHAPTER 21

The Two Traditions: the Hebraic and the Hellenic

Chaim Raphael*

> What we call culture may be defined as the locus of the meeting of literature with social actions and attitudes.
> LIONEL TRILLING, *A Gathering of Fugitives*.

> All the characters are on trial in any civilized narrative.
> WILLIAM EMPSON, *Milton's God*.

The most obvious quality common to all literature is that it is never just entertainment. Even when the author seems to be pitching what he is saying or writing at this level, a search or a battle—with moral overtones—is going on. The world around is being probed for what it may yield in terms of our deepest interests: our instinctive likes and dislikes, our fears, our hopes. Everything becomes relevant in this probe: the ideas or beliefs that have grown in us since childhood, the delights or tensions of private life, the drama of the public scene, and the ultimate paradox—that our capacity for casual pleasure is coexistent with a universal need to respond to the challenge of effort and danger. The author, however personal and original his treatment, has to speak to us in our own terms. The raw material that his imagination is shaping or re-shaping is the common tradition, without which he can have no contact with his audience.

At the superficial level, most people are content to feel that they have been born into, and remain part of, one fairly clearly defined tradition: their national culture; and this idea remains valid even when the national culture is supplemented by other powerful currents of feeling, such as might derive from being an ardent Catholic or Cornishman. If we dig deeper, it soon begins to emerge that our apparently "native" traditions have been

* Research Fellow in Jewish Social History, University of Sussex.

moulded over the centuries out of a constant flux of the human spirit, endless movements of people and their ideas, borrowing, and transmutation. However much we think for ourselves, we are drawing on concepts that have fought their way over centuries into our minds, proving their validity by their living quality, which becomes manifest as we apply them yet again to the problems and pleasures of daily existence.

For all of us in Western society, two ultimate sources are recognized as paramount, labelled for short as the Hebraic and the Hellenic. The most obvious aspect of this is the freedom with which we use phrases that immediately betray their origin, as when we talk of "a patriarchal figure" or "an Olympian look," "the patience of Job" or "the Oedipus complex." The influence is not, of course, merely a verbal one. It is true that we are always quoting, particularly in our use of Old Testament English. The King James (or Authorized) Version has enriched the language since 1611 with innumerable phrases that are now part of everyday speech: "the apple of my eye," "the skin of my teeth," "a lamb to the slaughter," "out of the mouths of babes and sucklings," and so on. But this, although obviously relevant, is more a result than a cause of the power over us of the Hebraic tradition. We draw on Shakespeare equally for the rightness of his words—"screw your courage to the sticking-place," "the crack of doom," "a man of my kidney," "jealousy . . . the green-eyed monster"— but with him, too, the words coming so readily to our lips are a kind of shorthand to the power over us of his imagination as a whole, with different emphasis, no doubt, in each generation.

Shakespeare, like all Western writers, reflects in turn the two primary traditions. In his plots, settings, characters, and rhetoric, the classical world, transmuted usually into its Roman form—"an eye like Mars to threaten and command," "sweeter than the lids of Juno's eyes"—is for him the natural language of poetry. The Hebrew influence, less pronounced in his verbal imagery, is identifiable at what one may fairly call the inner level: the psychological depth of his characters, their ambivalent motivations, the conflicts of love and jealousy, ambition and despair, the ultimate loneliness of man before his Creator. But although his influence can be traced back to the peculiar quality of Old Testament literature, it has found expression for 2000 years in the minds of people exposed equally to the Greek approach. The two traditions have coalesced as if they were parallel aspects of man's search for a philosophy that can stand trial in meeting our needs both as individuals and as members of society.

In one sense, the Greek and Hebrew views are alternatives; in another, they are two sides of the same search. Looking for a basic contrast, Joseph Needham says, in *The Grand Titration* (p. 290):

> For the Indo-Hellenic, space predominates over time. . . . The temporal world is less real than the world of timeless forms, and indeed has no ultimate value. . . . The most appropriate religion is therefore either polytheism . . . or pantheism. . . . For the Judaeo-Christian, on the other hand, time predominates over space. . . . The world era is fixed upon a central point which gives meaning to the process . . . hence the most appropriate religion is monotheism, with God as the comptroller of time and all that happens in it. It may seem other-worldly . . . but its faith is tied to the future as well as to the past. . . . It is thus essentially optimistic.

This key will certainly unlock some, though not all, of the doors to the two literatures. In its recognition of the Hebrew concern for progress, it is a useful corrective to the sterility implied in a form of the contrast put forward by Tarn and Griffith in their learned *Hellenistic Civilization*. Discussing there the two approaches to political freedom, they say (p. 226):

> To the Greek, freedom was an end, expressed in the free self-governing community, making its own laws, and worshipping what gods it pleased: while to the Jew it was a means, preventing interference with his devotion to a Law divinely given and unalterable by man.

The fact is that Hebrew "Law," though "unalterable," was an essentially dynamic force, a means for man's struggle within himself for the good life, and part of the process through which humanity moved toward the building of a perfect society. The Law called not only for its practice but also for its study. It was god-given, but man had to find ways of explaining it in terms of daily existence: it was a force through which men felt they were expressing their living interests as creatures of reason and conscience. In Holy Writ the most archaic myths had been given a moral interpretation: the teachers pursued this tirelessly, seeing God's Law as a starting point for endless re-interpretation.

In their earliest oral form, the two literatures had emerged from a common background, drawing on ideas, adventures, myths, and language that offer endless parallels. As the historical traditions of each people became formalized and their thought-styles took individual shape, their literatures were bent to different purposes: each yielded ideas of great symbolic power, linked expressly, it seemed, to its own "sacred" tradition. Yet these separate ideas were to flow into each other in later centuries as Western society fell more and more under the influence of the Near East.

Western man made his own amalgam of the traditions. Cain—originally the primeval "disturber" of society, branded for his own protection because of his magic skills or his violence—emerged to Western man as a Greek figure of Doom. His cry, "Am I my brother's keeper?" became the Hebrew call for social justice. In imagery, too, the two traditions were two sides of the same coin. To Keats, an instinctive Hellenist, his nightingale— "light-winged Dryad of the trees"—sings a song that Ruth might have heard as "she stood in tears amid the alien corn." Rembrandt, exploring the great dramas of the Old Testament, produces Bathsheba as a luscious Renaissance nude: his Aristotle, contemplating the bust of Homer, has stepped out of a synagogue in Amsterdam.

Although the ideas of both cultures had the innate character to become universal in their appeal, it is still a mystery how they broke through their kindred environments with such individual generative power. It hardly does more than move the mystery one stage along to argue as Toynbee does (e.g. in *The Crucible of Christianity*, p. 39) that the parallel creativity of Jews and Greeks arose from their similarity in living in poor rocky countries: "in both regions the parsimony of nature has been a permanent stimulus to human ingenuity." This must surely have applied to many others whose message did not survive. Nor (for the same reason) is it easy to agree with Toynbee that the passion of Hebrew faith is due to the fact that it was forged during the first great historic "bout of agony" in the Near Eastern world (from the 8th to the 6th centuries B.C.), whereas the Greeks, being spared this particular agony, were led instead into their famous "serenity." The mystery is easier to describe than to explain.

The special quality of the Hebrews' tradition lay in their belief—unique among all the surrounding cultures—that their own continually unfolding history enshrined a meaning that was crucially relevant to man's existence on earth. The literature of the Old Testament covers a vast variety of forms—narrative, epics, poems, laws, argument—but all are unified through this central idea. The Hebrews claimed to be able to follow their historic story, with its crucially important religious significance, from the beginning of time. They felt themselves re-affirming the ancient truths when they saw life flowing from a Creator who was the personification of Truth, Justice, and "Loving kindness," and who demanded the practice of these qualities from mankind. The Isaiah who cried: "Here am I: send *me*!" had, underlying his sense of dedication, a vivid, and to that extent authentic, folk-memory of Abraham, more than 1000 years before him.

In contrast, the Greek-speaking peoples, who migrated southward into the peninsula at the beginning of the 2nd millennium and became absorbed in to the splendours of the Mycenaean civilization (1400–1200 B.C.), carried no history with them in such conscious fashion. We know now that the sophisticated civilizations of the Near East had spread into the Aegean to lay a basis in the arts and sciences on which the Greeks were to draw so brilliantly; but there was no personally remembered link. For the Hebrews, the patriarchal age, and the period that followed the Exodus and culminated in the Monarchy, left a literary tradition of enormous power, reflecting not only their own adventures but the documented worlds of Mesopotamia, Syria, and Egypt, of which Israel was the bridge-land. For the Greeks, the absence of writings for this period leaves their world in shadow. There is no visible preparation, therefore, for the way Greek culture suddenly flared with the burst of imaginative splendour that was Homer, and then, some 300 years later, in the 5th and 4th centuries B.C., launched into an absolutely original exploration of man's potential as "the measure of all things," opening up every question to the power of man's reason in an effort to formulate a unifying view of natural law, and turning to philosophy, medicine, mathematics, poetry, the drama, sculpture, and architecture with an energy and self-confidence that was wholly unprecedented.

The contrast in their feeling about history remains, as Needham suggests, a valid dividing line between the two traditions. Although the Greeks, when they turned to the writing of history, made a leap forward as in so many other fields, their aim was "scientific"—to understand man in the variety of his social and political experience. To the Hebrews, the aim was to portray man as part of a developing story. Christianity took this over completely, with an expanded theology that stretched unbroken from Creation and original sin, through the Prophets and Christ, and on to the Last Judgment. Western society drew from both sources, finding in the literature of each tradition voices that spoke for different sides of our nature.

Inevitably, therefore, the stories move us in different ways. The Old Testament, despite the variety of its 39 books, is a closely integrated saga: each of its vast gallery of characters, from Adam and Eve to Malachi, lives for his own time, yet has visible links with all the others. Once involved, we are drawn on as if by a novel. The style changes, with straight narrative giving way to archaic epic, genealogy to drama, legal or moral rules to the most personal lyric poetry. Yet we read it as a unified revelation of life, earthy and human. With the Greeks, despite the savageries that crop up, the stories themselves lie around us with a kind of magic, a world that is symbolic rather than earthy. Human activity is described with infinite care and detail, corresponding to the smooth accuracy of Greek sculpture and the perfect proportions of Greek architecture. The gods, so close to man, are part of this world of "sweetness and light." The Hebrews are never at ease in this way. Even when a story or a character is sketched in a few sentences, we are caught up with a personal involvement. When God is thundering from Sinai, we share the perplexity—or terror—of those who hear it.

The Homeric heroes, it has been said, are fully open to view in all their actions and motivations. As Bowra puts it in *The Greek Experience* (p. 138), the Greeks were "not deeply interested in the hidden conflicts and contradictions of human character, and shrank from analysing themselves on any exacting scale." Delight in physical existence is everything to them. In contrast, the biblical characters are presented as men and women of mixed emotions: we see their thoughts and feelings at different levels: perhaps, more correctly, we intuit their internal conflicts with Fate and their fellow-men from the bald style of much of the narrative. Erich Auerbach has developed this idea in his book *Mimesis* (pp. 11–3), finding the biblical style "fraught with background," in which "conversation is only an interruption of the heavy silence." Whereas Odysseus is the same man at the end of his 20-year journey, a biblical character such as Moses or David goes through a whole experience of development that we, as readers, enter into completely. One could argue that this difference should not be exaggerated. The subtleties of biblical characters often arise only from the expressive brevity with which they and their speeches are recorded—so unlike the Greeks. Yet in some sense we can agree that it is the Hebraic tradition that has introduced into Western literature the theme of contradiction and multiplicity, with man picking his way between obedience and rebellion, desperation and hope. Certainly this is a more authentic view of the force of the Hebrew tradition than that presented by Matthew Arnold in *Culture and Anarchy*, where the label "Hebraism" is attached to a rather sour version of English Nonconformism. Not only is this "Hebraism" blind to beauty and therefore "Philistine" (another odd label), but its emphasis on personal conscience is disruptive of an established order in society! The fact is that although the prophets have stimulated rebels, the Bible has also been interpreted as a prop for the Establishment. Hellenism, in turn, in spite of its famed serenity, was the major influence on the romantic rebels of the 19th century. The contrasts lose validity if they are thought of as watertight.

Another apparent contrast lies in the settings of the Greek and Hebrew stories. In Greek literature, the interest centres on the affairs and thoughts of the ruling class. Society, with all its attendant soldiers, priests, and slaves, moves around this axis. In the Hebraic tradition, there is a sense throughout of the active involvement of the people; the social picture is mobile, and individuals come forward to be kings, preachers, leaders, rebels. The classical writers mainly address their social peers: the Hebrew (and later the Christian) writers tell their tale to Everyman. Yet these are not the ways in which the contributions of the two traditions emerged in Western society. From the peculiar circumstances of the small, self-contained city-state, the Greeks contributed to society the ideal (or working tool) of individual participation in government by every citizen. From the Hebraic tradition, the contribution was, paradoxically, the notion of the state's authority. The idea of "a holy nation" meant, to quote J. L. Talmon, "the total absorption of a whole people in the service of an impersonal ideal." Through its acceptance of the Mosaic code, the whole nation was involved in government and the rule of law. There is clearly a coming together here in the effects of the two traditions on Western life.

The two traditions were to irradiate each other later in many ways, and the reason, as mentioned earlier, is that both were drawing, albeit differently, on a background in which man had already marked out the significant steps for his future. Modern studies have enabled us to push farther and farther back into the early history of the Near East, and we can see now, with astonishment, that the empires that rose and fell as long ago as 3000 B.C. had created a variety of cultures of great sophistication. Although the ancient Hebrews are brought into the picture more directly because of the echoes of these empires in the Bible, the movement that can now be traced of Indo-European and Semitic peoples across the Mediterranean and Asia Minor in successive waves of conquest and absorption—accompanied by the exchanges of trade, language, and ideas implies the involvement, too, of the ancient Greek peoples. For example, the rich literature of ancient Ugarit, on the Syrian coast (unearthed from 1929 onward), not only parallels biblical myth and language, but establishes literary links between Homer and Mesopotamia, as Cyrus Gordon shows in *Before the Bible*. For trade and art it is enough to note that a wealth of 14th- and 13th-century Mycenaean pottery, and still older Minoan products, have been found all over Palestine and Syria. The stele of the Pharoah Meniptah, dated 1200 B.C., recording the invasion of Egypt by "the peoples of the sea," includes names indicating Lycians, Etruscans, Sardinians, and Achaeans.

What is even more significant is that we now see from many discoveries and decipherings how ancient in this area is man's involvement with a conscious, civilized attempt to understand his place in nature and society. Behind Homer and the Bible—which were once the twin ultimates, coming to us without any sure guidance as to where legend (centred on the 2nd millennium B.C.) ended and moved into history—we now have copious reflections of more ancient times: poems and stories that spring from and illuminate the human situation; and law books, diplomatic records, and historical writings that reflect the organization of society. Behind it all stands the immense achievement of this ancient world in every art-form. The writings do not speak, as the art does, with a "modern" voice, but they form a luminous background to the way in which the Hebrews and the Greeks, in their separate ways, broke out of their primitivism in the 1st millennium B.C. to deal so forthrightly with what seem to us the eternal human questions: the nobility and temptations of individuals, the aspirations and deceptions of society, the struggle for the expression of equity, law, and reason, the desperations of battle, anger, and love.

The links with earlier writings are particularly striking in the case of the Hebrew tradition, for here the crucial transformation happens, as it were, under our eyes. On almost every page the Old Testament offers details that find parallels or illustrations in the writings of other people in the area, echoing, often very closely, the widespread legends of Creation and Flood, law codes, myths, festivals and religious practices related to the sun and moon, storm, rain and fertility, the travels and settlements of peoples, their battles and treaties, their trade and social customs. Not only is the Hebrew of the Bible linked with the languages of the neighbouring countries, but the content, imagery, and rhythms of prose and poetry are constantly similar. Scholars are tireless in showing how this or that obscurity in the Bible text can now be explained in terms of some new discovery from a cognate culture.

By these standards the Hebrews are to be understood as a group of tribes living perilously, and without any special distinction, among the settled—and often mighty—cultures around them, adapting themselves to their ways, and rising to a brief period of limited territorial power under David, Solomon, and some of their successors. The only thing that this does not explain is how it was that this obscure people created *and preserved* a whole literature, a philosophy of life, a religious faith, a powerful ethic, and a will to live that transcended all their borrowings and obscurity. The key lies, as was suggested earlier, in the force they gave to their view

494

of history. Around 1800–1700 B.C. a tribal chieftain, remembered as Abraham, had moved from northern Mesopotamia into the land of Canaan and had fostered a distinctive cult of one protective God, peculiar to his people, incorporeal but all-powerful, the *fons et origo* of an ethical view of life. There was a covenant that Abraham's descendants would eventually achieve untroubled independence in this new land. Every folk memory and new experience was re-interpreted against the rock-like certainty of this covenant, as binding as the secular covenants of that age. The history of the tribe, as successive generations fought, travelled, and settled in many places, became *ipso facto* the story of their God's purpose for the Hebrews and for mankind.

It was a story first transmitted orally in epic verse (easy to memorize) and later in written records, all lost now but showing their mark clearly in the consecutive narrative that first began to be edited (in overlapping form) from the 10th century B.C. onward. In daily life the Hebrews had been for centuries part of the constantly changing Canaanite background —traders, raiders, mercenaries, settlers, and for a while some, at least, slaves in Egypt. The Exodus, and the ultimate settlement in the hill-lands of Palestine, gathered together and intensified the historic memories. Although their God was "King"—calling to mind the triumph of all God-Kings in the area in the annual (or cyclical) battle for fertility— he was never in peril, as these God-Kings were. He was the historic God of Abraham and Moses, whose real purpose was seen in man's unquenchable thirst for justice and love. The more parallels modern discovery produces to the biblical account of the customs, laws, myths, and poetry of the ancient Hebrews, the more remarkable is it that this background of myth and fertility rites could be infused by them at all stages with the single-minded ethical beliefs underlying their unitary view of the universe. "Nature," it has been said, "was de-mythed."*

---

* An illustration may help. The discoveries at Ras Shamra document the fertility rites of Ugarit, celebrating the annual triumph of Baal over the gods Sea and Stream—"the unruly waters"— his death, revival, and final victory over the god Mot (death or sterility), all reminiscent, of course, of the myths of Marduk, Attis, Osiris, and Adonis. The language of Psalm LXXIV, "Thou brakest the heads of the dragons in the waters. . . . Thou driedst up mighty rivers," is a remarkable echo (there are many others) of the actual language of the Baal epic. But in no sense was this to the Hebrew an annual dramatization of some struggle between coeval powers, with the issue in doubt. There was no pantheon of gods; only one, who is, in the same Psalm, the "king of old, working salvation in the midst of the earth." And of supreme importance, the Psalmist, only a few verses later, spells out with absolute clarity the moral purpose of this salvation: "O let not the oppressed return ashamed: let the poor and needy praise thy name." Another instance would be the detailed legal code of Exodus XXI–XXIII, which has many parallels with the Sumerian and Babylonian codes. But in the Bible, the principles of equity are infused with religion: "Keep thee far from a false matter; and the innocent and righteous slay thou not: for I will not justify the wicked." And there is always the unique appeal to the religious

Although, among the Hebrews themselves, the force of their tradition can be seen to have been powerful, there is still a paradox to be examined: that although the expositors of Hebraism were a small, weak people in contrast to the all-powerful Greeks, their tradition had a peculiar carrying power that transcended the weakness of its material base. The appeal of Hellenism, in its original and Romanized versions, perhaps needs little explanation. Carried everywhere through a mighty colonization, it celebrated man's existence with style, ease, and never-failing charm. Hebraism in itself could offer little of this. To follow the way in which it was ultimately fed into the common tradition, we need to unearth two different, though never entirely separate, processes: on the one hand, the development of Hebraism by the Jews themselves; on the other, the carrying of a form of Hebraism to the world through Christianity. Neither is a simple process. For odd historical reasons, Hebraism among Jews made its most significant impact on the Diaspora at large through an intense development in Babylonia. Christian Hebraism was swamped for centuries by Christian Hellenism. And the Jewish tradition itself bore the marks of successive confrontations with Greek thought.

The interactions were constantly changing. To the ancient Greeks, the Jews, when first met "officially" during Alexander's triumphal assumption of power in the Middle East (332 B.C.), were a small, unimportant tribe, gobbled up without even a battle and left free to worship their own gods in the tolerantly superior attitude that the Greeks had toward all "barbarians." At that point, the Jews equally had no quarrel with the Greeks, or at least not with their leader. They thought of him as the deliverer from their Persian overlords, as the incarnation in some providential way of their ideas of kinghood. Later Jewish legend envisaged an actual encounter with the hero, endowing him with a full understanding of the supreme power of Yahweh, whose humble servant he was. But this pleasant harmony was not to last.

Jews and Greeks had, of course, met before this dramatic confrontation. Greek influence had spread over the eastern Mediterranean, and farther, following the Persian wars in the first half of the 5th century B.C. Travellers, traders, and mercenaries had carried Greece with them wherever they settled; and although Judaea was, perhaps significantly, the only area without any Greek cities until the time of Herod, their influence must undoubtedly have been felt there. Earlier trading and travels had cast their shadow in biblical "memories." "Javan" (Ionia)

power of their own history. "Thou shalt not oppress a stranger: for ye know the heart of a stranger, seeing ye were strangers in the land of Egypt" (Exodus XXIII, 9).

appears in Genesis x as one of the seven sons of Japheth (son of Noah) and as the progenitor himself of four "sons," including "Kittim" (the Hittites). In all, 14 "grandsons" of Japheth are listed. "By these were the isles of the Gentiles divided in their lands; every one after his tongue, after their families, in their nations." In these extremely early memories of the Bible, "Javan" was probably vague in its connotation, and was perhaps still so to the author of Isaiah (LXVI), where the Hebrews who "escape" from the sinning community are threatened with being sent "unto the nations, to Tarshish, Pul, and Lud, that draw the bow, to Tubal, and Javan, to the isles afar off, that have not heard my fame, neither have seen my glory." In later biblical passages, however, as in Joel (III, 16), "Javan," to which the Jews are sold as slaves by Phoenicians and Philistines, sounds like an explicit place, presumably the mainland of Greece.

There are no correspondingly old references to the Jews in early Greek literature. The earliest historical writings—first of the fragmentary logographers toward the end of the 6th century B.C. and then, at a great bound, of Herodotus—concentrated on the mighty peoples: Assyrians, Persians, Egyptians. There was an interest, of course, in "oriental" religions, the chief gods of which were felt to parallel in function those of the Greeks themselves. The single-mindedness of the Hebrews about *their* god, unique and intolerant, must have seemed strange. Nevertheless the first surviving mention by Greek writers of Jewish religious practices, in the 3rd century B.C., after the direct encounter had been made, saw them not unfavourably as a race of "philosophers": "during the sacrifice they discuss the divine nature with each other." But as contacts deepened, the early acceptance became strained. The Greeks felt the Jews to be intolerant and inbred in their observances, utterly lacking the graceful scepticism that was a characteristic of true philosophers. The Jewish religious leaders, in turn, had become very aware of the gap between the Hellenistic culture and their own intense faith.

Oddly enough, the one open physical battle between "Greek" (in Syrian guise) and Jew—the War of the Maccabees, 166–4 B.C.—can be seen in retrospect to have been almost irrelevant in the long term to the battle of ideas. It had been the aim of Alexander the Great to harmonize, under a benign Greek patronage, the national differences (and theologies) of the world he had conquered, and to a great extent this had been achieved. The Jews were acknowledged to be somewhat of a sore thumb, sticking to their "superstitions" and showing reluctance to participate in the sports and other amenities of public life: but an accommodation had been made by allowing the Temple and the "teachers" of Palestine to continue as rallying points for Jewish identity. It was only when the Seleucid ruler Antiochus IV was encouraged (by bribes) to install a renegade High Priest and was led on by his own version of Hellenism to forbid many Jewish practices (including circumcision) and to try to install in the Temple the cult of Olympian Zeus (and of himself) that all sections of the Jewish community, except the most ardent Hellenizers, were stimulated to resist. In a series of brilliant campaigns, aided by the distractions of Antiochus in fighting also on other fronts (all vividly described in the Greek-style Books of the Maccabees), the Hebrews won, with the result that a Jewish dynasty, the Hasmoneans, appeared on the scene, and survived in one form or another until the final destruction of Jerusalem by the Romans in A.D. 70 But although the ardently religious Jews (the Hasidim) had lent full support to the Maccabees when the struggle first broke out, the Hasmonean dynasty that ensued soon lost its religious character. The genuine religious leaders, known to history as the Pharisees, felt no sympathy for the Greek-style politics of the dynasty, and turned back to their own studies and devotions in pursuit of the traditional faith.

These "guardians of the Law" were inevitably drawing on the Hellenistic background in thought and language; but "Javan" remained the symbol among them for what was utterly alien and hostile to the Hebrew tradition. At this point no one could have guessed that so much in later history was to be distilled from a mingling of these two disparate forces; yet even at that time there were clues to the coexistence or mutual accommodation that was to develop.

At the intellectual level, although apparently obsessed in a most un-Greek way with a narrow, inward-looking worship and blind adherence to a single sacred book, the Hebrews had already given evidence—and were soon to give more—of that inquiring and argumentative temper, linked to a reasoning and eclectic spirit, that was to distinguish them in later centuries. Their speculative powers were still concentrated on exposition of their holy Law; but in this there was already fierce argument reflecting ideas from Greece that were spreading all over the Near East. It is significant that in this intellectual groping there was no automatic division, based on social factors, between Hellenizers and their opponents. On the all-important issue of the possibility of an after-life and the implications of this idea for conduct on earth, the Book of Jubilees (from the 3rd or 2nd century B.C.) expressed views close to the orthodox Stoic position, reinforced by the Book of Ben Sira (beginning of the 2nd century B.C.), which argues explicitly against counting on resurrection. The Sadducees, when we see them emerging in the 1st century B.C., took this view: and, as the "ruling class," more likely to be Hellenizers, they might have been expected to be sympathetic to Greek ideas. In fact, however, they were narrow and inflexible, concerned only with a literalist view of the Bible. Their view of free will, for example, was Hebraic but rigid: the prophets had said that man had the choice between good and evil, and that was that.

In contrast, the Pharisees, their opponents, although socially distant from the Hellenistic rulers, were closer to them in the sense of being willing to give much freer rein to speculation. They could approve (as is reflected in the later-edited *Ethics of the Fathers*) the Stoic dictum of one of their early teachers, the 3rd-century Antigonus of Socho, that the just life had to be pursued for its own sake, regardless of reward in any life hereafter; but this did not rule out ideas on the after-life. If we are to read back into Pharisaic thought the varied ideas that emerged later in rabbinic teaching (as also in the teaching of Jesus), the immortality of the soul, although not biblical, was a potent element in their feelings. Their belief that the Holy Writ of the Bible demanded free-wheeling explication, drawing on linguistic parallels, legend, and allegory, allowed them to entertain much subtler views than those of the conservative Sadducees. On free will, they could argue that man was responsible for his actions and yet, paradoxically, subject to God's Providence—a view that had elements of the Stoic idea of predestination but was more imaginative in its influence. They could elaborate eschatological ideas on salvation in terms of a personal Messiah without letting this affect the attention they gave to the realities of day-to-day life. They could build a protective "fence" around the Law, calling for the most elaborate rules of practice, while interpreting these rules in terms of joyous spiritual experiences and an unshakable view of an ultimate ethical purpose. These are attitudes that emerged later but must have been a powerful element in the intense preoccupation with biblical study that had been building up ever since the return from the Babylonian exile.

The social "invention" that made this philosophizing attitude possible was the synagogue: a house of study and teaching as much as a house of prayer. From the time of Ezra, and probably even in the Exile, it had become the function of a special class to instruct the people (Nehemiah, VIII, 8) in their ancient scriptures. Readings were accompanied by homilies based on a widespread tradition of law, custom, and folk legend. The evidence for this powerful unwritten tradition has been detected by scholars in the contemporary Bible translations (Aramaic and Greek), in Josephus, in the Dead Sea Scrolls, and in other sources, all in line with the ultimate editing of the traditions centuries later in the rabbinic writings. The synagogue, apart from its more obvious purpose, was both a forcing-house for rational argument and a "parliament" for the discussion of what one must call, in modern terms, social welfare. Although it was not an academy in the Greek sense, and certainly not a theatre, it was the nearest the traditional Hebrews got to both, a place for personal challenge and excitement, as well as for folk-memory, wit, and entertainment. And although they would not have realized how much they owed to the Greek temper, their argument, as we see from the recording of it later, was often Socratic in kind, and their rules of deduction and inference as precise as in a Greek book of logic.

The passion for study had deep origins. The tribute to the role of Wisdom in God's scheme, as set out in the remarkable chapters VII and VIII of the Book of Proverbs, is thought from its language to have been stimulated by 7th-century-B.C. Canaanite influences, harking back in concept to the Ugaritic goddess of Wisdom in 15th-century-B.C. Ugaritic writings, though of course interpreted symbolically by the Jews of the synagogue. The concept of the *logos* as a philosophic approach to the power of God—so powerful later in Christianity—had also entered Jewish thought, albeit faintly, from Semitic rather than Greek sources.[1] From another angle, the content of study was already intensely humanist, anticipating a dominant trend of Hebraism in later centuries. To judge from the oral tradition as recorded in the Mishnah (2nd century A.D.) and later in the Talmud, the range of interest in the Beth Hammidrash (house of study) covered every field of human inquiry—law, medicine, astronomy, biology, history, and much more. Although there was no systematic ordering of these studies in the Greek style, the social importance of a fully accepted legal system, and the need of man to understand his material circumstances as well as his fate, were unifying elements in their thought.

The synagogue, with its accompanying study centre, was, above all, infinitely mobile. Every community of Jews, however small, had one: the social centre, and the locus of faith, pride, prayer, and argument. Because of this, the subsequent dispersions, which became the most important *political* factor in Jewish life and might have scattered the Jews into sterile oblivion—the "fossilized relic" conjured up so quaintly by Toynbee— had the opposite effect of carrying a positive and vibrant philosophy of life into the world.

When Alexander appeared in all his splendour in the Near East, the

Jews, then, were already much more than a small people living under subjection in their ancient land. They were widespread through many adjacent Mediterranean and Near Eastern countries and were later to spread and grow much more, so that by the beginning of the Christian era they were serving (as slaves), working (as farmers and artisans), trading, fighting, and (as we have seen) *worshipping* in every part of this world. In some places, notably Egypt and Mesopotamia, the settlement was in very large numbers; but even where the groups were small, they formed distinctive communities. That the Greeks had long since spread through or colonized this whole area is, of course, a commonplace. They left their mark everywhere in striking physical form, and laid the basis for the Roman take-over. The Jews left few physical marks; but their disposition in so many countries, and the way in which their separate view of life maintained itself, became highly important for the future.

As always in their history, the Jews clung to their beliefs against forces that might have been thought strong enough to swamp them. Scattered everywhere in the Greek world, they were all subject to its influence, whether conscious participants in Hellenistic culture or more parochial in their views. In the sophisticated atmosphere of Alexandria, the long-established Jewish community could produce a man such as Philo Judaeus (*c.* 20 B.C.–A.D. 50), in whose writings we see how a Jew versed in Greek philosophy could apply its techniques to a systematic presentation of Jewish ethical monotheism, taking the Bible (he knew only the Greek translation) as the word of God, but interpreting it allegorically in ways that would not have conflicted essentially with the less sophisticated allegorists among the rabbis. Philo's harmonization of Jewish faith with Greek thought of the 1st century B.C.—when it had already moved away decisively from its earlier rationalism and scepticism—was to be of great importance to the formulation of Christian thought among the Church Fathers, and was to survive as a major influence (allied with that of Plotinus) for many centuries.

The rabbinic tradition never knew Philo's writings; but even where the main object of the Jews was to concentrate on their own Torah they were living among Greeks, speaking Greek, and interpreting the Law in terms of the social and legal conditions of their neighbours. The result becomes particularly evident in the rabbinic writings of the early Christian centuries, as Saul Lieberman has shown in his *Greek in Jewish Palestine*. By that time there was even an "Academy of Greek Wisdom" under the auspices of the Patriarch, the aim being to facilitate a good understanding between the Jews and the government. Interpreters in the synagogue would translate from Aramaic to Greek for some, just as they would translate from Greek to Aramaic for others. Homer was read by some of the Jews, though with reservations: as Lieberman puts it, "The Jews enjoyed the charm of his style and plots, but certainly saw his mythology as mere fairy tales and as a good occasion for making fun of idol worship." A knowledge of Greek mythology must certainly have been in the air. Erwin Goodenough has indeed argued, in his monumental *Jewish Symbolism in the Greek and Roman Period,* that the decorations on early tombs and the elaborate figurative frescoes in the later Dura synagogue include many symbols of the Dionysus cult and of the widespread mystery religions, showing that these were live and meaningful for the Jews as early as pre-Christian days, which explains (in his view) how it was that Jewish Christianity could Hellenize so rapidly. Lieberman puts it more cautiously, but agrees that the cultural influence of Hellenism on the Jewish people was certainly greater than could be inferred from later rabbinic writings. Living and trading with the Greeks, the Jews "could not help admiring the beautiful and the useful: they could not fail to be attracted by the external brilliance and superficial beauty of Gentile life." The rabbis did their best to prevent the people from becoming thoroughly Hellenized, but could not be completely successful. In the cities, social life would lead to some forms of assimilation. In the country, peasants would adopt their neighbours' beliefs in magic, astrology, and other folklore.

But although the Jews absorbed much from the surrounding cultures, their vast dispersion also worked in the opposite sense, to encourage loyalty to their ancestral faith and to help them to forge new institutions to support it wherever they lived.

The dispersion of the Jews had begun in the 8th century B.C., when the Assyrian king Tiglath-Pileser had overrun Israel, the northern kingdom of Palestine (733 B.C.), carried off large numbers of its inhabitants, and installed in their place settlers from his other territories (II Kings xv). Much more significantly, the fall of the southern kingdom, Judah, to Nebuchadnezzar in the 6th century led to successive deportations (597 and 586 B.C.) to Babylonia, out of which developed an entire "Jewish-Babylonian" culture, immensely important for all later Jewish thought and for the carrying of Hebraism into the world. The image of the sadness of the Babylonian captivity has been largely determined by the lamentations and denunciations of the Hebrew prophets, and even more perhaps by one magnificent poem, Psalm CXXXVII ("By the rivers of Babylon"), surely one of the most affecting lyrics in all literature. From other sources,

502

however, we know that the Jews who settled in Babylonia took root and flourished. Under royal protection as exiles, they enjoyed special prerogatives. They practised their ancestral religion, administered their own internal affairs, engaged in normal occupations (agriculture and trade), and suffered few of the enslavements and persecutions that were their lot elsewhere. Although this material ease led to a certain cultural and social merging with the other inhabitants (which accounts for so much prophetic denunciation), the distinctiveness of a sufficiently strong remnant kept the Jewish faith alive with emphasis on what could function outside the Holy Land: the strict observance of Sabbath and festivals, circumcision, prayer (clearly separated for the first time from Temple sacrifice), and a keen interest in their holy writings, to which a new breed of scribes gave much attention. The freedom to return to Palestine (538 B.C.), even when reinforced a century later by Ezra and Nehemiah, was used by only a small minority.

The great majority of the exiles not only remained in Babylonia but established it as a centre of Jewish life and thought in some respects equal, or even superior, to that of the Holy Land itself.[2] In later centuries, under the successive rule of the Greeks, Parthians, Persians, and Arabs, the Jews of Babylonia had considerable freedom to develop their own institutions; they kept their adopted language (Aramaic) and took a lively part in political and military affairs. Like their brothers in Palestine, with whom they kept in close contact, they had welcomed Alexander's arrival on the Near Eastern scene and had even fought in his armies.[3] The dynasty under Seleucus Nicator that soon emerged in Babylonia was accepted by the Jews as a new era for reckoning time (*minyan shtarot—aera contractuum*). A similar *modus vivendi* prevailed under Parthian rule. The Jews were valued for their special skills as farmers, artisans, and financiers, and also as soldiers useful against unruly provincials or in major wars— as when the Parthians revolted successfully against Trajan (A.D. 115).[4] Their numbers were constantly swollen by the arrival of settlers from other parts of the Near Eastern world, particularly refugees from the wars with the Romans in Palestine. Their status was increased for many centuries to come by the granting of real authority to their own quasi-monarchical leader, the *Resh Galut* (Head of the Exile), whose family claimed descent from the house of David.

But it was the role they played in the development of scholarship, science, and philosophy that was most important for later history. Under Persian rule (from A.D. 226) they were subject to greater strain in their ordinary life, although the Persians were more tolerant to them than to the Christians. By now, however, the Jews of Babylonia had assumed almost paramount spiritual authority in relation to the Jews of Palestine and elsewhere. They acknowledged the special holy character of Palestine, but asserted their independence in scholarship and practice through their own much more powerfully established Academies. A sign of this is that when they produced their own recension of the whole oral tradition in the monumental Babylonian Talmud—a huge compilation of law, legend, thought, and argument—it became the standard source for all subsequent generations.

The conquest of the country in the course of the triumphant Arab expansion of the 7th century A.D. gave the Jews there, for three centuries at least, a still stronger base from which to carry the message of Hebraism into the world. The economy was prosperous, allowing them better living conditions and an open door to the professions. Responsive as Jews were everywhere to such opportunities, they began to find their way increasingly, with Arab scholars and scientists, into secular learning. The authority of their *Geonim* (supreme scholars) was now even more respected; and although this phase of Jewish-Babylonian leadership came to an end around A.D. 1000, the achievements until then proved momentous to the Hebrew tradition, and through that to Western thought.

It may seem a long journey from Nebuchadnezzar's Jewish captives "by the rivers of Babylon" in the 6th century B.C. to (let us say) the school of Christian Platonists in 17th-century England, who hung their harps on very different willows; yet the connection is clear enough. A major connecting link, though by no means the only one, was the familiarity of so many Jews with Arabic. From the 7th century onward, the studies of the Jews of Babylonia had peculiar carrying-power to the Arabic-speaking Jews living in Egypt, Spain, and other parts of the vast Arab-dominated world. This world in turn was to become the matrix of a cultural explosion, the first Renaissance—the rediscovery of many philosophical and scientific Greek writings (preserved by Syriac Christians), and the nurturing of this new learning in the background of an already scholarly culture. As a result, over a period of centuries, the Jews of this Arab world became the interpreters of a sophisticated tradition in which they took account not only of the influences that, over the course of more than 1000 years, had flowed into the Hebrew sholarship of the Babylonian Jews, but also of the philosophy, science, and medicine of the "lost" Greek thought. Both Arabs and Jews made powerful contributions of their own, especially in Arab Spain; but it was the Jews who, by virtue of their *lingua franca* Hebrew and their contacts in different countries, carried the "lost" books and contemporary Arab and Jewish studies to the Christian world. Translation was often from Arabic into Hebrew first, and then, perhaps in another place, from Hebrew into Latin. From the 11th to the 13th centuries particularly, it became a major Jewish activity, with profound effect on mediaeval thought and literature.

The absorption with the recovered Greek tradition was, of course, only one aspect of the brilliant civilization of this Arab world, which made its own independent contributions to architecture, agriculture, history, literature, the study of language, and indeed to all the graces of life except the figurative arts, which were forbidden by the Moslem faith. The Jews, until persecution excluded them, took part to the fullest possible extent; and it is interesting that in Spain particularly they were responsive, in a way unique for them, to the play of poetry, which the Arabs had developed with great subtlety, lyricism, and wit. The Jews, by adapting the cognate language of Hebrew to Arabic rhythms and style, virtually created a new kind of Hebrew literature, and certainly a new feeling, which could embrace the grandeurs and poignancies of the past (with constant "interior" quotation of the Bible and rabbinic lore) in harmony with a personal lyricism touching on every aspect of the present. The Jewish poets who took off on these flights of imagination were to a large extent the same scholars, philosophers, and scientists who were deeply involved in their more "serious" pursuits. There was a breadth of spirit in this that might have led Matthew Arnold to revise his view of Hebraism.

In Spain, of course, it was mostly in the south that this special involvement with the culture of the Arab world took place. It is hardly less important for Western history that the Jews were able to continue and intensify many aspects of this intellectual creativity in the adjacent Christian society of the central and northern parts of the peninsula, from which it could spread to southern France and across the Mediterranean to Italy. The Arab connection was all-important for the partial recovery of Greek thought; but there was also a golden age of philosophy and scientific development among Christians, through the links of Jewish participation, with momentous results for mathematics, astronomy, navigation, and exploration.

The Greek influence, always in the background, was a search for truth that was relevant to every aspect of life. In the field of philosophy, it was pursued most intensely as a tool for the justification of faith. The Greek sources here were largely such works of Aristotle as had become available and the neo-Platonic writings (rather than Plato himself, in the early stages). In this limited field, far from there being any essential conflict

505

between Hebraism and Hellenism, it was the common task of all scholars to harmonize the cool reasoning methods of Aristotle with the biblical account of God, the angels, and man, good and evil, sin and grace, matter and spirit. The philosophers—Arab, Jewish, and Christian—were all engaged equally in elaborating metaphysical constructions of the Universe and its purpose, dealing with "elementals," "emanations," "attributes," and the like, fitting them into great theological systems consistent with faith. From our present standpoint, the minutiae of the scholastic systems seem fantastic and even absurd; but they were satisfactory in terms of their age, and an inevitable stage in Western man's groping toward the freedom of thought that began to make itself more explicit in the second Renaissance, from the 15th century onward.[5]

In what became, from then, the full rediscovery of Hellenism, Hebraism paradoxically both suffered and gained in influence. It suffered, inevitably, as the philosophers and theologians turned away from scholasticism. If reason was to be given full rein, leaving theology to be satisfied only by faith, Maimonides (the paramount Jewish philosopher of the Arab period in the late 12th century) had almost as much to lose as Aquinas. But in the pursuit of what their "innate reason" could tell them, Renaissance philosophers found a new impulse for turning to Hebrew scholarship. Believing in Holy Writ by faith, they felt that if they turned away from scholastic interpretations of the Bible to the original words, their own reasoning powers might open up new understanding. The study of Hebrew and the rabbinic commentators became an essential step. Jewish mysticism (in the Cabbala and the Zohar) was pursued side-by-side with the rediscovery of Plato. Above all, the return to the literal words of the Bible, at a time when the new spirit had set men's reason free, seemed to endow writers, preachers, and artists with an intense feeling for the Hebrew past. Although it could not compare in range with the revival of the classical world, it spoke with a direct intimacy through which men identified themselves with the ancients of the Old Testament and the canons of their faith.

The pursuit of Hebrew studies, of which the Authorized Version of the Bible (1611) was one momentous outcome, was therefore more than a linguistic tribute to Hebraism. Although the Christian scholars had turned away from dry scholasticism, they found much that was illuminating in a poetic sense in the Hebraic scholarly tradition, especially as enshrined in rabbinic commentary. A British Platonist (or Plotinist), such as the 17th-century John Smith, could turn to the rabbis and quote with approval the distinction they made between the different degrees in which prophecy "flows in upon the minds of men." The highest degree is the *gradus mosaicus*, where divine knowledge is conveyed, as with Moses, "face to face with God," by direct illumination of the highest, or rational, faculty of the soul. This, he says, springs from the *Ruach Hakodesh* (Holy Spirit), which directly inspired such books as the Psalms or Job. He quotes Maimonides to illustrate how some of the anthropomorphisms of the prophets reflect a lower degree, at which reason is illuminated *in*directly, through the imagination. It is a strange experience to read the elegant English of the 17th century and to think back to the chains of thought that link its ideas, on the one hand with Plato in 5th-century Athens, on the other with—say—the outstanding Jewish philosopher of 10th-century Babylonia, the Gaon Saadya, who greatly influenced Maimonides.

The dispersion of Jews to Babylonia and all that it produced for the widespread influence of Hebraism was, of course, only one channel—though a very distinctive one—through which these traditions made their way into Western life. Infinitely greater for the effect it was to have on the carrying of Hebraism to the world was the dispersion around the Mediterranean shores, because this not only took into Europe many Jews who remained steadfast, but also laid a seed-bed for the flowering of a new faith, based on Hebraism, that was to sweep the whole continent. By a familiar paradox, however, the new religion was to take definitive shape by diluting its own original sources and taking over, to a large extent, the ideas and style of the world it conquered.

The dispersion around the Mediterranean had been stimulated as far back as the 6th century B.C. through Nebuchadnezzar's destruction of Jerusalem. Although the formal Diaspora was to Babylonia, many Jews (as Jeremiah records) had gone into Egypt, and there are legends of dispersion to even more distant lands. The return of exiles from Babylonia to Palestine did not put a stop to the impetus of dispersion. The lack of political independence led to sporadic revolts, followed by further deportations and voluntary emigration. In the almost continuous fighting of the 3rd and 2nd centuries B.C. in Syria and Asia Minor, thousands of Jews were made captive, enslaved, and then set free to settle in the lands to which they were transported. Their release was usually swift, partly—according to one view—because their unswerving attachment to their customs made them poor slaves. A more powerful factor was the ease with which they found co-religionists ready to pay their ransom. This responsibility toward fellow-Jews was always the highest duty; and the consequent reinforcement of settlement spread the communities everywhere.

The achievement of independence under the Hasmonean dynasty in the 2nd century B.C. did not arrest the movement; great hordes of Jewish captives after the wars against Vespasian, Trajan, and Hadrian (A.D. 70–135) swelled the numbers of Jews being transported even farther afield to Italy, Spain, and Gaul, where they ultimately founded communities. Nor was this the only stimulus. Jewish soldiers were in demand to garrison borders or fight campaigns in distant lands.[6] They were sought as colonists for sparsely settled areas, and offered special privileges to encourage their settlement in newly founded cities.[7] Although evidence of the numbers involved is scarce, one estimate[8] is that by the time Jerusalem was destroyed in A.D. 70 there were, in addition to one million Jews in Palestine itself, at least one million also in each of the countries of Egypt, Syria, Babylonia, and Asia Minor, to which must be added the numbers in other parts of Africa and Europe. Of particular importance for the later spread of Hebraism through Christianity, it is said that Jews formed about one fifth of the population of the Eastern Roman Empire.

The Jews, scattered as they were, maintained very strong links with the Jews of Palestine, contributing funds and sometimes rising to fight the ruling powers in sympathy with their brethren.[9] They were ardent believers in their ancestral faith and even propagandists for it, something that had rarely happened before and has never happened since. The freedom to practice their religion and even to win proselytes was not based on a comfortable social background, even though they prospered economically in the rich Greek cities of Asia Minor. Though "Greek" in many ways, the Jews' separatism and general dislike of the cults, pageants, and gymnastic displays around them earned antagonism and contempt, expulsions, and even massacres.[10] There were great strains in Alexandria, despite the fact that the Jews had put down deep roots in Egypt; and the extreme hostility there tended to be echoed elsewhere, even in fair-minded Rome, encouraging sporadic prohibition of Jewish rites. From the time of Claudius (in the middle of the 1st century A.D.), however, the older toleration by the Romans of the Jews, as of other oriental cults, reasserted itself. Jewish religious liberty was guaranteed, and the Jews even came to enjoy a special status.[11] The Roman authorities went to great trouble to make this policy work everywhere through the Empire, despite complaints and disorders in Alexandria, Antioch, and many of the cities of Asia Minor.

Against this background, conditions became helpful to the preaching and persuasion that led first to an active interest in Judaism itself and then to the momentous adaptation of this interest in the spreading of

Christianity. The Greek version of the Bible, available since the 2nd century B.C. and used everywhere, must have had great appeal; a strong factor also must have been the social framework of Jewish life: the gatherings in synagogues, the sense of self-discipline and confidence that was generated, the humanism of the ethical teachings, the happiness of Sabbath and festivals. All this, and probably also the sense of communal loyalty and family decency, must have been attractive to many, even if the majority of outsiders could find no interest in the peculiarities of the cult. Where Jews were active propagandists, they adapted their methods of persuasion to suit local conditions. They brought into play, for example, a specially designed literature, linking the stories of Bible heroes with the great geniuses of ancient Greece.

Although the Torah was the rock of faith for the Jews themselves, they were prepared not to insist on literal interpretation where necessary to make the Bible more acceptable to the uninitiated. Allegory was one of the methods used, as it had been by Philo. Gentiles could become, as it were, friends or associates of Judaism, working their way into full acceptance as its tenets took firmer hold. Some who joined the Jews were their former slaves. Others may have been attracted by the well-being of some of the Jews or by the privileges they enjoyed. Certainly the numbers of proselytes or associates increased rapidly, even though circumcision and the strict observance of the Law remained a barrier.

One of the privileges accorded to Jews was the recognition of the Jewish Patriarch in Palestine[12] as having authority to send envoys (or apostles) to maintain contacts with both the authorities and the Jews themselves. When some of the travellers began to come from the Holy Land on these visits with new, and less burdensome, interpretations of the Law, linked to stories of a new prophet, they found a very large audience already conditioned to a sympathy with the historical presentation and ethical beliefs of Judaism, and ready to receive it if the barriers could be lowered. The new faith was presented at first not as a refutation of Judaism but as its fulfilment, "the Law" being given a new meaning, the words of the new prophet echoing and amplifying the old. In addition, the new prophet expressed—as "the Saviour," and in the circumstances of his birth, death, and resurrection—ideas that were familiar elements in the background of the proselytes and associates.[13] It was almost entirely among them that the foundations of the new Church were established.

How far, it may be asked, did the Church carry Hebraism to the world? How far, in contrast, did it attempt to stifle or combat this influence both directly, through argument with and persecution of the Jews, and indirectly, through its gradual assumption of much of the Greek tradition, ascribing to this tradition some of the "chosen people" quality that had been the essence of Hebrew historicism, drawing on the Greek writings for heroes and imagery, and abandoning, through the Trinity, the infrangible monotheism around which the whole of Hebraism turned?

There can be no simple answer. In *The Early Church* Henry Chadwick says: "The translation of the Gospel into the religious language of the Hellenistic world was a task of great intricacy calling for the highest sensitivity and awareness of responsibility if its structure was not to be altered."[14] Dean Inge, some years ago, took a blunter view: "The Church was half-Greek from the first. . . . The accident of our educational curriculum . . . traces Christian dogma back to Palestine, with which it had little connection."[15] Certainly the Church, as it developed, went a long way from its early Hebraism, when the Apostle Paul would haunt the synagogues for what was, to begin with, his preferred audience, and found his spirit "stirred in him" to see Athens "wholly given to idolatry" (Acts XVII, 16). It is a far cry from this, which is entirely Old Testament in character, to the fully developed doctrines of Paul himself, summed up perhaps in the purely Platonic: "We look not at the things which are seen, but at the things which are not seen; for the things which are seen are temporal, but the things which are not seen are eternal." There is a sharp break, too, between the old idea of the "knowledge of God" as awareness, and "the knowledge of Christ," which meant for Paul: "that I be found in Him"—a concept close to ideas of the mystery religions. It is clear that, although Hebraism was carried to the world through the Church, it was done so in no simple or direct manner. As Christianity grew stronger, pagan cults would still be fiercely attacked, but their philosophic ethos would be less abhorrent than the "hypocrisy" of the Jewish Law, the guilt of the Jews at having put the Saviour to death, and their "wicked" blindness in continuing to refuse to accept Christianity as the true fulfilment. If evidence were needed, the denunciation of the Jews by their own prophets lay to hand: their wickedness in neglecting the inner moral teachings had been proclaimed from time immemorial. By the 2nd century, the uneasy accommodation that had existed between Jews, Christians, and less rigid groups among both of them gave way to direct and bitter hostility. By the 3rd century the Christians, despite the bouts of persecution they themselves suffered, were in a strong enough position to make many direct efforts to crush Hebraism. This was intensified once Rome was converted.[16]

But although the primary interest of the Church Fathers was necessarily (given the background) to explore the implications for Christianity of Greek philosophy, they combined this from the beginning with a continual reassertion of the essential bond of the Old Testament with the New, rejecting the wild attacks by the Gnostic heretics on "the Hebrew God." Although in their sermons and hymns they were willing to include some of the popular sentiment attached to the myriad local cults of paganism, they brought in at the same time not only the universalism of the Saviour, but also the names and stories of Old Testament heroes, who became, as it were, honorary members of the pantheon. In philosophic thought they made common cause with Platonic metaphysics and Stoic ethics. The God of Plato, properly understood, was the God of the Bible: Socrates was a premature Christian martyr. But to Justin Martyr (*c.* 100–165) the answer as to how the Greek sages had come to the "truth" was that they were already familiar with the Pentateuch. For Clement (d. 215), the symbol of the deification of life was Moses on Mount Sinai, or the Holy of Holies in the Tabernacle. Origen (d. 254) was particularly explicit in the value he put on the textual understanding of the biblical source. To this end, he compiled the Hebrew and various Greek versions into a text of six parallel columns (the *Hexapla*), partly to strengthen his hand for argument with the Jews and other non-Christians, but also in the belief that the very differences in the texts could help to uncover subtleties of interpretation and thus lead to the whole truth. The emphasis on the text was an approach destined to be revived some 1300 years later, when (as mentioned above) the Christian scholars of the Reformation also turned back to the minute study of the Hebrew Old Testament; but for most of the intervening period the direct intimacy and instruction that Reformation scholars were to find in Hebraism was very shadowy. The assumption of Roman power by the Church from the 5th century onward meant also the acceptance of the total classical inheritance, and serious exploration of Hebraism by the Western world was abandoned for several hundred years.

Yet something recognizable as purely Hebraic in source survived and flourished to become a prime factor not merely among the Jews but in all Western thought and action. The reason can only be that it appealed to some deep instinct in man. The odds were heavily against its survival. As literature in our modern sense began to stir in Europe in the early Middle Ages, the inspiration was overwhelmingly classical. The "romances" of 11th- and 12th-century France dealt with Greek, Roman, or Trojan heroes. The metaphysics of romantic love (as in the 13th-century

Roman de la Rose) stemmed from Ovid. For Dante, the classical world was an inseparable prior element in the Christian vision. For Boccaccio, the contemporary world had become entirely pagan: in style and feeling ("let the immortal gods bear witness") the stories were rooted in ancient times. As translation of the classics into conteporary languages gathered force from the 15th century onward, lyric poetry, epic, opera, and drama all drew on the world now revealed. Even when the subject-matter was "native," as (say) in Spenser's *Faerie Queene*, the tone was modelled on Homer and Virgil.

What had happened to the Hebrews? Living perilously and for the most part cut off from a normal economic life, they clung obstinately to their own tradition, as deepened predominantly by the Academies of Babylonia, founding schools in many parts of Europe, where they turned the Bible (and the commentaries) over and over ("for everything is in it"), and laying a strong basis for the future in grammatical and exegetical work. Although their leading scholars played an important part (as we have seen) in mediaeval philosophy and science, it was all incomprehensible to the conservative Jews, who sometimes turned on outstanding scholars (such as Maimonides) in painful episodes of heresy-hunting. To the Christian world it was the physical survival of the Jew, rather than his ideas, that was the factor to be reckoned with. He was a living reminder of the shadowy Old Testament and its patriarchs. The notion that society itself might be remoulded by specifically Hebrew ideas would have appeared strange.

It was the virtual rediscovery of the Bible in the Renaissance and Reformation periods, and its becoming available to a very wide range of people through translation, printing, and reading in churches, that changed all this. The Hebrew approach to life suddenly offered a form of experience that forced itself on the individual conscience. It was as if two separate stimuli, both centred on humanism, had now to be taken into account. At one level, man could lose himself in the Greek world of imagination, accepting that if his spirit was moved by heroism, poetry, and beauty, this was an expression of his highest nature. At another level, man was an individual spirit alone with his Creator. The life breathed into him was held on trust. He was at one with Creation only when he was aware at every moment that he lived for the glory of God.

It is a common misconception (as was suggested earlier) to ascribe the power of the Bible wholly to the magnificence of its language. It was the *content* of the Bible that gripped men's minds, as it had always done with the Jews themselves. In all its varied forms—narrative, poetry, and prophecy—it was a literature that conveyed emotion, drama, and a reverence for life in a voice of its own.

This is not to suggest that the awakening to Hebraism meant some weakening of the classical tradition. Some, then or later, certainly gave one or the other influence pride of place, but the characteristic position was to let the two traditions irradiate each other. Milton is a supreme example: *Paradise Lost* is built around a Hebraic theme and is full of biblical incident and argument; but even Milton, who knew Hebrew well, writes overwhelmingly in classical imagery. In the Garden of Eden

> . . . universal Pan,
> Knit with the Graces and the Hours in dance,
> Led on the eternal spring.

When Michael comes in to expel Adam and Eve, he wears "a military vest of purple" dyed by the Greek goddess of the rainbow: "Iris had dipped the wool." The battle scenes between the angels and the devils are derived from the battle of the gods in the *Iliad*.

The classical background was the source of instruction at school and men carried it with them in everything. Yet there is a sense in which the Hebraic tradition spoke to men with greater power. The classical literature, with all its imaginative colouring, was engrossing; but the Bible was "true." For some, this "truth" was taken quite literally; but even for those who preferred not to consider literal truth as a criterion, there was a form of direct communication in Bible stories and poetry that brooked no question. Bible characters came through as "real" people; the Psalms expressed feelings that mattered about God and nature; the thirst of the Prophets for the creation of a just world called for a direct response from anyone who listened. In the classical sources there was a vision of ordered beauty and rightness: in the Bible there was tension, argument, and aspiration. It harked back to something primitive and unfathomable; and there was a ring of authority in the ancient words.

Where did this authority come from? The Greeks, from the 6th century B.C., had daringly asserted that the material world, in all its aspects, was subject to an integrated system of laws that man could discover and understand. The Hebrews, centuries earlier, had decided that the universe was unitary in nature, created by a Being with a moral purpose. Throughout their history they had clung to this idea, building their own sense of brotherhood on it, but seeing their Covenant as a stage in the establishment of the universal brotherhood of man.

It is sufficient to state these two views of life to see how interrelated they are in the emergence of Western culture. They are referred to again and again in later volumes of this work, for in every great cultural epoch in Europe their similarities and contrasts have been discovered anew.*

References

1. There is an interesting discussion of this subject in ALBRIGHT, *From the Stone Age to Christianity*, pp. 371–4. See also his discussion of Iranian influences, pp. 358–67.
2. They regarded themselves as of purer Hebrew stock; the descendant of the Davidic house occupied an important position among them, and they claimed higher authority for their customs, biblical texts, and interpretations.
3. Josephus (A.D. 37–93), *Contra Apion* I, 22, tells us that these Jews refused on religious grounds to take part in Alexander's rebuilding of the destroyed Belus temple.
4. The "romantic" story of two Jewish Robin Hoods, Anilai and Sinai, is told by Josephus. They gathered a troop of freebooters and, after winning a battle against the Parthian rulers, were given territory that they ran as a robber-state. Another story is the conversion to Judaism (*c.* A.D. 40–50) of the little Parthian state of Adiabene, or at least of its rulers. Some of the Adiabene rulers fought in Jerusalem in the war against Vespasian, which ended in A.D. 70, and were taken to Rome as hostages. The Jews of Babylonia could not fight, as they wanted to, alongside their brothers in Palestine against Vespasian; but they expressed their feelings in helping to defeat Trajan during the Parthian revolt.
5. Of the writers in Arabic whose work in translation influenced the Christian world, the outstanding were the Jewish Isaac Israeli of Kairouan (*c.* A.D. 855–955); the Muslim Avicenna (980–1037), born in Persia; Avicebron (*c.* 1021–58), discovered in the 19th century to have been not an Arab but the Jewish poet Ibn Gabirol; and the Muslim Averroes (*c.* 1126–98) and the Jewish Maimonides (1135–1204), both born in Cordova. There were many others. See CHARLES and DOROTHY SINGER, "The Jewish Factor in Mediaeval Thought," in *The Legacy of Israel*, pp. 173–282.
6. Ptolemy I is said to have taken about 30,000 Jews with him to Egypt for this purpose (*Letter of Aristeas*, ed. Schmidt, p. 255; Josephus, *Antiquities* XII, 1). Tiberius sent 4000 Jews from Rome to Sardinia, ostensibly to wage a war (Tacitus, *Annales* II, 85) but perhaps also to expose them to its "deadly" climate.
7. Josephus, *Ant.* XII, 3; *Cont. Apion* II, 4.
8. A. EBAN, *My People* (London 1969), p. 104.

* See, for instance, Vol. III, "Humanism and Language;" Vol. IV, "Literature and Ideology;" Vol. V, "Poetry and Ideology."

9. There was an apparently concerted rebellion among the Jews of Libya, Egypt, Cyrene, and Cyprus in A.D. 115; it was linked with the Jewish supporters of the Parthian revolt. See C. RAPHAEL, *The Walls of Jerusalem* (London 1968), pp. 37–40.

10. *ibid.*, pp. 33–4, cites examples of mutual dislike. For a full picture, see T. REINACH, *Textes d'auteurs grecs et romains relatifs au judaisme* (Paris 1895).

11. There had to be special privileges because the ordinary religious liberty characteristic of much of the ancient world did not conform with the beliefs and practices of the Jews. Whereas the gods of other nations were quite tolerant of each other, the god of the Jews insisted on absolute monotheism from his followers. Judaism was technically a *religio licita*, but the Jews were regarded more as a *collegium* than a *religio*. As *peregrini* they had something akin to Roman citizenship and although their political status was shakier in the Greek cities, their communities were autonomous, with their own synagogues, burial grounds, and lay and religious heads, and they administered justice among themselves. They were exempt from some of the ordinary duties (e.g. military service) because these conflicted with their religious practices, and as a result of this they were liable to special taxes. The only religious practice that caused difficulty from time to time was circumcision. It was banned briefly at one time for Jews themselves, and when restored the practice was forbidden for proselytes.

12. Originally the Patriarch in Jerusalem; after A.D. 70, the Patriarch in Tiberias.

13. Against the widely held view that the doctrine of Jesus as the Saviour (*christos*—both "Son of Man" and "Son of God") was introduced, long after the crucifixion, by the Apostles in A.D. 30–50 or even later, ALBRIGHT, *op. cit.*, pp. 395–9, argues that "Jesus's messianic consciousness was the central fact of His life." The striking parallels with ancient Near Eastern religious ideas—the virgin birth of a god, his astral associations, birth among cattle, imprisonment, death, disappearance for three days, resurrection and exaltation to heaven—reflect the fact that, even before Jesus, the Old Testament was combed for passages with potentially messianic allusions tailored to widely held eschatological ideas; these, in turn, reached back to the framework of the cycles of Tammuz, Adonis, Attis, Osiris, and others. As Albright reasons, "The effective religious value to early Christianity of these superficial resemblances must have been very great, since these cycles had been gradually put into extraordinarily effective forms, all essentially alike in principle. The underlying dramatic forms which had swayed the religious emotions and impulses of the Near East for three millennia made the same psychological appeal to the multitudes of the 1st century A.D. as they had to their forefathers."

14. HENRY CHADWICK, *The Early Church* (London 1967), p. 14.

15. In a contribution to LIVINGSTONE (ed.), *The Legacy of Greece* (pp.

25–56), Inge wrote a lively account of the "complete" debt of the Church to Hellenism rather than to Hebraism: "The Christian Church was the last great creative achievement of the classical culture."

16. CHADWICK, *op. cit.*, pp. 170–1, says that the situation of the Jews tended to pursue "a zig-zag course." At times of strain and economic crisis, they were a scapegoat. There were only sporadic moves toward enforced baptism. The first really bad persecution came under the Visigoths in 7th-century Spain. JAMES PARKES, *The Conflict of the Church and the Synagogue* (London 1934), details the pronouncements and ordinances of the Church against the Jews that, in his view, sowed the seeds of mediaeval and later anti-Semitism.

Bibliography

W. F. ALBRIGHT, *From the Stone Age to Christianity*, 2nd edn (Baltimore 1957), relates the Bible to the neighbouring cultures, bringing in a vast range of archaeological and other material to support his view that Hebrew ethical monotheism, as transmitted by the Bible, took its form in very early times. On the same theme, Albright's *Yahweh and the Gods of Canaan* (London 1968) includes much literary analysis.

A. H. ARMSTRONG (ed.), *The Cambridge History of Later Greek and Early Mediaeval Philosophy* (Cambridge 1967).

E. AUERBACH, *Mimesis*, trans. by W. Trask (Princeton 1953).

E. BEVAN, *The Legacy of Israel* (Oxford 1927).

R. R. BOLGAR, *The Classical Heritage and its Beneficiaries* (Cambridge 1954), is illuminating on the classical tradition in the Middle Ages.

M. BOWRA, *The Greek Experience* (London 1957).

J. BRIGHT, *A History of Israel* (London 1960), is a straightforward account, including a sketch of the earliest history of the Near East.

T. H. GASTER, *Myth, Legend, and Custom in the Old Testament* (New York 1969).

E. GOODENOUGH, *Jewish Symbolism in the Greek and Roman Period* (Princeton 1954 ff.).

C. H. GORDON, *Before the Bible: the Common Background of Greek and Hebrew Civilizations* (London 1962).

F. C. GRANT, *Hellenistic Religions* (New York 1953).

S. LIBERMAN, *Greek in Jewish Palestine* (New York 1942).

R. LIVINGSTONE (ed.), *The Legacy of Greece* (paperback: Oxford 1962).

G. F. MOORE, *Judaism—in the First Centuries of the Christian Era*, 8th edn (Cambridge, Mass. 1958).

J. NEEDHAM, *The Grand Titration: Science and Society in East and West* (London 1969).

A. A. NEUMANN, *The Jews in Spain* (Philadelphia 1942).

M. NOTH, *History of Israel* (London 1960), is comparable with Bright but is more critical of biblical narrative.

R. M. OGILVIE, *Latin and Greek* (London 1964), considers the changing influence of classical authors on British thought from the 16th to the 20th century.

W. W. TARN and G. T. GRIFFITH, *Hellenistic Civilization* (paperback: London 1966).

A. TOYNBEE, *The Crucible of Christianity* (London 1969).

B. WILLEY, *The 17th-Century Background* (London 1934).

H. A. WOLFSON, *Philo: Foundations of Religious Philosophy in Judaism, Christianity, and Islam* (Cambridge, Mass. 1947).

CHAPTER 22

Retrospect

David Daiches[*]

"It was at Rome, on the 15th of October, 1764, as I sat musing amidst the ruins of the Capitol, while the barefooted friars were singing vespers in the Temple of Jupiter, that the idea of writing the decline and fall of the city first started in my mind." So Edward Gibbon recalled the moment when the first suggestion of writing what was to become his *Decline and Fall of the Roman Empire* entered his head. Looking back from the 18th century across what for him was the darkness of the Middle Ages to the high civilization of ancient Rome, Gibbon saw the decline of that civilization as the central problem in history. A civilized city and empire, adorned with arts and equipped with technology, representing the culmination of centuries of painful progress, had then declined and fallen, leaving to future generations the slow and painful task of fighting a way out of the new barbarism to something that they could, in their more complacent and optimistic moments, compare with Augustan Rome. We still call the earlier 18th century the Augustan age of English literature, for so they liked to think of themselves. "The Reflections of Horace, and the Judgments past in his Epistle to Augustus, seem'd so seasonable to the present Times," wrote Alexander Pope, "that I could not help applying them to the use of my own Country." So about 1736 he wrote his "First Epistle of the Second Book of Horace Imitated: to Augustus," one of his many imitations of Horace. Rome still provided models and standards.

But the reason why the decline of Rome haunted the imagination of the 18th century involved much more than the prestige of classical Latin literature. Throughout the Middle Ages Rome had been looked back to not only as the great and unique empire providentially ordained to receive, organize, and administer Christianity (that very function of the empire that for Gibbon was a main cause of its decline), but also as the home of the arts and sciences, the mother of technology in all that

---

* Professor of English, University of Sussex.

concerned buildings, roads, and aqueducts.* The latter particularly were of a quality quite beyond the reach of later times. It is important to remember that throughout the Middle Ages and well into the 18th century, superiority in this kind of engineering and design lay in the *past*. Roads and aqueducts in many regions of Europe were slowly decaying from their original Roman glory. The progressive decline of the roads built by the Romans in England—there is a classic account of the appalling state of English roads at the end of the 17th century in Chapter 3 of Macaulay's *History of England*—made visible to the eye the decline from Roman standards. The actual Roman roads were still there, getting visibly worse year by year. It has been said that one could have sent a letter from Rome to York more quickly in A.D. 200 than in 1700. So Rome was not just Virgil and Horace: it was civilization, with its efficiency and comfort.

The new science of the Renaissance and the flowering of literatures in the vernacular languages on classical models in Italy, France, and England encouraged the belief that in some respects at least the modern world had at last gone beyond the ancients, but the great 17th-century battle between the Ancients and the Moderns—that is, between those who believed in what was called the "Decline of the World" and those who believed in progress—was far from being a push-over for the Moderns. For the new science itself had been made possible by humanist progress in knowledge of the classical authors and languages, especially Greek. As long ago as 1914 Professor John Burnet remarked that "it is not sufficiently realized that one of the first aims of Humanism was the recovery of Greek science, and that it was the work done by the 15th-century humanists that alone made possible the scientific discoveries of the 16th and 17th centuries."[1] The printing, in the original Greek texts, of Euclid, Archimedes, and Hippocrates in the early 16th century, the re-establishment of contact with Pythagorean mathematics and astronomy, the rediscovery of certain neo-Platonic traditions in mathematical and astronomical thought, and the consequent overthrow of certain limiting mediaeval orthodoxies in scientific matters—all this shows that the new science of the Renaissance was the result of the re-establishment of direct contact with the ancient classical world. Francis Bacon himself, the prophet of the inductive method in science and the great enemy of authority and tradition in matters of scientific inquiry, attacked the concept of Aristotle as "dictator" as he attacked the scholastic philosophy,

* It is significant that Virgil's one image from technology should be connected with the use of cement. See the remarks on this subject, however, in Ch. 5, "The Latin Language."

but he never attacked the "Ancients," whom he believed to have possessed the ultimate secrets of the natural world, since lost.

In spite of the importance of Aristotle in late mediaeval thought, as a result of the work of the great 13th-century systematizers and synthesizers of thought, Albertus Magnus and Thomas Aquinas, it is Plato who is the dominating ancient philosophical influence on the literary mind of Europe. Plato came early into Christian thinking* through the work of St Augustine and Boethius as well as through the writings of the early-6th-century writer now known as Dionysius the Pseudo-Areopagite. This early Platonism is itself mediated through the thinking of Plotinus, the 3rd-century neo-Platonist. The effect of Platonism and neo-Platonism on the European imagination is a massive subject: Plato himself was the most literary and the most aesthetically seductive of the Greek philosophers in spite, paradoxically, of the abstract and mathematical nature of his thought. His distinction between knowledge and opinion, between what is eternal and wholly intelligible and what is discerned obscurely through local and temporal media, between given sense perceptions and the time-less reality to which they provide a clue for the instructed intellect, encouraged concepts of ideal excellence that can be seen working equally in poets and in philosophers. It was from Plato's view of eternal Forms reflected in natural phenomena that the mediaeval Christian view of Nature as a system of symbols ultimately derives. This view was as strong in the 17th century as in the Middle Ages: the mediaeval Bestiary, cataloguing the qualities of animals, helped men to understand the sig-nificance of animal imagery in Scripture, and the emblem books of the 16th and 17th centuries—and, indeed, some of the subtlest imagery of "metaphysical" poetry—derive ultimately from the same tradition.

Platonism and neo-Platonism flooded back into European thought, directly from the original sources, in the 15th and 16th centuries. As early as 1438 a scholar from Constantinople, Gemistus Plethon, lectured on Plato in Florence, and Platonism spread rapidly in Italy thereafter. Cosimo de' Medici, inspired by Gemistus, founded a new Platonic Academy in Florence and appointed his young protégé Marsilio Ficino as its head. Many of the Italian Platonists, including Ficino and Pico della Mirandola, combined Platonic, Plotinian, and Jewish Cabbalistic ideas in ways that may seem strange to us but that had significant effects on the literary imagination. Giordano Bruno, one of the most remarkable minds of the Renaissance, had his cosmological imagination stimulated by a reading of Plato and the neo-Platonists. He spent some time in England, and exerted

* See Volume II, "Christian Thought."

an influence on Edmund Spenser, whose *Four Hymns* show, in addition to Bruno's influence, that of Ficino as well as of Plato's *Phaedrus* and *Symposium*. Plato was a significant influence on 17th-century English theology, notably in the work of the so-called Cambridge Platonists, Ralph Cudworth, Henry More, John Smith, Benjamin Whitcote, Nathaniel Culverwell, and Peter Sterry. But it was on poets rather than on philosophers and theologians that Platonic influence was most apparent throughout Europe, particularly in England, and not only in the Renaissance. Shelley's *Defence of Poetry* is as essentially Platonic as Sir Philip Sidney's *Apologie for Poetrie* had been nearly 200 years before, and the central significance of Plato and Plotinus in the thought of W. B. Yeats is even more striking than the significance of Platonic and Pythagorean notions for the young Milton.

That the Roman Empire was the heir and the fulfilment of the civilization that had begun in Greece was the view of the Renaissance and of the 18th century. Its decline and fall represented a spectacular and unprecedented reversal in historical progress, as well as the loss of civilization itself. When Greek science and Roman technology were lost to the West, they went—the former to a greater degree than the latter—to the Arabs and from them to the Jews. (Walter Scott was quite right in *The Talisman* to show the Moslem physician as altogether in a superior class to the Western doctors of physic, just as he was right in *Ivanhoe* to show Jews in possession of medical skills that the ignorant and superstitious Christians could attribute only to witchcraft. Queen Elizabeth was not the only European monarch to have a Jew as her private physician.) Thus the Renaissance humanists re-established contact with scientific traditions of the ancient world that had bypassed the Christian Middle Ages to take refuge in Moslem Spain or in the brilliant multilingual and multi-religious court of Frederick II in Sicily, where Michael Scott and Jacob Anatoli translated astronomical and biological works from Arabic and Hebrew.

The early 17th century talked about the "Middle Age," but the early 18th century called it the "Middle Ages," a term that has stuck: both meant the period that stood between them and the classical world, an age that had to be deliberately undervalued and even ignored (as the "Dark Ages") by those who wanted direct access to "the glory that was Greece and the grandeur that was Rome." But in fact, of course, the Middle Ages had absorbed the classical world in its own way and made its own remarkable use of themes and traditions deriving from ancient Greece and (more especially) Rome. The late-12th-century *trouvère* Jean

Bodel divided the subject-matter of mediaeval romance into three categories: the "Matter of France" (Charlemagne and his knights), the "Matter of Britain" (Arthur and his knights), and the "Matter of Rome the Great." The third category represented the ancient classical world as seen through mediaeval eyes. This world, as it emerges in mediaeval literature, is not that of Homer or Pericles or Virgil; it is a mediaevalized ancient world that classical scholars today (as well as Renaissance humanists) would consider to be far removed from the mainstream of classical culture. The mediaeval writers were haunted by the story of Troy, but they did not get it from Homer: they got it from the 4th-century Latin writer Dictys Cretensis and the somewhat later Dares Phrygius, both of whom claimed to have been eye witnesses of the siege of Troy, the former on the Greek side and the latter on the Trojan. Virgil, the ultimate source of the Troy story as the Middle Ages knew it, was popularly regarded throughout the period as a "wizard" rather than a great poet. The *Aeneid* was the basis of a French romance, the *Roman d'Eneas* (*c.* 1160). But the Troy story as known to mediaeval writers derived essentially from the work of Dictys and Dares as worked up in the late-12th-century *Roman de Troie* by Benoît de Sainte-Maure, and, a century later, in the *Historia destructionis Troiae* by Guido delle Colonne. The "Matter of Rome" also included other stories of the ancient world—of Thebes, Alexander the Great, and Julius Caesar, among others. We can see in Chaucer's "Knight's Tale" how Greece was seen less as a period of history than as a group of legends concerning Greek historical and mythological figures who were conceived of as feudal lords with their retainers. As for the Trojan War, mediaeval Europe was on the side of Troy, and European countries liked to trace their origins—as the Romans themselves had done—to Trojan ancestors.

There is, of course, a paradox in the fact that the Renaissance humanists regarded themselves as having recovered the classical world and put it at the service of their own culture, whereas the Middle Ages, which in the humanist view blocked the light of the classical world, in fact used as its common learned and literary medium a language derived directly from that world. Mediaeval Latin, of course, is not Ciceronian Latin, nor is mediaeval Latin verse classical Latin verse. The centuries of experiment that "brought Latin verse back to the natural patterns of accentual or rhythmic metre, accompanied by sonorous and often intricate rhymes"[2] did not exclude imitations of Ovid or Horace in classical quantitative metres. But the new kind of Latin verse was a living poetry and it was a mediaeval Christian achievement, related to developments in vernacular verse-forms. Nevertheless, however changed and transmuted the classical legacy was in the Middle Ages, it *was* a classical legacy. Helen Waddell has pointed out that the 12th-century Latin lyric "seems as new a miracle as the first crocus; but its earth is the leafdrift of centuries of forgotten scholarship." She asserts what every student of the subject will echo: "There is no beginning, this side the classics, to a history of mediaeval Latin; its roots take hold too firmly on the kingdoms of the dead."[3]

It is no part of this essay's purpose even to sketch such a history. But we can at least note that much early Christian poetry took the form of biblical paraphrase in Latin hexameters, and as such "is a continuation of the antique rhetorical practice of paraphrase,"[4] and that there is a direct line between the metrical cadence (based on syllabic quantity) of artistic Latin prose of the ancient world, the development of the rhythmical (accentual) cadence in late antiquity, the later degeneration and then revival of that cadence or *cursus*, and developments in the rhythm and metre of both mediaeval Latin prose and mediaeval Latin verse.[5]

Of course, mediaeval literature is full of palpable misunderstanding of the classical world, not only in the most obvious anachronisms but also in innumerable details, some of which have their own creative function. Thus when Boethius quotes from a lost Aristotelian treatise a remark about the inner hideousness of the beautiful body of Alcibiades—*Alcibiadis pulcherrimum corpus*—mediaeval readers assumed that he must have been referring to some famous female beauty of antiquity.[6] She is the Archipiade of Villon's "Ballade des dames du temps jadis" (Ballad of the ladies of yore):

> Dictes moy où, n'en quel pays,
> Est Flora la belle Romaine,
> Archipiade, ne Thaïs . . .
>
> (Tell me where, and in what country, is Flora the beautiful woman of Rome, Archipiade [sometimes translated as Hipparchia], and where is Thaïs . . .).

Thus the mediaeval imagination, playing with orts and fragments of the classical world, builds its own symbolic world.

What the mediaeval imagination made of the classical world of Greece and Rome is readily seen in the work of Chaucer, who was master of what was known in his time of classical history, mythology, and literature. We see in Chaucer how the mediaeval imagination transmuted the image of Greece and Rome, mingling it with patristic thought, scholastic categories, and popular beliefs in a way that left a permanent impress on Western thought. Chaucer knew the *Aeneid*, as he knew Ovid's *Heroides* and *Metamorphoses*, Lucan's *Pharsalia*, Statius's *Thebaid*, Boethius's *De conso-latione philosophiae* (which he translated), Macrobius's commentary on the *Somnium Scipionis* of Cicero, and the Troy stories of Dares and Dictys. Of course he also knew much patristic literature, the Vulgate, the Latin liturgy of the Church, innumerable mediaeval romances, and a mis-cellaneous assortment of mediaeval scientific, religious, historical, and entertaining works. In the world that he and his contemporaries con-structed out of this sort of reading, "Pluto and his queene, Proserpina, and all hire fayerye" can meet in a walled garden

> So fair . . .
> That he that wroot the Romance of the Rose
> Ne koude of it the beautee wel devyse

and quote to each other "Jhesus, filius Syrak" (author of Ecclesiasticus) and "This Jew, this Salamon" (King Solomon). Or we might consider the significance of the Nine Worthies of mediaeval legend and romance, of whom three were Jewish, three classical, and three mediaeval: Joshua, David, Judas Maccabeus, Hector, Alexander the Great, Julius Caesar, Arthur, Charlemagne, and Godfrey de Bouillon.

If we put the Theseus of Chaucer's "Knight's Tale" beside the Theseus of Shakespeare's *A Midsummer Night's Dream*, and then try to relate them both to the Theseus of Euripides' *Hippolytus*, we get some indication of how the 16th century saw a classical world that had reached it via the Middle Ages. Chaucer's Theseus was a mediaeval "duc":

> Ther was a duc that highte Theseus;
> Of Atthenes he was lord and governour,
> And in his time swich a conquerour,
> That gretter was ther noon under the sonne.
> Ful many a riche contree hadde he wonne;
> What with his wisdom and his chivalrye,
> He conquered al the regne of Femenye. . . .

Theseus is here conceived of as a mediaeval ruler and warrior, known for both wisdom and chivalry. The land of the Amazons, which was one of his conquests, is here called "Femenye," a name that first appears in Old French and suggests a country inhabited by heroines of mediaeval romance. As for his being both wise and chivalrous, this is very far from the Greek legend, which attributes his success in slaying the Minotaur to the help of Ariadne, not to Theseus's own wisdom, and presents him also as one of the great cads of literature who deserted his helper when he had no further need of her. Euripides creates his Theseus by building on other aspects of the Theseus legend; he becomes a trapped and tragic figure who is manipulated by the irrational passions of others so as to deliberately cause the destruction of his own beloved son. Shakespeare's Theseus obviously descends from Chaucer's. He is "Duke of Athens," firm but just in his rule, chivalrous to his bride Hippolyta, and generously condescending to his loyal subjects: when Bottom and his humble friends offer to perform a play at the wedding celebrations of Theseus and Hippolyta, the master of the revels (a very Elizabethan officer) rejects the offer as absurd, but Theseus overrules him in words that are a model of royal graciousness:

> For never anything can be amiss
> When simpleness and duty tender it.

This is Queen Elizabeth, watching a masque or a play, a pageant or some pretentious and botched entertainment by humble folk presented to her on one of her many progresses from one great house to another; but it is rooted in a mediaeval notion of "gentilesse." The Thésée of Racine's *Phèdre**—a retelling of Euripides' *Hippolytus*—is a lost, bewildered version of Euripides' trapped character, but he lives in a world of high courtesy and lofty conceptions of honour that have more in common with the world of mediaeval *amour courtois* than with the world of the Greek imagination. In considering the image of the classical world in literature of the 15th and 16th centuries we must not forget Shakespeare's use of Plutarch and his fascination with such Roman characters as Julius Caesar, Mark Antony, and Coriolanus.

The humanists changed all that. They brought a fierce desire to cultivate what Erasmus called *bonae literae* and put their knowledge at the service of the vernacular languages of Europe. The Middle Ages had their own complex theories of rhetoric, deriving ultimately from classical sources, and rhetoric was one of the three subjects in the mediaeval *trivium*. But Renaissance Humanism—with its obsession with Cicero, and its distinction between good classical Latin and debased Latin—had other standards. The discovery in 1422 by Gherardo Landriana, Bishop of Lodi, in a dust-covered chest in the cathedral library, of Cicero's principal works on rhetoric, was an important moment in the history of prose style. Cicero's name had been known in the Middle Ages, and his *De inventione*

* For a discussion of Racine and specifically of *Phèdre*, see Vol. III, "Drama in England and France."

had been used often as a source of rhetorical theory and practice, but this was a youthful work, and the other work commonly studied with the *De inventione*, the *Rhetorica ad Herennium*, was attributed to Cicero quite erroneously. The discovery in 1422 of the *De oratore* and the *Orator* gave Cicero new prestige as the master of prose style, and although these works were not manuals of rhetoric but discussions of the nature and importance in society of rhetoric and of the orator, their recovery encouraged the humanists in their development of Ciceronianism, which is characterized by the view that Latin attained its ideal perfection at a specific period in history, that during this great period style was constant, that it is both possible and desirable to revive this model style by deliberate exercise, and that a single author can serve as a model, imitation of whose style will yield a range of expressiveness sufficient for all aspects of personal expression.[7] Of course, there were distinguished humanist opponents of Ciceronianism (notably Poliziano, 1454–94) who considered the imitators of Cicero to be "like parrots or magpies." "I am not Cicero. I am expressing, I think, myself."[8] Poliziano was a great Latinist who did not merely imitate Latin styles; he learned from the Latin poets to embody in his own Italian *ottava rima* a combination of flexibility, elegance, and lightness that provides a remarkable example of the vitalizing influence of the new Renaissance Latin scholarship on vernacular verse. Indeed, the influence of the Latin lyric was much more significant, especially in the development of native verse-forms, than imitation of Cicero.

In England, the combination of strength and grace that we find in the lyrics of Ben Jonson owes much to Catullus, Martial, and Horace; and Ben Jonson's influence runs through the Cavalier poets to the "reform of our numbers" in the latter half of the 17th century, and so to Dryden and Pope. The formalizing of mediaeval verse-forms in Italy, France, and England represents another interesting influence of classical Latin on Renaissance poetry. Petrarch, a pre-humanist or perhaps the proto-humanist in his enthusiasm for Latin, had given the sonnet (a mediaeval form) a new classical status, so that Petrarchism and the imitation of the Petrarchan sonnet were twin influences with classical Latin verse in much Renaissance lyric poetry all over Europe. Humanist poets wrote voluminously in Latin as well as in the vernacular, and the Renaissance Latin lyric is worth careful study on its own account, as also are the mutations and the influence on vernacular literatures of the pastoral poetry of Theocritus and Virgil.

We tend to think of the Middle Ages as the age of Latin, and of the Renaissance as the beginning of that pride in the vernacular literature that was to produce so many of the glories of national literatures throughout Europe. This is a justifiable view, but it is also true that the introduction of printing, coming at a time when humanist enthusiasm for Latin was running high, encouraged a kind of *Latinitas* different in nature but no less widespread than that of the Middle Ages. The first printed books in Europe were in Latin—it has been calculated that in Germany there were more books printed in Latin than in German until the middle of the 18th century—and the early printing of Latin grammars in large numbers led to an immense improvement in classical education and the strengthening of Latin as the literary language of Europe. The Latin grammar of the 4th-century Roman grammarian Aelius Donatus was a standard work in Renaissance Europe, as it had been in the Middle Ages, but the fact that it went into 360 editions in the first two generations of printing is testimony enough to the wider audience it now reached.

It was humanist influence that produced a suspicion of rhyme as a barbarous invention of the Dark Ages, and provoked some of the most extraordinary (and fortunately abortive) experiments in English verse in the late 16th century. Stimulated by his Puritan humanist friend Gabriel Harvey, Edmund Spenser tried out some quantitative English hexameters. "For why a Gods name may not we, as else the Greekes, haue the kingdome of oure owne Language, and measure of our Accentes, by the sound, reseruing the Quantitie to the Verse: Loe here I let you see my olde vse of toying in Rymes, turned into your artificial straightness of Verse, by this *Tetrasticon*. I beseech you tell me your fancie, without parcialitie.

> See yee the blindefoulded pretie God, that feathered Archer,
>   Of louers Miseries which maketh his bloodie Game?
> Wote ye why, his Moother with a Veale hath coouered his Face?
>   Trust mee, least he my Looue happely chaunce to behold.

Spenser here wants the accent to fall quantitatively, independently of the stress of the spoken word, so that the first two lines would scan thus:

> See yee the blindefoulded pretie God, that feathered Archer,
>   Of louers Miseries which maketh his bloodie Game?

Harvey, in his reply, complains about the inconsistency of the quantities, and produces a poem in hexameters, an address to a laurel tree encountered in a "goodly Kentish garden," that preserves the natural stress of the English words:

> What might I call this Tree? A *Laurell*? O bonny Laurell:
> Needes to thy bowes will I bow this knee, and vayle my bonetto:
> Who, but thou, the renowne of Prince, and Princely *Poeta*:
> Th'one for Crowne, for Garland th'other thanketh Apollo . . . .[9]

This is even more absurd and considerably less craftsmanlike than the Italian blank verse, deemed to be Virgilian, of Alemanni, Rucellai, and others.

These were blind alleys, but instructive ones. It is a different matter when we come to Milton's blank verse. Milton hesitated long before deciding to be an English rather than a Latin (and therefore an international European) poet. Like Harvey, but in a wider sense, he was a Christian humanist. When he chose a verse-form for his great Christian epic he naturally turned to the classics. "The measure is English heroic verse without rhyme, as that of Homer in Greek, and of Virgil in Latin; rhyme being no necessary adjunct or true ornament of poem or good verse, in longer works especially; but the invention of a barbarous age, to set off wretched matter and lame metre; graced indeed since by the use of some famous modern poets, carried away by custom, but much to their own vexation, hindrance, and constraint to express many things otherwise, and for the most part worse than else they would have expressed them."[10] In his lyric poetry Milton showed himself a master of rhyme; but it would not do for the epic.

The direct influence of classical metrics on English verse has not been happy, nor has it been significant. Tennyson was the last important poet to experiment with classical metres, but only as a *jeu d'esprit*. He wrote an ironic comment in hexameters on an attempt to translate Homer into English hexameters:

> These lame hexameters the strong-winded music of Homer!
>   No—but a most burlesque barbarous experiment.
> When was a harsher sound ever heard, ye Muses, in England?
>   When did a frog coarser croak upon our Helicon?
> Hexameters no worse than daring Germany gave us,
>   Barbarous experiment, barbarous hexameters.

He was better disposed to Latin lyric measures. He wrote a set of Alcaics in a poem to Milton:

> O mighty-mouthed inventor of harmonies,
> O skilled to sing of Time and Eternity,
>   God-gifted organ-voice of England,
>   Milton, a name to resound for ages; . . .

and he imitated Catullus in hendecasyllabics:

> O you chorus of indolent reviewers,
> Irresponsible, indolent reviewers,
> Look, I come to the test, a tiny poem
> All composed in a metre of Catullus,
> All in quantity, careful of my motion,
> Like the skater on ice that hardly bears him,
> Lest I fall unawares before the people,
> Waking laughter in indolent reviewers. . . .

But Tennyson's most classical-sounding poem is not written in a classical metre at all, although it has the effect of one. It is his address to Virgil:

> Roman Virgil, thou that singest
>   Ilion's lofty temples robed in fire,
> Ilion falling, Rome arising,
>   wars, and filial faith, and Dido's pyre. . . .
>
> I salute thee, Mantovano,
>   I that loved thee since my days began,
> Wielder of the stateliest measure
>   ever moulded by the lips of man.

And this reminds us that the 19th century had its own kind of deep allegiance to the classical world. Milton had exalted Republican Rome above the Empire, as more suited to his democratic Puritanism, just as the Roman classicism of the French painter David in, for example, *The Oath of the Horatii* derived from an admiration for what Arnold Hauser has called "the republican civic virtues."[11] Eighteenth-century Augustanism had its own more urbane relationship to the classical past. A crucial chapter in the history of European architecture from the 16th to the early 19th century concerns the impact, imitation, and modification of classical forms. Much of this history would be involved in a gloss on Pope's lines to the Earl of Burlington:

> You too proceed! make falling Arts your care,
> Erect new wonders, and the old repair,
> Jones and Palladio to themselves restore,
> And be whate'er Vitruvius was before.[12]

Architecture, like poetry, should follow classical models, in this case the rules of Vitruvius (born *c.* 88 B.C.) codified by the 16th-century Italian architect Andrea Palladio and adopted by the English architect Inigo Jones (1573–1652). The later 18th-century Hellenic revival, with which Johann Joachim Winckelmann's *Geschichte der Kunst des Altertums* (1764) is particularly associated and which influenced Goethe's doctrine of *Bildung* as developed in *Wilhelm Meisters Lehrjahre,* flows into the phil-Hellenism of the 19th century. Goethe, of course, had other classical interests, an effect of his crucial Italian journey in 1786. The *Römische Elegien* and the *Italienische Reise* show ancient Rome stimulating a creative writer at the end of the 18th century in a new way, and his drama *Iphigenie auf Tauris* applies an ultimately Hellenic concept of harmonious expression of essential humanity to the production of a non-tragic version of a Greek tragedy.

Phil-Hellenism was a European phenomenon, but nowhere was it more eloquently expressed than by Matthew Arnold, who, in *Culture and Anarchy* (1869), recommended for the health of English culture a strong dose of Hellenism (representing "spontaneity of consciousness") as a leaven for what he called Hebraism, the English emphasis on "strictness of conscience":

> The best art and poetry of the Greeks, in which religion and poetry are one, in which the idea of beauty and of a human nature perfect on all sides adds to itself a religious and devout energy, and works in the strength of that, is . . . of such surpassing interest and constructiveness for us, though it was,—as, having regard to the human race in general, and, indeed, having regard to the Greeks themselves, we must own,—a premature attempt, an attempt which for success needed the moral and religious fibre in humanity to be more braced and developed than it had been. But Greece did not err in having the idea of beauty, harmony, and complete human perfection, so present and paramount.[13]

Arnold's phil-Hellenism was based on a close knowledge of Greek literature in the original, especially of Homer and Sophocles, even though, like so many in his age, he romanticized 5th-century Athens, ignoring such uncomfortable facts as that its economy was based on slavery and its idealism oddly bound up with homosexuality. But at the beginning of the century John Keats had fallen for Greece with no better knowledge of Greek culture than that provided by the Elgin Marbles, the 16th-century George Chapman's translation of Homer, and Lemprière's *Classical Dictionary.* Keats's empathy with Greece was remarkable: he seemed to intuit some of the most profound realities of Greek civilization, and at the same time the thought of ancient Greece was bound up with a sense of loss, of the inevitable movement of time. The picture in the "Ode on a Grecian Urn" of the little Greek town, "emptied of its folk" to participate in a religious festival, is luminous and moving, yet equally moving is his sense of its location in the irrecoverable past:

> . . . and not a soul to tell
> Why thou art desolate, can e'er return.

Yet the urn itself perpetuates the spirit of the lost town, as the Elgin Marbles produce in the modern viewer both a sense of "Grecian grandeur" and an awareness of the erosion wrought by time:

> Such dim-conceived glories of the brain
>   Bring round the heart an indescribable feud;
> So do these wonders a most dizzy pain,
>   That mingles Grecian grandeur with the rude
> Wasting of old Time—with a billowy main—
> A sun—a shadow of a magnitude.

This sonnet, "On Seeing the Elgin Marbles," almost comes apart under the stress of Keats's endeavour to communicate simultaneously his sense of admiration and his sense of loss.

The phil-Hellenism of Keats's contemporary, Shelley, derived from a first-hand knowledge of Greek poetry (especially the tragic dramatists) and philosophy (especially Plato); but that of the third of the trilogy of second-generation English Romantic poets, Byron, was associated with political feeling in favour of the liberation of Greece from Turkish rule. Indeed, the word phil-Hellenism was originally coined to denote not so much lovers of Greek art and literature as champions of the Greek cause in the Greek War of Independence. The cause of Greek independence was championed by liberal elements throughout Europe, especially in England. It is thus no accident that the great 19th-century history of Greece was by George Grote, a philosophical radical of the school of Mill and Bentham and a passionate believer in the glories of Athenian democracy, whose account of the growth and decline of that democracy is the most eloquent and memorable part of the work. Grote's *History of Greece* (12 volumes, 1846–56) was largely responsible for the view of 5th-century Athenians as the best kind of English liberal democrats—a view that prevailed in British schools well into the 20th century. Grote himself called the mid-Victorian age "the age of steam and cant" that could be redeemed, for him no less than for Arnold, by Athenian example. Mr Crotchet, in Thomas Love Peacock's novel *Crotchet Castle* (1831), had already made the point:

> . . . where the Greeks had modesty, we have cant; where they had poetry, we have cant; where they had patriotism, we have cant; where they had anything that exalts, delights, or adorns humanity, we have nothing but cant, cant, cant.[14]

The phil-Hellenism of Walter Pater, at the end of the century, was of a different order, though in the same general tradition. Pater was a classical scholar, a life-long academic, whose imagination was as at home in ancient Greece as it was in the Renaissance (in its art, at least) and in 2nd-century-A.D. Rome, the setting of his novel *Marius the Epicurean* (1885).[15] But Pater's ancient world was filtered through his very special sensibility. On the whole the 20th century has been less interested in Greek culture in the Arnoldian sense than in ancient Greece as a source of myths and archetypes. James Joyce's *Ulysses* (1922) is a novel of 20th-century Dublin counterpointed to scenes and actions in the *Odyssey* in order to give it a mythic dimension. The Greek myths have been active in 20th-century literature in a variety of ways, and the themes of Greek tragedy have been repeatedly explored and re-developed. It was to Greek tragedy, too, that the most influential of all modern psychologists turned to find a name for the most discussed of all his diagnoses, the Oedipus complex.

We come back to Gibbon, pondering on the decline of Rome in the ruins of the Capitol on that October evening of 1764. Our historical purview may be wider now, and we no longer regard the decline and fall of the Roman Empire as the greatest of all historical problems. But in any case the problem, looked at from today's perspective, is less that Rome declined and fell than that long after its fall Rome and Greece influenced the thought, sensibility, and literature of the Western world in so many ways for so long a period. Again and again in the following volumes of this work we shall see classical literature fruitfully at work long after the eclipse of the societies that produced it.

References

1. JOHN BURNET, "Humanism in Education," *Essays and Addresses* (London 1929), p. 105.
2. G. F. WHICHER, *The Goliard Poets* (New York 1949), p. 2. See F. BRITTAIN, *The Mediaeval Latin and Romance Lyric to A.D. 1300* (Cambridge 1951), pp. 2 ff.
3. HELEN WADDELL, *The Wandering Scholars* (London 1932), p. ix.
4. E. R. CURTIUS, *European Literature and the Latin Middle Ages*, trans. by W. R. Trask (New York 1953), p. 148.
5. *ibid.*, pp. 151–2.
6. *ibid.*, p. 406.
7. See C. S. BALDWIN, *Renaissance Literary Theory and Practice*, ed. by D. L. Clark (Gloucester, Mass. 1959).

8. ANGELO POLIZIANO, *Opera* (Lyon 1537–9), I, 251; quoted by BALDWIN, *op. cit.*, p. 48. See also Vol. III, "Humanism and Language," for a general discussion of this topic.

9. The "familiar letters" between Spenser and Harvey, in which classical metres are discussed and their own efforts exhibited, are in *The Poetical Works of Edmund Spenser*, ed. by J. C. Smith and E. de Selincourt (Oxford 1929), pp. 623 ff.

10. *The Poems of John Milton*, ed. by J. Carey and A. Fowler (London 1968), pp. 456–7. The quotation is from Milton's prefatory note on his verse in *Paradise Lost*.

11. ARNOLD HAUSER, *The Social History of Art*, Vol. III (London 1962), p. 137.

12. ALEXANDER POPE, *Moral Essays*, Epistle IV, 191–4.

13. MATTHEW ARNOLD, *Culture and Anarchy* (London 1869), Ch. 1.

14. THOMAS LOVE PEACOCK, *Crotchet Castle* (London 1831), Ch. X.

15. See also Pater's essay on Winckelmann in *The Renaissance* (London 1873), in the concluding part of which he discusses Goethe and Hellenic culture.

Index

Page numbers in *italics* refer to items in the footnotes.

DATE DUE

JAN 5			
MAY 8 1985			
FEB 19 1987			